"This fresh and lucid work is written in an accessible style. Stevens presents a coherent history of apocalyptic and interpretive history, and places Revelation in its proper Jewish and Roman contexts. Through deep exploration and engaging analysis, the reader is invited to a Christocentric reading of Revelation in light of Jesus' incarnation and passion. This passion-millennial approach reconfirms Revelation's canonical place and authority. A 'must read' for scholars, clergy, and laypersons alike."

—**Renate Viveen Hood**
Professor of Christian Studies, The University of Mary Hardin-Baylor

"Gerald Stevens offers a reading of Revelation that confronts and counters centuries of misinterpretation; simultaneously, he demonstrates the relevance of the Apocalypse for every generation. Rooted firmly in the context of the Seer of Patmos and of the believers in the seven churches, the interpretation offered here is both a sound, credible exegesis of Revelation and an example of the faithful application of hermeneutics to a challenging text."

—**R. Warren Johnson**
Professor of Religion, East Texas Baptist University

"Gerald Stevens writes with students in mind. In a clear and understandable manner, Stevens makes the history of John's Apocalypse accessible from its apocalyptic origins, through its original context, and across its interpretation for twenty centuries. Stevens 'recanonizes' the historic message of Revelation rooted in the gospel message of the cross in a way that is significant, relevant, and largely unheard today."

—**Jeff Cate**
Professor of Christian Studies, California Baptist University

REVELATION

REVELATION

The Past and Future of John's Apocalypse

Gerald L. Stevens

PICKWICK Publications · Eugene, Oregon

REVELATION
The Past and Future of John's Apocalypse

Copyright © 2014 Gerald L. Stevens. All rights reserved. Except for brief quotations in critical publications or reviews, no part of this book may be reproduced in any manner without prior written permission from the publisher. Write: Permissions. Wipf and Stock Publishers, 199 W. 8th Ave., Suite 3, Eugene, OR 97401.

Pickwick Publications
An Imprint of Wipf and Stock Publishers
199 W. 8th Ave., Suite 3
Eugene, OR 97401

www.wipfandstock.com

ISBN 13: 978-1-62564-549-4

Cataloguing-in-Publication Data

Stevens, Gerald L.

    Revelation : the past and future of John's apocalypse / Gerald L. Stevens.

    xxxii + 633 p. ; 23 cm. Includes bibliographical references and indexes.

    ISBN 13: 978-1-62564-549-4

    1. Bible. N. T. Revelation—Criticism, interpretation, etc. 2. Bible. N. T. Revelation—Commentaries. I. Title.

BS2825.53 S77 2014

Manufactured in the U.S.A.

Cover Image: "Christ's Last Judgment" by Coppo di Marcovaldo, in the ceiling of the Battistero di San Giovanni, Florence, Italy. The imagery is allusive to Christ's last judgment parable of the sheep and the goats (Matt 25:31–46). At the right hand are the rewards of the saved as they leave their tombs; at the left hand, the punishments of the damned.

Dedicated to my students
past, present, and future

Credits and Permissions

In the pursuit of learning, we never walk alone, and we always stand on others' shoulders. This book is the result of many contributions, known and unknown, large and small, of many individuals over a lifetime. I thank students, colleagues, former teachers, pastors, family, friends, and Bible study leaders for their input into my understanding of God's Word. Especially assisting the production of this volume have been my wife, Jean M. Stevens, my legal counsel, Joseph W. Looney, and my doctoral assistant, Allyson R. Presswood.

Bar Kokhba Silver Tetradrachm, derived from Classical Numismatic Group, Inc., www://www.cngcoins.com. Used by permission. Creative Commons license. All rights reserved.

Bede, *On the Reckoning of Time*, illumination of folio 53r from MS Hunter 85. Used by permission of University of Glasgow Library, Special Collections. All rights reserved.

Cartography, unless indicated otherwise, is derived from *Accordance*, ver. 10.1.5. OakTree Software, Inc. 498 Palm Springs Drive, Suite 100, Altamonte, Fla. Used by permission. All rights reserved.

Codex Sinaiticus, Oxford University Press, Walton Street, Oxford, England OX2 6DP, for the image of Codex Sinaiticus on p. 561 from Helen and Kirsopp Lake, *Codex Sinaiticus Petropolitanus: The New Testament, The Epistle of Barnabas and the Shepherd of Hermas, Preserved in the Imperial Library of St. Petersburg, Now Reproduced in Facsimile From Photographs by Helen and Kirsopp Lake, with a Description and Introduction to the History of the Codex by Kirsopp Lake* (The Clarendon Press, 1911).

Die Luther-Bibel von 1534, Vollständiger Nachdruck, Taschen GmbH, Hohenzollernring 53, D-50672 Köln, Germany. Abbreviated as Taschen.

Credits and Permissions

Doré woodcuts, from *Doré's Illustrations of the Crusades, Gustave Doré*, 1997. Dover Publications Inc., 31 East 2nd Street, Mineola, N.Y. 11501. Used by permission. All rights reserved.

Douce Apokalypse (Ms 180) Illuminations, Copyright © *Akademische Drucku. Verlagsanstalt Graz,* Austria (ADEVA), A-8042 Graz, St. Peter Hauptstraße 98. Used by permission. All rights reserved. Abbreviated as ADEVA.

Hildegard, Antichrist illumination, *Scivias* 3.11, from Eibington Abbey codex 1, a modern copy of the lost Rupertsberg manuscript (late twelfth century). Scanned from the reproductions included in Lieselotte Saurma-Jeltsch's 1998 study, *Die Miniaturen im "Liber Scivias" der Hildegard von Bingen: die Wucht der Vision und die Ordnung der Bilder* (Wiesbaden: Reichert).

Joachim, *Figurae*, illumination of three ages, from CCC MS 255A fol. 7v. Used by permission of the President and Fellows of Corpus Christi College, Oxford. All rights reserved.

Koresh, David. Image available from Wikimedia, Creative Commons, taken to be in the public domain.

Late Great Planet Earth paperback cover, Taken from *The Late Great Planet Earth* by Hal Lindsey, with C. C. Carlson. Copyright © 1970 by Hal Lindsey. Use by permission of Zondervan. www.zondervan.com.

The New Scofield Reference Bible; Holy Bible: Authorized King James Version (Oxford University Press, 1967), image of the title page. By permission of Oxford University Press, USA. All rights reserved.

Photograph by Mark A. Gstohl, Copyright © 2014 Mark A. Gstohl, 3725 Tall Pines Drive, New Orleans, Louisiana. Used by permission. All rights reserved.

Photograph by Renate Viveen Hood, Copyright © 2014 Renate Viveen Hood, 3310 Elmer King Road, Belton, Texas. Used by permission. All rights reserved.

Photograph by Rzuwig, taken 2012, of ancient Perge main boulevard with canal available through Wikipedia Commons under the Creative Commons license.

Photographs, unless indicated otherwise, are by Gerald L. Stevens, Copyright © 2014 Gerald L. Stevens, 3777 Mimosa Ct., New Orleans, Louisiana. All rights reserved.

Photographs by Jean M. Stevens, Copyright © 2014 Jean M. Stevens, 3777 Mimosa Court, New Orleans, Louisiana. Used by permission. All rights reserved.

Roman merchant ship model, Science and Society Picture Library, Image #10422383, SCMG Enterprises Ltd., Science Museum Group, Exhibition Road, London SW7 2DD. Used by permission. © Science and Society Picture Library.

Scripture quotations unless marked otherwise are the author's own translation.

Scripture quotations marked (NRSV) are taken from the *New Revised Standard Version* (NRSV) Copyright © 1989 by the Division of Christian Education of the National Council of the Churches of Christ in the USA.

Scripture quotations marked (NASB) are from the *New American Standard Bible* Copyright © 1960, 1962, 1963, 1968, 1971, 1972, 1973, 1975, 1977, 1995 by The Lockman Foundation.

Scripture quotations marked (NIV) are from the *New International Version* Copyright © 1973, 1978, 1984 International Bible Society.

Smith illustrations from Uriah Smith, *Daniel and the Revelation: The Response of History to the Voice of Prophecy; a Verse by Verse Study of These Important Books of the Bible*. Nashville: Southern Publishing Association, 1897.

Vespasian Coin, sestertius, copper alloy, A.D. 71, obverse laureate Vespasian with reverse goddess Roma, AN0417709001. British Museum. Used by permission. © The Trustees of the British Museum.

Wikipedia Common images of Bede, Augustine, Book of Mormon, British Stamp Act, Czechoslovakia map, John Nelson Darby, Martin Luther, William Miller, Plague Victims, Charles Russell, Mount Carmel in flames, C. I. Scofield available through Wikipedia Commons under the Creative Commons license.

Wycliffe, John. Public domain. Image available at http://www.graven-image.co.uk/2011/09/wycliffe/

Contents

List of Figures • xiii
Preface • xxiii
Abbreviations • xxv

PART 1

Apollyon and Armageddon: Revelation's Apocalyptic Traditions and Their Interpretation in History

1 Tributaries of Tradition: Jewish Sources of John's Apocalyptic Traditions • 3

2 A Strong River: Historical Developments to the Reformation • 25

3 Swept Away Downstream: Reformation to the American Revolution • 53

4 A Mighty Flood: The Nineteenth-Century Deluge • 71

5 A Hermeneutical Swamp: Problematic Readings • 99

6 A Glassy Sea: Learning from History • 139

PART 2
Beyond Apollyon and Armageddon: Setting Hermeneutical Foundations for the Interpretation of Revelation

7 Interpretive Decisions: Genre, Prophecy, Judgments, Millennium • 145

8 Theological Decisions: Christology, Ecclesiology, Soteriology • 173

9 Contextual Decisions: Historical and Literary Settings • 201

PART 3
Apocalypse of Jesus Christ: Reading John's Vision of a Future Anticipated from the Past

10 Judgment of the Church: The Son of Man and His Churches • 249

11 Judgment of the World: The Sovereign God and His World • 377

12 Hope of Heaven: God and Christ and Their Victory • 525

Epilogue: The Future of John's Apocalypse • 569

Bibliography • 577

Scripture Index • 591

Ancient Documents Index • 607

Modern Authors Index • 611

Subject Index • 613

Figures

Figure P-1   Signorelli's Judgment Angels • xxii
Figure 1.1   Ishtar Gate of Babylon • 4
Figure 1.2   Jerusalem from the Mount of Olives • 4
Figure 1.3   Jerusalem Temple Model • 5
Figure 1.4   Signorelli's Resurrection of the Flesh • 6
Figure 1.5   Cyrus Cylinder • 6
Figure 1.6   Reproduction of a Qumran Scroll • 8
Figure 1.7   Tel Megiddo's Overview of the Jezreel Valley • 8
Figure 1.8   Alexander the Great Coin • 9
Figure 1.9   Damned Taken to Hell and Received by Demons • 10
Figure 1.10 Raphael Instructs Tobit on Demon Exorcism • 11
Figure 1.11 Domitian Coin • 12
Figure 1.12 Ephesus: Domitian Altar Frieze • 12
Figure 1.13 Smith: The Great World Kingdom Image • 13
Figure 1.14 Antiochus IV Coin • 14
Figure 1.15 Pompeii Fresco of Pig Sacrifice • 14
Figure 1.16 Roman Imperial Coins • 15
Figure 1.17 Jerusalem Bronze, 11 B.C. • 15
Figure 1.18 Qumran Caves • 16
Figure 1.19 The Burnt House • 17
Figure 1.20 Roman Civil War • 18
Figure 1.21 Damaged Jerusalem Street • 19
Figure 1.22 Judea Capta Sestertius • 19
Figure 1.23 Mamertine Prison Plaque • 20
Figure 1.24 Triumphal Arch of Titus • 20

xiv Figures

Figure 1.25 Arch of Titus: Jewish Menorah Relief • 21
Figure 1.26 Tributaries of Tradition • 23
Figure 2.1 Bar Kokhba Coin • 26
Figure 2.2 Chiliasm and Premillennialism • 27
Figure 2.3 Hierapolis of Asia Minor • 29
Figure 2.4 Frontinus Gate of Hierapolis • 29
Figure 2.5 Phrygia of Asia Minor • 30
Figure 2.6 Battle of Milvian Bridge • 31
Figure 2.7 Arch of Constantine • 32
Figure 2.8 Venerable Bede • 33
Figure 2.9 Saint Augustine in Prayer • 35
Figure 2.10 Colosseum • 36
Figure 2.11 Plague Victims Blessed by Priest • 38
Figure 2.12 Bede Illumination, *On the Reckoning of Time* • 39
Figure 2.13 Signorelli's Deeds of the Antichrist • 41
Figure 2.14 Louis IX Attacks Damietta, 1249 • 42
Figure 2.15 Hildegard Antichrist Illumination • 43
Figure 2.16 Joachim, Three Ages Illumination • 45
Figure 2.17 Douce Apocalypse at Rev 9:17 • 47
Figure 3.1 Czechoslovakia in 1928–1938 • 54
Figure 3.2 John Wycliffe (d. 1384) • 55
Figure 3.3 Martin Luther (d. 1546) • 56
Figure 3.4 New Testament Contents, *Luther Bible*, 1534 • 58
Figure 3.5 Angers Apocalypse Tapestry • 59
Figure 3.6 Rev 11 Illustration, *Luther Bible*, 1534 • 60
Figure 3.7 Rev 17 Illustration, *Luther Bible*, 1534 • 60
Figure 3.8 St. Lambert's Church Steeple • 63
Figure 3.9 Colonial Millennialism • 65
Figure 3.10 British Stamp Act • 67
Figure 3.11 Development of Traditions • 69
Figure 4.1 Book of Mormon Title Page, 1830 • 72
Figure 4.2 William Miller (d. 1849) • 73
Figure 4.3 Uriah Smith (d. 1903) • 77
Figure 4.4 "The World Tomorrow" Broadcast • 79
Figure 4.5 "GTA" Broadcasts • 81
Figure 4.6 Charles T. Russell (d. 1916) • 81
Figure 4.7 David Koresh (d. 1993) • 83
Figure 4.8 Mount Carmel in Flames • 84

Figures   xv

Figure   4.9   John Nelson Darby (d. 1882) • 85
Figure   4.10 Darby's Seven Dispensations • 87
Figure   4.11 Cyrus I. Scofield (d. 1921) • 94
Figure   4.12 *The New Scofield Reference Bible* • 95
Figure   4.13 *The Late Great Planet Earth* • 96
Figure   5.1   Example Modern Insecurities • 108
Figure   5.2   88 Reasons • 120
Figure   5.3   Smith Illustration A of Dan 12:4 • 133
Figure   5.4   Smith Illustration B of Dan 12:4 • 134
Figure   7.1   Revelation's Complex Genre and Corollaries • 146
Figure   7.2   Assyrian Winged Bull • 146
Figure   7.3   Woodcut of Rev 1 • 149
Figure   7.4   The Epistolary Binding of Revelation's Genre • 152
Figure   7.5   Ancient Corinth • 153
Figure   7.6   Ancient Ephesus • 154
Figure   7.7   Prophecy as Foretelling in Revelation • 157
Figure   7.8   Historicist Periodizing Methodology • 159
Figure   7.9   Composite Futurist Chart • 160
Figure   7.10 Idealist View • 161
Figure   7.11 Linear Judgments • 162
Figure   7.12 Telescopic Judgments • 163
Figure   7.13 Recapitulation Judgments • 164
Figure   7.14 Millennium Theories • 166
Figure   8.1   Herculaneum Eatery • 177
Figure   8.2   Cave Entrance at Panias • 179
Figure   8.3   Roman Soldiers • 184
Figure   8.4   Roman Merchant Ship • 187
Figure   8.5   Two-Age Jewish Apocalyptic • 194
Figure   8.6   Vasari's The Last Judgment • 197
Figure   8.7   Fresco of Fra Angelico • 199
Figure   9.1   Map of the Island of Patmos • 206
Figure   9.2   Panorama of Patmos • 207
Figure   9.3   Cave of the Apocalypse Mosaic • 209
Figure   9.4   Seven Churches • 210
Figure   9.5   The Aeneas Legend • 212
Figure   9.6   Zoilos Remembrance Monument • 213
Figure   9.7   Aphrodisias Theater and Temple of Aphrodite • 213
Figure   9.8   Aphrodisias Stadium and Bouleuterion • 214

Figure 9.9 Grave Stele, Supervisor of the Linen Workers • 214
Figure 9.10 Antonius Claudius Demetrious • 215
Figure 9.11 Claudia Antonia Tatiana • 216
Figure 9.12 Leading Citizen • 217
Figure 9.13 The Goddess Aphrodite • 218
Figure 9.14 Drawing of the Sebastion Entrance • 219
Figure 9.15 Sebastion of Aphrodisias • 220
Figure 9.16 Sebastion Friezes, North Second Story • 221
Figure 9.17 Sebastion Frieze, ETHNOUS IOUDAIŌN • 221
Figure 9.18 Emperor and Roman People • 222
Figure 9.19 The Goddess Hemera and the God Oceanus • 223
Figure 9.20 Roma and Earth and Victory of the Emperors • 224
Figure 9.21 Tiberius, Captive; Claudius Conquers Britannia • 225
Figure 9.22 Nero and Agrippina • 226
Figure 9.23 Claudius, Master of Land and Sea • 227
Figure 9.24 Imperial Cult Priest, Ephesus • 228
Figure 9.25 Temple of Trajan, Pergamum • 229
Figure 9.26 Dedicatory Imperial Inscription • 230
Figure 9.27 Apollo Playing Cithara • 230
Figure 9.28 Palatine Hill • 231
Figure 9.29 Goddess Roma Seated on Seven Hills of Rome • 232
Figure 9.30 Actor Dressed as Papposilenus • 235
Figure 9.31 Theater at Aspendos • 236
Figure 9.32 *Scaenae Fons* of Perge Theater • 237
Figure 9.33 Apocalypse Tapestry, Rev 13:1–2 • 240
Figure 9.34 Revelation's "Big Picture" • 243
Figure 10.1 Revelation, Act 1 • 249
Figure 10.2 Apocalypse Tapestry, Reader • 254
Figure 10.3 Victorious Hadrian (d. 138) • 269
Figure 10.4 Apocalypse Tapestry, Rev 1:9–20 • 273
Figure 10.5 Grammar and Structure of Rev 1:19 • 277
Figure 10.6 Seven Letters—Sevenfold Structure • 281
Figure 10.7 Seven Letters—Verse Structure • 282
Figure 10.8 Seven Letters—Contents • 283–86
Figure 10.9 Apocalypse Tapestry, Rev 2:1 • 287
Figure 10.10 Ephesus, Domitian Temple • 288
Figure 10.11 Ephesus, Domitian Statue • 288
Figure 10.12 Ephesus, Harbor Decree • 289

Figure 10.13 Polemaeanus, Proconsul of Asia • 289
Figure 10.14 Ephesus, Temple of Artemis • 290
Figure 10.15 Ephesus, Terrace Homes • 291
Figure 10.16 Colosseum of Rome • 295
Figure 10.17 Gladiator Mosaic • 295
Figure 10.18 Bronze Coin, Reverse of Roman Standards • 296
Figure 10.19 Gladiator Grave Stele • 296
Figure 10.20 Gladiator Graffiti at Ephesus • 296
Figure 10.21 Modern Izmir • 299
Figure 10.22 Fragments of the *Res Gestae Divi Augusti* • 299
Figure 10.23 Caesarea Maritima • 300
Figure 10.24 Sepphoris and Scythopolis • 300
Figure 10.25 Smyrna, Agora Arch and Keystone • 301
Figure 10.26 Damokkaris Inscription • 302
Figure 10.27 Smyrna Imperial Coin • 302
Figure 10.28 Synagogue Lintel Inscription • 304
Figure 10.29 Attalos III of Pergamum • 307
Figure 10.30 Pergamum, Temple of Trajan • 308
Figure 10.31 Pergamum, Zeus Altar Foundation • 308
Figure 10.32 Pergamum, Statue of Zeus • 309
Figure 10.33 Pergamum Zeus Altar, West Front • 310
Figure 10.34 Pergamum Zeus Altar Frieze, East Side, Hekate • 310
Figure 10.35 Library of Pergamum • 311
Figure 10.36 Asklepion Votive • 311
Figure 10.37 Asklepios Statue • 312
Figure 10.38 Asklepion of Pergamum • 313
Figure 10.39 Bithynia and Pontus • 315
Figure 10.40 Ancient Thyatira • 321
Figure 10.41 Pagan Worship • 323
Figure 10.42 Roman Bed • 327
Figure 10.43 Pompeii Amphorae • 329
Figure 10.44 Aphrodite Coin • 330
Figure 10.45 Aphrodite Figures • 331
Figure 10.46 Sardis Acropolis • 332
Figure 10.47 Sardis Synagogue • 333
Figure 10.48 Sardis Synagogue Items • 334
Figure 10.49 Sardis Synagogue Inscription • 334
Figure 10.50 Sardis Bathhouse Complex • 335

xviii Figures

Figure 10.51 Sardis Synagogue Courtyard • 335
Figure 10.52 Sardis Marble Hall • 336
Figure 10.53 Sardis, Temple of Artemis • 336
Figure 10.54 Sardis Priest Inscription • 337
Figure 10.55 Hills of Philadelphia • 342
Figure 10.56 Philadelphia, Saint John's Basilica • 344
Figure 10.57 Saint John's Basilica Inscription • 344
Figure 10.58 Seven Letters Chiasm • 345
Figure 10.59 Hour of Trial • 347
Figure 10.60 Didyma, Apollo Temple Aerial • 349
Figure 10.61 Didyma, Apollo Temple • 349
Figure 10.62 Apollo Temple Drawing • 350
Figure 10.63 Apollo Temple Workmanship • 350
Figure 10.64 Laodicea Stadium • 352
Figure 10.65 Laodicea, Syria Street • 353
Figure 10.66 Syria Street Tile Work • 353
Figure 10.67 Laodicea, Central Temple Complex • 353
Figure 10.68 Water Distribution Terminal 1 • 354
Figure 10.69 Terracotta Pipe System • 355
Figure 10.70 Colossae Tel • 355
Figure 10.71 Laodicea, West Theater • 356
Figure 10.72 Cliffs of Hierapolis • 356
Figure 10.73 Ancient Hierapolis Drawing • 357
Figure 10.74 Cliff View of Lycus Valley • 357
Figure 10.75 Frontinus Gate of Hierapolis • 358
Figure 10.76 Syrian Gate of Laodicea • 358
Figure 10.77 Imperial *Neokoros* Coin of Laodicea • 359
Figure 10.78 Priestess of Isis • 360
Figure 10.79 Medical Instruments • 361
Figure 10.80 Herculaneum, House of the Telephus Relief • 362
Figure 10.81 Herculaneum, House of the Black Salon • 362
Figure 10.82 Herculaneum, House of the Corinthian Atrium • 363
Figure 10.83 Herculaneum, House of the Saminte • 364
Figure 10.84 Herculaneum Worship Shrine • 366
Figure 10.85 Herculaneum, House of the Augustals • 367
Figure 10.86 Herculaneum Augustals Plaque • 367
Figure 10.87 Clothing Finery • 368
Figure 10.88 Herculaneum Triclinium • 370

Figure 11.1   Revelation, Act 2 • 377
Figure 11.2   Apocalypse Tapestry, Rev 4 • 381
Figure 11.3   Griffin Artwork • 383
Figure 11.4   Inscription, Praise of God Hymn • 384
Figure 11.5   Scroll in Hand • 386
Figure 11.6   Ancient Seals • 387
Figure 11.7   Apocalypse Tapestry, Rev 5:6 • 392
Figure 11.8   Douce Apocalypse, Rev 5:6 • 393
Figure 11.9   Roman Incense Altar • 396
Figure 11.10 Imperial Inscription, Sardis • 399
Figure 11.11 Judgment Cycle (Rev 6–20) • 401
Figure 11.12 Seals and Mark 13 • 402
Figure 11.13 Luther Bible, Rev 6:1–8 • 403
Figure 11.14 Apocalypse Tapestry, Rev 7:9 • 406
Figure 11.15 Apocalypse Tapestry, Rev 8:2 • 409
Figure 11.16 Trumpets and Egyptian Plagues • 409
Figure 11.17 Herculaneum, and Pompeii Victim • 410
Figure 11.18 Trumpets: Three Woes • 411
Figure 11.19 Apocalypse Tapestry, Rev 9:1 • 412
Figure 11.20 Apollo Inscription • 412
Figure 11.21 Hour of Trial • 417
Figure 11.22 Elijah on Mount Carmel • 418
Figure 11.23 Michelangelo's Moses • 418
Figure 11.24 Trumpet 7 and Dragon Cycle • 421
Figure 11.25 The Dragon Cycle • 422
Figure 11.26 Revelation 12 Intercalation • 423
Figure 11.27 Marriage of Zeus and Leto • 424
Figure 11.28 Douce Apocalypse, Rev 12:6 • 426
Figure 11.29 Douce Apocalypse, Rev 12:7 • 427
Figure 11.30 Rev 13 and Dan 7 • 431
Figure 11.31 Sea Beast Parody of Christ • 432
Figure 11.32 Apocalypse Tapestry, Rev 13:1 • 433
Figure 11.33 Land Beast Parody of Christ • 435
Figure 11.34 Apocalypse Tapestry, Rev 13:15 • 437
Figure 11.35 Apocalypse Tapestry, Rev 14:1–6 • 442
Figure 11.36 Second Angel's Babylon Announcement • 443
Figure 11.37 Luther Bible, Rev 14:14–20 • 446
Figure 11.38 Apollo Kylix • 450

Figure 11.39 Plague Parallels • 451
Figure 11.40 Pollio Aqueduct • 452
Figure 11.41 Aqueduct at Antioch of Pisidia • 452
Figure 11.42 Nymphaeum at Perge • 453
Figure 11.43 Trevi Fountain of Rome • 454
Figure 11.44 The Euphrates River • 456
Figure 11.45 Kidron Valley • 460
Figure 11.46 Bowl Judgments—Perspectives • 462
Figure 11.47 Claudius, Master of Land and Sea • 463
Figure 11.48 Babylon and Zion, New Jerusalem • 463
Figure 11.49 Theban Dionysus • 465
Figure 11.50 Luther Bible, Rev 17 • 466
Figure 11.51 Roman Gold Jewelry • 467
Figure 11.52 Pompeii Aristocratic Woman • 467
Figure 11.53 Injured Aeneas • 468
Figure 11.54 Hadrian Military Cuirass • 469
Figure 11.55 Domitian's *Damnatio Memoriae* • 470
Figure 11.56 The Seven Kings of Rev 17 • 471
Figure 11.57 Literary Form of Rev 18 • 475
Figure 11.58 Ephesus Ivory Panel Relief • 476
Figure 11.59 Luxuries of an Empire • 477
Figure 11.60 Roman Glass Perfume Bottles • 478
Figure 11.61 Relief of the Conquered Galatian • 479
Figure 11.62 Roman Glass Vase • 480
Figure 11.63 Douce Apocalypse, Rev 18:21 • 482
Figure 11.64 Roman Street Players • 483
Figure 11.65 Roman Millstone at Pompeii • 483
Figure 11.66 Roman Glass and Alabaster Krater • 484
Figure 11.67 Roman Bronze Lamp • 484
Figure 11.68 Roman Sarcophagus • 484
Figure 11.69 Parallel Structure • 491
Figure 11.70 Triumphal Quadriga (Horses of St. Mark) • 493
Figure 11.71 Gold Myrtle Wreath Crown • 493
Figure 11.72 Arch of Septimius Severus • 495
Figure 11.73 Olive Press • 496
Figure 11.74 Second Crusaders Find First Crusader Remains • 497
Figure 11.75 Douce Apocalypse, Rev 19:19 • 498
Figure 11.76 Luther Bible, Rev 20:2 • 503

Figure 11.77 Millennium Intercalation • 509
Figure 11.78 Gog and Magog as the Hour of Trial • 511
Figure 11.79 Douce Apocalypse, Rev 20:7–8 • 513
Figure 11.80 Apocalypse Tapestry, Rev 20:9–10 • 516
Figure 11.81 Judgment of the World • 518
Figure 11.82 Fresco of Christ's Judgment of the World • 520
Figure 11.83 Mosaic of Christ's Last Judgment • 521
Figure 12.1 Revelation, Act 3 • 525
Figure 12.2 Oceanus, Roman Sea God • 527
Figure 12.3 Apocalypse Tapestry, Rev 21:2 • 528
Figure 12.4 A Tale of Two Cities • 531
Figure 12.5 Relief of Assyrian Assault on Lachish • 532
Figure 12.6 Masada Fortress • 533
Figure 12.7 Roman Siege • 533
Figure 12.8 Triple Arch Gate of Thyatira • 534
Figure 12.9 Triple Arch Gate of Antioch of Pisidia • 534
Figure 12.10 Erastus Inscription at Corinth • 535
Figure 12.11 Babylonian Ziggurat Model • 536
Figure 12.12 Precious Stone Necklace • 537
Figure 12.13 Jerusalem Temple Model • 538
Figure 12.14 Sunrise on Cadillac Mountain • 539
Figure 12.15 Apocalypse Tapestry, Rev 22:1 • 541
Figure 12.16 Perge Canal • 542
Figure 12.17 Date Palms of Galilee • 543
Figure 12.18 Bronze Relief, Creation of Adam and Eve • 544
Figure 12.19 Epistolary Genre *Inclusio* • 547
Figure 12.20 Motif Connections • 548
Figure 12.21 *Cave Canem* • 552
Figure 12.22 Tomb of David • 553
Figure 12.23 Temple of Aphrodite • 555
Figure 12.24 Heavenly Rider Motif • 555
Figure 12.25 Herculaneum Fountain • 556
Figure 12.26 Ancient Scribes • 557
Figure 12.27 Church of the Holy Sepulcher • 559
Figure 12.28 Codex Sinaiticus at Rev 22:21 • 561
Figure 12.29 Berea Paul Shrine • 563
Figure 12.30 Paul and Laodicea • 563
Figure E-1 Revelation: A Three-Act Play of God's Judgment • 569

Figure E-2   Gladiator Helmet • 570
Figure E-3   Griffins Galore • 570
Figure E-4   Emperor Trajan (98–117) • 572
Figure E-5   Apollo Inscription • 573
Figure E-6   The Risen Christ • 575

FIGURE P-1. Signorelli's Judgment Angels. Signorelli's fresco masterpiece (1499–1502) depicting scenes of the Apocalypse in the chapel of the Madonna di San Brizio in Orvieto, Italy. This scene is over the doorway exiting the chapel nave back into the main auditorium of the Orvieto Cathedral. Tour guides love to point out the "death rays" of the angels of divine judgment, apparently under the spell of having seen one too many Star Trek movies. Signorelli's images and scenes, while a Renaissance masterpiece, inadvertently reveal the serious problem in art and in theology in trying to understand the operation of the judgment of God. The matter becomes acute in preconceived ideas of our own age that we unthinkingly and automatically import into our reading of the book of Revelation that take us so far afield of John's meaning we lose the canonical and gospel moorings of his message.

Preface

Over my years of teaching the book of Revelation, my students have begged me to write what I taught. "Why?" I protested. "We have great commentaries." I was quite serious. Twenty-five years ago we had a dearth of academic commentaries, but today, the plethora of resources is embarrassing. Their answer was disarmingly simple. "We do not want another commentary. We want your thoughts and reflections." I did not have an answer for that one. I do have some thoughts that they find challenging. I know because I see and hear their reaction in and out of class. Thus was born this publication. I capitulated.

I have two points about the book of Revelation. First, we must re-canonize the book. False prophets, failed prophecies, and feckless interpreters have made the book a joke for late night comedians, a word to be ignored, and the playground of fools. We have to be careful not to eviscerate the authority of the book with bogus "signs of the times" preaching that is oblivious to the history of the interpretation of the book, which shows without any question the absolute absurdity of such a superficial grasp of the meaning of the visions. We have to bring the authority of the book back, but I most certainly am not talking about making a movie about the hell of Antichrist nor the horrors of Armageddon. How do I envision reclaiming the authority of the book if we do not have the prophetic pyrotechnics of Jesus burning eyeballs out of their sockets with his thermonuclear power rays at the Second Coming? That is my second point.

If Revelation is not about the gospel, the book is not Christian. I insist that my students demonstrate New Testament concord with any interpretive scheme they put forward. I insist that if the book does not preach Jesus Christ crucified, its pages never should have found their way into the New Testament. Christ crucified is the only gospel—the only way, the only truth, the only life, and the only future. I tell my students the only future in Revelation is the future you can know from the past. I am not amillennial, premillennial, or postmillennial. I am passion-millennial. I will have to unpack the thought later in the book. You can get a sneak peak of the trajectory I will plot for the prophecies of Revelation in the two essays I wrote in the earlier publication that I edited.[1]

As I wrote previously, my journey into eschatology began as a teenager absorbing the dispensationalism of my first study Bible, the *Scofield Reference Bible*, and a Texas radio preacher telling me how the events in the news that week had fulfilled some end-time prophecy. This "signs of the times" reading of this week's headlines at first was exhilarating, especially to think that Antichrist already was out there just waiting for his apocalyptic moment in the sun. As the weeks and months passed, though, I began to perceive the buffoonery of constant revisions of what was said only a few weeks ago. My (dispensational) premillennial days of high school and college gave way to the amillennial days of seminary and ministry. (Full disclosure: the third option, postmillennialism, never had a rational chance in my thinking given the tragic realities of two world wars in the twentieth century and the horrors of the slaughter of millions by mustard gas, Holocaust ovens, and nuclear bombs.) When I returned to my alma mater to teach, my journey continued in reflecting on Revelation's visions. The history of interpretation makes me wonder if John never realized how encoding the gospel in apocalypse was going to spin so wildly out of hermeneutical control. Even so, I hope to show that Revelation is a great book with which to end the Bible. My own reading of John's Apocalypse is that he anticipates the church's finest hour. I hope to tell that story in this book.

Gerald L. Stevens
New Orleans, Louisiana
Easter 2014

---

[1] Stevens, *Essays on Revelation*.

Abbreviations

ANTC	Abingdon New Testament Commentaries
BEC	The Bible Exposition Commentary
BECNT	Baker Exegetical Commentary on the New Testament
BJS	Brown Judaic Studies
BNTC	Black's New Testament Commentaries
BRS	The Biblical Resource Series
CCSNS	Cincinnati Classical Studies, New Series
CIS	Copenhagen International Seminar
CJ	The Classical Journal
ESV	English Standard Version
EGT	The Expositor's Greek Testament
GNT^4	*Greek New Testament*, 4th Edition
HCSB	Holman Christian Standard Bible
HTS	Harvard Theological Studies
ICC	International Critical Commentary
IDB	*Interpreter's Dictionary of the Bible*
INTF	Institute for New Testament Textual Research
IVPNT	InterVarsity Press New Testament
JBL	Journal of Biblical Literature
JSNT	Journal for the Study of the New Testament
JSNTSup	Journal for the Study of the New Testament Supplement
JSPSS	Journal for the Study of the Pseudepigrapha Supplement Series
KJV	King James Version
LCL	Loeb Classical Library
NASB	New American Standard Bible
NBC21	New Bible Commentary: 21st Century Edition
NCBC	New Century Bible Commentary
NET	New English Translation
NICNT	New International Commentary on the New Testament

NIV	New International Version
NIVAC	The NIV Application Commentary
NJB	New Jerusalem Bible
NKJV	New King James Version
NLT	New Living Translation
NRSV	New Revised Standard Version
NTIC	The New Testament in Context
NTL	New Testament Library
NTM	New Testament Message: Biblical-Theological Commentary
OHE	The Oxford History of England
PBTM	Paternoster Biblical and Theological Monographs
PC	Proclamation Commentaries
PCCS	Paul in Critical Contexts Series
RBS	Resources for Biblical Study
SBG	Studies in Biblical Greek
SBLSS	Society of Biblical Literature Semeia Studies
SBLSymS	Society of Biblical Literature Symposium Series
SHBC	Smyth & Helwys Bible Commentary
SNTSMS	Society for New Testament Studies Monograph Series
SPNT	Studies on Personalities of the New Testament.
TCS	TEAMS Commentary Series
TJ	Trinity Journal
WBC	Word Biblical Commentary
WGRWSS	Writings from the Greco-Roman World Supplement Series

SCRIPTURE

OLD TESTAMENT

Gen	Genesis	Neh	Nehemiah
Exod	Exodus	Esth	Esther
Lev	Leviticus	Job	Job
Num	Numbers	Ps (*pl.* Pss)	Psalm (Psalms)
Deut	Deuteronomy	Prov	Proverbs
Josh	Joshua	Eccl	Ecclesiastes
Judg	Judges	Song	Song of Solomon
Ruth	Ruth	Isa	Isaiah
1–2 Sam	1–2 Samuel	Jer	Jeremiah
1–2 Kgs	1–2 Kings	Lam	Lamentations
1–2 Chr	1–2 Chronicles	Ezek	Ezekiel
Ezra	Ezra	Dan	Daniel

Hos	Hosea	Nah	Nahum
Joel	Joel	Hab	Habakkuk
Amos	Amos	Zeph	Zephaniah
Obad	Obadiah	Hag	Haggai
Jonah	Jonah	Zech	Zechariah
Mic	Micah	Mal	Malachi

New Testament

Matt	Matthew	1–2 Thess	1–2 Thessalonians
Mark	Mark	1–2 Tim	1–2 Timothy
Luke	Luke	Titus	Titus
John	John	Phlm	Philemon
Acts	Acts	Heb	Hebrews
Rom	Romans	Jas	James
1–2 Cor	1–2 Corinthians	1–2 Pet	1–2 Peter
Gal	Galatians	1–2–3 John	1–2–3 John
Eph	Ephesians	Jude	Jude
Phil	Philippians	Rev	Revelation
Col	Colossians		

Apocrypha

1–2 Macc	1–2 Maccabees
2 Esd	2 Esdras
Tob	Tobit

Pseudepigrapha

2 Bar.	*2 Baruch*
1 En.	*1 Enoch*
Jub.	*Jubilees*

Other Ancient Sources

Church Fathers

1–2 Clem.	*1–2 Clement*
Adv. Haer.	*Against Heresies*
Adv. Marc.	*Against Marcion*

Apology	*The First Apology*
Baptism	*On the Mysteries. II. Of Baptism*
Cat. Lect.	*Catechetical Lectures*
Dial.	*Dialogue with Trypho*
Embassy	*Embassy for the Christians (Presbeia peri Christianōn)*
Eph.	*To the Ephesians*
Mart. Poly.	*Martyrdom of Polycarp*
Panarion	*The Panarion of Epiphanius of Salamis*
Phil.	*To the Philippians*
Praes. Haer.	*De Praescriptione Haereticorum*
Quis Dives	*Quis Dives Salvetur*
Tr. John	*Tractates on John*

AUGUSTUS

Res Gestae	*Res Gestae Divi Augusti*

ARISTIDES

To Rome	*Encomium of Rome*

CICERO

Epis. Att.	*Epistulae ad Atticum*
Epis. Fam.	*Epistulae ad Familiares*

DIO CASSIUS

Dio Cassius	*Historia Romana (Roman History)*

EPICTETUS

Disc.	*The Discourses*

EUSEBIUS

H.E.	*Historia Ecclesiastica (Church History)*

HERODOTUS

Hist.	*The Histories*

HORACE

Car. Saec.   *Carmen Saeculare*
Epistles   *Epistularum liber secundus*

JERUSALEM TALMUD

Ta'anit   *Moed Ta'anit*

JOSEPHUS

Ant.   *Jewish Antiquities*
J.W.   *The Jewish War*

LACTANTIUS

Institutes   *Divine Institutes*
Persecutors   *On the Manner in which the Persecutors Died*

LIVY

Livy   *History of Rome*

MARTIAL

Epig.   *Epigrams*

PLINY THE ELDER

Nat. Hist.   *Natural History*

PLINY THE YOUNGER

Letters   *Epistulae*

PLUTARCH

Quaes. Gr.   *Quaestiones Graecae (The Greek Questions)*
Antony   *Life of Antony, Parallel Lives*

PROPERTIUS

Eleg.   *Elegies*

SIBYLLINE ORACLES

Sib. Or. *The Sibylline Oracles*

STRABO

Geog. *Geographica*

SUETONIUS

Dom. *Domitianus, De Vita Caesarum*
Nero *Nero, De Vita Caesarum*

TACITUS

Annals *The Annals of Tacitus*

VIRGIL

Aen. *Aeneid*
Ecl. *Eclogae*
Georg. *Georgics*

MUSEUMS

AAM	Antalya Archeoloji Müzesi, Antalya, Turkey
AMA	Aphrodisias Müzesi, Aphrodisias, Turkey
AMAC	Archeological Museum of Ancient Corinth, Greece
ASM	Attalos Stoa Museum, Athens, Greece
BHM	Burnt House Museum, Jerusalem, Israel
BMB	Bergama Müzesi, Bergama, Turkey
BML	British Museum, London, England
EMS	Ephesos Müzesi, Selçuk, Turkey
GPMM	Great Palace Mosaic Museum, Istanbul, Turkey
HAM	Hatay Archeoloji Müzesi, Turkey
HAMH	Hierapolis Archeoloji Müzesi, Hierapolis, Turkey
IAM	Istanbul Archeoloji Müzerleri, Istanbul, Turkey
IAMI	Izmir Archeoloji Müzesi, Izmir, Turkey
IMJ	Israel Museum, Jerusalem, Israel
KAM	Konya Archeoloji Müzesi, Turkey
LP	The Louvre, Paris, France

MCA	Museo Civico Archeologico, Orvieto, Italy
MMM	Manisa Müze, Manisa, Turkey
NAMA	National Archeological Museum of Athens, Greece
NNAM	Naples National Archeological Museum, Italy
PMB	Pergamon Museum, Berlin, Germany
ROM	Royal Ontario Museum, Toronto, Canada
SMS	Side Müzesi, Side, Turkey
TAM	Thessaloniki Archeological Museum, Greece
TMT	Tarsus Müze, Tarsus, Turkey
YMY	Yalvaç Müze, Yalvaç, Turkey

Part 1

Apollyon and Armageddon

Revelation's Apocalyptic Traditions and Their Interpretation in History

1

Tributaries of Tradition

Jewish Sources of John's Apocalyptic Traditions

HELPFUL IN KNOWING where you are is knowing where you have been. In interpreting the book of Revelation, a good question to ask is, Where have we been? Part 1 of this book seeks to answer this question. We want to explore the interpretation of the book of Revelation through the centuries in order to have some perspective on where we are today. Although John innovated numerous traditions in his composition, Jewish apocalyptic was his main source. Our focus first will be on Jewish historical periods that generated the primary sources of John's apocalyptic traditions. We then will survey major developments of John's apocalyptic traditions through the centuries.[1]

The mighty Mississippi River that divides the United States east and west and has had a major role in our nation's history is really the confluence of numerous tributaries. Likewise, the primary tributary flowing into John's apocalyptic is Jewish. Jewish apocalyptic developed in direct response to four dramatic periods in Jewish history. This history is tied up with the ebb and flow of four empires: Babylon, Persia, Greece, and Rome. These developments challenged Jewish

---

[1] The PBS video, "Apocalypse! The Story of the Book of Revelation," presents Revelation's apocalyptic traditions, their Jewish sources, and their interpretation and development throughout the church age. This video was produced right before the turn of the millennium, since so much attention was focused on millennial speculation at the time. The attention surrounding the turn of the millennium at the time actually is paradigmatic with one of the main problems of interpreting the book of Revelation—so much focus on a chronology trigger.

faith in God. Apocalyptic literature was an attempt to reassure Jewish faith by adjusting Jewish thought in the harsh light of new historical realities for the Jewish people. What were these developments following the history of these four empires?

BABYLONIAN PERIOD

The first development was the tragic loss of the Jewish state. In 586 B.C. the Babylonians destroyed both Jerusalem and its temple and sent the Jews into captivity. In this humiliating exile, the glorious kingdom of David had come to a bitter and cataclysmic end. Two powerful images in Jewish apocalyptic thought derive from this Babylonian period. One comes from the Jewish struggle upon return to rebuild their beautiful city of old, and the other image from exposure to Babylonian culture and thought.

FIGURE 1.1. Ishtar Gate of Babylon. This magnificent gate built by Nebuchadnezzar II in 575 B.C. is on the Processional Way through which statues of deities were paraded on New Years (PMB).

FIGURE 1.2. Jerusalem from the Mount of Olives. The view is of the old walls of the plateau on which the ancient temple stood.

New Jerusalem

As the Jews endured their exile, they mourned the loss of their nation, their homeland, and their way of life. "How deserted lies the city, once so full of people" (Lam 1:1, NIV). The total destruction of the city of Jerusalem and its great temple caused Jews to wonder, "Is all lost for us as a nation among the nations? Will we ever have another city and temple?" The prophet Ezekiel answers with a yes by realigning Jewish thought under the rubric of a "New Jerusalem" that would have its own equivalent new temple. Against the backdrop of Mosaic and Davidic traditions, however, Ezekiel's New Jerusalem was oddly configured, and his new temple was even more bizarre—not Mosaic in its architecture, personnel, or service. Ezekiel's prophetic visions were obtuse and entirely confusing to many Jews. Yet, in spite of these idiosyncrasies, Ezekiel's "New Jerusalem" image took traction in Jewish thought, inspired the imagination about a future place filled with God's presence in his city, and flowed into John's apocalyptic world.

FIGURE 1.3. Jerusalem Temple Model. Ancient Jewish temple mount as rebuilt by Herod the Great on scale of 1:50 (Holyland Model of Jerusalem, IMJ).

Resurrection

The prophet Ezekiel gave Jewish traditions another shot in the arm with his arresting vision of the valley of dry bones, Ezekiel's answer to the Babylonian exile (Ezek 37). The Jewish nation would reconstitute itself; i.e., the vision was about the Jewish nation, not individuals. The Persians conquered the Babylonian empire and brought Zoroastrian religion into Jewish thought with its already fully developed doctrine of resurrection. Jews began to synthesize Ezekiel's vision of dry bones with the Persian idea of the resurrection of individuals. We see Jewish resurrection ideas on their way to becoming doctrine in 2 Macc 7:14, "One cannot but choose to die at the hands of mortals and to cherish the hope God gives of being raised again by him. But for you there will be no resurrection to life!" Since 2 Maccabees is written by a Pharisee around 130–120 B.C., we are witnessing how the idea of resurrection especially found a home in the teaching of the Pharisees as reflected in the New Testament. Not all Jews, however, accepted such Pharisaic innovations. The Sadducees rejected this new teaching (cf. Acts 23:8).

FIGURE 1.4. Signorelli's Resurrection of the Flesh. Signorelli's masterpiece (1499–1502) from the frescos depicting scenes of the Apocalypse in the chapel of the Madonna di San Brizio in Orvieto, Italy.

PERSIAN PERIOD

The second historical development was the renewal of the Jewish state. Cyrus I of Persia had conquered the Babylonians in 540 B.C. In the Bible, he is described as God's anointed "messiah," according to Isa 45:1. Cyrus was lenient and allowed the Jews to return to their homeland.

FIGURE 1.5. Cyrus Cylinder. Records deeds of the Persian king Cyrus who repatriated displaced peoples, including Jews (BML). Credit: Renate Viveen Hood.

Jews who returned brought back with them their exposure to Persian religious thought, especially Zoroastrianism. Zoroaster was a sixth century B.C. Iranian prophet who attempted to reform Persian religion with an emphasis on a form of dualism and his own brand of monotheism. His teachings are thought to have had significant impact on the major Western religious traditions. In addition to developed reflections on resurrection doctrine, two other important Persian contributions were an emphasis on the religious metaphor of light and darkness and a dramatic story of the final apocalyptic battle between the forces of good and evil that eventuates in the arrival of the kingdom of God on earth.

Light and Darkness

The language of light and darkness was a central feature of Zoroastrian religion due to its dualism. This symbolism integrally was tied to the concept of earth as a cosmic battleground between good, the forces of light, and evil, the forces of darkness. While the concepts of light and darkness can be found as religious metaphor in many religious writings around the world, the key in the Zoroastrian framework is the use of this metaphorical language to describe opposing forces of good and evil in a cosmic conflict worked out on the stage of human history that will continue worsening until consummated in a final war that brings about a new age. While Jewish religious thought properly is not dualistic, the ideas of two ages, an age of evil followed by an age of good, of cosmic conflict of opposing forces of good and evil, and of a final battle, can be traced in Jewish writings that emerge during this time of exposure to Persian thought flowing into the first century. One can note how John styles his first vision of the Apocalypse as a vision in the night, with his seven lampstands, which are the churches. The only light in the dark world of pagan empire comes from Christ and his churches (Rev 1:9–20).[2]

Final Battle

One of the most enduring images that developed in apocalyptic literature to fire human imagination is that of the Zoroastrian final battle, or, as Saddam Hussein described the original Gulf War of 1991, "the mother of all battles." Zoroaster invented apocalyptic war language, which then flowed into many streams. His language of apocalyptic war seems evidenced particularly at Qumran, a Jewish sectarian group that

---

[2]See Stevens, "A Vision in the Night," *Essays on Revelation*, 1–15.

separated from what they considered to be Jerusalem's corrupt temple cultus in the Roman Period. Their martial document, *The War of the Sons of Light and the Sons of Darkness*, details that final apocalyptic showdown. This battle would feature the inhabitants of Qumran as key participants. Their priestly army would bring in the kingdom of God by defeating pagan oppressors of Israel and purifying the corrupt Jerusalem cult and its worship. They decided the Jewish revolt that broke out against Rome in A.D. 66 was their anticipated final battle. They marched out of their desert commune in battle array to defeat, with God's expected intervention, the advancing Roman legions under Vespasian coming down from Galilee. They were slaughtered out of human memory until their scrolls were rediscovered nearly two thousand years later bringing to light their community and their story.

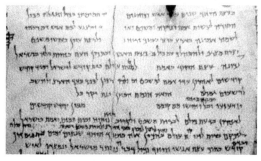

FIGURE 1.6. Reproduction of a Qumran Scroll. (Qumran National Park, Israel).

In Revelation, this war imagery acutely and powerfully is summarized in one famous word that has entered into the mainstream of American popular jargon—Armageddon (Rev 16:16). Tour groups to Israel often are taken to the top of Tel Megiddo to be told with dramatic flair the Jezreel Valley or Plain of Esdraelon before them is to be the scene of the "greatest battle of all history."

FIGURE 1.7. Tel Megiddo's Overview of the Jezreel Valley. This valley is the supposed location of the final showdown of God and evil, Revelation's battle of Armageddon.

In contemporary popular culture, one has the fictional efforts of the "Left Behind" series of Tim LaHaye and Jerry Jenkins, which has garnished significant commercial success dramatizing this supposed end-time plot of Antichrist and his war with Christ. The series even has been transformed into cinematic drama.³ Of course, LaHaye and Jenkins did not invent the modern prophecy novel genre. Already in the 1930s we have publication of a similar piece in Oilar's novelette, *Be Thou Prepared, for Jesus is Coming*.⁴

GREEK PERIOD

The third development was Hellenism. Alexander the Great (336–323 B.C.) conquered the world with his armies and revolutionized society and culture with his cosmopolitan vision. Alexander thought all civilization should be Greek ("Hellenistic"). Alexander's "Hellenism" eventually became a giant social, religious, and cultural melting pot in which various traditions, including those of the Jews, began to interact together.

FIGURE 1.8. Alexander the Great Coin. Imaged in lion's mane as a conqueror (PMB).

Ideas that percolated in this potent brew included angels and demons on the Greek side and images of empire on the Jewish side.

Angels and Demons

The book of *1 Enoch* is a composite Hellenistic Jewish work, but its main traditions can be dated back to about 250 B.C. Enochian traditions illustrate new and developing Jewish ideas in the interaction with Hellenistic traditions. One such tradition is the development of a sophisticated hierarchy of angels and their story world. In one legend a head angel is cast down to earth. Such an idea is reflected in John's Red Dragon cast down to earth (Rev 12:9). Another tradition involved

---

³LaHaye and Jenkins, *Left Behind: A Novel of the Earth's Last Days*, 1995; cf. *Left Behind: The Movie*, directed by Victor Sarin, 96 minutes, 2000. Nicolas Cage and Lea Thompson star in the 2014 remake, *Left Behind*, directed by Vic Armstrong.

⁴Oilar, *Be Thou Prepared, for Jesus is Coming*, 1937. See the discussion in Boyer, *When Time Shall Be No More: Prophecy Belief in Modern American Culture*, 106.

the idea of devils. These stories feature a dramatic victory of God over forces of evil, along with a concrete idea of heaven and hell.

FIGURE 1.9. Damned Taken to Hell and Received by Demons. Luca Signorelli's masterpiece (1499–1502) of frescos depicting scenes of the Apocalypse in the chapel of the Madonna di San Brizio in Orvieto, Italy.

Pharisees in Jesus' day, for example, had absorbed and developed angelic traditions during the intertestamental period and effectively communicated these ideas to the general Jewish populace in popular Pharisaic literature, such as the book of Tobit, written in the second century B.C. As the story is told, Tobit is the father of Tobias, who has to send his son on a journey of which Tobias is unacquainted with the way. So, Tobias has to find a guide. God sends an angel for this task, but Tobias seems unaware of the special identity of his chosen companion: "So Tobias went out to look for a man to go with him to Media, someone who was acquainted with the way. He went out and found the angel Raphael standing in front of him; but he did not perceive that he was an angel of God" (Tob 5:4).

In this narrative, God's angel Raphael, whom Tobit believes is his kinsman Azariah, instructs Tobit in making a potion from the organs of a fish Tobit just caught. This potion is for the exorcism of a demon and healing of eyes. The language of exorcism and healing suddenly sets us up on familiar ground. Such topics are dominant features of our Gospel stories. This episode is given prominent early position in Tobit's trip, because he will need the potions later. So, the story illustrates a clear trajectory in our Jewish traditions that will become integral to the story of Jesus and the early church.

FIGURE 1.10. Raphael Instructs Tobit on Demon Exorcism. Painting exposed to heat and humidity in an exterior hallway (San Marco Convent, Florence, Italy).

Here is this interesting narrative from the book of Tobit.

> Then the young man went down to wash his feet in the Tigris river. Suddenly a large fish leaped up from the water and tried to swallow the young man's foot, and he cried out. But the angel said to the young man, "Catch hold of the fish and hang on to it!" So the young man grasped the fish and drew it up on the land. Then the angel said to him, "Cut open the fish and take out its gall, heart, and liver. Keep them with you, but throw away the intestines. For its gall, heart, and liver are useful as medicine." So after cutting open the fish the young man gathered together the gall, heart, and liver; then he roasted and ate some of the fish, and kept some to be salted. The two continued on their way together until they were near Media. Then the young man questioned the angel and said to him, "Brother Azariah, what medicinal value is there in the fish's heart and liver, and in the gall?" He replied, "As for the fish's heart and liver, you must burn them to make a smoke in the presence of a man or woman afflicted by a demon or evil spirit, and every affliction will flee away and never remain with that person any longer. And as for the gall, anoint a person's eyes where white films have appeared on them; blow upon them, upon the white films, and the eyes will be healed" (Tob 6:3–9, NRSV).

Another example that shows these broader ideas in the culture taking root in Jewish tradition is the concept of Abaddon, the place of death and destruction (Job 26:6; 28:22; 31:12). Abaddon personified becomes a satanic, demonic figure of destruction in Jewish traditions. John takes up this Jewish figure for use as a destroyer image in Revelation, but John strikingly renames Revelation's correlate with the "Apollyon" appellation, which is made up, but probably based on the Greek verb for "destroyer" (*apollymi*). In Revelation's story he is the destroyer angel of the Abyss (Rev 9:11). Whatever the derivation, John's designation comes off as a deliberate, almost provocative, play on the Greek name Apollo, the Greek god whom the Roman emperor Domitian claimed to be, or to be related to, among other gods as well, such as Minerva.

FIGURE 1.11. Domitian Coin. Minerva with long spear, victory shield on the ground. A thunderbolt in her right hand represents divinity, closely associating Domitian with the gods (HAM).

FIGURE 1.12. Ephesus: Domitian Altar Frieze. Evidence for the emperor cult in Ephesus, this frieze is part of the base of the altar for the worship of the emperor Domitian in Ephesus (EMS).

Images of Empire

The biblical book of Daniel, irrespective of the arguments of date, clearly is written for the context of the Maccabean Revolt (167 B.C.). This revolt represented the Jewish struggle against the enforced

Hellenism of Syrian overlords.[5] Daniel is important for understanding the on-going development of apocalyptic traditions, especially the idea of God's sovereignty over pagan world empires. The story is a dream.

In the story, the Babylonian king, Nebuchadnezzar, had had a disturbing dream. The central feature in Nebuchadnezzar's dream was a colossal statue of mixed material composition; none of his soothsayers could divine the dream. Daniel, however, illuminated by God's wisdom, was able to give the king the interpretation. The dream was the story of four successive world empires (Dan 2:31–45), beginning with Nebuchadnezzar's own kingdom. The end of the story was the coming of God's own kingdom, which would break into pieces all the previous kingdoms and would stand forever. This dramatic, colossal statue depicts God's sovereignty over all pagan empires. Daniel's imagery of the shattered statue evoking the end of world empires (and, hence, logically, the end of history) is meant to communicate that the time of the oppressed people of God would come. God's dominion over the kingdoms of the world would be established.

FIGURE 1.13. Smith: The Great World Kingdom Image. An illustration in Uriah Smith's 1897 Adventist publication, *Daniel and the Revelation: the Response of History to the Voice of Prophecy*.

Daniel's message to faithful Jews of God's ultimate sovereignty, even over pagan world empires, as set in the context of Babylon's King

---

[5]The issue of the historical context of Daniel and the application of its prophecy, especially the dispensational perspective, will be treated later in the discussion.

Nebuchadnezzar (605–562), came home to Jews living in Judea in the enforced Hellenism of the Syrian king Antiochus IV Epiphanes (175–164 B.C.). This king was infamous among Jews, especially due to his claim as *Epiphanes* ("God manifest"), that is, the visible representation on earth of the gods (1 Macc 1:10). He minted coins with this claim. Jews among themselves changed one letter of the name to convert this title in derision to *Epimanes*, which meant "mad man."

Antiochus IV also was infamous for his sacrifice of a pig on the Jewish altar in Jerusalem to enforce his Hellenization in 167 B.C. This pagan sacrilege left the Jewish altar desolate for three years until reconsecrated by Judas Maccabeus in 164 B.C. (1 Macc 4:36–61). The literal three years of abomination became a symbolic three and a half year period in Jewish apocalyptic literature on the symbolic pattern of half of a significant number (as in 2 Esd 14:12; Dan 7:25; 12:7).

FIGURE 1.14. Antiochus IV Coin. Zeus seated, holding Nike and scepter. The inscription is BASILEŌS ANTIOXOU, THEOU EPIPHANOUS, NIKĒPHOROU (HAM).

Daniel's message, whether to Jews oppressed by pagan kings like Nebuchadnezzar or by Antiochus IV, is the same: hold fast, God will deliver, and soon. Jewish apocalyptic forever would carry Daniel's heritage of Jewish rejection of all pagan empire claims to ultimate power and authority.

FIGURE 1.15. Pompeii Fresco of Pig Sacrifice. Pig sacrifice was a standard part of religious ritual in many Hellenistic religions in the Greco-Roman world (NNAM).

The spirit of King Nebuchadnezzar and the Syrian Antiochus IV would be revisited in later Roman emperors such as Caligula (37–41), Nero (54–68), and Domitian (81–96). No matter how powerful their earthly throne nor majestic their present rule, the apocalyptic response to such sovereign claims of all pagan kings was consistent and clear: ultimate destiny is under God's sovereignty as Lord of Lords. In apocalyptic images of empire, the statue always is shattered: "Fallen, fallen is Babylon the Great!" (Rev 18:2).

FIGURE 1.16. Roman Imperial Coins. Left to right: Caligula, 37–41; Nero, 54–68; Domitian, 81–96 (MCA, PMB).

ROMAN PERIOD

The fourth development was Roman patronage. As the Jews under the Maccabees were regaining their independence from the Syrians from 167–140 B.C., the shadow of Rome already was advancing on the entire Mediterranean world. The Maccabean dynastic heirs were the Hasmoneans (140–37 B.C.), who had to deal with this rising Roman power now controlling events in Judea (1 Macc 14:40–41). They ruled as client kings under a Roman patronage system. Thus, rulers in Judea had to show loyalty to Rome. This Roman client kingship came to fullest expression in the reign of Herod the Great (37–4 B.C.) after transition from the Hasmonean to the Herodian dynasty. Some Jews supported Roman patronage, particularly Sadducees, with their vested interests in preserving the political status quo as a way of maintaining their key institution of the temple in Jerusalem. Other Jews, on the other hand, despised Herod as a usurper to the Jewish throne and Herod's Roman overlords as the epitome of pagan empire attempting to rise up against God's sovereign claims over Israel and the nations.

FIGURE 1.17. Jerusalem Bronze, 11 B.C. Rome gave client kings the right to mint coins. Herod the Great minted this coin a few years before Jesus was born (PMB).

Roman Collusion

For some Jews, the Jewish temple in Jerusalem no longer was a sign of God's presence in Israel. Rather, the temple and its Saducean controllers were a sign of collusion with Roman overlords. Jews protested. One such protest movement was Qumran. These desert dwellers had separated themselves from Jerusalem and its elite, priestly cultus. They followed a charismatic leader, the Teacher of Righteousness, about a century and a half before the time of Jesus. Among their library of writings, known as the Dead Sea Scrolls, their commentary on the prophet Habakkuk illustrates an important "pesher" method that all readers of Revelation would do well to understand. This way of reading the text is simple: contemporize the prophetic text by completely ignoring the original historical context of the prophet and his audience. Instead, simply equate *any* given prophetic text with *any* current news. In this way, the inhabitants at Qumran could convert any verse in Habakkuk into today's news about the Romans and their lackeys, the Hasmonean client kings so despised who controlled the high priesthood. In terms of Revelation's apocalyptic traditions, one can witness this "pesher" way of reading today's headlines back into prophetic texts repeating itself over and over throughout the centuries of church history, and especially today on Internet websites.[6]

FIGURE 1.18. Qumran Caves. The Dead Sea Scrolls were discovered in the caves surrounding the settlement at Qumran. The center entrance in this picture is to Cave 4, the most famous, repository of 200 books and fragments, of which 122 were biblical.

Other protests against Roman patronage were registered by John the Baptist and Jesus. John preached national repentance out in the

---

[6]For more on this "pesher" style hermeneutic at Qumran, consult Klein, Blomberg, and Hubbard, *Introduction to Biblical Interpretation*, 27–28.

desert, probably because he rejected the city of Jerusalem as polluted by the presence of a pagan occupying army, and Jerusalem's temple as polluted by the service of a fully corrupt priesthood that offered daily sacrifice on behalf of the Roman emperor and Saducean high priests who had sold their souls to Rome under Annas and his family. Jesus as well made a dramatic and prophetic condemnation of the temple's Saducean authorities by throwing out their money changers, whose commercial activities in the Court of the Gentiles not only lined Saducean pockets but, as well, polluted any chance for Gentiles to worship the God of Israel in an honorable place of sanctity and holiness. In the face of Jewish collusion with Roman overlords, both John the Baptist and Jesus preached an apocalyptic message of the imminent, in-breaking kingdom of God. While neither John the Baptist nor Jesus show any direct dependence on the Dead Sea Scrolls, the Scrolls illustrate similar reaction and revulsion on the part of some Jews to the detested Roman occupation of Judea and all Jewish groups in collusion with their Roman patrons.

First Jewish War

Jews eventually revolted against Rome in the First Jewish War (A.D. 66–70). Jewish rebels in Jerusalem threw out the Saducean high priests and installed their own. The purification of Jerusalem and her priesthood was on, as in the days of old with the famous warrior Judas Maccabeus.

FIGURE 1.19. The Burnt House. Excavated 1969–1982, this priestly home near the ancient Jerusalem temple belonged to the wealthy Kathros family and was destroyed by the Romans in the final conflagration a month after the destruction of the temple and Lower City. The Romans killed the last surviving remnants of the wealthy aristocrats of the Upper City, who already were ravaged by disease and starving to death, and burned everything in a furious fire (BHM).

With the outbreak of hostilities, some Jews naturally concluded the final battle had arrived that presaged the arrival of God's kingdom on earth. God and his holy angels would defeat

Israel's enemies. Inhabitants at Qumran were convinced the final war was on, but were wrong. Though annihilated as a Jewish sect, they left the power of their apocalyptic light and darkness language, with its images of a final conflict fought by God against all evil forces arrayed against God's people, to be absorbed and invoked by later apocalyptic writers, including the Jewish authors of *2 Baruch* and 2 Esdras—and John of Patmos. With its "pesher" method of interpreting the prophets in light of contemporary events, Qumran reflects the perpetual apocalyptic impulse to make one's own time the end time. In a way, they are precursors of historicist periodizers and futurist "signs of the times" preachers beguiling gullible audiences but constantly contradicted.

FIGURE 1.20. Roman Civil War. Imperial coins of Galba, June–January, 68–69, Otho, January–April, 69, and Vitellius, April–December, 69 (PMB).

General Vespasian conducted most of the campaign against the Jews in Judea on behalf of Emperor Nero. However, Nero's suicide in 68 threw Rome into political chaos. Civil war ensured among three successive emperors in eighteen months (Galba, Otho, and Vitellius). Vespasian's eastern legions, however, acclaimed him as emperor. He returned to Rome, ousted Vitellius, and started a new dynastic imperial family. His son, General Titus, was left to finish the siege of Jerusalem. The city resisted to the point of severe famine and desperation, but finally fell in the spring of A.D. 70 with great loss of life. Still visible today is the street damage in the southwest corner of the ancient walls where paving stones on the street below were crushed by the falling upper structures of the temple walls near Robinson's Arch. This destruction is silent testimony to how truly horrible the final end of Jerusalem and its temple must have been. Thousands of Jews were killed in those last, desperate hours. Jesus' words, "not one stone will be left here upon another," tragically were fulfilled.[7]

---

[7] Matt 24:2; Mark 13:2; Luke 21:6.

FIGURE 1.21. Damaged Jerusalem Street. First Jewish War damage still visible today.

FIGURE 1.22. Judea Capta Sestertius. Judea captured by the Romans; obverse: laureate head Vespasian; reverse: JVDEA CAPTA; date palm emblem of Judea center; bound Jew, left; mourning Jewess seated right. Struck to commemorate the Roman victory in First Jewish War; extremely rare (MCA).

Jerusalem fell in part because she was in chaos inside the walls of the city. Various factions of Jews vied for power and fought amongst themselves for control of the city. Simon ben Giora was one of these factional leaders. Simon fought on for a brief time in the Upper City even after the capture of the Lower City and the temple. Eventually, he was captured in the final days of the city's destruction by the Romans. He was taken to Rome, led in a triumphal march, and then executed. The Jewish menorah and other spoils of the temple were paraded down Rome's streets and carved into the Arch of Titus.

FIGURE 1.23. Mamertine Prison Plaque. Roman incarceration often was a temporary holding cell awaiting execution. War prisoners were held, then humiliated in chains in the Roman general's victory parade down Rome's streets, then executed. On this plaque is the name Simon ben Giora, Jewish Zealot leader inside Jerusalem in the First Jewish War, who was captured, taken to Rome, paraded, and executed.

FIGURE 1.24. Triumphal Arch of Titus. This arch at one end of the Roman Forum near the ancient Colosseum celebrates the Roman victory over the Jews in the First Jewish War under the Roman general Titus in the spring of A.D. 70.

FIGURE 1.25. Arch of Titus: Jewish Menorah Relief. Roman war booty from the First Jewish War included precious items from the Jewish temple. One notable item was the Menorah, depicted here as part of the triumphal parade in a relief on the interior of the Arch of Titus.

Many Christians at the time interpreted the destruction of Jerusalem and its temple as the apocalyptic prelude to the kingdom. This judgment of God meant the end of the world was just around the corner. Luke writes Luke-Acts to suggest something else is going on with the "kingdom of God" that requires a gospel mission (Acts 1:6–8).

Jews also struggled to interpret the significance of these dramatic and life-changing events. The postwar period of A.D. 70–100 also saw a flurry of new Jewish apocalypses trying to interpret the disastrous results of the First Jewish War. A good example is 2 Esdras.[8] Often quoted in the early church fathers, received as Scripture in the Ethiopian Orthodox Church, and preserved in Roman Catholic traditions, the text was included in early King James editions. Stylistic patterns in 2 Esdras reoccur in Revelation. Note this symbolic language:

> But if the Most High grants that you live, you shall see it
> thrown into confusion after the third period;
>   and the sun shall suddenly begin to shine at night,
>   and the moon during the day.
>   Blood shall drip from wood,
>   and the stone shall utter its voice;
>   the peoples shall be troubled,
>   and the stars shall fall.
> And one shall reign whom those who inhabit the earth do not
> expect, and the birds shall fly away together; and the Dead Sea

---

[8]Naming conventions for this work are confusing because of the complex history of composition and the transmission in Latin versions across the centuries. All or parts of the work have received designations of *2*, *3*, *4*, *5*, or *6 Ezra*. The designations 2 Esdras or *4 Esdras* derive from Latin traditions related to the work of Jerome, which came into English Bible translations.

shall cast up fish; and one whom the many do not know shall make his voice heard by night, and all shall hear his voice. There shall be chaos also in many places, fire shall often break out, the wild animals shall roam beyond their haunts, and menstruous women shall bring forth monsters. Salt waters shall be found in the sweet, and all friends shall conquer one another; then shall reason hide itself, and wisdom shall withdraw into its chamber (2 Esd 5:4–9, NRSV).

Another example of the shared imagery between the Jewish apocalypse of 2 Esdras written within the same timeframe as the book of Revelation is the symbolic use of the number seven. Even a cursory reading shows the author of 2 Esdras's penchant for the symbolic use of seven (cf. 7:80, 91, 101; 9:23).

A final example of shared imagery is use of a woman as symbol for a city. In 2 Esdras, the visionary is confronted by a strange woman in an open field. Ensuing conversation with her makes clear that the burden of the conversation is the fall of Jerusalem and the destruction of its temple (10:20–21). Dramatically, this strange woman suddenly is transformed before the seer's eyes into that glorious city (10:27). In Revelation, likewise, a woman is a symbol for a city, but, in this case, a negative symbol. She is "Babylon," the mother of harlots. So, the genus of the old empire, eternal nemesis of Judaism, literarily rises again. Daniel is reprised. This evil "Babylon" is destroyed by God precipitously (Rev 14:8; 16:9; 17:5; 18:2, 10, 21).

John of Patmos

John of Patmos is another negative reaction to Roman patronage, but from within the Christian world of the late first century. We have clear evidence for the pervasive presence of the imperial cult in the provinces of Asia Minor where we find all of Revelation's seven churches. Significantly, emperor worship in these provinces had grown dramatically under Vespasian's second son, Domitian (d. 96).[9] In the context of the popularity of the emperor cult in Asia Minor at this time, John interpreted conditions in his own churches in western Asia as rank compromise with Rome and intolerable. We will illustrate the Roman imperial background and John's imagery at a later stage of the book.

---

[9]See the excellent summary in Johnson, "Confronting the Beast: The Imperial Cult and the Book of Revelation," 130–41.

John's powerful imagery applied to Rome, but his point actually was not Rome. The Inaugural Vision of the Son of Man and the seven lampstands (Rev 1:9–20) makes clear his point was the church. As the following history of interpretation will show, John was the victim of his own success. As the writer of an apocalypse, he had mastered allusion, symbol, and metaphor. Unfortunately for John, the images of his visions that fired the imaginations of later readers were not those of the Son of Man and the lampstands. Rather, they were those of the beasts, Apollyon, Armageddon, and millennium. John's visions were interpreted as suggesting that the fall of Rome was imminent. The failure of this expectation might explain why the book of Revelation was ignored almost completely in Christendom in its area of origin in the east for almost a hundred years. Ironically, attention in the east was by the heretic Montanus (A.D. 172) in his failed attempt to predict the "New Jerusalem" arriving near Pepuza in Phrygia of Asia. While John made clear the beast was Rome, to read him canonically, we have to recognize he was talking more about the church than about the beast.

Tributaries of John's Apocalyptic Traditions			
Period	Development	Sources	Ideas
Babylonian Exile	Destruction	Ezekiel	• New Jerusalem • resurrection
Persian Return	Restoration	Zoroaster	• light/darkness • final battle
Greek Conquest	Hellenization	Daniel	• angels/demons • empire images
Roman Empire	Patronage	2 Baruch 2 Esdras	• collusion • First Jewish War

FIGURE 1.26. Tributaries of Tradition. Major Jewish apocalyptic traditions deriving from four major periods of Jewish history flow into the writing of John's Apocalypse.

SUMMARY

Numerous tributaries flow into John's powerful apocalyptic river. Various empires against which Jewish history was written became the watersheds for these tributaries of apocalyptic developments in Jewish thought. The tragic loss of the Jewish state in the Babylonian period produced the powerful and evocative imagery of a New Jerusalem and resurrection. The renewal of the Jewish state in the Persian period saw Jews returning to their homeland impacted by the symbolic language of light and darkness and an apocalyptic war decisively concluding the spiritual struggle of good and evil. Hellenism's global spread in the Greek period permeating every element of society introduced highly developed ideas of angels and demons and inspired Jewish images of pagan empire overthrown by God's sovereign power. Rome eventually became the supreme embodiment of that pagan empire. Her seductive patronage system was despised by various groups of Jews who struggled against this collusion with Rome that was embedded into the very fabric of Jewish political and religious life. The struggle exploded into the First Jewish War and the cataclysmic destruction of Jerusalem and her temple by the Romans—as had happened with the Babylonians—inspiring the production of numerous Jewish apocalypses in response.

Onto this storied and dynamic literary stage our John of Patmos emerges writing his own visions. We watch him incorporating these Jewish apocalyptic traditions, but he does so in such bold and radical strokes. He is unconstrained, fully innovating their use for his own purposes according to his Christian conviction and his laser focus on the Christ event. He writes to meet the needs of beleaguered churches of Asia Minor hard pressed internally by heresy and externally by emperor worship. That original historical context gave the visions their original historical meaning. John's visions, however, took on a life of their own in the interpretive history of Revelation long after the original seven churches and their very real struggles had faded from our memory. The inevitable appropriation of John's apocalyptic traditions for new challenges of later generations continued after John. To that strange and fascinating story we turn in the following chapters.

2

A Strong River

Historical Developments to the Reformation

JOHN NEVER MAY HAVE REALIZED the massive interpretive floodgates he would open with his heavily symbolic portrayals of controversy with heretical teachings and compromise with the Roman emperor cult in first-century Asia Minor churches. The simple truth is, he spoke beasts into existence and released them on Christian imagination for millennia. Wainwright distinguishes interpreters and prophets of the Apocalypse. Interpreters are those attempting to understand contents. Prophets, on the other hand, are those who inspire movements.[1] As we survey these interpreters and prophets, our focus will be on the principal developmental periods in which apocalyptic traditions that John bequeathed to the church sprang forth in vigorous, new forms.

DEVELOPMENTAL PERIODS

Patristic Apocalyptic

Understanding the period of patristic apocalyptic requires that we clarify the concept of chiliasm.[2] Ancient chiliasm of patristic writers must be distinguished from the premillennialism of post-Reformation writers. Patristic chiliasm is a literal understanding of the millennium

---

[1]He provides an excellent summary of the history of Revelation's interpretation in the first part of *Mysterious Apocalypse*, "Part One: The Millennium and History," 21–103.

[2]The word "chiliasm" derives from the Greek word for thousand (χίλιοι, *chilioi*).

as evidenced in those second to fourth-century Christian writers with a focus on speculations about the materialistic aspects of a millennial reign of Christ, often based on the imagery of Isa 66. A good example would be Justin Martyr's (d. 165) following comments:

> as the elders who saw John, the disciple of the Lord, related that they had heard from him how the Lord used to teach in regard to these times, and say: The days will come, in which vines shall grow, each having ten thousand branches, and in each branch ten thousand twigs, and in each true twig ten thousand shoots, and in each one of the shoots ten thousand clusters, and on every one of the clusters ten thousand grapes, and every grape when pressed will give five and twenty metretes of wine. And when any one of the saints shall lay hold of a cluster, another shall cry out, "I am a better cluster, take me; bless the Lord through me." In like manner [the Lord declared] that a grain of wheat would produce ten thousand ears, and that every ear should have ten thousand grains, and every grain would yield ten pounds of clear, pure, fine flour; and that all other fruit-bearing trees, and seeds and grass, would produce in similar proportions.³

This chiliasm of early church fathers should be distinguished carefully from later Reformation views referred to as premillennialism for at least three reasons.

FIGURE 2.1. Bar Kokhba Coin. Simon bar Kokhba was hailed as messiah, "son of a star," (Num 24:17) by Rabbi Akiba, the most famous rabbi of the day. Silver tetradrachm; obverse: temple façade, ark of the covenant inside, star above; reverse: lulav with etrog (Classical Numismatic Group, Inc.).

1. *Traditionally*, chiliasm is Jewish in origin. Patristic chiliasm is the influence of hyperliteralistic and obsessively materialistic strands of Jewish apocalyptic traditions that fueled failed Jewish insurrections, such as the Bar Kokhba revolt of A.D. 133–35. Jews swore off apocalyptic literature after this failed revolt. The only reason

---

³Justin Martyr *Dial.* 33.3.

we have Jewish apocalypses is because Christians preserved them. Post-Reformation premillennialism, though literal like chiliasm, does not wade in the stream of these particular Jewish apocalyptic traditions. Since the post-Reformation construct does not derive directly from these Jewish apocalyptic traditions, this form of millennialism is not inherently hyperliteralistic nor obsessively materialistic like patristic chiliasm.

2. *Hermeneutically*, chiliasm anticipates only *one* future advent of Christ and the tribulation *before or after* the millennium. In stark contrast, all forms of post-Reformation premillennialism teach a tribulation period *before* the millennium.[4] Further, one mutation of premillennialism from the nineteenth century teaches *two* future advents: one advent is secret (the so-called "rapture"), and the other is public before the millennium ("second coming").

3. *Historically*, chiliasm is a patristic phenomenon from the period of the early church fathers. Premillennialism, on the other hand, is a sixteenth-century phenomenon from the period of the Anabaptists of the Radical Reformation eventually finding permanent root in American apocalyptic in writers such as Joseph Priestly (d. 1804), Edward Bickersteth (d. 1850), and Thomas Birks (d. 1883).[5]

FIGURE 2.2. Chiliasm and Premillennialism. Historically, these two eschatological constructs derive from two entirely different periods of church history.

Thus, in short, second-century chiliasm and sixteenth-century premillennialism, traditionally, hermeneutically, and historically are not the same animal, although they both center on the basic idea of a "literal" thousand year reign of Christ on earth.[6]

---

[4] Hence, the "pre" in premillennial for some systems not only is about the sequence of the second coming, but, in fact, also about the sequence of the tribulation. When distinctions are made about the timing of the second coming within this tribulation scheme, one encounters "pre-tribulation," "mid-tribulation," and "post-tribulation."

[5] Cf. Wainwright, *Mysterious Apocalypse*, 81–82.

[6] In millennial arguments the term "literal" is rendered useless by linguistic ignorance and rhetorical abuse. Postmillennialism is just as "literal" as premillennialism.

Further, just positing evidence of a generalized literal concept of the millennium in the early patristic fathers is not enough to establish a continuous *historical* line from second-century chiliasts to the post-Reformation premillennialists. The desire to assert such a connection often is based upon the attempt to build a canonical argument that the chiliasm of early church fathers, who were close historically to the teaching of the apostles themselves, inevitably has to be, by default, the apostolic view of the millennium, hence, inspired and authoritative. Thus, if post-Reformation premillennialism is in the direct, continuous, historical line of chiliasm, then premillennialism has to be the apostolic—read, only correct—understanding of the millennium. Yet, even *if* such a theoretical historical line could be established, however unlikely, we still would have the more pressing hermeneutical issue of having to critique the traditions of the church fathers. Just because the church fathers taught something does not, *de facto*, make that teaching apostolic. Especially is this hermeneutical caution necessary when what is asserted about particular New Testament passages only can be *inferred* between the lines of admittedly ambiguous texts, none of which are as explicit in and of themselves as the eschatological superstructures built upon them.

Chiliastic Apocalyptic (c. 130)

A review of the writings of the early church fathers does not reveal significant development of Revelation's traditions. These writers are acquainted with Revelation, but show hyperliteralism and apologetic use. A curious historical irony is that John's apocalyptic writing was ignored almost completely in Eastern Christendom, its place of origin, for almost a hundred years. The church at Rome was a different story.

Our earliest testimony of acquaintance with the book shows up in the West. Papias (c. 130), the bishop of Hierapolis and connected to Rome's patriarchate, apparently knew the work, according to both

---

The existence of the church on earth is just as "literal" for a postmillennialist as the existence of a Jewish nation in ancient Judea is for a premillennialist. Likewise, the reign of the church on earth is no less literal for a postmillennialist than the reign of a king on a throne in Jerusalem is for a premillennialist. In postmillennialism, the reign of Christ simply is not conceived in *monarchial* terms, that is, in terms of Jewish nationalism, with its incumbent political and militaristic overtones.

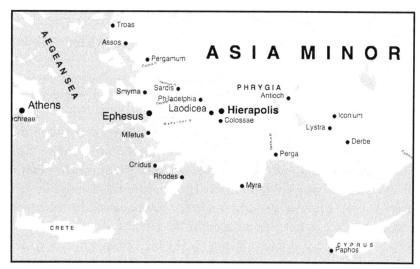

FIGURE 2.3. Hierapolis of Asia Minor. Papias (c. 130) was bishop of Hierapolis. The city was connected to the patriarchate in Rome. Epaphras, Paul's associate in the work in Ephesus, apparently helped establish the church in Hierapolis (Col 4:12–13).

Irenaeus (d. 202, *Adv. Haer.* 5.33.3–4) and Eusebius (d. 339, *H.E.* 3.39. 12). Papias seems to have focused mostly on advancing the literal character of the millennial reign. Justin Martyr (d. 165, *Dial.* 80–81),

FIGURE 2.4. Frontinus Gate of Hierapolis. Erected by Julius Frontinus in honor of emperor Domitian, c. A.D. 83, so often misnamed Gate of Domitian. Led to the main street of the city, which was a thermal spa built by Eumenes II, king of Pergamum in the Lycus valley near Colossae and Laodicea. Remains of the main street are first century. The bishop Papias hailed from this city.

an early apologist in Rome who was martyred, referred to the work, but only to buttress apologetic arguments defending the doctrine of resurrection and the concept of a thousand-year reign in a restored Jerusalem. Irenaeus (d. 202, *Adv. Haer.* 5.32–36), bishop of Lugdunum (Lyon) in France, also understood Revelation's millennial reign literally. As with Justin, Irenaeus's emphasis was on the materialistic aspects of this millennial period. These early church fathers are called "chiliasts," from the Greek word for a thousand. The chiliasm of these early church fathers tended to show hyperliteralistic and materialistic readings into the concept of the millennium of Rev. 20:4, as well as the New Jerusalem of Rev. 21:2. For example, Tertullian (d. 220) reported that pagan Roman soldiers had recurrent visions of the heavenly New Jerusalem in suspension above the city of Jerusalem that would appear and then vanish over a period of a number of days (*Adv. Marc.* 3.24.4).

These hyperliteralistic tendencies can be understood within the context of persecution and martyrdom in the Roman Empire. The images of Revelation provided an assured future hope for the faithful in the midst of dire circumstances. The hyperliteral readings in part were a direct function of mental relief of severe social distress. Such readings were not, however, necessarily the product of considered exegetical and historical interpretation of the texts from which they derived.

Montanus Apocalyptic (c. 172)

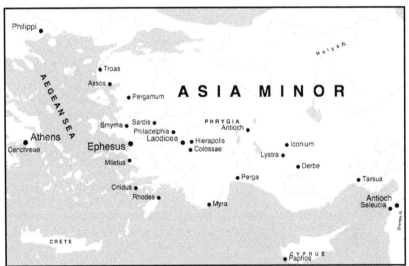

FIGURE 2.5. Phrygia of Asia Minor. The territory of Phrygia in Asia Minor is where the prophet Montanus was active. The exact location of the ancient town of Pepuza, the city he predicted would be the location of the New Jerusalem, is lost in obscurity.

The first extended development of Revelation's traditions is in the teachings of Montanus (c. 172), a prophet in the Roman province of Phrygia in Asia Minor. Unfortunately for Revelation's reputation, this development, while initially tolerated, eventually was to be declared heretical. Montanus was declared a heretic on the basis of his strange teachings about the new revelatory activity of the Spirit, as well as announcing New Jerusalem's imminent arrival in Pepuza. Montanus interpreted a serious plague of his day as a sign of the end. He is our first signal of the serious use of Revelation in Christian circles after its composition for interpreting current events through various visions. Montanus, then, begins a long line in the history of the interpretation of Revelation of the struggle to interpret and apply John's visions. The book of Revelation's authority came under attack by the "Alogi" and Gaius of Rome (c. 210); they were attempting to undercut the obvious pneumatic excess of the Montanist movement by denying to them their main text. The story of Montanus is a harbinger of Revelation's future canonical and interpretive history: a book that always is highly controversial in its attempted contemporary application even from the first sustained use of which we have record in Christendom.

Constantinian Apocalyptic (d. 337)

FIGURE 2.6. Battle of Milvian Bridge. Constantine defeats Maxentius. Painted by Giulio Romano (1520–24) and held in the Apostolic Palace, Vatican City, Rome.

The next serious development of Revelation's traditions was catalyzed by Constantine. Diocletian's successors vied for control of Rome after he stepped down, but focus was on the two generals, Constantine and Maxentius. Constantine won the decisive Battle of Milvian Bridge in 312. He attributed the victory to the sign of the cross, converted, and declared Christianity legal in the Edict of Milan in 313. Overnight, the world was turned on its head: former enemies were declared allies. Suddenly, interpreting Rome as the beast of Revelation, formerly so pertinent and powerful under the persecutions by a succession of cruel

Roman emperors, no longer was tenable. How did the church react to this stunning, unexpected development? Various options were taken.

FIGURE 2.7. Arch of Constantine. The Arch of Constantine, spanning the Via Triumphalis and situated between the Colosseum and Palatine Hill, was erected by the Roman senate to commemorate Constantine's victory at the Battle of Milvian Bridge (312). After this victory, Constantine issued the Edict of Milan (313), which changed the interpretation of Revelation overnight.

Greek Orthodox. In the Eastern Church, Revelation simply was ignored. The content already was considered too radical and violent; the visions were too obscure and dangerous; heresy too easily lurked in the murky depths of its thought. A Syriac translation of the book of Revelation did not exist until the sixth century, half a millennium after the book was written! We do have a few Eastern writers, such as Oecumenius (unclear date) and Andreas, bishop of Caesarea in Cappadocia (d. 637), who did write commentaries on Revelation contemporizing the book in plagues, natural disasters, and politics. This meager result in the Eastern Church is ironic, since the book had its origins in the East (Asia Minor). Even today the Greek Orthodox Church does not use Revelation for doctrine or liturgy. The book is in the canon but hardly is treated with any canonical authority.

Roman Catholic. The church in the West, in contrast, found itself unable to let go of the book so easily. The most important consideration was the book already was well on its way to canonical status, even though questioned in the Eastern patriarchate. Necessity is the mother of invention. New hermeneutical strategies arose in response to the surprising, unexpected historical realities of this post-Constantine era, both focused rhetorically on reconfiguring the *topos* of time.[7] The two strategies were deferred timing and symbolic timing.

---

[7] *Topoi*, a term originally derived from rhetoric, are commonplace themes, ideas, or recurring elements in literature. A powerful way to analyze apocalyptic thought is to gain an understanding of the basic *topoi* of this genre of literature. Time is one of the basic *topoi* of apocalyptic thought.

Deferred timing.[8] This strategy was simple: maintain the reading of the millennium as literal and earthly, but *defer* the timing. If one could shift timing of prophecy fulfillment by centuries, one effectively could eliminate or defuse contemporary agitation. One starts counting from creation. The idea was to elaborate an "in the year of the world" concept of religious time (*Anno Mundi*), with its related "sabbatical" millennium, based on the analogy of the seven days of the creation story in conjunction with Ps 90:4 (a day as a thousand years). Current history was interpreted as in the "sixth millennium"; one only needs to calculate the beginning of creation to anticipate the end of the world, that is, the beginning of the "seventh millennium" (also, "sabbatical millennium"). The accepted calculation placed the seventh millennium not beginning before A.D. 500, which, at the time of Constantine, was almost two centuries away. Now, you have to admit, two centuries seemed like a long time at the time. Time, however, just has this infuriating way of marching on, in spite of our calculations.

FIGURE 2.8. Venerable Bede. From the Nuremberg Chronicle, 1493 (CLVIIIv), ancient illustrated world history.

This deferred time solution, of course, was an interim strategy only. The effort worked only until the year A.D. 500 actually became imminent. Then, counterproductively, the solution itself eventually spawned even more intense apocalyptic fervor. Recalculation was necessary. The English monk Bede (d. 735) came to the rescue. Bede reset the beginning point and recalculated the end. He thus came up with a new date of A.D. 800. His recalculation, however, played right into the hands of the political maneuverings of Charlemagne (d. 814), the French ruler who consolidated the Carolingian dynasty of his father by uniting all Euro-

---

[8] A brief summary of this strategy is found in O'Leary, *Arguing the Apocalypse: A Theory of Millennial Rhetoric*, 48–50. O'Leary's resource for this material is Landes, "Lest the Millennium Be Fulfilled," 137–211.

pean kingdoms under his control. Charlemagne declared himself emperor, that is, the *de facto* heir of Rome and her traditions. He strategically set his imperial coronation for Bede's millennially significant year of A.D. 800. Political realities after Charlemagne, however, eventually forced the Carolingians to recalculate the end once again. The new strategy was a new calculation of the beginning of the "sixth millennium," which now was declared to start with the Incarnation. Thus, the dawn of the "seventh millennium" of religious history gained a nice symmetrical appeal of coinciding with a millennium of world history, the historical Christian millennium. The new, new date was the millennial year A.D. 1000. We will discuss this first Christian millennium shortly.

Clearly, all such time deferred strategies were of temporary value only. Time persistently always caught up, inevitably forcing inventive recalculations. History's reality always seems to be causing perpetual millennial recalculations. (Yet, the other side of the coin is, millennial calculators never seem to tire of recalculating!) Though such deferred timing schemes were popular interpretive strategies for some leaders post-Constantine, the ultimate ineffectiveness and hidden dangers of deferred timing, so easily seen in historical hindsight, were not lost on others, such as Augustine, who opted for a more effective strategy.

Symbolic timing. The second hermeneutical strategy to rework Revelation's visions in response to empire developments under Constantine was to refuse to capitulate to reading the millennium as literal or earthly (i.e., as monarchy). Rather, one could insist on a symbolic reading. Though he had precursors and drew upon a number of interpretive traditions of his time, Augustine (d. 430), the great scholar of the West, was the powerful force in church history for the adoption of a new symbolic approach for reading Revelation's images. Augustine, as representative of the Western Church, championed the traditional authority and apostolic authorship of Revelation. Because of Constantine, however, Augustine was forced to liberate Revelation from a literal interpretation of its visions and images. Such images in days past so easily were seen fulfilled in the evil empire of Rome, but now, such readings no longer made any sense. The former villain, Rome, suddenly now was aligned with the church. In an audacious move, Augustine painted Rome as the hero, not the villain. Since Rome now supported, protected, and nurtured the church, Rome *must* be the hero. To accomplish Rome's rehabilitation, invoking an interpretive sleight of hand, Augustine simply remapped the apocalyptic images of Revelation onto the terrain of the Christian life, thereby rubbing Rome as the beast completely off John's apocalyptic canvas.

In fact, Augustine was following the "spiritual" or "timeless truth" interpretive traditions that had been developing down in the Alexandrian school led by Origen (d. 254) and Dionysius (d. 265). Augustine read the millennium of Rev 20:4 as a heavenly reality, not earthly, simply another way to describe the "New Jerusalem" of Rev 21:2. Augustine allegorically read Christian life into this heavenly reality. Thus, the "first resurrection" of Rev 20:5 Augustine interpreted as an allegory of Christian baptism. Again, the "millennium" of Rev 20:4 became an allegory for Christ's present reign in the church (following Tyconius, d. ca. 400). Augustine adopted the recapitulation theory of Victorinus (d. 304), who taught that the famous triadic series of judgments of Revelation's seals, trumpets, and bowls do not progress linearly; rather, they recapitulate the same truths for dramatic emphasis. Thus liberated from Revelation's beast image, Rome, the "eternal city," could stand for the strength and stability of the church.[9]

FIGURE 2.9. Saint Augustine in Prayer. By Sandro Botticelli, 1480, Chiesa di Ognissanti, Florence, Italy.

<u>Last Emperor Myth</u>. After this rehabilitation by Augustine, the Roman empire, through its emperor, proved useful in interpreting an entirely different apocalyptic tradition from the Pauline material. The emperor and the empire were the power restraining the appearance of the Antichrist,[10] fulfilling the Pauline teaching of 2 Thess 2:6–7. This

---

[9] Eusebius the church historian systematically interpreted Constantine's empire as fulfillment of the millennium promise; cf. Chilton, *Visions of the Apocalypse*, 38–44.

[10] "Antichrist" is a legendary individual who is the Satanic embodiment of evil at the end of time. McGinn, *Antichrist*, traces the legend's origin and development. For the intertestamental Jewish precedents, cf. Lorein, *The Antichrist Theme*.

perceived season of Antichrist's restraint led to the myth of the "Last Emperor." The Last Emperor was that Roman emperor who would be the last emperor immediately prior to the revelation of Antichrist. The myth of the Last Emperor had a long, rich, and complex tradition in European history, being appropriated by Charlemagne and the Carolingians, and later figuring significantly into both French and German history, especially under the German king Frederick II (d. 1250).

City of God. Unfortunately, history cuts no slack at any point for interpreters of Revelation. For Augustine, "eternal Rome" was sacked by Alaric I and the German Visigoths in 410. Rome had not fallen to an enemy for nearly 800 years, so the whole world was shocked by the news. Most histories of Rome mark this event as one of the major milestones toward the fall of the Western Roman Empire. In addition to reconfiguring the millennium, Augustine also had to transmute the "eternal city" that had had its literal correlate for a thousand years in the city of Rome into the eternal "City of God," that had its spiritual correlate in heaven. Spiritual Rome replaced real Rome. *C'est la vie*.

FIGURE 2.10. Colosseum. Rome's glory had stood for centuries, which left the aura in the public mind of her absolute invincibility. Invading Germanic tribes proved otherwise, to the shock of the whole world.

Augustine's interpretive ploys with the millennium and the City of God came at great cost, as the maneuvers drained both Revelation and history of all apocalyptic meaning. Revelation's loss of its apocalyptic voice also was the loss of its immediacy and urgency. The book conveniently could be shelved as playing second fiddle to the truths already revealed in other New Testament documents. Revelation might bark in its fearsome visions, but the book no longer had any interpretive bite for contemporary events. The end, whatever that was, for Augustine was a galaxy far, far away.

Council of Ephesus (431). The Western Church canonized Revelation but could not control its interpretation. Three problems were evident. First, the hedonistic excess of chiliast millennial imagination embarrassed later church leaders. Second, the Montanus heresy had demonstrated early in the book's interpretive history what maverick movements such literal readings could inspire. Third, Constantine had turned the religious world on its head, and Rome no longer was the persecutor of the faithful. As a result, traditional literal readings of the beasts and Babylon as prophecies of Rome's demise seemed falsified by history almost overnight. No wonder that the Council of Ephesus formally declared certain literal readings of the millennium heretical. Many currents were flowing into their deliberations. For example, one tributary was philosophy, which played a significant role. In terms of heresy, gnostic dualism and spirit emphasis already had seized hold and sterilized Christian eschatology. Add to that serious mix Platonic dualism, which depreciated matter and, therefore, all elements of the physical world, then any expectation of a literal, millennial kingdom clearly would be completely unacceptable, sure evidence of an inferior philosophy.[11] For these reasons and others, an allegorically symbolic interpretation won the day in the Western Church. Augustine's thorough-going system became known as amillennialism. This view would rule the mainstream interpretation of Revelation for another thousand years. Quite the accomplishment for one theologian!

Minority reports did appear along the way. These would include deferred timing schemes, especially those surrounding the career of Charlemagne, as well as developments with the Crusades, Joachim of Fiore, and radical fifteenth-century European movements that were the precursors to the radical Anabaptists of the Reformation. Even so, Augustine's amillennialism arguably has been the most successful of all schemes of interpreting Revelation in church history.

Millennium Apocalyptic (A.D. 1000)

The next significant development for interpreting Revelation's traditions was tied to the arrival of the first Christian millennium. Yet, we

---

[11]See Chilton, *Visions of the Apocalypse*, 29–34.

must ask, If the book of Revelation's images had been remapped from the plane of history to the inner life of the believer, why would the arrival of any historical point be imbued with any interpretive significance? "Elementary, my dear Watson." Though Augustine's spiritual interpretation of Revelation came to rule the church in official circles, Augustine's scholastic erudition on Revelation failed to rule popular imagination. (So what's new?) Pictures are worth a thousand words. Christian art in the Dark Ages continued to depict Revelation literally for the great masses of believers, even though at times grotesquely. Aesthetic value aside, this art informed the thinking of the uneducated masses. Art is interpretation, and in this apocalyptic art, Revelation retained its potency for absorbing and explaining current events.

One great example is the worldwide bubonic plague of 541–543. This epidemic wiped out as much as one-third to one-half of Constantinople's entire population and struck the rest of Europe severely as well. Another bubonic plague outbreak in 1346–53 became known as the "Black Death" and reduced the entire human population on earth by a third. Revelation's visions of plagues witnessed in art clearly were

FIGURE 2.11. Plague Victims Blessed by Priest. Blessing of disfigured monks, titled, "Omne Bonum," by the painter James le Palmer, London, 1360–75, in the British Library. As a thought experiment, take the current world population, reduce by a third, and see what equivalent cities would have to disappear to be like the "Black Death" plague that decimated all of Europe in the 1300s.

being fulfilled. Such art helped maintain the sense that Revelation's visions had *something* to do with external *historical* events, not just Augustine's interior spiritual life of the believer. Also, deferred timing schemes inherently fed into these popular apocalyptic expectations based on more literal readings of Revelation.

Bede (d. 735)

The English monk Bede (d. 735) unwittingly added to this literal understanding of Revelation that contemporized the meaning by application to current historical events and figures, probably not in a way intended by Bede himself. Bede wrote a commentary on Revelation, but this work was not really his main contribution to the popular imagination. (His commentary was nothing more than allegory along typical lines of the patristic traditions following in the path of Augustine.)

More importantly, Bede was a philosopher of time. He calculated the age of the earth by adding up all the biblical generations. He wrote about time and bequeathed to the church a clearly articulated concept of linear history, as well as the crucial phrase, *Anno Domini*, "in the year of the Lord." This "year of the Lord" concept transmuted the older "in the year of the world" philosophy with its "sabbatical" millennium correlate into a philosophy of time that was more directly connected to the First Advent of Christ. These concepts about time fired popular imagination. Time could be conceived as marching on toward its appointed, sovereign end as decreed by the sovereign Lord Jesus Christ. The English monk Bede, then, along with his "sabbatical" millennium precursors, are

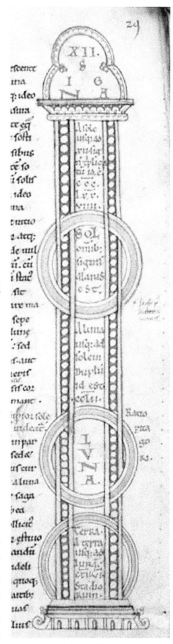

FIGURE 2.12. Bede Illumination, *On the Reckoning of Time*. From folio 53r, University of Glasgow, Special Collections (Sp coll MS Hunter 85).

the beginnings of that *ad infinitum* series of all end-time calculators whose entire eschatological theory hinges on one simple principle: add the days, know the time. The theory begs indulgence for ignoring its fatal flaw: when history falsifies the math, what artificial device can be invented to manipulate the rules right in the middle of the calculations such that one plus one no longer is two?

Adso of Montier-en-Der (d. 992)

Adso was a French monk who wrote a narrative of Antichrist in the then popular "lives of the saints" form that hit the Medieval best-seller list. This "life," however, was more like a "saint in reverse," a point-counterpoint of the life of Jesus. In the words of one scholar, Adso "marks a major moment in the history of the Antichrist legend."[12] His work is important as a window into the evolving traditions creating the fictitious legend of Antichrist. He provides the first complete summary of that developing legend in its incarnation in his day. Adso is evidence for how firmly fixed is this Antichrist legend with the book of Revelation, even though John never once mentions the name.

Adso discusses many features that were to became a permanent part of the Antichrist legend. He also reveals the continuing impact of Jewish apocalyptic traditions, finding Antichrist forecast in infamous rulers of the past, such as Antiochus IV, Nero, and Domitian. On the negative side, he shows the Antichrist-as-Jew, born of the tribe of Dan association that already had become integral to the myth in Europe. In Adso we also see the merging of Pauline teaching in 2 Thess 2:3 on the "man of lawlessness" and a great apostasy with this Antichrist legend, conflating disparate eschatological traditions in the apostle Paul, the author of 1 John, and the Seer of Revelation. Finally, in Adso's narrative we see a perpetuation of the "Last World Emperor" legend, the popular myth of Europe's heritage as the last surviving vestige of the Roman empire, whose last ruler would unite Christians to defeat Muslims as the prelude to the final revelation of Antichrist and the end-time drama. Though not so well known to the general reading public in America, this French monk and his letter documenting the life of Antichrist is crucial to the story of the development of the Antichrist legend and of traditions related to the book of Revelation.

[12] McGinn, *Antichrist*, 101. For Jewish precedents, cf. Lorein, *The Antichrist Theme*.

This Antichrist portrait as point-counterpoint to the life of Jesus becomes a fixed part of the Antichrist legend and inspired the luminary Renaissance artist Signorelli when he adorned frescos of the Chapel of the Madonna di San Brizio with his images from John's Apocalypse. His most famous image in the entire set is of Antichrist as Jesus' evil demonic twin into whose ears Satan whispers his words of deceit to preach to the people. In sum, Adso in responding in a letter to a request from Gerberga, wife of Louis IV of West Francia, to help her understand the figure of Antichrist demonstrates how the Antichrist myth is like a great eschatological snowball picking up everything on its way down the hill of history.

FIGURE 2.13. Signorelli's Deeds of the Antichrist. Luca Signorelli (1499–1502). Chapel of the Madonna di San Brizio, Orvieto, Italy.

Sylvester II (d. 1003)

Popular thinking about time was the fuel for the fire of high anticipation that "something wonderful is about to happen" as the momentous first Christian millennium of the year A.D. 1000 approached. As Sylvester II became pope in 999, the countdown to the millennium and the return of Christ was thought to have begun. The belief widely held was that in Sylvester II's last mass of 999, Christ would emerge on earth to reveal his glory and reign, making manifest to all the world the premier "year of the Lord" as calculated by the calculators. Most fittingly, the completion of the historical church millennium would inaugurate the dawning of the divine royal millennium. Sylvester II celebrated the last mass of 999, of course, without even the slightest manifestation of some special "year of the Lord." Christ did not return, and many believers were quite disappointed and disillusioned. While the highly anticipated first millennium return of Christ never materialized, one can trace in this intense millennial fever that passed unrelieved in A.D. 1000 the undying desire in the popular imagination to bring Revelation down to earth on some concrete date. To that flippant desire many a false prophet has catered shamelessly.[13]

Crusade Apocalyptic (A.D. 1095)

The next significant development of Revelation's traditions relates to the Crusades. Jerusalem had fallen to fierce Muslim onslaught by 638. The faithful were succumbing to the infidels with quite breathtaking speed. All of the Christian world seemed to be falling into chaos. In 1071 the Seljuq Turks controlled areas around Jerusalem. They then cut off all pilgrim routes to the city. This Turkish action provoked Pope Urban II (d. 1099) to issue his call to take back Jerusalem in 1095, inaugurating three centuries of Christian Crusades. When crusader armies of the First and Second Crusades were moving down the Rhine River valley in Germany, anti-Semitic mob violence broke out in the effort to kill Jews in the final conflict leading to the capture of Jerusalem and the return of Christ. Towns all along the Rhine saw killings of thousands of Jews. In this way, apocalyptic thought during the Crusades found itself reinforcing the sad history of centuries of Christian anti-Semitic activity.

FIGURE 2.14. Louis IX Attacks Damietta, 1249. Woodcut by Gustave Doré (d. 1883).

Hildegard of Bingen (d. 1179)

Hildegard was a German abbess. She was a talented poet, composer, artist, and visionary. The Benedictine Abbey of St. Hildegard in Rüde-

---

[13]See the critique in chapter 6; cf. Wainwright, *Mysterious Apocalypse*, 89–103.

sheim am Rhein honors her life and work. Her claim of divine visions officially was ratified at the time by the archbishop of Mainz. Her visions were recorded down by the order of the archbishop.

FIGURE 2.15. Hildegard Antichrist Illumination. From *Scivias* III.11 (Rupertsberg MS). Antichrist, monstrous beast, church born, attempting to ascend to heaven.

Hildegard was the first to draw a picture of Antichrist, featured in the illuminations in the *Scivias*, which detailed her visions.[14] In this

---

[14]*Scivias* III.11, Rupertsberg MS. The Latin term *Scivias* is shorthand for *Scito vias Domini*, and means, "Know the ways of the Lord."

picture, the upper left panel shows the five beasts representing the five ages immediately prior to Antichrist's arrival. The lower panel on the left shows Antichrist as a despicable beast who devilishly raped the church and then was born from her. His monstrous head is emerging from the woman figure representing the church. The top right panel shows that the church will recover from this assault and eventually be taken by her bridegroom, Christ. The lower panel on the right has Antichrist trying to ascend to heaven on his mountain of dung, but he is struck down by Christ.

In several ways, the figure of Antichrist in the presentation of Hildegard takes on similar legendary features as seen in the teachings of Adso: Antichrist is the reverse of Christ.

> He will show them his treasures and riches, and allow them to feast as they will, confirming his teaching by deceitful signs so that they think they need not restrain or chastise their bodies in any way. He will command them to observe circumcision and the Jewish laws and customs, but will alleviate for them as much as they want the stronger commands of the Law, which the Gospel, by worthy penance, converts into grace. And he will say, "When anyone is converted to me, I will blot out his sins, and he shall live with me forever." He will throw out baptism and the Gospel of My Son, and scorn all the precepts handed down to the Church. And he will say, with devilish mockery: "See what a madman that was, Who through His falsehoods decreed that the simple people should observe these things!"[15]

What is clear in this quote is that what most bothered Hildegard was the corruption of the church internally by its own ministers abusing this institution of Christ. Her desire for reform and purification found voice in apocalyptic, and to this end apocalyptic traditions such as Antichrist were harnessed. The voice of ministers in her own world who did not restrain the flesh and corrupted the church were simply intimations of the evil to come and to be embodied in the figure of the Antichrist, who would advocate a licentious lifestyle.

At the same time, again, as illustrated in the quote above, though depicting Antichrist as born from the church, Hildegard subtly also associated Antichrist with things Jewish. He would attempt to enforce

---

[15] *Hildegard of Bingen: Scivias*, 504.

Jewish laws and customs on believers. Effectively, intentionally or unintentionally, Hildegard characterized Jews as potential followers of Antichrist and enemies of Christ, since Antichrist would promote Jewish customs. Thus, in Adso, Hildegard, and others of this time, we see Christian Antichrist slander in its initial stages towards becoming a *topos* of apocalyptic discourse.

Joachim of Fiore (d. 1202)

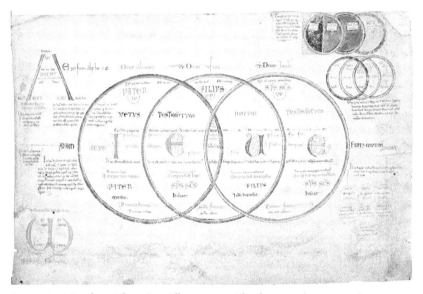

FIGURE 2.16. Joachim, Three Ages Illumination. The three overlapping circles represent Joachim's periodizing scheme of the three ages of Father, Son, and Holy Spirit. From Joachim's *Figurae*, Oxford, Corpus Christi College, MS. 255A, fol. 7v.

Joachim was an Italian monk in the monastery of Corazzo south of Rome. At first finding the book of Revelation altogether obscure and impenetrable, he finally had a flash of insight to read the book literally taking his cue from the Holy Trinity to read the book as disclosing history in three ages. Each historical period has a direct relationship to the mystery of the Trinity: (1) the first age is God the Father and the period from creation through ancient Israel characterized by human obedience to God's rules; (2) the second age is God the Son and the period from King Josiah through the present church when humankind becomes the son of God; (3) the third age is God the Spirit and the period of the future and direct communion with God, which is imminent, to begin in 1260.[16] Instead of the second coming inaugurating this third age, this third period would begin on its own as a new epoch of peace and harmony in which freedom would reign, actually rendering the presence of the church superfluous. This last statement of imminence is the most audacious, as Joachim thereby directly is contradicting Augustine and the longstanding teaching of the church that the end was far, far away. Thus, Joachim represents the survival of deferred timing schemes with their inherent periodizing of history. They survive in this period of the Crusades, even against the powerful symbolic timing scheme of Augustine's amillennialism. Joachim's theories, however, were declared heretical at the Synod of Arles in 1263. His historical periodizing would have to await the Reformation.

Signs of the Times. All history periodizers like Joachim naturally talk "signs of the times." The whole point of inventing periods of history is to show how you are at the precipice of the "final days." Joachim's monastic influence is readily apparent in his own description of the final period of the Spirit, for this age is eerily like—surprise!—a monastery. In fact, the monastic order of the church brings about the necessary purification of the church preparatory to this final period and itself is one of Joachim's "signs of the times."

Joachim's other sign of the times was the Crusades. For him, the Crusades were the sure sign of that global conflict between God and Satan (i.e., Christians and Muslims). Without doubt, Joachim taught, the Crusades would conclude in the climactic Battle of Armageddon. God (crusader knights) would win. Joachim concluded Revelation's "beast with seven heads" could be mapped on the timeline of history as seven historical kings infamous for their persecutions of Christians, from Herod the Great's slaughter of Bethlehem's infants at the birth of Jesus down to the current Muslim leader, Saladin (d. 1193).[17] Joachim confidently taught that numerical calculations could establish the precise timeframe of end-time events (shades of Bede). From the birth of Christ to the end of the world would be 1,260 years (using the 1,260 days of Rev 12:6). Thus, the end is about 80 years away into the future

---

[16] His was an add the days, know the time variety. He read the "one thousand two hundred and sixty days" of Rev 11:3 and 12:6 as predicting 1260 years after Christ.

[17] For analysis of the Muslim interpretation of Revelation in thirteenth-century England, including the Douce Apocalypse, see Lewis, *Reading Images*, 223.

of the next century—just conveniently far enough into the future for Joachim that he does not have to contemplate bearing responsibility when his predictions are falsified.

FIGURE 2.17. Douce Apocalypse at Rev 9:17. Illumination of Ms. 180, Douce Apocalypse, at Rev 9:17 (*circa* 1270). The two-hundred million strong army sweeping across the dried Euphrates River pictured in this British manuscript as Muslim warriors (ADEVA).

The sudden rise of the Mongol Empire under Genghis Khan (d. 1227) complicated this thirteenth-century European apocalyptic plot. Once again, history was recalcitrant, refusing to bend to current end-time storylines. Initially, the Mongols were thought to be the answer to the threat of Islam, but when they slaughtered Christians just as indiscriminately as Muslims, opinions changed. Then they were Gog and Magog presaging the arrival of Antichrist (Ezek 38:2; Rev 20:8).[18]

Thus, similar to Hildegard, Joachim's eschatological burden is ecclesiastical, the internal corrupt condition of the church. Also, like Hildegard, he thought the church would find its way to purification—whatever that should look like. From such ecclesiastical burden we can learn a lesson. Putting aside the method of periodizing of history with its accompanying "signs of the times" rhetoric, the interpretive intuition of Hildegard and Joachim that Revelation ought to be read in a way to challenge the church to achieve her mission in history is an important lesson and an enduring legacy for how to read the book.

In eschatological constructs, Joachim of Fiore is the first serious minority report to Augustine not tied directly to the popular opinions

[18]McGinn, "Moslems, Mongols, and the Last Days," 149–57.

of the masses, who never really were on board Augustine's neutered apocalyptic. Joachim helped preserve a literal reading strategy. He also rejected Victorinus's recapitulation idea, adopted by Augustine, that Revelation's visions do not advance in time but recapitulate the same truths. Joachim's distinctive contribution was forever burning into apocalyptic imagination even against the interpretive authority of the Roman Catholic Church the idea that the images of Revelation are not only literal but also a linear map of the progress of church history.

Periodizing Precipice. This linear history method can be seen in modern times, for example, in the desire of dispensationalists. They trumpet a "literal" interpretation and agree that the seven letters of Rev 2–3 have application historically to seven actual churches in first-century Asia Minor. Simultaneously, though, they want to assert these same letters also are intended as prophetic metaphors for marking the seven periods of church history.[19] Of course, by design, we always are in the seventh period, the "Laodicean Age" of a lukewarm church bent on apostasy, regardless the century the dispensational writer happens to be (nineteenth, twentieth, or twenty-first). Funny how, throughout the centuries of interpretation, no historical periodizer from the time of Constantine, through Joachim, Ribera, the Reformers, to today ever proposed a historical sequence and concluded they were in the *middle* of their periodic scheme! *The goal of any periodic scheme is to convince readers that they are standing on the precipice of history, not to know history.* Any indiscriminate bundle of "signs of the times" then can be thrown in as lagniappe "confirmation" of an already decided historical "fact." The "signs of the times" do not actually have to be exegetically correct or even logically consistent. Any "sign" is "believable" because *belief in the arrival of the end already is established as a presupposition of the argument.*

SUMMARY

A history of the interpretation of Revelation turns on the significance of the idea of the millennium and millennial constructs to interpret the idea. The circumstances leading up to the Reformation generate the development of one of the most successful millennial constructs in

---

[19] Cf. *The New Scofield Reference Bible*, 1353.

church history, that of Augustine's amillennialism. Revelation already is problematic in the generations immediately following its original production for churches in Asia Minor. Even in the second century, the hyperliteralism and materialism of the chiliasm of early church fathers reflected more the traditions of Jewish apocalyptic than New Testament teaching. Montanus is an early harbinger of the pneumatic excess and maverick interpretation that will vex Revelation's future.

Constantine is a historical watershed in the interpretation of Revelation. The Edict of Milan illustrates the stress actual history places on any hermeneutical construct for interpreting the book. Rome overnight went from beast to beauty. The interpretation of Rome as the enemy portrayed in Revelation's vivid visions had to be abandoned in a moment. Three solutions surfaced: ignore the book, deferred timing, and symbolic timing. The Greek Orthodox solution of circumscribing the book and ignoring its use at least has relieved their history of the misery of its abuse. Deferred timing was not as successful, as any scheme to periodize history in order to defer the timing of a literal fulfillment is overtaken by the inexorable advance of history, and the fever for fulfillment inevitably is rekindled. Symbolic timing was Augustine's imminently successful solution enshrined in amillennialism.

Revelation began to be mixed with other interpretive streams of the New Testament. One idea that facilitated a particular mixing of Paul and John derives from Augustine. After Augustine rehabilitated Rome as a positive rather than a negative image for interpreting Revelation, then Rome could be read positively into other apocalyptic texts, such as the Pauline "man of lawlessness" and the "apostasy" in 2 Thess 2:6–7. The prelude to the appearing of the "man of lawlessness" would be the last in the sequence of emperors of the Roman Empire, or, in the case of European history, the claim to be the legitimate inheritors of Rome's legacy. Thus was born the enduring European idea of the Last Emperor myth. John's visions conflated with other eschatological material spontaneously generated altogether new traditions. When historical Rome was sacked, Augustine had to transmute his use of the idea of historical Rome as the eternal city into a symbolic City of God.

By the fourth century, the literal interpretation of Revelation is reeling. The book has endured excesses of chiliastic materialism and Montanus spiritualism and taken a blow to the literal solar plexus by

Constantine. The die was cast for the Roman Church to declare all literal readings of Revelation heretical in the Council of Ephesus and canonize Augustine's amillennialism. The literal approach is down on the mat, but not out. Artistic endeavors and independent interpreters keep the literal approach on life support.

Art in the Middle Ages was impervious to the interpretations of Augustine, always opting for some literal depiction of the visions and imagery of Revelation. The subject was current historical events, such as the bubonic plague, which kept the literal approach alive in spite of all the efforts of the Roman Catholic hierarchy. The English monk Bede kept deferred timing schemes going as well by transforming the original "in the year of the world" calculations to "in the year of the Lord" calculations. Such calculation constructs brought the faithful to a fever pitch at the accession of Pope Sylvester II, whose last mass of 999 was supposed to usher in the fated Christian millennium. Talk shows, mass media, and publications anticipating the year 2000 seem to suggest the church never recovered from this original millennial "great disappointment."

Antichrist becomes a full legend. Adso is clear evidence by his time that Antichrist is a bona fide Hollywood star, a cardboard cutout superglued onto Revelation's pages. He now has a history. His story has plot and characters. The paradigm for developing the Antichrist legend is simple: reverse all the major elements of the story of Jesus. All of this Antichrist detail, and yet this character now crucial to the on-going interpretation of the Apocalypse as far as Adso is concerned never is mentioned even once by John. Revelation never will extract its interpretation from this Antichrist legend. The strangest irony of the interpretation of Revelation is that a book that John thought would reveal Jesus Christ (Rev 1:1) has instead provoked the invention of a character about whom we supposedly know more than Christ himself.

Hildegard gives us the first known artistic representation of the Antichrist. Her fiery apocalyptic preaching and teaching was aimed at ecclesial reform. Her burden, like Joachim of Fiore's, was that the church internally was corrupt, impoverished spiritually, and missing her mission. She rightly saw Revelation addressing such situations.[20]

---

[20]Chilton, *Visions of the Apocalypse*, 70–73, reminds us that critique of the papacy, especially among the Franciscans, was going on long before Wycliffe and Luther.

After the staggering blow of Constantine to the interpretation of Revelation, historical developments continued to force interpretive mutations. Another watershed in Revelation's interpretation was the Muslim onslaught, which, after sweeping over many regions of the eastern world, threatened to overrun all of Western Europe as well. After the interpretive collapse of Rome as the beast of Revelation with political developments under Constantine, Revelation's beast imagery in the Medieval period once again was easy to read as having a clear historical correlate. Antichrist now wore a turban. This imagery fed into the Crusades. Joachim of Fiore could see the battle of Armageddon on the near horizon of his own history as a pitched conflict between Christians and Muslims. His calculations were literal, linear, and easy. He periodized history and decided 1260 was the date. All such periodizing schemes use "signs of the times" rhetoric. Since belief that the end is near is presuppositional, the choice of any particular sign is completely irrelevant. Muslims or Mongols, any sign will do.

Christian apocalyptic tradition cannot be exculpated from anti-Semitism. Jewish pogroms along the Rhine River during the First and Second Crusades is an overt example. Latent attitudes, however, are conveyed by describing Antichrist as from the tribe of Dan or saying Antichrist will teach Jewish traditions. Such speech is only a subtle form of Antichrist slander, in this case used in service of anti-Semitic tendencies. Antichrist slander will become a *topos* of apocalyptic rhetoric. Whomever you oppose is Antichrist. In this speech you can vilify and demonize whomever you like. Wycliffe and Luther picked up and sanctioned this abusive Antichrist slander. The new target was the pope. Because of certain Reformers, papal Antichrist slander will become a rhetorical pattern permanently ingrained in certain forms of Protestant apocalyptic discourse, and a characteristic identifying mark of Protestant interpretation of Revelation.

3

Swept Away Downstream

Reformation to the American Revolution

A<small>LTHOUGH WE ARE BITING</small> at the bit to race into the Reformation era, because matters really start heating up here hermeneutically, we have to set up this story with historical precursors that anticipate this watershed in the use of Revelation's apocalyptic traditions. These precursors are the Hussites, the Taborites, and John Wycliffe.

REFORMATION PRECURSORS (1400s)

The Hussites

Developments of the Reformation were presaged already in the 1400s with the story of the Hussites, a movement in the Czech Republic's Bohemia province in central Europe. This province is in the western region of the Czech Republic that cuts into the interior of the eastern part of Germany. The Hussites were followers of John (Jan) Huss, a priest whose reformist ideas anticipated Luther, Calvin, and Zwingli. As master at Charles University in Prague, Huss focused on opposition to the two basic medieval institutions of European feudalism and the Roman Catholic Church, both formidable opponents. His ideas on the church and the Eucharist were considered radical and heretical. The pope launched five crusades against Hussite followers (known among Roman Catholics as the Hussite Wars), but was defeated every time. John Huss was burned at the stake in 1415, but the movement he started continued in various Hussite groups, some of whom were quite radical and apocalyptic in their views, such as the Taborites.

FIGURE 3.1. Czechoslovakia in 1928–1938. Bohemia is in the western part of former Czechoslovakia, now the Czech Republic.

The Taborites

The Taborites centered in the Bohemian city of Tabor. They were one of the radical offshoots of the Hussite movement during the Hussite Wars. Their concerns were focused on religious issues of the church and social issues of the peasantry, which already pointed respectively to later developments under Martin Luther and Thomas Müntzer in Germany (and even later in the classless society ideals of twentieth-century communism). The Taborites declared the imminent arrival of the millennium, which would be facilitated by their war on all non-Taborites. The story is tragic. After a brief interval of twenty years, 13,000 of 18,000 Taborite troops were slaughtered by the armies of the Czech king Sigismund in the Battle of Lipany in 1434.

This disastrous defeat ended the radical Taborite movement, but their violent heritage hovered like an ominous shadow over Europe's history into the next century. Their millennial eschatology anticipates the premillennial Reformation eschatology that becomes firmly fixed in many Protestant readings of Revelation. Riding strong interpretive currents already part of medieval history, but redirecting the object of Antichrist slander, Reformers found one sure way to fight the pope is to call him Antichrist and declare the end of the world.

John Wycliffe

The Roman papacy by now had been embroiled in political, military, and religious controversy for centuries. Thoughtful believers yearned and prayed earnestly for reform of the institution and the church. The thoughts of John Wycliffe (d. 1384) on the matter anticipated serious interpretive developments in the Reformation. He was an Oxford scholar who advocated Bible translation into vernacular English. He also agitated for papal reform, setting high hopes upon the election of Pope Urban VI (d. 1389) as so-called "reform pope." Urban VI, however, quickly proved to be a poor choice, and the papacy devolved into open schism. Rebelling French cardinals elected Clement VII (d. 1534) to replace Urban VI. The collapse of Wycliffe's reform hopes that he had placed in Urban VI later turned him against the papacy. He decided the papal institution irredeemably was corrupt and declared the papacy to be Antichrist. His followers were known as Lollards. Luther also turned to Revelation's images to fight his battles with the papacy, and brought Wycliffe's papal antipathy and Antichrist slander into the Protestant mainstream.

FIGURE 3.2. John Wycliffe (d. 1384). "Morning star of the Reformation" for desiring papacy reform and to translate the Bible into common English.

REFORMATION (1500s)

Martin Luther

The next significant development of Revelation's traditions resulted from Reformation politics. Here, even before we start, we must mourn the loss of symbolic reading that was the inevitable consequence of the politics of protest. Clearly, Protestants in their protest against the Roman Catholic Church could not countenance Augustine's allegorical, amillennial approach that had been the mainstay of Catholic reading for a millennium. Falsely equating allegory with metaphor, Protestant interpreters permanently seared out of the interpretive conscience any metaphorical reading of Revelation as automatically suspect, an incalculable loss to appropriate reading of Revelation's apocalyptic genre.

Symbol and metaphor are fundamental to apocalyptic writing and a key component in reading Revelation. Even though Luther read Revelation literally in contrast to Augustinian allegory of interior Christian life, he still knew quite well that the words were symbol and metaphor. Regrettably, Luther's Protestant heirs did not always nuance their own literal reading with Luther's hermeneutical sophistication.

The Reformation crystalizes in the critique of the German monk Martin Luther (d. 1546), whose reaction against the sale of indulgences in 1516 generally is taken as the formal beginning of protest against the church and attempts at reform. Luther is an important figure in the development of Revelation's apocalyptic traditions for at least four reasons. First, Luther revived the old historical periodizing scheme for interpreting the visions. Second, Luther's heavy use of his Antichrist slander sanctioned this type of ill speech for all later generations of Protestants and created a *topos* of political and religious rhetoric in all later use of Revelation's apocalyptic traditions. Third, Luther's work illustrates the power of images for the promotion of apocalyptic ideas. Finally, Luther exposes a certain Reformation naïveté about the violent tendencies lurking in unbridled use of apocalyptic rhetoric.

FIGURE 3.3. Martin Luther (d. 1546). From a painting by Lucas Cranach the Elder.

Periodizing Revived

Luther at first had no use for the book of Revelation. In the preface to Revelation in the first edition of his German translation of the Bible (1522), Luther spoke bluntly his own opinion that the Apocalypse was "neither apostolic nor prophetic," and he went on to complain, "I can in no way detect that the Holy Spirit produced it."[1] He thought the

---

[1] Das ichs wider apostolisch noch prophetisch hallte . . . und aller din ge nicht spuren kan das es von dem heyligen geyst gestellet sey. *Luther's "September Bible" in Facsimile*; cf. *Luther's Works*, 398.

images were much too obscure to fulfill the gospel mandate to preach Christ clearly, and that was reason enough to be uneasy with the book. His sense was, "Christ is neither taught nor known in it."[2] He later changed his mind as his conflict with church authorities continued to grow. Even while Luther read the book as images and figures, he still presumed the images and figures to be a prophetic prospect of history, thus reviving historical periodizing schemes long suppressed by the church-approved amillennial reading.

Luther periodized history in Revelation's visions in the following manner. He understood the seal judgments beginning in Rev 6 to be bodily afflictions of those persecuted for belief in Christ across all of church history and happening all the time. He then took the images of Rev 7–8 as spiritual heresies afflicting the church, assuming trumpet angels to be evil. The first angel portends Tatian; the second Marcion, the Manichaeans, and Montanus; the third Origen; and the fourth Novatus and the Donatists. The last three trumpet angels are further distinguished as woe angels that portend first Arius, then Mohammed and the Saracens, then the papal empire. The interlude of the mighty angel with the bitter book in Rev 10 anticipates the false teaching of the papal office, and Rev 11 pictures a counterfeit church of external holiness but internal corruption. The first beast of Rev 13 is restored Roman imperial power aligned with the second beast, which is the papacy and its idolatries, monasteries, sainthood, pilgrimages, purgatory, indulgences, and celibacy. Luther clearly has Rome and the papacy in his crosshairs. In Rev 15–16 the visions move on to the bowl judgments of which the image of frogs portends sophists such as Faber, Eck, and Emser. The destruction of the papacy is envisioned in Rev 17–18, and their forces are sent reeling in Rev 19. A recapitulation of evil occurs in Rev 20, in which Gog and Magog are the Turks, but they too are destroyed, and the lake of fire consumes all beasts and all evil.[3] Luther demonstrates that periodizing is easy, because you start with what you already know in what history already has transpired up to your time, and then you distribute that history in any manner you desire across the entire loom of Revelation's fabric.

[2] Das Christus drynnen wider geleret noch erkandt wirt. *Luther's "September Bible" in Facsimile*; cf. *Luther's Works*, 399.

[3] *Luther's Works*, 401–09.

Antichrist Slander

Luther's use of Revelation for political broadsides against the pope is a premier feature of his appropriation of Revelation's apocalyptic traditions. Key to his success was that Luther was able to surf the publishing wave created by the new Gutenberg printing press, so was able to disseminate his thoughts to the masses rather quickly. One important publication was his German translation of the Bible. He relegated the Apocalypse to secondary status in the first edition in 1522, and even in subsequent editions continued to suggest the book was of secondary value by not numbering the book and including in a subgroup.

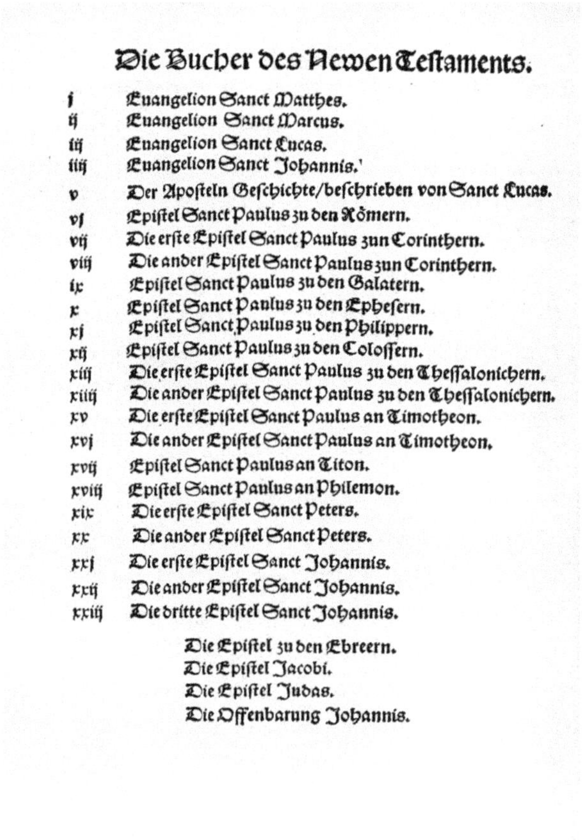

Die Bucher des Newen Testaments.

j	Euangelion Sanct Matthes.
ij	Euangelion Sanct Marcus.
iij	Euangelion Sanct Lucas.
iiij	Euangelion Sanct Johannis.
v	Der Aposteln Geschichte/beschrieben von Sanct Lucas.
vj	Epistel Sanct Paulus zu den Römern.
vij	Die erste Epistel Sanct Paulus zun Corinthern.
viij	Die ander Epistel Sanct Paulus zun Corinthern.
ix	Epistel Sanct Paulus zu den Galatern.
x	Epistel Sanct Paulus zu den Ephesern.
xj	Epistel Sanct Paulus zu den Philippern.
xij	Epistel Sanct Paulus zu den Colossern.
xiij	Die erste Epistel Sanct Paulus zu den Thessalonichern.
xiiij	Die ander Epistel Sanct Paulus zu den Thessalonichern.
xv	Die erste Epistel Sanct Paulus an Timotheon.
xvj	Die ander Epistel Sanct Paulus an Timotheon.
xvij	Epistel Sanct Paulus an Titon.
xviij	Epistel Sanct Paulus an Philemon.
xix	Die erste Epistel Sanct Peters.
xx	Die ander Epistel Sanct Peters.
xxj	Die erste Epistel Sanct Johannis.
xxij	Die ander Epistel Sanct Johannis.
xxiij	Die dritte Epistel Sanct Johannis.

Die Epistel zu den Ebreern.
Die Epistel Jacobi.
Die Epistel Judas.
Die Offenbarung Johannis.

FIGURE 3.4. New Testament Contents, *Luther Bible*, 1534. Notice the four unnumbered and physically separated books at the bottom demoting Hebrews, James, Jude, and Revelation to secondary status, similar to the Apocryphal books (Taschen).

Later, however, Luther found a powerful propaganda tool against the Roman papacy in the beast imagery of the Apocalypse. He thereafter embraced Revelation for polemical use. In stark contrast, John Calvin (Jean Chauvin, d. 1564) had no use for John's Apocalypse and never changed his mind about the book. Tellingly, Calvin wrote commentaries on every book of the Bible but Revelation.

Apocalyptic Art

FIGURE 3.5. Angers Apocalypse Tapestry. The famous Apocalypse Tapestry on display in the Chateau d'Angers at Angers, France. Commissioned by Louis I of Anjou, produced 1377–1382, woven in Paris by famous French artist Nicholas Bataille.

Luther's interpretations of Revelation's images might not have had the enduring effect they achieved without Lucas Cranach the Elder (d. 1553) and Albrecht Dürer (d. 1528), Renaissance artists who provided illustrations for Revelation. Dürer widely was regarded as the greatest German Renaissance artist. We noted the lack of reaction to Augustine's spiritualized apocalyptic among common people, who found inspiration through the Dark Ages in various forms of apocalyptic art. In fact, Revelation was so amenable to picturing that its scenes already by the Middle Ages could be recognized and interpreted independently of the text. The Apocalypse Tapestry in Angers is a magnificent French tapestry 78 feet wide and 20 feet high that has a series of panels depicting 90 scenes from the Apocalypse, but no text.[4]

---

[4] Cf. Camille, "Visionary Perception and Images of the Apocalypse," 280.

60 REVELATION: THE PAST AND FUTURE OF JOHN'S APOCALYPSE

FIGURE 3.6. Rev 11 Illustration, *Luther Bible*, 1534. The beast who opposes the two witnesses, featured wearing the famous triple tiara of the papal crown (Taschen).

FIGURE 3.7. Rev 17 Illustration, *Luther Bible*, 1534. The harlot riding the seven-headed beast, featured wearing the famous triple tiara of the papal crown (Taschen).

So, fast-forward to the Reformation, and you know the rest of the story: a picture is worth a thousand words. Dürer's woodcuts are some of the most enduring images of Revelation of all time.[5] They are ubiquitous in publications related to Revelation. Because of Luther's vitriolic rhetoric against the Roman Catholic papacy, forever etched onto dramatic images of Revelation by artists of the day, various streams of Protestantism probably never will extirpate from their apocalyptic imagination the Antichrist slander in this image of the pope as Antichrist and lackey of Satan. Such papal Antichrist slander, for example, is particularly pervasive in the Seventh-day Adventist literature of the nineteenth and twentieth centuries.[6]

Radical Rhetoric

Thomas Müntzer (d. 1525) was a German cleric initially attracted to Luther's reform movement. What drove Müntzer, however, was not theological reflection, like Luther, but his overwhelming interest in the economic oppression of German peasants by upper class landholders. This economic struggle caused Müntzer to skew religious reflection into social cause. Müntzer eventually led the Peasants' Revolt (1524–1525) in Thuringia, which was an unmitigated disaster. Five thousand unarmed and untrained peasants died, slaughtered on the field of battle when Müntzer's promised apocalyptic intervention of God never materialized. The tragic fate of the inhabitants of Qumran going out to meet Vespasian's Roman legions in the First Jewish War is reprised.

Indeed, Marxists of the twentieth century claimed in Müntzer's preaching, writing, and revolt both the prototype and the paradigm in their struggle for a classless society in modern Europe. Taking his cue from apocalyptic periodization of history schemes (shades of Bede and Joachim), Karl Marx secularized the periods into a series of stages of class struggle that would become communism's total victory. During communist control of East Germany, a great circular monument was erected in the very field of Müntzer's final conflict. This edifice has a gigantic painted diorama on its inner wall aggrandizing Müntzer and the peasants' story. In the communist portrayal of Müntzer's revolt,

---

[5] A good discussion of reasons why is in Camille, "Visionary Perception," 283–89.

[6] Or, in other traditions, combined with a very healthy dose of misogyny, as in Dave Hunt, *A Woman Rides the Beast: The Roman Catholic Church and the Last Days*.

Revelation's visions were hijacked into images of secular class struggle. This radical apocalyptic rhetoric that can be hijacked by any group for any cause and later turn on a dime into violence is one of the most infamous legacies of the Reformation and Revelation.

Radical Anabaptists

The most famous apocalyptically-inspired civil disobedience in the Reformation was the Münster Rebellion of the radical Anabaptists.[7] French and German popular imagination was prepared for radical thought by the ravages of bubonic plague and excessive taxes levied for defense against Turkish expansion into Europe. Such conditions led to general social and political unrest. Into this social unrest came Melchior Hoffmann (d. 1543), who was rebaptized as an Anabaptist, but seemed to stir trouble almost anywhere he traveled. Luther was alarmed at the constant disruption to social peace Hoffmann's presence inevitably seemed to create, not to mention their more mundane differences on the theology of the Eucharist. Luther seemed unaware, however, that his own apocalyptic rhetoric had loosed the beast.

Anabaptists appropriated earlier Taborite eschatology, most particularly with convictions of being on the edge of the end and wanting to help bring New Jerusalem down to earth to inaugurate that second coming and millennial reign. Using the book of Revelation, Hoffmann taught that papal Rome was the Babylon of Revelation and Strasbourg, France was the New Jerusalem. Strasbourg, however, was uncooperative. Strasbourg authorities rejected Hoffmann's offer to be the New Jerusalem. Instead, they arrested Hoffmann. His influence thereby was reduced considerably, but he still inspired others.

Hoffmann's premillennial ideas inspired Jan Matthys (d. 1534), a Dutch Anabaptist who himself decided that Münster, Germany was to be the New Jerusalem (convenient, since French leaders in Strasbourg did not appear to be too cooperative with the Anabaptist program for locating New Jerusalem somewhere in Europe). Unlike Hoffmann's poor reception over in Strasbourg, a small group in Münster favorably received disciples of Matthys.

---

[7]Hard to keep distinguished is the name of a man, Müntzer, the German cleric of the Peasants' Revolt, and the name of a city, Münster, the German town made infamous by the Radical Anabaptist rebellion of Matthys and Bockelson.

Catholics and other citizens were driven out of Münster, and a new civic council set in place. Catholics, however, fought back. They laid siege to the town, and Matthys was killed in one of the skirmishes. John Bockelson (also called John of Leyden, d. 1536), a disciple of Matthys, thereafter took control. Conditions inside the city soon spiraled out of control. Bockelson declared polygamy the social norm and himself the king of this New Jerusalem. Eventually, this "king" was to be captured, tortured, and killed. His body and those of two other leaders were left to rot in cages outside the steeple of St. Lambert's Church in Münster, Germany. The cages remain to this day. Both Müntzer's Peasants' Revolt and the Münster rebellion of the Radical Anabaptist movement, led by men such as Hoffmann, Matthys, and Bockelson, show the radical possibilities in all millennial rhetoric.

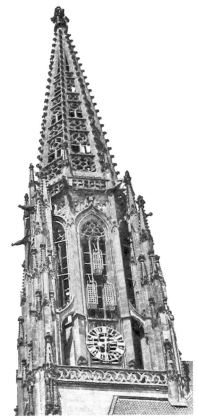

FIGURE 3.8. St. Lambert's Church Steeple. The three cages are in the middle directly above the clock. Credit: Mark A. Gstohl.

What we learn from radical Anabaptists related to the use of Revelation is that we do not have to have the direct persecutions of an empire as in the days of John in Asia Minor to have the fertile soil for acceptance of radical apocalyptic preaching. All we need is general social anxiety (such as the bubonic plague and its social upheaval) and strong political and military fears (such as the Muslim onslaught) to have an audience not only mentally and emotionally primed to hear our newest speculation about the end, but to believe. Fast-forward to the social upheavals of the hippie generation and the Cold War era of communist Russia in the American twentieth century, and you have the formula explaining the success of Hal Lindsey's dispensationalism.

Catholic Reaction

Catholics were not going to play possum to Protestant antipapalism. They either dished back more of the same by turning the tables and identifying Protestants with the beasts and frogs and judgments, or by changing the prophecy fulfillment timeline. Rather than periodizing history up to the present like Protestants, they pushed the fulfillment to either extreme of future or past, creating futurism or preterism.

Futurism

One extreme of the timeline of history is the end out there in the future. The prophecies could be interpreted as not yet fulfilled and awaiting a special time. This approach to prophecy most is associated with Francisco Ribera (d. 1591), a Jesuit professor at the University of Salamanca. He proposed Revelation's 1260 days were not equivalent to years, as in Protestant historicism. Instead, they were real days and pictured a 3.5 year period just prior to the second coming of Christ at the end of history. This view became known as futurism. A supreme irony in the history of interpretation of Revelation is that a Catholic invention for interpreting Revelation as prophecy in order to counteract Protestant antipapalism by a curious twist of fate later became a core fixture of certain streams of Protestant interpretation.

Preterism

The other extreme of the timeline of history is the past. The prophecies could be interpreted as already fulfilled. This approach most is associated with the Jesuit Luis de Alcazar (d. 1613). For Alcazar, Rev 4–19 is the story of the church under Jewish and pagan persecution. Constantine conquers the beast by conversion, the angel who binds Satan in Rev 20 and inaugurates the millennial reign of the church. This view became known as preterism. The preterist view also was adopted among some Protestants who did not have a vested interest in demonizing the pope. Among these Protestant interpreters would be included Hugo Grotius (d. 1645) and Henry Hammond (d. 1660). Reacting to Reformation developments with Revelation, Catholics invented futurism and preterism, but these approaches took on a life of their own as they were swept away downstream.[8]

---

[8] For further analysis, see Wainwright, *Mysterious Apocalypse*, 61–66.

COLONIAL APOCALYPTIC (1700s)[9]

The next significant development of Revelation's traditions is in the ideology of the New World coming out of colonial Europe. About a hundred years after Germany's Peasants' Revolt, various Protestant groups in control in England were making conditions most dangerous for dissenters, including the Puritans, who were trying to purify the Church of England (separated from Rome in 1534 by King Henry VIII) from what they considered lingering vestiges of Roman Catholic "popery." The Puritans advanced the idea of a "Holy Commonwealth," a covenant pact between God and state that would be the foundation for an established church under Puritan ideals of morality and ethics. These are the root ideas of civic millennialism that become the foundation to developing a new eschatological construct that would become known as postmillennial eschatology.[10]

FIGURE 3.9. Colonial Millennialism. Europeans sailing to America brought their own civic millennial ideas foundational to the development of the new eschatological construct of postmillennialism.

Puritan Apocalyptic

America from its very beginnings was born in apocalyptic language and has continued to this day to use this language to interpret its history. The Puritan reform movement failed in England, which

---

[9] Cf. Boyer's *When Time Shall Be No More*. Boyer shows prophecy belief has played a significant role in forming American public attitudes on a wide range of issues.

[10] Cambridge theologian Joseph Mede (1586–1639) infused Puritan thought with a literal, immanent millennium; cf. Chilton, *Visions of the Apocalypse*, 80–86.

remained Episcopal, but Puritans brought their ideals of a Holy Commonwealth to the New World with the eager anticipation of a New World order. Puritans did not call America "the New World" simply because they had not seen the continent before. (Now, have you ever wondered why so many colonial names have the word "new" in them, such as New England, New Jerusalem, New Bedford, etc.?) All such names meant they anticipated actually establishing a New World, with God and human government in covenant. America would become the "righteous nation" God always had desired the people of God to be. Puritans read Revelation's millennium even more literally than did the second-century church fathers Papias, Justin Martyr, or Irenaeus, who thought God himself would have to bring in the millennium. Puritans were confident *they* would bring in the millennium, literally, on God's behalf. The New World opening up in the American colonies was the sure sign of the inauguration of that grand earthly enterprise. New England literally would become Jesus' city "set on a hill" not hidden under a bushel (Matt 5:15), the New Jerusalem of Rev 21:10. As one example, Cotton Mather (d. 1728), the brightest mind of all American Puritans, preached confidently that the American world was on course for transformation into the Holy City, which Christ's return would celebrate. The revival preaching of Jonathan Edwards (d. 1758) in the context of both of the Great Awakenings (1720s–1740s; 1795–1835) continued to promote and popularize this civic millennialism of the Puritans.[11] The colonial period is the heyday of postmillennial thought in America.

Revolutionary Apocalyptic

The Puritan heritage already was losing its governmental grip during the lifetime of Cotton Mather, but the apocalyptic formulation of the civic discourse was an abiding contribution of the Puritans to the American Revolution. Revolt from the tyranny of England's colonial empire was fueled by apocalyptic language. King George III quickly became the target of Antichrist slander when he was declared to be the Antichrist. Paul Revere (d. 1818) said the revolutionary fight really was a struggle against the beast of the Apocalypse. The Stamp Act of 1765 proved this apocalyptic equation for Revere and others. The

---

[11]Cf. Boyer, *When Time Shall Be No More*, 68–74.

British government passed a law requiring the appropriately-stamped piece of paper for all types of commercial activity in the American colonies. Clearly, American colonialists interpreted the British Stamp Act imposed upon colonies as the sure mark of the beast in Revelation.

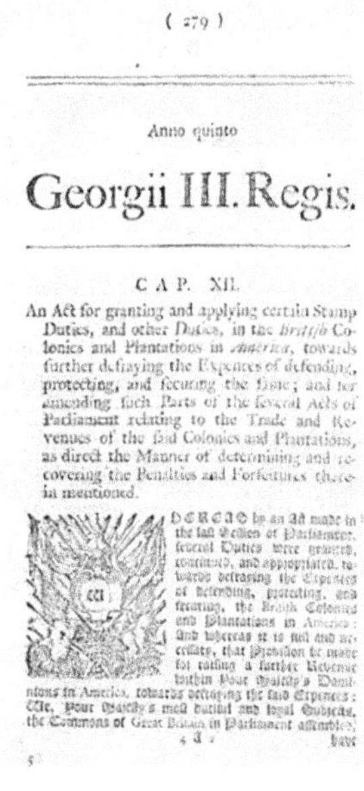

(279)

Anno quinto

Georgii III. Regis.

CAP. XII.

An Act for granting and applying certain Stamp Duties, and other Duties, in the British Colonies and Plantations in America, towards further defraying the Expences of defending, protecting, and securing the same; and for amending such Parts of the several Acts of Parliament relating to the Trade and Revenues of the said Colonies and Plantations, as direct the Manner of determining and recovering the Penalties and Forfeitures therein mentioned.

WHEREAS by an Act made in the last Session of Parliament, several Duties were granted, continued, and appropriated towards defraying the Expences of defending, protecting, and securing, the British Colonies and Plantations in America: And whereas it is just and necessary, that Provision be made for raising a further Revenue within Your Majesty's Dominions in America, towards defraying the said Expences: We, Your Majesty's most dutiful and loyal Subjects, the Commons of Great Britain in Parliament assembled,

FIGURE 3.10. British Stamp Act. Newspaper post of Stamp Act (Library of Congress), interpreted by colonials as the mark of Revelation's beast.

This civic millennial language of the colonial period carried over into political and religious discourse into the next century. A common assumption surfacing in sermons and speeches was that America had a special role in God's plan and would come to realize a millennial destiny. Dramatic changes, such as the American and French political revolutions, the religious awakenings, and more were interpreted as divine preparation for this destiny. Zion, New Jerusalem, would be built in America. Even up through the Civil War, this civic millennialism is written clearly into public discourse and hymnody. Julia Ward Howe's (d. 1910) "Battle Hymn of the Republic," written specifically as a marching hymn for federal troops in the Civil War, is direct: "Mine eyes have seen the glory of the coming of the Lord."[12] Late in the nineteenth century factors inevitably arose to quench this civic postmillennial fervor, but its millennial rhetoric itself had been established firmly as central to American civic and political discourse. This trail of millennial rhetoric is evidenced from President Woodrow Wilson's (d. 1924) energetic support of the League of Nations after World War I to Ronald Regan's (d. 2004) "evil empire" declaration of Soviet Russia during the Cold War.[13]

[12]First appearing on the front page of *The Atlantic Monthly*, February 1862. The melody preexisted as an 1850s campfire spiritual usually traced back to William Steffe.

[13]Used in a March 8, 1983 speech to the National Association of Evangelicals in Orlando, Florida after Soviet fighters shot down Korean Air Flight 007 for violating Soviet air space, purportedly not knowing the target was a commercial flight, just west of Sakhalin Island in the North Pacific. All 269 passengers and crew perished as the plane spiraled into the sea, including U.S. Congressman Larry McDonald.

SUMMARY

Augustine's amillennial construct finally meets its match. The Reformation inaugurates premillennialism, a second major paradigm shift in the strategy for reading Revelation, which turned on its head to a literal reading. The tragic Taborite violence attempting to bring in the millennium was an early precursor to the Reformation's premillennial construct, which also revealed the potentially radical trajectory of a literal reading like premillennialism. Reformers such as Luther seemed little aware of the radical potential in their apocalyptic speech. Corruption in the Roman papacy, already infamous by the time of Wycliffe, triggered this paradigm shift. His desire for reform foundered. He turned to papal Antichrist slander substantiated by a premillennial construct that was precursor to Luther, Rome, and Revelation.

Luther is a watershed both for the Reformation and for Revelation. He revived historical periodizing schemes. He sanctioned Antichrist slander. He proved art as a premier interpretive technique. He unleashed radical apocalyptic rhetoric. Luther's teaching permeated and dominated the religious world due in part to the newly-invented printing press and the power of art. Revelation always inspires art as a premier venue because Revelation fundamentally is symbolic.

Radical potential in premillennial thought plays out in Thomas Müntzer's social activism and peasant rebellion and in radical Anabaptists, such as Hoffmann, Matthys, and Bockelson. The Anabaptists were clear that Montanus was wrong. New Jerusalem was in Münster, Germany, not Pepuza, Phrygia. (Later, we will find out Salt Lake City, Utah is the real deal.) Reformation hermeneutics illustrates how a general climate of social upheaval, along with any perceived, national political threat, become key ingredients for popular acceptance of apocalyptic rhetoric in any generation.

Catholics react to Protestant pope bashing. They reciprocate the rhetoric or invent new views to prophecy fulfillment. They reject Protestant periodizing. They focus on either past fulfillment (preterist), interpreted as Constantine, or future fulfillment (futurist) interpreted as a brief period immediately prior to the second coming. Protestants, unperturbed, keep bashing and periodizing.

Colonial Europe and America produced the third paradigm shift in the eschatological construct for reading Revelation. The shift was born in Puritan ideas of God and government that they brought with them to America. The New World was new not only in undiscovered territory but also in prophetic fulfillment. America with her incredibly rich natural resources and near limitless land had to be the beginnings of New Jerusalem on earth. Apocalyptic formulations were bred into civic discourse and political speech so early in the country's history that American political rhetoric and stump speeches always evoke millennial ideas. America has her millennial destiny to embrace.

Development of Apocalyptic Traditions to the Crusades			
Patristic	Constantine	Millennium	Crusades
100–300s	300s	1000	1000–1200s
• Chiliasm: ⟩ literal reading ✦ hyperliteral ✦ martial messiah ✦ materialistic ⟩ Jewish traditions • Montanism: ⟩ literal reading ⟩ early aberrations ⟩ canonical problems	• Timing Schemes: ⟩ deferred timing ✦ literal reading ✦ periodizing (A.D. 500) ~Anno Mundi ~Last Emperor ⟩ symbolic timing ✦ symbolic reading ✦ timeless truths ✦ recapitulation • Augustine ⟩ amillennialism ⟩ City of God ⟩ Council of Ephesus	• Bede: ⟩ deferred timing ✦ literal reading ✦ periodizing (A.D. 800) ~Anno Domini ~new calculations ⟩ Charlemagne • Adso: ⟩ Antichrist legends ⟩ anti-Semitism • Pope Sylvester: ⟩ periodizing (A.D. 1000) ⟩ common beliefs ⟩ imminence fever	• Anti-Semitism • Hildegard ⟩ literal reading ⟩ periodizing (A.D. 1160) ⟩ church renewal ⟩ Antichrist legends • Joachim of Fiore ⟩ literal reading ⟩ periodizing (A.D. 1260) ⟩ church renewal ⟩ signs of the times ✦ monastic orders ✦ crusades

Development of Apocalyptic Traditions to America			
Reformation	Colonial America	Industrial America	Modern America
1500s	1600–1700s	1800s	1800–1900s
• Luther: ⟩ literal resurgence ⟩ premillennialism ✦ periodizing return ✦ Antichrist slander ✦ apocalyptic art ✦ radical rhetoric ⟩ Radical Anabaptists • Catholic Reactions: ⟩ reciprocal rhetoric ⟩ deferred timing ✦ futurism (Ribera) ✦ preterism (Alcazar)	• Puritans: ⟩ New World ideas ⟩ civic millennialism ⟩ postmillennialism • Revolutionary War: ⟩ Antichrist slander ⟩ millennial rhetoric ✦ national destiny ✦ political discourse	• Mormonism: ⟩ civic millennialism ⟩ postmillennialism • Millerism: ⟩ Millerites ✦ false predictions ✦ new innovations ~invisible return ~three advents ⟩ Adventists (White) ⟩ Splinter Adventists ✦ Worldwide C/G ✦ Jehovah's Witness ✦ Branch Davidians	• Darbyism ⟩ seven dispensations ⟩ two covenants ⟩ great parenthesis ✦ futurism ✦ secret rapture ✦ three advents • American Features ⟩ imminence theme ⟩ signs of the times ⟩ aberrant teachings ✦ multiple advents ✦ maverick schemes ✦ dual covenants

FIGURE 3.11. Development of Traditions. Tracing the main lines of developments over the centuries with John's apocalyptic traditions concluding with the story in America.

4

A Mighty Flood

The Nineteenth-Century Deluge

THE IMPACT OF THE CENTURY following the American Revolution on Revelation's apocalyptic traditions hardly can be overestimated. Apocalyptic imagination goes into overdrive. Radical paradigm shifts dramatically altered Revelation's interpretive landscape. These shifts parallel new religious movements in America that left their enduring mark on the nation's apocalyptic discourse. Three movements in the 1800s are notable in this regard.

MORMONISM

The first nineteenth-century movement is Mormonism (The Church of Jesus Christ of Latter-day Saints), which has everything to do with the biography of Joseph Smith, Jr. (d. 1844). In his very early years as a young boy, Smith was caught up in the highly charged atmosphere of religious revivalism in New York. As a young teenager, he claimed to have experienced a life-changing vision of God and Jesus Christ. Subsequently, according to Smith, the angel Moroni told him that he would reconstitute the true church of Jesus Christ on earth, all others being irredeemably corrupted by false doctrine. Moroni, the last of the ancient prophets, led Smith to find golden tablets the angel had buried fourteen centuries earlier in a hill in Palmyra, New York. These golden tablets purportedly recorded the history of the American Indians, revealing them to be decedents of Hebrews who had sailed the Pacific to the New World. Smith claimed to have translated the tablets. This work became the Book of Mormon, which is the inspired text of the Mormon religion. As Smith attempted to establish a community of followers, he met significant resistance in each place he settled. Eventually, this persecution would push the movement westward until they were outside the current United States boundaries in what is today's Utah.

Mormon apocalyptic thought reflects the religious age in which the movement was born. Mormon leaders echoed the civic millennial language of the postmillennialism common in their day. Hence, America was destined to become the

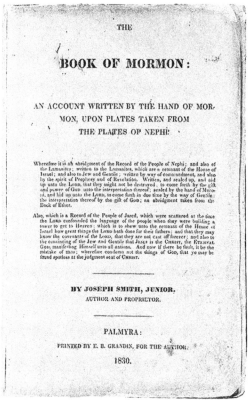

FIGURE 4.1. Book of Mormon Title Page, 1830. Title page of an 1830 copy of the book of Mormon held in the Library of Congress.

location of Zion on earth. The New Jerusalem would be established soon. Facing persecution at every stage of their journey, Smith led his Mormon followers ever westward in search of the New Jerusalem for the true church. Smith was murdered by a mob in Carthage, Ill., but a bright and capable Brigham Young (d. 1877) arose to assert leadership over the main group, continuing the trek westward across America looking for the spot of New Jerusalem. New Jerusalem finally was sighted in the hinterlands of Utah, eventually becoming today's Salt Lake City. (Montanus and Matthys would just have to get used to the idea.) Today's "Mormon Trail" traces this migration and is a part of the United States National Trails System. Because of their numbers globally, the Church of Jesus Christ of Latter-day Saints remains a bastion of postmillennialism.

MILLERISM (ADVENTISM)

The second nineteenth-century movement is the Millerite movement, or, more accurately, the Millerite fiasco. This movement has two historical stages: (1) the first stage of the original movement that failed, and (2) the second stage of the surviving remnant that succeeded. The second stage involves the morphing of the original failed movement into today's Seventh-day Adventists, who have themselves fragmented into numerous splinter groups, including the Waco disaster.

First Stage—Original Millerites

FIGURE 4.2. William Miller (d. 1849). Baptist prophecy preacher good in math not prophecy.

William Miller (d. 1849) made spectacular and dramatic eschatological calculations. Millennial belief in America surged in the 1800s, and Miller rode the wave. He was the equivalent of a combined Bede and Joachim of Fiore on steroids. Miller interpreted Revelation with the book of Daniel. Miller's calculations showed Daniel's two thousand three hundred year apocalyptic clock (2300 days, Dan. 8:14) had started ticking in 457 B.C., calculating the time of the issuance of the decree to rebuild the temple in Jerusalem by Artaxerxes I. That gives the year 1843. In 1839 Joshua Hines put his printing press at Miller's disposal to propagate Miller's calculations. "Something wonderful" was in the air again (shades of the year 1000). Estimates of about 40,000 to 50,000 believers were drawn from all walks of life to hang their eschatological beliefs on Miller's star. They were known as Millerites. Miller refined his calculations down to the month. He declared the end of the world and the second coming of Jesus Christ would happen somewhere in the window between March 21, 1843 and March 21, 1844 in the Gregorian calendar. The date came and went. What to do? Mathematics to the rescue. A slight adjustment on the Jewish side from a rabbinic to a Karaite calendar moved the date one month into April. Unfortunately, that date failed too. Time has this infuriating habit of blithely marching on. What to do? Keep the faith, man!

A hallmark of believing in "the end" is the obstinate refusal to accept history's stark falsification—even in the face of total, public humiliation. Like a dishonest Enron accountant, you cook your books. Miller cooked the prophetic books. He "found" a mistake in his time-calculation formula and simply recalculated. Miller decided he forgot to account for the one-year shift caused by the transition from 1 B.C. to A.D. 1. (What?) In any case, the new date was only months away, in October 1844. (Funny how *every* recalculation ever suggested always pushes the date *forward*, never backward! Wonder why?)

True believers rallied to Miller's new October 1844 date. Farmers failed to harvest crops. Bankers cashed out earnings. Businessmen quit jobs. October 1844, however, came and went. In contrast to the first and second failed-date fiascos, the disillusionment among Millerites this third time around was intense and deeply traumatic. Many were in financial ruin. This third prophecy failure among Millerites was truly "apocalyptic" (at least world changing) and became known as "The Great Disappointment." Disenchanted Millerites now left the movement by the thousands. Miller himself died only five years later.

Miller's prophecy movement, however, did not die. One might wonder how, in the face of such brutal historical contradiction and embarrassing false prophecy, the movement possibly could survive. Be assured of one lesson learned from Revelation's interpretive history: end-time belief ultimately is immortal. Some Millerites survived by: (1) adjusting their teaching—even inventing new eschatological doctrine—so that they could (2) adjust their time, and finally, in terms of public discourse, by (3) adjusting their rhetorical strategy. All groups preaching end-times imminence since then have learned these lessons well. They have honed these strategies to a fine science. Adjust your teaching, adjust your time, adjust your rhetoric. These deceptive and dissimulating strategies continue unabated to this day. The Millerite failure, oddly enough, was a successful rhetorical lesson learned for later end-time prophecy preaching going into the twentieth century.

Adjustment 1: New Teaching (Heavenly Tabernacle)

The care and feeding of apocalyptic faith knows no end to ingenuity and innovation. Some Millerite believers *still* hung on, even *after* the so-called "Great Disappointment" of 1844. What was their solution to this extraordinary problem of historical falsification? New doctrine!

Out of thin air they audaciously invented a bold, new doctrine of a *prophetic heavenly tabernacle visit*. Millerites now claimed that Jesus really *did* come in October 1844. (Now you see him; now you don't.) How? Well, certainly not in the way that they had anticipated. History was too obvious for that fiction. They suddenly claimed that Jesus' prophetic itinerary had changed (not only rewrite history but rewrite core beliefs). Jesus' return to earth included an unexpected stop along the way, shorter than expected, that is, not all the way down to earth. Jesus got only as far as appearing in the heavenly tabernacle, which, of course, no one actually could witness, so disproof now was impossible (brilliant stroke) creating an "invisible coming," which happened in 1844, as predicted. This invisible coming to the heavenly tabernacle was the *first stage* of the second coming and what Miller unknowingly really had calculated. The *second stage* of the second coming is Jesus still returning to earth. That event still is "nigh, even at the door."

Adjustment 2: New Timing (Third Advent)

In this way, by inventing a new *two-stage second coming* (first time in Christian thought), true Millerite believers could continue in the hunt for the second coming—*second stage*, that is. What Millerites really invent is a *third* coming of Christ (incarnation, heavenly tabernacle, millennium). In between the heavenly tabernacle stop and the complete return to earth is a short period that continues to the present time that can anticipate the end at any moment. We already have had over 160 years of this unwavering "imminence" preaching since the 1800s! (Of course, the elephant in the room is, when is "near" no longer near?)

To buttress the anticipation during this interim time between the heavenly tabernacle stop and the picking back up of Jesus' return to earth, Millerites preached irrefutable "signs of the times"—as do all literal readers with linear historical countdown schemes (add the days, know the time)—always showing that this event of the second stage of the return was near, very near, even at the door. This invention of an invisible part of the second coming was a shrewd move, as the strategy helped anesthetize Millerite memory of the "Great Disappointment." This strategy propped up faith in "imminence" preaching by relieving the fatal blow delivered by historical falsification. So, they adjusted their teaching so that they could adjust their timing and obdurately kept preaching "signs of the times."

Adjustment 3: New Strategy (Precisely Imprecise)

The third key to survival for Millerites besides adjusting their teaching and their timing was an adjustment in their rhetorical strategy, that is, how they preached the imminent return of Jesus. To stay in business with Millerite prophetic believers and still remain unexposed as false prophets, Millerite preachers now learned to avoid being concrete about the date. They learned to be careful only *to insinuate* "nearness," without getting caught by too much specificity, as did Miller himself. To insinuate nearness without explicitly saying "now," Millerites learned to make subtle, leading suggestions supposedly adding up the "signs of the times," but then stopping just short of an actual concrete date prediction, with a "you do the math" knowing wink and a nod to the listener. The Millerite listener, fully understanding what had been insinuated, made the calculation, watched for the date, then became confused by historical falsification. Afterwards, the Millerite preacher simply published another book, making subtle shifts in calculations, and comforted the prophecy believer that they misunderstood matters somehow. Any false prophet in this way can become invulnerable to historical falsification. Thus, even though unequivocally falsified *three times* in 1844, the Millerites movement survived in some form.

The Millerite failure was crucial in the evolution of American prophecy rhetoric. Later American prophecy chasers learned how to be precisely imprecise. This "precisely imprecise" rhetorical strategy has been perfected by subsequent "imminence" preaching in America, especially among Adventists, Jehovah's Witnesses, Dispensationalists, Pentecostals, and others even into the twentieth and twenty-first centuries.[1]

Second Stage—Seventh-Day Adventists

A persistent remnant of this original nineteenth-century Millerite movement reincarnated itself as the Seventh-day Adventists, so, effectively becoming the second stage of the original Millerite movement. The Seventh-day Adventist movement inextricably is tied to Ellen G. White (d. 1915). White in her young life had an intense religious experience in a Methodist camp and later became a Millerite. She turned

---

[1] Cf. O'Leary on Hal Lindsey, *Arguing the Apocalypse*, 208–18.

out to be the key figure stepping into the gap of the Millerite "Great Disappointment," with a series of trance states that produced heavenly visions coming not long after. The visions functionally reinterpreted the October 1844 experience, and some Millerite followers ascribed the gift of prophecy to White. White wrote extensively and picked up the broken pieces of the Millerite movement. Millerites who refused to cry "uncle" to history's stark and brutal falsification of the original movement now followed White. They eventually became known as "Seventh-day Adventists."

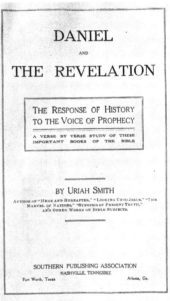

FIGURE 4.3. Uriah Smith (d. 1903). Nineteenth-century Adventist leader who wrote *Daniel and the Revelation*, the classic text on Adventist eschatology.

Uriah Smith (d. 1903) held positions in Adventist leadership in the Adventist general conference, taught at Battle Creek College, and contributed to the *Review and Herald* (*Adventist Review*) for many years. Smith wrote the classic text on Adventist eschatology, entitled *Daniel and the Revelation*. The book is a verse-by-verse commentary on these two prophetic texts. For writers such as Smith, the emphasis on "seventh day" in the title is the Adventist teaching that worship on Sunday, the first day of the week, is the mark of the beast (Rev 13:16). Like radical Protestant teaching, Smith taught the Antichrist will be a Roman Catholic pope. The papacy is fingered by Smith as the power that has spread this "strong delusion" of Sunday worship to all Christendom. True worship of God happens on the only day recognized by God in the Law, the Sabbath, the seventh day of the week. Thus, all Protestant, Roman Catholic, Greek Orthodox, and Russian Orthodox churches, and any other group calling themselves Christian, but not worshipping on the seventh day of the week, will be in jeopardy of falling under the influence of the enforced Sunday worship during the end-time program of the Protestant beast and papal Antichrist.[2]

Third Stage—Splinter Adventists

Adventist groups have a history of splintering into numerous fringe groups. Historically, all these splinter Adventist groups are the third stage ripple effect in history of the original failed Millerite movement. Each splinter Adventist group is tied to a distinct personality as leader. Three significant splinter groups are: (1) Herbert W. Armstrong's Worldwide Church of God with its strange British-Israelism doctrine; (2) Charles T. Russell's Jehovah's Witnesses with their failed 1914 end of the world prediction and their deep suspicion of all organized religion (ironically, like theirs is not), as well as all human government; and (3) David Koresh's Branch Davidians, who left an indelible mark on United States history in the infamous Waco, Texas disaster.

Armstrong: Worldwide Church of God

Herbert W. Armstrong (d. 1986) is one famous example of a splinter Adventist group. Armstrong, originally a businessman in advertising, was reached by the Adventist seventh-day worship argument in the 1920s. Even though at one time accepted as an Adventist minister, Armstrong eventually was defrocked due to his eccentric teachings. Forming his own group, Armstrong secured a fifteen-minute spot on a radio station (KORE, Eugene, Ore.) and organized as the "Radio Church of God" (1934). This initial fifteen-minute radio spot grew into "The World Tomorrow" broadcast and its associated "The Plain

---

[2]Smith makes an attempt to distinguish unwitting participation in Sunday worship of countless generations of believers through the ages from the end-time apostasy of Sabbath violation that is an *intentional* following of the beast's *enforcement* of Sunday worship. This distinction supposedly absolves all Christendom of the error up to the point of Antichrist. Cf. Smith, *Daniel and the Revelation*, 596–607.

Truth" magazine, reaching a worldwide audience. Taking his cue from his broadcast success, Armstrong later renamed his organization "The Worldwide Church of God." The "world tomorrow," of course, is the global monarchy Jesus will establish from his throne in Jerusalem after Apollyon, Antichrist, and Armageddon—God's government on earth.

Armstrong's innovative "The World Tomorrow" radio program evolved into a television broadcast of the same name. Armstrong is the first apocalyptic prophet fully to recognize, embrace, and successfully martial the power of public broadcasting through the new mediums of radio and television to persuade millions. His son, Garner Ted (d. 2003), became the "face" of this new television venue and seemed to be heir apparent of the media empire.

> **"The World Tomorrow" on YouTube**
>
> Not to be confused with:
> - "Tomorrow's World," end-time series by Richard Ames, Charlotte, NC
> - "The World Tomorrow," 2012 television program series of political interviews hosted by WikiLeaks founder, Julian Assange

FIGURE 4.4. "The World Tomorrow" Broadcast. Old television series by Herbert W. Armstrong.

Herbert Armstrong, like all Adventists from whom he derived his eschatological impetus, was persuaded biblical prophecies were being fulfilled in the historical events surrounding his own lifetime. History was on the edge of the end. As herald of the gospel of God's kingdom on earth in this momentous time, Armstrong was the end-time Elijah, or perhaps not. Armstrong left the "Elijah" theme he promoted about himself and his age ambiguous (precisely imprecise). History did not oblige. In any case, the Elijah tease was just a sideshow in his teaching.

The odd teaching that most quickly identifies "Armstrongism" is "British Israelism." Armstrong's was an Americanized subspecies of this tradition. The key to unlocking all biblical prophecies about the future, Armstrong taught, lay in establishing the unrecognized, true identity of Great Britain and America. This identity was—hold your breath—Davidic, no less! Armstrong read promises to David about establishing David's earthly throne as immutable and continuous in history. David was promised a dynasty that would be a continuous, unbroken historical stream. Through imaginative, inventive readings of a conglomerate of specific Old Testament texts, Armstrong traced this historical stream. He included ideas of the Abrahamic birthright of Ephraim and Manasseh, the "lost ten tribes" of northern Israel after Assyrian exile, and Jeremiah's postexilic survival and protection of the daughters of King Zedekiah in Mizpah. Armstrong read other biblical references as pointing to the "northwest" quadrant of the world from Jerusalem. Geographically and miraculously, these lined up perfectly, he asserted, with the British Isles. So, Scripture pointed to the significance of Great Britain in the biblical horizons of great empires and the Davidic dynasty. To these British Isles the Davidic dynasty preserved in Zedekiah's daughters secretly emigrated.[3] Here in the British Isles this true Davidic dynastic line survived, just as prophesied to David, through the centuries.[4] Through its relationship with Great Britain, the American nation thus inherits a central role in end-time prophecy.

You may have noticed Jesus Christ has not been mentioned in this British Israelism drama. What about Jesus Christ in this scheme? Oh, Jesus? He was the promised fulfillment of an entirely *different* set of Abrahamic promises. We are talking only the Ephraim, Manasseh side of the Abrahamic birthright legacy. Go figure.

In later years the Armstrong organization was rocked by scandals moral and financial, as well as Armstrong's failed prophecy regarding the year 1972. Armstrong was forced to disfellowship his intended heir, son Garner Ted, but the reason never publicly was given. In the process of this intense infighting, rumors were rife about adultery and gambling on one side, with countercharges of serious sexual impropriety on the other.

Garner Ted seemed nonplussed enough over the entire matter to form his own media organization, "The Church of God International," locally based in Tyler, Texas. He was mediagenic, with a relaxed style of delivery on the pattern of a talk show host, and comfortable around cameras and microphones. Garner Ted continued a teaching ministry with a weekly television broadcast and supporting literature until he

---

[3] Of course this Davidic emigration to the British Isles had to be secret, because the event is non-historical. Such "secrecy" teaching is similar to the Millerite solution to solve the failed prophecy of the coming of Jesus by inventing the "secret" visit of Jesus to the heavenly tabernacle before continuing on his way to earth. Here's a clue: any prophecy teaching that invokes an element of secrecy is a sure tip-off to non-historical eisegesis and hermeneutical sleight of hand.

[4] Sounds weirdly similar to tracing the supposed family line of Jesus through all of European history in the fictional plotline of Dan Brown's *The Da Vinci Code*, 2003.

died in 2003. His organization continues to broadcast shows previously recorded by Garner Ted, but another personality has not come forward to take the media helm.

Numerous Armstrong splinter groups have arisen; most have derived from this period of family scandal and failed prophecy. The splinter groups usually include modified forms of "Church of God" in their name, even though other denominations also use this title. The common inclusion of "Church of God" in all these off-shoots actually codes an exclusivist belief that any particular splinter Armstrong group is the only true church on earth.

> Garner Ted Armstrong on YouTube
> Search: jimc1596
>
> video and audio messages from the GTA archives

FIGURE 4.5. "GTA" Broadcasts. An old television series by Garner Ted Armstrong.

Russell: Jehovah's Witnesses

FIGURE 4.6. Charles T. Russell (d. 1916). Publisher, leader of Bible Students groups.

A second splinter Adventist movement notable in American history is tied to the personality of Charles T. Russell (d. 1916). In his formative years, Russell could not abide the traditional church's doctrine of hell and left the church a skeptic until reclaimed for eschatology by some Adventists. With the injection of this new Adventist teaching, Russell grew into an intense Bible student, self-taught, and began his own calculation career on the time of the end. His followers formed Bible Students societies. He was a prolific writer; he founded the Watchtower Bible and Tract Society, which became an eminently successful publication venture whose main focus is promoting the imminent return of Christ (16 million copies, 35 languages, 2,000 newspapers initially carrying Russell's sermons). Russell's prophetic calculations caused him to conclude the "invisible return" of Christ (Russell's version of the Adventist "heavenly tabernacle" teaching) actually happened in 1874, not 1844 as Miller had calculated. The start of WWI was the beginning of the end of the world. Russell predicted Jesus' final return to earth (*third* advent) would be 1914. Jesus' return would provoke Armageddon, the final conflict between good in capitalism and evil in communism (or socialism, take your pick). Russell's movement survived the exposure of Russell as a false prophet after the critical date of 1914 came and went (the indomitable spirit of prophecy belief—not even undeniable historical falsification counts).

Russell's successor, Joseph F. Rutherford (d. 1942), gave Russell's original lay movement its name. Rutherford was enamored with the name Jehovah. Rutherford taught that "Jehovah" was the "true" God, known only by that name, and only Jehovah's witnesses the one true church. Organized religion of any form and denominations of any kind are all tools of Satan to deceive the world. Political parties and all governments are tools of Satan too (no flag saluting, no military service). Rutherford warned to be on the lookout on the watchtower of time. The end is perpetually "near."

Thus, in Russell and Rutherford and the Jehovah's Witnesses we have new Adventist *calculations* of the end, but not any substantially new eschatological teachings developing Revelation's traditions. We do note how Russell took Luther's cue and used the power of print to its fullest extent. Adventist-inspired counter-movements, such as in Armstrong and Russell, were teaching future prophets of Revelation the power of modern media for rapid and wide dispersion of new and controversial teachings. The Internet now has democratized the process to anyone with a computer.

Koresh: Branch Davidians

A third Adventist splinter group made famous in more recent memory was the "Branch Davidians" at the Mount Carmel compound near Waco, Texas. They were under the leadership of David Koresh, whose real name was Vernon Wayne Howell (d. 1993). The story is somewhat convoluted. The Branch Davidians can be traced back to an Adventist splinter group originally led by Victor Houteff (d. 1955). Adventist leadership had rejected Houteff's reform efforts, so he and his wife, Florence, formed their own group, which seems to be the constant saga of Adventism. They then established a compound called Mount Carmel, near Waco, Texas. Florence assumed leadership of the group after her husband died. Florence predicted the return of Jesus for April 22, 1959. After this prophecy failure, the group splintered even further. The family of Lois Roden and her son George Roden had control of the compound for some time, but conflicts between George Roden and Vernon Howell, who had joined the group, eventually led to Vernon gaining complete control of the compound.

FIGURE 4.7. David Koresh (d. 1993). Leader of the "Branch Davidians" at Waco, Texas.

In 1990 Howell legally changed his name to David Koresh. The David part of the name was an assertion of a claim to the biblical Davidic line. The Koresh part of the name was a transliteration of the name of the Persian king Cyrus, notable for allowing the Jews to return to their homeland. Koresh claimed to be appointed to a messianic role. He taught that he and the 144,000 would gather at Jerusalem in preparation for the imminent end-time saga. He then decided the story would center in Waco, Texas, and, ominously, renamed Mount Carmel as the "Ranch Apocalypse." The group began to get in trouble with law enforcement officials over allegations about child abuse and statutory rape at the compound, but access to the compound was denied. Eventually, the U.S. Bureau of Alcohol, Tobacco, and Firearms also became involved. Negotiations, however, were not successful, and the Bureau decided to take action.

Unfortunately, when agents of the ATF raided the compound on Feb. 28, 1993 in a show of force, four federal agents and six Branch Davidians were killed in the ensuing gun battle. The unsuccessful raid led to a standoff between the federal government and Koresh and his Branch Davidians penned up in the compound. The Federal Bureau of Investigation now had become entangled in the siege, which went on for several months. Koresh interpreted these events as the beginning of the battle of Armageddon. The standoff ended in a disastrous conflagration of the compound when FBI agents moved in on the center April 19, 1993. Almost eighty people died in the tragic fire, including women and children, historically reprising Qumran and Müntzer.

84 REVELATION: THE PAST AND FUTURE OF JOHN'S APOCALYPSE

FIGURE 4.8. Mount Carmel in Flames. The David Koresh tragedy of April 19, 1993.

DARBYISM (DISPENSATIONALISM)

The third nineteenth-century movement radically altering America's apocalyptic landscape and Revelation's interpretation is Darbyism or dispensationalism. This movement provides us with the most dramatic and extensive development of Revelation's traditions since Augustine and Luther—quite an accomplishment, to be sure. We will survey the history and teachings of this significant movement with a view to its popular writers, because these publications have impacted the general take on Revelation of the person in the pew and on the street. What is amazing is constantly to encounter the almost complete ignorance of the general American populace that this eschatological view is no older than the American Civil War.

Origins—Plymouth Brethren

Darbyism has roots in the Plymouth Brethren movement in Ireland and England in the first half of the nineteenth century. By the early nineteenth century, after the failure of postmillennial constructs of American revolutionary and colonial history, traditional Protestant denominations and clergy generally ignored the teaching and preaching of prophecy and the second coming of Christ. One exception to this prophetic apathy in church hierarchy was what came to be known as the Brethren movement originating in Dublin, Ireland in the 1820s. This lay movement felt the Church of England and her ministers had become corrupt and untrustworthy. Members of the movement in the main distrusted denominational clergy and eschewed any semblance of hierarchical authority. They did not even want to give themselves a name, claiming to be just believers strictly following the Bible alone. The "brethren" designation was inspired by the general term used in the Bible to make reference to all believers.

With this distrust of hierarchy and the established church, the inevitable result was that any Brethren cell easily accepted the teaching of any charismatic or assertive lay leader who would step into this gap. The usual focus of their meetings and assemblies was upon biblical prophecy. The only approved reading of any prophecy, in a move that fundamentally denied sound hermeneutical principles, was a "literal" interpretation. Brethren teachers were quick to criticize any figurative reading as "spiritualizing" the text. Of course, rhetorically, this charge of "spiritualizing" was no more than a disguised attack on legitimate figurative readings for literature using figurative language. The movement quickly spread to Plymouth, England, from where the group got the other part of its name.

Americanization—J. N. Darby

John Nelson Darby (d. 1882), was a former cleric of the Church of Ireland (Anglican). He soon became the premier personality driving the Brethren movement in the Plymouth area (hence, "Plymouth Brethren"). Darby was assertive in his teachings and aggressive in his leadership. He ruthlessly attacked anyone who had the audacity to disagree with his particular teachings—even ejecting out of the fellowship former close associates and friends who had become increasingly uncomfortable with his unusual teachings and had tried to speak out against him. Opposition, however, continued.

FIGURE 4.9. John Nelson Darby (d. 1882). Father of the new dispensationalism invented in the mid-1800s.

When reaction against Darby became too problematic for his ongoing leadership in Plymouth, Darby looked to the fertile prophetic soil of America to transplant his distinctive brand of the Brethren movement overseas in the 1860s. Here was a new and charismatic prophecy speaker with unheard-of eschatological teachings to titillate the American public arising at the perfect time to fill the prophetic gap left by the failed Millerite movement in its 1844 "Great Disappointment" debacle. As he traveled the American countryside, Darby gave numerous lectures, led Bible studies, and conducted Bible conferences disseminating ideas that became the hallmark of a new eschatological system that eventually came to be called "dispensationalism." What were these new, never before heard teachings of Darby? The question is a little hard to answer, simply because the construct works more as an entire system together and not on any one particular thought. The following seem to be the main innovations.

Seven Dispensations

The name of the movement is derived from its own odd periodization scheme of biblical history. The scheme is odd for several reasons. First, the scheme is not based on any cycle of visions in Revelation. Second, four of the seven periods are derived from just the first twelve chapters of Genesis alone. Third, each of the so-called dispensations are based on idiosyncratic readings of singular verses in the Bible. Fourth, one dispensation is derived from a term literally mentioned in the entire Bible only twice in one paragraph. Fifth, the dispensations serve only to support a deficient understanding of salvation. That is, even though Darby's new dispensational teachings echoed the periodization of history schemes already seen, Darby's dispensations were presented by way of supporting a radical and aberrant soteriology. Darby asserted the dispensations were divinely ordained periods of human history in which humanity was given an express revelation of the will of God to which humanity was to respond with faith. Judgment would differ in each dispensation according to whatever conditions God set for that dispensation. The bottom line for this complete rewrite of salvation history is that every dispensation expresses a new and different basis for salvation. This seriously flawed soteriology was one of the main criticisms Darby got from the very beginning even from some of his closest friends back in Plymouth, England before Darby even came to

America. To be blunt, Darby's novel presentation of "dispensations" of salvation history theologically better can be described as multiple "salvation systems"—and even Darby's closest associates in Plymouth perceived that clear theological aberration right away.

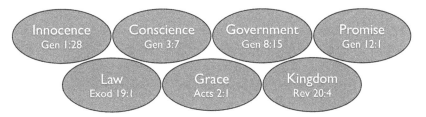

FIGURE 4.10. Darby's Seven Dispensations. Another historical periodizing scheme, but not based on the cycle of visions of Revelation and functionally supporting multiple salvation systems.

Scofield later codified Darby's dispensations as seven: innocence (Gen 1:28), conscience (Gen 3:7), government (Gen 8:15), promise (Gen 12:1), law (Exod 19:1), grace (really the church, Acts 2:1), and kingdom (Rev 20:4). For example, acceptability before God in the dispensation of law had a *Mosaic legal condition* to salvation. In the dispensation of grace, acceptability has a *Christocentric faith condition* to salvation. In the future kingdom, acceptability before God will have a *messianic legal condition*, that is, a more perfect legal condition available under Messiah than was available under Moses. The description of these dispensations even among dispensationalists themselves has had to be modified significantly in response to searing criticism. Note carefully the dramatic difference in two editions of the Scofield Bible. As one compares the 1917 and 1967 Scofield editions, one quickly sees the attempt by the editors of the newer edition to fend off the critics in the note at Gen. 1:28, which is the note that first introduces discussion of dispensations. The note now has this curious asseveration: "These different dispensations are not separate ways of salvation." In a similar way one again has this disavowal: "such stewardship is not a condition of salvation."[5] Simply asserting "not separate ways of salvation" does not make them not separate ways of salvation. They are. If you have "dispensations" that are concrete historical periods in which God in each of the periods has responded to humans in salvation *differently*, you have taught *different* (multiple) salvation systems.

[5] *The New Scofield Reference Bible*, 3.

Two Covenants

Darby's dispensational teaching is only one component of his radically new understanding of prophecy. The dispensations are an exotic and interesting facet, and a strange doctrine unknown to the whole church for thousands of years. More importantly, though, these dispensations really are meant to service a cardinal doctrine in Darby's scheme. Darby's cardinal teaching upon which his entire dispensational system is based is his covenant distinction between "Israel" and the "church." By making these covenant distinctions between Israel and the church, Darby could assert that Israel and the church represent two different people of God with two different covenants and two different tracks in salvation (and, likewise, in prophecy). In fact, one might could go so far as to charge that *Darby's entire dispensational system is sublimated to, and developed solely for the purpose of supporting this distinction between the two mutually exclusive entities of "Israel" and "the church."*

So how did Darby define "Israel"? Darby clearly thought of Israel as a *national* entity with an *exclusive and eternal* covenant for political supremacy over the nations of the world in the end time that will be lived out on earth. What then is the "church"? A footnote in prophetic history. In stark contrast to Israel's glorious and status-filled prophetic future, the church is only the result of Israel's rejection of her Messiah in his First Advent, an unnecessary historical accident, a prophetic "parenthesis" in Israel's story, a diversion to the real drama of Israel. The church resulted as an afterthought to God's original plan for Israel for national and political supremacy among the kingdoms of the world. The church's consolation prize for not really being a key player on the stage of eschatology is that she gets to convert Gentiles. Thus, during the church's measly existence as a prophetic parenthesis in the countdown to worldwide Israeli military supremacy and political empire, she can at least provide an opportunity for Gentiles to be saved. That God never intended Israel to be about saving Gentiles despises texts such as Gen 12:3; Isa 42:6; 49:6; 60:3; Luke 2:32; Acts 9:15; 15:14; Rom 11:26; 15:10; and Eph 3:6. Dispensationalists teach the church's role is completely separate from Israel's, and, prophetically, not nearly as significant. What about the millennial reign? Only for Israel, Darby said. Darby did offer the church the consolation prize of an eternal reign in heaven, but, as far as Darby was concerned, the church does not get to participate in Israel's thousand year reign on earth.

One Great Parenthesis (Futurism)

"Nearness" preaching always ignores the big elephant in the room: the awkward embarrassment of two millennia of church history without the return of Christ. The purpose of any periodizing scheme today is an attempt to deal with this embarrassment, which inherently contradicts any emphasis on imminence. Today's periodizer assumes certain historical events have to transpire, then comes the end, and I am at the end. Any armchair prophet can take the timeline of history, divide into any arbitrary number of periods (Bede's seven, Joachim's three, etc., take your pick), then take a history book and distribute the events already known to have occurred across these arbitrary periods, but always so as to make your own day the last. After two millennia of church history, Bede's old device of add the days, know the time now has become assume the end, divide the time.

Darby's third innovation was his ingenious way of duping his audience about the elephant in the room. He did so by completely bypassing the periodizing scheme that had been the literalist go-to strategy for this problem for centuries. Darby invented an interpretive device that simply erased two thousand years of church history and the non-event of the return of Christ. This radical rewriting made the church's two thousand years absolutely meaningless in the prophetic scheme, but apparently for Darby that was a sacrifice worth reinvigorating "imminence expectation" about the return of Christ. In effect, Anglican Darby suddenly canonized the Catholic Ribera's futurism.

Darby's revisionist church history was accomplished by a bold manipulation of a passage in Daniel inventing a transparently non-literal interpretation that denied the literal meaning of the text to import an alien meaning the text does not actually communicate. The passage is Daniel's famous seventy weeks to Israel's Messiah bringing in "everlasting righteousness" (Dan 9:24). Darby insisted that Daniel intended his readers to pick up on a pause in the divine clock between the sixty-ninth and seventieth weeks. Numerous critics have noted this supposed "pause" is nowhere explicitly stated or implied in the actual Daniel passage. The movement from week sixty-nine to seventy reads exactly as does any previous week in Daniel's sequence. If any so-called "pause" existed between weeks sixty-nine and seventy, then this invisible, silent, unspoken, unacknowledged pause could not be denied between *any* of the seventy weeks in the entire sequence, not just the last one. So, the assertion of a "pause" in Daniel's sequence from week sixty-nine to week seventy is completely arbitrary, logically inconsistent, and unabashedly self-serving to an interpretive scheme.

This asserted prophetic pause in Daniel's prophecy of the seventy weeks became dubbed the "great parenthesis." Such a "parenthesis" in church history is neither known to the apostles of the Lord, nor any of the church fathers, nor the great minds of the church applied to this passage for two millennia. Thus, the "great parenthesis" really turns out to be the extraordinary embarrassment of the "great ignorance." Darby knew that his teaching on Dan 9:24 would be a huge offense for what was implied about all the church theologians to his day. He thus attempted to mitigate this great ignorance of the church implied in his "great parenthesis" artifice by a patent interpretive hubris that takes the breath away. He simply explained Daniel's prophecy was "sealed" till the generation of the end-time, based on Dan 12:9. That end-time generation would have the veil of mystery lifted off crucial prophetic texts such as Dan 9:24—and Darby was the man. *Ecce homo*.[6]

We can use a football game analogy to see where Darby put the church on stage of prophetic time and what role he assigned to her in the end-time drama. Darby's end-time drama is like a cosmic football game. The real game is played by the real home team—national Israel. The first half is Israel's history up to Messiah. After Israel's rejection of Messiah comes the halftime show. Into this halftime pause in Israel's game, the church band comes out on the field to play. The church has nothing to do with the points on the scoreboard, or the real outcome of the game. The church just entertains the crowd for a while and then exits the field of play. After the halftime pause, the crowds of history, duly distracted from Israel's national game by the entertaining and energetic, but eschatologically insignificant, historical movement of the church, then would watch the church band leave the field, and the real game with the home team, Israel, the future world empire, would continue. God, the eschatological referee, would blow the whistle, and the second-half kickoff would restart the end-time game with Israel, the recent halftime show of the church a quickly fading memory.

---

[6]Incredible to think that Darby was claiming an interpretive brilliance and insight greater than the combined intelligence of Irenaeus, Tertullian, Origen, Jerome, Augustine, Thomas Aquinas, Luther, Calvin, Zwingli, Wesley, and so many more.

Secret Rapture

The second-half kickoff event was Darby's fourth extraordinary and daring eschatological innovation after the "great parenthesis" reading of Dan 9:24. Darby taught that this kickoff to the (supposedly) delayed last week of Daniel would be the "secret rapture" of the church, which, since all prophecies necessary to be fulfilled before the rapture takes place are in place, could be at any moment. Darby's supposed "secret rapture" teaching ostensibly is derived from Paul's statement in 1 Thess 4:17. Paul taught that believers would be "caught up in the clouds" to meet the Lord in the air. The verb in this verse translated "caught up" (KJV, NRSV) is rendered in the Latin Vulgate, the official Bible of the Roman Catholic Church, as *rapio, raptum*, "snatch," from which is derived our English word "rapture."[7] After the church is so-called "raptured," the divine eschatological clock for Israel begins ticking again, and Daniel's seventieth week unfolds in that final seven-year period of tribulation for the world. At the end of this tribulation, Christ returns for the second stage of the second coming. Without any doubt, this novel, any-moment "secret rapture" teaching at the time Darby introduced the idea was an unknown concept in the language of Christian eschatology until voiced by Darby—once again, neither known to the apostles of the Lord, nor any of the church fathers, nor the great minds of the church for two millennia—either invented by Darby himself or snatched from elsewhere. Dispensationalists do not feel the extraordinary weight of this critique of two thousand years of Christian interpretation because they dismiss this observation with the most preposterous claims.

Take Hal Lindsey, for example. Lindsey, taking Darby's cue, uses Dan 12:9, the "sealing up" of Daniel's prophecy to the time of the end, as meaning that what Daniel wrote would be a complete mystery and senseless until the end-time generation. So, what kind of interpretive hubris then would countenance this following slam by Lindsey on millennia of Christian interpreters? "Christians after the early second century spent little time really defining prophetic truth until the mid-

---

[7]A most curious irony of history is that a main tenet of dispensationalism, today a dominant strand of modern evangelical eschatology, is dependent for its name on terminology from the Roman Catholic Latin Vulgate.

dle of the nineteenth century."[8] You have *got* to be kidding me. Our current survey of the history of the interpretation of Revelation has shown this balderdash to be absolute, total falsification.

What Darby really invents with his so-called secret rapture of the church, similar to Adventists, is a *third* advent of Christ (incarnation, secret rapture, millennium). Darby's "secret rapture" of the church is nothing more than another "invisible coming" equivalent to Adventist teaching of the invisible coming of Jesus to the heavenly tabernacle in 1844 (or Russell's 1874).

Because Darby emphasized the authority of the Bible and a literal reading of prophecy, his system became the darling of evangelical fundamentalism. Further, his futurist teaching on a national Israel was in the spirit of the age. This jingoistic rhetoric easily resonated with the American Zionist movement that was picking up steam politically in the late nineteenth century.[9] In addition, Darby's clearly maverick and idiosyncratic eschatological teachings regarding a "great parenthesis" in Daniel's prophecy of the seventy weeks and the associated cousin teaching of an any-moment "secret rapture" of the church—unheard of in all the ages of the church—also was in the very spirit of the age. Nineteenth century America spawned the most rampant apocalyptic expectations ever seen—the most furious flurry of wild speculations that an ever increasing industrial and secular society could provoke when challenging the bedrock tenets of American pietistic religion. In the end, Protestant eschatology bought stock in Catholic futurism.

Historical Animosity

Dispensationalism, though going through attempted reforms in the twentieth century, still continues to emphasize the "great parenthesis" teaching of Daniel's prophecy, with the "invisible coming" aberration

---

[8]*Late Great Planet Earth*, 181.

[9]The movement's official beginning as a political force usually is assigned to Theodore Herzl and the 1897 World Zionist Congress meeting in Basel, Switzerland. For the political marriage of American Zionism with American fundamentalism, especially in the twentieth century, see Grace Halsell, *Prophecy and Politics: Militant Evangelists on the Road to Nuclear War*. An interesting fresh perspective on President Truman's decision to recognize the state of Israel after hard Zionist lobbying by his lifelong friend, Eddie Jacobson, is given by Michael Beschlos, *Presidential Courage: Brave Leaders and How They Changed America 1789-1989*.

on the second coming of Christ, ironically dubbed the "rapture" of the church. The imminence of Christ's return perpetually is propped up through indefatigable "signs of the times" preaching that never is dissuaded by historical falsification. Dispensationalists of the Darby variety, in fact, despise history. The true facts of history, as for Miller, Russell, and others, are inconvenient annoyances that disturb the hermeneutical equilibrium of a contrived prophetic system. The attitude clearly is along the lines of, "Don't confuse me with the facts; my mind is made up."

Darby's own words give one of the most telling examples of his dispensational animosity to the real facts of history. In a comment on Rev 4:1, Darby injected a revealing note. This verse opens with John's invitation through a heavenly voice to "come up here"; that is, John is introduced to a vision of heaven. Darby pours into this verse his entire futurist system of interpreting all of Revelation from this point forward as events yet to occur. What is really bizarre, however, is how in a footnote on this verse Darby launches out into a philosophically twisted false dichotomy between "prophecy" and "history," setting these up as supposedly opposing ideas. "Prophecy," Darby asserted, is the mind of God, history written in advance, knowledge of the future that has divinely-inspired authority. Hence, only the one who has ascertained correctly divine "prophecy" can write true "history." Darby then defines "history" as mere human invention, the propositions of human ignorance, a futile attempt to know the mind of God. Most people would be in disbelief that Darby, after setting up this false and absurd dichotomy, then actually dared in print to acknowledge: "I do not admit history to be, in any sense, necessary to the understanding of prophecy. . . . I do not want history to tell me Nineveh or Babylon is ruined or Jerusalem in the hand of the Gentiles."[10] Any sense of logic here is twisted into a pretzel of epistemological contradictions. Declaring invalid any attempt at knowing "history," how can any "prophetic" interpretation, which is supposed to be "history written in advance," be confirmed or disconfirmed? Worse still, any objection to Darby's convoluted interpretation of "prophecy," that is, any objection to his dispensational futurist approach to Rev 4:1 and all chapters forward

---

[10] *The Collected Writings of J. N. Darby*, 2:272.

blatantly is declared an attack upon the inspiration of the Bible. When divining the meaning of "prophecy" is the issue, Darby already has declared "no contest." Darby has the mind of God; objectors do not. Futurist interpretation in this way is insulated from the facts of history and rendered impervious to criticism. Dispensationalists who follow Darby in such inherently contradictory argumentation and distorted ideology truly despise the facts of history.

American Dominance

With such an idiosyncratic and aberrant teaching innovated after two thousand years of church history, what put dispensationalism onto its trajectory of dominance in America and then to the evangelical world? Cyrus I. Scofield (d. 1921) almost universally is credited with this feat. When one is apprised of Scofield's continually notorious personal life, even after conversion, laced as this story is with sorry episodes of liquor, gambling, forgery, divorce, jail time, and the like, this feat is even all the more astonishing.

FIGURE 4.11. Cyrus I. Scofield (d. 1921). Creator of the *Scofield Bible*, teaching Darby's dispensationalism.

Scofield Reference Bible

Scofield had absorbed dispensational teaching from James H. Brookes (d. 1875), the famous minister of Walnut Street Presbyterian Church in St. Louis, who for years was president of the Niagara Bible Conference. Scofield's legal training and legislative experience in Kansas qualified him for detail and argument, and he put this training and experience to good use in compiling a system of notes for teaching a correspondence Bible course. These teaching notes essentially became the foundation for a unified, global system of Bible reference notes that evolved into *The Scofield Reference Bible*, first published in 1909, with a revised and updated edition in 1917, and again in 1967.

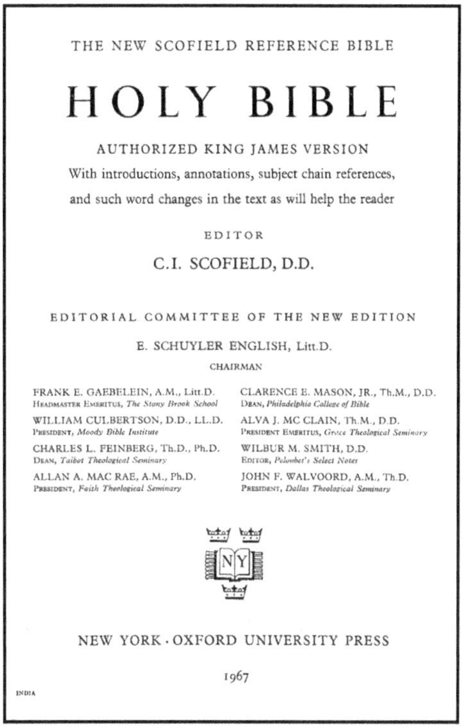

THE NEW SCOFIELD REFERENCE BIBLE

HOLY BIBLE

AUTHORIZED KING JAMES VERSION

With introductions, annotations, subject chain references, and such word changes in the text as will help the reader

EDITOR

C.I. SCOFIELD, D.D.

EDITORIAL COMMITTEE OF THE NEW EDITION

E. SCHUYLER ENGLISH, Litt.D.
CHAIRMAN

FRANK E. GAEBELEIN, A.M., Litt.D.
HEADMASTER EMERITUS, *The Stony Brook School*

WILLIAM CULBERTSON, D.D., LL.D.
PRESIDENT, *Moody Bible Institute*

CHARLES L. FEINBERG, Th.D., Ph.D.
DEAN, *Talbot Theological Seminary*

ALLAN A. MAC RAE, A.M., Ph.D.
PRESIDENT, *Faith Theological Seminary*

CLARENCE E. MASON, JR., Th.M., D.D.
DEAN, *Philadelphia College of Bible*

ALVA J. MC CLAIN, Th.M., D.D.
PRESIDENT EMERITUS, *Grace Theological Seminary*

WILBUR M. SMITH, D.D.
EDITOR, *Peloubet's Select Notes*

JOHN F. WALVOORD, A.M., Th.D.
PRESIDENT, *Dallas Theological Seminary*

NEW YORK · OXFORD UNIVERSITY PRESS

1967

INDIA

FIGURE 4.12. *The New Scofield Reference Bible.* A new edition continuing to promote a novel, nineteenth-century eschatological scheme (by permission of Oxford University Press, USA).

The first publication of the *Scofield Reference Bible* in 1909 launched Darby's new dispensational teaching into evangelical orbit. The *Scofield Reference Bible* has become the most successful reference Bible publication of all time. Multiple editions have sold millions of copies. With Scofield's organized, systematized, integrated set of dispensational notes in an apparatus at the bottom of each page of the inspired text, this novel publication well exceeded initial expectations and did more than any single person to propagate Darby's dispensationalism in America. Uncritical readers of Scofield's notes were not advised alternative interpretations existed, nor that the eccentric eschatological ideas promoted were less than seventy years old when first published. Nor were they cautioned not to read the notes as inspired as the inspired text.[11]

Scofield Institutionalized

This novel and radical Scofield system was institutionalized by Lewis Sperry Chafer (d. 1952) when he founded Dallas Theological Seminary (1924). Chafer founded this institution to inculcate dispensational eschatology exclusively. Chafer served as president until his death. Other academic notables in the twentieth century are John Walvoord (d. 2002), Dwight Pentecost, and Charles Ryrie.

[11]My primary study Bible in my high school years was the *New Scofield Reference Bible.* I cut my eschatological teeth on its dispensational system and naïvely thought everyone held these beliefs to be the self-evident prophetic truth of God's Word.

Scofield Popularized

FIGURE 4.13. *The Late Great Planet Earth*. Popularizing dispensationalism in America. (Image used by permission from Zondervan).

A Dallas Seminary graduate, however, excelled them all in commercial success and in popularizing dispensational teaching for general public consumption in the twentieth century. He rode the wave of general political and social upheaval of the hippie generation and Cold War fears. On the heels of the 1967 Six Day War between Israel and an Arab confederation of Egypt, Jordan, Iraq, and Syria, Harold Lee ("Hal") Lindsey published *The Late Great Planet Earth* (1970), written in a popular and folksy newspaper style for the masses energized by the "Jesus Movement" of colleges and universities in the late 1960s and early 1970s. The book, translated into fifty-four languages with thirty-five million copies, is still in print.

While attempts to respond to strong criticism of dispensational teaching from Reformed theologians and others has produced some revisionist efforts such as "progressive dispensationalism,"[12] the main Darbyite teachings, in fact, are still solidly in place today, as one easily can determine in general conversation with the person in the pew of a dispensational preacher. The only matters that actually have changed are some of the "signs of the times," which, of course, have to be updated for every new generation.[13]

---

[12] Blaising and Bock, *Progressive Dispensationalism: An Up-to-Date Handbook of Contemporary Dispensational Thought*.

[13] For a website with resources critiquing dispensational theology, one might consult http://www.monergism.com/thethreshold/articles/topic/dispensationalism.html.

SUMMARY

Almost all popular preaching on the second coming of Christ in the twentieth and twenty-first century in America, especially that which is disseminated through mass media, including television programs, radio talk shows, mass-marketed publishing, Internet websites, audio and video, and other methods, flows from three nineteenth-century movements in America, two that were homegrown, and one that was transplanted from Britain: Mormonism, Millerism (Adventism), and Darbyism (Dispensationalism). Characters might change, but the plot remains the same in variations, adaptations, and splinter groups.

These three American movements have left two main deposits on Revelation's apocalyptic traditions. The first deposit is a distinct and easily recognizable rhetorical strategy. The second deposit is theological aberration necessary for supporting novel eschatological schemes. The rhetorical strategy is to attempt to induce "imminence" expectation artificially propped up by "signs of the times" preaching. The true *modus operandi* of this preaching is anti-historical, since transparent historical falsification occurs, but is denied. Theological aberrations are numerous, but salient teachings from which most other deviations derive, or from which necessary implications are deduced, can be reduced to four. The first two are shared in common, but the last two are distinctively dispensational.

1. *Multiple advents.* American systems are forced to invent multiple advents, that is, some artifice of splitting up the second coming of Christ into multiple comings. Usually, the strategy involves arbitrarily creating *three advents* of Christ instead of the apostolic teaching of two, which translates into a two-stage second coming of Christ. Never a thought is given to how strange that multiple second comings of Christ went unrecognized by the apostles and then for two millennia of Christian theology.

2. *Invisible advents.* The invention of a two-stage second coming of Christ always involves inventing some form of *invisible coming*—whether of the heavenly tabernacle variety of Adventism or the secret rapture variety of dispensationalism. The "invisible advent" breaks up the traditional teaching of the second coming into two distinct stages separated in time but not evidenced in fact. This invisible coming construct is an imperative presupposition of pro-

posing three advents. Any first stage of the Second Advent *must be invisible* because this first stage in no way can be *historical*. Rather, this teaching is a *theoretical construct* that cannot be demonstrated in any historically verifiable way. Impossibility of proof is true for Adventists and beside the point for dispensationalists.

3. *Great parenthesis.* Dispensationalism particularly invents a *great parenthesis* idea in the interpretation of Dan. 9:24 to explain away two millennia of church history in the non-event of the return of Christ. This entire construct is fundamentally flawed, being pulled out of thin air exegetically. The construct also has the inevitable consequence of rendering the entire church age an eschatological joke on behalf of a future Israeli political empire. The total absence of sound ecclesiology is shocking.[14]

4. *Covenant distinctions.* Dispensationalism also invents *covenant distinctions* between Israel and the church, both in prophecy and in salvation. These distinctions are buttressed by an elaborate periodization of history into arbitrary and idiosyncratic dispensations. Unsuccessful efforts to mitigate these teachings by progressive dispensationalists really have more demonstrated that Darby's system is pretty much all or nothing. Cut one thread, and the whole hem falls out.

Finally, in retrospect, no significant development of Revelation's traditions has manifested itself in almost the last hundred years. We still are riding in the wake of these nineteenth-century movements. However, given Revelation's historical track record since the days of Montanus, this status quo of the stagnation of apocalyptic imagination should not be expected to continue indefinitely. The power of Revelation's apocalyptic imagery to fire the imagination, inform millennial movements, and frustrate apocalyptic interpreters should not be underestimated—in any generation.

---

[14]A necessary corollary would be the schizophrenic messiah, one that conforms to the humility of the First Advent, and the other that conforms to secular concepts of an earthly regent whose rod of iron is not nails in hands and feet but a scepter with which to beat. We will discuss this perversion of messianic consciousness later.

5

A Hermeneutical Swamp

Problematic Readings

OUR SURVEY OF THE HISTORY of Revelation's interpretation has been all too brief. A plethora of interpreters, prophets, and movements have gone unmentioned. We hope, however, at least to have traced out the main lines of options available to us along with suggesting a few of their inherent weaknesses. We hesitate, however, to move on into the book of Revelation without addressing a few of the more egregious interpretive errors that openly flaunt sound hermeneutical principles, duplicitously ignore constant historical falsification, and perpetually fill the popular press. Four problematic readings are addressed in this chapter: insistence on a literal dictum, desire for setting dates, advocating a schizophrenic messiah, and espousing signs of the times.

LITERAL DICTUM

A dispensationalist hermeneutical mantra is that interpreters should "take the plain, literal sense unless the literal sense makes no sense"—which actually makes no sense.[1] Two considerations are paramount. First, this rule completely begs the question of the fundamental nature of apocalyptic literature. Second, those who most insist on this dictum seem oblivious to how dangerously close they are sailing to the shoals of subjectivity from which they think the mantra delivers them.

---

[1] E.g., Lindsey, *Late Great Planet Earth*, 50, who is quoting Cooper, *When Gog's Armies Meet the Almighty in the Land of Israel*; Lindsey, however, gives no actual page number for the quote.

The emphasis on the "literal" interpretation of prophecy is linguistically naive.[2] Failure to apply proper interpretive method leads to capricious interpretive abuse. Sound principles of interpretation do distinguish prose and poetry. The literal and the figurative do not read the same, yet those most insisting on the literal dictum want to say they do. Such reading constantly conflates figurative and referential language in Scripture. What results is interpretive chaos. One insists on a "literal" (referential) understanding of one phrase in one clause, but then proffers a metaphorical meaning for a following phrase in the very next clause, without even a hermeneutical hiccup.

The rhetoric slamming any other interpretation besides a literal one has changed over the centuries. In the nineteenth century, the term of aspersion was "spiritualizing." If you read the text figuratively, you were "spiritualizing" the text, which was grossly bad. The *term de jour* in the twentieth century became "allegorizing," even though the interpretation being opposed really had not one whit to do with true allegorical methodology. Hal Lindsey wrote, "The real issue between the amillennial and the premillennial viewpoints is whether prophecy should be interpreted literally or allegorically."[3] Here one encounters not only an ignorant equating of reading figurative language figuratively as "allegorical" methodology, but also a dismissive speech that is belied by the writer's own practice. "Literal," as practiced by Lindsey and others, is an interpretive strategy of convenience, as we shall see.

For example, notice how Scofield's original notes at Gen 1:16 had to be changed because they were so egregiously allegorical. Gen 1:16 is about the creation of the sun and moon ("two great lights"). The editors of the *New Scofield Reference Bible* silently and with no fanfare dropped Scofield's original note entirely.[4] The original 1909 and 1917 editions preserve Scofield's original assertion that the sun was a "type" (read, "allegory") of Christ, who would take on this character of blinding light at the Second Advent, but now, even while the sun is not seen fully, light still exists, just so Christ is not seen fully, but his light exists and will be seen in its fullness in the Second Advent. Likewise, Scofield unquestionably "spiritualized" the lesser light, the moon, as a "type" of

---

[2]The problem becomes acute in discussion of "signs of the times."
[3]Lindsey, *The Late Great Planet Earth*, 176.
[4]*The New Scofield Reference Bible*, 2.

the church, because the moon reflects the greater light of the sun, like the church reflects the greater light of Christ.⁵ Such hermeneutical nonsense is "allegory" as rich as the master Augustine himself could muster. No surprise Scofield's ridiculous note at Gen 1:16 eventually was dropped completely in modern editions of the Scofield Bible.

Principle of Genre

Observing literary genre is a premier principle of hermeneutics. The primary feature of apocalyptic literature is its symbolic character. Any apocalyptic literature by its very nature lives and breathes symbol and metaphor. Reading apocalyptic literature otherwise is just literarily ignorant. Insisting on a literal reading of apocalyptic literature is dead wrong, begs the question of sound interpretation, and errantly denies observing the fundamental hermeneutical principle of genre applied to apocalyptic literature.

Revelation is apocalyptic literature. Few would deny this literary feature of this book. Even Luther was able to recognize that Revelation keeps company with other apocalyptic writings. In fact, he was careful to point out the book's close affinities to 2 Esdras, a Jewish apocalypse written at almost the same time as Revelation.⁶ Earlier in chapter 1 we used 2 Esdras as an example of the highly symbolic language Jewish apocalypses used, as well as the symbolic significance of numbers.

Luther also discussed three types of prophetic literature of the kind that foretells the future. The first simply expresses itself in plain words. The second uses words, but then also offers the interpretation. The third type, Luther observed, "does it without either words or interpretations, exclusively with images and figures, like this book of Revelation."⁷ Even Luther, the father of Protestant literal reading of the Bible, was fully aware that you do not read Revelation as literal, even if his heirs failed to heed his hermeneutical insight.

Simply taking a figurative approach to Revelation, however, is no panacea for interpretation. Just saying what the symbols figure is itself

⁵*The Scofield Reference Bible* (1917), 2.

⁶*Luther's Works*, 398.

⁷Die dritte die es on wort odder auslegung mit blossen bilden und figuren thut wie dis Buch der Offenbarung. *Die Luther-Bibel von 1534*, CLXXX, recto. Cf. *Luther's Works*, 400.

a rollercoaster ride in the history of interpretation. By the Medieval period, the general lines of approach are evident, as illustrated in the interpretation of the Seven Seals. The seal judgments figure: (1) Christ, (2) the church, or (3) history. The christological reading has two basic patterns. One pattern is using the seven seals to read ways the Old Testament was prefiguring Christ. The other pattern is using the seven seals to read the life of Christ from incarnation to ascension. The ecclesiological reading is assigning elements of spiritual life, both of the believer and of the church, to each of the seals. The historical reading is periodizing history. The periodizing reading has two basic patterns. One pattern is using the seven seals to trace past and present history. The other pattern is using the seven seals to trace a future end-time scenario.[8] Thus, simply acknowledging Revelation's genre does not guarantee an easy path to a proper reading, but one has a better start.

Shoals of Subjectivity

The literal dictum yields a false sense of immunity from subjectivity. As commonly applied, the "rule" involves both circular reasoning and a fundamental *non sequitur* of logic. A hidden question that is begged is, Just who judges what is "sensible"? The answer is the interpreter, of course. Thus, such a dictum still is subservient to the interpreter's own preunderstandings and fallacious assumptions. The result is that the interpreter can usurp the text's authority, which makes the text a slave to the interpreter's own "sensibility." All interpreters do this to some degree.[9] When prophetic texts in particular are on the table, however, classic dispensationalists, especially of the Hal Lindsey variety, just deny culpability, apparently assuming immunity from interpretive subjectivity by advocating this dictum. A literal mantra does not save the interpreter from sinking on the shoals of subjectivity.

A literal reading certainly failed the Ethiopian eunuch in Acts 8:28–34. This eunuch could read with "common sense" the prophet Isaiah's Servant Song about someone who suffers (Isa 53:7). Common

---

[8] An excellent resource, including translations of pertinent original Medieval Latin texts, is Gumerlock, *The Seven Seals of the Apocalypse: Medieval Texts in Translation*.

[9] Cf. Fee and Stuart, *How to Read the Bible for All Its Worth*, 19–20. On the crucial role of preunderstanding, see Klein, Blomberg, and Hubbard, *Introduction to Biblical Interpretation*, 154–68.

sense dictated that the passage could be about the prophet Isaiah himself or possibly someone else. These common sense options, however, still left the eunuch without a clue as to the prophetic text's christological, figurative meaning until Philip drew the figure around Jesus of Nazareth's suffering and death. Nothing in a literal "common sense" reading of Isa 53:7 was of any assistance to the eunuch to know the passage was about Jesus. Even pointing to crucifixion is not enough in and of itself. After all, thousands of Jews were crucified in the time surrounding the life of Christ.[10]

Confused Literal Semantics

Prophecy can be literal, but *literal is more than referential.* Even when read literally, how does one know when to read a prophetic image referentially or figuratively? If we read about a great army invading on horses (Ezek 38:15), is that a great army invading on horses, or the mechanized land forces of a modern army?[11] If we have the military weaponry of bows and arrows (Ezek 39:3), are those bows and arrows, or the weaponry of modern infantry?[12] If we read about God making a mighty shaking of the earth and pouring down torrential rains, and hailstones, fire, and sulfur (Ezek 38:18–32), is that a divine mighty shaking and hailstones, fire, and sulfur, or is that the use of tactical nuclear weapons?[13] Yet, turn right around in almost the same breath and find blood standing to the horses' bridles for two-hundred miles (Rev 14:20), and suddenly, that is just simply blood standing to the horses bridles for two-hundred miles. In the blink of an eye we have forgotten that this supposed Armageddon scene already has been pitched as a modern, mechanized army with tactical nuclear weapons. If one has warriors on horses, warriors with bows, heavenly hailstones, fire, and sulfur, and so on, are those referential, or figurative? Both referential and figurative readings are *literal* readings of the text.

---

[10] As by Cleopatra's son, Alexander, who crucified 800 at one time, or by the Roman general Varus, who crucified 2000 in putting down a revolt; cf. Josephus *Ant.* 13.14.2; 17.10.10.

[11] Lindsey, *Late Great Planet Earth*, 157.

[12] Ibid., 160–61.

[13] Ibid., 165–66.

The salient question of language is, when do we know the difference between referential and figurative readings within the same context? Or, do we allow the excuse that a figure of speech was "the best the ancient prophet could manage" with his limited first-century military vocabulary attempting to describe scenes of modern military warfare? How do we know the prophet even *saw* scenes in the first place, especially when he does not say so? In fact, in this particular instance, this prophet says only that he was an *auditor* of God's *speech* (Ezek 38:17), not an observer of a scene. The true issue for interpretation is not an insistence on the clear, literal sense. The literal sense is clear, but the interpretive meaning, whether referential or figurative, is not. This literal or figurative ambiguity was the dilemma of the Ethiopian eunuch, and our dilemma as well.

A classic illustration of the literal versus figurative conundrum is Lindsey's reading of Zech 14. The prophet describes in 14:12 a plague striking those who have fought against Jerusalem: their flesh is consumed away while standing, their eyes consume away to their sockets, and their tongues consume away in their mouths. Lindsey offered a moment of revelation to his readers: "A frightening picture, isn't it? Has it occurred to you that this is exactly what happens to those who are in a thermonuclear blast? It appears that this will be the case at the return of Christ."[14] Strange that in Zechariah's words in 14:12 we have an "exact" description of thermonuclear war, when down only three verses later in Zech 14:15 we have the main transportation in this thermonuclear enemy camp comprised of horses, mules, camels, and donkeys. I guess the donkey is toting the nuclear warhead.

Another good example is, again, imagery from Zech 14. The Lord goes forth to fight Israel's enemies and stands on the mountain before Jerusalem, the Mount of Olives, which then splits the mountain in two (14:4). Lindsey joins this text with Acts 1:11, the angels' remonstrance to the disciples who are staring into the heavens after the ascension of Jesus. Lindsey concluded that Jesus will come back to the Mount of Olives, which is his understanding of the angels' words "as you have seen him go."[15] He then proposes that this return literally splits the

---

[14] *Late Great Planet Earth*, 175.

[15] The question is the adverbial meaning of the phrase "as you have seen him go," which just as well could be an adverb of *manner* as an adverb of *place*.

mountain, as Zechariah "prophesied." Finally, rendering this whole affair even more marvelous, an amazing realization takes hold of the Jews, Lindsey asserted. "The believing Jewish remnant in Jerusalem will rush into the crack . . . They will know this prophecy and realize that this great cavern has opened up for the Lord to protect them from the terrible devastation that He is about to pour out upon the godless armies all around. It will be used as a type of bomb shelter."[16] To add scientific aura to the whole interpretation, Lindsey dons the mantle of a scientist and refers (only obliquely, with zero documentation—"it was reported to me") to seismic studies of some oil company that "discovered a gigantic fault running east and west *precisely* through the center of the Mount of Olives. The fault is so severe that it could split at any time. It is awaiting 'the foot.'"[17] So, an unnamed, unknown oil company with an undocumented, unpublished seismic study seals the authenticity of Lindsey's exegesis of Zech 14:4?

Contradictory Literal Application

Sometimes the inane duplicity of this literal mantra can be witnessed in surprisingly self-incriminatory comments that in the same breath without even a moment's hesitation are self-contradictory. Take, for example, the following amazing series of interpretive assertions about the "four horsemen of the Apocalypse" based upon Rev 6 that were spoken in an interview given for A&E Television Networks:

> I don't believe they are allegorical. I don't believe they are metaphoric [sic]. I believe they are factual. I believe that there will be four horsemen of the Apocalypse that will represent four different, specific times of terror that will come upon the earth in rapid succession.[18]

---

[16] I swear, I am not making this up. *Late Great Planet Earth*, 175. Nothing could more closely evoke the paranoia of the Cold War and the "duck and cover" drills for elementary school children of the 1950s.

[17] Ibid., 174 (emphasis added). The allusion to "the foot" is to the return of Jesus to the Mount of Olives. Notice how Lindsey adroitly slips in that word "precisely" again into his apocalyptic rhetoric. He seems incurably enamored with "precisely" lingo. One must not forget the original audience upon which he honed his rhetorical skills as a minister for Campus Crusade for Christ—college and university campuses of the 1960s.

[18] John Hagee, "Countdown to Armageddon," 2004.

Quite breathtaking in its self-contradictory expression, this statement bends language backwards upon itself. If these four horsemen are not "allegorical," not even "metaphoric" [sic], *then they must be referential: they are four horsemen*. The language then is telling us about four men riding four horses on the terrestrial plane of earth. Yet, in the same breath as denying they are "allegorical" or "metaphoric" [sic], comes the contradictory assertion that the four horsemen are *not* four literal horsemen, but, in fact, "represent" something! So, the four horsemen are *not* actually horsemen riding. They are "specific times of terror." So, the real meaning (read, metaphorical) that is hidden in the figure of four horsemen is "times of terror." How can language that assuredly is *not* "metaphoric" [sic] simultaneously be metaphorical? In "representing" something other than the simple referential sense, by definition the language is figurative! This Orwellian double-speak is blatant abandonment of the highly-touted "literal" meaning. We have *denied* metaphor in one breath only to *use* metaphor in the next breath to explicate the meaning! The "literal" dictum as popularly trumpeted is smoke and mirrors exegesis of the biblical text.

SETTING DATES

The issue here for the reader of popular books on Revelation is not really about any date in particular. The issue is whether a false prophet can persuade you. The real game in town is rhetorical strategy. The false prophet has to develop rhetorical strategies to persuade belief in the arrival of the end-time. The prophet presumes the end-time, then goes about trying to prove what is presumed to a captive audience. We need to address the underlying motivational strings pulling these date-setting end-time puppets.

Playing to the Audience

We have to keep in mind that all of this end-time dating game from Montanus to Joachim of Fiore to Millerites to Darby is simply pandering to the audience. That is the nature of the beast. Interpreters of Revelation always will have to judge how to construe the realities of Revelation's appropriate interpretation in the context of popular demands for relevance, especially when those popular demands sacrifice without a moment's reflection both historical tenability and hermeneutical integrity for the cheap change of a fleeting emotional charge that "something wonderful is about to happen." Even a thousand years after the first Christian millennium, expectations for the year 2000 revealed that, fundamentally, the general public always is primed for apocalypse, and commercial profit beckons the prophets. Most of the time, prophets of the end walk a short plank, except for the Mayans. Prophets are vexed trying to reconcile their millennial traditions and end-time prognostications with the harsh realities of history.

Protean Quality

One fundamental datum of apocalyptic rhetoric Boyer styled as "the protean quality of the biblical apocalypses."[19] The rhetoric can take on literally any form, like the cyborg assassin in the "Terminator" movie series. Apocalypses also inspire indestructible end-time belief that always rises from the ashes of failed prophecy. After a survey of apocalyptic interpretation through the centuries, Boyer asked this penetrating question: "If the prophecies can be applied with equal validity to *any* historical situation, what becomes of their status as a divinely inspired foretelling of *specific* events?"[20] This is one great question.

All such apocalyptic prophets of doom prey on the insecurities of any given age. In the twentieth and twenty-first centuries, all kinds of social and political instability have haunted our worries about what the future might bring. We could make up a list that potentially could be endless. Even just a few years ago, the "Y2K crisis" was huge in the popular press. The acronym stands for "year two thousand." To have been such a cause of anxiety and alarm in the media and on the news prior to the turn of the millennium, the fast-fading memory of this crisis is amazing. The crisis was the fear that a time-keeping glitch in notating the year with only two digits, not including the century with four digits, in the clocks of computer chips running 90% of the world's personal computers would cause entire systems of computers around the world to crash with the change of the millennium moving from 1999 to 2000. The global computer failure would domino as disastrous failures in world banking systems would create the perfect storm for Antichrist to seize total control of the world market. Or, at least such a

---

[19]Boyer, *When Time Shall Be No More*, 80.
[20]Ibid., 77.

scenario was clear to Grant R. Jeffrey prior to the new millennium when he wrote *Final Warning: Economic Collapse and the Coming World Government*. Funny, Jeffrey no longer advertises this book on his website, but he does have a number of new publications bartering his brand of futurism for your entertainment.

An even newer modern technology haunt is RFID, which stands for "radio frequency identification," a new technology for microchips that emits radio waves that can be read at a distance. This technology already has been fingered as the undoubted mark of the beast. Jeffrey, of course, having so quickly forgotten his Y2K warnings of the end, makes the paranoia palatable in his *Surveillance Society: The Rise of Antichrist*. Jumping on the bandwagon, we have Katherine Albrecht and Liz McIntyre, *The Spychips Threat: Why Christians Should Resist RFID and Electronic Surveillance*. Seems like almost every new piece of technology since the Gutenberg printing press has been announced as the potential "mark of the beast" by someone. Websites that promise to be rapture ready, or provide daily prophecy updates, or offer media end-time ministries all sell this snake oil.

FIGURE 5.1. Example Modern Insecurities

• AIDS	• international terrorism
• biometric cryptology	• Internet
• CNN (modern media)	• megalomaniac dictators
• collapse of family values	• nuclear bombs
• computer chips	• pestilence
• earthquakes	• RFID
• European Common Market	• Roman papacy
• famine	• universal bar code
• gay rights	• war rumors
• genetic engineering	• wars
• genocide	• women's liberation
• global warming	• World Council of Churches
• holocaust	• world wars
• influenza pandemic	• Y2K crisis

Whatever worries us greatly from today's headlines can be promoted as prophetic fulfillment. Contemporary end-time prophets proclaim their prescient knowledge of the end to tantalize crowds of religious

5—A Hermeneutical Swamp   109

but anxious onlookers who are searching for external routes of escape from life's harsh, confusing, and seemingly insoluble problems. These sterile and impotent prophetic insights instantly die the death of a thousand falsehoods and fall to the ground, lifeless. Yet, like the Phoenix, they rise from the ashes of the last failed prediction. We still have yet to learn that "signs of the times" rhetoric can be manipulated and morphed into an infinite variety of forms to meet popular anxiety of any kind in the face of stressful contemporary realties of any age.

End-time Tease

Thus, we can hold the popular imagination spellbound with verifiable "signs of the times." The real trick for maintaining these deceptive illusions about knowing the future and avoiding instant falsification is to learn to be precisely imprecise. Predict the time, hit the light, and die the prophetic moth's dance of death. On the other hand, suggest only that we're "close," constantly weaving near the light without ever actually touching the light, and live the prophetic moth's innuendo waltz in perpetuity. In reality false prophets constantly adjust their prophetic calculations like an Enron accountant cooking the books. Finally, after the false prophet dies, the unceasing predictions that the "end" is "close" slip off into far horizon of forgotten interpretive history, like a rudderless ship drifting quietly into the sunset. No worries, mate—except for the poor blokes you suckered into buying your book who are left behind in the wake of your departure, trying to pick up the broken prophetic pieces in the futile attempt to keep intact what they had equated as their faith but in reality was your eschatological hard sell of cheap trinkets and beads.[21]

In reality, setting dates, or even pretending to know proximity, is the sure sign one does not have a clue. This rhetoric is no more than a prophetic strip tease. Worse, however, is setting up a failed prophecy and then either changing its parameters so that all can "recalculate," or quietly ignoring the tempest one has stirred up as if the words never were spoken. Internet web pages are a great place to hide these sins. Just pull the failed prophecy down to pretend one never uttered such

---

[21]For a technical rhetorical analysis of this phenomenon of apocalyptic discourse based on the ordering *topoi* of time, evil, and authority, see O'Leary, *Arguing the Apocalypse*, 20–60.

lying words. These days, with the technology of HTML code, modern end-time prophets never have to be responsible or accountable for what they say. Here today, gone tomorrow—and we are not talking the rapture.

SCHIZOPHRENIC MESSIAH

A deficient eschatology can impact negatively other areas of Christian thought, such as ecclesiology or Christology. For example, how would one have to picture Messiah in Darby's dispensational scheme? If the second coming is to establish a national Israel as just one more empire among the world's empires (only this time Israeli), one would have to succumb to some unusual teaching that distanced the First Advent messiah from the Second Advent messiah. These two messiahs would have to be different in character and personality, since the historical picture actually revealed in Jesus Christ in the First Advent is a person of humility, suffering, and death. Such a crucified Christ does not fit a hyperliteral reading of Old Testament prophecies about war and conquest when taken as messianic or eschatological. To hide this strangely schizophrenic Christ, one would need to invent two messiahs, craftily disguised under the metaphor of "two portraits" of one messiah. If these two messiahs are the same person, then we have a schizophrenic messiah who really cannot make up his mind how to conquer evil.

Lindsey proposed just such a scheme.[22] His christological double-take on messiah is classic Orwellian double-speak in theological dress. Christological and soteriological implications of these "two portraits" of messiah, if accepted without theological reflection, are immense and staggering. The preeminent implication is that the cross of Christ did not, in fact, deal decisively and finally with evil in the world. The cross becomes a second-class soteriological effort that failed to achieve what the apostles claimed. The crucified messiah's soteriological job is left unfinished on the cross. A final climactic battle, Armageddon, is necessary to consummate what Calvary did not finish—God's ultimate dealing with evil in the world. This "Armageddon" battle, of course, especially as popularly dramatized in numerous books and movies, is

---

[22]Lindsey's "Two Portraits," *Late Great Planet Earth*, 28–29. Cf. *New Scofield Reference Bible*, 1161.

nothing less than an unapologetic remake, in modern props and costume change, of the ancient Zoroastrian apocalyptic final war of good and evil. This remake is supposed to be based scripturally upon particular texts in the Jewish prophets that evoke militaristic imagery, but, these prophets we are assured, without doubt did not prophesy to their own generation with this imagery. Surprising how Zoroaster's eschatological solution comes home to America with a vengeance, facilitated by an unchallenged schizophrenic messiah tradition.

That some future battle of Armageddon is the real locus of where God decisively eliminates evil in the world allows the fox back into the christological henhouse, and classic dispensationalists seem happy to oblige the fox. *In so doing, they have revived and sanctified a first-century Jewish expectation of a military messiah resoundingly rejected by Jesus.* If a military messiah was unacceptable for Jesus in the first coming, why would such a Christology be acceptable for him in a second coming? In fact, the Jewish public was offended by Jesus' teaching of a non-military messiah. These distorted expectations are precisely why the loud "hosannas" of a triumphal entry of the king into Jerusalem so quickly were drowned out by "crucify him" in less than a week (Matt 21:9; Mark 11:9–10; 15:13–14; Luke 23:21; John 12:13; 19:6).

Three times the Jews tried and failed to bring in the kingdom of God by martial violence. The first-century Jewish expectation of a military messiah that Jesus confronted and rejected had its historical matrix two centuries before in the Maccabean Revolt against Syrian Hellenization (Mattathias and Judas, Jonathan, Simon, 167–140 B.C.). This Maccabean Revolt was the first of three historical efforts by Jews to bring in the kingdom of God by the violence of martial action. The second effort that reprised the original Maccabean Revolt was the First Jewish War fought by Zealots such as John and Simon against the Romans (A.D. 66–70), which Jesus himself predicted would happen and resulted in the loss of nationhood and the destruction of the temple. The third major effort by Jews at martial violence to bring in the kingdom of God was Rabbi Akiba's messianic protégé Bar Kokhba in the final rebellion against Rome of the second Jewish War (133–35). All martial violence paths to the kingdom failed, and Jesus himself rejected the very essence of that way of "thy kingdom come."

The apostolic teaching in the New Testament is that the cross is the ultimate revelation of Messiah's true and eternal character—where thorns are the "crown" and a cross is the "throne." This Messiah came onto the stage of history as a complete shock to popular expectations that forever will be a scandal to the Jews and foolishness to the Greeks (1 Cor 1:18–25). Further, this eternally cruciform shape of messianic identity is the consummate revelation of God (Heb 1:1–4; 1 Pet 1:20; Rev 5:5–6). No other messianic identity awaits revelation to the world. If Christ awaits from heaven to vanquish his enemies with future thermonuclear blasts, the humility of the cross is a historical sham. A two-messiah Christology has to deny the Pauline scandal of the cross, since such a Second Advent messiah is undoubtedly so completely other—a glorified military conqueror that sets about vanquishing pagan armies with his power rays (see image, p. xviii).

A theologically schizophrenic Christ is precisely what one will find among dispensationalists of the Lindsey variety. The first coming messiah is a servant king, messiah-the-humiliated. The second coming messiah, however, is wholly other. He is as a military king, messiah-the-humiliator. Lindsey is clear on this point.

> When Jesus came the first time it was not to judge the world, but to save it. He came as the Lamb of God who gave His life to take away the sin of the world. The one thing that God has established for man to do is to believe in His Son as Savior. When Jesus returns the second time it will be as a lion to judge those who rejected the free gift of salvation from sin. Man will have completely demonstrated his worthiness of judgment.[23]

One easily could be distracted by the seriously perverted theodicy propounded here in the completely specious argument on the tail end that humanity really needed an extra two millennia of rampant evil to demonstrate a worthiness of divine judgment. No attempt at theodicy could be more lame.

More to the point, instead of Lindsey's schizophrenic picture, his "two portraits" of messiah, as clearly laid out above, what we actually encounter in the New Testament, especially in Revelation, is a *merged picture*, a proclaimed Davidic lion that when visualized instantly is presented as a slaughtered lamb (Rev 5:5–6). When Lindsey asserts that Jesus' first coming "was not to judge the world," one almost has the feeling that the Gospel of John simply has not been read at all. The

---

[23] *Late Great Planet Earth*, 174.

Johannine proclamation of *salvation that simultaneously is judgment* that comes into the world through the cross (John 3:19; 5:22–30; 9:39; 12:31; 16:11) is conveniently ignored or critically disavowed. John's merger of judgment and salvation into one seamless garment, revealed by Jesus' death on the cross, Lindsey unceremoniously rips apart, splitting up christological functions across time. Lindsey thus creates two different christological functions tied to two different historical events, not one christological truth tied to one historical event.

Further, the bad Christology dominos into defective soteriology. A bifurcated Christology *allows for a different type of salvation at the end than one has at the cross*. Lindsey is clear about this matter too: "According to Zechariah, 'all nations will be gathered against Jerusalem to battle.' The Jews who live in the area will be on the verge of annihilation when God will give them supernatural strength to fight. Then the Lord will go forth to fight for them and save them."[24] Proper exegetical and theological reflection on the implications of such an interpretation ought to encourage one to step back from the text, take a breath, and seriously rethink the matter. Bearing a sword is the way God wins? The crux of the meaning of the cross is at stake. Christ will behave tomorrow when he comes like he did yesterday when he came. A defective ecclesiology also is a consequence. Not getting messianic consciousness correctly means not getting church destiny correctly.

SIGNS OF THE TIMES

The focus in "signs of the times" preaching often is on a select set of biblical texts purported to apply to the end of time. They are offered as "proof" that the second coming of Christ is "near." The basic method reincarnates and promotes the classic "pesher" method of Qumran. Prophetic fulfillment is ripped from today's headlines, just like an episode of CSI.[25] That is, no matter what generation the interpreter happens to be in, his or her particular generation uncannily always is right on the edge of the end-time drama. A common tactic is to claim news-

---

[24]Ibid. Again, Lindsey's constantly tendentious argumentation is clear. He never even asks *whether* Zech 14 is to be read eschatologically in the first place. Old Testament texts constantly are heisted for eschatological use.

[25]CBS's "Crime Scene Investigation" series. Their marketing spot uses the tag of "ripped from today's headlines." Sounds just like current prophecy chasers.

paper headlines as prophetic "fulfillment," historical proofs showing that we have entered this end-time stage of history.[26]

We now turn to a few illustrative texts used to "prove" the arrival of the end in popular press and media. While "chosen" biblical texts have a tendency to vary across time and speakers, we only need to deal with a few to expose quickly the charade being played with the reader. The following popular passages are heisted from their historical and exegetical moorings in Scripture and are enough to demonstrate the non-existent exegetical or logical basis in the use of such passages as supposed "proof" that the end-time drama is on.

Example 1: "this generation" (Matt 24:34)

One common text often used in "signs of the times" preaching is Jesus' statement about "this generation" not passing away until "all these things" are fulfilled (Matt 24:34; Mark 13:30; Luke 21:32). Matthew 24 is a great passage to illustrate the problem of the language of prophecy, especially since we are confronted in this passage with the broader terms of the coming of the Son of Man, the sun and moon darkened, stars falling, and the powers of heaven being shaken. The problem of whether the literal sense is intended as referential or figurative especially applies to Jesus' eschatological discourse on the Mount of Olives recorded by all three Synoptic Gospels. The question is how to interpret the eschatological language. When we hear that the "stars fall from heaven," do the stars fall from heaven, or do we have to do with some other meaning? Fortunately, the meaning of Jesus' prediction about the temple's destruction no one argues. Here, the temple's destruction is the temple's destruction for virtually all interpreters. (At least we have one hermeneutical reprieve in the passage.)

Mark and Luke's Version

Mark and Luke indicate that the time of fulfillment of the matters that the disciples had asked about (destruction of the temple) was close enough that the generation of the disciples hearing his teaching would witness the fall of Jerusalem and the destruction of its temple. The most straightforward interpretation is that this prophecy was fulfilled exactly as Jesus had predicted in Titus's destruction of the temple in

---

[26]Google "signs of the times," and websites instantly pop up that offer daily updates.

A.D. 70. At least on this point, then, "this generation" in both Mark and Luke clearly refers to the disciples' own generation.

The problem is, in Mark and Luke the disciples ask *only* about the destruction of the temple. That is, both Mark and Luke restrict the disciples' question about "when" to the immediate prediction Jesus had made about the temple's destruction (cf. Mark 13:4; Luke 21:7). Neither one has anything about "the end of the age." Luke's context could not be clearer that the Jewish War against Rome is meant by Jesus, when Luke makes explicit the intended meaning is the siege of Jerusalem by the Romans with the clarifying words, "When you see Jerusalem surrounded by armies, then know that its desolation has come near" (Luke 21:20).

The difficulty is, even though the disciples' question in Mark and Luke is singular, simple, and clear, in answering that question, Jesus has included apocalyptic language and imagery. Is Jesus' apocalyptic language an unexpected jump to the end of time, or the inclusion of end-time teaching without an end-time question? Possibly. Yet, one other possibility would be to understand that Jesus is appropriating eschatological language, which always bears the undercurrent of divine judgment, not to complicate a simple historical answer to a simple historical question but to assist the church in interpreting the fall of Jerusalem as the judgment of God. That is, the apocalyptic language is in service to a pedagogical purpose. Jesus was teaching the future church that Jerusalem did not fall simply because the Jews rebelled and the Romans responded. Jerusalem fell because God judged the Jewish nation for rejecting the Messiah. In this reading, the apocalyptic language Jesus used about the temple's destruction is understood as metaphorical, not referential, and still applies to the destruction of the temple in A.D. 70.

We have precedent for this way of reading Jesus' apocalyptic language here in Mark and Luke in Luke's later presentation of Peter's use of Joel 2:28–32 in his explanation of the Pentecost phenomena (Acts 2:14–21). Peter's Joel quote includes the apocalyptic wording about the sun turned to darkness and the moon to blood, even though what has been described by Luke in the historic events of Pentecost does not have any referential correlates to these astronomical events. Clearly, Peter has taken Joel's words about these astronomical events metaphorically. One could speculate that Jesus' own manner of teaching about the temple's destruction is what taught Peter this way of reading Joel. Thus, John of Patmos using astronomical events to present realities about Jesus does no more than Peter did at Pentecost.

Matthew's Version

While the above interpretation might be a viable one in terms of Mark and Luke, Matthew's version does seem to muddy the Synoptic waters. In Matthew's version, the disciples *do* ask an additional question about the "end of the age." Our first clue is to notice that only Matthew has the disciples' question split into multiple parts like this, with secondary questions about the sign of Jesus' coming and the end of the age (Matt 24:3). Why would Matthew *include* these secondary questions if both Mark and Luke *omitted* them? Not because Matthew wanted to teach about the end of the age but Mark and Luke did not.

Rather, reading all the three Synoptics *together* might supply the answer. In a post-resurrection setting, Mark and Luke were well aware that the disciples' equation of Jesus' prediction about the destruction of Jerusalem with the end of the age was ill informed both historically and theologically. Mark and Luke, therefore, omit the inference by the disciples that the destruction of Jerusalem would be the end of the age. In contrast, Matthew includes the questions to show how Jesus corrected the ill-informed theology. Both Mark and Luke make clear that Jesus modulated the eschatological judgment language of the coming of the Son of Man to apply to the Roman destruction of Jerusalem and its temple. In this way, Jesus anticipated and authorized the church's later interpretation of Jerusalem's destruction as a divine act of God in history, just as Jerusalem's destruction by the Babylonians centuries earlier had been a divine act of God in history. The implication, then, in the canonical context of both Mark and Luke, is that even though Matthew acknowledges the secondary questions of the disciples about the end of the age, a concordant Synoptic reading makes clear that *the disciples themselves have equated the fall of Jerusalem with the end of the age, not Jesus.*

Were the disciples right to make this equation? Not according to Mark and Luke's version of this Olivet Discourse. Further, one could point out that even after the resurrection the disciples remain in a fog about how to correlate their previous preunderstandings about the meaning of "Israel" and "kingdom" in the light of the new realities brought about by the completely unexpected events of Jesus' death and resurrection. Even after the resurrection, they still ask the bumbling question: "Lord, will you at this time restore the kingdom to Israel" (Acts 1:7)? Luke will take twenty-eight chapters in Acts to answer this question. Luke will lay out carefully in the ministries of both Peter (Acts 1–12) and Paul (Acts 13–28) how this old pattern of Jewish nationalism for framing up what is happening in Jesus Christ, long nurtured in popular Jewish thought for almost two centuries by nostalgia for the glory days of the Maccabean Revolt, no longer works for understanding old questions and old answers, whether "Israel" or "kingdom." Instead, the word from Jesus is, "You will be my witnesses . . . to the uttermost parts of the earth." Gospel witness is Jesus' answer to the disciples' Jewish nationalism (Acts 1:8). Thus, Acts 1:8 is Luke's equivalent to Matthew's "Go, therefore, and make disciples" (Matt 28:19).

Dispensational Version

The dispensational twist on Matt 24 depends upon the importation of Darby's "great parenthesis" eisegesis into Matthew's context. In such a dispensational scheme, Jesus meant for the apostles to fast-forward their understanding not only past the obvious destruction of Jerusalem, which was the immediate point of their question, but even past two millennia of a long halftime show of the church to the real game of Israel-the-empire at the end of time. The apostles were supposed to understand the statement about "this generation" really to be not the common sense meaning of *their* generation (shows you how far a dispensationalist really intends to abide by a common-sense driven literal approach). Rather, Jesus suddenly without clutching shifts gears to the "terminal generation" that presages the so-called "secret rapture" of the church before the seven-year tribulation period that ends time and culminates in Christ's second (*third*) coming. Such an elaborate eschatological scheme, however, in no way is spelled out so explicitly in this passage in Matthew on its own. This scheme for interpreting Matt 24 is totally dependent upon asserting the so-called "great parenthesis" in Daniel's seventy prophetic weeks suddenly applies. So they weave together multiple scriptural texts into an entire system that is inserted unilaterally into Matt 24. Since all dispensationalists are obligated to prove their current generation is the "terminal generation," otherwise their entire eschatological scheme has no point, then once they say who the "terminal generation" is, the interpretation can be falsified by history. Once falsified, the previous interpretation has to be changed by mutating the meaning rather than convert to, God forbid, another millennial construct. How do they mutate meaning? Well, watching Hal Lindsey contort himself worse than Cirque Du Soleil performers on this very point over the decades is the best answer and better entertainment than the prophecy channels on cable.

What if—purely for the sake of argument—we say that Jesus in Matt 24 was forecasting two millennia into the future in answering a simple question by the disciples about his prediction of the temple's destruction? Are we getting straight talk from Lindsey about how to understand "this generation" within that scheme? The answer clearly is, "absolutely not."

Lindsey's own dissimulation on "this generation" is cloaked in a rhetorical strategy of constantly manipulating the math. In the three decades since *Late Great Planet Earth* was published, *Lindsey has offered up four vastly different approaches to "this generation,"* continually forced to stretch the meaning as time has marched on and exposed his faulty hermeneutic. What is the end result? Lindsey has fudged the figures, grossly inflating his original forty year definition by a whopping 150% to the figure of one hundred years in just three decades. How "precise" is that? The general reading public has been duped about how to do the math of a "biblical generation" for those who are supposed to be the "terminal generation." Painfully obvious is that the math of a "biblical generation" has changed dramatically in the three decades following the publication of *The Late Great Planet Earth* in 1970. Let us follow the trail of those answers over time.

Answer 1: Forty years. Lindsey's first operative interpretation was clear and unequivocal: "a generation is something like forty years."[27] Notice in this important calculation establishing the length of "this generation" in Matt 24:34 that not the slightest allusion or suggestion is even hinted that the calculation factor is other than the figure of forty years. Even Lindsey's attempt to hedge a bit with the expression

---

[27]Lindsey asserted in 1970: "A generation in the Bible is something like forty years. If this is a correct deduction, then *within forty years or so of 1948*, all these things could take place," *Late Great Planet Earth*, 54 (emphasis added).

"or so" tagged on the end does not help. This "or so" amount has to be less, and on the rules of logic, significantly less, than the larger matrix of forty years itself. Again, the contingency of the auxiliary verb "could" in "could take place" is only a thinly disguised and superficial cover belied rhetorically by the actual precision of the argument being made. (Forty years of an end-time "window of imminence" is only 2% of the entire two thousand years since Jesus' First Advent.) As he discussed the meaning of "this generation," notice that Lindsey naturally slipped into his favorite "precision" language with his misleading expression, "world events which are *precisely* predicted."[28] We soon will learn with his treatment of "this generation," Lindsey loved to assert "precisely" but constantly avoided real precision—a transparent sign of rhetorical bait and switch.

Lindsey's math has been falsified historically *twice* already. The first falsification was 1988. The date of 1988 (1948 + 40) was a known data point among Lindsey disciples and many other end-time chasers in the 1970s.[29] Lindsey had a failure of nerve after his bold declaration.

Answer 2: Forgotten years. Lindsey's first strategy going into the 1980s was to try to soft pedal his former bold specificity about "this generation." In his following publication, *The 1980's: Countdown to Armageddon*, he simply failed to mention "forty years" anywhere in the book. He erased the specific mention of the figure of forty years clearly set forth in *Late Great Planet Earth*. Perhaps he was hoping his audience might forget his figure, like testing the publication waters to see if that earlier reference simply could be forgotten.[30] Lindsey, however, could not stem the flood of pent-up audience demand for specificity that Lindsey himself had unleashed in the 1970s in *Late Great Planet Earth*. The strategy of *Countdown to Armageddon* did not work. A more effective rhetorical strategy had to be devised to defuse audience discontent. Lindsey's ingenuity was up to the task.

---

[28] *Late Great Planet Earth*, 41 (emphasis added).

[29] I know; I was one of them. We also have Edgar C. Whisenant's widely distributed publication, *88 Reasons Why the Rapture Could Be in 1988*. Whisenant calculated that the Jewish festival of Rosh Hashanah in 1988, September 11–13, would be the exact date; 300,000 copies were given freely to pastors; over four million copies were sold in bookstores and other outlets. He recalculated numerous times, immediately retrying for October 1988, then 1989, 1993, and 1994 (apparently his last attempt).

[30] Cf. Lindsey, *The 1980's: Countdown to Armageddon*, 162.

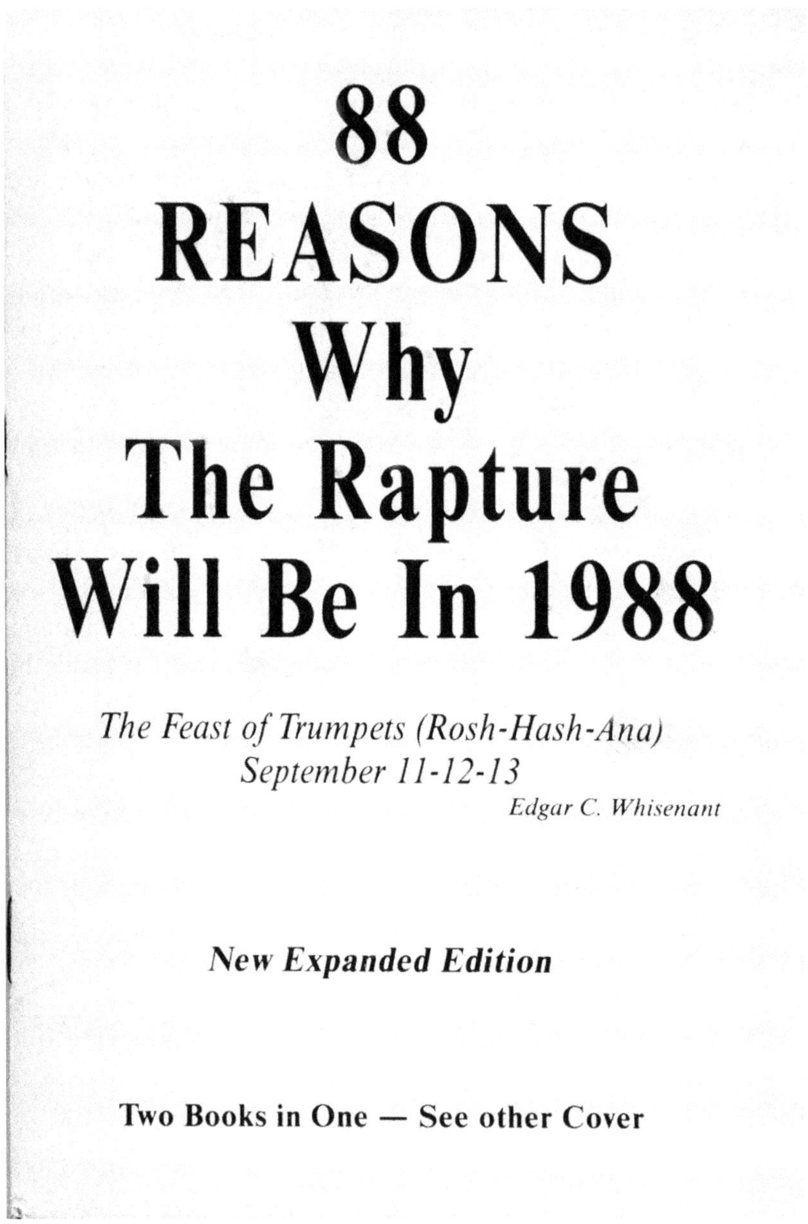

88 REASONS Why The Rapture Will Be In 1988

The Feast of Trumpets (Rosh-Hash-Ana)
September 11-12-13

Edgar C. Whisenant

New Expanded Edition

Two Books in One — See other Cover

FIGURE 5.2. 88 Reasons. The publication *88 Reasons Why the Rapture Will Be in 1988* by Edgar C. Whisenant illustrates how the 1980s were flush with end-time predictions and apocalyptic zeal due to the forty year generation calculation after the creation of the secular state of Israel by the United Nations in 1948. None were so audacious and specific as Whisenant, who repeatedly recalculated at least three more times. Not as successful a publishing venture as Hal Lindsey, but the date-setting mentality and the falsified result are the same.

Answer 3: Fudged years. The failure of the 1988 prediction was a serious blow. What to do? Change the math. Lindsey's next strategy in the 1990s was *to shift the calculation starting point*. Lindsey fudged the math. Under even more intense scrutiny and criticism in the passage of time after the failed 1988 expectation, Lindsey capitulated. He finally put forward an entirely new hermeneutic: *he shifted the starting date for calculating the 40 years of "this generation" from 1948 to 1967*. He shifted the starting point *nineteen* years, almost *half* the duration of the original calculation! "I have begun to see," Lindsey wrote rather coyly nearly a quarter century after *Late Great Planet Earth*, "that the recapture of Jerusalem was much more important than even the taking and re-establishing of the nation of Israel."[31] Really? Wow! What a seismic shift in a calculation starting point for such understatement! Of course, one would not want to draw too much attention to this matter of prophetic *mea culpa*. Alas and alack! History eventually falsified even this newly recalculated scenario (1967 + 40 = 2007). Lindsey should have studied more earnestly the history of interpretation of Revelation. As Roman Catholics learned in their own eschatological calculations post-Constantine, all deferred timing schemes at best are only a temporary solution to the popular clamor for specificity and imminence.

Answer 4: Foobar years. Thus, Lindsey still would have to cook the prophecy books *again a third time* like a really bad accountant, after 2007, unless something more ingenious and resourceful could be done now to settle the matter permanently—at least for Lindsey's own lifetime. What to do? Why, not only can you *change the starting point*, while you are on a roll in massive manipulations despising historical falsification, how about just *changing the entire equation*? Yes, one could completely rewrite the equation for a "biblical generation" like a computer programmer's foobar variable that can mean anything the programmer desires. That will change the math. Lindsey unilaterally decided to declare abruptly, without offering any exegetical warrant, that a "biblical generation" no longer was a clear and unequivocal time of forty years, as in his first publication in the early 1970s. Suddenly, Lindsey expanded the elusive figure to *double or more in length, even up to one hundred years!* In crying "uncle" to history, Lindsey finally

---

[31] Lindsey, *Planet Earth—2000 A.D.*, 173.

has been forced to assert, "A biblical generation is somewhere between 40 and 100 years."[32] Goodness. That audacity is mind-boggling. Any mathematician would consider changing calculations by up to 150% a significant adjustment to any formula! Shades of William Miller still haunt the hunt for the end-time calculus that makes a joke of the text.

This duplicitous extension gives Lindsey plenty of room not to have to worry about any future additional adjustments. He now has the great prophetic luxury of avoiding being around when falsification is reprised for the third time.[33] No median adult alive today will be around then to confront the failed calculation; Lindsey certainly will not be. He is home free now on his interpretive journey with the meaning of "this generation"—both in prophecy and in publication. Once again, Lindsey may have achieved the appearance of precision, perhaps satisfying his commercial coterie for the time being, but such an appearance is deceptive and illusory; this too shall pass. The date will vaporize in the searing heat of inevitable historical falsification, probably with no notice at the time whatsoever due to lost memory. Lindsey's device is an old trick learned from Joachim of Fiore's handling of Rev 12:6 and the 1,260 days equals 1,260 years, which put the matter eighty years into Joachim's future when calculated from Joachim's *new* starting point (compare Lindsey) of the birth of Christ. Joachim died in 1202. He did not have to face the failure of his new "window of imminence" calculation in 1260. Neither will Hal Lindsey now, even though he already has been falsified *twice*, in eerie historical parallel to William Miller, but admittedly without the nineteenth-century prognosticator's fanfare and drama. History resoundingly has shown Lindsey's constantly shifting hermeneutic on "this generation" in Matt 24:32 to be a fairy tale. Lindsey no more knows how to do the math on "this generation" than the man in the moon.

Example 2: "Shall a nation be born at once?" (Isa 66:8)

Another "signs of the times" text is Isa 66:8. Isaiah asks, "Shall the earth be made to bring forth in a day? Shall a nation be born at once?" This passage is said to be a prediction of the action of the United Nations in voting to create the modern secular state of Israel in one day in May

---

[32] *Planet Earth—2000 A.D.*, 5.

[33] 1988, 2007, and, now, 2067 (1967 + 100).

1948. The United Nations action was anticipated in Great Britain's 1917 Balfour Declaration calling for a national home in Palestine for the Jewish people. Both the Balfour and United Nations declarations were born in the cataclysmic geopolitical changes of the twentieth century's two world wars, which included World War I's collapse of the four imperial dynasties of Germany, Russia, Austria-Hungary, and Turkey. Such changes brought on revolution and political chaos (such as the Bolsheviks in Russia and the Nazi Socialist Party in Germany), and deep social unrest across Europe. These strong European social and political currents flowed directly and inevitably into World War II. Into this highly volatile geopolitical and social mix were poured the incendiary issues of Jewish Zionism and the Jewish Holocaust.[34] Did Isaiah anticipate this 1948 United Nations declaration? Hardly.

Deliberate Misquote

Right off the bat we have to point out that Isaiah's question is completely and deliberately misquoted in two crucial ways when used for "signs of the times" proof. First, Isaiah does *not* use the verb "reborn," as in the misquote, "A nation shall be *reborn* in a day." By substituting a verb Isaiah did not use, the meaning of the text deliberately is manipulated to conform more congenially to the intended interpretation. Second, the misquote rips the question from its literary context and flips the original meaning on its head by turning what was a question into an indicative assertion. Isaiah's original rhetorical question is jammed into an indicative declaration of one line. ("A nation will be reborn in a day.") This misquote of Isaiah is an act of interpretive violence because Isaiah is made to say the *opposite* of what he meant in the original context. What did Isaiah really say?

We ought to be obligated to lay out systematically the poetic lines in the Hebrew of Isaiah's carefully crafted verses in Isa 66. Even a cursory glance shows that Isaiah's context is a rhetorical question of two finely-balanced poetic lines of Hebrew. This question itself is in the context of a string of questions. A study of the original Hebrew easily demonstrates in the context of Isa 66 that in this string of questions

---

[34]As crudely, callously, and inhumanely expressed by Jack Van Impe in alluding to a future Jewish holocaust, "the Jews have been steadily marching toward Hitler's ovens ever since the fall of their beloved city in A.D. 70." *Israel's Final Holocaust*, 51.

Isaiah uses the irony of the obvious, and his whole series of rhetorical questions, including the one in consideration, expects a "no" answer in each and every instance.

Figurative Flip Flop

Besides the deliberate misquote that makes Isaiah say exactly opposite of what he meant, a second observation is the flip flop from figurative meaning to literal meaning in the same breath. Upon what principle do we jump instantly from weeks and days as metaphors for years in prophetic "end-time" lingo to the word "day" in Isa 66:8 meaning just one twenty-four hour day in a supposedly "end-time" prophecy? So, Daniel's "weeks" in Dan 9:24 "clearly" are *metaphorical* years, but Isaiah's "day" in Isa 66:8 is supposed to be *a literal twenty four hours*— and both are supposedly "end-time" texts? How convenient! Where comes the exegetical prowess to jump back and forth from figurative to referential like that? Who gets to make uncontrolled, capricious interpretive jumps regarding time references in eschatological texts?

Botched History

Why is Isaiah's original historical context completely ignored? Ignoring the original historical context is just bad exegesis. The salient hermeneutical question is, how would these rhetorical lines first have been read and understood for those in Isaiah's original audience?

One simple contextual observation is that the lines in question are in a poetic series of questions, asked rhetorically, to which the expected answer in each case is "no!" "Who has heard such things? Who has seen such things?" Isaiah asks (Isa 66:8a). To what "things" does he refer? The "things" are specified in the immediately preceding lines in the context: "Before she was in labor, she gave birth" Is that possible? Of course not! "Before her pain came upon her she delivered a son." Is that possible? Of course not! Then Isaiah continues the rhetorical flourish without pause: "Shall the earth be made to bring forth in a day?" The answer is no, of course not—not in the face of Israel's denuded forests and destroyed croplands in the wake of Babylon's armies! "Shall a nation be delivered in one moment?" No, of course not, not in the wake of Babylon's ferocious sack of the city!

So, whereas Isaiah's *poetic irony* does dictate a brief period of time within the context of preposterous rhetorical questions, the point is not *that* a nation will be "reborn" in a moment; rather, no matter how long Israel struggles to reestablish her national existence in the hard times of postexilic realities returning to a destroyed Jerusalem, faithful Jews will be those who have the tenacity to hang on within Jerusalem's ruins, who believe that God, in spite of all appearances, will be with Israel and will bring her back to national life. This faith is a powerful faith, a faith like Isaiah's, and a faith that ultimately will lead to Messiah. This faith trusts the covenant God to bring life out of absolute destruction and death, which is precisely what God accomplished with Messiah when Israel did bring forth the redeemer. Out of the absolute destruction and death of the cross and a cold, dark tomb, God brought forth life and an eternally secure destiny of God's people.

Thus, the legitimate, historical context of Isa 40–66 is the return from Babylonian exile. Isaiah's series of questions in Isa 66 is addressing the difficulties confronting the ragged remnant returning to the ruins of Jerusalem and its temple leveled to the ground by the armies of Babylon in 586 B.C. Will the walls go back up in a day? No, of course not. Rebuilding Jerusalem is not magic. Will the returning Jews go to bed one night, and the next morning find the temple in all of its original Solomonic glory in downtown Jerusalem? No, of course not! Raising the temple again is not magic. These are hard matters for the returnees as they walk through the ruins of their former life now cataclysmically destroyed, a severe challenge to faith in God. Those who believe, as does Isaiah, that the God of creation *can* make new heavens and a new earth, a new day for a renewed Israel after the total devastation of the Babylonian exile (Isa 65:17), can see in these impossible circumstances of the return from exile the salvation of God. For one who holds this kind of faith in God, Isaiah promises that, in God's hands, Jerusalem's future holds the promise of eventual succor for the physically and spiritually parched returnees:

> *Rejoice with Jerusalem, and be glad for her,*
>   *all you who love her;*
> *rejoice with her in joy,*
>   *all you who mourn over her—*
>   *that you may nurse and be satisfied*
>   *from her consoling breast;*
> *that you may drink deeply with delight*
>   *from her glorious bosom.* (Isa 66:10–11, NRSV)

Thus, even a simple exegetical overview shows that Isa 66:8 *means the opposite* of what is claimed. The United Nations vote in 1948 creating a modern secular state propped up by imperialist superpowers in no way is "fulfillment" of Isaiah's so-called "prophecy." For this nonsense, one must first deliberately misquote the text and then illegitimately apply a "pesher" ripped from today's headlines to makes the text say opposite its original meaning. This is raw interpretive violence.

Example 3: "valley of dry bones" (Ezek 37)

Another text used to "prove" the end-time drama is on, similar to Isa 66, is Ezekiel's valley of dry bones vision in Ezek 37. This text too supposedly is prophetic of the United Nations vote to create the secular state of Israel in 1948, another variation of reading twentieth-century headlines as prophecy fulfilled. In his own context, Ezekiel envisions two interconnected realities: (1) a *spiritual rebirth* of the nation (Ezek 37:23) as the only solution for (2) *postexilic Israel* in the withering realities of having suffered the wrath of God in the loss of nationhood and consequent Babylonian exile. True to form, "signs of the times" interpreters simply ignore the original context entirely.

Lindsey, for example, trying to squeeze Ezek 37 into his modern Israel dispensational construct, attempted to distinguish a "physical restoration" and a "spiritual restoration" of Israel. He offered no exegetical argument for this assertion.[35] The reason is clear. Any such distinction is specious and alien to this passage, solely derived from the preexisting commitment to the dispensational scheme of national Israel and a prophetic end-time game for Israel's own world empire. Lindsey is oblivious to Ezekiel's fundamental point in the valley of dry bones imagery: the spiritual failure of Israel to be faithful to the covenant created the wrath of exile in the first place, so Ezekiel was insisting *no return from exile has any purpose whatsoever, postexilic or end-time, without the prior reality of right relationship to God*. In fact, dispensationalists are loathe to admit that prior to 1948, *most dispensational writers insisted that Jewish conversion must precede any realization of Jewish nationhood*, which they found a compelling reason for evangelistic mission among Jews! Examples are Arno C. Gaebelein (d. 1945) and William E. Blackstone (d. 1935). In New York, Gaebelein

---

[35] Lindsey, *Late Great Planet Earth*, 48.

worked to evangelize Jewish immigrants to that city, and in Chicago, Blackstone made personal contributions to the work of the Chicago Hebrew Mission, today's American Messianic Fellowship.[36]

Further, Lindsey also claimed that he had studied commentaries from Christian scholars as far back as 1611 who gave testimony to the expectation that the Jews would be returning back to Palestine as a part of God's prophetic end-time action. Disingenuously, however, the only examples he proffered were two dispensational writers of the nineteenth century! Lindsey's extravagant overstatement is that he had "found that *many scholars* clearly understood that the Jews would return to Palestine and re-establish their nation before the Messiah would come."[37] Then, without whispering a word about even one of these so-called "many scholars" that provided a trail all the way back to 1611, Lindsey *instead quoted two nineteenth-century dispensationalists,* John Cumming (1864) and James Grant (1866). With nothing more to offer, Lindsey marooned his readers in nineteenth-century Darbyism.

The idea of a return of the Jews to the Holy Land was innovated by the most radical of the post-Reformation premillennial prophets and prophetic movements. Their conflicts were with the English King and Parliament in groups such as the Ranters, Levellers, Diggers, and Quakers. All proclaimed the imminent millennium would arrive in England. Lindsey apparently does not seem to want to be associated in print with this radical English heritage, although he finds convenient claiming their interpretive traditions. Worth hearing one more time is Wainright's discussion of the matter.

> A characteristic of English prophets in the mid-seventeenth century was their favorable attitude toward the Jewish people. They predicted the return of the Jews to the Holy Land and their conversion to Christianity, and they tried to make these predictions a reality. The Ranter John Robbins made a fruitless attempt to recruit an army of 144,000 to liberate the Holy Land from the Turks. Thomas Tany, another Ranter, who claimed to be a descendent of Aaron, announced that he was to lead the Jews back to Israel. Having been commanded in a vision to slaughter every member of Parliament, Tany drew his sword in

---

[36] This Blackstone is not the famous eighteenth-century English jurist.

[37] *Late Great Planet Earth*, 49 (emphasis added). Scholars? Who are they? What are their academic credentials? Many? Where are they?

the House of Commons. Nobody was killed, but Tany was committed to prison. He later drowned in an attempt to make the journey to the Holy Land.[38]

In addition, Boyer points out that the English Puritans channeled this Jewish return concept from the English dissenter controversies to the New World of the American colonies. One example is Increase Mather's *The Mystery of Israel's Salvation Explained and Applyed* (1669).[39] Seems as though dispensationalists simply are ready to depend upon modern institutions such as the United Nations to do for them what the Ranters could not do for themselves, and then claim such secular, human action as the work of God, like the conquistador de Soto (d. 1542) planting the Spanish flag on the shores of Florida and claiming such sixteenth-century imperial seizure of territory the act of God. Israel today is avowedly secular, not religious—in other words, as far from Ezekiel's postexilic spiritual ideals as can be conceived. The ability to produce the secular state of Israel no more represents God's will or God's plan than Abraham's ability to produce Ishmael as his firstborn progeny by his own schemes was God's will or God's plan.

Instead of "prophecy" of events more than two millennia distant, Ezekiel was addressing issues for Israel after the Babylonian debacle, just like Isaiah. Neither Isa 66 nor Ezek 37 are about the United Nations and 1948, or the Israeli Six Day War of 1967 for that matter. No "generation" of forty years post the 1948 event, implying 1988, nor the Six Day War of 1967, implying 2007, has any biblical end-time significance on any concocted eschatological "time line" of God. Historical exegesis of Isaiah and Ezekiel exposes current calculations involving the secular state of Israel as eschatological mythology. In reality, such a soothsayer is a dead man walking prophetically. He already has been falsified, twice, if anyone is counting.

Example 4: "earthquakes," etc. (Mark 13:8)

Another "sign" often used as "proof" we are the "terminal generation" actually is a set of related ideas: earthquakes, famines, and plagues, along with the twin thought of wars and rumors of wars (Luke 21:11; Matt 24:7; Mark 13:8; cf. Matt 24:6). None of these predict the end.

---

[38] Wainwright, *Mysterious Apocalypse*, 93.
[39] Boyer, *When Time Shall Be No More*, 182–83.

A Whole Lot of Shaking Going On

An asserted increase in the number or severity of earthquakes is a perennial favorite as a pointer to the "terminal generation" and the end. The only problem is, for anyone who actually would do due diligence on their homework to find out, seismologists will be happy to give statistics to anyone who asks that demonstrate how earthquakes in the twentieth century were not any more prevalent than in any other century, nor was their severity particularly notable. In fact, the largest earthquakes on record did not even happen in the twentieth century.

One of the largest earthquakes ever known was the 1755 Lisbon earthquake. Estimated at magnitude 8.7 or more on the Richter scale, the Lisbon quake struck on the morning of Nov. 1, 1755, with an epicenter in the Atlantic Ocean about 125 miles west-southwest of Cape St. Vincent. This quake probably was the most destructive and deadliest ever recorded. The entire port of Lisbon, Portugal was virtually destroyed, killing upwards of 100,000 people. As the quake developed over a period of twenty to thirty minutes, residents rushed in panic to the harbor area to avoid collapsing downtown buildings, and, to their utter amazement, saw nothing but the seafloor and the washed-out remnants of centuries of lost cargo and shipwrecks. As the population amassed at the harbor staring in disbelief, suddenly, without warning, the monstrous tsunami raised up by the earthquake finally arrived on its hurling landward journey, crashing in and totally engulfing the entire harbor and town. In areas not flooded by the tsunami waters, fires raged uncontrolled for days. The Lisbon quake is credited with seriously disrupting Portugal's colonial ambitions. In England, John Wesley convinced Londoners of the 1750s that the Lisbon quake was a clear sign of God's displeasure with sinners.[40]

The Plague of Plagues

Closely associated as sure factors in the "signs of the times" game are famines and plagues. While famines can capture the headlines and, predictably, the attention of end-time prognosticators, the frightening specter of plagues and diseases proves a more virulent attraction for

---

[40]See de Boer and Sanders, *Earthquakes in Human History: The Far-Reaching Effects of Seismic Disruptions*. A good web resource on seismology specifically related to earthquakes is http://www.norsar.no/index2.html.

these perennial purveyors of doom. Plagues conveniently are defined as "diseases that cannot be cured" and AIDS cited as the fulfillment.[41] What can be said about the typical rhetoric of such prognostications about plagues and the like? They are arguments of convenience.

For example, how does one come to a definition such as "diseases that cannot be cured" of the word translated as "plague" in the first place? The word for "plague" in the commonly-used passages (Luke 21:11; Matt 24:7; Mark 13:8) simply means a widespread, contagious disease. Nothing in the Greek word's linguistic or semantic domain means "incurable." Forget that the Black Death plague during the Dark Ages of Europe met the definition of a "disease that cannot be cured" and literally wiped thousands of European towns and villages completely out of existence. The modern disease of AIDS, though deplorable and sad in each fatal case, does not even come close as a percentage of the total world population to the Black Death in the Dark Ages of Europe. So neither in kind, scope, nor consequence does AIDS have any unique or even distinctive profile that would set this disease out as a clear "sign" of any eschatological significance. Further, just because a cure has not been found does not mean a cure will not be found. Then, when a cure is found, AIDS suddenly, given the "incurable" definition, no longer is a "sign of the times"? "Now you see it; now you don't." Nice sleight of hand.

Misquoting Jesus

Jesus actually taught the *opposite* about the experience of earthquakes, famines, plagues, wars, and rumors of wars than the end-timers claim. Jesus said such disasters would occur, but not to let anyone make anything of them, because, clearly, with all such disasters, "the end is not yet" (Matt 24:6). How much more transparent can Jesus' teaching be? Jesus said unequivocally that earthquakes, famines, and pestilence, along with wars and rumors of wars are *not* a sign of the end; rather, *they are signals of the continuation of life's struggles:* "You are going to hear about wars and rumors of wars: see that this does not trouble you: for all these things inevitably will happen, *but the end is not yet.*" (Matt 24:6; emphasis added).

[41]Hagee, "Countdown to Armageddon," 2004.

Further, even the meaning of "the end" itself has to be inferred in this context. In mentioning earthquakes and the rest, is Jesus referring to the destruction of Jerusalem and the end of the temple, or the end of time? At this point in the dialogue, Jesus was not far along in the discussion. Thus, the contextual meaning of "the end," at least at this point in Matt 24:6, would seem to be related much more to the question about the temple's destruction than already picking up the second question, that is, assuming even that Jesus accepted the Jewish nationalistic assumptions hidden in the second question. However, even if "the end" here were taken as a premature reference in the current discussion by Jesus to the end of time, the qualifier "not yet" still would apply. The so-called "signs" supposedly indicative of some end-time scenario *are rejected as such by Jesus himself.*

Example 5: "knowledge will be increased" (Dan 12:4)

Another text used to insinuate we are on the edge of history, Dan 12:4, reads, "many shall run to and fro, and knowledge shall be increased" (KJV). This "knowledge shall be increased" idea today is read as veiled reference to the Internet. Knowledge explosion of the Internet? Are you kidding? Who cut their college history class? So, the knowledge explosion that brought Europe out of the Dark Ages apparently does not count? Neither does the knowledge explosion of the Enlightenment that set the stage for all modern philosophy and science today, including the machines that are foundational to the Internet? The incredible and stunning results of the Gutenberg printing press just do not count? What a biased and historically ignorant perspective! Since we did not live those times, we simply do not evaluate properly their true impact on the human psyche and human history. Proposing that the Internet is the first time humans have experienced a "knowledge explosion" is simply naive and fundamentally ignorant of the history of Western Europe, not even counting the entire scene of the Orient.[42] In addition, the present Internet will look primitive some time in the future. Modern computers never were conceived as possible for any

---

[42] On the extraordinary explosion of knowledge with the Gutenberg printing press, see Eisenstein, *The Printing Revolution in Early Modern Europe*. On the intellectual foundation of the Internet actually being based on the Gutenberg printing press, see Hauben, "The Expanding Commonwealth of Learning: Printing and the Net."

individual to own. Only governments and universities had the financial means to afford them. These were institutional behemoths that took up entire rooms. Old 1950s films and photographs show a room full of banks of tall metal cabinets with their spinning magnetic tape spools a foot each in diameter. These black and white images look so backward and primitive today! Yet, at the time, they were so *avant-garde*, promising incredible calculation power. That entire room of 1950s computer hardware, by the way, could not even begin to calculate what the least expensive iPad in the lap of an elementary school child can perform today. The plot of the famous science fiction movie "Terminator" is based on an interconnected computer network Skynet becoming self-aware and going rogue on the military establishment and taking control of the world. Be assured that the Internet of today will appear mere child's play at some point in the future. Do not get too enamored with yourself or your times.

The attempt to find fulfillment of Dan 12:4 in technology of the writer's time is pathetic. I have an Adventist volume in my library that is over 115 years old. The author pointed to the telegraph, the trolley car, the suspension bridge, electric lighting, the steam railway, the typewriter, and the phonograph—all elements of the new industrial revolution into which he was caught up and with which he clearly was impressed. These were all signs marking out the "present age" (read, industrial revolution) as the one presaging the end.[43] The one item, however, that always puts a smile on my face to read is his reference to "modern artillery." His climaxing example is a canon guarding New York harbor, which he describes in dramatic fashion: "At Sandy Hook, guarding the entrance to New York harbor, is a monster breech-loading canon 49 feet in length, weighing 130 tons, capable of throwing a projectile, over five feet in length and weighing 2,400 pounds, a distance of twenty miles."[44] Though quite quaint now, be assured true "believers" then were in awe and fully assured with a vision of this canon that Daniel's vision of the end was "nigh, even at the doors" (Mark 13:29, KJV). One only can wonder. Who shall smile, quaintly bemused, reading our own technological prognostications a century from now?

---

[43] Smith, *Daniel and the Revelation*, 332-36.
[44] Ibid., 332.

FIGURE 5.3. Smith Illustration A of Dan 12:4. An illustration of the phrase "many shall run to and fro" from Dan 12:4 in a late 1800s Adventist commentary by Uriah Smith. The general idea is the burgeoning technology of travel, communication, and knowledge within the industrial revolution of the nineteenth-century United States. (See Industrial America in the table, "Development of Traditions," p. 69, Figure 3.11.)

FIGURE 5.4. Smith Illustration B of Dan 12:4. An illustration of the phrase "knowledge shall be increased" from Dan 12:4 in a late 1800s Adventist commentary by Uriah Smith. The general idea is the burgeoning technology of travel, communication, and knowledge within the industrial revolution of the nineteenth-century United States. (See Industrial America in the table, "Development of Traditions," p. 69, Figure 3.11.)

Example 6: "they ... will see" (Rev 11:9)

As one last example of seeing "signs of the times" coming together is the assertion that the death of the two witnesses according to Rev 11:9, assumed to be two end-time figures, must be witnessed by the "whole world simultaneously." The inference is that such a viewing could not possibly be fulfilled until satellites and CNN news. The only problem is, these assertions fall completely off the table of sound exegesis and hide faulty assumptions that are "read into" the text. They make false inferences that clearly are not what the text actually says.

First, the invented adjective "whole" or "all," as in "whole world" is nowhere to be found in this passage. Literally, the Greek of this text is straightforward. The text reads: "Those from peoples and tribes and tongues and nations will see." "All" is not used at all! That this viewing is broad based of many people is clear. That this is "all" is eisegesis. So, to infer that the "whole world" or "all the world" must witness this event is off the beam and reading into the text an important but non-existent adjective qualifier that distorts the meaning of the text.

Second, the declaration made in the passage itself is only that the onlookers "will see" the dead bodies. Not one word is given about *how* they will see, or even less, that the seeing must be *simultaneously*. An American president lying in state in the capital rotunda, with thousands of mourners from around the world silently slipping by the flag-draped casket, would fully satisfy the intent and meaning of "those from peoples and tribes and tongues and nations will see." This text in its basic sense entails absolutely no demand for satellites, CNN news, the whole world, or simultaneity. Such a reading of Rev 11:9 as "the whole world simultaneously" is completely bogus, both for misquoting the text and for false inference.

"Signs" Ambivalence

One more observation about signs of the times should be made. What is striking about modern dispensational writers in regard to "signs of the times" is their ambivalence in exactly how to position their own stance with regard to any particular "sign," or, in other cases, the positive or negative value in their appraisals of social reform or political activism. With any particular issue, they know not whether to trumpet its praise or castigate its vanity. In the Cold War period, for example, the effort to pursue nuclear non-proliferation and the buildup of American military might in the Reagan era could be trumpeted as a way to keep America strong and in the game of holding back the forces that Antichrist would assemble against Israel. Or, that same effort could be denigrated as a denial of the inevitable march to Armageddon.[45] Either way, any such effort, movement, or event can be read as a "sign of the times" and heralded as the sure indicator of the millennial Advent, even when we are not sure how we feel about the topic itself politically or socially. This mercurial perspective is quite strange in the light of the bombastic preaching that uses these very "signs" as infallible proofs of the end.

Signing Off

One common feature of modern teaching and preaching about the second coming of Christ is the use of the invented construct, "signs of the times," to "prove" the end is near. These "signs" are based on deliberately misquoted Scripture, questionable presuppositions, faulty exegesis, distorted facts, or false information. Further, this sad "signs" obsession systematically and seemingly intentionally ignores the long history of finding dubious "signs of the times" in *any* generation from the teachings of Montanus on. The real point is not whether any one set of "signs" in any given generation is correct. Given enough time, the statistical odds will *have* to work in your favor. The point, rather, is rhetorical: all you need to do with any talk of "signs" is persuade the audience. The trick is to use whatever is highly feared in the political and social discourse of the day, whether Saladin and the Muslim onslaught, Communist Russia and the threat of nuclear war, or Osama bin Laden and the threat of global terrorism, strike a chord of fear that resonates with the needs and anxieties of the audience, and then speak boldly and convincingly, and you usually can cross the goal line of public persuasion. To be sure, the actual exegetical legitimacy of your purported "sign" simply does not matter at all for your "sign" to work persuasively with your audience. That is why the craziest and wackiest "signs" one can imagine can be read in a pamphlet, heard on the radio,

---

[45]Boyer, *When Time Shall Be No More*, 252, pointed to a typical example in Lindsey the Cold War ideologue versus Lindsey the thoroughly consistent premillennialist.

or viewed on some cable channel. The only question is, Is someone in the audience persuaded? That is all that matters. Suggest only that we are "close," constantly weaving in, around, and near the blazing light of Revelation's visions without ever actually touching the light, and live the prophetic moth's innuendo waltz in perpetuity, as long as you can get your listener to write that check to support this vital end-time ministry or buy your most recent end-time book, which, unfortunately, you will have to revise soon.

An excellent study of dispensationalism in America is Weber's *On the Road to Armageddon*. Weber covers the history, inner logic, popularization, the alignment of major twentieth-century events with prophetic beliefs (albeit constantly adjusted to fit), and the close but complicated relationship with Jews and modern Israel. Weber's thesis is that dispensationalists now have moved from being just observers to being political participants to the dangerous precipice of turning their protean predictions into self-fulfilling prophecies.

SUMMARY

Reading Revelation is perhaps the most acute hermeneutical challenge of all of Scripture. The first challenge is coming to grips with the genre of apocalyptic literature. First-century readers were well trained in this style of writing, because such books were on their bookshelves at their local Barnes and Noble. Unfortunately, modern readers, especially of the Protestant variety, never even have known about the existence of 2 Esdras, much less read the work. Thus, we talk about Revelation being "apocalyptic," but have not a clue what that is supposed to imply about reading the book.

One implication of reading apocalyptic genre is its fundamentally symbolic world, which is figurative in meaning. Thus, claiming to read the Bible "literally" if applied to apocalyptic symbolism but without distinguishing literal as referential and literal as figurative is ignorant, creates chaos of meaning, and offers no immunity whatsoever from subjectivity. Even a literal reading must pay due regard to figurative meaning. By default, symbols are read figuratively, so Revelation's symbolic language even when read literally must be read figuratively.

Reading Revelation figuratively, however, simply brings in the interpreter's presuppositions of how to figure the figures. Thus, if one presupposes that the figures are realities of spiritual life, then one plays the game of reading what spiritual life event onto what figure. On the other hand, if one presupposes that the figures are periods of history, then one plays the game of periodizing what history on what figure. No matter what total history is in view or how many periods to subdivide that history, the end game always is to place oneself in the last period so as to be able to say, "Game over, man!" Again, if one presupposes the history is future judgment, then the periods simply are shifted forward to that future, but one then has to invent an escape route to avoid the consequences of that judgment. Or, one could not periodize at all and just assume to be at the cusp of realizing whatever positive future Revelation's figures have in mind in our town.

History is the great falsifier, whether setting dates or preaching signs. Setting dates is a sure sign one does not have a clue. Preaching signs is commercially profitable, but a sham and a shame. History has proven infallibly that signs of the times are worthless. False prophets, however, have no honor and no shame. The Internet has exacerbated the problem exponentially. The signs game more reveals the present than the future. Signs rhetoric exposes problems of the age and what worries people the most. Prophets of the end prey upon these fears and sadly turn them into tremendous commercial profit, even though the end never comes.

The problem with bad eschatology is its negative impact on other Christian doctrine. Three areas critically affected are Christology, ecclesiology, and soteriology. One prominent christological distortion is a strange conviviality with a schizophrenic messiah who cannot make up his mind how he is going to deal decisively with evil, whether by dying on a cross or by thermonuclear war. Such a distortion actually resurrects the old Jewish expectation Jesus himself rejected of a martial messiah who brings in the kingdom by violence. This bifurcated Christology allows for multiple paths of salvation, depending on which messiah you follow. One saves you by dying for you. The other saves you by blasting your enemies with his power rays. The implications also are dramatic for the church. Not understanding the scandal of the cross as the essence of Jesus' messianic conscience also distorts ecclesiology. What is the historical destiny of the church? What does the rapture really teach? A cross for Jesus but not the church?

6

A Glassy Sea

Learning from History

ALL RIVERS EVENTUALLY FLOW into the vast sea. Having traced this complex history of the interpretation of Revelation, we now have arrived at the point of the present. Time to ask where we have been and what we have learned. In this brief chapter, we want to summarize the main directions in history we have seen the apocalyptic traditions John used have taken after John. We then suggest some main areas we need to study in order to get a handle on interpreting this book.

We have traced the Jewish tributaries of John's apocalyptic traditions that he used innovatively and powerfully to address the needs of churches in first-century Asia Minor under social, religious, and political pressures due to heresy within and imperial ideology without. He draws upon existing Jewish apocalyptic traditions innovatively for his own purposes. His visions become a strong river of interpretation after John that flows in directions he might never have anticipated. His opening vision of the Son of Man standing among the lampstands he might have taken as the most important, since he gave this vision first, but history has shown no one really picked up on his favorite image of the Son of Man. Instead, one image alone that John offered late in his drama pushes the wall of water down the canyon of interpretive history—the millennium. Entire eschatological constructs have been built on this solitary image mentioned in only one passage in the entire Apocalypse. One might suspect John would have been confused, even dismayed, had he known about this strange choice later prophets and interpreters seized upon to focus a search for Revelation's meaning.

Chiliasm is one of the early millennial constructs. This view was influenced by Jewish apocalyptic ideas of a literal, earthly kingdom, but including a hyperliteral twist, with a strong dose of materialism. The beast for centuries clearly was Rome. The reward for faithfulness under the spell of this beast would be reigning in the superabundance of that earthly millennial paradise after Rome is ruined, destroyed by a martial messiah on the Jewish pattern of a Simon bar Kokhba type rebellion and victory. The millennial kingdom probably will be centered in Jerusalem. History, however, completely undercuts the power of the Rome-is-the-beast construct after Constantine. Thus, monumental interpretive adjustments have to be made.

The new millennial construct is amillennialism. Revelation's imagery is moved from exterior history to interior spiritual life. This view is hugely successful for many, but not for all. The church, even with her amillennial construct, still cannot seem to control strong literal currents of interpretation even after Rome no longer is the beast. One clear stream of interpretation that reveals the lack of ability of the church to control Revelation's interpretation is the Antichrist legend. The ever-developing legend of Antichrist shows the power of popular imagination for creative inventiveness to write entire plotlines for Revelation with characters alien to John's imagery. The legend of Antichrist, an infamous character John never mentioned, grows into a full-fledged biography and drama by Medieval centuries inextricably mixed with Revelation's imagery.

A premillennial construct erupts among Reformers. This new construct releases with full force again a literal approach that has been dammed up by the church for centuries. Periodizing, once a maverick scheme of those swirling in the small eddies of the main current, such as Bede and Joachim of Fiore, now is adopted wholesale and partnered with this premillennialism. Premillennialism, with its supporting prop of a periodizing of history to prove the last days have arrived, becomes a standard Protestant way of handling the visions of Revelation as prophecy. Thus, after the Reformation watershed, interpreters are swept away downstream along the two main currents of symbolic and literal readings of Revelation.

A postmillennial construct rises up rather suddenly among the colonialists settling uncharted, vast expanses of a New World. Once again, unexpected historical developments are transmuting Revelation's traditions. America changes everything. A new day dawns in the colonial heartland, with her vast and rich natural resources and seemingly unlimited land. A New Jerusalem here and now is no longer a dream that must await some far off future. The new day inspires a new millennial construct, postmillennialism. Its civic millennial rhetoric forever becomes embedded into the national psyche and into political speech. The naïveté of this initial colonial optimism is exposed by the pragmatics of actual government, and, later, a savage civil war.

Three nineteenth-century movements in America represent Revelation's traditions overflowing in a mighty flood that sweeps all away downstream, tumbling completely out of control. One is Mormonism, a postmillennial revival, but based entirely on an alien scriptural text that fosters unheard of, ahistorical ideas about the Hebrews, American Indians, and America's millennial destiny. New Jerusalem is Salt Lake City. The second movement is Millerism, not a beer fad, but a failed date-setting fiasco that swept along thousands in its wake, but that unbelievably survived as Seventh-day Adventism preaching signs of the times "nearness" for almost 150 years now. Adventists, however, splinter when they sneeze, so they have spawned Jehovah's Witnesses, Worldwide Church of God, Branch Davidians, and numerous other mutations. The third movement is Darbyism, better known as dispensationalism, whose name is a tip-off to theological aberrations so extraordinary not even the original Plymouth Brethren group of its origins could countenance the teachings, yet still, once transplanted to America, conquered almost the entire evangelical world through the Scofield Bible that organized, systematized, and propagated the new eschatology in an elaborate note apparatus.

Interestingly, no new eschatological construct for understanding Revelation has arisen since the 1800s. This one observation reveals the fundamental centrality of nineteenth-century America for the history of the interpretation of Revelation. Today, in print and media, we are witnessing an unending repetition of the same interpretive traditions already set in play by Joseph Smith, William Miller, and John Darby, exacerbated by desire for notoriety or commercial gain. Seeing how the general American public has been duped by all this, spending millions of dollars along the way, frankly is depressing.

The end result of these American traditions after a century and a half of the nonsense is Revelation has been turned into a farce and its warnings of judgment a fodder for jokes for late-night comedians. Unrecognized is that the problem is not "pagans who just don't believe the Bible." The problem is false prophets who just don't understand the Bible. So-called prophets of Revelation are saying stupid things about the book and never being held accountable. The comedians are right. Revelation, as popularly understood, is a joke. What an ignominious end for such a masterful and powerful book. After two thousand years, that is where we are here in America.

So, where in the world do we go from here? The history of the interpretation of Revelation certainly gives a reasonable person cause for pause. We have been all over the map. Why even try? Perhaps because the book is in the canon? That might be a good place to start. Now, we could take the Greek Orthodox route: have the book in the Bible but refuse to base any doctrine or liturgy on its verses. That approach at least avoids the Excedrin headache of what to do with the millennium. The church in the West, however, never was able to let go of the book so easily the way the Greek Orthodox church did, so still is haunted by their canonical intuition the book has more to offer. Even when a Reformer such as Luther complains he can detect nothing of the Holy Spirit in the book and that the book says nothing of Christ, he will not have the audacity actually to refuse to translate the book for his own German Bible.

That the book is in the canon actually is our main clue how to proceed from here and how to begin to interpret the book. Luther was wrong. John's Revelation *is* inspired of the Holy Spirit and the book says *everything* about Christ. However, the interpretive burden is on us to prove this assertion. We must contextualize this assertion within the canon of the Gospels. The Gospels are our lodestone for knowing who Jesus is as the Messiah of God. If our interpretation is to have genuine validity that will stand the test of time, we must not base our approach on wild schemes of an unknown, unknowable future. We will use the history of interpretation as our GPS to map out directions we do *not* want to go, because they already have proven—repeatedly—to be false or misguided. We are trying to get to that serene, glassy sea near the divine throne (Rev 4:6; 15:2).

Part 2

Beyond Apollyon and Armageddon

*Setting Hermeneutical Foundations
for the Interpretation of Revelation*

7

Interpretive Decisions

Genre, Prophecy, Judgments, Millennium

READING REVELATION REQUIRES major interpretive choices even before beginning. This requirement is the burden of being confronted by two millennia of interpretive traditions already pushing us hard from behind before we even open up the book. Some of the most urgent questions focus specifically on four problem areas that incessantly demand our attention, insisting that we answer these questions even to begin: (1) how to handle the complex genre, (2) how to historicize prophetic fulfillment, (3) how to sequence the judgment cycles, and (4) how to understand the millennium. We need to make some fundamental interpretive decisions on these four problem areas. We start with the question of genre, because that is the most important interpretive decision to make about any piece of literature. Fortunately, John actually helps us out here. He seems to give intentional signals at the very beginning of Revelation to clue the reader that he is mixing genre on purpose.

CONQUERING GENRE

The first few verses of Revelation indicate its form is a complex mix of three genres. The work is styled as an apocalypse in Rev 1:1, "Apocalypse of Jesus Christ." The work is styled as a prophecy in Rev 1:3, "the words of this prophecy." Finally, the work is styled as an epistle in Rev 1:4, "John, to the seven churches." Thus, John signals Revelation has a hybrid genre. Each has two major implications for interpretation.

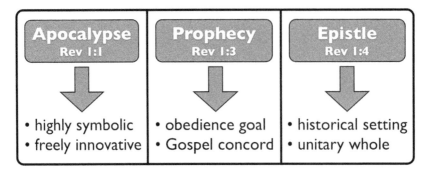

FIGURE 7.1. Revelation's Complex Genre and Corollaries.

Apocalypse

Revelation's apocalyptic genre has two important corollaries for interpretation. Apocalyptic is (1) highly symbolic and (2) freely innovative. This genre seems the least understood of the three.[1]

Highly Symbolic

In all apocalyptic literature, images flash across the screen for their emotional power. Images likewise are symbolic; they are "commentary" on some human reality.

In a world without TV media appearances, Twitter, talk shows, YouTube, and blogs, such that your only "commentary" was in carved images, the symbolic was the norm. Human kings and their empires often took on animal characteristics in the ancient world as political propaganda. Using an animal form is called zoomorphism. Everyone knew that no such

FIGURE 7.2. Assyrian Winged Bull. Empire propaganda carved forever in stone (BML).

---

[1] A good introduction is Murphy, *Apocalypticism in the Bible and Its World*.

exotic creature as a winged bull who had lion claws and a human face existed. All knew the symbolism was about a king whose armies could sweep down on you like an eagle suddenly snatching prey in its talons. They knew the symbolic meaning that attempting to resist such a king would be like facing down a raging bull, or being savagely mauled by a wild lion. A winged bull was empire propaganda.

These wild images come in visions and dreams. They are intentionally fantastic, unreal, weird. An eagle has three heads, and a lion speaks with a human voice. Cosmic disturbances in sun, moon, and stars portray gods in the heavens leaving their thrones and going into action. Earthly disturbances (terror, tumult, and abnormalities) are just mirror reflections of heaven's happenings. Angels execute the divine will. Beasts are kings and their kingdoms. A woman is a city. The visceral impact of this drama was felt emotionally, not just for rational contemplation. Thus, apocalyptic is highly symbolic, a normal way of "thinking" in the ancient world.[2]

Numbers appear for their symbolic power. That is why certain numbers are repeated over and over. Seven churches, seven spirits before the throne, seven seals, seven trumpets, seven bowls, and on and on the number resounds across the pages of Revelation. Why seven? The number became hugely popular in Jewish apocalypses due to the original seven days of the creation story. The number seven came to represent rich theological reflections such as God in his sovereignty, divine completion, or divine fulfillment. In Jewish apocalypses, the length of messiah's reign was a different period of time in each apocalypse. The length of the reign never was read referentially, always symbolically. In 2 Esdras, for example, the reign is 400 years, a period clearly patterned on the time of Israel's Egyptian slavery.[3]

Thus, numbers in Revelation are literal, but typically they are not referential. For example, the 144,000 in Rev 7:4 is not referential. The number is a symbolic expansion by the same number as the twelve tribes of Israel (12x12=144). This is the whole company of the people of God represented as the fullness of Israel. Likewise, the number 666

---

[2]Not like moderns are not just as subject to the evocative power of beast imagery. Hollywood has made a mint on the beast rising up out of the depths, whether deep sea, deep space, or deep time, as in movies such as "Jaws" (1975), "Alien" (1979), and "Jurassic Park" (1993).

[3]2 Esd 7:28.

of the beast in Rev 16:18 and the 1,000 year reign of the saints given in Rev 20:4 are figurative, not referential. Numerology is the study of the symbolic significance of various recurring numbers in apocalyptic.

Freely Innovative

The symbolism of apocalyptic also is freely innovative. Authors used symbols out of a stock barrel of images, like graphic artists buying a DVD "image collection" of royalty free "stock" images to use as they wish for their own artistic purposes. Just because a previous apocalyptic work used a stock image with a certain figurative meaning does not bind any later apocalyptic author exclusively to that usage or meaning. Just because Daniel uses imagery of four beasts coming up out of the sea to represent four separate empires does not bind John slavishly to that usage. In fact, John freely innovates Daniel's imagery, morphing the figures into an entirely different meaning. Daniel presents a lion, a bear, a leopard, and a ten-horned beast (Dan 7). John merges all four beasts into *one* beast that has characteristics of all four (Rev 13). Further, for Daniel, the ten horns of the fourth beast are ten kings of the Seleucid dynasty who each rule sequentially. In stark contrast, John's ten kings rule *simultaneously* with his one beast. The book of Daniel does not interpret Revelation, as many end-timers are prone to assert. The tail does not wag the dog. Rather, John interprets Daniel. Innovative use would apply to the famous "four horsemen of the Apocalypse" in Rev 6, which is built on Zech 6, or the dirge of Babylon's doom in Rev 18, which is built on Isa 27, Isa 43, and Jer 51, or the new heaven and new earth in Rev 21, which is built on Isa 66.

The same would be true of the use of non-biblical traditions as well. Use of non-biblical traditions does not mean we then have to think of such traditions as inspired. Paul quoted from the Greek poet Epimenides in Acts 17:28. That does not make Epimenides inspired. Epimenides just was useful to Paul's point. John uses the Greek Leto myth to develop the dragon story in Rev 12, not because the Greek myth is inspired, but because the story involves the birth of Apollo, the dragon slayer, and Emperor Domitian claimed to be Apollo. John is not sanctifying the Leto myth. He is just scoring a point with his audience. Asia Minor readers would get the allusion because they lived the story. He is saying that the realities that are encountered in that myth are realities that the story of Jesus has circumscribed. Jesus is the real dragon slayer, not Domitian. The things that people are talking about in this myth have happened in the real life of Jesus Christ. So, whatever the source of the imagery, whether biblical or non-biblical, we have to allow apocalyptic authors to be freely innovative with their source material, as they clearly are inclined in this genre of literature.

How will we know what John means if past usage is not an infallible guide to John's meaning? Sometimes, John will tell us directly. In the opening vision, he talks about seven stars in the right hand of the Son of Man. He talks about seven lampstands where the Son of Man stands. He then tells us in Rev 1:20 the seven stars are the angels of the seven churches previously introduced in 1:11, and that the seven lampstands are the seven churches. These seven congregations will have letters sent to them in the following chapters (Rev 2–3). Not too difficult. When he does not directly tell us, what he explicitly has said functions as a guide for the meaning of imagery to come. If the drama of Revelation starts with a vision of the crucified and resurrected Messiah reigning over his seven churches, sending them letters and judging them with both commendation and condemnation on what currently is taking place in their congregations, then *these opening chapters and churches have to be a clue to the rest of the book.*

FIGURE 7.3. Woodcut of Rev 1. An illustration of the vision of Christ in the 1522 Luther Bible (Taschen).

What guides John as he freely innovates the apocalyptic imagery he has inherited, both biblical and non-biblical, is his focus on cross and Christ. He has his mind fixed on the core of the gospel story, the death, burial, and resurrection of the Son of Man, who now is present in power to all the churches. This focus he makes absolutely clear in the opening vision of Revelation. His vision, he says, is from "Jesus Christ." How does John then choose to describe this Jesus? What is most on John's mind when he thinks of this Jesus? Apollyon? No. Armageddon? No. John clarifies, "the faithful witness, the first born of the dead, and the ruler of the kings of the earth" (Rev 1:5). Faithful witness is the cross. First born of the dead is the resurrection. Ruler of the kings of the earth is the ascension. You cannot get more gospel than that. Further, John's own testimony is, "To him who loves us, and released us from our sins by his blood" (Rev 1:5). Such a soteriological confession has a vision of Calvary at its heart. The cross is John's definitive theological affirmation of how God has chosen to deal decisively with evil in the world. John will put all his apocalyptic imagery through the refracting lens of the gospel. No gospel? Then no apocalypse, no drama, no story, no Revelation of Jesus Christ.

Prophecy

Revelation's prophetic genre has two important corollaries for interpretation. First, prophecy's goal is practical, the obedience of God's people. This goal implies that prophecy is more about forthtelling the present than foretelling the future. Second, New Testament prophecy to be legitimate must show New Testament concord. This concord is a canonical issue.

Obedience Goal

Prophets speak God's word to God's people to call them to obedience right now, as in, "Choose you this day whom you will serve" (Josh 24:15, KJV). Prophecy's burden is not the future but the present. Little of what prophets spoke had to do with a far off future. The future they pointed to was the near future of God's imminent judgment. The Jewish nation had broken covenant with God and would be judged soon. A prophet preached to call for repentance. Assyria and Babylon are coming, sent by God to judge an unrepentant Jewish nation. Prophecy is more present than future. Paul speaks of prophets in New Testament churches, and regulates their activity.[4] Where are all these

---

[4] Cf. 1 Cor 12:28–29; 14:29, 32, 37.

prophets? Where is all their material? We do not have the huge bulk of the prophetic sayings of these early churches because *those* prophecies were for *those* churches in *their* historical setting. Prophecy is for now.

This sound understanding of the prophetic office is more in line with John's intent in labeling his work as a "prophecy" (Rev 1:3). His burden is to call God's people living in the churches of first-century Asia Minor to faithful obedience. To those businessmen powerfully seduced by Roman imperial propaganda to buy into the Roman world system and its values, to those believers sorely tempted to compromise their confession by participating in the Roman emperor cult, John, like Joshua, draws a line in the sand, "Choose you this day whom you will serve." To those following the idolatries of Jezebel (Rev 2:20) or heeding the doctrine of the Nicolaitans (Rev 2:15), John is demanding, "Choose you this day whom you will serve." At the level of prophecy, Revelation is about faithful obedience in Asia Minor under Domitian, Jezebel, and the Nicolaitans. To insist Revelation has a first-century hermeneutic is not to be preterist. That insistence is being faithful to the very essence of prophetic genre. Further, Revelation is epistolary, and that genre unquestionably nails exegesis to the first century. Their call to faithfulness in their context is our clue as to how Revelation might be read faithfully and prophetically in the church today.

Gospel Concord

The prophecy genre in the context of the New Testament canon also means we must be quite careful to interpret the book of Revelation in canonical concord, that is, staying true to the gospel, whose essence is preserved in the four Gospels. Revelation will not tell you anything about Jesus you do not already know in the four Gospels. So, anything said about Revelation that does not square with the four Gospels is flat wrong. If Revelation is going to be prophetic, the book has to be in concord with the prophetic New Testament.

Lack of true gospel concord is where we really go wrong with the book of Revelation. We are not careful to read the book in concord with the Gospels. We wind up with schizophrenic messiahs, multiple salvations, invisible comings, and a church who, at the end, fails in her historical mission. Revelation presents us with a canonical decision, not that we have to decide whether the book is inspired, but whether we are going to read the book as gospel canon. Only if Revelation is interpreted in conformity to the gospel will the book ever be genuinely authoritative for the church and profitable for the future. With our eyes off the gospel, we start saying crazy things about what Jesus is going to do at some future Armageddon, inexplicably oblivious all the while how such "pictures" flat do not square with the Jesus known in the Gospels. In so doing we eviscerate the book of its gospel core and make a joke of canonical concord. For a book that we supposedly are taking as inspired and authoritative, we really wind up de-authorizing and de-canonizing its visions with a perverted word that truly is not the Word of God made flesh. Luther's words come back hauntingly, almost prophetically: "Christ is neither taught nor known in it."

FIGURE 7.4. The Epistolary Binding of Revelation's Genre.

Epistle

The epistolary genre becomes clear in the epistolary format to which John shifts in Rev 1:4. He identifies the sender and then the receiver, the traditional first two beginning elements of the letter form. Then, to show how this epistolary form is meant to be a global structure for the entire work, John ends Revelation like an epistle. In fact, he actually invokes the sense of a typical Pauline letter conclusion with a standard Pauline grace benediction, "The grace of our Lord Jesus Christ be with all of you" (Rev 22:21). So all visions of Revelation are "sandwiched" by this epistle genre. The epistle binds both apocalypse and prophecy together, so epistolary genre circumscribes the meaning of the entire work. Why did John do this? A brilliant literary stroke because of what the epistle genre tells us about a document's interpretive sense. Epistle genre tells us the work has a specific historical setting and is to be interpreted as a unitary whole.

Historical Setting

First, the epistle genre means the work is to be interpreted within a specific historical setting. A letter's meaning is grounded in the his-

FIGURE 7.5. Ancient Corinth. The imposing Acrocorinth in the background is a monolithic rock that is the backdrop to the foreground of the first-century ruins of ancient Corinth and the famous Laechean Road leading into the city from its busy harbor port.

torical context surrounding the letter's production. For example, one never would think of trying to interpret Paul's letter to the Corinthians without first studying the ancient city of Corinth. One would want to understand its ancient setting, its history, culture, and commerce. How did Paul start the church? On what missionary journey? Under what conditions? What was the significance of his appearance in the court of the proconsul Gallio? So, every letter has historical specificity that contextualizes its meaning.

If John wraps his visions in a letter envelope, he is doing so as a deliberate act of genre mixing. He wants to make clear *the primary sense of his work is to be found in his own historical setting.* This setting is tied to the seven churches in first-century Asia Minor. These are real churches with real problems right now and Revelation is written to address these needs of the seven churches of Asia Minor. This observation is not really taking a so-called "preterist" approach to Revelation. This is simply paying attention to the genre in which John wrote and giving John the right to do whatever he wants with his own piece of literature. If Daniel wrote an apocalyptic piece so as to "seal up" its meaning, John makes explicitly clear with his global epistolary structure surrounding his visions that he never intended to write like Daniel. In contradistinction to any "sealing up" or obfuscation of his meaning so as to be reserved only for an elite audience of the future,

John wrote clearly and dramatically to his own first-century audience. What he meant for the seven churches would not have to await some future setting two thousand years later.

What is the historical setting of these seven churches? We can read between the lines of the church letters to get an idea. John's first-

FIGURE 7.6. Ancient Ephesus. The façade of the Library of Celsus at the bottom of Curetes Street leading to the upper city and intersecting the Marble Way leading to the theater where the silversmiths rioted against Paul in a general mob action (Acts 19:23–40). John confronts a group called the Nicolaitans in the letter to Ephesus in Rev 2:6, 15.

century context is persecution. What specific kind is unclear. Whether this persecution is state sanctioned, which is unlikely, or simply civic mob action, like the silversmith's riot against Paul in Acts 19:23–40, but indulged by the provincial authorities, or what exactly, we do not know. Fact is, Antipas already has paid with his own life (Rev 2:13). That single incident could be read as a harbinger and raise ominous prospects about the future for believers in Asia Minor. So, one part of Revelation's setting is persecution, perceived or real.

Another part of the historical setting of Revelation is heresy. Some are provoking compromise, such as Jezebel. False teachers are invoking errant doctrine, such as the Nicolaitans. They all are creating serious problems for faith and practice. The church in Asia Minor is under duress both externally and internally. The visions of Revelation primarily address this specific historical setting. Just like Paul wrote to Corinth, John writes to seven churches in Asia Minor pressured from within and without. That setting is why John has such emphasis on personal testimony, the witness theme of the Apocalypse: "And they overcame him by the blood of the Lamb, and by the word of their testimony; and they loved not their lives unto death" (Rev 12:11).

Unitary Whole

Second, the epistle genre means the work is to be interpreted as a unitary whole. One would not dare to attempt to explain the meaning of Rom 11:26 without first putting this verse in its immediate context of the three chapters of Rom 9–11. Further, even the three chapters of Rom 9–11 would not have their proper meaning without a careful study of the entire movement of Rom 1–11.

Likewise with Revelation. The work is written as one integrated piece of literature whose various parts work together and interpret one another. The Inaugural Vision of the Son of Man (Rev 1:9–20) lays the theological foundation for the judgment of the church in the following Letters to the Seven Churches (Rev 2–3). The connection is clear, because Christ is characterized in each letter by an allusion to an element of the Inaugural Vision. The Vision of Heaven (Rev 4–5) then lays the theological foundation for the judgment of the world in the seal and trumpet judgments that follow (Rev 6–11). The connection is clear, because the Lamb introduced in Rev 5 is the one who starts the whole cycle rolling by opening the seal judgments in Rev 6.

Further, all imagery is sublimated to gospel truths and made to resonate within Revelation in sympathetic vibrations. The Son of Man of the Inaugural Vision (Rev 1:13) already has been typed as one who sheds his own blood because he is a faithful witness (1:5). John signals that martial imagery, such as Jewish tradition in the "lion of Judah" is to be transmuted into gospel truth as the image of a slaughtered Lamb (Rev 5:5–6). So, the martial imagery in Revelation is not referential but figurative. Martial imagery figures gospel truths. Here in Rev 5:5–6 is where popular Armageddon interpreted as referential martial imagery meets its own hermeneutical Waterloo.

In terms of soteriology, the image of a slaughtered Lamb of Rev 5:5–6 also makes transparently clear that if redemption is pictured in Revelation, the blood in the imagery will be Jesus' own blood. This truth of Jesus' shed blood already has been insinuated in the prologue characterization of Jesus in Rev 1:5. Thus, when the rider on the white horse appears from heaven in Rev 19:13, universally taken to be Jesus Christ, and his robe is baptized in blood, that is not the blood of his enemies; that is his own blood. Thus, any image finds its true meaning in the corporate whole of Revelation, as does the warrior image in Rev 19 reaching all the way back to Christian hermeneutic in Rev 1 and 5.

Or again, this rider on the white horse treads the winepress of the fierce wrath of God, indeed. Yet he strikes down the nations with a sword that goes out of his mouth (Rev 19:15), which is a most odd weapon with which to fight some supposed thermonuclear war. The sword is not referential, but figurative, and is the same sword already seen in the Inaugural Vision of the Son of Man (Rev 1:16). This sword pictured coming out of the mouth is the precise reason why this rider in Rev 19 is called the Word of God (Rev 19:13). If any war is pictured in Revelation that war is a war of words—a war of witness, of confession, of testimony, of obedience to God. The war is won on the paradigm of Jesus as presented in the four Gospels and, indeed, in the rest of the New Testament—faithful testimony, even to the point of death (Rev 12:11).

HISTORICIZING PROPHECY

The next interpretive decision we have to make is how to historicize the prophetic fulfillment. This choice is forced upon us by interpreters who focus on foretelling. We have suggested Revelation's burden is forthtelling. Revelation is not just prophecy. John mixed three genres deliberately. He sublimated apocalypse and prophecy to epistle. The epistle genre frames the other two and controls their meaning. John signals that his apocalyptic symbolism and prophetic figures are to be read from within his own first-century historical setting. Like letters, Revelation is "occasional literature." The writing is occasioned by specific, historical circumstances and directly addresses those readers and their needs in that setting. Thus, our interpretive approach derives from observing John's creative use of literary genre and compositional structure. The epistle frame is intentional on John's part to say that the bulk of the prophetic material he is composing in Revelation is in the mode of forthtelling, not foretelling.

Much of the history of interpretation of Revelation has ignored this epistolary frame of the book, simply assuming Revelation to be nothing but foretelling. Even Luther assumed Revelation is foretelling: "Another kind foretells things to come which are not previously contained in Scripture."[5] However, even if we ignore John's definitive epistolary frame, asserting Revelation is foretelling prophecy raises two further hermeneutical problems. We do not know where in the book prophecy begins, nor when in time prophecy applies.

First, *where* in the book does the foretelling begin? That is, how do we decide precisely what passages are foretelling? Seems a simple question, but no one can agree. Some say in the Letters to the Seven Churches in Rev 2–3 (Adventists). Some say at Rev 4:1, when John is told to "come up here." This is when John begins seeing the future (Dispensationalists). Some say with the Seal Judgments starting in Rev 6 (Luther and later Reformers). And so on. The point is obvious. We cannot have real confidence in any of these assertions. The choice of where to begin is patently arbitrary. If John had intended foretelling, he did a poor job making clear just where to start for his readers.

Second, *when* in time is that foretelling fulfilled? That is, if some of Revelation's prophecy is about history, what history? Again, no one can agree. Even if we assume any one of these foretelling schemes of where to begin reading Revelation as foretelling, we still would have to decide at what point on history's timeline—past, present, future—is the fulfillment. Logical options are four: past, present, future, or none of the above. These four options have been given names.

———— Timeline of History ————▶

Idealist		
Preterist	**Historicist**	**Futurist**
Past	Present	Future
70, 95, 313	Western History	"End Times"

FIGURE 7.7. Prophecy as Foretelling in Revelation.

Preterist

The preterist approach assumes the prophecies have been fulfilled. The concept is tied to three possible historical settings: (1) John wrote

---

[5]Etliche weissagt von Künsstigen dingen die nicht zuuor inn der Schrisst stehen. *Luther Bible*, 1534; cf. *Luther's Works*, 400.

about the watershed moment for Judaism in the destruction of Jerusalem in A.D. 70; (2) John wrote about his own setting of Domitian and Asia Minor in A.D. 95; (3) John wrote about the watershed moment for Christianity in Constantine and the Edict of Milan in A.D. 313.

The preterist view has difficulties. First, as explained already, John probably did not write Revelation as foretelling in the first place. Second, that John wrote about A.D. 70 and Jerusalem's destruction requires an unnatural extension of the symbolic as a metaphor of a metaphor. The beast is Rome is Jerusalem. Such a reading of symbolic language is convoluted and more confuscates the way symbols work than makes clear what John meant. Third, if John wrote to prophesy about A.D. 95, Domitian, and the Roman empire, those prophecies failed. In fact, this reading as within John's own context is actually the most natural one, if foretelling is the deal, but, at the same time, also is the reading that so bothered so many about Revelation as foretelling; sensing failed prophecy is what in part set up the canonical difficulties of the book. Fourth, applying Revelation to Constantine also does not work, because Rome was not destroyed. No reading of the total destruction of Babylon in Rev 18 makes any sense if "Babylon" in reality continues to rule an empire long afterwards. Fundamentally, any of the preterist readings of Revelation ignores the lack of early canonical attestation that Revelation suffered. If Revelation were interpreted as clear prophecy fulfilled, as all preterist views suggest, the book's authority never would have been so questioned, as happened in its long journey into the canon. Fifth, the preterist view mitigates the biblical word of universal, final judgment.

Historicist

The historicist approach assumes the prophecies outline western civilization. The key is to periodize that history already transpired up to the time of the interpreter to produce the impression the interpreter's generation is the last. *All historicist views presume the last generation.* Whatever number of periods—three, five, seven, whatever, take your pick—the interpreter always will end up at the end—pure magic! No matter where counting starts (creation, Cyrus, Christ, etc.), or what the momentous time (Constantine, Muslims, Mongols, Turks, Israel, Russia, China), Revelation "proves" your generation is the last. Funny how that works. The historicist approach is transparently tendentious, completely unconvincing, and little more than self-serving hermeneutical hocus pocus. The history of interpretation is littered with these schemes: Bede, Hildegard, Joachim of Fiore, Luther, Millerites, Adventists, Jehovah's Witnesses, Worldwide Church of God, Dispensationalists. For prophecy in Revelation, they are a dime a dozen.

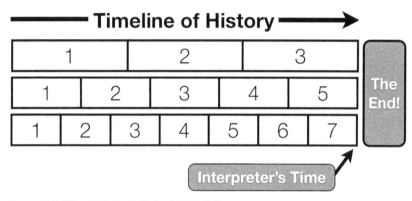

FIGURE 7.8. Historicist Periodizing Methodology.

The historicist view has difficulties. First, John probably did not write as foretelling. Second, the methodology is totally arbitrary and patently self serving. The mathematical odds that the "last age" always is the interpreter's, no mater what century over the last two thousand years, is astronomical. Third, the view is grossly biased. No accident western writers view only western history. The book of Revelation is a front to explain western civilization. Oriental history does not even get a footnote in these schemes. Christianity in half the world has no eschatological significance for the coming of the kingdom of God. Really? Fourth, the view has no relevance to the original readers; their reading of the book was a waste of their time and no consolation.

Futurist

The futurist approach assumes the prophecies have yet to be fulfilled. The concept is tied to a future historical setting, often called the "end times," with one distinctive associated time of brief duration called the "tribulation period." This approach is well known even in the general public due to the immense popularity of dispensational publications. With this particular variety an end-time plot has developed that plays out the conflict between an Antichrist figure and those 144,000 Jews who have gotten saved during the tribulation period when all heck is breaking loose in the world. The church, in the meantime, has been raptured out of history, so is sipping her end-time tea watching all this from heaven's balcony. The Jews would be totally annihilated save for the second coming of Christ with his thermonuclear death rays that blast Antichrist and his minions off the face of the earth. That is why you do not want to be left behind. Graphic charts on the Internet are crammed with the intricacies of various theories about the tribulation period that Revelation is supposed to detail. They are so convoluted and complicated they leave the mind spinning. Such charts also reveal the total absence of sound principles of interpretation exacerbated by infinite ingenuity on what Bible verses to include as prophetic of the "end times" and shoehorn somehow, somewhere into the chart.

The futurist view has difficulties. First, as for the other two, John probably did not write as foretelling. Second, futurists beg the ques-

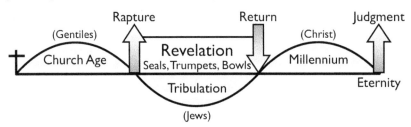

FIGURE 7.9. Composite Futurist Chart. Composite chart, simplified, summarizing main ideas of general end-time scenarios. Specific details, components, vary wildly.

tion of knowing the time. Regardless of what they say, they pretend to know that time. They disavow that they know the time, but they imply they know the time by the very act of writing, for they have no other reason for writing than on the assumption the end time has arrived. They then imply with every statement that they know the time. They never *say* now is the time, but they constantly *imply* now is the time. Otherwise, you never would hear from them. Third, this approach, as typified by Adventists, Jehovah's Witnesses, Worldwide Church of God, and Dispensationalists, is rife with defective doctrines of soteriology, ecclesiology, and Christology. These problems already have been discussed. Fourth, futurists play an interminable game of "signs of the times" rhetoric ripped from today's headlines that has nothing to do with genuine signs or eschatological times. "Signs of the times" preaching is pure gimmickry. The goal is to persuade an uncritical audience, which, given America's rampant scriptural ignorance, general gullibility, pervasive conspiracy mindset, and widespread fears of social and political disruption, is not that hard. Fifth, we do not have to wait with a clock ticking down to an arbitrary point to reach the last generation for God to show up in judgment in history. Sixth, this view renders Revelation absolutely meaningless to the original readers.

Idealist

The idealist approach assumes the prophecies always are fulfilled. The concept is not tied to any historical setting. The key is to emphasize the symbolic value of Revelation's language as addressing the conflict of good and evil in any generation and every generation. Believers are always in tribulation and always are fighting the beasts of their age that oppose God and his purposes. An advantage to this approach is to simplify Revelation's dense imagery to a singular concept that is easy to understand, simple to preach, and always true. The approach also can give better consideration to prophecy as forthtelling, which works more in tune with John's unusual genre mixing and epistolary frame.

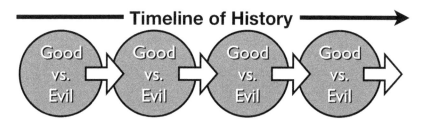

FIGURE 7.10. Idealist View. This view is not tied to a particular historical setting. The emphasis is on the symbolism of the on-going struggle of good and evil in the world.

The idealist view, however, has difficulties. First, the view has an inadequate philosophy of history. History has no purpose and no goal. History just repeats itself in an indefinite cycle of good versus evil. A biblical viewpoint on the meaning of history starts with the creation story. The creation story clearly presents a divine purpose in ordering and structuring creation and a divine intent for bringing that creation to an intended goal or destiny. That destiny was interrupted by the fall of Adam and sin. Biblical evidence points to a grand salvation story that centers in Christ and ultimately will end history and consummate creation (Rom 8). Second, the idealist view has an inadequate concept of evil. The problem of evil never is resolved. Therefore, God is not truly sovereign, because God never decisively wins.

SEQUENCING JUDGMENTS

The next interpretive decision we have to make is how to sequence the judgment cycles. Revelation has a famous triad of judgments: seven seals (6:1—8:1), seven trumpets (8:2—11:19), and seven bowls (15:5—16:21). Each series of seven judgments is a judgment cycle. The three judgment cycles combined result in a total of twenty-one judgments. How are we supposed to conceptualize the progress of these twenty-one judgments? Three theories have been proposed.

Linear

The linear theory assumes the judgments are a chronological sequence of twenty-one historical judgments following one right after the other. This view usually goes hand-in-hand with the historicist and futurist approaches. The issue revolves around the assumption that Revelation is foretelling. The preterist and idealist do not really have to struggle with this problem *de facto*.

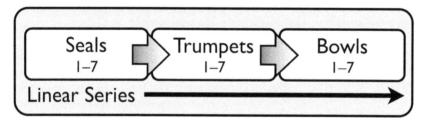

FIGURE 7.11. Linear Judgments. The judgments are assumed to be a continuous, unbroken sequence documenting a series of historical events.

The trick for the historicist is to nail what continuous series of historical events are prefigured in the sequence of the seals, trumpets, and bowls. John may not have meant a straight sequence of historical judgments in the first place. Yet, even assuming he did, no one has a real clue what judgment goes with what historical event. Centuries of the historicist approach have been an abject failure. Assignment of any particular judgment to any particular event is a study in capricious subjectivity. Thinking someone could hit just the right combination is like saying a monkey at a keyboard poking mindlessly away, at some point, given enough time, just might type a line of Shakespeare.

Futurists have a better time of application, because they are not constrained by real history. They invent their own fabricated plot of the seven-year tribulation period and then say the seals, trumpets, and bowls go there. The judgment cycles fit nicely as a linear sequence, because no history has transpired, or even can, to falsify the theory. Thus, futurists conveniently escape being falsified by history, because they are ahistorical in their eschatological inventions about the judgment cycles on a historical timeline that does not exist. Theoretically, history could play like one of the futurist dramas, but, hermeneutically, entertaining that discussion is like asking how many angels can dance on the head of a pin. We are so far removed from sound interpretation and what John likely meant as to be near meaningless.

Telescopic

The telescopic theory is linear, only slightly modified. The basis is the literary observation that the seventh in each series of the seals and trumpets does not actually portray a judgment. Instead the last in the series introduces the next series. Thus, the seventh seal is simply si-

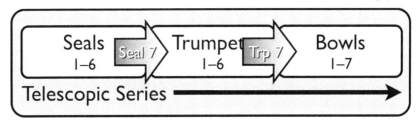

FIGURE 7.12. Telescopic Judgments. A simple variation of the linear view, but making the literary observation that the seventh judgment is introductory to the next series.

lence in heaven (Rev 8:1). The seventh trumpet is simply singing, first in heaven, then by the twenty-four elders, followed by a brief vision of heaven opened, revealing the ark of the covenant in the temple, with lighting, thunder, earthquake, and hail (Rev 11:15–19). So the seventh seal seems a transition to the seven trumpets, and the seventh trumpet seems a transition to the seven bowls. Thus, each series telescopes out into the next series, which connects all three as a unified whole. The literary observation of the seventh in each series as a way to connect all three cycles together is noteworthy. Logically, however, the telescopic theory is just a variation of the linear theory, only that nineteen judgments result instead of twenty-one. Since the telescopic theory is just a linear variation, this approach is subject to the same weaknesses as the linear. Applying what series of historical events is involved is an exercise in arbitrary subjectivity.

Recapitulation

Victorinus of Pettau (d. 303) in reacting against the literalism of the chiliasts already had decided that the judgment cycles in Revelation were not a linear series. Instead, he observed that the cycles seem to recapitulate the truth of judgment intensifying to a climax. The chorus of a modern, popular song has a similar movement. A song progresses through each verse only to get back to the chorus, which emphasizes the main point of the song. Likewise, the judgment cycles progress through a series only to get back to the chorus, the truth that God is sovereign over creation and history and ultimately judges all things. Recapitulation is not redundant repetition. In fact, judgments in each cycle are described quite differently. Each cycle is distinctive. Yet, all the cycles work in concert to increase the intensity, gaining dramatic momentum, enhancing the overall impact. The progression of the cycles is not linear. The progression is acceleration, like a centrifuge.

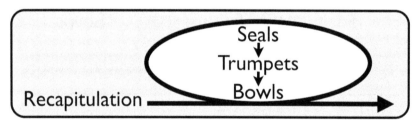

FIGURE 7.13. Recapitulation Judgments. The theory that the seals, trumpets, and bowls judgment cycles do not progress chronologically in time but dramatically in intensity.

What literary elements suggest the judgments recapitulate? First, the three series are interlocked. This interlocking is the insight upon which the telescopic theory is built: the last in the prior series does not actually present a judgment, but, instead, seems intended to introduce the next series. The literary observation is fundamentally sound. The point here is simply deducing a different purpose for the interlocking. The purpose is dramatic intensification. Second, the percentage of destruction in each cycle increases: in the seal judgments, one fourth; in the trumpets, one third; in the bowls, total. Again, this increasing percentage of destruction creates a dramatic intensification. Third, the seal and trumpet series each seems to present a climactic ending in its sixth judgment. If you did not have the following series, you would not suspect the previous cycle was unfinished. Notice in the following the dramatic opening of the sixth seal, which provides every sense the judgments have climaxed, and that all is being consummated.

> When he opened the sixth seal, I looked, and there came a great earthquake; the sun became black as sackcloth, the full moon became like blood, and the stars of the sky fell to the earth as the fig tree drops its winter fruit when shaken by a gale. The sky vanished like a scroll rolling itself up, and every mountain and island was removed from its place. Then the kings of the earth and the magnates and the generals and the rich and the powerful, and everyone, slave and free, hid in the caves and among the rocks of the mountains, calling to the mountains and rocks, "Fall on us and hide us from the face of the one seated on the throne and from the wrath of the Lamb; for the great day of their wrath has come, and who is able to stand?" (Rev 6:12–17, NRSV)

The reader would have no impression this description is not the end. Yet, the narrative continues. The blowing of the sixth trumpet likewise is climactic (Rev 9:13–21). Four angels bound at the Euphrates River are released, which apparently makes way for an invading army. An unbelievably huge two-hundred million strong cavalry rides onto the stage with fearsome descriptions of riders and horses. A third of humankind is killed. In both of these descriptions of events related to the sixth seal and to the sixth trumpet, one has the impression that this judgment cycle has reached its climactic end, and no judgments are to follow. The drummer rolls the toms and slams those symbols with a decided finality, and yet, the song goes on to another verse. Not until the bowls is the judgment series finally consummated with language of totality and, hence, finality: "seven angels with seven plagues, which are the last, for with them the wrath of God is ended" (Rev 15:1). So the three judgment cycles are connected, intensified, and concluded.

Augustine picked up and used Victorinus's recapitulation theory as a part of his development of his revolutionary amillennial interpretation of Revelation. However, one needs to be cautious about assuming that just because Augustine incorporated recapitulation into his amillennial construct means they are inseparable. The recapitulation theory can stand on its own independently of amillennialism.

The recapitulation approach suffers none of the weaknesses of the linear or telescopic views. This theory is not undermined in its hermeneutical integrity by the empty exercise of mapping out history up to the completely arbitrary point in time of the interpreter. This theory also provides an integrative literary reading of Revelation that emphasizes a literary purpose in Revelation's mysteriously repeating cycles of judgment. Further, the theory maintains concord with the essence of apocalyptic literature as a symbolic genre, that is, using the dramatic for its evocative power to provoke an emotional response. By the time the bowl series has arrived, the reader has been brought to a cathartic experience about the consummative, inescapable judgment of God.

INTERPRETING MILLENNIUM

The next interpretive decision we have to make is how to interpret the millennium. One central image throughout the history of the interpretation of Revelation is the millennium. In *Mysterious Apocalypse*, Wainwright's thesis is that the central and controlling task assumed by both interpreters and prophets of the Apocalypse throughout the history of the church is attempting to understand and apply John's millennial imagery, which occurs only in Rev 20:4–6 in all the Bible.

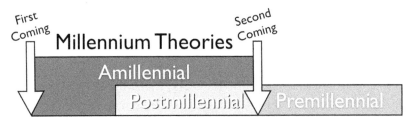

FIGURE 7.14. Millennium Theories. Millennium theories try to understand the nature of a reign mentioned in only one place in the Bible in Rev 20:4–6, as well as its relationship to the timing of the second coming of Christ.

Wainwright's proposal that the controlling task historically for understanding Revelation is interpreting the millennium is echoed in the use of prefixes to this key term to distinguish major eschatological theories. Important to understand is that the prefix characterizes not only a way to construe a theory of the *timing* of the second coming of Christ in relationship to the millennium, but also how to conceive the very *nature* of the millennium itself, that is, what is the character of this reign? Three major eschatological theories have evolved over the centuries trying to answer these questions and are coded with prefixes to the word millennialism.

These prefixes need to be understood in terms of the petri dishes of church history in which they were cultured. Amillennialism, as an example, is a *pre-Reformation development with Roman Catholic roots* that formalizes the increasing reactions to the gross excesses of early patristic chiliasm, as well as attempting to respond to the new political and religious realities for the Roman empire and for Christianity after Constantine's Edict of Milan. Premillennialism and postmillennialism, on the other hand, are *post-Reformation developments with Protestant roots*. Premillennialism has Reformation origins with a surge in Anabaptist movements; these ideas eventually migrated across the Atlantic in various forms, but none more successfully than a variant called dispensationalism. Postmillennialism has particular focus in English dissenter groups that also transplanted to America in the heady days of colonial optimism and utopianism that the new world of America really was about to blossom profusely into the kingdom of God.

Amillennialism

Amillennialism arose in response to Constantine and to the abuses of patristic chiliasm. Augustine took his cue from Tyconius's playbook and abandoned a literal reading of John's millennial imagery for a symbolic reading. The problem with Augustine's symbolic reading is not that he is reading symbolically. The problem is the allegorical way in which Augustine simply asserted *what* was symbolized without any real exegetical work to establish the context of Rev 20. He arbitrarily assigned the thousand years to be symbolic of the entire church age, whatever its length. Further, the kingdom is personal. The "reign" is in the church in the hearts of believers who confess Jesus as Lord in this life. Images such as the second resurrection then are mapped out onto the life of the believer. Finally, in terms of the second coming, amillennialism construes Christ's second coming as concluding a *symbolic ecclesiastical* millennium of the entire church age.

Premillennialism

Premillennialism arose in the renaissance of literal readings among Reformers. This construct reads the millennium as a literal reign of a literal thousand years. The reign, however, is construed like a typical European monarchy. That is, the reign is conceived in earthly and monarchial terms, and Jerusalem will be its capital. Premillennialism construes Christ's second coming as inaugurating a *literal monarchial* millennium at the end of history. This view has two major problems. One is the theologically faulty paradigm for the nature of the kingdom. The other is the literal reading itself.

First, the premillennial view coming out of Reformation Europe is built on the paradigm of a European monarchy. Nothing we read in the Gospels, however, even faintly suggests Jesus is interested in such a kingdom. In fact, when Jesus tells Pilate, "My kingdom is not of this world" (John 18:36), he is not saying his kingdom is going to be like Pilate's but just is not here yet. So, the premillennial view has a faulty theology of the nature of the kingdom.

Second, the so-called literal reading despises the actual context of Rev 20. That is, the literal reading, quite frankly, is just dishonest. You cannot just arbitrarily pick and choose bits and pieces of a verse as both literal and metaphorical at the same time in the same verse, or just completely ignore what the text literally says. For example, what John *actually* says is that only those who *did not worship the beast and his image* participate in the millennial reign. This fact is obfuscated in many of the so-called "literal" schemes. Further, only those *specifically martyred* for their testimony participate in this reign. Thus, if you lived faithfully in these times, but were not martyred, you are not on the invitation list. Pushing even further along literal lines, not even all martyrs get to participate. Of those who were martyred, *only martyrs who specifically were beheaded* get to be a part of the millennial reign (Rev 20:4). That is what John *literally* says. No literalist literally sticks to the text John actually wrote. The so-called literal reading of the millennial reign is duplicitous, ideological, and exegetically unsound.

Postmillennialism

Postmillennialism arose in the "new world" optimism characteristic of colonial America. This construct reads John's millennium as a literal reign on earth. In contrast to premillennialism, the reign is construed as the reign of the church. This view theoretically has a little more in its favor than does the premillennial, since the kingdom conception as related to the church is more along New Testament lines. For postmillennialists, the church brings New Jerusalem down to earth as a result of her successful gospel mission. Postmillennialism then construes Christ's second coming as either inaugurating or concluding a *literal ecclesiastical* millennium at the end of history.

Practically, however, postmillennial movements have worked out inevitably married to one particular civic municipality or government that never fulfills the initial optimism, but rather becomes government as usual, only clothed in religious trappings. Further, the idea that the church will be successful with her gospel mission in conquering the world seems biblically naïve. That perspective really does not seem to square with the biblical picture of evil as unrelenting, unimaginably destructive, demonic forces let loose on the world—a great red dragon with horrific evil billowing out from deep within a profoundly wicked, deeply incorrigible heart.

SUMMARY

We have to read Revelation trying to balance a complex mix of three genres—apocalypse, prophecy, and epistle—because this is the way John composed the work. Each genre has two interpretive corollaries.

Revelation as apocalypse is to be read symbolically. At the same time, John innovates christologically whatever source imagery he uses. Revelation as prophecy is to be read as forthtelling. John is preaching the present, not prophesying the future. He is challenging churches of Asia Minor to faithful witness in a fearful time. Yet, he preaches the present in such a way as to reveal the future, if one knows how to look into the past. Prophetic concord with the New Testament gospel will reveal the interpretive lens for seeing that future. The Jesus of the Gospels will not be a different Jesus in the Revelation. Revelation as epistle is to be read historically. John has his eye on first-century Asia Minor and so should the interpreter. Revelation in part interprets itself as a unitary whole. Earlier images inform the meaning of later images.

Historicizing the prophecy of Revelation begs the question of foretelling and ignores the basic problem that John's language is in no wise historical. That is why no one can get a handle on *what* history if Revelation is a prophetic forecast of a particular history. The failure of all attempts to historicize the "prophecy" of Revelation over thousands of years of interpretation is patent proof the entire effort is off the beam hermeneutically. All foretelling schemes are crippled by their inherent arbitrariness and founder on the facts of history, or invent ahistorical plots of the future John would not recognize. Revelation is neither preterist, historicist, futurist, nor idealist.

Attempting to sequence the judgments chronologically is vain, since this effort is part and parcel to the fatally flawed historicizing approach. Trying to make the triad of seals, trumpets, and bowls a linear walk down history lane is futile. However, the telescopic view seizes upon a valid observation about the unusual function of the seventh seal and seventh trumpet. Recapitulation, once extracted from Augustine's amillennial construct, has a robust interpretive capability to provide a satisfying explanation of the literary features of the judgment cycles, and can incorporate easily the telescopic view's observation of the linking function of the seventh seal and seventh trumpet.

Millennium imagery begs the question of the nature and timing of the kingdom of God. Premillennialism is unsatisfactory, assuming a European monarchy paradigm for the reign of the Messiah, which is theologically suspect. Premillennialism automatically prejudices literal readings by the force of its own hermeneutical tradition from the Reformation. Literal readings are fine for literary contexts that clearly are historically driven by the contextual clues of historical details. A literal reading of Rev 20, however, clearly is prejudicial, since a literal reading does not give due deference to Revelation as apocalypse, and is trying to force itself onto the text in spite of the absence of the very historical details that are the contextual clues to reading a text literally in the first place. A reading of Rev 20 does not have to do violence to Revelation's apocalyptic genre for the ideological sake of sustaining a literal reading at all costs, despising the immediate context.

Postmillennialism is more theologically informed of the nature of the kingdom as connected to the church, but is naïve about the depth and power of evil in the world. The optimism of the view does not square with the reality of church history. Further, the view also never has worked practically at any point in history in experimentation with actual civic incorporation.

Amillennialism also is not a satisfactory reading of Rev 20. The problem is not its symbolic approach, but assuming what is symbolized. Augustine's allegorical figure of interior spiritual life is not based on contextually driven observations, more eisegesis than exegesis. Any interpretation of an image as unique to all of Scripture as is the millennium must be driven contextually for a sound analysis of the figure. The immediate context is absent any historical detail, so the millennial reign clearly is meant to be symbolic. That interpretive approach is the most defensible exegetically. However, the problem is in determining contextually what John meant to symbolize.

8

Theological Decisions

Christology, Ecclesiology, Soteriology

Reading Revelation requires major theological reflection. Besides eschatology, which we dealt with in part in the previous chapter, three other areas seem to percolate to the surface constantly as we have reviewed the history of interpretation. These areas overlap in their functions, but classically break out as Christology, ecclesiology, and soteriology. We often do not stop to contemplate the theological inferences to be drawn from the "pictures" of Jesus, or the church, or salvation we are painting with our eschatological schemes. We need to reflect on these areas at some length to get a New Testament picture. Our principal focus will be the Gospels, as this is the core tradition from which all else flows in the New Testament.

CHRISTOLOGICAL REFLECTION

Who is Jesus? Seems a simple question, right? Not really, because what you say about Jesus in the end-time plot you concoct answers this question before you realize what you have done. The problem is, more often than not, you change the answer we get in the Gospels. The Gospel of Mark is a good example, because the identity of Jesus is a major theme in this Gospel. Mark then intertwines this identity theme with his second major theme, the failure of discipleship, to create a powerful ending. The question of the identity of Jesus is answered by the suffering Son of Man. The issue of the failure of discipleship is answered by suffering discipleship.

The following is a full discussion of this development in Mark. Why go to the trouble? Is not this book about Revelation? Yes, and that *is* the point. We insist that Mark's "Son of Man" perspective in his Gospel is absolutely essential to understanding Revelation, because Jesus is presented right off the bat in the Apocalypse as one like a "Son of Man" (1:13). Thus, we must establish canonical concord between Mark and Revelation, or Revelation is not prophetic in the New Testament sense and never should have been canonized. *We need to know who Jesus is before wrongly using Revelation to say who he is not.*

Jesus' Identity in Mark

Mark immediately develops the question of the identity of Jesus. He announces this issue up front in the very first verse, and then advances the question raised by using elements in the plot.

Announced up Front

The identity of Jesus is announced at the very beginning of the Gospel. Mark opens with "Jesus Christ, Son of God" (1:1). This is an unusual opening, because instead of a sentence to begin the narrative, this opening is more a title. The title itself has narrative significance. The title grabs the reader's attention two ways. First, with the title itself the crucial issue of the Gospel is inaugurated. This crucial issue is the theme of Jesus' identity. The theme of Jesus' identity is established by the omniscient narrator's voice. This narrator's voice identifying Jesus as the Son of God is validated and affirmed by the heavenly voice, not once, but twice later in the Gospel. The first divine affirmation is at the baptism of Jesus: "And a voice from heaven came: 'You are my beloved Son; in you I am well pleased'" (1:11). The second divine affirmation is at the transfiguration of Jesus: "And a voice came from the cloud: 'This is my beloved Son; listen to him!'" (9:7). Second, the reader's attention is grabbed by the unusual beginning right away because no one in the first-century world would confess anyone else but the emperor of Rome as the son of the divine. The first-century reader instantly would recognize that this Gospel is demanding a confessional response. To call Jesus "Son of God" allows no middle ground or room for political correctness. Either Jesus is the Son of God, or the emperor is. Choose you this day whom you will serve. So, the identity of Jesus is announced up front as the crucial issue of this Gospel, and this identity of Jesus in particular requires a confessional response. Thus, before we leave the first verse of this Gospel, a confessional decision is demanded of the reader.

Advanced by Plot

The identity of Jesus announced up front then is advanced by the plot in three ways: through Mark's "messianic secret" motif, through questions that characters in the drama ask, and through accusations that are made. Six early episodes reveal these interactive elements.

- In the wilderness temptation (1:12–13), Jesus hears the voice of Satan tempting him, trying to derail Jesus' public ministry before that ministry can begin. The issue is Jesus' identity. The temptation is about trying to redefine Jesus' messianic consciousness.

- In the demon exorcisms (1:24–25, 34), the demons cry out the identity theme: "We know who you are! The Holy One of God!" Jesus commands silence, which is Mark's "messianic secret." While the spirit world instantly recognizes and confesses Jesus' divine sonship, humans have difficulty with Jesus' identity. The disciples will have to grow into their understanding of how Jesus being Son of God relates to Jesus being Messiah. Jesus has a unique understanding of his messiahship, which is his own messianic consciousness. Since this messianic consciousness is not anything anyone would have expected, Jesus will have to bring the disciples along in their own understanding.

- In the healing of the paralytic (2:7), Jesus makes the bold declaration, "Your sins are forgiven," which, of course, is a divine prerogative only. Educated scribes naturally object, and in so doing, ask the identity question: "Who is this who speaks this way?" Humans are having a hard time catching on to Jesus' identity and its meaning.

- In the casting out of the demons (3:22), the scribes attempt to shame Jesus with their bold declaration: "He has Beelzebub!" In so doing they unwittingly admit that Jesus has divine powers. Jesus destroys their assumption about his alliance with the devil with disarmingly simple logic: "How can Satan cast out Satan?" The issue of Jesus' identity continues to push forward.

- In the storm at sea (4:41), Jesus asks the disciples, "Why are you so fearful?" This question puts in bold relief their inability to see Jesus for who he really is. So, they ask the question of identity: "Who is this that even the wind and the sea obey him?"

- In the encounter at Caesarea Philippi (8:27), Jesus now brings the identity question to a crisis moment in the plot, because he asks his own disciples: "Who do people say that I am?" Their answers reveal that the general public does not have a clue as to Jesus' identity: "Some, John the Baptist; others Elijah; some, one of the prophets."

So, in multiple ways of plot development in what various characters say and do, Mark keeps hammering home this question of the identity of Jesus in the first half of his Gospel. While he announces right up front for the reader that Jesus is the "Son of God," curiously, this very identity is what humans in all categories—the general populace, educated scribes, even his own disciples—continually seem to fail to grasp as the story moves along.

Failure of Discipleship in Mark

With this question of Jesus' identity theme he intertwines the second, that of the failure of discipleship. Mark is brutally blunt about Jesus' disciples. We need to hear Mark's point, and not confuse his picture with that of Matthew, Luke, or John. Each Gospel writer has distinct perspectives. Mark focuses on a *pre-resurrection* perspective of Jesus and his disciples; the others focus on a *post-resurrection* perspective. These two perspectives are not contradictory. Both are correct, but we have to be sure to keep them in literary context, which means letting Mark say what he says about the disciples without watering down his pre-resurrection perspective with post-resurrection realities. Mark's point will be the harsh truth of discipleship failure, which is his second theme. He advances this theme in three narrative cycles, of several chapters each: the Feeding Miracle (Mark 6–8), the Confession at Caesarea Philippi (Mark 8–10), and the Passion (Mark 11–16). We overview these three narrative units to establish Mark's crucial theme.

Feeding Cycle (Mark 6–8)

This cycle is kicked off by a stunning miracle as Jesus feeds five thousand (6:30–44). This food episode launches a narrative series of stories related to that event that draw out its significance. The first is walking on water (6:45–52). The question of Jesus' identity surfaces: "It's a phantom!" in 6:49. Jesus gets in the boat, the storm ceases, and they are astounded. Then, Mark has this unusual statement: "for they did not understand about the loaves, but their hearts were hardened" (6:52). The "hardened hearts" statement is unusual. A strange way to describe the disciples, right? Why the hardened hearts? What are they obstinate about? The disciples do not get who Jesus is or what he has come to do, not because they did not witness a miracle like a messiah might perform, but because they are going to refuse to accept the kind of Messiah Jesus teaches he is.

FIGURE 8.1. Herculaneum Eatery. Herculaneum, along with Pompeii, was one of two sister cities destroyed by the eruption of Mount Vesuvius in A.D. 79. This fast food eatery open to the main street served up hot food daily from the inset clay warming pots and fresh-baked bread stored on the shelves behind.

The next story developing the theme is another feeding miracle, this time of four thousand (8:1–10). The point will be that in the last two miracles, Jesus has shown the power to feed nearly ten-thousand people. He has no problem providing food. Immediately after this second feeding miracle is the story of a boat ride across the lake (8:14–21). The disciples were unprepared for food; they brought no bread with them; they have only one loaf on board (8:14). The backdrop is two feeding miracles in which Jesus had fed thousands by multiplying loaves. In this context, why in the world would the disciples wonder about having enough bread? Jesus seizes the moment to teach with a metaphor that is going to allude to his own messianic consciousness: "Beware the leaven of the Pharisees" (8:15). Jesus' disciples do not perceive the meaning of the metaphor, and Jesus then confronts their unbelief in 8:17–18: "Why are you talking about having no bread? Do you still not perceive or understand? Are your hearts hardened? Do you have eyes and fail to see?" Jesus then reviews the miracles with them, and asks with exasperation: "Do you not *yet* understand?" The disciples do not understand because they more are trying to box Jesus into their own preunderstandings of who messiah is and what messiah should do—just like the Pharisees. At this point, their understanding of messiah is more determined by what they have been hearing the Pharisees teach in their synagogues than what they have been hearing Jesus teach, which he uses to put his miracles into the context of his messiahship. Note Mark's subtle point that the disciples are said to have eyes, but fail to see. Having eyes but not seeing is the very point of the next miracle of the blind man at Bethsaida.

Mark's strategy here is to structure his narrative to establish the metaphorical connection between physical sight and spiritual insight as crucial to his storyline about the disciples. This storyline will be played out immediately in the following narrative of the healing of the blind man at Bethsaida. The astute reader needs to be sure to connect the story of the healing of the blind man as itself the prelude to the story of Peter's so-called confession at Caesarea Philippi.

Confession Cycle (Mark 8–10)

Bethsaida Healing. This cycle is kicked off by the healing of the blind man at Bethsaida (8:22–26). Literarily this story functions as a prelude to the story of Peter's so-called confession at Caesarea Philippi. The blind man's miracle of sight must take place in two stages, key to Mark's use of the miracle. Mark already has been clear to say that in some cases, Jesus has difficulty performing miracles, and that unbelief is the obstacle Jesus has a hard time overcoming in these cases (6:4–6). The healing of the blind man at Bethsaida is a difficult healing that has to take place in two stages. The first stage is one of minimal sight. The blind man sees, but not clearly. The movement of people around him is only "like trees walking" (8:24). The second stage is one of full sight. The blind man now sees clearly, because he "saw every man clearly" (8:25). Mark's point is parabolic of the disciples' two-stage perception of the true meaning of Jesus' messiahship. The first stage is their false expectation. They follow Jesus, but are hindered in their faith by false messianic expectations, just like the general public around them at Caesarea Philippi. The second stage is genuine faith, the realities of a life following the true Messiah, who is the suffering Son of Man.

FIGURE 8.2. Cave Entrance at Panias. A natural cave and fresh water spring in this rock outcropping gave rise to the worship of the nature god Pan. Herod the Great built a temple to Augustus here, and Herod's son Philip enlarged the site and renamed the city Caesarea in honor of Augustus. Philippi was added to the name to distinguish this city from the Caesarea on the seacoast his father Herod the Great had built earlier.

Peter's Confession. Peter's confession follows the blind man story (8:27–38). This story splits Mark in half, as Jesus now turns from a general ministry to focus particularly on his disciples. Jesus begins to teach the disciples the true meaning of his messiahship. To start off the second half of the Gospel, Jesus asks the provocative question that, once again, raises the issue of his identity. The question is crucial, because *who you say Jesus is determines how you will follow him*. The nature of your answer determines the shape of your discipleship. The question of Jesus' identity is framed in two parts. The context is significant. Caesarea Philippi is ancient Panias, a cult center of a cave and spring dedicated to the nature god, Pan, and a later center of idolatry.

First, Jesus asks generally in 8:27: "Who do people say that I am?" The answers the disciples give reveal the general confusion about his identity. Second, Jesus then turns specifically to the disciples to see if they can cut through the fog of this general confusion in 8:29: "But who do *you* say that I am?" Peter responds: "You are the messiah!" One would think that is a correct answer, but not in Mark. Remember that Mark's perspective is pre-resurrection. Two narrative indications make clear that something is amiss with Peter's answer. First, Jesus has to go into an immediate teaching session. After Peter says "messiah," Jesus immediately shifts the discussion to "Son of Man." This Son of Man teaching is the first of Mark's "passion predictions" (8:31–38). In this passion prediction, Jesus completely rewrites the story of Messiah as popularly conceived in the first century. Jesus defines who he is by redefining who Messiah is. Son of Man reveals Jesus' own messianic consciousness. He redefines Messiah as Son of Man who suffers and dies. Messiah does not "fight and win," like some Judas Maccabeus or Simon bar Kokhba. Instead, Messiah suffers and dies.

Jesus personalizes the consequence of understanding Messiah in this radically new way of a suffering Son of Man. Not only does Jesus have a cross as his destiny, the disciples too have a cross as their destiny. Jesus challenges his disciples to "take up your cross" (8:34). The first point here is to observe that the nature of messiahship determines the nature of discipleship. Who you say Jesus is determines how you will follow him. The second point is to note that the pronoun "your" in "your cross" is *plural* in the Greek. That means in this context that *cross-bearing is corporate,* not individual. Therefore, in the teaching of Jesus, taking up a cross is a destiny for a group to embrace, not just an individual. Was Peter on board this suffering Son of Man way of defining messiahship?

No. When Peter hears Jesus attempting to modulate expectations of Messiah into a suffering Son of Man paradigm, he immediately has the extraordinary audacity to rebuke Jesus (8:32). Imagine that! A dunderhead follower of Jesus trying to tell Jesus what he must do to fulfill his messianic mission! Mark carefully notes that Jesus observes the reaction of the other disciples, because they will follow Peter when Jesus is gone, so Peter will determine the entire direction of the church after Jesus (Matthew's perspective, which is post-resurrection, Matt 16:17–19). At this point, however, since Peter is rejecting Jesus' Son of

Man teaching, Jesus is forced publically to rebuke Peter with one of the sternest warnings in the New Testament: "Get behind me, Satan!" (8:33). The same voice Jesus heard in the wilderness tempting him to embrace an alternate path for Messiah Jesus now hears again from his own disciple. In Peter's rejection of the Son of Man, Jesus hears the voice of Satan about messianic destiny. Further, if Peter does not get Messiah right, the church will not.

Peter's rebuke of Jesus about the Son of Man develops Mark's failure of discipleship theme. Jesus' earlier question to the disciples in the boat, "Do you not *yet* understand?" continues to reverberate in the narrative. Thus, Peter's so-called confession at Caesarea Philippi is not a full confession of genuine faith. Peter is only partially "seeing" Jesus for who he really is, since, even though Peter wants to identify Jesus as Messiah, Peter does not fully realize what kind of Messiah Jesus will be. Like the two-stage healing of the blind man at Bethsaida, for the miracle of deeper spiritual insight, Peter will have to have the death and resurrection of Jesus applied before he truly will see clearly the significance of Jesus as a suffering Son of Man type of Messiah.

Jesus then promised the disciples that some of them would not taste of death until they "see that the kingdom of God has come with power" (9:1). In Mark's Gospel, seeing the "kingdom of God has come with power" has to be some event entirely other than the second coming of Jesus, because Jesus is explicit that this truth is for his original disciples. One way to see this fulfilled is in the transfiguration event to come in only a few days. Yet, the transfiguration has no theological significance without the passion of Jesus. The "listen to him" divine command of the transfiguration is about Jesus' passion prediction. Thus, even in Mark, glory and passion cannot be separated as if two different realities. They are one and the same. One cannot see Jesus' glory until one sees the passion, seeing Jesus die on a cross and being raised from the dead. Jesus spoke this coming of the kingdom of God truth again to the high priest just before crucifixion. The high priest had asked Jesus directly if Jesus was the Messiah. Jesus responded unequivocally: "I am; and 'you will see the Son of Man seated at the right hand of Power,' and 'coming with the clouds of heaven'" (14:62). So, the Son of Man "coming with the clouds of heaven" at least for the high priest here in Mark's Gospel is something other than the second coming. John in the Apocalypse is going to center squarely on this gospel idea in his own use of the coming on the clouds tradition (Rev 1:7).

The Transfiguration. Since this Son of Man teaching about the role of the Messiah is so radical, could Jesus possibly have misunderstood? In typical Jewish pictures of messiah, he is conquering warrior. He is the lion of the tribe of Judah. How does Mark make clear that Jesus absolutely is to be believed here? Mark uses the transfiguration of Jesus, which Mark carefully notes took place just six days later, to emphasize the divine affirmation and approval of this radical Son of Man Messiah taught by Jesus (9:1–32). The divine voice affirming his sonship and commanding disciples to "hear him" is pointedly saying to Peter that Jesus' Son of Man teaching just given at Caesarea Philippi is not up for discussion in the coffee shops of Capernaum. Being able to "see" Jesus in all his messianic glory will require looking from the perspective of the foot of the cross.

The transfiguration event is followed by Mark's second passion prediction (9:30–32), repeated by way of literary emphasis. Jesus is not kidding about the suffering Son of Man as the definition and destiny of Messiah. Unfortunately, the failure of discipleship theme continues to develop as well. To show how decidedly the disciples were missing the Son of Man point of self-sacrifice, they ask a question of self-serving in the very next verse in 9:33: "Who is the greatest?" Could Mark be any more blunt about the disciples' obtuseness?

The third of Mark's three passion predictions occurs against the context of the request by James and John to Jesus for seats of honor in glory (10:32–34). Mark uses this request once again to emphasize that true discipleship is self-sacrifice and death. The path to transfiguration glory comes only through the cross—a point sorely misunderstood by the disciples before the death and resurrection of Jesus.

Passion Cycle (Mark 11–16)

Mark's passion cycle is kicked off by Jesus' triumphal entry into Jerusalem, beginning the fateful last week of his life, works through the garden of Gethsemane, Peter's denials, the centurion's confession, and then the empty tomb. Here, Mark brings to a climax the two themes he has been developing all along since the first verse of his Gospel: Jesus' identity and discipleship failure.

Triumphal Entry (11:1–11). Jerusalem has symbolic significance, both in the history of Israel, and in the story of Messiah. Jerusalem represents the fateful destiny of the suffering Son of Man where the passion predictions will be fulfilled. The crowds shout "Hosanna!" which is yet again another errant confession in the Gospel based on false messianic expectations. Who you say Jesus is determines how you will follow him. The false basis of these Davidic expectations of a conquering lion of the tribe of Judah, military messiah are foreshadowed in the healing of blind Bartimaeus (10:46–52). Once again, as with the two-stage Bethsaida healing as prelude to Peter's confession at Caesarea Philippi, Mark uses the technique of a healing of sight as a prelude to interpret the significance of the following passion story. Bartimaeus cries out to Jesus as son of David to have mercy on him, insistently trying to get Jesus' attention even as the crowd tries to dissuade him. Jesus stops and responds. Bartimaeus is told: "Your faith has healed you" (10:52). Bartimaeus after regaining his sight followed Jesus "on the way"—and Jesus was going to the cross. Mark implies a true confession of Jesus as a Davidic Messiah will be not in the self-serving ambitions of a crowd ready to throw off the yoke of Roman oppressors by insurrection, but in genuine faith of a disciple who follows Jesus to the cross. Mark in parabolic form shows where true sight is gained for any true disciple—at the foot of the cross. The cross of Christ is the point of revelation about Jesus' identity for a true disciple. Who you say Jesus is determines how you will follow him.

Garden of Gethsemane (14:50). Peter's misunderstanding of Jesus' identity as Messiah in his so-called confession at Caesarea Philippi and the overall theme of discipleship failure are now woven tightly together by Mark. The sad truth of Peter's errant confession is now brought home in the Garden of Gethsemane on the night that Jesus was betrayed by one of his own. Judas was not the only betrayer. When the crowds come to arrest Jesus, Peter reveals the hidden martial definition of messiah he has been harboring all along. Peter draws a sword—his false messianic idea openly revealed. Peter is now ready to rebuke Jesus again by reinventing Jesus as a new Judas Maccabeus for a new day against the Romans (cf. John 18:10). Peter's idea of messiah, again, is rejected. When the disciples see that Jesus refuses to take a martial path to his messianic destiny, they all abandon him. Mark says rather sadly: "All forsook him and fled" (14:50). Just five words, but these words bear the entire load of Mark's theme of discipleship failure, the nadir of this narrative theme. Here in the garden truth lays exposed in raw reality. The dramatic pathos of Jesus' total abandonment will be given the deepest voice in Jesus' own cry from the cross: "My God, my God, why have you forsaken me?" (15:34).

Peter's Denials (14:66–72). Mark's theme of the utter failure of discipleship is brought home acutely and personally for both Peter and Jesus. Peter has to deny he follows Jesus to the little servant girl, because she serves the high priest, and word would get back immediately to the very one who had orchestrated Jesus being crucified. Peter does not want to embrace the destiny Jesus has embraced. Peter is not ready to follow a Son of Man who suffers and dies as his Messiah, his lion of the tribe of Judah.

A Centurion's Confession (15:39). Upon witnessing the death that Jesus died, the Roman centurion at the foot of the cross confesses: "Surely this man was the Son of God!" In the entire Gospel, since Jesus was announced as the Son of God in the very first verse, this word is the first full confession as the divine Son of God from human lips, and those lips are the lips of a pagan Gentile, no less, not any of the followers of Jesus! Here is a loyal centurion serving in the armies of the emperor of Rome, supposed son of the divine, confessing that Jesus is the true Son of God. Mark's irony here is extraordinary. A Roman *centurion's* confession is the apex and climax of the identity of Jesus theme in Mark's Gospel! Gentiles "see."

FIGURE 8.3. Roman Soldiers. Gigantic monument relief on the tomb of Tiberius Flavius Miccaulus, Prafectins and Priest, 1st cent. B.C. (IAM).

Empty Tomb (16:1–8). Mark has an unexpected ending, almost anticlimactic. Our earliest and best manuscripts clearly indicate that the Gospel ends at 16:8.[1] This ending, however, seems oddly abrupt, especially since Mark includes no resurrection appearances of Jesus, a standard feature of all the other Gospels.[2] Let us assume the ending is a literary one, intended by Mark, once again to invoke dramatic irony. So what happens? Well, the angels give a direct, clear command that the women disciples having witnessed the empty tomb are to "go and tell" (16:7). As a direct command from angels, this word acts as divine command. However, ironically, the women fail to obey. Mark starkly states: "They said nothing to anyone, for they were afraid" (16:8). The women's failure to obey is the last word of the Gospel. What is up with that? Yet another episode of discipleship failure. They are commanded to go and tell. They tell no one.

In this case, though, here at the end of the Gospel, we note this episode of discipleship failure happens *after* the resurrection in the narrative plotline. What is Mark's challenge? Even *after* witnessing the resurrection, disciples can fail to live up to the expectations of a community whose identity is defined by a suffering Son of Man. If we assume Mark's historical context is in Rome, this last word in his Gospel could have been a powerful word to persecuted Christians in Rome. Even after the resurrection, confessing who Jesus is has to play out in contemporary discipleship for the whole community of Christ. So, in the ears of readers of Mark's Gospel in Rome, the question of Jesus to his disciples at Caesarea Philippi still echoes hauntingly: "But who do *you* say that I am?" The call of the first passion prediction to Jesus' original disciples to "take up *your* cross and follow me" heralds forth in the heart of Rome as the lions roar. Who you say Jesus is determines how you will follow him. The Seer of Revelation will issue a similar challenge to persecuted believers in Asia Minor under the rule of Domitian, but his vernacular will be apocalypse.

---

[1] The ending of Mark's Gospel is complicated by multiple variations, but the best evidence is that 16:9–20 was a later addition by scribes who conflated elements from the other Gospels and Acts to remedy what was felt to be an abrupt ending.

[2] Conjectures would include Mark never finished the manuscript, or he finished the manuscript, but the ending was damaged and lost, and so forth.

ECCLESIOLOGICAL REFLECTION

What is the mission of the church? Seems a simple question, right? Not really, because what you say about church in the end-time plot you concoct answers this question before you realize what you have done. The problem is, more often than not, you change the answer we get in the Gospels. The publication of Luke-Acts is a good example, because the identity of the church is a major theme in this Gospel and its sequel in Acts. We can begin by asking, What is the book of Acts in the first place?

Luke and Acts

The first observation to make about how Luke proceeds is to state the obvious: Luke did not consider the gospel story to be finished by ending where the others do. Luke does not end his Gospel with post-resurrection appearances proving Jesus is alive and a "go and tell" commission of some sort (Mark 16:8; Matt 28:18–20; John 20:21). Instead, Luke keeps going. He writes Acts. He connects the two as a seamless, unified product. The prologue to Acts picks up the earlier volume of Luke (Acts 1:1). The gospel story is not finished with Jesus' death and resurrection. Luke extends the definition of a gospel by writing Acts. In writing Acts, he considers that he still is writing the story of Jesus. In this way, the subtitle of his Gospel would be like "The Story of Jesus, Part 1: How the Gospel Got Started." Then, the subtitle of Acts would be, "The Story of Jesus, Part 2: How the Gospel Became the Church." So Luke's story of the church in Acts is his continuation of the story of Jesus in his Gospel.

Simeon's Prophecy (Luke 2:25–35)

One of the ways Luke works his gospel story of Jesus this way into a two-volume production is by introducing themes into the first volume that do not get fulfilled until the second volume. One of these themes comes to light early in the Gospel in Luke's Nativity. Simeon speaks a prophecy in the temple about the child Jesus (Luke 2:25–35). God had promised Simeon that Simeon would not see death until he had seen God's Messiah (Luke 2:26). Simeon sees Jesus, takes him into his arms, and prophesies that the child will be "a light of revelation to the Gentiles" (Luke 2:32). Simeon's prophecy, however, never is fulfilled in the Gospel. To consummate this prophecy, Luke has more to write.

The fulfillment of Simeon's prophecy awaits Acts 9, the story of Saul and the Damascus Road. Ironic that a "light from heaven" strikes Paul blind (Acts 9:3). A disciple in Damascus named Ananias is told this Saul will "bring my name before Gentiles," and Saul sees again when Ananias lays hands on him (Acts 9:15–17). Paul retells this story in Acts 26. He mentions how he came to understand he was being sent to the Gentiles, and says, "to open their eyes so that they may turn from darkness to light" (Acts 26:18). What happened to Saul on the Damascus Road, moving from darkness to light, blindness to sight, becomes the paradigm of Paul's ministry to the Gentiles. The mission and work of the apostle Paul in Acts is the fulfillment of Simeon's prophecy that Messiah would be a "light of revelation to the Gentiles" in Luke. Thus, the entire last half of Acts, sixteen chapters, is devoted to showing the fulfillment of Simeon's prophecy at the beginning of

FIGURE 8.4. Roman Merchant Ship. Model of typical corn galley bound for Rome. About 90 feet long and hauling 250 tons, they were powered by a central mast sail and small headsail on a heavy spar raking overextending the bow, essential for steering. Paul traveled on such ships; cf. Acts 27:2; 28:11 (Science and Society Picture Library).

Luke. This prophecy means Messiah's significance is gospel witness, and that is the church's mission. Luke's kingdom language works in concert with Simeon, Jesus, Paul, and the Gentile mission.

Kingdom Language

Even though explicit kingdom language is infrequent in Acts, Luke prominently positions kingdom language with high literary visibility at the beginning and at the ending of Acts. He also puts this language in the mouths of prominent players in the Acts drama, which adds to the sense of the significance in the use of the terminology. Below are the eight references to the kingdom in Acts.

- "And to whom he presented himself alive after his passion by many proofs, through forty days appearing to them and talking about the things related to the kingdom of God" (Acts 1:3)
- "When therefore they had gathered together, they were asking him and saying, 'Lord, is this the time you are restoring the kingdom to Israel?'" (Acts 1:6)
- "But when they believed Philip, who was proclaiming the good news about the kingdom of God and the name of Jesus Christ, they were being baptized, both men and women" (Acts 8:12).
- "As they were strengthening the souls of the disciples, they were exhorting them to remain in the faith, and, 'Through many tribulations we must enter the kingdom of God'" (Acts 14:22)
- "And after he entered in the synagogue, he was speaking out plainly over the course of three months, arguing and persuading concerning the kingdom of God" (Acts 19:8)
- "And now, behold, I know that all of you no longer will see my face, among whom I went about preaching the kingdom" (Acts 20:25)
- "Now after they had set a day, they came to him at his residence in great numbers, to whom he was expounding, testifying to the kingdom of God, persuading them concerning Jesus from the law of Moses, and the prophets, from morning until evening" (Acts 28:23)
- "Preaching the kingdom of God and teaching the things concerning the Lord Jesus Christ, with all boldness unhindered" (Acts 28:31)

Kingdom Framing. Two features related to these passages jump out right away. The first is Luke's bracketing of the entire narrative of Acts with kingdom language. Similar to how John frames Revelation with the epistolary genre, Luke frames the book of Acts with the language of the kingdom of God. The first mention is part of the note about Jesus' teaching for forty days after the resurrection and then the disciples' kingdom question that precipitates a statement of Luke's witness theme of Acts (1:3, 6). The last mention is part of Paul's teaching in Rome, which actually is the last verse of Acts (28:23, 31). So, Luke literarily is "framing" the kingdom question with the narrative of Acts itself. The narrative, then, is used to define the kingdom of God.

Ecclesiological Pattern. The second feature to note about these references is that, in the Acts narrative, anytime the kingdom of God is mentioned, that reference always is connected directly to mention of Jesus' name or the early church's gospel mission and preaching in that name. In this way, Luke builds his association of kingdom and the nature and mission of the church. Notice that the mention of kingdom language related to the evangelist Philip's work immediately is equated with preaching the name of Jesus Christ, followed by notation of the early church rite of baptism. This is an ecclesiological initiation emphasis. Notice as Paul and Barnabas are exhorting converts on the first missionary journey to persevere in the faith, they teach that *present* tribulations are the path into the kingdom. This is an ecclesiological eschatology emphasis. Notice that Paul's synagogue preaching to Jews in Ephesus on the third missionary journey incorporates kingdom language, but this language is tied to the life, death, and resurrection of Jesus. Paul's kingdom preaching is reprised in the Miletus speech to the Ephesian elders at the end of the third missionary journey. This is an ecclesiological mission emphasis. Finally, Luke concludes the entire narrative of Acts with Paul preaching the kingdom of God both in the synagogue and in general. Luke states that this kingdom preaching of Paul always is "concerning Jesus." By the time we finish Luke's Gospel we already have been appraised that the phrase "concerning Jesus" is about the events directly related to the life, death, and resurrection of Jesus. Thus, we conclude that by constructing his kingdom references with this constant ecclesiological association, Luke reinterprets Jewish kingdom language, modulating the meaning to a higher ecclesiological key. Luke is careful to make clear by how he has constructed Luke-

Acts that the church's gospel mission and preaching about Jesus grew directly out of the mission of Jesus. Further, Luke says this movement of the gospel story from the mission of Jesus to the mission of the church was at Jesus' own direction in the power of the Holy Spirit. Thus, for Luke, the essence of the kingdom of God after the resurrecttion and ascension of Jesus is in the nature and mission of the church.

Disciples' Question. This ecclesiological pattern of Luke's kingdom language throughout Acts is what provides an exegesis of the disciples' question to Jesus at the beginning of the Acts. Even after forty days of intense post-resurrection training on the kingdom of God (Acts 1:3), the disciples still have trouble getting their minds around Jesus' own messianic consciousness, which, in the storyline in Acts, is going to evolve into the early church and her gospel mission. They ask a question about the kingdom framed in terms of Jewish nationalism: "Lord, is this the time when you will restore the kingdom to Israel?" (Acts 1:6). In this question we learn the *second* major issue the disciples had to rethink completely about Messiah and his kingdom. The first issue, the identity of Messiah as suffering Son of Man, we learned from Mark. The second issue, that of the nature of the kingdom of God now revealed as the church and her suffering gospel mission, we learn from Luke. If the new wine of Messiah as suffering Son of Man broke all the old wineskins of the disciples' old messianic thinking patterns, the same ever more was true about the kingdom of God. If Messiah radically is redefined as the suffering Son of Man, logically, the kingdom of this same Messiah likewise radically must be redefined as the suffering mission related to this suffering Son of Man. This process of redefining the kingdom Luke begins immediately in Acts with Jesus' redirection of this kingdom question of the disciples.

Jesus's response is curiously ambiguous. He does not say yes, and he does not say no. Instead, he almost puts them off. He tells them they do not know the times or periods of the Father's choosing (Acts 1:7). As Luke will make clear with his contextualization of kingdom language in his narrative development of Acts, this response is another way of saying softly without strong remonstrance that the disciples still misunderstand the very essence of the messianic kingdom. Jesus replaces the disciples' Jewish nationalism with a concept of expanding waves of global gospel witness empowered by the Holy Spirit. Jesus responds, "Rather, you will receive power after the Holy Spirit has come upon you, and you will be my witnesses, in Jerusalem, and all Judea and Samaria, even until the uttermost places of the earth" (Acts 1:8). This word, "you will be my witnesses," redefines the essence of the kingdom of God. That essence is not Jewish nationalism, but gospel witness. This witness is defined by the church's preaching of Jesus, embracing a global mission that takes the message to the heart of the empire, and from there to propagate to the whole world. In fact, this mission is the very point of Simeon's prophecy about the significance of the child Jesus as a "light of revelation" and the journeys of Paul.

In all of this, we note that Luke's presentation lends no support for a "holy land" theology, nor does the rest of the New Testament for that matter. This "holy land" aberration is prominent among dispensational preachers and drives intense political lobbying in zealous support of the secular state of Israel. Burge offers a careful critique of "holy land" theology in a study of Old Testament promises related to Israel and the land carried on through the intertestamental period and into the New Testament.[3] Burge notes, "To fight for holy territory, to defend the land as a divinely appointed duty, is to regress utterly in the most miserable way."[4] To the point, Revelation offers no support to "holy land" theology and its related eschatological schemes. While "land" ($g\bar{e}$, γῆ) occurs 82 times in Revelation, not even once does the term ever mean the Holy Land. Thus, "There is no sense in Revelation that Christians are to invest in or to fight for the restoration or preservation of Jerusalem in the climatic scenario of the Last Days."[5]

Pentecost Fulfillment. Jesus promised the Spirit to empower this global mission of witness. The Spirit came at Pentecost. Luke parallels the baptism of Jesus, with its descent of the Spirit to empower Jesus for his mission in the world, with the event of Pentecost, with its descent of the Spirit to empower the church for her mission in the world (Luke 3:21–22; Acts 2:1–4). The manifestation of this power was the ability to speak the languages of the world to those pilgrims assembled for the feast from around the world. The miracle meant that everyone could hear and understand the message of "the great deeds of God." In the Gospel context of Luke, these great deeds would be none other

---

[3] Burge, *Jesus and the Land: The New Testament Challenge to "Holy Land" Theology.*
[4] Ibid., 107.
[5] Ibid., 106.

than the essence of the gospel, the death, resurrection, and exaltation of Jesus, which Peter makes clear in his speech explaining the event to the amazed crowds (Acts 2:22–36). The only reason to speak the languages of the world is if you have a story to tell. Pentecost is the realization of the early church of her mission and destiny that transformed an upper room prayer meeting into global gospel witness.

By the three elements of his kingdom language framing of Acts, his ecclesiological pattern describing that kingdom, and his Pentecost narrative, Luke has made clear the nature and mission of the church. The church in her nature reflects Jesus and the pattern of his life. Further, the shape of this pattern will include persecution and death. Just as the life of Jesus does not reach its destiny and purpose until a specific moment in time, so too the church does not reach her destiny and purpose until her own historical denouement. This moment will be the church fulfilling the mission challenge of Jesus to take up a cross as he did. The church's mission is to preach the gospel to all the world at all cost. Luke's point is, on the pattern of the life of Jesus, the church will have to die to fulfill her mission. If the church is raptured out of the world, her historical mission and destiny in the world as defined by Jesus and made clear by Mark and Luke is aborted. God did not rapture Jesus, and he will not rapture the church.

Pauline Concord. Luke's perspective paralleling the life of the early church with the life of Jesus is echoed in the apostle Paul. Paul spoke of bearing the "brand marks of Jesus in my body" (Gal 6:17). He spoke of being "crucified with Christ" (Gal 2:20). He spoke of "completing what is lacking in Christ's afflictions for the sake of his body, that is, the church" (Col 1:24). A statement of "completing what is lacking in Christ's afflictions" is not as much a substitutionary metaphor for individuals as an expiry pattern for the church. Paul suggests the cross of Christ has not been consummated. Some future reality historically yet remains to "complete what is lacking in Christ's afflictions." Paul thus teaches the church incarnates the body of Christ in the world, and the full design and effect of Christ's cross is not realized until the church fulfills her mission. The death of Jesus reverberates historically in the story of the church. Luke makes clear in his version of Jesus' challenge to "take up a cross" not only that every believer is called to this ecclesiological mission and destiny, but every day holds the promise of its possible consummation (Luke 9:23). John in writing his Apocalypse is on board Luke's Gospel way of configuring the nature and mission of the church. In his hymn celebrating the defeat of the great dragon, John writes of believers, "But they conquered him through the blood of the Lamb, and through the word of their witness, and they did not love their lives even to the point of death" (Rev 12:11). That is John's equivalent to the gospel call of Jesus to "take up your cross" and the apostle Paul's echoing call to "complete what is lacking in Christ's afflictions." The church must walk the way of the cross. That is her eschatological destiny. Her future is in her past.

SOTERIOLOGICAL REFLECTION

What is the essence of salvation? Seems a simple question, right? Not really, because what you say about salvation in the end-time plot you concoct answers this question before you realize what you have done. The problem is, more often than not, you change the answer we get in the Gospels. The Gospel of John is a good example, because the question of salvation is a major theme in this Gospel. John even concluded, "Now, these things have been written in order that you believe that Jesus is the Messiah, the Son of God, and that by believing you might have life in his name" (John 20:31).

Salvation and Eschatology

Eschatology often is defined as "the study of last things." Usually this is explained as topics such as the second coming of Jesus, resurrection, wrath of God, last judgment, eternal life, and so forth. Of course, all this is to be awaited out there in the future. Or, maybe not. The Gospel of John acts like a funny mirror at the state fair on these concepts, because the apostle John speaks of them as realities in the present tense: "Whoever believes in the Son has eternal life; whoever disobeys the Son will not see life, but wrath of God abides on that person" (John 3:36). Thus, the apostle John speaks of topics that are supposed to be about "last things," such as eternal life or wrath of God, but as present realities of human experience. These "last things" experiences are realized already in the present. What is going on here? Why cannot John make up his mind whether eschatological realities are present or future? To answer this question, we need to summarize the traditional Jewish two-age apocalyptic view.

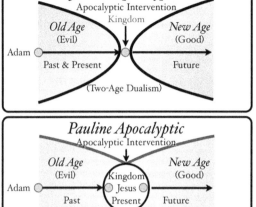

FIGURE 8.5. Two-Age Jewish Apocalyptic. Adapting the traditional Jewish conception of the coming of the kingdom as one historical event that separates the two ages to the Christian conception of the two ages in part overlapping as a result of the coming of Jesus, in which some future realities are presently realized, but the fullness of the kingdom awaits a future point in time.

Jewish apocalyptic had envisioned two ages, a present age of evil kicked off by Adam's sin, and a future age of good kicked off by the apocalyptic inbreaking of God's kingdom. Usually, this inbreaking kingdom of God was understood as brought about by God's Messiah. The typical plot involved military conquest and overthrow by Messiah of pagan oppressors of God's chosen people, such as Rome. Christian believers such as Paul, who were Jews, seemed to have adapted this traditional two-age view due to the realities of the coming of Jesus and the complex teachings of kingdom realities spoken as present now and kingdom realities as yet to be fulfilled. The Jewish view of two distinct ages was modified by Paul and others. The two ages now seemed to overlap in this present time. The old age presently is coming to an end, but not yet completely. At the same time, the new age is coming into being, but not yet consummated. We see different views about the connection of Jesus' life and issues of eschatology in various Gospels.

Inaugurated Eschatology

The apostle John seems more focused on the "now" part of kingdom reality. John's way of writing about future eschatological realities in the present tense is labeled "realized eschatology." This present tense perspective is in contrast to a "futurist eschatology." As the name suggests, this perspective understands eschatological realities only in the future. The futurist idea, naturally, comes directly out of sayings of Jesus that seem to suggest awaiting something to arrive as a future event, such as when the Son of Man "comes in the glory of his Father with the holy angels" (Mark 8:38). Another example is how Matthew seems to emphasize a future day of judgment (Matt 10:15; 12:36). The apostle John, in contrast, says, "Now is the judgment of this world: now the prince of this world will be cast out" (John 12:31).

This tension of present versus future realization of eschatology, John's Gospel versus Matthew or Mark, scholars have resolved by the concept of "inaugurated eschatology." This view says both present and futurist views are right in part. Jesus inaugurated the coming kingdom in his life, death, and resurrection. He brought about some of the realities of the future kingdom into present experience, such as forgiveness of sins and the Holy Spirit. So, some eschatological realities are realized now, at least in inaugural form. Though inaugurated, however, the fullness of this kingdom not yet is consummated. The consummation awaits future events, such as the second coming, resurrection, and judgment. Inaugurated eschatology sometimes is labeled a "now-not yet" approach. The kingdom is both now (realized) and not yet (future) at the same time. The kingdom is inaugurated.

We present the inaugurated eschatology construct to show one way to integrate the duality of the seemingly contradictory elements of both present and future dimensions to salvation that are inherent in the Jesus tradition preserved in the Gospels. This view is a helpful way to try to nuance the complexities of New Testament teaching on salvation. The point is that all New Testament writers have to be read with some sophistication in terms of their eschatological perspectives. The perspective of one writer, while true, is not necessarily the whole picture. New Testament authors have nuanced their discussions in the light of historical realities, what really happened when Messiah finally came. Each have their own points they wish to emphasize. Our canonical burden is to treat eschatological realities of the kingdom of God revealed in the New Testament in such a way as to integrate both present and future perspectives together and to show as we do so how these work together consistently and harmoniously. One task is the need to integrate salvation into eschatology.

The Future of the Past

Whatever salvation is, that reality has past, present, and future tenses attached in the New Testament, and all three tenses are conceived as one continuous process.[6] Whatever salvation is out in the future, that salvation already has been secured by an event in the past, the cross of Christ. Our future is in our past. Paul expresses this truth to the Thessalonians, when he assures them: "For God has not destined us for wrath but for obtaining salvation through our Lord Jesus Christ, who died for us, so that whether we are awake or asleep we may live with him" (1 Thess 5:9–10). The future, that is, "obtaining salvation," is determined by the past, "who died for us." Further, Paul makes clear that whatever salvation is out in the future, that salvation will continue to have a cruciform shape.

So, a comparison with Paul shows that the Gospel of John has an important contribution to make to our eschatological understanding of salvation. Paul agrees with John that in Jesus, eternal life is secured now, because the cross is an accomplished fact (John 1:29). John expresses this truth differently than Paul. The apostle John's preferred language is glory. For John, the life, ministry, and death of Jesus is the future glory of God already touching earth (John 1:14; 2:11; 12:23; 13:31; 21:19). We can ask, what is out there in the future? The apostle John answers with his realized eschatology. In effect, he is saying, "Whatever is out there in the future, I know by the glory I saw revealed in Jesus Christ on the cross that that future day will look like the cross" (John 1:14).

The art of the Renaissance depicting Jesus in glory after the resurrection regularly shows him with crucifixion scars, even though the resurrection promise for believers is for a glorified body (1 Cor 15:42–53). Renaissance resurrection imagery perhaps is based on an assumption about the nature of Jesus' glorified body made from the doubting Thomas episode (John 20:25–29). This assumption may or may not be correct, since whether Jesus was in a transitional state prior to full glorification for the sake of disciple recognition is unclear. In any case, Renaissance imagery of the glorified Jesus showing crucifixion brand marks in his body perfectly captures the theological

---

[6]For example, even in the same letter Paul can use multiple tenses for salvation. Cf. Rom 5:9; 8:24; 13:11. Also, cf. Phil 2:12; 1 Thess 5:9.

dimension that molds the cross and resurrection into one indivisible theological truth.

John's perspective of realized eschatology we can take as our theological clue: our future is in our past. At the same time, in the final analysis, the question the apostle John is trying to answer is not actually about peeping into the future. What question is he really answering? A question about the past.

FIGURE 8.6. Vasari's The Last Judgment. Detail of the masterpiece by Giorgio Vasari (d. 1574) on the dome of the Duomo in Florence, Italy. Illumination of divine glory showcases crucifixion details of the nail-pierced hands and the sword-pierced side.

How Does God Conquer Evil?

The Bible story of salvation is about God conquering evil in the world. Adam sinned, and through Adam sin entered and then reigned in the world, because all sin (Rom 5:12). Adam's sin created an old age of sin and death. In the context of this biblical storyline, the salient theological question posed by the last book of the Bible is, Just how *does* God conquer evil? If the revelation of God in Jesus Christ is our guide (Heb 1:2), and if the apostle John is right that our future is in our past, then God does not conquer evil with Uzi submachine guns, M1A2 Abrams tanks, F22 Raptor jets, B2 stealth bombers, thermonuclear bombs, or supernatural, eyeball-frying power rays. If God had wanted to conquer evil with an army of angels, he would have sent them. God did not send an army of angels. That method would have been brute force. He did not choose to conquer evil with brute force. Brute force is no victory. The result of force is only cessation of hostilities, not resolution of hostilities. If one wins only by brute force, one does not truly win. That is the message of the cross, and that message scandalizes any who assume that the only true way of winning is by the path of brute, overwhelming force. In the light of the cross, such an idea seems barbaric, human contrivance, and definitely not what God revealed in Jesus. Only in Christ is our enmity with God consummately resolved (Rom 5:10). So, instead of inflicting brute force, God sent his Son to die on a cross to endure brute force.

We have to wrap our minds around the cross of Christ as the apocalypse of the way God saves, of how God conquers evil in the world. The cross teaches that a suffering Son of Man is God's glory manifested on earth, God's way of conquering evil in the world. The cruciform shape of salvation never is not true (Gal 6:14). Any other path to salvation is not the New Testament message (Gal 1:7–8). Thus, Christ coming in flames of fire to render vengeance on those who do not know God (2 Thess 1:7–8) is an apocalyptic framing that *must* be sublimated theologically to the message of the cross. Paul's message *is* sublimated even in this context in the very next verse (2 Thess 1:9): the only punishment that is meted out is framed as separation from God's presence. Further, this separation is the result of rebellion against God due to refusal to believe in God's Messiah. To write any other script of the future in which God's Messiah does not win by dying and God's salvation is secured by any other path than by the glory of bearing a cross is unthinkingly to create a schizophrenic messiah who simply cannot make up his mind how he wants to conquer evil. This problem bewitches all conceptualizations of Jesus' "coming in glory." The first coming did not cut the mustard on evil.

Thus, for New Testament authors and the issue of salvation, the past controls the future. Looking at the cross, you are looking into the future. The cross is how God conquers evil. We must be careful to read Revelation in this way if we are to establish the canonical concord of the Apocalypse with the rest of the New Testament, especially John's Gospel. We must be diligent to preserve the canonical status of the Apocalypse. Therefore, be careful what you say is Armageddon, as you may be preaching another gospel. Does the second coming suddenly concede brute force? Does God capitulate the cross?[7]

FIGURE 8.7. Fresco of Fra Angelico. The Dominican friar Fra Angelico (d. 1455) meditates clinging to a vision of Jesus on the cross. Fra Angelico was an early Renaissance artist who was beatified by Pope John Paul II in 1982. San Marco Cloister, Florence, Italy.

---

[7] A good discussion for a more general audience addressing canonical issues in end-time scenarios that lose a New Testament focus on the cross is given by Larry Helyer and Ed Cyzewski, *The Good News of Revelation*. Each of five sections has two chapters. The first chapter is a dramatic vignette of first-century fictional characters reminiscent of Longenecker's *The Lost Letters of Pergamum*. These stories help dramatize topical issues to be discussed in the following chapter. I could argue issues of apostolic authorship, literal millennium, or antichrist lingo, but the overall presentation is rich with sound theological insight and superb christological focus.

SUMMARY

Besides eschatology, three other major theological areas always keep surfacing in various ways that need reflection when contemplating the "picture" of Jesus we are painting on an apocalyptic canvas such as Revelation. These areas are Christology, ecclesiology, and soteriology.

Who is Jesus? Mark's Gospel helps answer the question, because his entire plotline is driven by that question. Of course he is Messiah, but what kind of Messiah? Suffering Son of Man was Mark's answer. Take up your cross daily is the discipleship implication of this answer.

What is the church? Luke's two-volume production of Luke-Acts helps answer this question. The church is the on-going story of Jesus after the resurrection, the kingdom community of the called reflecting the life and death of Jesus in a global mission of the gospel. Preach the gospel faithfully is the discipleship implication of this answer.

What is salvation? John's Gospel helps answer this question. The apostle John teaches that any tense in which you conceive salvation, you have to be thinking of the crucifixion of Christ. The future of the kingdom, however you write the plot, has to have a cruciform shape. The future is in the past is the discipleship implication of this answer.

The kingdom of God manifested itself as a person, not a place. We are obstinate in receiving this revelation. We refuse to associate the kingdom with a person, like the disciples at the beginning of Acts. Thus, to talk about the kingdom being "near," or arriving "soon," as does John of Patmos, just does not compute in our eschatological schemes, because we refuse to embrace that the kingdom is a person. When that person arrives on any scene, the kingdom has come.

9

Contextual Decisions

Historical and Literary Settings

EPISTOLARY FRAMING INDICATES a specific historical setting for the Apocalypse. This setting has been alluded to multiple times in the course of the discussion of the history of interpretation. In this unit, typical historical issues such as date and authorship are summarized, but only briefly. Detailed arguments are left for the commentaries.[1] The student of Revelation should supplement this discussion with extensive reading in critical commentaries; various arguments for other positions are easy to access and consider. Fortunately, the burden of Revelation's message can be canonized and treated soundly without the need for absolutely resolving all the questions that can be raised by historical issues, because regardless of Nero or Domitian, the beast is Rome. Decisions made here do impact the sense of where John is going in what he writes. So, these questions do matter, and, eventually, every interpreter of Revelation must take off along one of the runways the results herein will dictate. The purpose here is to overview the historical and literary settings.

HISTORICAL SETTING

The main information around which discussion of historical setting is generated is the intended audience, the seven churches in the province

---

[1] Of the more recent commentaries, Beale, *Revelation*, has an excellent introduction, being extensive, thorough, balanced, and fair.

of Asia Minor, directly addressed in letters in Rev 2–3. This context is quite explicit. This context also is quite significant, because the churches at Smyrna and Thyatira might not have come into existence until later in the first century, which clearly would favor a post-70 date.[2]

Date

Persecution is in the context, whether real or perceived.[3] Antipas has been killed (Rev 2:13), and martyrs cry out from under the altar for their blood to be avenged (Rev 6:10). Two settings most often are proposed, Nero (54–68) and Domitian (81–96), because these emperors had known negative interactions with Christians. Nero blamed the fire of Rome on Christians, and Domitian interrogated the family of Jesus, executed Flavius Clemens, and Pliny implies recantation of Christian confession in the time of Domitian.[4] Nero's setting is unlikely, being too early and too restricted (not supported by the canonical history of Revelation and restricted to the city of Rome itself, not the provinces). Domitian is highly favored along converging lines of evidence, but most especially due to patristic evidence in Irenaeus, who says Revelation was "seen" toward the end of Domitian's reign.[5]

Internal evidence seems more to favor the later date context. This evidence would include local conditions evidenced in the seven letters.

---

[2] Polycarp *Phil.* 11.3; Epiphanius *Panarion* 51.33.1; cf. Beale, *Revelation*, 16–17.

[3] For perceived crisis, see Collins, *Crisis and Catharsis*. The question of persecution involves consideration of degrees of accommodation and assimilation into the culture and the level of suspicion or disdain experienced, and whether sporadic or organized, local or state sponsored.

[4] For Nero, see Tacitus *Annals* 15.44. For Domitian, the traditional commentary view is based on *1 Clement*, Pliny's letter to Trajan (A.D. 112), Ignatius of Antioch, and Hegesippus. Domitian's reign radically was reassessed as caricatured and vilified by later Roman court historians serving political propaganda purposes, suggesting no persecution of Christians occurred; e.g., Jones, *The Emperor Domitian*; Thompson, *The Book of Revelation*. The arguments have forced serious reevaluation of Domitian's reign. However, concluding no persecution at all existed is overcooked, swinging too much the other way. Cf. deSilva, *Seeing Things John's Way*, 50–55.

[5] *Adv. Haer.* 5.30.3. "For that was seen no very long time since, but almost in our day, towards the end of Domitian's reign." Surprisingly the evidence of Irenaeus goes strangely without comment by Smalley in his attempt to revive a Vespasian context and prewar setting of A.D. 64–70. Smalley, *The Revelation to John*, 2–3. Smalley also does not explain Revelation's unexpected focus in Asia Minor for a prewar John in Judea, nor that a church at Smyrna or Thyatira possibly did not even exist prewar.

Also, we have the likelihood of a post-A.D. 70 matrix both for the use of "Babylon" as a cipher for Rome and for the broad circulation of the *Nero redivivus* myth that apparently drives the imagery of Rev 13 and 17.[6]

Early dating arguments simply are not as persuasive. Attempts to use the sequence of emperors in Rev 17 for dating are doomed from the start. Besides the question of whether John even intends a referential meaning, the process is confounded by two major issues: (1) we do not know where to start (Julius Caesar, Augustus, or elsewhere); and (2) we do not know what to do with the Roman civil war, when Rome endured three emperors in a year and a half after Nero's suicide without an heir, which threw Rome into political and military chaos (Galba, Otho, Vitellius). Whether to count the civil war emperors as three, or as one composite, or even ignore them totally in the count is completely arbitrary. The measuring of the temple in 11:1–2 does not prove the Jerusalem temple is still standing, since the specifics of those measurements comport with Ezekiel's eschatological temple (Ezek 40–48), not the Jerusalem temple.

Heresy also is in the context, but not helpful for the question of date. The false prophetic leadership of Jezebel has created a problem at Thyatira related to some type of fornication and idolatry (Rev 2:20). The doctrine of the Nicolaitans is a problem at both Ephesus and Pergamum (Rev 2:6, 15). The teaching of Balaam, which also relates to food sacrificed to idols and fornication on the pattern of Jezebel, has corrupted the church at Pergamum (Rev 2:14). While all these are explicit statements, they are not helpful for dating the book. How much of the descriptions are metaphorical (even the name "Jezebel"), and exactly what is referenced, simply are not clear.

Authorship

The Western church clearly assumed that John the apostle was author of Revelation. Our earliest evidence is in Justin Martyr (d. 165).

---

[6]Cf. Reddish, *Revelation*, 16. Rumors followed Nero's suicide that he either really was not dead and was hiding out in Asia Minor waiting for his chance to retake Rome, or had died but miraculously come back to life to haunt Rome. A similar conspiracy theory was reprised after WWII with the rumors following Hitler's suicide of his actual survival and hideout in the German community in Brazil after the war, which fueled Ira Levin's *The Boys from Brazil* thriller novel.

> And further, there was a certain man with us, whose name was John, one of the apostles of Christ, who prophesied, by a revelation that was made to him, that those who believed in our Christ would dwell a thousand years in Jerusalem; and that thereafter the general, and, in short, the eternal resurrection and judgment of all men would likewise take place.[7]

Most church fathers in the West repeat or enhance in minor ways this John the apostle tradition.

The Eastern church, however, disagreed. The Montanist heresy, a second-century Asia Minor movement based on Revelation, was the inoculation in the East that immunized thought against the book of Revelation. The book was considered too obscure and dangerous, and already proven to have spawned heresy. Cyril of Jerusalem (d. 386), bishop of Jerusalem and a church theologian, enumerated accepted books to be taken as inspired and authoritative but did not include Revelation. Cyril went on to castigate all other books he had left off his list, including the book of Revelation: "But let all the rest be put aside in a secondary rank. And whatever books are not read in Churches, these read not even by thyself, as thou hast heard me say."[8] Not only does he not regard Revelation authoritative, Cyril also is clear he does not even think the book is of any benefit for private reading. Eusebius indicates the split between East and West on the book of Revelation by putting Revelation on both his accepted and disputed lists.[9]

A rare voice in the West arguing against the apostle John as author of Revelation was Dionysius of Alexandria (d. 265), who had excellent facility in the Greek language. Dionysius actually went to the trouble to perform a careful analysis of the Greek of the Gospel and epistles and Revelation. He made multiple converging observations:

- the lack of explicit self-reference to the author's own name in *any* of the other literature ascribed to the apostle John

- the absence of known patterns of self-reference by the apostle as the beloved disciple, as in the Gospel, or as an eyewitness, as in 1 John

---

[7]*Dial.* 81.4. Confusion was raised by Eusebius about a supposed second John the elder at Ephesus, but most conclude Eusebius probably misunderstood a statement by Papias.

[8]*Cat. Lect.* 4.36.

[9]*H.E.* 3.25.2–4.

- that the name John was extremely common in later Christian generations in honor of the legacy of the apostle, so could be anyone

- that the ideas, vocabulary, and even arrangement of words in Revelation are totally alien to the apostle, with entire categories of common words and phrases that are well known to be theologically crucial to the apostle missing entirely in Revelation

- the extraordinarily contrasting symbolic thought world of Revelation versus either that of the Gospel or of the epistles, which never even allude to having visions or dream states by the author

- the Greek of the apostle shows hardly any example of the constant barbarism, solecism, and vulgarism of the Greek of Revelation[10]

Dionysius concluded the author of the Apocalypse simply could not be the same as the author of the Gospel and epistles. If the apostle John wrote the Gospel and epistles, he did not write Revelation. If the apostle John wrote Revelation, he did not write the Gospel and epistles. Dionysius explicitly affirms the canonical status and authority of Revelation. He simply rejects that the author is the apostle John and confesses the book is too dense in meaning for him to comprehend.[11]

Dionysius's observations are persuasive and cannot be ignored. One is reduced to attempting to establish some other basis for the bad Greek of Revelation, such as the solecisms are deliberate, or elicit Old Testament rhetorical strategy. Radically different conceptual worlds, ideas, and vocabulary have to endure serious leveling, almost bulldozing, by pointing out "so much in common." Such efforts in no way offset what these pieces of literature do *not* have in common.[12] Dionysius's arguments are simple, straight-forward, and decisive. We might put the matter this way. If Revelation had come to us anonymously, never in a million years would the thought have occurred to anyone to suggest, "Hey, you know, I think the author of the Apocalypse and the author of the Gospel of John are the same person."

The author of Revelation is John, not the apostle, a local prophet active in churches in Asia Minor whose authority has been challenged

---

[10] H.E. 7.25.7–27.
[11] H.E. 7.25.4.
[12] Cf. Beale and Smalley, as well as Bauckham's *Climax of Prophecy*.

seriously by contrary prophets in these churches, eerily reprising the challenges the apostle Paul had to confront in Galatia and at Corinth. Also similar to Paul, he senses the foundation of apostolic tradition has been undermined alarmingly by false teachings he considers not only heretical but hazardous to the health of his Asia Minor churches. Thoroughly versed in the Old Testament, but not the Greek language, his thought world is visionary, his literature apocalypse. All this combines to become the intense mix of Revelation, a work unparalleled in Christian literature. Somehow, we are supposed to understand.

Patmos

John indicates he was on Patmos, an island off the western coast of Asia Minor in the Aegean Sea of the Dodecanese complex of islands, opposite Miletus and not far down from Ephesus (Rev 1:9). The island is a little over 17 square miles, and Eastern Orthodox heritage includes the Monastery of Saint John the Theologian and the Cave of the Apocalypse, declared World Heritage Sites by UNESCO in 1999. Two considerations require comment. One is the nature of John's presence on the island, and the other is the nature of Patmos itself.

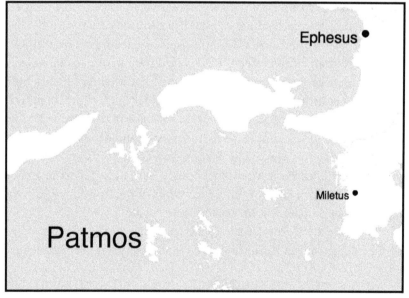

FIGURE 9.1. Map of the Island of Patmos. Approximately 17 square miles, the island is in the northern region of the Dodecanese complex off the coast from ancient Miletus.

FIGURE 9.2. Panorama of Patmos. Eastern Orthodox heritage on the island includes the Monastery of Saint John the Theologian and the Cave of the Apocalypse.

John and Patmos

First, what is the nature of John's presence on the island? Is he there voluntarily or against his will? In the immediate context, John identifies himself as a "brother" and "fellow-sharer in the tribulation and kingdom and endurance in Jesus" (1:9). Words such as tribulation and endurance suggest a context of some duress. The duress seems related to the kingdom, and John is not the only one affected. John then gives the reason for his presence on Patmos: "because of the Word of God and the testimony of Jesus." What is unclear in the "because of" wording is whether John is on Patmos of his own will. On the surface, this causal clause does not have to suggest anything more than a preaching circuit. However, the preposition *dia* (διά) used in 1:9 regularly in its other occurrences in Revelation means result not purpose. In addition, the immediate context of duress, and the wider context of persecution in the document for this same phrase (Rev 6:9; 20:4), seem to suggest John was not on Patmos by his own desire.

Thus, church tradition decided that John was *exiled* to Patmos.[13] John does not explicitly say he was exiled. The tradition probably is based on the supposition a reader might make from the wording in Rev 1:9 in its immediate context and in the context of Revelation as a whole. Banishment or exile to an island was typical Roman juridical policy. However, a study of Roman policy shows that the majority of those so punished were men and women of wealth and influence, such as the members of the imperial family, Republican senators, orators, philosophers, ladies of rank, and so forth.[14] Social status at least gave

---

[13] So Tertullian, "remitted to his island-exile." *Prescription Against Heretics*, 36.

[14] Braginton, "Exile Under the Roman Emperors," 391.

Roman citizens the possibility of preferential treatment and judicial deference, which translated into exile not execution. That John would have this kind of elite social status and garnish preferential treatment is unlikely. So, while we could accept church tradition that John could have been exiled to Patmos, we still would have to wonder why Rome would bother. Why he would receive not only this degree of attention but preferential treatment from Roman jurisprudence is an enigma.[15]

Clement of Alexandria said that on the "tyrant's death" (presumably Domitian), John returned to Ephesus.[16] Rescinding decrees at the death of an emperor was standard action for Rome, so had John been banished by Domitian, a return to the mainland at the beginning of Nerva's reign (96–98) would be reasonable. Irenaeus even said that John lived into the reign of Trajan (98–117).[17] Clement and Irenaeus, as do all those connected to Rome, assume the John of Revelation is the apostle John. A return to Ephesus after Patmos would make sense to them, since the church tradition is that the apostle John ministered in Ephesus for a long time. However, John of Patmos does not have to be the apostle John, and we really do not know where John went after Patmos in the first place. He never said where he was when he wrote. Further, we can note that none of the traditions about John the apostle locate him anywhere outside of Ephesus, and they especially do not associate him with an itinerant ministry among multiple churches in disparate urban centers. Even in tradition, the apostle's locale profile does not meet the implicit profile of the author of the Apocalypse.

Other church tradition was that John had a personal scribe. His name supposedly was Prochorus. John dictated as he saw his visions. Prochorus wrote. So the tradition goes. The name Prochorus has New Testament connection as one of the seven chosen to serve tables in Acts 6:5. In church tradition, he became Saint Prochorus and worked with Peter. Tradition is mixed on whether Peter or John consecrated Prochorus bishop of Nicomedia in Bithynia.

The legendary character of Prochorus as John's scribe raises the question, What did John see? How did he see? How did he write? We

---

[15] Also, would an Asian official have legal jurisdiction over Patmos? Hemer, *Letters*, 27–29. Further, what if John himself *fled* to Patmos to avoid attention for a time?

[16] *Quis Dives* 42. Cf. also Eusebius *H.E.* 3.20.9.

[17] *Adv. Haer.* 2.22.5. Repeated by Eusebius *H.E.* 3.23.3.

already have written how we cannot parse out what John saw. He saw, but we read. So, we have to have a literary approach.[18] In any case, the Prochorus scribal fiction memorialized in the mosaic over the Cave of the Apocalypse entrance on Patmos has a problem in the Greek of Rev 1:9. John says that he "*was* on the island" (emphasis added). The verb is past tense. John no longer is on the island when he writes. So, even if exile put him on the island, as in church tradition, he no longer is on the island when he composes this unique piece of literature.

FIGURE 9.3. Cave of the Apocalypse Mosaic. The visitor to the traditional Cave of the Apocalypse on the island of Patmos is greeted by this mosaic over the doorway entrance to the cave. Pictured is John's scribe, Prochorus, seated and writing as John, turning toward heaven, views the visions and dictates to Prochorus what he sees.

Rome and Patmos

Besides the reason for John's presence on Patmos and the nature and timing of his composition, the other element requiring comment is the nature of Patmos itself. The problem that confronts us is that the tradition of exile to Patmos often is accompanied by other ideas that historically are not likely. Two of these in particular are problematic. One idea is that the tiny island of Patmos was used by Rome as a penal colony.[19] Another idea, in evidence with Victorinus (d. 303), was that

---

[18]Stevens, "A Vision in the Night," *Essays on Revelation*, 4–13.

[19]Ramsey, *Letters*, 85. Known islands used for exile in the Aegean Sea were Gyarus, Donusa, and Amorgus; Tacitus *Annals* 4.30.

Patmos was used as a Roman quarrying center.[20] No first-century evidence, however, exists to corroborate either of these two assertions, so both must be considered unlikely.

Recipients

John identifies the recipients as seven churches in Western Asia Minor: Ephesus, Smyrna, Pergamum, Thyatira, Sardis, Philadelphia, and Laodicea (Rev 1:4, 11). The names as listed show a general circuit.

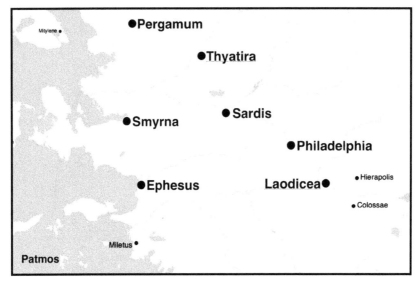

FIGURE 9.4. Seven Churches. The cities of the seven churches of Asia Minor addressed in the book of Revelation. Thyatira and Philadelphia were only minor municipalities.

Actually, understanding these cities becomes a major obstacle to interpreting Revelation. We read as twenty-first century urbanites in a post-industrial world. As Johnson pointed out, "the preindustrial *polis* was a radically different social institution."[21] Even social space was organized according to social status and to benefit the urban elite who ruled the city.[22] Further, the careful reader will see evidence of how

---

[20]Victorinus asserted John "was in the isle of Patmos condemned to the quarries by Domitian Caesar." *Erat in insula Pathmos in metallo damnatus a Domitiano Caesare.* Victorinus *Scholia in Apocalypsin.* 10.11. Repeated by Eusebius *H.E.* 3.23.6.

[21]Johnson, "Urban Persons: City and Identity in the Book of Revelation," 102. This excellent article shows the value of social perspective for understanding Revelation.

[22]Dramatized nicely by Longenecker's fictional *The Lost Letters of Pergamum.*

John incorporated elements of each local situation into each letter.[23] In a society in which personal identity was defined by group identity, believers faced daily pressure to show conformity to groups that constituted the city's identity: "citizens, worshippers of the patron divinities, participants in the trade guilds that promoted the material prosperity of the *polis*, participants in the patron/client relationships that formed the fabric of society, etc."[24] The social, commercial, and political pressure to compromise Christian beliefs would have been intense.

Asia Minor provinces under Domitian had healthy relationships with Rome and were prosperous. They supported the emperor cult here as strongly as anywhere in the empire. S. R. F. Price examined the presence and distribution of imperial altars, imperial temples, and appointment of imperial priests in Asia Minor. All seven cities evidence at least one of these elements, and Ephesus, Smyrna, Pergamum, and Sardis have all three of them.[25] Pressure to conform was indirect. The patronage that affected choice of prefect of Rome's praetorian guard more than military ability mediated pressure outside Rome through ruling provincial elites, who likewise were indebted to Rome for their power and position.[26] Patronage exploited even commercial activity.

> How Rome benefited from this commercial arrangement is clear; how provincial proponents of imperial power benefited is also comprehensible. The materials that filled the ships described by Petronius were mined, harvested, and manufactured in provincial cities and loaded in provincial harbors, often onto ships owned by non-Romans. Wealth was available to those who served as agents in this commerce. Gaining the confidence of Rome through participation in the imperial cult was a useful means to ensure continued rewards from this mercantile system; loyal subjects of the emperor would be perceived as more trustworthy and more deserving business partners. The common people in the provinces (who comprised more than ninety percent of the population) had less to gain from worshipping the emperor, but they were dependent upon elite patrons who could persuade them to bow before the imperial

---

[23]See Hemer, *Letters to the Seven Churches.*

[24]Johnson, "Urban Persons," 113.

[25]Price, *Rituals and Power,* 252–60, 264–65. Cf. Fig. 1.12, p. 12, showing the frieze on the base of the imperial altar to Domitian in Ephesus.

[26]Bingham, *The Praetorian Guard,* 28; cf. Fig. 9.24, p. 228, local imperial cult priest.

altar. This seemingly irresistible veneration of the emperor was one of the more insidious aspects of the imperial cult that allowed Roman imperial priorities to control people at all levels of society.[27]

The imagery of Babylon's fall in Rev 18 is based thoroughly on Roman commerce—fabulous empire wealth flowing into the heart of insatiable Rome—so described by Petronius, to whom Johnson referred.[28]

Aphrodisias

Aphrodisias, about 19 miles west of Denizli (near ancient Laodicea of the seven cities), illustrates Roman imperial propaganda advancing the goals of Rome through local provincial elites.[29] This ancient city's remains are the epitome of the imperial message and Roman support.

FIGURE 9.5. The Aeneas Legend. Three panels in the legend of Aeneas: (1) divine conception by Aphrodite; (2) flight from Troy with son, Lulus; (3) final arrival in Italy (AMA).

Roman Legend. In Roman legend, the Trojan hero, Aeneas, was the son of the goddess Aphrodite, born from divine conception of the goddess with the prince Anchises. Aeneas escaped the destruction of Troy by the Greeks with his son, Lulus. His journey as a brave refugee brought him to Rome, where he and his son would become the forebears of Julian and Augustan families. Aphrodisias was named after Aphrodite, the mother of legendary Aeneas, progenitor of emperors.

[27]Johnson, "Confronting the Beast," 137.

[28]Ibid., 136. Cf. Petronius *Satyricon* 119.1–12.

[29]Another fine resource is deSilva, *UnHoly Allegiances*. Galinsky, *Augustan Culture*, prefers *auctoritas*, "authority" (prestige, influence toward one's will), to "propaganda."

Thus, Roman origin legends meant the city of Aphrodisias always held high status and favored relationship with Rome for its namesake.

FIGURE 9.6. Zoilos Remembrance Monument. Part of a massive monument complex commemorating the Aphrodisias patron Gaius Julius Zoilos (AMA).

Patronage. Gaius Julius Zoilos, a former slave in the house of Augustus, was freed and returned home to Aphrodisias, where he became a wealthy, enterprising businessman who maintained close, powerful relations with Rome due to his imperial family connections. He brandished his power and social status through benefactions to his home city. He was patron to the city theater construction (7,000 capacity), the north portico, the north agora, and the temple of Aphrodite, with its elaborate colonnaded court framed by an impressive two-story façade on the east side and extensive porticos on the other three sides.

FIGURE 9.7. Aphrodisias Theater and Temple of Aphrodite. Major benefaction to the city of Aphrodisias by the patron Zoilos, who had strong ties to the imperial family.

FIGURE 9.8. Aphrodisias Stadium and Bouleuterion. The Aphrodisias stadium held up to 30,000 spectators and shows the impact of trade guilds on social life. Statues honoring local patrons of Aphrodisias garnished the entrances to the bouleuterion, often emphasizing connection to Rome, imitation of Roman style, and the status of priest of the imperial cult.

Stadium. The stadium at Aphrodisias was 886 feet long with 30 tiers of seats holding up to 30,000 spectators and is the best preserved in the ancient world. Inscriptions in stadium seats show reserved places for various trade guilds, such as the Association of Tanners and the Association of Goldsmiths, as well as for individual citizen elites not only of Aphrodisias but of surrounding towns. The near end of the stadium later was modified for Roman-style spectator sport, gladiatorial combat.

Bouleuterion. The entrances to the bouleuterion (council chamber) were lined with statues of patron benefactors of the city. One of these patrons was Antonius Claudius Demetrious, who is depicted wearing civic dress and a heavy, priestly crown ornately decorated with a bust of Aphrodite and the Roman emperors. Another statue is of Claudia Antonia Tatiana, with hair imitating the empress Julia Domna, and the god Eros at her side. The plinth is signed by the master craftsman, Alexandros, son of Zenon, indicating the expense of these public honorariums.

FIGURE 9.9. Grave Stele, Supervisor of the Linen Workers. This workman had achieved significant social status and business clout in Aphrodisias as supervisor of the linen workers guild. He would represent the kind of citizen who would have had a reserved seat at the stadium (AMA).

9—Contextual Decisions 215

FIGURE 9.10. Antonius Claudius Demetrious. Honored by the city of Aphrodisias at the entrance to the bouleuterion. Civic dress, heavy priestly crown, decorated with bust of Aphrodite and Roman emperors (AMA).

FIGURE 9.11. Claudia Antonia Tatiana. Statue adorning one of the entrances to the bouleuterion of Aphrodisias. Roman aristocratic hairstyle in deliberate imitation of empress Julia Domna. A small figure of the god Eros was at her side. Work signed by master craftsman, Alexandros, son of Zenon (AMA).

FIGURE 9.12. Leading Citizen. A member of the social elite class and aristocrat of first-century A.D. Aphrodisias. Portrayed wearing a priestly crown, so in the cult service of a patron god of the city (AMA).

FIGURE 9.13. The Goddess Aphrodite. Best preserved statue of the goddess Aphrodite in Aphrodisias, from the bouleuterion. Head veiled, with heavy symbolic casing in multiple rows of images, including the famous sculpture of the three Graces, the sun and moon gods, Aphrodite on the seat of a goat, and Eros figures making sacrifice (AMA).

FIGURE 9.14. Drawing of the Sebastion Entrance. Architectural schematic depicting the view of the grand entrance into the three-tiered, open courtyard of the Sebastion temple complex (AMA).

Sebastion. The Sebastion was the cult center of the worship of the Roman emperor. The architecture was designed foremost to provide ostentatious, public display of standard Roman imperial propaganda. The "storyline" of the friezes and statuary aggrandized the power of Rome and the mighty expanse of her empire. Rome's obvious success was because the emperors enjoyed the divine favor of the gods. Her victories were inevitable. Resistance was futile. Besides, Rome did the world a great favor in subduing the barbaric hinterlands and bringing peace, stabilization, civilization, commercialization, and the benefits of world empire to all peoples. "You should be grateful we conquered you" was part of the message.

FIGURE 9.15. Sebastion of Aphrodisias. One corner of the ruins of the sebastion sanctuary for emperor worship in Aphrodisias has been reconstructed to suggest the original three-tiered portico flanking the inner courtyard. Nearly 70 reliefs illustrative of Roman imperial propaganda were discovered in this area.

The friezes on the second story of the north Sebastion featured a series of fifty personifications of places and people from East Africa to Western Spain. They were designed to look like statues between the columns of the portico. These friezes represented conquered territories and peoples subjugated by the overwhelming, irresistible power of Rome. Inscriptions on the frieze statue bases identified the conquered: Andizeti, Arabs, Besse, Bosporans, Callaeci, Crete, Cyprus, Dacians, Dardani, Egyptians, Ethiopians, Iapodes, Judeans, Phaeti, Piroristi, Sicily, Trumpilini, and more. In effect, this series was a visual listing of the extraordinary expanse of the Augustan empire. Some of the selections specifically were chosen to emphasize the wilder people on the edges of the world, barbarians, uncivilized. Few of the inhabitants of Aphrodisias even ever had heard of some of them. The grand scale and emotional impact must have been stunning. Message received.

9—Contextual Decisions 221

FIGURE 9.16. Sebastion Friezes, North Second Story. A series of 50 personifications of conquered peoples from East Africa to Western Spain. The four represented here are the Pirousti, Dacian, and Besse peoples, and the island of Crete (AMA).

FIGURE 9.17. Sebastion Frieze, ETHNOUS IOUDAIŌN. Inscription of one more conquered nation in the north second-story series, the Jewish people (AMA).

The friezes of the third story of the south Sebastion focus on the Roman emperors and their imperial victories shown in concert with Olympian gods. The symbolic message here is clear: the emperors are today's powerful warring deities and are mixed with the old gods as near-equal partners. The superscription of the entire series is *Theoi Sebastoi Olympiori*, or "Olympian Emperor Gods." The principal emperors depicted are Augustus, Tiberius, Claudius, and Nero, because their most important activities were their victories over barbarians. So, we visualize and vicariously experience emperors in their signature victories: Claudius is conquering Britannia (the furthest west), and Nero is conquering Armenia (the furthest east). The style is imitative, Romans affecting the Greek heroic style.

One frieze depicts the emperor and the Roman people. The emperor is shown in the classic Greek style as naked warrior. He is being crowned by Romans, personified, wearing a toga, the stately civilian dress of Roman citizens. The crown is an oak wreath, which is the civic crown (*corona civica*), which is awarded for saving citizens' lives. The emperor sets up his battlefield trophy as a sign of victory. Beneath him in humiliation pose is the pathetic image of a kneeling, anguished, barbarian woman captive. In this way, the "message" of the imperial political agenda is symbolized figuratively in images that have no need for a prose explanation of the drift of the message. Symbols, figures, and images are a normal way of "talking."

FIGURE 9.18. Emperor and Roman People. Gratitude to heroic emperor civilizing barbarians, protecting Roman citizens' lives (AMA).

FIGURE 9.19. The Goddess Hemera and the God Oceanus. Hemera left, Oceanus right. Both are framed with billowing cloak behind the head, a symbol of a divine epiphany to mortals. These gods served Roman imperial ideology (AMA).

Another frieze is of the goddess Hemera (Day). The style is "still action," as she steadies a dramatic billowing cloak framing the head. Use of a billowing cloak behind the head was the standard figure for a divine epiphany to mortals. Why would the Romans be interested in the gods Day and Night? They had political interest, not religious. These gods proved useful for advancing imperial propaganda. They became stock images in Roman friezes for signifying the eternity of the Roman imperial rule. "Eternal Rome" is still an expression used even today. One could move from a temporal point to a terrestrial point. In a similar vein, the mutual depiction of the bearded god Oceanus alongside the goddess Earth again was a Roman imperial line for representing the empire as without end over land and sea.

One of the standard Roman goddesses was *Dea* Roma, the city of Rome, with the city of Rome itself a symbolic representation of the entire empire. By picturing *Dea* Roma together with a fecund Earth, one could represent earth's fertility and abundance as in the control of and administrated by the wise stewardship of Rome. In this particular frieze, Roma holds a spear and wears a crown in the form of a city wall (symbolic of civilization). Earth reclines, half naked, leaning on fruit and holding a cornucopia of fruit, indicating abundance and fertility. An innocent child climbs the horn wisely provisioned and secure.

FIGURE 9.20. Roma and Earth and Victory of the Emperors. Imperial ideology of Rome as wise manager and protector of earth's abundance, and of the prominent victory theme common in so much Roman imagery (AMA).

Another frieze is titled "Victory of the Emperors" (*Nike Sebastin*). This frieze, another "still action," pictures the goddess Victory as she swoops across the panel bearing a military trophy on her shoulder. This image is meant to convey one of the most prominent themes of Roman imperial ideology—victory. This victory theme was a key *topos* of imperial rhetoric. Rome and her legions were victorious on the field of battle. Conquering by force of military supremacy was the constant story of the Roman empire and her continual expansion to global domination, and Rome never let you forget that story. Her generals were honored with grand victory parades, or triumphs, in the heart of Rome with thousands to witness and laud success on the field of battle. Simon ben Giora, one of the Jewish Zealot leaders, was paraded down Rome's streets before his execution at Titus's triumph after Titus defeated the Jews in the First Jewish War.[30] This victory rhetoric provides background to John's "conquering" language, as in the seven letters ("to the one who conquers," 2:7, 11, 17, 26, 28; 3:21).[31]

---

[30] See Fig. 1.23, p. 20.

[31] See the excellent discussion in Horn, "Let the One Who Has Ears," *Essays on Revelation*, 175–87, for four important terms telling the story of Revelation: almighty, conquer, throne, and lamb. Each of these have imperial ideology in view.

FIGURE 9.21. Tiberius, Captive; Claudius Conquers Britannia. Every generation of emperors continues Rome's victorious conquest theme (AMA).

From generation to generation, the Roman emperors never fail in their military task as successful generals on the field of battle to vanquish their enemies and conquer and civilize barbarian hinterlands of a world empire. In a frieze about the reign of Tiberius (14–37), the emperor is depicted next to one of his captives in the Greek heroic style of the naked warrior. He stands frontally, in a pose of total dominance, holding spear and shield and wearing a cloak and sword strap. Beside him stands a captive barbarian, intentionally rendered at half size as a sign of humiliation and shame. The prisoner wears cloak and trousers, but has his hands tied behind his back, signifying captivity.

In another frieze again symbolizing a victorious conquest theme, Claudius (41–54) is depicted in heroic Greek style as naked warrior, wearing helmet, cloak, and sword-belt. He is captured at the moment he is about to deliver the death blow to this slumped female figure representing all of Britannia. She is styled bare-breasted in imitation of the legendary Greek Amazon myth.

Another of the imperial friezes shows Agrippina (d. 59) crowning her young son Nero (54–68) with a laurel wreath. Nero is styled in high honor, since he wears military armor and the cloak of a Roman commander, and with a helmet at his feet. The early reign of Nero universally was praised as a time of peace and prosperity. He was under the tutelage of the Stoic philosopher, Seneca (d. 65), for political matters and the prefect of the Praetorian Guard in Rome, Burrus (d. 62), for military matters. Nero's early reign widely was associated with the sun god Helios. The frieze of Nero and Agrippina is interesting for its timing, because its production had to be before A.D. 59, when Nero had his mother Agrippina murdered and got rid of both of his advisors. Even though the story of the emperors has such mundane matters as intrigue for accession to the imperial throne, the Roman imperial ideology ignored these realities and continued to propagandize conquered peoples with their alternate version of the "glory" of the imperial world.

FIGURE 9.22. Nero and Agrippina. Young Nero ruled well with mother's supervision and advisors Seneca and Burrus (AMA).

One last example from the imperial friezes is Claudius as master of land and sea. In this frieze Claudius is depicted as a god striding confidently forward in an intimidating divine epiphany, signified by the drapery that is billowing behind his head just like in the depiction of the gods when they manifest themselves to mortals. A figure is emerging from the ground and gifts Claudius with a cornucopia of fruits of the earth. The symbolism is clear: the emperor god is worthy of worship because he guarantees prosperity of land and sea. The image is remarkable for illustrating how in the outlying provinces of Rome, and most especially in the eastern province of Asia of the seven churches, the Roman world view not only is accepted but advanced. The emperor's role as universal savior and divine protector is affirmed enthusiastically and vigorously promoted by the local elites such as at Aphrodisias. Considering this city was only a short distance from both Laodicea toward the east and Ephesus toward the west, both addressed in John's letters to the churches, the pervasive presence of the Roman imperial world and its ideology is transparent.³²

FIGURE 9.23. Claudius, Master of Land and Sea. Claudius is depicted in a divine epiphany (billowing drape framing the upper torso). The divinely appointed role emphasized in this frieze is as master of land and sea. Therefore, the emperor also is the guarantor of abundant prosperity for all under his domain (AMA).

LITERARY SETTING

The most important observation to make about Revelation's literary setting is its mixed genre. The fusion of apocalypse, prophecy, and epistle requires balancing six interpretive corollaries, which seriously complicates the hermeneutical task. Besides genre, already discussed, four other elements of literary setting come into play reading this text.

Subversive Rhetoric

John writes against the background of Roman empire as illustrated at Aphrodisias. He rejects Rome's claims to sovereignty, power, and the

---

³²Galinsky, "The Cult of the Roman Emperor: Uniter or Divider?" 2–6, cautions not to conceive the imperial cult in monolithic, undifferentiated terms, such as suggested in "*the* imperial cult." Rather, local practices varied; the imperial cult was more a civic activity amalgamated into existing local religious, social, and economic structures. Much depended on patronage, social advance, and local elites. Cf. Spaeth, "Imperial Cult in Roman Corinth," 77. Care also must be taken not to conceive that Jews or Jesus followers responded in a monolithic manner to imperial cult interactions. Cf. White, "Capitalizing on the Imperial Cult: Some Jewish Perspectives," 188–89; Carter, "Roman Imperial Power: A New Testament Perspective," 142.

divinely appointed throne; he rejects propaganda of Augustan peace through victorious conquest; he rejects Rome's ill-gotten wealth; he rejects Rome's claims of empire benefits (law, stability, art and architecture, civilization). John instead sees the brutalization of peoples, the raping of earth's resources, and idolatry. Rome is after Rome's glory alone. Rome represents the perversion of an insatiable appetite for pleasure. John believes God is the true sovereign and is on his throne, so Rome is judged already. John writes subversive imperial rhetoric in imagery throughout the Apocalypse.

Kingdom of Priests

John declares Jesus' kingdom is priestly. Jesus himself offers the ultimate and true sacrifice ("by his blood," Rev 1:5). All Jesus' followers become a kingdom of priests to God (Rev 1:6), not just the socially elite. John universalizes that priesthood that Rome had reserved exclusively for elite provincials, the wealthy and politically connected, such as Zoilos in Aphrodisias and other social aristocrats in Asia Minor. Cities vied with each other to be designated with the status of *neōkoros* (νεωκόρος), "temple warden," or keeper of the imperial temple. Serving in

FIGURE 9.24. Imperial Cult Priest, Ephesus. Note the prominently displayed imperial cult ring of a proud, high status, aristocratic family of Ephesus (IAMI).

the imperial cult priesthood was a great honor. Ephesus, Smyrna, and

Pergamum achieved the honor of this high status, and their elite citizens competed to serve in the imperial priesthood.³³

FIGURE 9.25. Temple of Trajan, Pergamum. On the highest point atop the acropolis of Pergamum stand the remnants of the magnificent imperial cult temple of Trajan.

God the Almighty

Emperors in their imperial inscriptions liked to style themselves as the *autokratōr* (αὐτοκράτωρ), or "self-powerful one." John coyly speaks of God in Revelation with a term he reserves exclusively for the divine, *pantokratōr* (παντοκράτωρ), that is, "all-powerful one" ("Almighty" in our English translations).³⁴ That labeling was a clear shot across the emperor's bow that real authority and power in this world belonged to God alone.³⁵ God is the only sovereign who truly is sovereign. Against imperial propaganda, God rules over day and night, not Rome. God rules over earth and sea, not Rome. One sees the inscriptional remains of this imperial nomenclature all over what used to be ancient Asia Minor, now only relicts of a lost empire, display pieces in museums.

---

³³Cf. Burrell, *Neokoroi*.
³⁴Nine times in Rev 1:8; 4:8; 11:17; 15:3; 16:7, 14; 19:6, 15; 21:22.
³⁵Cf. Rev 4:11; 7:12; 11:17; 12:10; 15:8; 19:1.

FIGURE 9.26. Dedicatory Imperial Inscription. Probably part of a dedicatory monument to the emperor cult, this inscription's first two lines are, AUTOKRATORI KAISARI, "to the Emperor Caesar" (AAM).

Apollyon

Another example of John's subversive imperial rhetoric is his styling of the king of the bottomless pit in Rev 9:11. John first presents this king as the recognizable, standard Jewish figure of Abaddon, a traditional place of the dead like Sheol, but later personified into a character called "Destruction" in Jewish literature. John, however, in his own innovative, calculating way, subversively changes the characterization of this traditional Jewish figure into "Apollyon," which appears to be a word play on the Greek verb whose root meaning is "destroyer" (*apollymi*, ἀπόλλυμι, Rev 9:11). Few first-century readers could miss this crafty allusion playing off the name for the Greek god Apollo, whom the emperor Domitian claimed to represent. Rome is "Destroyer" not Protector.

FIGURE 9.27. Apollo Playing Cithara. From Miletus (IAM).

Seven Hills of Rome

John images a beast with seven heads that are seven hills (Rev 17:7–9). First-century readers hardly could miss the seven hills as a symbol for Rome, the city famously set on seven hills in ancient literature. We see this reference in multiple ancient Roman authors in prose and poetry.

FIGURE 9.28. Palatine Hill. On the right of the Roman Forum in this image, Palatine was one of the famous "seven hills of Rome." The emperor's palace here overlooked the forum, triumphal arches, temples, and senate house (Colosseum in background).

Horace wrote, "to sing their song to the gods, who have shown their love for the Seven Hills."[36] The seven hills formulation also appeared on imperial coins. Thus, this epigrammatic concept was well known in the first-century world and became a stock figure of Roman imperial propaganda. John's innovative imagery is treating Rome as the new "Babylon"—easily equated, since Rome and Babylon were the only two empires in history to destroy Jerusalem and the Jewish temple.

---

[36]Horace *Car. Saec.* 7. See also, Pliny *Nat. Hist.* 3.66, *conplexa montes septem*, "surrounding the seven hills"; Virgil *Georg.* 2.535; *Aen.* 6.784, *septemque una sibi muro circumdabit arces*, "she encloses her seven hills in single wall"; Martial *Epig.* 4.64, *Hinc septem dominos videre montis*, "Hence, see the seven mountains"; Propertius *Eleg.* 3.9. Cicero *Epis. Att.* 6.5, " when leaving the city of seven hills."

FIGURE 9.29. Goddess Roma Seated on Seven Hills of Rome. Vespasian sestertius, copper alloy, A.D. 71, laureate Vespasian; reverse: goddess Roma seated on seven hills of Rome with the Tiber River flowing under her feet; a smaller image of legendary she-wolf that suckled Romulus and Remus, founders of Rome (© British Museum).

Old Testament

Revelation makes more use of the Old Testament than any other book of the New Testament. Clearly, the author was saturated with Old Testament traditions in both Hebrew and LXX forms. The usage, however, is unusual. John never makes a direct quote. Instead, he makes allusions. One hears more like Old Testament echoes; some are loud, some soft. Throughout the Apocalypse one hears echoes from the five books of Moses, Judges, Proverbs, Song of Solomon, Job, Psalms, Daniel, Ezekiel, and Isaiah. He seems to borrow content, sequences, and themes. The plagues of the exodus, the geometry of the temple, the call experience of prophets, historical judgments of nations and of Israel, visions of seers, the holy mountain, hieratic ritual, tabernacle furniture, the garden of Eden, famous characters, and more constantly are bubbling up to the surface of Revelation.[37]

Unfortunately, this allusion pattern complicates a literary analysis of Revelation. John may have made allusions deliberately. Or, his imagery might simply reveal a stream of consciousness of a mind so absorbed in Old Testament traditions he just habitually and naturally expresses himself this way. Further, pinpointing the exact source of the allusion not always is clear. He never footnotes an exact reference.

---

[37]One of the best recent discussions is Beale, *Revelation*, 76–99.

Even with Old Testament allusions, John has been, true to form, innovative. He is not cut and paste. Often, he inverts usage, both in temporal sequence and in meaning. What is applied to the distant future John takes as present reality, or what is applied to Israel John applies otherwise.[38] Even his very first verse innovates Daniel's distant future defeat of cosmic evil (Dan 2:28–29, 45), because what Daniel was to seal up, John now opens up.[39]

John baptizes everything to Christ. This style includes the use of inaugurated eschatology in which fulfillment in the Christ event transforms concepts of salvation and judgment. We should not let the Old Testament context overwhelm John's carefully crafted christological fulfillment. A good example is John's apparent allusion in Rev 19:13 to Isaiah's image of Yahweh the divine warrior returning from battle on behalf of Israel, whose clothing is sprinkled with the blood of Israel's Edomite enemies (Isa 63:1–6). John's warrior in Rev 19:13 transforms entirely the appropriation of Isaiah's imagery christologically.

- First, John *reverses* the sequence. This warrior has soiled garments *before* the battle even is described. The *battle already has been fought* even though the imagery is about going out to do battle. Irony here signals this battle has an alien quality unlike "normal" battle scenes. Another indicator of a post-battle reality is the white horse, which was the customary mount for victors in Rome's sacred games, not generals on the field of battle.[40]

- Second, John *changes* the verb. The verb used for the soiled garment in Isa 63:3 is נזה, *nzh*, "sprinkle," "spatter." The verb John uses, however, is βαπτίζω, "baptize," a game changer. Irony again signals that he is transforming Isaiah's imagery. This rider is not "sprinkled" or "spattered" with blood as in Isa 63's slaughter of enemies. This robe is "baptized" in blood—drenched, completely soaked. Here, John is

---

[38]John's allusions in Rev 1:5–7 to Daniel's vision of the future judgment of the Ancient of Days (Dan 7:13) and Zechariah's promise to Israel that her enemies will not overwhelm God's purposes for his people (Zech 12:10–14) is a classic appropriation of both a distant future temporal sequence into the present and of promises for Israel for followers of Jesus. See Stevens, "Vision in the Night," 11–13.

[39]What was distant future in the Old Testament horizon is present reality for John. Cf. Smalley, *Revelation to John*, 9.

[40]See the description in Suetonius *Nero* 25.1.

drawing on gospel imagery, the significance of the question of Jesus to his disciples when alluding to his death by crucifixion, "Are you capable of being baptized with the baptism with which I am baptized" (Mark 10:38)? The blood is not the blood of enemies. The blood is this warrior's own blood. This alien imagery comports with the figure of Jesus in Revelation. Jesus is the one who has "freed us from our sins by his blood" (1:5); the Son of Man who suffers and dies (1:13); the Lion of the tribe of Judah who is a "slaughtered Lamb" (5:6) who "by your blood" ransomed for God (5:9); the one whose gives followers victory "by the blood of the Lamb" (12:11). John simply could not be more clear. We should not allow Isaiah's sense to overwhelm John's christological transformation.

- Third, John *names* the warrior. This warrior is called "Faithful" and "True" and "the Word of God" (Rev 19:11, 13). These titles echo the opening of Revelation in which Jesus is described as the "faithful witness" (1:5) and with the Inaugural Vision of the Son of Man who has a sharp, two-edged sword coming "out of his mouth" (1:16) and who in the seven letters calls himself the "Amen, the faithful and true witness" (3:14). The titles in Rev 19, then, resonate with the witness theme throughout Revelation, and this witness theme is reflected in Jesus' followers, most especially in hymns that celebrate the victory of followers who have conquered "by the word of their testimony" (12:11). If any war is depicted in Revelation—and we would have to include the war mentioned only once, Armageddon (16:16)—John signals that this war is a war of words—confession, testimony, and witness. John explicitly says that this warrior smites the nations with a "sharp sword that proceeds out of his mouth" (19:15). No tanks, no guns, no lasers, no nuclear warheads, but a sword out of the mouth. In fact, a sword out of the mouth is the only offensive weapon ever associated with Jesus in Revelation. Any other picture of the conduct of this war is fundamentally wrong and theological distortion. In this way, John is countering imperial propaganda that has perverted all of first-century society. Notice that Babylon is condemned for her "sorcery" in 18:23. Remains of Aphrodisias are a prime example of what that sorcery is comprised. In fact, John's warrior is multi-named: he also has a secret name, a name that no one knows but the warrior himself

(19:12). This idea comes from ancient magic in which power was believed resident in certain names. A sorcerer could increase power by accumulating names of power to invoke more potent spells. The "secret" name of this warrior means Babylon's sorcerers never will know or use this warrior's name in their attempts at incantations. This warrior's secret name, therefore, breaks the spell of Babylon's power. John claims that gospel witness exposes Rome's pretentious, presumptuous, and false imperial hubris. Not Claudius, not Nero, not Domitian, only Jesus is true "Lord of Lords and King of Kings" (19:16).

So, whatever the Old Testament allusion, John's point is christological and assumes post-resurrection reality. Not maintaining John's christological perspective destroys his New Testament concord and paints an image of Jesus completely unrecognizable from the Gospels.

Drama

Oddly enough, reading Revelation just might be the wrong approach. John's Apocalypse probably was meant to be a visceral experience, more moving than contemplated, more felt than formulated. We have to remember the original audience first *heard* the book, and John has this reality in mind as he writes (Rev 1:3). Revelation is like good drama and likely should be read so. Raquel points out not all John's hearers would have been as intimately acquainted with the details of his Old Testament allusions as John was. His audience would not, however, need to be for Revelation to fire imagination, fill senses, and evoke response. Characteristics of Roman productions and the content of Greek compo-

FIGURE 9.30. Actor Dressed as Papposilenus. Papposilenus, oldest of the Silens, leads retinue of Dionysus, in whose cult the Greek theater developed. Sheepskin, with coat around hips, wearing theater mask (PMB).

sitions, Raquel says, are evident in the Apocalypse. Like Romans used plays to advance philosophical, religious, and political agendas, John has his own counterpoint take on Roman politics, religion, and society. Raquel also points out that staging Revelation as drama lets an audience capture more of its original emotional impact and realize more effectively contrasts between the vision of the world the Romans projected and the vision Christ realized.[41]

FIGURE 9.31. Theater at Aspendos. Ancient Aspendos in Pamphylia, Asia Minor, on the Eurymedon River about 10 miles inland from the Mediterranean Sea, has the best-preserved theater of antiquity, seating 7,000 and 315 feet in diameter. This theater is one of few with the *scaenae fons* (backdrop) remaining intact. Post holes on the upper level held masts for the *velarium* (awning) shading spectators.

Dramatic Production

After reviewing first-century drama in terms of the physical layout of the stage and the elements of Greco-Roman plays, Raquel then overviews Revelation presented as drama. She identifies characters, theme, plot, setting, and structure.[42] Finally, Raquel effectively sets out the details of presenting an actual contemporary performance of Revelation, specifying the support staging for the production, with schematic

---

[41] See the excellent article by Raquel, "Revelation as Drama," 156–58. The most thorough-going effort to undertake Revelation as performance drama in the past is in the work of John W. Bowman; cf. Bowman, "Revelation," IDB, expanded more fully in *The Drama of the Book of Revelation*.

[42] Raquel, 162–66.

diagrams to illustrate, and providing a running outline of the seven acts with guidance for director, producer, and actors.[43] Raquel's essay shows the promise of Revelation read as drama. Reading her neatly organized, creative performance helps visualize the possibilities.

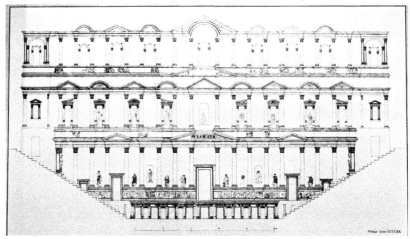

FIGURE 9.32. *Scaenae Fons* of Perge Theater. An artist's depiction of the backdrop, or *scaenae fon*s, of the theater at Perge in Pamphylia (AAM).

Antichrist Character

One famous character is missing from Revelation's drama. His name is Antichrist. You may have met him before. He's a pretty popular fellow in futurist dramas. Amazing how legend can take a single sheet of blank paper and cut out an intricate origami masterpiece never seen in the original. As we saw in our history of interpretation, already by the time of Adso the Antichrist legend in Medieval Europe had grown into a full body armor "Iron Man" apocalypse movie star better than Marvel Comics could conjure, even with elaborate Hollywood CGI special effects. One never ceases to be amazed how flights of fancy in apocalyptic traditions evolve out of one single verse of Scripture, or at most, a few, and those often are in the same solitary paragraph—an entire doctrine with extraordinarily elaborate details, no less! We see this phenomenon with ideas such as the millennium, Armageddon, and Antichrist. What is the real story of Antichrist? Most certainly not what you probably think.

[43] Ibid., 166–74.

The term "antichrist" occurs in only four verses in all of Scripture, and all four are in 1–2 John (1 John 2:18, 22; 4:3; 2 John 7). How about we let the author of these epistles tell us what he means by the figure—because he does. The two verses of 1 John 2:18–19 teach four major truths about the figure of "antichrist" completely ignored in the popular Antichrist legends. The Antichrist you know is not biblical.

- First, John's *realized* eschatology is unquestionable; the last hour is present: "Little children, it is the last hour." Futurism not even in the slightest is on the horizon for this statement. John's "antichrist" teaching is in the context of this realized eschatology.

- Second, John's *exclusive* teaching is for his own community: "just as you heard that antichrist is coming." This specialized tradition and technical terminology is not found in any other early Christian community or literature. Paul's "man of lawlessness" in 2 Thess 2:3 does not qualify. Paul is precise. He emphatically does *not* say "antichrist." Further, Paul's context is crucially different on multiple counts. The most important is, Paul speaks of the future, but John the present. Paul expressly says the "man of lawlessness" has *not* arrived, but John expressly says the "antichrist" *has* arrived.

- Third, John's *multiple* number of "antichrists" is explicit: "and now many antichrists have come about." John's teaching of "antichrist" is a conceptual role to be fulfilled, not the name of one person.

- Fourth, John's *identification* is about heretical teachers. John identifies precisely who are the multiple "antichrist" figures in the very next verse: "They went out from us" (1 John 2:19). These separatists are known heretics formerly aligned with John's churches but now separated in their own communities. They teach a false Christology, which dominos into their ethical and pneumatic aberrations. John denies their false teachings forcefully: "Who is the liar except the one who denies Jesus is the Messiah" (1 John 2:22)? Again, he says, "and every spirit that does not confess Jesus is not of God, and this person is of the antichrist, which you heard that it is coming, and now is in the world already" (1 John 4:3). This "antichrist" is the spirit of heresy. John restates the "antichrist" teaching in the second letter: "For many deceivers are gone forth into the world, even they that confess not that Jesus Christ comes in the flesh. This one is the deceiver and the antichrist" (2 John 7). Once again, this teaching is about a *present* situation among *multiple* individuals who teach or affirm christological *heresy*. Context makes clear the concept is the heresy of false Christology that denies Jesus as having come in the flesh. Many persons can fulfill the role of directly opposing Jesus through heretical teachings—the essence of John's "antichrist." For John, being "antichrist" is being "anti-Jesus" in Christology.

Four verses in two Johannine epistles is the sum total of what the Bible has to say of "antichrist." The teaching is this: exclusively Johannine, now present in John's community, multiple persons teaching heresy. The legendary character "Antichrist" never appears in the real drama of Revelation. John the Seer never even uses the term. The figure is a wild fantasy of apocalyptic imagination having accrued personhood, personality, and plot over multiple millennia of mythical evolution, but one for whom John writes no script in his play.

The problem with obsessive focus on the Antichrist character is more serious than believing a myth. Antichrist is a distorted caricature that, while supposedly personifying evil, trivializes evil into a comic-strip character. Antichrist also exteriorizes evil "out there," allowing a dissociation from our own persons. We think whatever the problem of evil is, that is the Antichrist and has nothing to do with us. Antichrist legend is a projection of the Satan any human soul can incarnate. Antichrist mythology anesthetizes conscience by distracting us from looking in the right direction for what is wrong with the world and preventing us from dealing with evil where evil truly resides (Jas 1:14).

Structure

The structure of Revelation is an Excedrin headache. Consult the critical commentaries. Immediately, you are in a morass. Some outlines even have arranged the entire book as one gigantic chiasm.[44] Some

---

[44]The name chiasm comes from the Greek letter chi, which looks like an "X." The outer points of the two legs of the letter can be arranged variously, such as A1, A2, B1, B2 or A1, B1, B2, A2. Symmetry is the point. If A1 is a scene with angels, then A2 is some similar scene with angels. Or, if B1 has a central feature of a command, then B2 will have a command element. Ancient writers arranged material this way to aid the hearer in following the "flow" of material through recognizable elements of symmetry.

240 REVELATION: THE PAST AND FUTURE OF JOHN'S APOCALYPSE

truth is found in almost any outline. Yet, Revelation's structure always is complicated by material hard to "fit" nicely.

Almost any outline of Revelation has weaknesses. We can try to perceive chiasms. We can try to take linguistic cues (repeated phrases, for example, such as "and I saw," or "a sign appeared," etc.). We can try to take numeric cues, such as series of sevens. But the devil is in the details, and, in Revelation, the details are the devil. Most outlines work but also do not work.

For example, the order in which the new characters of Dragon (Rev 12), Beasts (Rev 13), and Babylon (Rev 17) are introduced is the reverse order they are destroyed: Babylon (Rev 18), Beasts (Rev 19), Dragon (Rev 20). That order is an easy chiasm to see in the structure. Beginning in Rev 12, then, specific new characters are introduced that drive the drama and run throughout the following chapters.

FIGURE 9.33. Apocalypse Tapestry, Rev 13:1–2. John, on the left, views the red dragon standing on the shore of the sea giving the beast from the sea his authority by the icon of a scepter (Angers, France).

At the same time, these same chapters (Rev 12–20) have "interludes," "breaks," or "interruptive" elements—interpreters struggle for the proper term. Thus, the straightforward introduction of the Dragon and Beasts in Rev 12–13 that will be completed with the new character of Babylon in Rev 17 is "interrupted" by a vision of Zion and the 144,000 (Rev 14). This Zion vision clearly is meant to tie the material all the way back to the "interlude" after the Seal Judgments (Rev 6) of the sealing of the 144,000 (Rev 7). Further, the Zion vision itself immediately is followed by a Harvest Judgment vision in the same chapter that calls on one "like a son of man" to take his sickle and reap. This phrasing clearly alludes to the opening vision of the Son of Man (1:9–20). These "interruptions" in the story of the Dragon and Beasts continue. The Zion and Harvest visions, which seem to tie back into earlier material in Rev 1–11, then are followed by the Bowl Judgments (Rev 15–16). Only after the three "interruptive" visions of Zion, Harvest, and Bowls is the character of Babylon finally introduced in Rev 17. Clearly, this character works in concert with the Dragon and the Beasts of Rev 12–13, but we do not get to this character for a while. Thus, while we have clearly marked new characters in the drama of Dragon, Beasts, and Babylon that begin to be introduced in Rev 12, their "story" is "interrupted" by a complicated series of other visions worked into the plotline that interconnect with earlier material in Rev 1–11. Outlining these "interruptive" elements logically is hard. Charles asserted the entire work disparate material hopelessly disarranged.[45]

Not only that, knowing how the new Dragon material of Rev 12–20 should "outline" with the earlier material of Rev 1–11 itself is problematic. Even similar items between Rev 1–11 and Rev 12–20 do not function in the same way. For example, the seven Bowl judgments seem related to the earlier judgment cycles of the seven Seals and seven Trumpets, Literarily, however, they are not treated the same. The Seals and Trumpets are essential to Rev 1–11. They function as literary devices that drive the drama forward. The Bowls, on the other hand, are not essential to Rev 12–20 and do not drive the drama forward. They are secondary to the Dragon plot. The reader could jump from the end of the grape harvest judgment scene (Rev 14:17–20) to the beginning of the Babylon story with the angel's invitation, "Come, I will show you the punishment of the great harlot, who sits on many waters" (Rev 17:1), and hardly skip a beat. The reader easily would read the judgment of the winepress of God's wrath in Rev 14 as being detailed more fully in the judgment of the harlot Babylon in Rev 17. If the Bowls were not there in Rev 15–16 between the winepress of God's wrath and the judgment of harlot Babylon, they simply would not be

---

[45]R. H. Charles, *Revelation*, ICC, 1920.

missed.[46] What the Bowl judgments *do* tell the reader is that the entire judgment cycle is coming to a *literary* end with the story of the harlot Babylon, because these judgments are specified explicitly as the last: "seven angels with the seven last plagues because with them the wrath of God is finished" (Rev 15:1). So, the Bowl judgments do have literary function: they alert the reader to the conclusion of the entire judgment series. Yet, even if connected as a similar series of seven, the Bowl judgments have a different literary *function* in their context than do the Seal and Trumpet judgments. They are necessary but not essential. How, then, should the *secondary* literary function of the Bowl judgments in Rev 12–20 be represented in an outline in contrast to the *primary* literary function of both the Seals and Trumpets in Rev 1–11?

However, we do not have to despair completely. At least we still can see the "big picture" of the structure of Revelation. Certain large aggregations of material are recognized in some way in almost every outline of Revelation. After an obligatory Introduction (1:1–8) and Conclusion (22:6–21), then the major blocks would be the following:

- Vision of Son of Man (Rev 1)
- Seven Letters (Rev 2–3)
- Vision of Heaven (Rev 4–5)
- Judgment Cycle (Rev 6–20)
- Vision of Victory (Rev 21–22)

Notice how John strategically has placed major visions as prelude to major judgment cycles. The preludes have theological function. John uses each vision to lay down a theological foundation upon which the following judgments are based. The Vision of the Son of Man prepares for the judgment of the church that follows in the seven letters. The Vision of Heaven prepares for the judgment of the world that follows in the Judgment Cycle. The book climaxes in a Vision of Victory in which God's sovereignty is realized fully and all God's creative and redemptive purposes are consummated.

---

[46]Once again, ability to "drop out" material and not miss a beat is another literary clue that John's imagery is meant to be experienced cumulatively, as in a drama. He writes to recapitulate judgments for dramatic intensification, not to lay out a linear progression of judgments through time.

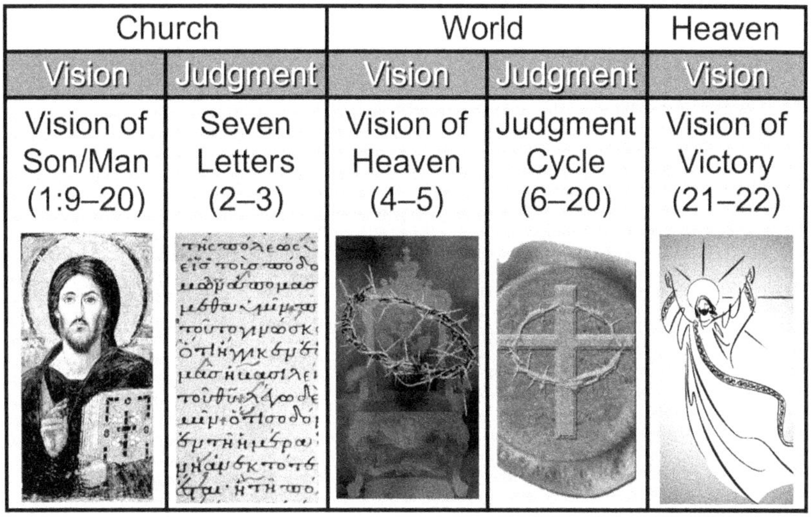

Church		World		Heaven
Vision	Judgment	Vision	Judgment	Vision
Vision of Son/Man (1:9–20)	Seven Letters (2–3)	Vision of Heaven (4–5)	Judgment Cycle (6–20)	Vision of Victory (21–22)

FIGURE 9.34. Revelation's "Big Picture." Details of outlines of Revelation vary, but the basic building blocks of material showing the "big picture" most would agree on.

SUMMARY

Two aspects of setting needed to be covered to round out the frame for interpreting Revelation under construction. One is the historical setting, specifically date, authorship, and the social setting of the seven churches. The other is the literary setting, specifically use of the Old Testament, drama, and structure. The approach has been to provide a general overview, depending on more details for the arguments pro and con and other options in the critical commentaries.

In terms of the historical setting, the most frequently suggested dates have hovered around Nero and Domitian. The later Domitian date is the clear favorite. The reason for this preference is transparent: the composite accumulation of evidence, both historical and patristic, favors Domitian much more. The desire to establish John the apostle as author prior to Gospel and epistle production may unconsciously control the desire to argue an earlier date even in spite of the actual historical evidence available. Use of various internal matters, such as the sequence of kings in Rev 17, inherently involve arbitrary decisions rendering the argumentation specious and highly tendentious and no help. Persecution is in the context, but without sufficient information to localize in time.

The author is John, clearly identified multiple times at both the beginning and the end of the work (Rev 1:1, 4, 9; 22:8). The problem is which John. The Eastern church pretty much ignored the book from the beginning, or actually proscribed its reading or use as too dangerous or radical. This historical phenomenon renders the reception of Revelation in the East ironic, since the book is rejected by those in its very region of origin, but accepted by those outside its origins in Rome. The Eastern church has little conviction that John the apostle wrote the book. They would have little argument upon which to stand to reject the book if they felt the apostle had written the book.

The Western church, in contrast, from at least Justin Martyr on always understood John the apostle as the author of Revelation. The Western tradition was that the apostle John had a long ministry in Ephesus after the First Jewish War. Since one of the seven letters in Revelation was addressed to Ephesus, and the author's name in the work is given as "John," and the tradition in Rome was that the apostle John long was in Ephesus, then, *voila!* John the apostle obviously is the "John" of Revelation. The one dissenting voice otherwise in the circle of the Roman patriarchate was that of Dionysius of Alexandria, one of a decreasing number of early church fathers still knowledgeable about the Greek language. Dionysius concluded from a study of the Greek of Revelation that the author of the Apocalypse and the author of the Gospel simply could not be one and the same person on many counts. His arguments never have been confuted. They either are ignored or tacitly admitted. When admitted, however, the burden is immediate to invent some intentional contrivance on John's part to overcome the huge obstacle of the grammar, syntax, language, and thought-world of the Apocalypse versus that of the Gospel. These contrivances are unnecessary.

The author of Revelation is an itinerant prophet of Asia Minor named John active in the life of multiple congregations, whose experience is visionary, whose thought world is apocalyptic, and whose language is symbolic. He is disturbed by problems of heresy within and pressures of Rome without. He writes to meet these crises in his Asia Minor churches.

John is on Patmos because of his faith and his preaching of Jesus. Church tradition of John's exile could be correct, but might be no more than supposition from various statements in Revelation itself.

Against church tradition is general Roman policy that invokes banishment principally for the social elite and politically connected, a status for which not even John the apostle would qualify. The tradition of Prochorus, John's supposed scribe on Patmos writing down visions as John sees them and dictates, is legendary only. We do not know where John was when he wrote the Apocalypse, but his own description is unequivocal that he no longer was on Patmos at the time. Primary evidence does not exist to support the idea that Patmos was used as a Roman penal colony in the first century, nor that the Romans maintained a mining operation on the island at any time.

The recipients were seven churches in Asia Minor. Our challenge in understanding them is divesting ourselves of our post-industrial and differently structured societal concepts with their own implicit value systems dictating structures of behavior, public and private, political and religious. We have to work to appreciate more deeply the pressures to conform felt by first-century believers in a world sold out in Asia Minor particularly at every level of society to the pervasive and persuasive Roman imperial propaganda.

John's rhetoric is subversive. He undermines imperial propaganda about Rome, her emperors, and her empire. He does this often with titles. Everyone in Jesus' kingdom is a priest, not exclusively the social elite and politically powerful in collusion with Rome. God as Almighty subverts the emperor as self-mighty. Domitian is Destroyer Apollyon, not the god Apollo. Rome's seven hills support a harlot not an empire.

The use of the Old Testament is unusual. Direct citation does not occur, but allusions are pervasive throughout the text. The Old Testament provides themes, content, even sequences. The allusive nature, however, sometimes renders unclear the literary strategy. John freely innovates even temporal sequences and meaning. John baptizes all to Christ. His meaning is christological and in concord with the Gospels.

While Revelation by genre is not drama, the message without doubt is dramatic. One even can convert what John has written into a drama. Since drama connects with an audience more powerfully and emotionally, reconfiguring Revelation as a drama may communicate John's message to a modern audience more effectively and more like the original audience would have experienced the book. The reader needs to be alert that images pile up on top of each other in Revelation, not to be confusing, but to be dramatic and intensify the effect on the audience. This unusual feature of Revelation's imagery as intended for cumulative impact is probably why outlines of Revelation struggle to show the logic. Revelation has more emotion than logic. Revelation has no Antichrist—such a character is never mentioned, not seen nor heard anywhere in the book. The Antichrist legend is a fabled fiction invented in unbridled speculations that have accumulated over several millennia. As popularly conceived, he does not exist and certainly has no role in Revelation.

Attempting to outline Revelation's structure is not compliant to detail. The logic is illusive. All outlines have strengths and weaknesses. However, the book does have a macro structure that most recognize. Two main visions are prelude to two main judgments. The visions lay out the theological foundation for the judgments that follow them. One series judges the church. The other series judges the world. The book climaxes with a vision of heaven in which all God's sovereign purposes are realized.

Part 3

Apocalypse of Jesus Christ

Reading John's Vision of a Future Anticipated from the Past

10

Judgment of the Church

The Son of Man and His Churches

I OFTEN HAVE TOLD MY STUDENTS that if they get the first chapter of Revelation correctly, they have mastered the rest of the book. The reasons are two. The introduction (1:1–8) reveals the christological key, and the Inaugural Vision (1:9–20) reveals the hermeneutical key for the rest of the Apocalypse. The first vision of ancient apocalypses was the most important one. The opening vision set the interpretive stage for all the other visions to follow. John's vision of the Son of Man, positioned first, is the most important vision in all the Apocalypse. At least, that seems to be what John thought he was doing. Later readers failed to take his cue.

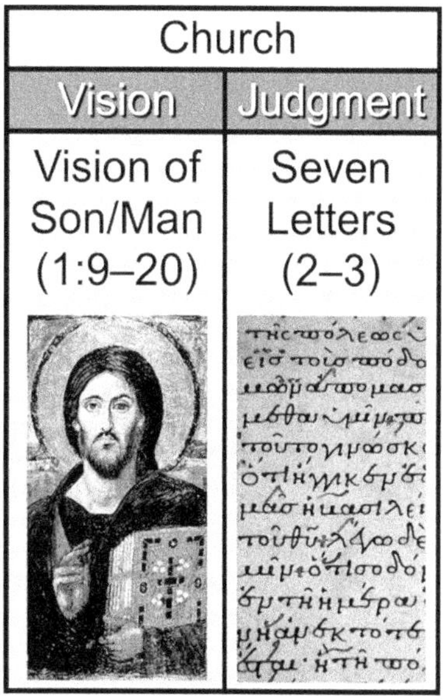

Church	
Vision	Judgment
Vision of Son/Man (1:9–20)	Seven Letters (2–3)

FIGURE 10.1. Revelation, Act 1. The Son of Man and His Churches.

After an introduction, the first act in John's drama has two scenes, a vision and its related judgment cycle. The vision is of the Son of Man who stands among seven lampstands, which are the seven churches. The following judgment cycle, based on the Inaugural Vision, is a composite series of seven letters written to these seven churches in which the Son of Man comes in judgment in his piercing assessments.

INTRODUCTION (1:1–8)

The introduction, sometimes called the prologue, has several functions. The introduction establishes the genre of the writing, which is a hybrid trifold mix that requires a difficult balancing of six interpretive corollaries. The introduction showcases the visionary experience of the author, which sets him apart as a New Testament writer.[1] Also, the introduction validates his authority to write with a commission from God. Finally, the introduction is our christological key to Revelation. This christological function is our present focus.

Christological Key

Christology is the heart of the introduction. John writes in such a way as to make Christ central to the introduction and realities surrounding the story of Jesus the most defining characteristics of the introduction. This christological theme has defining characteristics in the opening verses of Revelation clarifying that this vision is about Jesus, signed by symbols, kept by obedience, soon to take place, addressed specifically, and authorized divinely.

About Jesus

The vision is Jesus. John's first words are "Revelation of Jesus Christ." In case anyone had any doubt about what Revelation's surreal visionary drama reveals, John erases the ambiguity immediately. What is revealed is not the future. What is revealed is Jesus. John does not write, "Revelation of the future." What he says is, "Revelation of Jesus Christ." The preposition "of" communicates two truths. If one says, "This is a painting *of* Van Gogh," one could mean a painting *by* Van Gogh, or one could mean a painting *about* Van Gogh. With "of Jesus Christ" John means both. He intends to say that the Apocalypse both is *from* Jesus and the Apocalypse is *about* Jesus. From Jesus is spelled

---

[1] John's sense of deeper spiritual awareness ("in the Spirit," 1:10) can be compared to Stephen, who also sees heaven opened and the Son of Man seated in power (Acts 7:55–56). Paul saw the resurrected Jesus (Acts 9:1) and apparently himself had visions in an ecstatic state (1 Cor 12:2). On vision reports, see Humphrey, "In Search of a Voice," 144. None of these experiences, however, resulted in such a complex literary production as we have in the book of Revelation. No one wrote autobiographically in depth and detail the content of their visions. Revelation is unique in the New Testament.

out in the first verse: "The revelation of Jesus Christ, which God gave him to show his servants what must soon take place; he signified by sending his angel to his servant John" (1:1). About Jesus is played out in the Inaugural Vision of the Son of Man that immediately follows the introductory verses: "and in the midst of the lampstands I saw one like the Son of Man" (1:13). So the book of Revelation is from Jesus and is about Jesus. The apocalypse is Jesus. John saw the Son of Man, not future time. Any future in Revelation would be because Jesus is the future. *Knowing who Jesus is, then, is the interpretation of Revelation.*

John characterizes this Jesus in Rev 1:5–6. The characterization is christological to the core and permeated with gospel truth.

- Jesus is "faithful witness." This witness is epitomized in the Gethsemane prayer that led to the cross. This path intimates what is ahead for believers and for the church. Witness, with its cousin idea of testimony, will become a major theme in Revelation.

- Jesus is "firstborn of the dead." This birth is a resurrection life that leads to heaven. Whatever the terrors to be faced in this judgment drama, the end of the story is a vision of heaven. Jesus conquers the death Rome deals. For Jesus, "firstborn" is primogeniture rights, his messianic inheritance, which he shares with his followers.[2]

- Jesus is "ruler of the kings of the earth." This rule is ascension glory, already realized, through which God controls all history and our destiny through what the incarnate Son accomplished in his life and death and what he will accomplish in his church. Jesus does not await a future event to reign.[3]

- Jesus is the one who "loves us." This love expresses the heart of the covenant-keeping God. This love assures believers in duress in Asia Minor they are not forgotten. Their struggle has purpose and destiny in defining the present reality of the kingdom of God.

- Jesus is the one who "freed us from our sins." This freedom is the explicit act of God's covenant love. Redemption is integral to the story of God's people. The premier redemption narrative in the Old

---

[2] Cf. Ps 88; 89:7; 37.

[3] As in Ps 89, which Jews interpreted messianically. John envisions Jesus as the ideal Davidic king.

Testament is the story of the exodus from Egypt after a series of devastating plagues. Exodus typology permeates Revelation's judgment cycle imagery, especially in the trumpets (8:2—11:19) and the bowls (15:5—16:21). Several truths define this redemptive action in Revelation. First, this freedom already is achieved. Whatever future believers can expect already has been secured by the past. Second, this freedom is freedom from sin, that is, has sacerdotal function. Jesus is priest. In this sacerdotal imagery, Revelation's language reflects the thought world of the book of Hebrews.

- Jesus frees believers "by his blood." The cross is the apocalypse of God's love. This blood language early in the book is crucial, because this concept here at the beginning of Revelation provides the reader the hermeneutical key for the blood theme in the entire book. The word blood is used 17 times in Revelation. All occurrences but one of blood in Revelation are tied to the experience of Jesus and his followers, not those rejecting the gospel.[4] Almost exclusively, the term blood has Christian focus in Revelation and refers to the reality of redemption coming through Jesus' death, or to the reality of persecution of Jesus' followers.

- Jesus has made believers "a kingdom, priests." Jesus' kingdom is a *priestly* kingdom—not military or political! This priestly nature of Jesus' kingdom has numerous implications for interpretation.

    First, priestly imagery ought to control how to conceptualize all martial imagery in the Apocalypse. Revelation is not a reprise of Qumran. John does not expect his church members to go out as if to fight advancing Roman legions expecting some apocalyptic inbreaking of the kingdom of God only to get slaughtered. To suggest any such actual military action as part of the plan of God for God's people to conquer evil in the world—whether now or in a fabricated seven-year "tribulation" period of the futurist scenario—is a perversion of everything for which Jesus lived, taught, and died. That unquestionably *is* another gospel. We are priests who live by self-sacrifice, not by slaughtering others. This priestly character is inherent in Jesus' response to Pilate that Jesus' kingdom is "not of

---

[4]Lamb, 5x (1:4; 5:9; 7:14; 12:11; 19:13); martyrs, 5x (6:10; 16:6; 17:6; 18:24; 19:2); elements, 6x (6:12; 8:7, 8; 11:16; 16:3, 4); unbelievers, 1x (14:20).

this world" (John 18:36), that is, the world Augustus had created into which Jesus was born. Otherwise, Jesus would take the way of the Roman world that had put Pilate in his position of power and authority—the route of Roman imperialism, a violent path of brutal conquest subduing so-called "barbarians." Jesus does not feign to be another Roman general setting up his battlefield trophy, pushing his victim to the ground in abject humiliation by a heel on the neck, parading the streets of Rome, then executing his captives at the end of the parade in a rank domination display of summary execution. Jesus refuses to aspire to such a Roman vision of kingdom nor to conquer in this Roman way. His followers are to take his lead. A priestly kingdom was to be Israel's destiny in order to reveal God to the world.[5] Followers of Jesus fulfill this role. If Jesus achieved his "victory" by losing, that is, by dying on an imperial cross, by what path, then, do the seven churches "win" against this same empire? No surprise that each of the letters to the seven churches ends with the same promise, "to him who conquers" (2:7, 11, 17, 26; 3:5, 12, 21). John probes believers to ask: Just how does this "conquering" of the church take place? John has answered decisively in 12:11.[6] The "rapture of the church" then "great tribulation" script rips the very heart out of John's message and is christologically bankrupt. *Second*, all are priests in Jesus' kingdom, not just the social elite of Roman life. John universalizes priesthood, which radically shatters the paradigm of Roman patronage in the provinces. *Third*, Jesus' kingdom is forever, as John expresses in his benediction: "to him be glory and dominion forever and ever" (1:6). John's "forever" is the ultimate put-down of Roman imperial pretense. You never will see a relic inscription in a museum to a long lost Jesus kingdom.

Signed by Symbols

The vision is signified. John uses the Greek verb *sēmainō* (σημαίνω), which means "sign" or "signify." Translations often render as "made it known" (1:1). John says the visions were "signed" to him, and so he is

---

[5]Exod 19:16. The exile meant that the nation of Israel failed this mission (Exod 24:4–8; Isa 43:10–13).

[6]Which is in canonical concord with Matthew's conclusion (Matt 28:19), Luke's beginning (Acts 1:8), and Peter's summary (1 Pet 2:5–10).

"signifying" the vision to his audience, that is, using sign language. His images are his sign language to the spiritual realities he contemplated. Images have symbolic function. With his *sēmainō*, John indicates the language of Revelation is not referential. The language is symbolic.[7]

Kept by Obedience

The vision is kept. In his first benediction, John announces he is writing a prophecy and says, "Blessed is the person who reads aloud the words of the prophecy, and blessed are those who hear and who keep the things written within" (1:3). So, John does not write prophetic words to facilitate future voyeurism. They are to reinforce present obedience. They are words to be kept—now. John later plays out the challenging implications of a prophetic benediction in the words of Jesus recorded in letters to the seven churches in the following two chapters. Jesus' imperative commands ring out a constant call in the Seven Letters how to keep the words of the prophecy in the challenge John had issued by pronouncing his benediction:

FIGURE 10.2. Apocalypse Tapestry, Reader. Gothic canopy, prophet's headdress, turning page (Panel 3, Scene 26, Angers, France).

- "remember," "repent" (Ephesus, 2:5)
- "beware," "be faithful" (Smyrna, 2:10)
- "repent" (Pergamum, 2:16)

[7] Kraybill, *Apocalypse and Allegiance*, 34–37, has a helpful discussion of sign theory (semiotics) related to Revelation.

- "hold fast" (Thyatira, 2:25)
- "wake up," "strengthen" (Sardis, 3:2)
- "hold fast" (Philadelphia, 3:11)
- "buy from me," "listen" (Laodicea, 3:18, 20)

Words to the churches in the Seven Letters (Rev 2–3) are matters to keep, not to discuss. John is forthtelling, not foretelling. Jesus is not advising the seven churches what to do in two thousand years. If the churches do not heed these warnings, Jesus no longer will support or associate with them or empower them by his indwelling presence. He will remove their lampstand (2:5). If the church had not heeded these words and had not been obedient to them, the light of witness would have gone out in Asia Minor. Fortunately, believers in Asia Minor were faithful. That is why we have the book of Revelation in the first place. One way for the church to appropriate the book of Revelation in the present is to make the past obedience and faithful witness in the face of superpower ideology and social control a guiding paradigm.

Soon to Take Place

The vision is soon. "What must soon take place," John says (1:1). Do we need to say soon means soon?[8] John images realities that *presently* are confronting first-century Asia Minor believers. John is calling for their obedience and faithful witness. John concludes Revelation with the same message of "soon." The angel repeats this imminence theme at the end of the book: "to show to his servants what must soon take place" (22:6). Jesus emphatically reaffirms in 22:7 the angel's word: "Behold, I am coming soon!" From the very beginning to the very end of the drama, the word "soon" hovers over the entire Apocalypse and gives the visions their urgency and potency. Otherwise, the script is a charade and John's message pointless to the original audience.

Interpreters have to attempt a Texas two-step to obviate John's transparent meaning with "soon." (The awkward stumbling around is obvious.) Perhaps these vain efforts are because we suffer a failure of nerve? How is a "prophecy" of destruction fulfilled if the Roman em-

---

[8]Just in case one might want to opt for "quickly" (adverb of manner) rather than "soon" (adverb of time) for the *tachei* (τάχει) adverb, John repeats two verses later, in unequivocal terms, "for the time is near" in 1:3.

pire continued for centuries after John penned his visions? The real question is how divine judgment works.

Addressed Specifically

The vision is addressed. "John to the seven churches that are in Asia" (1:4). These churches are enumerated in 1:11. You are reading someone else's mail, not yours. Revelation is timely communication from God's prophet to God's people to address them in their hour of need. Thus, all of Revelation is about these seven real churches of Asia Minor. The Seven Letters are about the seven churches. The vision of heaven is about the seven churches. The vision of judgments is about the seven churches. The dragon, beasts, and Babylon are about the seven churches. The rider on the white horse is about the seven churches. The millennium and Gog and Magog are about the seven churches. The final vision of heaven is about the seven churches. Revelation is about the seven churches. John unequivocally says so at the beginning of the drama. Revelation is not a mythology conjuring a legendary and unbiblical Antichrist character in some fictive future nuclear meltdown. The world may undergo a nuclear meltdown, but that will not be Armageddon. That will be human depravity and gross stupidity. Revelation is a prophetic call to obedience to seven churches of Asia Minor.

Authorized Divinely

The vision is authorized. The revelation is from God. God regularly is referenced obliquely in Revelation: "the one who is, who was, and who is to come" (1:4). This title suggests eternity. Rhetorically, this titling strategy forces contemplation of the imperial claim to divinity. God's eternal sovereignty is proclaimed against the paltry efforts of Roman emperors to enforce sovereignty over humanity, which efforts always are limited in time. No emperor is forever. Every throne any human ever has occupied has been vacated. That is God's judgment. Thus, the "coming" of God is his coming in judgment on every human pretense to sovereignty, whether this be Augustus, Tiberius, Claudius, Nero, Vespasian, Titus, or Domitian—or anyone else. The world belongs to God, not Rome. God calls himself the "Alpha and Omega ... the Almighty" (1:8). Combining first and last letters of the alphabet means the summing up all words in between as well. Of all words to be said about rule and authority, God will have the last word, not the Roman emperor. God is the Almighty.

We note that John's title "who is, who was, who is to come" is used multiple times in Revelation (1:4, 8; 4:8; 11:17; 16:5). John, however, changes the last two to just "the one who is and who was." The "is to come" part is dropped off, because judgment has been realized. God the Almighty has had the last word, not the emperor. This distinct phrasing of the divine nomenclature is John's subtle way to signify that each judgment cycle is to be considered conclusive; therefore, the judgment cycles are recapitulative. Even the rhetoric of the divine name reinforces this purpose in the judgment cycles.

Second Coming Allusion

John already has been making Old Testament allusions. We have passed by these to get to this most obvious reconfiguration of Old Testament texts here in 1:7–8. John's handling of these passages is his way of signaling how he will use the Old Testament as background for signing his visionary experience. His allusions also set the profile of his understanding of how the second coming of Jesus flows out of the first coming of Jesus. Notice how, in the literary flow, the realities of the first coming (1:1–6) set up the allusion to the second coming (1:7–8). Thus, John's view is that the first coming reveals the very character and essence of the second coming. Without John's incarnational frame, his perspective on the second coming theologically is misunderstood. In Revelation, the second coming *consummates what has been inaugurated*. That is, the second coming does not contravene the cross; the second coming concludes the cross. Any futurama drama of the second coming of Christ coming out of Revelation must grapple with this truth. The way John will develop the drama, *the church will be essential to the realization of this theological trajectory*.

John's Allusions

John's allusions both combine and innovate on Daniel, Zechariah, and Ezekiel. "He is coming with the clouds" is rich with echoes of the Son of Man's enthronement in Dan 7:13, which in Jewish traditions had been understood as an event of the end of days. "Every eye will see him" echoes Zech 12:10 as Israel mourns the one pierced. The end-time defeat of nations echoes Ezek 38–39, which already had entered the stream of Gospel traditions (Matt 24:30). For John, Daniel is realized and Ezekiel universalized.

John's appropriation has been to claim that Daniel's prophecy is realized in Jesus' enthronement. In effect, John takes the theological value of Luke's ascension story and uses apocalyptic language to invest that ascension story with messianic prophetic significance. What for Daniel was future for the Son of Man, for John by the reality of the resurrection is present for Jesus. Jesus now sits at the right hand of the Father.[9] The reality of the incarnation fulfills the burden of messianic expectation from the Old Testament. The ascension glory of the reign of Jesus is wrapped up in the story of the church for Luke in Acts and in the story of the seven churches for John in Revelation.

John appropriates Ezekiel, but then innovates in the process by universalizing from just Israel mourning to "all tribes of the earth" mourning. The seeing is not sight, but perception, the same vision the disciples had to obtain to understand the nature of the messianic role Jesus came to fulfill in the plot of Mark's Gospel. In the Gospels, John 19:37 applies the same Ezekiel text to the events at the cross. Roman soldiers serving their Roman empire witness the death of Jesus and thereby gain depth of insight into the true Son of God and a different kingdom. The vision of the cross provokes two responses: a response of disobedience, which sets up fear of impending judgment at the coming of Jesus, and a response of faith, which sets up expectation of salvation at the coming of Jesus.

God's Affirmation

A divine proclamation in 1:8 concludes the proleptic presentation of the second coming using Old Testament allusions. God affirms that the sum of Christ's messianic actions in the incarnation is what Daniel and Ezekiel meant. Christ's incarnation is the end of days.[10] Christ's coming is God's coming, and Christ's coming is God's judgment.

In this divine affirmation, God proclaims himself as the Alpha and Omega. Alpha is an allusion to the beginning, so resonates with the creation story (Gen 1:1). Revelation being placed at the end of a

---

[9] As in the vision of Stephen (Acts 7:55–56).
[10] Rom 3:21; Heb 1:1–2; Acts 2:16–21.

canon that begins with Genesis is soundly theological: God is sovereign and consummates what he initiates. Eschatology is nothing more than creation theology's last chapter. God controls all in between this Genesis beginning and Revelation end. This control includes the seven churches of first-century Asia Minor. Revelation's last scenes proclaim this Alpha and Omega title (21:6; 22:13).

God also is the "Almighty." This title has dual function. The title undergirds the idea of the Lord of history's sovereignty as Alpha and Omega. God has the power to effect his will over his creation.[11] The title also fires a direct broadside against Roman imperial propaganda. The emperor may style himself as "self-powerful" in Roman imperial inscriptions, but God as true sovereign is "all powerful."

Summary

The prologue, or introduction, of Rev 1:1–8 offers the christological key to the central theology of the book. John is focused on gospel truths in the core of the story of Jesus. These gospel truths are fine-tuned to a persecution setting.

INAUGURAL VISION (1:9–20)

The introduction moves directly into the Inaugural Vision of the Son of Man. Like a president setting up the major themes of his presidency through his inaugural address to the nation, John's Inaugural Vision is setting up the major themes of his entire book with this address to the churches. Interpretation of Revelation derails immediately by ignoring the significance of beginning the drama with this scene. With its message of God's sovereignty in Christ versus Roman emperors, "John's opening vision contains the heart and kernel of the whole of the Revelation. The rest of the prophecy unfolds the significance of this vision of Christ, and how the destiny of his people find fulfillment."[12] The central vision of Revelation is this Inaugural Vision. Its central context is the church. Its central figure is the Son of Man.[13]

---

[11]The truth that God as creator means God is consummator is seen multiple times in Revelation (cf. 4:11; 10:6) and is the very essence of the new heaven and new earth vision at the end (21:1).

[12]Beasley-Murray, *Revelation*, 70, by way of referring to Lohmeyer.

[13]See Stevens, "One Like a Son of Man," 16–17.

Hermeneutical Key

The most important literary clue John has given to us from within his structure for how to interpret his Apocalypse is the opening vision. Opening visions always are the most important. They set the context. They set the audience. They set the plot. As the opening vision of Revelation, the vision of the Son of Man is the most important in all the Apocalypse, because this passage controls the interpretation of all subsequent visions in Revelation. Thus, this Inaugural Vision is our hermeneutical key to John's entire visionary experience and the heart of what he has to prophesy.

John's Commissioning (1:9–11)

Community Identification. With the opening identification "brother . . . fellow-sharer" (1:9), John indicates shared community. John here develops his kingdom theme from his introduction. This corporate feature is important. What applies in Revelation has a corporate and ecclesiological profile. The shared experience is "the persecution and kingdom and patient endurance." One Greek article controls all three nouns, which, being translated means, they all three together function as one composite reality. The kingdom is comprised of persecution, and the persecution is comprised of patient endurance. This persecution and its need for patient endurance seems to be the result of witness ("on account of the Word of God and the testimony of Jesus"). Believers are reigning through their faithful endurance in their present witness. John does not here speak of a future tribulation for which the church has to wait; he speaks of a present tribulation the church now endures. This kingdom imagery concords with Paul's own framing for believers in Antioch of Pisidia at the conclusion of the first missionary journey in Acts: "We must go through many tribulations to enter the kingdom of God" (Acts 14:22).

Yet, at the same time, while present reality, these elements each also have a future reality in Revelation. The tribulation is now (2:9), but also future (7:14). The kingdom is now (1:6), but also future (11:15). The perseverance is now (2:2), but also future (13:10). This duality implies the church has some unfinished business to fulfill. This trio of persecution, perseverance, kingdom characterization dovetails into the christological paradigm John will develop for the church.

Christological Paradigm. John circumscribes the entire experience that characterizes himself and his churches as "in Jesus" (1:9). This focus shows identification with Christ. Jesus' suffering becomes the church's paradigm. The reality is eschatological. The gospel call of Jesus to "take up a cross" shapes the church's eschatological destiny. The "testimony of Jesus" is both the witness Jesus gave (1:5, 16) and the witness Jesus receives (1:2). The context is forensic and anticipates Roman jurisprudence similar to Pliny's letter to Trajan asking what to do about those informed on as Christians in Bithynia, a province in northern Asia, and implying recanting the faith on the part of some as far as twenty years earlier, which would be in the time of Domitian.[14] Whatever human courts declare about those who testify to Christian faith, God will provide eschatological vindication.

Judgment Context. John tells the tale in the shadow of Old Testament commissioning. The "voice like a trumpet" (1:10) evokes Moses on Sinai (Exod 19:16) and Jewish theophany language, such that when John is commissioned to "write in a book," he evokes God's charge to prophets in their testaments of judgment against Israel (Exod 27:14; Isa 30:8; Jer 37:2). John insinuates judgment to come, which becomes the "big picture" outline of Revelation we have drawn: judgment of the church (Seven Letters, Rev 2–3) and judgment of the world (judgment cycle, Rev 6–20). The judgment happens in the literary product itself.

John is "in the Spirit," which is a heightened spiritual awareness. The exact circumstance of his physical or mental state is impossible to know. The point, however, is simple. Whatever state he is in, he is capable of receiving divine communication.

John's phrase, "on the Lord's day," has been misrepresented by futurists as indicating John's time machine teleportation to the future to witness the events of the "Day of the Lord." A parallel idea is that he was so overwhelmed by modern warfare—the supersonic jets, massive tanks, helicopter gunships, and nuclear holocaust—he just did the best he could manage with his limited vocabulary and primitive first-century knowledge of ancient warfare to try to describe the terrifying scenes he saw. Supposedly, that is why the imagery of Revelation is so bizarre. Actually, no. Revelation's imagery is "bizarre" only if one is

---

[14]Pliny *Letters* 10.96; cf. Ferguson, *Backgrounds*, 594–95.

unacquainted with the genre of first-century Jewish apocalypses to see how stereotypical and predictable John's images actually are.

John's phrase "on the Lord's day" actually is not even in the same form as the expression in the Old Testament prophets for the "Day of the Lord."[15] John's adjectival form is the same as Paul's expression for "the Lord's supper" (1 Cor 11:20). John's meaning is the day that belongs to and is dedicated to the Lord, like Paul's meaning is the supper that belongs to and is dedicated to the Lord. Not to pick this up is to miss a counterclaim on John's part in the context of the imperial *Sebaste*, the first day of every month that belongs to and is dedicated to Caesar.[16] Because of Jesus' resurrection on the first day of the week, early believers rapidly began speaking of Sunday as the "Lord's day." Pointedly, John receives his vision on the "Lord's day," the day dedicated to Jesus because of his resurrection, the true "ruler of the kings of the earth" because he is "firstborn of the dead" (1:5).[17]

Local Reality. John is told to write to "seven churches" (1:11). We do not need to allegorize these as seven stages of church history, which John never in any way insinuates and is exposed as false interpretation and a perennial abject failure in the history of interpretation. But why seven? Late first-century Asia Minor had more Christian communities than seven! John uses seven as symbolic of *all* the churches of Asia. The church universal and for all time is implied. Why use *these* seven? Probably two reasons: they best summarized conditions about which John had grave concerns for all the churches, and they were within the orbit of his itinerant ministry and prophetic authority.

Jesus' Appearance (1:12–16)

John sees Jesus. He signs four truths about Jesus in his appearance. John signs to us who Jesus is, where he is, how he is clothed, and what he looks like. The truth who he is—his identity—signs the fulfillment

---

[15] John's phrase is *en tēi kyriakēi ēmerai* (ἐν τῇ κυριακῇ ἡμέρᾳ), which is adjectival. The LXX expression is the standard noun form, *ē ēmera kyriou* (ἡ ἡμέρα κυρίου). The adjective form *kyriakos* simply never is used for the prophetic "Day of the Lord" in the LXX, the New Testament, or the early church fathers.

[16] Hemer, *Letters*, 31, 223. For numerous inscriptions illustrating the use of the adjective form *kyriakos* related to imperial rule and the emperor, cf. Deissmann, *Light from the Ancient East*, 361–62.

[17] Similar to Paul's quote of Roman creedal tradition in Rom 1:3–4.

of his messianic role. The truth where he is—his presence—signs what Jesus is doing post-resurrection. The truth how he is clothed—his functions—signs how Jesus fulfills his messianic functions of priest and king. The fourth truth, what he looks like, is John's way to signify how Jesus perfectly fulfills his identity, presence, and functions.

Who he is. This truth is one of identity. John turns to see the voice speaking like a trumpet, which imagery will play out later in the Trumpet judgments, and sees "one like a Son of Man" (1:13). The background is the Ancient of Days imagery of Dan 7 and 10, which is judicial, in whom John sees Jesus as the fulfillment as the latter-day, divine judge. Jesus is judge of the church in the Seven Letters (Rev 2–3), and judge of the world beginning with the seven seals (Rev 6–9) in which judgment occurs in historical forces unleashed by Messiah.[18]

John, however, also innovates Daniel's Ancient of Days judicial figure with the realities of the gospel. Son of Man is Jesus' favorite self-designation, used by Jesus to refer to himself more times than all other titles combined. In merging Daniel's imagery with his own teaching, Jesus generates a composite picture of one whose profile is heavenly origin, suffering ministry, redemptive death, and resurrected glory.[19] Jesus is judge, but his judgment is alien to Jewish expectation. Jesus took the traditional Jewish Son of Man language and transformed its imagery into one of suffering death. This passion image becomes the passion story of all the Gospels. Mark most brings this passion truth into its sharpest focus in his Gospel, as we already have seen. The nature of discipleship is determined by the nature of Messiah. Who Jesus is defines his followers. What is true for Jesus is true for believers. Jesus as Son of Man means the church's destiny is passion. If the church is in persecution, she is fulfilling her destiny.

Where he is. This truth is one of presence. Jesus is among the lampstands (1:12). Lampstands and stars are the only light at the beginning of this vision. Thus, the vision is a vision in the night. The world lies in darkness, and the only light comes from Christ and his churches.[20] In the Jewish context, lampstands evoke imagery of the

---

[18] Allusively reprising the storyline of Dan 10:21—12:13.

[19] The literature on the Son of Man terminology is immense. For a brief summary, see Stevens, "One Like a Son of Man," 18, n. 10.

[20] Stevens, "One Like a Son of Man," 19. Cf. Robbins, *Revelation*, 44.

presence of God.²¹ In a prophetic context, Jesus' presence among the lampstands suggests reversal of the curse of "Ichabod."²² Jesus among the lampstands signs the dynamic presence of Jesus among believers and is the functional equivalent of Luke's Pentecost, which for Luke is fulfillment of Joel's latter-day out-pouring of the Spirit. Jesus' presence in the church through the Spirit is the foundation of all prophetic activity of the church and of John's itinerant ministry among the seven churches. That Jesus stands among the lampstands is the basis of John's ministry and Jesus' judgment of the church. John has made an important connection for believers: *who* Jesus is determines *where* he is. The persecuted Son of Man sustains his persecuted churches by his presence among them. Unlike the Jerusalem temple destroyed by the Romans and its menorah light extinguished and taken to Rome to be part of Titus's triumph, the light of God's presence in the church never will be overcome.²³

How he is clothed. This truth is one of function. He is clothed in a robe to the feet and a golden sash about the waist (1:13). Clothing indicates function, and the robe and the sash indicate two interrelated functions.

First, Jesus wears a robe. Driven by the dual context of the temple allusion in the lampstands and the hieratic prologue language of "freed us from our sins" (1:5) and "made us ... priests" (1:6), the robe is priestly attire.²⁴ The hieratic function is salvation. Israel's priestly function is fulfilled in the person of Jesus. This priestly role of Jesus is highlighted in the book of Hebrews, whose author, as does John, also connects the priestly function to the community maintaining their

---

²¹From the seven constantly burning wicks of the tabernacle to the seven-branched menorah in the Solomonic temple (Exod 25:31–40).

²²Ichabod's mother went into shock and premature labor at his birth upon hearing her husband (Phineas) and father-in-law (Eli) had died and the Ark of the Covenant had gone into Philistine captivity; his name was explained as, "the glory has departed from Israel" (1 Sam 4:21).

²³See Fig. 1.25, p. 21.

²⁴Context entirely contradicts Aune's charge that a priestly view is "unfounded," *Revelation 1–5*, 93–94; A number of scholars do not see priestly allusion; cf. Resseguie, *The Revelation of John*, 76; Beasley-Murray, *Revelation*, 66–67; Osborn, *Revelation*, 89. Others do; cf. Beale, *Revelation*, 208; deSilva, *Honor, Patronage, Kinship, and Purity*, 309, n. 37; Smalley, *The Revelation to John*, 54.

confession.²⁵ Forgiveness of sins was to be a hallmark of the messianic age in traditional Jewish expectation, and this message was central to the ministry of Jesus and early Christian preaching: "For he delivered us from the authority of darkness, and transferred us into the kingdom of his beloved son, in whom we have redemption, the forgiveness of sins."²⁶

Later imagery in Revelation of priestly linen is derived from this Inaugural Vision of the Son of Man. White linen becomes symbolic of the purity of God's people and of their righteous deeds. The Lamb's bride is so clothed because of her purity and righteous deeds (19:8). The Rider's armies are so clothed also (19:14), which means this army is a priestly army, not a typical army.²⁷

Second, Jesus wears a sash. Driven by the dual context of the title God the "Almighty" (1:8) and the royal prologue language of "ruler of the kings of the earth" (1:5) and "made us a kingdom" (1:6), the sash is kingly attire.²⁸ The sash represents royal power and authority, as in Isaiah's prophecy of making Eliakim master of Hezekiah's palace.²⁹ The kingly function is judgment. The seven Bowl angels each wears a golden sash, a direct connection to the clothing of the Son of Man in this Inaugural Vision. So, in pouring out the Bowl judgments, these angels act in the power and authority of the Son of Man.

Kingship in Israel failed. The king was to represent God to Israel and Israel to God.³⁰ Tragically, the story of wickedness, idolatry, and court corruption as told in Kings and Chronicles ends with the final assessment: "The LORD, the God of their ancestors, sent persistently to them by his messengers, because he had compassion on his people and on his dwelling place; but they kept mocking the messengers of God, despising his words, and scoffing at his prophets, until the wrath of the LORD against his people became so great that there was no

---

²⁵Heb 4:14; 7:27; 9:12, 26; 10:2, 10. Cf. Rom 6:10; 1 Pet 3:18.

²⁶Col 1:13–14; cf. Matt 6:12; Acts 2:38.

²⁷Perhaps the imagery is inspired by Daniel's description of the wise as "refined, purified, and cleansed" (Dan 11:35). Other New Testament writers described their ministries as priestly service to God (Rom 15:16).

²⁸Cf. Murphy, *Fallen Is Babylon*, 90. The priest had a sash, but the color was blue, purple, and crimson, not gold (Exod 39:29).

²⁹Job 12:18; Isa 22:20–22.

³⁰1 Sam 8:7; Ps 2:6–7.

remedy" (2 Chr 36:15–16, NRSV). God had to come in judgment. The Northern Kingdom disappeared into Assyrian captivity. The Southern Kingdom only barely survived its Babylonian exile. This historical disaster left hanging Nathan's promise to David of an eternal Davidic throne (2 Sam 7:16).

After the exile was no better. The Hasmonean dynasty that came out of the Maccabean Revolt was completely Hellenized and became thoroughly perverted by Roman patronage. The Hasmoneans even attempted to combine the offices of priest and king, but the office was open to the highest bidder under Syrian control, and to the best client king under Roman patronage. The Herodian dynasty that followed the Hasmoneans was worse, more Roman than Jewish, more murderous than all.[31] One of Herod's sons, Archelaus (d. 18), was so wicked even the Romans had to banish him to Gaul. One of Herod's grandsons, Agrippa I (d. 44), killed James the son of Zebedee in Jerusalem and imprisoned Peter (Acts 12:1–17). Even to the end, as Jerusalem was going down in flames, both rebel Zealot leaders each in turn claimed to be king of Israel.[32] The way the story played out, kingship was a curse on Israel.

Even as the people cried out for a king like the other nations, God knew that "Sin would consume the kingship, and kingship would consume Israel."[33] God knew he would have to send a redeemer to deliver Israel from the curse of kingship. The Messiah that God sent marked God's greatest judgment against Israel's kingship, for Messiah was the antithesis of any who ever occupied Israel's throne.[34] The eternal Davidic kingdom Nathan promised really was not established by David. That kingdom was established by Messiah. Jesus plays on this irony in his question that baffled the scribes: "How can the scribes say that Messiah is the son of David? David himself declared by the Holy Spirit, 'The Lord said to my Lord, "sit at my right hand, until I put your enemies under your feet."' David himself calls him Lord; so

---

[31] Executing as many as forty-five of the royal Hasmoneans; cf. Burge, Cohick, and Green, *The New Testament in Antiquity*, 39.

[32] Josephus *J.W.* 2.7.8; 4.9.3. For detailed filling out of this tragic storyline of Israel's kingship, cf. Stevens, "One Like a Son of Man," 23–28.

[33] Stevens, "One Like a Son of Man," 27.

[34] This judgment is anticipated in the cleansing of the temple episode (Mark 11:15–18; Matt 21:12–27; Luke 19:45–48; John 2:13–22).

how can he be his son?" (Mark 12:35–37). The only true king that ever occupied Israel's throne according to the divine intention for Israel's kingship, and the only one who could establish that throne forever according to Nathan's prophecy, was Jesus, the true lion of the tribe of Judah (Rev 5:5).

With his imagery of the clothing of the Son of Man, John has fused the two functions of priest and king in one person. The failed attempt by the Hasmonean dynasty to combine the roles of priest and king in Israel was realized in Jesus. The enthroned Jesus now has all authority in heaven and earth.[35]

What he looks like. This truth signifies how Jesus perfectly fulfills the other three truths—his identity, presence, and functions. The features are seven in number to symbolize that Jesus perfectly fulfills his suffering identity as Son of Man, glorified presence in the church, and messianic functions of priest and king.

- head and hair: white (1:14), symbolic of heavenly origin, eternity, purity, and allusive to Daniel's Ancient of Days and judgment:

    > As I watched,
    > thrones were set in place,
    >   and an Ancient One took his throne,
    > his clothing was white as snow,
    >   and the hair of his head like pure wool (Dan 7:9, NRSV)

    John develops the features of Jesus so closely related to God as to be difficult to distinguish, and this is the reason Revelation is said to have a "high Christology."[36] Even Jesus' titles, such as the "First and Last" (1:18), echo divine titles, as in "Alpha and Omega" (1:8). John is declaring that the divine judgment Daniel anticipated would be executed by the Ancient of Days is realized in the Son of Man.

- eyes: flame of fire (1:14), allusive of infallible insight, omniscient knowledge. Fiery eyes was a frequent metaphor in Greek and Latin literature, especially in descriptions of the gods, among others.[37] The penetrating vision of the Son of Man reveals even the deepest and darkest secrets. Revealing secrets of the heart was part of the

---

[35]Cf. Matt 28:16–18; Eph 1:20–21; Phil 2:9–11.

[36]Cf. John 1:2; 3:13; Col 1:17; 1 Thess 4:16; Heb 4:15; 7:24–26, 28; 2 Pet 1:1.

[37]Aune, *Revelation 1–5*, 95.

ministry of Jesus and a function of the Holy Spirit in the church, and is reflected by the author of Hebrews: "No creature is hidden from his sight, but all things are open and laid bare to the eyes of him with whom we have to do" (Heb 4:13).[38] The eyes coordinate with the judgment theme of the first feature. Thus, when this one says, "I know," as in the letters to the churches, then he knows. The churches are commended for their good, but warned about the bad. The judgment of the Ancient of Days arrives in the moment the letters from the Son of Man first are read aloud to each church. The backdrop would be unjust administration in the Roman imperial system. Not only were the social elite immune in their patronage system, bribes to local Roman officials were rife and expected.[39] Jesus sees all and judges rightly without prejudice, a threat to those who do evil, but a consolation to those who do good. As the Chronicler said, "For the eyes of the Lord move to and fro throughout the earth that He may strongly support those whose heart is completely His" (2 Chr 16:9, NASB). Paul encouraged believers at Corinth, "be steadfast, immovable, always abounding in the work of the Lord, knowing that your toil is not in vain in the Lord" (1 Cor 15:58).

- feet: burnished bronze (1:15), allusive of strength and stability. The Son of Man is unmoved wherever he plants his feet. In this vision, he is standing among the lampstands. He will not be removed from his churches. Persecution with its dire straits for believers does not mean their security in Christ is challenged. Even martyrdom is not the last word, not for One who has the power of resurrection (1:5). Jude's doxology reflects this thought, "to him who is able to keep you from stumbling, and to make you stand in the presence of his glory blameless with great joy" (Jude 24). Ephesians too has its own echo in the words, "be strong in the Lord, and in the strength of his might" (Eph 6:10). Imperial statues of victorious Roman generals often depicted the conquered under the foot of the general, as in a famous statue of Hadrian. When the typical statuary pose of a conquered people is under the foot of the victor, this image of the Son of Man with feet of burnished bronze is counter propaganda.

---

[38] Cf. John 1:48; Luke 11:17; Acts 5:1–10.

[39] Even the Judean governor Felix anticipated a bribe from Paul (Acts 24:26).

FIGURE 10.3. Victorious Hadrian (d. 138). Traditional ceremonial military cuirass and conquest and subjugation pose; the humiliated, shamed barbarian in disproportionate size under foot (IAM).

- voice: sound of many waters (1:15), allusive of majesty and absolute authority. Many waters would be like the crashing of sea breakers against the cliffs of Patmos when enraged by a storm. Who can be heard above the roar? When Jesus speaks, the cosmos listens. What the Son of Man says, no one contradicts. A similar biblical metaphor is divine thunder, as Israel heard at Sinai (Exod 19:16), or in response to Jesus' prayer (John 12:29). In an eschatological context, "an hour is coming and now is, when the dead shall hear the voice of the Son of God, and those who hear shall live" (John 5:25), and Paul's revelation, "for the Lord himself will descend from heaven with a shout, with the voice of the archangel and the trumpet of God" (1 Thess 4:16). The words of Jesus that John has preserved by writing Revelation, both to the church (Rev 2–3) and to the world (Rev 4–20), are authoritative decrees that never will be remanded. In the context of ancient Roman imperial propaganda revealed in inscriptions, coins, statuary, and architecture, John's description of the Son of Man is subversive rhetoric.[40]

- right hand: seven stars (1:16), later identified as the seven angels of the seven churches (1:20). The stars are seven because the churches are seven. The Bible is saturated with imagery of the right hand.[41] The general meaning in this biblical imagery is strength, security, and positions of honor. The meaning of stars is in concert with the lampstands to imply a vision in the night. The world lies in darkness. The meaning of the stars as seven angels is inconclusive. The reason is because the association between particular churches and angels is unique in the New Testament, and even in Revelation is restricted to this Inaugural Vision and the addressee elements of the following

---

[40] Similarly on Rome and Caesar's unique place and universal message in antiquity, cf. Wright, *Paul and the Faithfulness of God*, 1318. We illustrated imperial ideology at Aphrodisias. To pursue the topic in depth with copious illustrations, see Zanker, *The Power of Images in the Age of Augustus*. The impact upon religion is explored by Elliott, *The Arrogance of Nations*, 124–25. For a challenge to American ideology, see Kraybill, *Apocalypse and Allegiance*.

[41] Inheritance blessing (Gen 48:14); receiving ram's blood (Exod 29:20); swearing an oath (Dan 12:7); the place of honor by the king (1 Kgs 2:19; Ps 16:11; 45:9; 110:1; Matt 26:64; Luke 22:69; Acts 2:33; 7:55; Rom 8:34; Eph 1:20; Col 3:1; Heb 1:3; 8:1; 10:12; 12:2; 1 Pet 3:22); God's security (Ps 16:8; 139:10); God's salvation (Ps 17:7; 20:6; 60:5; 108:6; 138:7); God's righteousness (Isa 41:10); God's power (Exod 15:6; Deut 33:2; Ps 18:35; 44:3; 60:5; 63:8; 73:23; 80:17; 89:13; 98:1; 118:15; Isa 48:13; 62:8; Acts 5:31).

Seven Letters.[42] Without New Testament parallels, we are left to argue whether metaphorical of pastors.[43] At the same time, John has an abiding interest in prophetic leadership and related functions of testimony and witness (1:3, 9). At the end of the vision, when John faints as dead, he specifically says the *right hand* of the Son of Man raised him up (1:17). This is the hand with the seven stars, which are seven angels. John perhaps uses this action as a literary clue that angels of the churches are connected to church prophets. Polycarp, bishop of Smyrna, in his martyrdom was characterized as an angel: "for they were no longer men but already angels."[44] Note that an angel mediated the original vision of Revelation to John (1:1). Held in the strong, right hand of the Son of Man, local prophets faithful to God in their testimony about Jesus insure the church's prophetic mission and destiny sustained by the mediation of angels. As Oden noted, "Thus the Spirit protects the continuity of the Word in history, ensuring that the whole church does not at any given time completely err, and that it does not err in the foundation."[45] John's aim is on Jezebel and the Nicolaitans to expose their false witness.[46]

- mouth: sharp, two-edged sword (1:16), martial imagery allusive of war, but "out of the mouth" means not a normal war. Rather, this is a war of words, of witness and testimony. Sword imagery in biblical contexts normally implies a word of judgment.[47] John uses martial imagery throughout Revelation, but some interpreters do not pick up that John's rhetoric is subversive.[48] This sword is not in hand, as in normal warfare. Rather, this sword is out of the mouth, which makes all attempts to represent this artistically somewhat clumsy.

---

[42] After a long excursus on the matter of angels of the churches here in Rev 1:20, Aune comes to no conclusion, but says the question "continues to be a major problem in the interpretation of Revelation," *Revelation 1–5*, 108. For other New Testament references not covered by Aune, see Stevens, "One Like a Son of Man," 33, n. 48.

[43] Since every other occurrence of angel is reference to divine beings in Revelation, trying to read angel as metaphorical is an uphill battle. However, an integral connection to the prophetic office of the church and her prophets may be in mind.

[44] *Mart. Poly.* 2.3.

[45] Oden, *The Rebirth of Orthodoxy*, 46.

[46] deSilva, *Seeing Things John's Way*, 331.

[47] Hanson, *The Wrath of the Lamb*, 166–67.

[48] Cf. Barr, "The Lamb Who Looks Like a Dragon," 205–06.

The only weapon in this war is words. Isaiah confirms this way of framing the conflict, as the expected Davidic ruler will "strike the earth with the rod of his mouth" and will vanquish the wicked "with the breath of his lips" (Isa 11:4, NRSV).[49] This conflict is of witness and testimony, the claims of Caesar versus the claims of Christ. The sword coming out of the mouth of the Son of Man is the theological equivalent of Jesus' penetrating question to his disciples in Mark 8:29—"Who do you say that I am?"—now addressed to believers in late first-century Asia Minor. John's sword has two characteristics. Being sharp, the sword cuts through anything, including Roman imperial propaganda, as in Virgil's almost euphoric celebration of the world Augustus created as savior and peacemaker.[50] Being two-edged, the sword cuts two ways, negatively as judgment, but positively as salvation.[51] John's use here echoes that in Hebrews, "For the Word of God is living and active and sharper than any two-edged sword, and piercing even as far as the division of soul and spirit, of both joints and marrow, and able to judge the thoughts and intentions of the heart" (Heb 4:12). With this "sword out of the mouth" imagery in the Inaugural Vision of the Son of Man, we can read ahead to be sure we make the connection John intended with the rider on the white horse in Rev 19. Note that this rider "judges and makes war" (Rev 19:11), but he is entitled the "Word of God" (19:13), not "Whack 'em Dead Warrior." This rider is no Mel Gibson of "Braveheart" fame. Instead, this warrior is given the description "from his mouth comes a sharp sword" (19:15), which is how those defeated are slain "by the sword of the rider on the horse, the sword that came from his mouth" (19:21). What kind of a war is that?

- face: sun in its strength (1:16), allusive of glorious power and deity. The sun shining in its strength is the sun in the brightest part of its heavenly circuit. Do not miss the drama of this feature. This feature

---

[49]Isaiah's imagery in Isa 11:4 and John's imagery in Rev 1:16 echoes in the unusual description of the destruction of the lawless one in 2 Thess 2:8, "whom the Lord Jesus will destroy with the breath of his mouth."

[50]*Ecl.* 4. Ferguson pointed out the "almost 'messianic' aura that surrounded the expectations of people in the Augustan age," *Backgrounds of Early Christianity*, 114. Cf. Horace, *Epistles* 2.1.15; Perriman, *The Coming of the Son of Man*, 163.

[51]Cf. Reddish, *Revelation*, 41.

is a sudden and stunning reversal of the Inaugural Vision's opening setting in darkness—lampstands and stars. The Bible is replete with images of light, radiance, and glory for deity, and the New Testament decidedly moves in this direction in descriptions of Jesus.[52] A similar appearance is given to believers in glorification.[53] Looking Jesus in the face, seeing him for who he really is, transfigures the reality of this life.[54] The light of Christ overcomes any darkness.

FIGURE 10.4. Apocalypse Tapestry, Rev 1:9–20. The Son of Man on a throne in front of seven candles, which are the seven churches. He is arrayed in white for purity, with a priestly robe and kingly golden sash. Stars in his right hand, book in his left, sword in his mouth, he is allusive of a regal judge, Daniel's Ancient of Days, which will tie into the great white throne. John is lying prostrate (Panel 1, Scene 3, Angers, France).

Thus, in sum, with white head and hair and eyes like a flame of fire, Jesus is Lord of judgment. With feet of burnished bronze and a

---

[52] Moses coming down from Sinai (Exod 34:29–35), Jesus' transfiguration (Mark 9:3; Matt 17:1–2), and Paul's Damascus Road (Acts 9:3–5). Colossians affirms of Jesus, "in him all the fullness of deity dwells in bodily form" (Col 2:9), to which thought Hebrews adds, "he is the radiance of his glory and the exact representation of his nature" (Heb 1:3). Finally, we have the imagery in 2 Thessalonians of Jesus returning "in flaming fire" (2 Thess 1:7).

[53] Believers are transformed "into conformity with the body of his glory" (Phil 3:21) and have the promise that "he has glorified us to share in the inheritance of the saints in light" (Col 1:12; cf. Col 3:3–4). On deity, see Resseguie, *The Revelation of John*, 79.

[54] In a similar vein, cf. Robbins, "Only as Christ is seen for what he really is can anything else be seen in true perspective," *The Revelation of Jesus Christ*, 45.

voice like many waters, Jesus is Lord of strength. With a hand holding seven stars and a mouth with a sword, Jesus is Lord of witness. With a face shining like the sun, Jesus is Lord.

Jesus' Self Description (1:17–18)

John faints at Jesus' feet. Such a post-visionary faint is a typical pattern in apocalyptic literature at receiving an Inaugural Vision: the visionary receives a vision, falls prostrate, receives strengthening by the angelic mediator, then has further visions. John's addition of "as dead" is an interesting wrinkle. This distinction has drawn the attention of some commentators about the possibility that John intends this to be read as parabolic action giving a resurrection picture. While such a meaning is possible, the rhetoric seems a little more subtle than characterizes John in general.

Jesus reassures John. John specifically notes that Jesus puts his *right* hand on John, which, in the Inaugural Vision just related, is the hand that holds the seven stars that are going to be identified in 1:20 as the angels of the seven churches. A connection could be inferred, then, between John and the meaning of the stars that are angels. The stars (angels) have to do with the prophetic office and the leadership of the seven churches. A possibility exists, then, that the stars/angels represent the local leadership in these congregations that are in John's camp versus those of the Jezebel, Nicolaitans persuasion.

Jesus predicates himself with "I am" statements (1:18). His self identification is in terms of attributes of God from the Old Testament. As "first and last," echoing the name of God in 1:8, Jesus, like God, is both the beginning and the end, therefore in control of all in between, which would include Domitian and Asia Minor.

Jesus adds, "the living one," which seems a tad tautological in the context of actually talking to someone. (Give the thought a moment.) This is theology in the making, not casual conversation. That is, this typical Jewish way of describing God now is the truth of resurrection folding back from the end of time into time because of history. All that resurrection doctrine promises about future judgment, vindication, and blessedness already is present reality in the person of Jesus. "Done deal," in our vernacular.

To insure this "life" is not framed as the kind of life one might expect as a citizen of Domitian's Roman empire and under Roman patronage, the gospel storyline is brought to bear. This "life" is restated more explicitly as "I was dead, and, behold, I am alive forever and ever," echoing the "firstborn of the dead" (1:5) in the prologue. While "alive forever" pertains exclusively to God in Revelation,[55] the previous description, "I was dead," never is true of God. This reality is history, Jesus' incarnation, death, and resurrection, made explicit. This "life" related to Jesus has infinitely deeper, richer quality and eternal consequences, nothing like any patron of the Roman empire could promise, much less actually provide.

Jesus enhances the truth about the power of life resident within him and available to believers by adding, "I have the keys of Death and of Hades." Hades is the Greek equivalent of the Hebrew "Sheol," the place of the dead, but only a shadowy existence not well defined or elaborated in Jewish thought. Since creation indicates God intended life and Eden, these are the enemies of God. They become actual characters in Revelation's drama destined for judgment (20:13–14). Death is the portal and Hades is the destination that circumvents God's creative will for humans.[56] However, these characters are made to give up their captives and then consigned to the lake of fire. Persecution might incur loss of this life but never will impact that life under God's sovereign control. Ultimate sovereignty belongs not to the one who can kill and deliver one over to the power of Death and Hades, but to the one who can control the ultimate outcome and keep one out of the lake of fire.[57]

Since Jesus has the keys of Death and of Hades, he has the power to be the "ruler of the kings of the earth," as declared in 1:5. The title suggests one of the plotlines in Revelation. Kings of the earth will set themselves in opposition to Jesus, because humans like to pretend to be sovereign, and when they do, set themselves to oppose the One who can challenge their claim. All such opposition will be judged. So, in Revelation's drama, rebellious kings of earth are destroyed.[58]

---

[55] Rev 4:9; 15:7.

[56] Against Aune's contention that the popular Asia Minor myth of Hekate who held the keys to the gates of Hades is in view, cf. Stevens, "One Like a Son of Man," 38, n. 68.

[57] A compatible thought is Paul's description of Death as the last eschatological enemy to be overcome in 1 Cor 16:15. Cf. Murphy, *Fallen Is Babylon*, 95.

[58] Rev 6:15; 10:11; 16:12, 14; 17:2, 9, 12, 14, 18; 18:3, 9; 19:18, 19.

John's Commission (1:19–20)

The command, "Therefore, write" (1:19), forms an *inclusio* with the earlier command, "write what you see" (1:11) and marks off the vision of the Son of Man as a distinct literary unit. After being revived, John is recommissioned, which reaffirms his prophetic authority. The logical "therefore" looks backward in several ways.

First, the backward glance is to the one speaking having the keys of Death and Hades, therefore write. Regardless the consequences of the Roman imperial system, write. Do not fear death, for the one giving the commission has overcome that enemy. Second, the key of the Inaugural Vision of the Son of Man has been granted, therefore write. In the avalanche of visions to come, write. Do not fear interpreting the drama, for reminders of the opening vision will provide guideposts along the way. Third, you are God's prophet for God's time, therefore write. Even in the face of serious challenges confronting the churches of Asia Minor, write. All the churches of Asia Minor need to hear the prophetic word—from the very large and wealthy congregations to the small and poverty stricken; from the troubled and persecuted congregations to the spiritually lukewarm without any sense of conflict; from the outwardly active but spiritually static congregations to the faithful few ready for even greater opportunities; even the doctrinally pure but evangelistically challenged congregations—they all need to hear the prophetic call to obedience.

The commission to write grammatically has three objects: (1) the things you saw, (2) the things that are, (3) the things that are going to happen. The problem is how to interpret the three elements. The issue is significant, since many use the grammar to develop an outline of the book.[59] Two basic options are structural and non-structural.

Structural. The direct objects identify the book's structure in a temporal sequence. One variation is that the three direct objects are a three-part outline of the book. The "things you saw" is the Inaugural Vision in Rev 1:9–20. The "things that are" are the Seven Letters in Rev 2–3. The "things to be" are the visions of Rev 4–22. The view ignores the Greek grammar of the tense of "things you saw," which

---

[59]One of the most extensive discussions is in Beale, *Revelation*, 153–77, which has good content, but is somewhat convoluted and not lucidly organized.

more likely refers to the entire content of the book.⁶⁰ The second variation recognizes that the verbal aspect of "things you saw" anticipates the entire book, but the effort still is made to make the other two direct objects temporal, such that "things that are" is Rev 1–3, and the "things to be" is Rev 4–22. The fatal flaw of any iteration of a temporal view is the constant mixing of past, present, and future tenses we see throughout Revelation. Revelation's tenses simply are not homogenous in any of its parts as a temporal view would require.

Non-structural. The non-structural option is that Rev 1:19 does not reflect the chronological structure of the book's content. Rather, John's grammar expresses some other literary feature of the book or of the nature of his visions themselves. Three main variations of a non-structural view are centered on the concepts of simultaneity, eschatology, or genre.

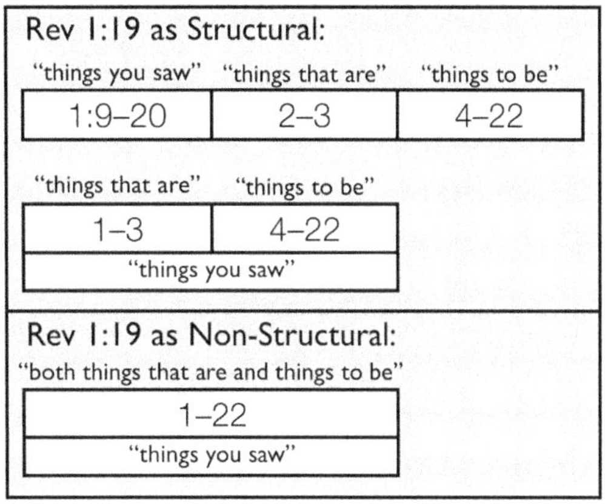

Rev 1:19 as Structural:		
"things you saw"	"things that are"	"things to be"
1:9–20	2–3	4–22

"things that are"	"things to be"
1–3	4–22
"things you saw"	

Rev 1:19 as Non-Structural:
"both things that are and things to be"
1–22
"things you saw"

FIGURE 10.5. Grammar and Structure of Rev 1:19.

Simultaneity. This view recognizes present tense and future tense in the expressions of the second and third direct objects, but not as the structural sequence of the book. Rather, drawing upon the grammar of the linked conjunctions, this view understands the direct objects to express simultaneity in all the visions: the visions both are true now and will continue to be true into the future.⁶¹ Thus, the first direct object ("things you saw") overviews the entire book. Then, the other two direct objects ("things that are" and "things to be") also overview the entire book, but from a dual perspective of what was confronting the churches in first-century Asia Minor, and from the perspective of si-

---

⁶⁰The verbal aspect of the second aorist tense *eides* (εἶδες) as undefined reflects the perspective of surveying the whole of an action. Cf. Stagg, "The Abused Aorist," 222–31; Porter, *Verbal Aspect*, 182–88; Fanning, *Verbal Aspect*, 97; McKay, *A New Syntax of the Verb*, 46.

⁶¹The conjunction sequence *kai . . . kai* (καί . . . καί) taken as "both . . . and."

multaneously what will be issues confronting the church throughout the church age.

<u>Eschatology</u>. This view puts emphasis on John's perspective as informed by Dan 2. The prophet Daniel anticipated the "last days" when God's kingdom would be realized. For Daniel that reality was off in the future. Because of the incarnation, Daniel's future John takes as his present. John takes Daniel's "after these things" which are in the "last days" and makes them equivalent to his "these things," that is, all his visions, which are kingdom truths realized in Jesus, at least in inaugural form. Thus, John's third direct object, "after these things" is his inaugurated eschatology, the fulfillment of Daniel's eschatological "last days" in Dan 2:28–29, 45, taken as inaugurated by Jesus. Revelation portrays present eschatological fulfillment of Daniel's "last days," which is expressed in all three tenses throughout Revelation.

<u>Genre</u>. The three object clauses do not describe the timing of the visions but the literary nature of the visions as apocalyptic genre. The first object, "what you have seen" is reference to the visionary experience itself, the fundamental basis for writing apocalyptic literature. The second object, "things that are," is reference to "what they mean," "the realities to which the visions point figuratively." The third object, "things to be," is reference to the eschatology of apocalyptic, whose topic is the "last days" and the arrival of the kingdom of God. Since Jesus has come to establish the kingdom of God, the last days are here and will be consummated by Jesus in the future.

Non-structural views have stronger viability simply on the distribution of tenses in Revelation alone. They also are more faithful to the apocalyptic genre of the literature. In fact, the non-structural views are not exclusive. All three reinforce each other. One rises above the other simply depending upon the emphasis sought. Thus, we conclude that Rev 1:19 is not intended by John as a structural outline of the book.

Old Testament prophets wrote to inscribe words of judgment to come. John writes similarly. As he writes, God's words of judgment come down on the church and on the world. As with Old Testament prophets, the judgment is in the literary product itself. In John's case this is the book of Revelation.

After the recommission to write about the visions he received, John is told the "mystery" of the Inaugural Vision (1:20). The word for the "mystery" (*mystērion*, μυστήριον) occurs only in Daniel in the Old

Testament.⁶² Mystery in Daniel relates to the ability to interpret obscure dreams as the actions of a sovereign God in history. Similarly, the sovereign God has acted decisively in history in Jesus, and John has had a vision about that action. John is told the core truth of the Son of Man vision is the seven stars and the seven lampstands. The seven stars are angels of the seven churches (prophetic leadership aligned with John), and the seven lampstands are the seven churches. John is interpreting Jesus as the fulfillment of Dan 7 and 10.

Summary

The Inaugural Vision in Rev 1:9–20 offers the hermeneutical key to the symbolic imagery of the book. The point of this symbolic imagery is to declare that God is sovereign over his creation. God has chosen to express his sovereignty through sending his Messiah. The events of the incarnation revealed that Christ has chosen to express his lordship in the figure of the Son of Man, which combines the image of Daniel's Ancient of Days and judgment with an ironic fulfillment in suffering and dying. The point of the spear of Christ's lordship as Son of Man in the present time is the church in her faithful witness in persecution.

Thus, through a seamless christological movement from the prologue (1:1–8) to the Inaugural Vision (1:9–20), John in the first chapter of Revelation reveals that the book's imagery and symbolism will focus on Christology (Son of Man) and ecclesiology (seven churches) in order to present the grand drama of soteriology (how God conquers evil). With the context of the Inaugural Vision's revelation of the Son of Man being his presence among the lampstands, which, to leave absolutely no confusion whatsoever, John explicitly indicates are the seven churches of Asia Minor, then John is making clear that the church is the context for all of Revelation. In short, for John, Daniel's "last days" expectation boils down to the seven churches and their prophetic leadership. Revelation is all about the seven churches. The inference we will draw from John's literary design is that realities in play with these seven churches John is presenting as the paradigm for the historical denouement of the church age, when the church reprises in history what the story of the Son of Man revealed in time.

⁶²Dan 2:18, 19, 27, 28, 29, 30, 47, all in eschatological contexts. Outside of Daniel in the Catholic canon, the word occurs only in the later books of the Apocrypha.

SEVEN LETTERS (2:1—3:22)

Literary Analysis

In form and content, the letters really are prophetic judgment oracles, which fulfills John's characterization of Revelation as a "prophecy" (1:3). In form, each letter has a prophetic opening in a typical formula of prophetic oracles often used in the LXX translation.[63] In content, each letter is comprised of prophetic judgment exhortations. Further, the identification of the one speaking uses characteristics of the Son of Man given in the Inaugural Vision, with each particular characteristic tailored to the needed word to that specific congregation. So, Ephesus hears now that the one speaking is he "who holds the seven stars in his right hand, who walks among the seven golden lampstands" (2:1). With these direct, linguistic ties back to the Inaugural Vision, the letter recipients know without any doubt that the one addressing them authoritatively with the prophetic "Thus says" is the glorified Son of Man speaking divine oracles of judgment, taking on his eschatological role as the Ancient of Days, executing judgment on his church. The eschatological judgments happen in real time the moment the letters first are read to these seven congregations. Thus, the letters actualize the Son of Man's judgment, expressing God's sovereignty through a reigning Lord. That this judgment of the seven churches by the Son of Man in these Seven Letters has in view the entire literary scope of all Revelation's visions is confirmed by the repetition of the "coming soon" theme of the Seven Letters in the conclusion of the book (22:7), as well as repetition of the promised "reward" for faithfulness theme of the Seven Letters at the end (22:12). This literary framing of beginning and end using themes from the Seven Letters rebuts the view that the absence of the word "church" in Rev 4–22 implies the absence of the church.[64] No one wants to use the exact same argument to insist that

---

[63]"Thus says," *Tade legei*, Τάδε λέγει. Cf. Exod 4:22; Josh 7:13; Judg 6:8; 1 Sam 2:27; 2 Sam 7:8; 1 Kgs 11:31; 2 Kgs 2:21; 1 Chr 17:7; 2 Chr 11:4; Isa 1:24; Jer 2:2; Ezek 4:13; Dan 14:34; Amos 1:6; Obad 1; Mic 2:3; Nah 1:12; Hag 1:2; Zech 1:3; Mal 1:4.

[64]An argument from silence supposedly proving the "rapture" has occurred in 4:1 and the rest of Revelation is all about one brief moment at the end of history of a seven-year period called the "Great Tribulation." Hermeneutically, this argument sorely begs the question of original meaning and leaves no way for the original readers to "keep" the prophecy as commanded in the first place (1:3).

because God never explicitly is identified as the "one sitting upon the throne" that God is not sitting on heaven's throne.

In structure, the letters are uniform. All letters display the same sevenfold division: address, identification, account, assessment, exhortation, promise, call. Often these structural elements are easy to spot, even in English translation, because they are so stylistically formulaic. The address always is: "To the angel of the church in . . . write." The identification is strongly formulaic, using the prophetic oracle introduction, "Thus says," followed by literary allusions to the previous Son of Man vision. The account has the recurring verb, "I know," often in the form, "I know your works," or variations. The assessment usually is notated by an adversative conjunction followed by the first person, "But I," and variations. The exhortation is marked by second person plural imperative verbs, such as "remember," "repent," "do," that offer ways to remedy the deficiencies noted in the prior assessment section. The promise uses a form of the verb for "conquer," either as "The one who conquers," or as "to the one who conquers," followed by imagery with eschatological nuance. The concluding call is rigidly formulaic: "Let the one who has an ear hear what the Spirit says to the churches." The call, however, is varied on a 3/4 pattern into which John often breaks his seven sequences. That is, in the first three letters, the call is before the promise section, but in the last four, the call is after.

Seven Letters—Seven-fold Structure	
1. Address	"To the angel of the church in . . . write"
2. Identification	"Thus says," with Son of Man allusions
3. Account	"I know your works" (minor variations)
4. Assessment	"But I" first person assessment
5. Exhortation	"Remember," etc. imperative verbs
6. Promise	"The one who conquers" ("To the one")
7. Call	"Let the one who has an ear hear . . ."

FIGURE 10.6. Seven Letters—Sevenfold Structure.

The exegetical significance of this uniformity is that the Seven Letters are to be interpreted as one complete literary unit, a unitary whole, not individually. No letter ever had a separate existence apart from this group of seven in Revelation, nor was any letter ever sent individually to any congregation. Thus, though each letter addresses a particular congregation with exhortations that are tailored to that congregation, all the letters are meant for all the congregations. This unitary purpose of all Seven Letters working together is confirmed by the verbatim conclusion shared by all the letters, each ending with the exact same appeal and expressed in the plural: "Let the one who has an ear hear what the Spirit says to the *churches*."[65] Each letter is heard by all. The letters mutually interpret each other and work in concert. What the Son of Man says to one church, he says to all the churches. The number seven universalizes the message to any church in any age and every church in every age, but most especially to the church confronted by Gog and Magog at the end of the ages.

	Ephesus	Symrna	Pergamum	Thyatira	Sardis	Philadelphia	Laodicea
	Rev 2				Rev 3		
1. Address	1	8	12	18	1	7	14
2. Identification	1	8	12	18	1	7	14
3. Account	2–3	9	13	19	1	8	15
4. Assessment	4	10	14–15	20–23	2	9–10	16–18
5. Exhortation	5–6	10	16	24–25	3–4	11	19–20
6. Promise	7b	11b	17b	26–28	5	12	21
7. Call	7a	11a	17a	29	6	13	22

FIGURE 10.7. Seven Letters—Verse Structure.

Our procedure in the following discussion will be to survey each of the letters to the seven churches but not for intense, word-for-word exegesis. Rather we will emphasize their interlocking intratextuality to make the point about their unity. The following tables outline the content. More could be said with details in any individual letter, but for these details, the reader is directed to the superb critical commentaries we now have available, as well as numerous ancillary publications, some of which show up in the following footnotes.

[65] Emphasis added; cf. Rev 2:7, 11, 17, 29; 3:6, 13, 22.

	EPHESUS	SMYRNA	PERGAMUM	THYATIRA	SARDIS	PHILADELPHIA	LAODICEA
ADDRESS	2:1 "To the angel of the church in Ephesus write:	2:8 "And to the angel of the church in Smyrna write:	2:12 "And to the angel of the church in Pergamum write:	2:18 "And to the angel of the church in Thyatira write:	3:1 "And to the angel of the church in Sardis write:	3:7 "And to the angel of the church in Philadelphia write:	3:14 "And to the angel of the church in Laodicea write:
IDENTIFI.	'The words of him who holds the seven stars in his right hand, who walks among the seven golden lampstands.	'The words of the first and the last, who died and came to life.	'The words of him who has the sharp two-edged sword.	'The words of the Son of God, who has eyes like a flame of fire, and whose feet are like burnished bronze.	'The words of him who has the seven spirits of God and the seven stars.	'The words of the holy one, the true one, who has the key of David, who opens and no one shall shut, who shuts and no one opens.	'The words of the Amen, the faithful and true witness, the beginning of God's creation.
ACCOUNT	2:2 "'I know your works, your toil and your patient endurance, and how you cannot bear evil men but have tested those who call themselves apostles but are not, and found them to be false; 2:3 I know you are enduring patiently and bearing up for my name's sake, and you have not grown weary.	2:9 "'I know your tribulation and your poverty (but you are rich) and the slander of those who say that they are Jews and are not, but are a synagogue of Satan.	2:13 "'I know where you dwell, where Satan's throne is; you hold fast my name and you did not deny my faith even in the days of Antipas my witness, my faithful one, who was killed among you, where Satan dwells.	2:19 "'I know your works, your love and faith and service and patient endurance, and that your latter works exceed the first.	"'I know your works; you have the name of being alive, and you are dead.	3:8 "'I know your works. Behold, I have set before you an open door, which no one is able to shut; I know that you have but little power, and yet you have kept my word and have not denied my name.	3:15 "'I know your works: you are neither cold nor hot. Would that you were cold or hot!

FIGURE 10.8. Seven Letters—Contents.

	EPHESUS	SMYRNA	PERGAMUM	THYATIRA	SARDIS	PHILADELPHIA	LAODICEA
ASSESS.	2:4 But I have this against you, that you have abandoned the love you had at first.	2:10 Do not fear what you are about to suffer. Behold, the devil is about to throw some of you into prison, that you may be tested, and for ten days you will have tribulation.	2:14 But I have a few things against you: you have some there who hold the teaching of Balaam, who taught Balak to put a stumbling block before the sons of Israel, that they might eat food sacrificed to idols and practice immorality. 2:15 So you also have some who hold the teaching of the Nicolaitans.	2:20 But I have this against you, that you tolerate the woman Jezebel, who calls herself a prophetess and is teaching and beguiling my servants to practice immorality and to eat food sacrificed to idols. 2:21 I gave her time to repent, but she refuses to repent of her immorality. 2:22 Behold, I will throw her on a sickbed, and those who commit adultery with her I will throw into great tribulation, unless they repent of her doings; 2:23 and I will strike her children dead. And all the churches shall know that I am he who searches mind and heart, and I will give to each of you as your works deserve.	3:2 Awake, and strengthen what remains and is on the point of death, for I have not found your works perfect in the sight of my God.	3:9 Behold, I will make those of the synagogue of Satan who say that they are Jews and are not, but lie—behold, I will make them come and bow down before your feet, and learn that I have loved you. 3:10 Because you have kept my word of patient endurance, I will keep you from the hour of trial which is coming on the whole world, to try those who dwell upon the earth.	3:16 So, because you are lukewarm, and neither cold nor hot, I will spew you out of my mouth. 3:17 For you say, I am rich, I have prospered, and I need nothing; not knowing that you are wretched, pitiable, poor, blind, and naked. 3:18 Therefore I counsel you to buy from me gold refined by fire, that you may be rich, and white garments to clothe you and to keep the shame of your nakedness from being seen, and salve to anoint your eyes, that you may see.

FIGURE 10.8. Seven Letters—Contents.

10—Judgment of the Church 285

	EPHESUS	SMYRNA	PERGAMUM	THYATIRA	SARDIS	PHILDELPHIA	LAODICEA
EXHORT.	2:5 Remember then from what you have fallen, repent and do the works you did at first. If not, I will come to you and remove your lampstand from its place, unless you repent. 2:6 Yet this you have, you hate the works of the Nicolaitans, which I also hate.	Be faithful unto death, and I will give you the crown of life.	2:16 Repent then. If not, I will come to you soon and war against them with the sword of my mouth.	2:24 But to the rest of you in Thyatira, who do not hold this teaching, who have not learned what some call the deep things of Satan, to you I say, I do not lay upon you any other burden; 2:25 only hold fast what you have, until I come.	3:3 Remember then what you received and heard; keep that, and repent. If you will not awake, I will come like a thief, and you will not know at what hour I will come upon you. 3:4 Yet you have still a few names in Sardis, people who have not soiled their garments; and they shall walk with me in white, for they are worthy.	3:11 I am coming soon; hold fast what you have, so that no one may seize your crown.	3:19 Those whom I love, I reprove and chasten; so be zealous and repent. 3:20 Behold, I stand at the door and knock; if any one hears my voice and opens the door, I will come in to him and eat with him, and he with me.

FIGURE 10.8. Seven Letters—Contents.

	EPHESUS	SMYRNA	PERGAMUM	THYATIRA	SARDIS	PHILDELPHIA	LAODICEA
PROMISE	2:7 To him who conquers I will grant to eat of the tree of life, which is in the paradise of God. [Note: comes *after* Call]	He who conquers shall not be hurt by the second death. [Note: comes *after* Call]	To him who conquers I will give some of the hidden manna, and I will give him a white stone, with a new name written on the stone which no one knows except him who receives it. [Note: comes *after* Call]	2:26 He who conquers and who keeps my works until the end, I will give him power over the nations, 2:27 and he shall rule them with a rod of iron, as when earthen pots are broken in pieces, even as I myself have received power from my Father; 2:28 and I will give him the morning star.	3:5 He who conquers shall be clad thus in white garments, and I will not blot his name out of the book of life; I will confess his name before my Father and before his angels.	3:12 He who conquers, I will make him a pillar in the temple of my God; never shall he go out of it, and I will write on him the name of my God, and the name of the city of my God, the new Jerusalem which comes down from my God out of heaven, and my own new name.	3:21 He who conquers, I will grant him to sit with me on my throne, as I myself conquered and sat down with my Father on his throne.
CALL	2:7 He who has an ear, let him hear what the Spirit says to the churches.'	2:11 He who has an ear, let him hear what the Spirit says to the churches.'	2:17 He who has an ear, let him hear what the Spirit says to the churches.'	2:29 He who has an ear, let him hear what the Spirit says to the churches.'	3:6 He who has an ear, let him hear what the Spirit says to the churches.'	3:13 He who has an ear, let him hear what the Spirit says to the churches.'	3:22 He who has an ear, let him hear what the Spirit says to the churches.'"

FIGURE 10.8. Seven Letters—Contents.

FIGURE 10.9. Apocalypse Tapestry, Rev 2:1. Seven angels appear from the top of each church. Churches imagined in medieval style. The first-century context likely would have been smaller gatherings in the homes of local church patrons, such as Lydia's home in Philippi that accommodated the apostle Paul and his companions on the second missionary journey (Acts 16:14–15). Lydia was a business woman from Thyatira, one of Revelation's seven churches. From Col 4:16, Paul apparently wrote a letter to Laodicea, another of the seven churches (Panel 1, scene 2, Angers, France).

Ephesus (2:1–7)

Ephesus vied with Smyrna and Pergamum as the greatest city of Asia Minor and is the most visited ancient site in Turkey for her remains. Ephesus was a strong center of the emperor cult, having the earliest temple to any emperor, and later funding from her great wealth the massive temple complex in the upper city dedicated to the Flavian dynasty and completed during the reign of Domitian, just before John probably wrote Revelation. The supporting arches for the foundation of this structure are still a central feature of the upper city. A colossal statue of a Flavian emperor (Titus or Domitian) was positioned prominently in this temple complex to project the imperial ideology upon all citizens. The head and forearm have survived and are on display in the Ephesos Museum in the nearby modern city of Selçuk. The terrace homes along the hillside of Curates Street reveal extraordinary Roman villas palatial in size and beautiful in architecture, full of frescos, mosaics, and marble. Such wealthy Romans would have been the families of Ephesus vying for civic honor in service to the imperial cult. The proconsul of Asia resided in Ephesus as the administrative center.

FIGURE 10.10. Ephesus, Domitian Temple. Remains of the north façade and supporting arch structure for the foundation to the temple of Domitian.

FIGURE 10.11. Ephesus, Domitian Statue. Remains of the colossal statue of Domitian that was part of the imperial cult temple at Ephesus (EMS).

FIGURE 10.12. Ephesus, Harbor Decree. A decree by the proconsul Lucius Antonius Albus (146–147) pledging to maintain Ephesian harbor dredging, which was absolutely essential for the operation of the busy port to maintain its commercial dominance in Asia. Still, heavy silting of the harbor and major earthquakes eventually caused the city to be abandoned (EMS).

FIGURE 10.13. Polemaeanus, Proconsul of Asia. Proconsul of Asia about a decade after John wrote Revelation, Tiberius Julius Celsus Polemaeanus (105–07) was wealthy and popular because of his generous and numerous benefactions to the city. His loyalty to Vespasian during the Roman civil wars (68–69) gained him promotion to senatorial class, then consul, then finally proconsul under Trajan. The Library of Celsus at the bottom of Curetes Street takes its name from this proconsul, built as an honorary mausoleum to hold his sarcophagus by his son Julius Aquila Polemaeanus (IAM).

Ephesus had the great temple of Artemis (Diana). This temple was one of the seven wonders of the ancient world. The silversmiths trade guild had a robust business in silver figurines for this goddess. When Paul brought his gospel to the city on his third missionary journey, he had significant success. Associates even reached surrounding regions.[66] Paul's success, however, inspired the silversmiths' riot due to their loss of business. This intersection of gospel and commerce at Ephesus already in Paul's ministry is an ominous forecast of a brewing storm for the seven churches—the storm of commerce and cult.

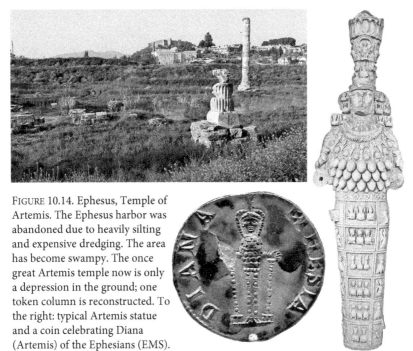

FIGURE 10.14. Ephesus, Temple of Artemis. The Ephesus harbor was abandoned due to heavily silting and expensive dredging. The area has become swampy. The once great Artemis temple now is only a depression in the ground; one token column is reconstructed. To the right: typical Artemis statue and a coin celebrating Diana (Artemis) of the Ephesians (EMS).

According to church tradition, the apostle John relocated in the city of Ephesus as a refugee from Judea after the First Jewish War. He was reputed to have lived many years after the war. With the mission work of the apostle Paul and the ministry of the apostle John, Ephesus was a church that had the benefit of learning their Christian traditions from two of the greatest apostles of the early church. Ephesus would be keen on apostolic doctrine. This church would have little patience for alien teachings or new doctrines.

---

[66]Cf. Luke's version in Acts 19.

FIGURE 10.15. Ephesus, Terrace Homes. Marble, mosaics, frescos, and more adorn these palatial homes that spill down the hillside into Curetes Street. These families would have supported and promoted the imperial cult and Roman imperial ideology.

Ephesus Identification (2:1)

The identification ties to the Son of Man vision and the one who holds the seven stars in his right hand and walks among the lampstands. The seven stars probably are an allusion to Ephesus having the privilege of great prophetic leadership, having been blessed to have not one but two famous apostles in her history, both the apostle Paul, who established the church, and the apostle John, who migrated from Judea to Ephesus after the Jewish War and spent many years ministering in that city according to church tradition. The church in Ephesus knows Christian doctrine well, and the reigning Christ dwells in her midst.

Ephesus Account (2:2–3)

The account is positive; the assessment negative. Positively, Ephesus is enduring patiently—not to be read as passively. Patient endurance is having your shoulder under a heavy load yet bearing up over time. The heavy load is false prophets, whose false doctrine is putting the church in duress to expose and counter. Often quoted in this context is Ignatius (d. 108), bishop of Antioch, who wrote letters on his way to martyrdom in Rome. One of these letters was to the Ephesians, in which Ignatius commended them: "But I have learned that certain people from there have passed your way with evil doctrine, but you did not allow them to sow it among you. You covered up your ears in order to avoid receiving the things being sown by them."[67] Revelation is about a war of words. How one testifies to Christ is how one wages that war. Opposing false doctrine is one of the crucial battlegrounds. Many antichrists have gone out into the world, and one key area of doctrinal distortion is Christology. This testimony of Jesus Christ is what landed John on Patmos.

Ephesus Assessment (2:4)

Negatively, Ephesus has abandoned her first love. John's meaning is clarified in Revelation. Love as a noun in Revelation is used only here and in 2:19 (Thyatira) in a context of works in combination with faith, service, and patient endurance. Thus, in 2:19 love is a work or deed to be done that has ties to service and patient endurance. As a verb, love is a sacrificial action of Jesus Christ on behalf of his community (1:5; 3:9; 20:9). For all believers, love is a measure of the depth of their commitment to their word of witness (12:11). Thus, John sees love as the faithful action of believers that reflects the faithful action of Christ. Christians are to reflect Christ, who was faithful in his witness to God, even to the point of death (1:5). Faithful witness marks a follower of Jesus. John prophetically is charging that Ephesus internally might be expert at exposing false doctrine in her midst, but externally she is faltering by failing to give priority to public testimony. She compromises the fruit of her strong doctrine with her anemic witness.

Ephesus Exhortation (2:5–6)

The exhortation is to "remember" and "repent." The caution for not doing so is the threat of removal of the lampstand. Removal of the lampstand is a basic "going out of business" banner for the church. The lampstand is a metaphor for the light of witness to the truth about Christ a church proclaims in her own setting. No light is no church. The first-love issue is truly serious and a deep crisis. To do the works she did at first perhaps means to have the kind of witness in which all

---

[67]Ignatius *Eph.* 9.1.

the residents of Asia are hearing the word of the Lord, miracles are being performed, and sorcerers are burning their magical books.[68]

Ephesus is commended for hating (i.e., refusing to perform) the works of the "Nicolaitans." The Nicolaitans are mentioned only twice in Scripture (here and Pergamum, 2:15), so we hardly know anything about them. Interestingly, both cities where they are mentioned set historical precedent in the development of provincial emperor worship. Ephesus was one of the first two cities successfully to petition Caesar Augustus to build a cult temple to the deceased Julius Caesar.[69] Pergamum, however, was one of the first two cities given permission to build a cult temple to a *living* emperor, that is, to Augustus himself, in 29 B.C.[70] Those who served imperial cult activities became a special class of high honor in ancient society, the *augustales*, for which aristocratic families in Asia competed intensely. So Ephesus and Pergamum, where we hear of the activity of the Nicolaitans, both are distinguished as the first Asian cities initiating and aggressively pursuing emperor worship as civic policy cemented by Roman patronage in the building of temples for the worship of Roman emperors.

More imperial cult temples in Asia followed. Smyrna, another of the seven churches, already had been the first city to build a temple to the goddess Roma during Rome's early struggles with the Carthaginian empire (195 B.C.). Smyrna later was the second city in Asia to gain permission to build a temple to a living emperor, to Tiberius.[71] Ephesus followed up with a third temple to living emperors (A.D. 89–90), this time dedicated to the "revered ones," presumably the Flavian dynasty of Vespasian (69–79), Titus (79–81), and Domitian (81–96).

We have to understand that political allegiance moves quickly to religious worship in the first century, unlike in the United States with its separation of church and state, a political doctrine unknown and inconceivable in John's first-century world. We need to listen with first-century ears to hear how the language that honors Christ in Revelation is the subversion of the language honoring Caesar integral to this imperial cult patronage system. Imperial ideology propagan-

---

[68]Cf. Acts 19:10–20. See pp. 562–64 for a possible connection to the apostle Paul.

[69]Dio Cassius 51.20.6–8. The other city was Nicaea.

[70]Tacitus *Annals* 4.37. The other city was Nicomedia.

[71]Tacitus *Annals* 4.55–56; approved in A.D. 23; constructed by A.D. 26 or 27.

dized the benefits of Rome as worthy of worship. One premier benefit was the Roman peace. Augustus claimed to bring peace to the world by ending the two-hundred year period of Roman civil wars, as well as conquering barbarian territories, such as Gaul and Spain. In gratitude and to honor the emperor, the Roman senate completed the "Altar of Peace" (*Ara Pacis*) dedicated to Augustus in 9 B.C.[72] When we hear of the many hymns in Revelation sung to divinity, we are hearing John's counterpoint to the professional male choirs (*hymnōdes*) serving the imperial cult, meeting monthly for banquets, celebrating various imperial calendar items, such as birthdays of the emperors, and using crowns, incense, lamps, and other accouterments of worship.[73]

In the context of compromised witness, a good guess is that the Nicolaitans at Ephesus and Pergamum have urged compliance with imperial ideology and emperor worship as simply smart politics and good business. John knows better and calls them out on their fundamental compromise of Christian witness. The Achilles heel of Christ and culture is Christ enculturated. While Ephesus has rejected as bad doctrine the Nicolaitan compromise of assimilating imperial ideology, she also may have lost her first love of fervent witness in the process and become too passive in public testimony in trying to cope with the pervasive influence of imperial ideology deeply embedded into Asian society. To have even the best of doctrine but no witness is to sacrifice the mission of the church and her destiny. The Nicolaitans, then, are literarily meant as the paradigmatic antithesis of Antipas.

Ephesus Promise (2:7b)

The promise is "to the one who conquers." This theme is universal. Note that every single church receives this same promise "to the one who conquers." In this way John signals that this theme is for the church universal. This theme also is crucial. This theme gets at the heart of answering the question of how God conquers evil in the world. God will conquer evil in the world though the church as the church fulfills her mission and destiny in the world. The church will

---

[72] See the excellent discussion in Kraybill, *Apocalypse and Allegiance*, 57–59.

[73] Cf. Friesen, "The Beast from the Land," 104–13. This imperial ideology and its professional cultic choirs is the context for Luke's presentation of the angels' chorus singing "and on earth peace" (Luke 2:14).

consummate what Jesus inaugurated. "Take up your cross and follow me," Jesus said (Mark 8:34). The church reflects the pattern of Jesus' life, Luke said (Acts 2:1–4). We must complete what is lacking in the Christ's afflictions, Paul said (Col 1:24).

FIGURE 10.16. Colosseum of Rome. Rome's grand amphitheater was built during the Flavian dynasty by Vespasian and Titus using slaves from the Jewish War and funded by treasures from the Jerusalem temple. Shown is the complex underground system of passage ways, storage rooms, loading docks, and animal pens underneath the arena floor serving the activity above. This is where gladiators awaited their entrance.

FIGURE 10.17. Gladiator Mosaic. Floor mosaics of the Great Palace of Constantinople, seat of the Eastern Roman Empire. Two *venatores* are fighting a tiger. Morning animal contests excited the crowd for the afternoon gladiatorial combat. Christians condemned to the arena usually died by wild animals. Paul uses the idea as a striking metaphor in 1 Cor 15:32 (GPMM).

John's conquering language is subversive rhetoric undermining the imperial ideology of conquest, a favorite theme of statues, reliefs, and coins of the Roman empire. This Roman conquest, however, is by Roman legions, by force and violence, subjection, threat, intimidation, war, and destruction, a blood lust reenacted across the empire in the public spectacles of staged gladiator contests in Roman amphitheaters.

FIGURE 10.18. Bronze Coin, Reverse of Roman Standards. (COSXVII = Domitian's 17th consulship.) Standard on the left is a *manus* (hand), below which is a crossbar for hanging wreaths. Center is the *aquila* (eagle) of the legionnaires. Right is a *vexilloid* (flag form). Military standards were extremely important, and troops went to great lengths to protect or recover them in battle. Standards were revered, almost worshipped, and were central to religious festivals, anointed with sacred, expensive oils and decked out in garlands (HAMH).

FIGURE 10.19. Gladiator Grave Stele. The first ever discovery of a gladiator graveyard was found in 1993 at ancient Ephesus, holding 67 individuals, aged 20–30. Analysis of bones and injuries reveals new insights into how gladiators lived, fought, and died. This grave stele in the courtyard of the Ephesos Müzesi marked the grave of a gladiator named Hippolytos. His large shield, visored helmet, shin grieves, and angled sword shows he was a *thraex* gladiator, normally paired in combat with a *murmillo* gladiator. Gladiatorial extravaganzas were expensive and required funding by wealthy civic patrons. The terrace homes on Curates Street in Ephesus have gladiator graffiti (see below), showing the huge popularity of gladiators and gladiatorial games among Roman aristocrats (EMS).

FIGURE 10.20. Gladiator Graffiti at Ephesus. A terrace home (Fig. 10.15) shows this graffiti likely celebrating gladiatorial heroes who fought in the arena not far away down the street known as the Marble Way that corners into Curetes Street at the Library of Celsus.

The gladiator games reenacted rituals of life and death, themes that are core to the gospel message. In addition, these games were dedicated to the gods, including a sacred meal shared by the gladiators the night before the public spectacle. The beginning of the games were marked with ceremonial prayers invoking the gods and ritual acts of sacrifice. The games were the grandest of pomp and pageantry and entertainment conceivable. Patrons all over the empire poured their vast wealth into sponsoring these coveted games. If John does not offer a different conquering narrative, and only changes the names but not the plot, then he simply has capitulated to Roman ideology.[74]

In fact, John's conquering narrative *is* radically different. John agrees with the gospel witness that the cross is the apocalypse of God's way of conquering. That is why the exchange between Jesus and the Roman governor, Pilate (John 18:36), the representative of imperial ideology of conquest, is crucial for understanding Jesus' perspective. Jesus conquers by dying, but his death is unique. A gladiator who lost was expected to die "like a true Roman" by showing courage without fear in the face of imminent death, thereby denying death its power over human thought. Jesus' ritual moment in time, however, releases a redemptive power that eternally transcends death like no gladiator's death ever could, regardless of how bravely enacted, because Jesus' death unleashes resurrection power. Jesus' death is the one true ritual of life and death for humanity. Roman ritual is but a cheap imitation and gross perversion of true conquering by the Lord of resurrection.

In Roman society, the promise for a victorious gladiator in the amphitheater or general on the field of battle was the adulation of the crowds and the fame that followed in this life. John depicts the reward for believers who "conquer" in each letter in eschatological terms, and thereby points to the reality of another life rather than the expectation of reward in this life. This view is reflected in Christian martyrologies: "with the eyes of their heart they gazed upon the good things which are reserved for those who endure patiently."[75] For the Ephesians, the reward is the "tree of life, which is in the paradise of God" (2:7). "Paradise" is a loan word for the royal gardens in the palace of the Persian

---

[74]For more on the ceremonial and religious significance of the games, see Kraybill, *Apocalypse and Allegiance,* 112–14. Today's end-timers capitulate to Rome's ideology.

[75]*Mart. Poly.* 2.3.

king. The Jews assimilated this word during the exile to imagine the garden of Eden. The word became symbolic of future life in the kingdom of God. Eden imagery surfaces here by way of the Bible's grand story: the God who creates is the God who consummates. God will fulfill all his purposes in the cosmos. He is the Lord of life.

Ephesus Call (2:7a)

Promise and call sections are swapped in the first three letters. The last four letters end with promise, then call. The call section is formulaic, highly stylized, and verbatim in each letter. The pattern is from the Old Testament, picked up and used by Jesus in the Gospels.[76]

The phrase "let the one who has an ear" is singular and may hold a double entendre. One meaning is that this address is to the one who is listening to Revelation being read in the church. Another meaning could be John himself. He was to be sure to fulfill his prophetic office by hearing these words of Jesus and writing these judgment oracles to the seven churches. By extension, this call could include the prophetic leadership in the seven congregations, who are enjoined themselves to fulfill their prophetic office by supporting John's position in this war of words. Even the conclusion to Revelation revisits this idea of the enclave of God's true prophets guiding the church. Not only is John reminded that the God of the vision also is the Lord of the spirits of the prophets (22:6), but the interpreting angel attending John appeals to a coalition in mission not only with John but also including "your brothers the prophets" (22:9).

The call is plural: "to the churches." So, every letter is meant for every church. John intends a composite picture of the message of Jesus to his churches to emerge from hearing all these letters as a group.

Smyrna (2:8–11)

Smyrna, like Ephesus, was a port city on the western coast of Asia with long loyalty to Rome and strong emperor sympathies. She was the first city ever to build a temple to goddess Roma (195 B.C.) and the second city of Asia after Ephesus to boast a temple to a living emperor (Tiberius). Trade and commerce in the Roman empire was prospered by the security and stability generated in the wake of imperial conquest.

---

[76]Cf. Isa 6:9–10; Matt 13:9–17; Mark 4:9; Luke 8:8.

In his testament to his own life accomplishments published in inscriptions throughout the empire, Augustus boasted of ending piracy on the high seas, and his contemporaries agreed this feat set the stage for the robust growth of commerce in the Roman empire.[77]

FIGURE 10.21. Modern Izmir. Ancient Smyrna lies under modern Izmir. The city was destroyed in the devastating earthquake of A.D. 178. The city was rebuilt under the auspices of the emperor Marcus Aurelius (d. 180).

FIGURE 10.22. Fragments of the *Res Gestae Divi Augusti*. One of the surviving copies of the "Deeds of the Divine Augustus," a first-person account by Augustus of his life and accomplishments as Rome's first emperor. The funerary inscription, preserved in several copies across the empire, epitomized the essence of Roman imperial ideology that became standard for generations (YMY).

In gratitude, those who profited demonstrated veneration for the emperors as faithful clients to their supreme patron. No wonder, then, that Herod the Great, a client king of Rome ruling in Judea, built a temple to the emperor to greet all those coming into the harbor of his newly constructed Caesarea Maritima (Caesarea by the Sea). Caesarea had all the standard features of Roman life, such as an aqueduct, theater, residential palace, and hippodrome right on the shoreline.[78]

[77]Augustus *Res Gestae* 25, his autobiography on his accomplishments particularly related to establishing the empire. Cf. Strabo *Geog.* 3.2.5; Epictetus *Disc.* 3.13.9.

[78]Cf. Kraybill, *Imperial Cult and Commerce*, 117–21.

FIGURE 10.23. Caesarea Maritima. Herod the Great's seaport named for his patron, the emperor. Surviving aqueduct, harbor storage facilities, and shoreline hippodrome.

Other cities throughout Judea and its surrounding territories had the imprint of Rome. Sepphoris, only four miles from Nazareth where Jesus grew up, was enlarged in typical Roman fashion into the capital of Galilee by its ruler, Antipas, son of Herod the Great. A leading city of the Decapolis region near Galilee was Scythopolis (the ancient Beth Shean), which, even though a predominately Gentile city with strongly Hellenistic culture, had a large Jewish presence too.

FIGURE 10.24. Sepphoris and Scythopolis. Beautiful floor mosaic in an aristocratic home in Sepphoris near Nazareth (left), and colonnaded street of Scythopolis (right).

The opulent wealth of Rome was notorious. Probably no greater example in the first century would have been the infamous Nero. His lavish and senseless expenditures nearly bankrupted the empire. He threw banquets in which walkways were strewn with millions of rose petals for their aroma when crushed. He never traveled without hundreds of carriages and horses shod with silver. Most notorious was his Golden House (*Domus Aurea*) built after the fire of Rome near where the Colosseum later would stand. A statue of himself in the vestibule of this house was 120 feet high. The entire structure was overlaid in gold, gems, and mother of pearl. He had numerous banquet halls whose ceiling panels were made of pure ivory and designed to rotate open to shower flowers on guests below and to reveal hidden pipes custom designed to mist perfumes down to those sumptuously dining. The main banquet hall was circular and even more inventive, perched on a mechanism that rotated continuously day and night.[79] Rome's wealth and her emperors regularly helped cities destroyed by earthquake rebuild, as Marcus Aurelius after the A.D. 178 event at Smyrna.

FIGURE 10.25. Smyrna, Agora Arch and Keystone. The reconstructed second arch of Smyrna's western agora features a keystone with an image of Faustina (d. 175), wife of emperor Marcus Aurelius (d. 180). The keystone establishes the time frame for when Rome rebuilt Smyrna after the devastating second century earthquake. The effort to rebuild Smyrna illustrates not only Rome's huge wealth, but also the municipal dependency of most provincial cities on Rome's munificence. Most citizens would have no problem at all in showing civic gratitude for Rome's patronage through the worship of the emperor cult. To refuse to do so was considered the height of impiety and impropriety.

[79] Suetonius *Nero* 31.1–2.

FIGURE 10.26. Damokkaris Inscription. A benefactor of Smyrna after the A.D. 178 destruction received this memorial stone. The inscription reads: "Praise to Damokkaris, O Judge Damokkaris famous with his skill! This success also belongs to you: After the mortal disasters of an earthquake, with a very diligent effort, you succeeded in the making of a city out of Smyrna again."

FIGURE 10.27. Smyrna Imperial Coin. Issued twenty years after the devastating tremor that leveled the city, this imperial coin minted at Smyrna (198–202) shows the goddess Victory placing a laureate wreath of victory on the emperor's head to show gratitude and to celebrate the supreme patron of the empire (PMB).

The Jewish community always had been strong in Smyrna. At the end of the first century as John composed Revelation, he was aware of growing tensions between followers of Jesus and the synagogue. The rejection of the preaching of Jesus as Messiah by this time had become fairly hardened, if not earlier. These early signs of animosity John had witnessed were harbingers of trouble to come. By the second century, strife had grown so dramatically that Jews in Smyrna were key in the martyrdom of Polycarp (d. 155), the famous bishop of Smyrna, whom Irenaeus (d. 202) himself as a young boy had heard speak.[80] Tertullian claimed Polycarp was appointed as bishop by John the apostle.[81]

[80] The story with emphasis on martyrological themes is the *Martyrdom of Polycarp*.
[81] Tertullian *Praes. Haer.* 32.2.

Smyrna Identification (2:8)

The "first and last" is from 1:17 of the Inaugural Vision in Jesus' self identification to John. As an echo of the divine "Alpha and Omega" title of 1:8, the close association of Jesus and God in Revelation continues. The Ancient of Days continues in his judgment assessment of the church. Similarly, "who died and came to life" is from 1:19 of the Inaugural Vision and reflects the sacrificial theology of 1:5. The identification is a potent reminder from the passion story of Jesus and Pilate that Rome does not have the last say on life. The reminder is pertinent to Smyrna, because their story is poverty and persecution. Since the martyrdom of Polycarp of Smyrna will become a permanent part of church tradition, the letter seems eminently qualified to speak to the needs of this congregation both presently and in her near future. The letter to Smyrna and her history fulfills the opening words "what must soon take place" (1:1) "for the time is near" (1:3).

Smyrna Account (2:9)

Smyrna's "I know" account immediately takes note of the dire straits of believers in this city: they are in "tribulation." They do not have to wait two thousand years to be in the "tribulation"! This tribulation has two characteristics. These characteristics seem to suggest the nature of the problem when seen in the light of the realities of imperial worship and its unavoidable connection to commercial activity.

One characteristic of the tribulation is "poverty." Inability to be viable commercially in a wealthy and commercially prosperous city simply means believers at Smyrna do not play the Roman patronage and imperial cult game required to be commercially prosperous. They refuse to compromise their confession of Christ as Lord to make the token signs of imperial fealty by burning incense to the genius of the emperor. As a result, they suffer greatly for this choice of conscience.

Later in Revelation, imperial commerce, embedded patronage, veneration, and worship will become the central focus in depicting the corruption and destruction of the harlot Babylon (Rev 17–18). Smyrna believers, probably reduced to poverty for their non-compliance with pervasive imperial ideology, will experience an emotional catharsis as the visions of Revelation climax in the dirge of Babylon's destruction.

In contrast to their meager present circumstances, believers in Smyrna actually "are rich" because they have not sold their souls nor their consciences to the lust for acquisition and aggrandizement, like Nero, nor have they invested in a greed that strips the planet of her resources for an elite, single-digit percentage of the global population. Those hearing Revelation read will learn that believers in Laodicea, in contrast, have not been as wise nor faithful as those in Smyrna.

Another characteristic of tribulation in Smyrna is "slander." They suffer in public discourse. Their reputation in the eyes of the city elite is smeared, because, as "atheists," they invite the wrath of the gods on Smyrna.[82] This public opposition most especially finds support in the synagogue. Jewish opposition reveals false Jewish identity for John. Jesus is the Jewish Messiah. True Jews respond in faith to the gospel. Jesus is the litmus test of Judaism. That synagogue leaders reject the Messiah's gospel infers imminent divine judgment. John's epitaph, "synagogue of Satan," is particularly harsh rhetoric to be sure, but no harsher than Jesus' own addressing of his premier disciple similarly ("get behind me, Satan!") when his suffering Son of Man identity for Messiah has been rejected (Mark 8:33). Further, we do not know what derogatory terms Jews themselves called followers of Jesus in Smyrna, nor under what circumstances denunciations of believers were being made to local authorities. Exaggerations might parallel the apostle Paul's experience in Thessalonica as locals punched Roman patronage buttons of civic leaders (Acts 17:6). John's synagogue title here seems intended as an ironic play on a typical inscription over the lintel of synagogue entrances announcing "Synagogue of the Hebrews."

FIGURE 10.28. Synagogue Lintel Inscription. "Synagogue of the Hebrews" (AMAC). Credit: Jean M. Stevens.

---

[82]Rejection of the gods everyone else believed in was equivalent to "atheism" in the ancient world view. Christians were full of such "abominations." Cf. Tacitus *Annals* 15.44; Justin Martyr *Apology* 5; Athenagoras *Embassy* 3. For what particular reasons would Christians be accused of cannibalism, business disruption, incest, anti-family communes, being unpatriotic, being antisocial, and causing disasters?

Smyrna Assessment (2:10)

Believers in Smyrna are in trouble, but Jesus forecasts even more trouble. "The devil will throw you into prison," he warns. Two important pieces of information are revealed in this statement. First, this prediction actually is a commendation. Jesus already knows that even with intense commercial, social, and religious pressures in Smyrna, believers there will not compromise. Instead, they will endure even harsher opposition. They will be faithful witnesses, the principal mission and calling of believers in Revelation (12:11). They are not in jeopardy of losing their lampstand, as is the present threat for Ephesus.

Second, Smyrna is the first occurrence of the character of Satan or the Devil in Revelation, who later takes center stage as the great red Dragon in Rev 12:9. The church's true opposition is the Devil. People are but pawns. Satan is the story behind the story. The story of Satan creates a duality of earthly and heavenly dimensions in the story of the church in the world. Dual dimensions will cause John to construct his Apocalypse with dual story lines that will overlap simultaneously. To envision this duality, John first tells the story of God and his Christ at the surface level of earthly history through the Seal and Trumpet judgments (Rev 6–11). John then rewinds and retells the same story but from a cosmic perspective of the heavenly forces that actually drive the earthly plot, the story of the Dragon and his beasts and the Bowl judgments (Rev 12–20). Greek intuition reflected in ancient mythology that connected events on earth with happenings on Olympus is not totally off base. The crux is monotheism and motives. So, God and his Christ and the Dragon and his beasts are distinct but interconnected plotlines of the same story. Three interconnected judgment septets of Seals, Trumpets, and Bowls are distributed unevenly across two major plotlines of God and his Christ and the Dragon and his beasts.

Jesus does not promise to make things better, but he does promise to make believers stronger. Their ordeal is for "ten days," which, at a minimum, at least means a duration that has an end. When going through trouble knowing an end is in sight is helpful. Whether a literal or figurative ten days is unknown. If figurative, whether a brief time, or a presumptive ten years, just cannot be determined. Designating a specific ten-year period in the history of Smyrna to which this refers is a completely arbitrary exercise of pure speculation on the part of the interpreter.

Smyrna Exhortation (2:10)

Believers in Smyrna now are exhorted to "be faithful unto death." No rapture here! This exhortation invokes the destiny of the church. Any other end-time scheme aborts the mission given by Jesus to Smyrna, the seven churches, and all churches. What Jesus says to one church, he says to all. Faithfulness to fulfill this commission garnishes the victory crown all contestants in stadiums and arenas fought to win in the first-century Roman world. This crown, however, does not fade or disintegrate to dust, but is the "crown of life." This life would have to be the resurrection life that Jesus alone can offer that is unlike any other known to human experience, the central message of the gospel. Thus, death is defeated, the true conquest of Jesus, and he offers this victory to his own. No judicial decree of death from Rome ever can put the final period on the sentence of a believer's life, only a temporary comma. Jesus controls the final script, regardless the signature of a Roman governor. That is the promise of the millennial reign.

Smyrna Promise (2:11b)

Promise reinforces exhortation. Those who "conquer" ("faithful unto death") are promised they "never will be harmed by the second death." The "second death" terminology is unique to Revelation in the New Testament, so its meaning must be inferred.[83] The second death:

- threatens the seven churches (2:11); present decisions have eschatological repercussions. Faithful witness now may mean death, but martyrs by definition show deliverance from the second death, the only death that truly need be feared.

- has its antidote in resurrection; resurrection hope sustains faithful witness and is prelude to participating in the millennial reign of the saints (20:6). Effective witness now is the resurrection power of the future reaching back into time in the lives of believers.

- is the lake of fire (20:14; 21:8); today's decisions and actions constitute the great white throne of judgment. This lake of fire is John's final word on the ultimate status of evil in the cosmos.

---

[83]The term occurs only four times in Revelation (2:11; 20:6, 14; 21:8). John probably is drawing on the Jesus tradition preserved in Matt 10:28; Luke 12:4 (fearing not those who kill the body but the one who can destroy both body and soul in Gehenna).

Spiritually, the lake of fire is that reality to which sinful, incorrigible, unrepentant beings willfully have consigned themselves beyond which the redemptive efforts of God completely and eternally cease and to which no appeal ever can be made.[84] Smyrna is the counterpoint to Ephesus. Smyrna has *not* lost her first love. Smyrna does not bow to Caesar to do business with the world. She is in tribulation as a result, impoverished and slandered, but she is rich in future dividends and will be vindicated by the Ancient of Days in the end.

Pergamum (2:12–17)

FIGURE 10.29. Attalos III of Pergamum. Willed his kingdom to Rome (HAMH).

Pergamum was fortunate to have a peaceful transition into the Roman empire when its king, Attalus III, willed his Asia Minor kingdom to Rome at his death in 133 B.C. because he had no male heirs. Pergamum briefly was capital of Asia until that honor was granted to Ephesus. Pergamum, like Ephesus and Smyrna, was a center of the prized imperial cult, the first city to build a temple to a living emperor as early as 29 B.C. Later an imperial temple was constructed at the very top of Pergamum's ancient acropolis dedicated to Trajan, an imposing monument over the entire city, parts of which still stand today.[85]

Another monumental construction was the Zeus Altar, built by King Eumenes II (d. 159 B.C.) on a southern terrace of the acropolis majestically commanding both east and west approaches to the city. The Zeus Altar was visible for miles along the main trade routes into and out of the city. The base of the altar consisted of an outstanding frieze in high relief depicting the Gigantomachy, or battle between the

---

[84]Philosophically, we can drink down a whole pot of coffee and never resolve whether annihilationism or eternal punishment is implicit in this metaphor. John's point is: (1) embraced willfully and (2) entered irrevocably. (Characters never reappear.)

[85]See Fig. 9.25, p. 229.

Giants and the Olympian gods, considered to be one of the greatest artistic masterpieces of the Hellenistic Age. Part of the west front of the altar was excavated and taken to Berlin to become the centerpiece of the Pergamon Museum. All that remains today on the Pergamum acropolis is the foundation to the altar.

FIGURE 10.30. Pergamum, Temple of Trajan. Perched on the crest of the acropolis are the remains of Trajan's Temple. The Asklepion center of the famous physician Galen (ca. 200), who attended emperor Marcus Aurelius (d. 180), is in the valley below.

FIGURE 10.31. Pergamum, Zeus Altar Foundation. This terrace held a commanding view of two major valleys and trade routes leading into Pergamum. The reconstructed altar is housed in the Pergamon Museum in Berlin.

10—Judgment of the Church 309

FIGURE 10.32. Pergamum, Statue of Zeus. This finely rendered marble statue from the second century A.D. of the supreme god Zeus was found in the ancient acropolis of Pergamum. The statue illustrates the high regard for Zeus in Pergamum not only in the decades immediately following the book of Revelation, but also for most of Pergamum's history. Pergamum was famous for its great altar to Zeus (PMB).

310 REVELATION: THE PAST AND FUTURE OF JOHN'S APOCALYPSE

FIGURE 10.33. Pergamum Zeus Altar, West Front. Reconstruction of the west front of Pergamum's famous Zeus Altar showing the base with its stunning Hellenistic masterpiece of the Gigantomachy frieze in high relief (PMB).

One element of fame for Pergamum was her reputation as a city of learning and arts. She developed a tradition as a cultural center and was noted for the adoption of Greek realism with natural movement, detailed anatomy, and exaggerated facial expressions to reveal strong emotion. The Altar of Zeus is the most stunning example of the high achievement of this tradition for its dramatic, dynamic high reliefs.

FIGURE 10.34. Pergamum Zeus Altar Frieze, East Side, Hekate. The three-headed goddess Hekate, with her Molossian dogs in fierce combat with the giants Klytios and Otos (PMB).

Related to Pergamum's development as a cultural center was her boast of one of the largest libraries in the ancient world, second only to the library at Alexandria, Egypt. The expansion of the library was the work of King Eumenes II (d. 159 B.C.). Pergamum is credited with advancing the use of parchment (leather) for book copies rather than the more fragile papyrus (paper). The library was said to have 200,000 volumes, but no content record survives.[86]

FIGURE 10.35. Library of Pergamum. This is the general area the German excavation team thinks is the location of the famous library of Pergamum in the mid-plateau of the acropolis near the temple of Athena. A statue of Athena stood in the main reading room. The library reputedly had 200,000 volumes, but no catalogue of holdings was preserved.

Another Pergamum claim to fame was its Asklepion center. An asklepion was an ancient medical center built in honor of the god of healing, Asklepios. Such centers often were connected to a sacred water spring, which provided the water used for healthy drinking and in medicinal rituals. A temple to Asklepios offered worship rituals. Activities included mud baths, herbal remedies, massages, and musical concerts. The look and feel almost might be similar to a modern spa. A premier part of these compounds was the sleep center. Patients would spend the night, hoping to have a dream, or even have contact with Asklepios.

FIGURE 10.36. Asklepion Votive. Grateful supplicants of the god Asklepios gave votive offerings, often of the body part healed. This inscription is, "To Asklepios, Savior, Fabia Sekounda, according to her strong desire" (BMB).

[86]Plutarch *Antony* 58.5.

The center was supplied with harmless snakes during the night. Patients interpreted contact by a snake to be a visit by the god Asklepios, who was there to inspire a dream. These dreams were thought to reveal the remedy for a malady. Priests the next day interpreted the dreams to determine a key to healing the patient's complaint. The famous physician Galen (ca. 200) was born in Pergamum and learned the medical arts in the Asklepion. He became famous for his treatment of gladiators, and might have treated gladiators from nearby Ephesus. Galen was the most accomplished physician of the ancient world. His writings and ideas dominated the practice of medicine up until the Renaissance. Galen also was imperial physician to emperor Marcus Aurelius (d. 180), known to American audiences as the emperor in the movie "Gladiator." Many testimonials of healing are preserved in inscriptions set up as stone monuments and in thousands of votive offerings. These votive offerings often were in the form of body parts that have some direct or indirect connection to the nature of the particular healing requested. A votive ear might represent hearing, or earache, or infection, for example.

FIGURE 10.37. Asklepios Statue. The snaked-curled staff of Asklepios became the symbol of modern medicine. Two of his daughters' names, Hygeia and Panacea, have provided medical terms used still today: "hygiene" and "universal remedy." A famous Asklepion healing center was near Pergamum (NAMA).

FIGURE 10.38. Asklepion of Pergamum. Two circular buildings in the schematic are the Temple of Telesphorus (Sleeping Center) left, and the Temple of Asklepios, right. The square was colonnaded on three sides; Odeon (musical theater) is upper right.

Pergamum Identification (2:12)

The tie to the Inaugural Vision is the "sharp, two-edged sword." John cuts straight to the heart of the matter: the power of the gospel versus imperial and pagan propaganda, Christ's truth for the world's lie.

Pergamum Account (2:13)

The focus is location. Jesus knows "where you dwell." He knows this because he stands among the lampstands. This location has a key feature, "where Satan's throne is." This location is crucial. We learn two elements about Satan's power and authority. First, Satan does not rule from heaven. Satan rules only on earth. Yet, earth already has a ruler over its kings, Jesus (1:5). Therefore, Satan's power is limited. So, if good and evil are locked in combat in Revelation, the struggle is uneven. John does not offer up cosmic dualism as in Zoroastrianism, nor does he offer up a Gigantomachy of the equally matched Giants and Olympian gods as in Greek myth.

Second, Satan's throne is where evil's power is localized on earth, and that is Pergamum for John. The thought may be more conceptual than architectural.[87] Pergamum is the seat of Satan's power because Pergamum is the epitome of Greco-Roman idolatry. This city's insidious combination of both supreme devotion to the emperor cult and supreme expressions of Hellenistic paganism puts Pergamum at the point of Christ's sword in John's view. With its famous library, famous school of art and sculpture, and famous healing center all cloaked in pagan belief and myth, and its multiple imperial temples adorning her magnificent acropolis, this city is symbolic as the apex of imperial ideology and idolatrous paganism in Asia Minor, the poster child of all that is wrong in John's world. While all the churches in Asia Minor have to deal with a pervasive Greco-Roman idolatry and imperial cult, none are as potent as Pergamum—where Satan's throne is.

This assessment that Pergamum is the seat of Satan's power is further established not only in general in the city and its culture but in the only named martyrdom in Revelation: "Yet you are holding fast to my name, and you denied not your faith in me even in the days of Antipas my faithful witness, who was killed among you, where Satan lives." Antipas is described exactly like Jesus as "faithful witness" (1:5). Thus, John makes Antipas the paradigm of those who "keep the things written in" John's prophecy. "Keeping the things written" clearly means faithful testimony in a place dangerous for faith. Antipas also is the reason why John announces at the beginning of Revelation, "for the time is near" (1:3). Antipas is the reason why Pergamum is "where Satan dwells" and "the time is near."

"Holding fast" the name probably alludes to an official refusal to recant the faith. Pliny the Younger (d. 112), a governor of Bithynia, sought legal counsel from the emperor Trajan (d. 117) for Christians.

---

[87]Some have conjectured "Satan's throne" is allusion to the great altar of Zeus at Pergamum perched on a high terrace of the acropolis and visible for miles from multiple directions. This connection is feasible and would provide a strong contrast to the gospel. However, such a connection not only is not necessary, but may actually reduce the broader application John seems to have intended by pinpointing Pergamum with this "throne of Satan" characterization.

FIGURE 10.39. Bithynia and Pontus. The governor of Bithynia on the southern coast of the Black Sea immediately to the north of the province of Asia was Pliny the Younger.

Pliny's legal letter to Trajan is extraordinarily revealing not only about inherent Roman suspicions but about early Christian practices as well. Due to its significance, the text is reproduced in full.

> It is my practice, my lord, to refer to you all matters concerning which I am in doubt. For who can better give guidance to my hesitation or inform my ignorance? I have never participated in trials of Christians. I therefore do not know what offenses it is the practice to punish or investigate, and to what extent. And I have been not a little hesitant as to whether there should be any distinction on account of age or no difference between the very young and the more mature; whether pardon is to be granted for repentance, or, if a man has once been a Christian, it does him no good to have ceased to be one; whether the name itself, even without offenses, or only the offenses associated with the name are to be punished.
>
> Meanwhile, in the case of those who were denounced to me as Christians, I have observed the following procedure: I interrogated these as to whether they were Christians; those who confessed I interrogated a second and a third time, threatening them with punishment; those who persisted I ordered executed. For I had no doubt that, whatever the nature of their creed, stubbornness and inflexible obstinacy surely deserve to be punished. There were others possessed of the same folly; but because they were Roman citizens, I signed an order for them to be transferred to Rome.
>
> Soon accusations spread, as usually happens, because of the proceedings going on, and several incidents occurred. An anonymous document was published containing the names of

many persons. Those who denied that they were or had been Christians, when they invoked the gods in words dictated by me, offered prayer with incense and wine to your image, which I had ordered to be brought for this purpose together with statues of the gods, and moreover cursed Christ—none of which those who are really Christians, it is said, can be forced to do—these I thought should be discharged. Others named by the informer declared that they were Christians, but then denied it, asserting that they had been but had ceased to be, some three years before, others many years, some as much as twenty-five years. They all worshipped your image and the statues of the gods, and cursed Christ.

They asserted, however, that the sum and substance of their fault or error had been that they were accustomed to meet on a fixed day before dawn and sing responsively a hymn to Christ as to a god, and to bind themselves by oath, not to some crime, but not to commit fraud, theft, or adultery, not falsify their trust, nor to refuse to return a trust when called upon to do so. When this was over, it was their custom to depart and to assemble again to partake of food—but ordinary and innocent food. Even this, they affirmed, they had ceased to do after my edict by which, in accordance with your instructions, I had forbidden political associations. Accordingly, I judged it all the more necessary to find out what the truth was by torturing two female slaves who were called deaconesses. But I discovered nothing else but depraved, excessive superstition.

I therefore postponed the investigation and hastened to consult you. For the matter seemed to me to warrant consulting you, especially because of the number involved. For many persons of every age, every rank, and also of both sexes are and will be endangered. For the contagion of this superstition has spread not only to the cities but also to the villages and farms. But it seems possible to check and cure it. It is certainly quite clear that the temples, which had been almost deserted, have begun to be frequented, that the established religious rites, long neglected, are being resumed, and that from everywhere sacrificial animals are coming, for which until now very few purchasers could be found. Hence it is easy to imagine what a multitude of people can be reformed if an opportunity for repentance is afforded.[88]

---

[88]Pliny *Letters* 10.96. Cf. http://www9.georgetown.edu/faculty/jod/texts/pliny.html for the text above; accessed 31 Mar 2014. "Twenty-five years" is a modern, speculative emendation to the Latin text. The Latin text actually reads "twenty years."

This crucial letter reveals many important elements of the legal status of Christianity, its current social setting out in the provinces, and its worship practices. Important for our purposes are the following:

- Legal policy in Roman law regarding Christians had not yet been established.
- The name Christian alone is not a crime but already seems on its way due to general public and official Roman attitudes.
- Persistence in Christian confession meant death.
- Pressure came from the general public, not Roman officials.
- Recantation was through indexes of imperial cult practice, pagan religions, and cursing Christ's name, which for some already had happened twenty years before, which would be during the reign of Domitian. This evidence is key for the background of Revelation.
- Christian meetings were classed as political associations. This classification makes problems for assembly and worship inevitable.
- Christian faith had spread beyond the large metropolitan areas in significant numbers with broad demographics, and the practice of pagan idolatry duly had been impacted.
- Pliny considered measures he had taken to be successful in checking the pernicious "superstition" for the time being.

Kraybill points to the word Pliny uses for the oath he compels those recanting their faith in Christ to take. This word is *sacramentum*.

> In discussing the oath, Pliny uses the Latin word *sacramentum*, a term the Roman army used for the oath of allegiance to the emperor. By the end of the second century, and perhaps sooner, the early church also used *sacramentum* to mean baptismal vows. At their initiation into the church by baptism, believers pledged allegiance to Jesus Christ and to the high ethical standards of the gospel. Joining the church was every bit as comprehensive a commitment as joining the army of Caesar.[89]

Antipas could have been the victim of mob action ignored by public officials. At the same time, he potentially could represent one of

---

[89]Kraybill, *Apocalypse and Allegiance*, 78.

those who refused to recant before government officials in the action to which Pliny alludes in his letter to Trajan that happened in the time of Domitian. Whatever the exact cause of his death, whether mob action or government verdict, Antipas reveals "where Satan dwells" for any perceptive believer and functions as a weathervane pointing where the wind is blowing and a storm is brewing out on the dark and ominous horizons of John's prophetic thoughts.

Antipas is the only other personal name besides John and Jesus in Revelation that is not a character of the Old Testament, an angel, or a metaphor.[90] Such a curiosity raises the question why. Why this one particular person? Of course, he is notable as a martyr, but John did not actually have to mention any particular name, just the fact of martyrdom would have been sufficient for the point. Antipas may have been a leader at Pergamum, even one of the prophets. Probably the martyrdom of Antipas shocked the community of believers in Pergamum and caught them by surprise. They were reeling to try to understand. In the meantime, prophetic leadership at Pergamum may have attempted to find safe houses until the attention of authorities was directed elsewhere, similar to Peter going to the house of Mary after surreptitiously being released from the prison of Herod Agrippa, and Polycarp being urged to take up residence out of the city in an outlying village.[91] For himself, John may have gone to Patmos on his own initiative as a safe house until matters became less volatile in Pergamum. While in hiding on the island, John received a vision from Jesus that helped him assimilate and process the Antipas event as not an anomaly but a trajectory. The vision gave John the "big picture" of the Dragon and his beasts at work "where Satan's throne is," and John was sounding a clarion call to all the churches of Asia Minor of what he had come to understand about the Antipas incident at Pergamum.

Pergamum Assessment (2:14–15)

Antipas has been faithful, but John still has reason to worry. The Nicolaitans are active at Pergamum like at Ephesus (2:5–6), and Ephesus

---

[90]Cf. Satan (2:9, 13, 24; 3:9; 12:9; 20:2, 7); Balaam and Balak (2:14); Israel (2:14; 7:4; 21:12); Jezebel (2:20); David (3:7; 5:5; 22:16); Judah (5:5); the Twelve Tribes (7:5–10); Wormwood (8:11); Abaddon and Apollyon (9:11); Michael (12:7); Moses (15:3).

[91]Acts 12:12; *Mart. Poly.* 5.

already had lost her first love. We learn a little more about the teaching of the Nicolaitans by John's analogy to Balaam. The narrative is Num 22–24. Balaam had turned Israel to idolatry and immorality, and those factors John sees for the church at Pergamum. Food sacrificed to idols most likely is the context of pagan religions that conducted feasts after sacrificial rituals left most of the animals intact. Other religions made mockery of morality. Even Pliny noted the peculiar behavior of believers in making a pact "to bind themselves by oath, not to some crime, but not to commit fraud, theft, or adultery, not falsify their trust, nor to refuse to return a trust when called upon to do so."[92] We have noted how trade guilds controlled almost all business and commerce and venerated their supreme patron the emperor. These guilds also held monthly feasts that included ritual worship of local patron deities to insure success of future business.

We can note how the letters become more and more integrated into one literary whole the further we progress through their contents. Pergamum is connected in content to both previous letters. The connection to Ephesus is through the Nicolaitans. We were just given a name in the letter to Ephesus, but now we are told more about what problem the Nicolaitans present in what they teach. Pergamum also is connected to Smyrna through the rhetoric of Satan. Just as Smyrna has a synagogue of Satan, Pergamum is where Satan's throne is. This flexible Satan rhetoric is helpful to show that John is not singling out Jewish communities everywhere, but only in specific locales in which synagogue leadership has been particularly vicious in opposition to the gospel. The later history of Smyrna's Jews lived up to John's fears in the story of the martyrdom of Polycarp of Smyrna. Even though the Sabbath, Jews participated in gathering firewood for the burning at the stake.[93] Opposition to the gospel that has potential to become lethal is the key to John's Satan rhetoric. Anyone can fill that role, and John calls out everyone moving in that direction from his perspective.

Pergamum Exhortation (2:16)

Pergamum's exhortation is pointed: "Repent, or I am coming to you soon." The second coming of Jesus at the end of time reflected in Rev

[92] Pliny *Letters* 10.96.5.
[93] *Mart. Poly.* 13.

1:7 is anticipated proleptically in the coming of Jesus throughout time. When the Lord of the second coming arrives at any moment in time, judgment happens. "Soon" means soon; soon means for those who are hearing Revelation when first read aloud to the seven churches. Without repentance, Jesus makes war "with the sword of my mouth." The gospel adjudicates the truth of Christian confession and the lie of the Nicolaitans. As John later says, "in their mouth no lie was found; they are blameless" (14:5). True believers do not participate in idolatrous pagan feasts, live immorally, venerate the emperor, or curse Christ, and those who do are hypocrites when they show up for church.

Note that Jesus makes war "against them." The pronoun shift is significant. Jesus means the Nicolaitans. Unrepentant Nicolaitans do not belong to Christ. They are alien to Jesus, what John the apostle would call antichrist. Indeed, many antichrists have gone out into the world. Jesus makes war though the book of Revelation itself. When the book is read, those who hear are blessed, as promised in the opening to the Apocalypse in 1:3, because Nicolaitan heresy no longer can hide behind false prophets but is exposed by true prophets such as John in the light of gospel truth. Indeed, Revelation is a war of words.

Pergamum Promise (2:17)

Pergamum is the last letter for the sequence of call, then promise. The last four letters have promise, then call.

The eschatological theme for Pergamum is "hidden manna," a deliberate choice that picks up on the wilderness theme of the Balaam allusion in the Assessment. This divine food provided by God to sustain his people in their wilderness wanderings is a deliberate contrast to the idol food eaten by the Nicolaitans. God's food is hidden in the gospel message and picks up on the Jesus tradition of Jesus as the "bread of life" (John 6:35, 48). God will sustain believers in Pergamum in their wilderness wanderings through paganism with the gospel faithfully preached by God's prophets such as Antipas, who sealed his message with his life, and John, who sealed his message with his book.[94]

---

[94]Jews had a tradition that the memorial pot of manna in the ark (Exod 16:32–34) was saved by Jeremiah before the temple's Babylonian destruction and buried to be revealed by the future messiah (2 Macc 2:4–8). John *possibly* could be alluding to this Jewish tradition, but the interpretation offered above is more contextually driven.

Another eschatological symbol is the "white stone." We have lost the meaning. A white stone had many associations and connections in the ancient world. Consult the critical commentaries for the options. The white stone has a "new name no one knows." Names are part of Revelation's symbolic universe, such as Abaddon, Apollyon, Armageddon, Babylon, Wormwood, Zion, and Gog and Magog. How most of these symbols work in their context is not too difficult to ascertain. However, this "new name," as with the "white stone," is not entirely evident in meaning. Seeing how John is in tune with the local context in each church, a reasonable interpretive suspicion is that something particular in the Pergamum context is at play, but that element now is lost in time.[95]

Thyatira (2:18–29)

FIGURE 10.40. Ancient Thyatira. In the center of downtown Akhisar are the ruins of ancient Thyatira. Partial excavation was done in 1974–75. Ruins are typical of west Anatolian cities of the Roman empire. Colonnaded street of Ionic and Corinthian style capitals with various buildings, shops along sides. Ancient sources indicate the road had 100 pillars decorated with 25 Eros statues. Road is Hekaton style. A Roman basilica is the main artifact, typical brick and plaster construction of late Roman period with central nave and apses, on the pattern of traditional agora basilicas.

This city bordering Lydia and Mysia was renamed by Seleucus I in 290 B.C. on a derivative of the Greek word for "daughter" upon learning

---

[95]Smalley, *Revelation*, 71, noted that the dual imagery of manna (Jewish) and white stone (Hellenistic) is further evidence John is writing to mixed congregations.

his wife had born him a daughter. The letter to Thyatira is the longest letter, which is odd, since Thyatira is an insignificant "frontier town." On the junction of three roads to Pergamum, Sardis, and Smyrna, the main function of Thyatira was as a military outpost, but without an acropolis for defense, easily taken. The garrison practically served as a warning of an invading army approaching Pergamum. Thyatira is a mere smudge on the map, but the longest letter! What is up? We may have literary evidence that John has arranged these letters in a chiasm, whose central axis would be this middle letter, hence the importance of Thyatira, not to Asia Minor, but to John. Trade guilds and Jezebel are going to be the key to understanding the centrality of this letter in the seven letter series.

Trade guilds were a central feature of Roman economy.[96] Rome herself had as many as eighty trade guilds.[97] Their main purpose was to provide laborers in an occupation political voice to advance the cause of their trade and social function for identity and community. A sense of community was so important in the ancient world that this value is inscribed on tombstones with expressions such as "brothers of the bronze guild" or "mates of the marble-workers."[98] Community was established by monthly meetings to recline and dine in meeting halls, in restaurants, or in patrons' homes. Guilds had patron gods, and their monthly feasts included pagan sacrifices. Monthly meetings began with prescribed rituals and veneration to statues of patron deities and imperial family members. Coins illustrate integral connection between guilds and cults, and cult practices were part of monthly meetings. Feasts often ended in debauchery. Even without the Roman empire, trade guilds and their patron deities were imperative to retain a job.

Failure to participate in these monthly fellowships was a huge social affront and entirely unacceptable and would generate serious consequences, even being shunned from the guild. To be shunned from a guild would be a catastrophic life event. Not only would one face a lost social identity as a social outcast but lost business income as well. Lost income would become failure to pay taxes. Failure to pay

---

[96] Cf. Thomas, "A Sociological Analysis of Guilds in First-Century Asia Minor" as an excellent resource on this topic.

[97] Abbott, *The Common People of Ancient Rome*, 218.

[98] MacMullan, *Enemies of the Roman Order*, 174.

taxes would incur being turned over to authorities. "To be excluded from such a group would be dishonorable and therefore emotionally and financially devastating. For the most part, one who had no group affiliation was a social outcast."[99] Thus, while we may have little evidence of any government sponsored "persecution" of believers in first-century Asia Minor, the situation is more complex than that. How to construe the idea of "persecution" is not so clear cut when one takes into consideration the potentially severe, life-altering consequences of a definitive Christian confession among the debauched pagan guilds of Thyatira.

FIGURE 10.41. Pagan Worship. Ram and draped garland indicate a sacrificial altar in Thyatira. Inscription below right indicates a sacred precinct of worship at Thyatira. Below left is the Isis temple at Pompeii, the only temple completely reconstructed after the A.D. 62 earthquake before the eruption of Mount Vesuvius buried the city in A.D. 79, showing the high esteem of mystery religions.

Thyatira's trade guilds were strong and dominant. We can document more guild names from Thyatira than any other city of Asia.[100] Thyatira's claim to fame was its dyeing industry as a center of the indigo trade, a blue dye extracted from plant matter and a luxury item for both Greeks and Romans. The synthetic substitute today makes

[99]Thomas, "A Sociological Analysis of Guilds in First-Century Asia Minor," 112.

[100]Ramsey, *Letters*, 324–25, catalogues wool-workers, linen-workers, outer garment makers, dyers, leather-workers, tanners, potters, bakers, slave-traders, and bronze-smiths. In terms of a robust economy, these would just be an illustrative sampling.

blue jeans. We know one business person in the purple cloth trade from Thyatira by name in the New Testament. She is Lydia, described by Luke as a "worshipper of God," who encountered Paul on the second missionary journey while she apparently was conducting a business trip to Philippi. Lydia was converted, and then subsequently offered herself as Paul's patron in hospitality (Acts 16:14–15).

Thyatira Identification (2:18)

"Son of God," the only occurrence of this title in Revelation, is one of the few times in the Seven Letters when an identity feature is not taken directly from the Inaugural Vision. The letter itself will reveal multiple reasons for this identification pertinent to Thyatira. This title probably is counter-propaganda to one of the local guild deities, Apollo Tyrimnaeus, as well as to the imperial propaganda of the emperor as "Son of Zeus." Further, given that all trade guilds had an associated patron deity, an even broader scope for this title would be to strike at the heart of what power genuinely binds humans together into shared community. True social identity in this life is in the church, not the trade guild. True ruling divinity in this world is Christ, not Caesar.

The identity then takes a turn back to the Inaugural Vision, "eyes like a flame of fire . . . feet like burnished bronze." The eyes of Jesus have piercing insight into the fidelity of faith. Compromise with cult might be hidden from the church but is easily visible to the Son of God. The burnished bronze term is allusion to a unique bronze trade guild product, and the bronze trade guild god is Apollo Tyrimnaeus.[101]

Thyatira Account (2:19)

As always, Christ knows. His knowing at Thyatira is accurate because of his eyes like a flame of fire and his standing in their midst. Their "works" are detailed as "love, faith, service, and endurance." These four elements sound generic, but actually are direct counterpoints to later descriptions of Jezebel and her activity. Love contrasts Jezebel's adultery. Faith contrasts Jezebel's unrepentant heart. Service contrasts Jezebel's pagan ritual. Endurance contrasts Jezebel's cultural compromise. In challenging contrast to Ephesus, then, who has lost her first love, Thyatira's "latter works exceed the first."

---

[101] Hemer, *Letters*, 116.

Thyatira Assessment (2:20–23)

We finally meet the problem at ground zero—"Jezebel." The name is metaphorical.[102] This pagan Phoenician queen of Israel's King Ahab was a thorn in the side of Elijah for introducing worship of the pagan god Baal into Israel's royal court. She had Naboth murdered to get his vineyard for unhappy Ahab (1 Kgs 21). Jehu answered the question of peace with the retort, "What peace can there be, so long as the many whoredoms and sorceries of your mother Jezebel continue?"[103]

The new "Jezebel" at Thyatira has corrupted Jesus' church just as the old Jezebel had corrupted Ahab's court. The "practice immorality" charge seems to be the problem of the trade guilds with their monthly feasts, and the "fornication" could be physical as the debauchery these feasts were notorious for becoming but also could be metaphorical for eating food sacrificed to idols, so participation in pagan idolatry. The problem of Jezebel has the appearance of another formulation of the Nicolaitan doctrine met at both Ephesus (2:6) and Pergamum (2:15), but that doctrine now is embodied in a named person.[104]

Jezebel calls herself a prophetess. She is attempting to subvert the present leadership. John later labels her doctrine as "the deep things of Satan" (2:24). Unclear is whether this expression is chosen by John on the fly or claimed by Jezebel herself as teaching the "deep things of God." If her own rhetoric, she might be claiming to go beyond the apostolic tradition to a deeper understanding of the gospel in lobbying for participation in the guilds. John puts a twist of irony on the claim: her teachings really are the deep things of Satan. This Satan rhetoric is the story behind the story again. When the synagogue opposes the gospel in ways that can become lethal, as at Smyrna, or when paganism and imperial cult are fused together into a lethally potent cultural mix, as at Pergamum, or a false prophet has set up shop in the church in ways that utterly corrupt and are lethal to the integrity of the gospel and the survival of the church, John is sure Satan is at work

---

[102] Seriously, given the biblical storyline, who would name their daughter Jezebel?

[103] 2 Kgs 9:22 (NRSV). The tragic summary of Ahab's reign is: "Indeed, there was no one like Ahab, who sold himself to do what was evil in the sight of the Lord, urged on by his wife Jezebel" (1 Kgs 21:25, NRSV).

[104] The house church setting would mean no more than 20 or 30 members at the most, so everyone would recognize the metaphorical reference instantly.

to destroy the church and the message she preaches. Perceived lethal threat to gospel and church is the core of John's Satan rhetoric.

How did she insinuate herself into a leadership role at Thyatira? Thomas offers insight from a sociological perspective. Similar to the original Jezebel being part of the elite class of Israel, this Jezebel could have been part of an elite class in Thyatira's social structure.

> This classification alone would have qualified her for a position of great magnitude in the guilds. As a patroness or benefactor to one of the non-elite social or trade collegia, she would have had access to other areas of society, including the church of Thyatira. This explanation would offer a plausible scenario for her to be converted to Christianity by a non-elite member of the church of Thyatira. Her status in the city also might answer the question of why some members of the church of Thyatira tolerated her teachings and even, to a great extent, followed them. The possibility of expelling Jezebel from the church at Thyatira would have been financially devastating for the members of the church who might have participated in her guild.[105]

Thomas shows that assuming Jezebel is a patroness to a trade guild is a reasonable assumption given the likely social dynamics the scenario at Thyatira suggests. In that high-status role, Jezebel would have "almost immediate power and a voice" upon her conversion into the church at Thyatira.[106] The only problem is, she teaches heresy. In the apostle John's terms, she is another antichrist gone out into the world in these last days. Jezebel needs to know that only Jesus is the true "Son of God" and ultimate patron of life at Thyatira, not the emperor and his embedded patronage system that drives business at Thyatira.

The problem of false prophets becomes a major theme of the Judgment Cycle (6–20). One of the fearsome characters in the second part of the Judgment Cycle (Rev 12–20) is the beast from the land, the false prophet serving the beast from the sea (Rev 13). The activity of these beasts becomes the figure of the great whore of Babylon in Rev 17. Jezebel's judgment announced here in the letter to Thyatira anticipates Babylon's judgment in Rev 18. Thus, the entire Judgment Cycle with its climax in the destruction of Babylon dramatically is meant to bring home the point for believers in Thyatira about Jezebel. This pro-

---

[105]Thomas, "A Sociological Analysis of Guilds in First-Century Asia Minor," 130.
[106]Ibid., 147.

phetess of Thyatira incarnates the beast from the earth who causes the worship of the first beast from the sea, which is the abomination of Babylon. This integration of the Judgment Cycle into the Seven Letters shows how the visions of Revelation are meant to dramatize the issues of the seven churches of Asia Minor.

Jezebel has been given time to repent, but she has refused (2:21). Perhaps local prophets had warned her she was teaching heresy. The repentance theme of the Seven Letters is crucial for understanding the judgments of the Judgment Cycle. They are not punitive. They intend repentance. God never judges such that he is not trying to save. The repentance theme is dominant in the Seven Letters, the verb occurring eight times in two chapters.[107] The theme also surfaces at key points in the Judgment Cycle, and the related theme of the failure of repentance suggests why the lake of fire will become inevitable in the drama.[108]

FIGURE 10.42. Roman Bed. A finely crafted Roman bed from the second century B.C. The basic style of Roman beds remained pretty much the same for centuries. They had the general form of a chase lounge. An elevated and inclined front portion was a simple design to accommodate leaning and resting as much as to use the bed for sleeping. John uses bed as a metaphor for illicit teachings (LP).

Building upon the immorality metaphor, Jezebel is judged with the sin she sins. She is thrown on a bed, but this is not the harlot's bed of pleasure; this is a bed of distress (2:22). "I will strike her children with death" is severe; however, a chance for repentance already has been refused. Within a larger context of all the letters taken as a group, the meaning here could be metaphorical, that is, alluding to the same reality as the "second death" at Smyrna (2:11). This is not physical death. This is the death that really matters.

Another internal indication that the Seven Letters are written as an integrated unit is the consequence of the judgment of Jezebel and

[107]Rev 2:5, 2x; 2:16; 2:21, 2x; 2:22; 3:3, 19.
[108]Rev 9:20, 21; 16:9, 11.

her followers: "and all the churches will know" (2:23). In whatever he does, how Jesus judges Jezebel will be apparent to all the churches of Asia Minor. What Jesus says to one church, he says to all. What will be known is that "I am the one who searches minds and hearts, and I will give to each of you as your works deserve." Heretics and hypocrites who are trying to worship both Caesar and Christ will be exposed. This exposure fits the identification of the one who has eyes like a flame of fire and emphasizes the need for the interior reality of faith.

Thyatira Exhortation (2:24–25)

Believers at Thyatira are to "hold fast." They are to persevere in their apostolic teaching and witness. They are to do like Smyrna, refuse to compromise, refuse to learn the deep things of Satan, that is, Jezebel's errant teaching and bad advice about trade guilds and pagan practice. How long are they to hold fast? "Until I come," Jesus says. If we put the emphasis on the coming part, this statement could be framed as inaugurated or futurist eschatology. If futurist, the coming is a future event to be awaited (Gog and Magog, Rev 20). If inaugurated, the coming is a judgment realized now in the context of the forces of history that the One who is the beginning and end controls and directs to achieve the divine purpose in all things (Babylon, Rev 18).

However, the emphasis in the thought "until I come" could be on the adverb, "until." The thought would be the call for eschatological perseverance that is imperative for the preaching of the gospel during the church age under social, political, and religious duress.

Thyatira Promise (2:26–28)

The last four letters have promise, then call. Every promise section has a formulaic conquering theme with eschatological nuance. Thyatira's promise is for the one who "continues to do my works to the end," which reiterates the exhortation to hold fast. "My works" is refusing Jezebel's cultural compromise. "To the end" is the coming of Jesus just referenced (in history, believer's death, or at the end of history). The promise, then, begins by reiterating the exhortation to persevere in the faith.[109] Resist Jezebel and her children decisively. To what reward?

---

[109]Not addressed is the question of apostates who later repent that later vexed the church. Easy to be confessional when the confessional crisis has passed.

In expressing the reward, John combines both Jewish and Roman traditions. The Jewish tradition is messianic. The Roman tradition is militaristic. They interact together to complete John's imagery.

The first part of the promise uses Jewish tradition. The allusion is to Ps 2:9: "You shall break them with a rod of iron, and dash them in pieces like a potter's vessel" (NRSV).[110] The Ps 2 background is a royal enthronement psalm used for the installation of a new king on the Davidic throne. The language in the psalm of God's adoption of the new king as his own son later became messianic in Jewish thought and anticipated the messianic kingdom. This messianic background would tie into the letter's identification of Jesus as "Son of God." Aptly, as Beale points out, the letter that begins with the royal title "Son of God" ends with allusion to a royal messianic psalm.[111]

FIGURE 10.43. Pompeii Amphorae. Amphorae bottles discovered in the ruins of Pompeii used in the commercial sea trade of wine and oil across the Roman empire. Elongated shapes with pointed bottoms were an ingenious method of storage in multiple rows in the latticework of curved boat hulls, almost as seen stacked here. A Pompeii street sign (right) embedded into a corner wall indicates a *themopolium*, the ancient fast food establishment (see Fig. 8.1, p 177). "Image signs" at major street intersections in Pompeii were for an illiterate population to navigate their way. Note the pole and rope transport of the amphora supported on the shoulders of two men.

To persevere in the faith garnishes "authority over the nations." An interpretive choice has to be made whether to allow this idea to be controlled by political and military concepts of European monarchy imported into the context or by the context as developed in the letter to Thyatira. So, once again we are asking, What is the nature of the kingdom Jesus advanced? We would argue that a contextually driven

---

[110] Consult the critical commentaries for the problem of the verb as "break" or "shepherd" in the quotation in the LXX versus the Masoretic text.

[111] Beale, *Revelation*, 226–27.

interpretation would see this bold "authority over the nations" as the authority of gospel truth over all enculturated pagan worship in any community that shatters all idolatrous claims to worship and veneration. That is the issue of Jezebel, trade guilds, and pagan practice in Thyatira. Believers in Thyatira are promised they will have "authority" over Jezebel and her children, who are functionaries of the Roman empire and its idolatrous commercial structures, by their faithfulness to apostolic tradition and gospel truth. In this way they rule with an "iron rod" (2:27) because gospel truth does not bend to pagan compromise. They rule as when "clay pots are shattered" could be allusion to vessels of commercial enterprise, such as the amphorae carrying wine and oil across the Roman empire.[112] The authority given to Jesus by the Father is the authority of the gospel, which Jesus has entrusted to the apostles, and the apostles have entrusted to the generations that followed them, including believers in Thyatira (2:28).[113]

The second element of the promise uses Roman tradition. The one who "conquers" is given "the morning star" (2:28). The morning star is Venus, brightest object in heaven after the sun and moon. This star reaches its maximum brightness just after sunset or before sunrise. Venus as the Greek Aphrodite is part of the myth of Rome. Aphrodite is the divine mother of Aeneas who fled the destruction of Troy and founded the Roman people.[114] As a result of this legend of Roman origins, Aphrodite became integral to Roman life even at the personal

FIGURE 10.44. Aphrodite Coin. From Laodicea, A.D. 139-44. Dolphin in lower right is association with the imperial family (PMB).

---

[112]Allusion may also be to ancient ritual ceremony among conquering kings who enacted a shattering of clay vessels in the presence of the vanquished ruler. However, the more immediate context in Revelation seems to be Rome's commercial enterprise.

[113]Even as Paul validated to the Corinthians the gospel they had received from him (1 Cor 15:1-11).

[114]See the material on Aphrodisias; for Aeneas legend, cf. Fig. 9.5, p. 212; for temple of Aphrodite, see Fig. 12.23, p. 555; for statue of Aphrodite, see Fig. 9.13, p. 218.

level. Images of Aphrodite retrieved from homes and private life from decorative statuary to small worship shrines are common finds. At the level of the Roman state, Roman generals gave loyalty to Venus. She was the bright star presaging the morning of battle. The victorious generals Sulla, Pompey, and Caesar all built temples to Venus in pious gratitude for battle victories. The Roman Forum has the remains the temple of Venus Genetrix, whom Julius Caesar claimed as a personal divine ancestress.[115] Roman legions carried the sign of Venus on their sacred standards, and Roman coins often were of Venus (Aphrodite).

FIGURE 10.45. Aphrodite Figures. Left is Aphrodite and Eros statuary that graced one of the Roman terrace homes of Ephesus (EMS). Right is a small terracotta worship shrine of Aphrodite in a traditional divine epiphany scene of billowing drape (TMT). Such Aphrodite figurenes could be found in almost all Roman homes.

The clue to Jesus' meaning about being given the morning star comes from the only other allusion to Venus imagery in Revelation, which occurs at the very end of the book. The conclusion to Revelation has several ties back to the promise sections of the Seven Letters (an indication of the importance of the Seven Letters to the exegesis of the book). In the closing lines of Revelation Jesus titles himself as the "bright morning star" (22:16), explicitly echoing the letter to Thyatira. Thus, what Jesus actually promises believers in Thyatira is himself. He

[115]Dio Cassius 43.22.1–2.

is both the promise of victory on the day of battle and the reward for victory. In this way, Jesus is the kingdom come.

In combining Jewish imagery of the messianic king and Roman imagery of the victorious general, the promise to Thyatira offers the true "Son of God" and the supreme ruler of the kings of the earth who transcends every pretense of the military emperor who rules Rome. In faithfully worshipping Christ, Thyatira conquers Caesar. Even if believers are martyred, as with Antipas at Pergamum, they win. In fact, martyrdom is the very seal of victory, the proof until the resurrection that the beast from the sea did not win the battle for the allegiance of the human heart, like Venus had Rome's heart.

Sardis (3:1–6)

FIGURE 10.46. Sardis Acropolis. A view from the Marble Hall past the synagogue to the mountains which created the impregnable fortress of the Sardis acropolis.

Sardis often is described as a city of faded glory because the age of the Lydian dynasties who used to rule the area long had past. Commercial importance was built on a gold trade. Sardis had a strong and socially prominent Jewish population. An element in the letter may have local reference to infamous incidents in the history of Sardis. Her acropolis fortress was considered impregnable. Yet, twice in her history, Sardis was captured by surprise. The acropolis was scaled by stealth, and no guard was watching. The Lydian King Croesus was surprised by Cyrus and the Persians in 547 B.C.[116] For a second time in her history, the city was taken by surprise by the Seleucid king Antiochus III in 214 B.C.[117]

FIGURE 10.47. Sardis Synagogue. The ancient synagogue excavated at Sardis was found to be 197 x 59 feet and is estimated at capacity to be able to hold 1,000 people.

Outstanding to this site is the largest Jewish synagogue ever discovered outside of Palestine. The main hall could accommodate an enormous crowd. Beautiful flooring has elaborate mosaics in detailed geometrical patterns. Some lower wall portions have been restored to show decorative marble inlays, again in geometric patterns. Several aspects of the Sardis synagogue are unusual. Some features illustrate the significant presence of Jews in the upper elite of the rich and powerful.

- First, the synagogue apparently was not gender segregated, since the interior walls were not accommodated with wall benches for sitting, as was usually the case in synagogues, and the meeting hall had no balcony, which normally functioned to segregate women.

[116]Herodotus *Hist.* 1.79–84.
[117]Polybius *Histories* 7.15–18.

- Second, the synagogue incorporates some unusual non-Jewish items recycled from other buildings and shrines, prominently displayed, that indicate strong acculturation to Roman life. Two of these items are an eagle table and a pair of back-to-back lion statues. The supports of the eagle table have reliefs of eagles, traditional symbols of Rome, adapted from a previously existing Roman monument. The lions are sixth-century B.C. sculptures similar to those used in Cybele monuments. The table and lions displayed on site are reproductions. The archeological museum at Manisa has the originals.

FIGURE 10.48. Sardis Synagogue Items. The eagle table and double lion pairs shown are the on-site reproductions. Eagle relief detail below is the original in the Manisa Müze, Manisa, Turkey.

- Third, the high social and political status of Jews in Sardis is indicated by inscriptions in the synagogue that document at least eight donors to the city, including city counselors (a status position that required great wealth to hold), a procurator, and imperial financial administrators. Jews at Sardis were not just part of the city. Jews at Sardis included wealthy aristocrats of elite social and political classes who controlled power, politics, and economy.

FIGURE 10.49. Sardis Synagogue Inscription. One of the inscriptions on the synagogue support lintel indicates Jewish patrons who donated to the needs of the city, including city counselors, one procurator, and several imperial financial administrators.

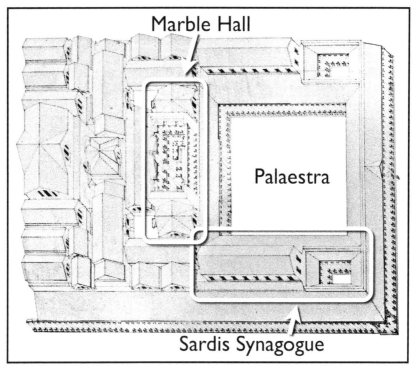

FIGURE 10.50. Sardis Bathhouse Complex. The largest diaspora synagogue ever found is prominently situated in the city center integrated into the bathhouse complex.

FIGURE 10.51. Sardis Synagogue Courtyard. The Marble Hall of the bathhouse is visible through an interior doorway of the Sardis synagogue's outer courtyard.

- Fourth, the synagogue not only occupies a premier location in the very center of the city, but architecturally is integrated directly into the famous "Marble Hall" bathhouse complex and comprises the entire left wing of the *palaestra* exercise field in front.

FIGURE 10.52. Sardis Marble Hall. The most dramatic feature of ancient Sardis is the Roman bathhouse, originally covered entirely in marble, called the Marble Hall.

FIGURE 10.53. Sardis, Temple of Artemis. The temple of Artemis, situated prominently on the Sardis acropolis, later included worship of Zeus and then the imperial family in the Roman Period. The temple eventually was quarried for later building projects.

Sardis also had a typical pagan environment, both in the worship of Artemis and Zeus in the Hellenistic period, and in the worship of the imperial family in the Roman period. Sardis gained the prestigious title of *neōkoros* (temple warden of imperial worship), and its temple complex on the top of the acropolis was remodeled to serve this new status. The original Artemis/Zeus temple was converted into a most unusual double-building design, with the worship of Artemis and Empress Faustina (d. 140) on one side, and the worship of Zeus and Emperor Antoninus Pius (d. 161) on the other. In later centuries after this pagan worship was suppressed and the temple fell into disuse, its structures were quarried for materials for other building projects. Hardly any of the original construction remains to be seen today.

Sardis Identification (3:1)

The two elements of the identification derive from both the prologue and the Inaugural Vision. The first as "seven spirits of God" is a literary tie back to the prologue (1:4), which is a symbol for the fullness of the Holy Spirit. The second, "who holds the seven stars in his right hand," is a literary tie back to the Inaugural Vision (1:16) and is similar to the identification to Ephesus (2:1). This similarity again shows the interconnectedness of the Seven Letters as one complete literary unit to be interpreted as a whole. The two elements mutually reinforce one another. The spirit of prophecy reflects the presence and activity of the Holy Spirit (22:6). Those held in the right hand are the local prophets of the seven churches. Thus, their work and ministry is at the will and discretion of the Holy Spirit. The identification, then, is constructed to emphasize God's divine sovereignty over the churches as the One who both sustains and directs all the churches through the local prophetic leadership. Without that divine directive, the church at Sardis is lost.

FIGURE 10.54. Sardis Priest Inscription. Letter of an imperial priest from Sardis to the proconsul of Asia Minor about A.D. 189 indicating the close relationship of empire and religion (MMM).

Sardis Account (3:1)

The "I know your works" formulaic phrase is judgment coming down on Sardis at the moment the letter first is read to the congregation. No church is spared the penetrating gaze of the all-knowing, all-seeing eyes of Jesus. The church has a name of being alive, but they are dead, Jesus says. This status is a precarious spiritual state. They are worse off than Ephesus, who has lost her first love but is not described as dead. The church is participating in a dangerous illusion. Some may even be on the way to the second death from which faithful Smyrna is preserved. If their lampstand already has not been removed, an action with which Ephesus has been threatened, the moving van is pulling up in the driveway at Sardis.

Sardis Assessment (3:2)

Sardis is to "wake up." This warning may be allusion to the history of the city twice conquered by surprise in the sleep of night. Sardis can wake up if she will "strengthen what remains and is on the point of death." Apparently all is not lost in this congregation. A few embers in the grey coals barely show a spark of life that could be fanned to flame.

The problem is explained as her "works are not perfect." These works are defined in the Seven Letters. They are:

- the toil and patient endurance that is bearing up for the name of Jesus as preached in the apostolic gospel and not growing weary in the face of heresy (Ephesus)
- enduring tribulation, poverty, and slander from opponents that publicly and maliciously shame and dishonor believers (Smyrna)
- holding fast the name and not denying the faith in dangerous public confession (Pergamum)
- showing true love, faith, service, and perseverance in a pervasively pagan culture (Thyatira)

Sardis has compromised her witness. She probably seeks a low public profile with only a token confession of faith. Perhaps the church has become as acculturated to life in Sardis as was the synagogue. Trying to "fly under the radar" of the notice of civic officials is sabotaging this church's actual mission. She should depend more on the Holy Spirit.

Sardis Exhortation (3:3–4)

By now, Sardis is absolutely clear what remedial actions she can take. She is to "remember then what you received and heard; obey and repent." Remembrance of what they "received and heard" would be a return to their baptismal confession on the basis of the fundamentals of gospel faith in a suffering Son of Man and his call to take up a cross and follow him. If they "repent," they will change their witness and reject compromise with their pagan culture.

If Sardis refuses to make changes, but instead, continues to insist, "What problem?" this church will meet a similar fate as this city—a surprise visit by one who comes "like a thief, and you will not know at what hour I will come to you." This statement echoes gospel traditions about the teaching of Jesus.[118] As with the kings Cyrus I and Antiochus III, another king will come and take the church by stealth precisely when they think all is well and are sleeping soundly. The question, as usual, is whether this coming is historical or eschatological. Inaugurated eschatology is a "both and" solution that is probably the best way to frame most of the statements of the "coming" of Jesus in the Seven Letters. Without the threat having some present reality for the seven churches, the coming rhetoric is little more than "blowing smoke" for the original audience. Local prophetic leadership in each of the seven churches would be emboldened by receiving Revelation if they took with due seriousness that the message had come directly from Jesus. Jesus would "come" in the form of local prophets being encouraged to toe the line of gospel truth and gospel testimony after the reading of Revelation in the seven churches. This coming like a thief theme, as well as the clothing theme in the promise section to follow, together integrate the letter to Sardis into the Judgment Cycle through theme repetition. Note how explicitly immediately prior to the imagery of Armageddon in the pouring out of the sixth bowl, John writes:

> "Behold, I am coming like a thief! Blessed is the one who stays awake and is clothed, not going about naked and exposed to shame." And they assembled them at the place that in Hebrew is called Armageddon" (16:15–16).

[118] Cf. Matt 24:42–43.

John explicitly has made clear by this "in your face" literary repetition directly out of the letter to Sardis just prior to using the Armageddon figure that this Armageddon is the battle Jesus is fighting for the truth of the gospel in Sardis (and churches like Sardis). Why is no Armageddon battle actually described? Because the battle recapitulates Rev 3:1–6 and a church almost dead. The ecclesial situation is dire.[119]

A "few" in Sardis have not "soiled their clothes." The metaphor is common enough in ancient literature for unethical or immoral behavior or character. In a Christian context, though, the imagery possibly could have baptismal imagery in mind in addition.[120] In any case, in both the Old Testament and in Revelation, stained garments are metaphorical for idolatry.[121] If the church functionally can be described as dead, then these few really have to be few indeed. These few "will walk with me" because they walk the path the suffering Son of Man walks in faithful testimony, and they eventually will be glorified with him. They will be dressed "in white" because they are "worthy." That is, they gave testimony to the truth of the gospel in an evil world. Ancient sacrificial ceremonies in both pagan and imperial worship included the wearing of white robes, and wearing white robes becomes a key symbol in Revelation of the redeemed.[122] Faithful witness translates into future fellowship. Present perseverance is future worthiness.

Sardis Promise (3:5)

Faithful witnesses will be clothed "in white" in eternity because they did not soil their garments by compromise of the gospel in history. The reward is to share the righteous glory of Christ, whose face is like the sun shining in its strength (1:16).

---

[119]Even if a futurist has made the journey this far into this book, which might be doubtful, they probably are struggling seriously now. I understand. I have been there.

[120]Ancient baptismal practice in the church fathers seems to include stripping off old garments as a symbol of shedding an old way of life to walk in a new way of life. Cf. Cyril of Jerusalem *Baptism* 2. How far back this fourth-century practice can be read into the traditions of the early church, and how widely practiced in the various regions of the established church, is ambiguous.

[121]Cf. Isa 65:4 (LXX); Rev 14:4.

[122]The literary development can be traced in the following series of passages: Laodicea (3:18); the twenty-four elders around the throne (4:4); martyrs are given white robes (6:11); the great multitude before the throne of God and the Lamb (7:9); the Lamb's armies (19:14).

The second reward is, "I will not blot your name out of the book of life." Imagery from Daniel may be in play here.[123] Ancient cities maintained registers of their citizens. Paul used his Roman citizenship as a protective mechanism in the story in Acts 22:25. The book of life later is associated with the Lamb as a key symbol in the Dragon half of the Judgment Cycle.[124] Within Revelation, the intentional contrast would be the books used later in the judgment of unbelievers (20:12).

While John does not explicitly tell us the Lamb's book of life is the Apocalypse itself, the nature of the beginning and ending of this book may imply this connection. First, from the very beginning, the reader is told this book comes directly from Jesus (1:1). Jesus immediately is seen as the Gospel figure of the Son of Man in the Inaugural Vision that John then transforms into the Lamb imagery of the vision of heaven (5:6) that he uses throughout the rest of the book.

Second, Revelation has a peculiar emphasis on itself as a book and as a prophecy that is repeated multiple times in Rev 22:7–19.

- "See I am coming soon! Blessed is the one who keeps the words of the prophecy of this book" (22:7).

- "but he said to me, 'Do not do that! I am a fellow servant with you and your fellow prophets, and with those who keep the words of this book. Worship God!'" (22:9)

- "And he said to me, 'Do not seal up the words of the prophecy of this book, for the time is near'" (22:10).

- "I warn everyone who hears the words of the prophecy of this book: if anyone adds to them, God will add to that person the plagues described in this book" (22:18).

- "If anyone takes away form the words of the book of this prophecy, God will take away that person's share in the tree of life and in the holy city, which are described in this book" (22:19).

These words of command and admonition at the end of Revelation are explicit that the Apocalypse itself and how one responds to the book are divine judgment enacted. Thus, the Lamb's "book of life" could be

---

[123]Cf. Dan 7:10–12; 12:1–2.
[124]Rev 13:8; 17:8; 20:12, 15; 21:27.

seen as the book of Revelation itself. These seven "letters" actually are judgment oracles that assess present spiritual realities within the seven churches and exhort repentance and promise life in each conclusion. Revelation is the Lamb's "book of life" because the book brings life to those who hear and heed the words of the book, and words of blessing for "keeping" what is written, both from John and from Jesus, form a grand *inclusio* for the book:

- "Blessed are those who hear and keep what is written" (1:3).
- "Blessed is the person who keeps the words of the prophecy of this book" (22:7).

To "keep" Revelation, then, is to transform John's prophecy into the Lamb's book of life.

The third reward is, "I will confess that person's name." This reward is the heavenly counterpart to the present crisis in the seven churches. The confession of Jesus has a dual reality: a present confession by believers of Jesus and a future confession by Jesus of believers. This confession is allusion to the Jesus tradition.[125] One can note how a "name" theme is prominent in this letter, and this prominence may reflect how bearing a Christian name is becoming a distinct challenge for witness in Asia Minor.

Philadelphia (3:7–13)

FIGURE 10.55. Hills of Philadelphia. The ancient site of Philadelphia is on the slopes of Mount Tmolus near the modern city of Alaşehir in the valley below.

Attalus II (d. 138 B.C.) named Philadelphia in honor of his love for his brother and heir, Attalus III (d. 133 B.C.), who then bequeathed the Pergamum kingdom to Rome when he died without an heir. The city was at a commercial trade junction between roads running to Smyrna and Pergamum, so caught all trade running the length and width of

---

[125] As in Matt 10:32.

the Asian province. Philadelphia itself had an agrarian economy of grapes producing wine and flocks producing textiles and leather.

Like numerous cities in Asia Minor at the time, Philadelphia was destroyed by the cataclysmic earthquake in A.D. 17. She was rebuilt by imperial money. Strabo in particular comments on how the frequency of earthquakes shaking and destabilizing the buildings of Philadelphia all the time caused the people to live more outside the city as farmers than in the city.[126] Outside the book of Revelation, her only claim to fame in Christian history was receiving a letter from Ignatius (ca. 108), bishop of Antioch, on his way through Asia Minor to martyrdom in Rome. Ignatius's letter warns against accepting Judaism, apparently indicating the Jewish community in Philadelphia still impacted the church.[127] In later history the city became a *neōkoros* of the imperial cult under the emperor Caracalla (d. 217). As all the cities of former Asia, Philadelphia succumbed to Islam in the Muslim onslaught of the eighth and ninth centuries. Modern Alaşehir means "city of Allah."

Philadelphia Identification (3:7)

The identification "Holy One and True" is not derived from the inaugural vision, but instead, is a divine attribution by the martyrs under the altar in the fifth seal (6:10). Isaiah may have coined the title "Holy One of Israel" (Isa 22:22). The name of God is intended by John. The emphasis on "true" in the seven letter context of constant concern about faithful testimony and the Philadelphian context of Jewish opposition probably means Jesus as the true Messiah, not a false Jewish pretender. The second element is "the one who has the key of David." This image seems to echo the Inaugural Vision "key" imagery (1:18). The allusion was to King David's palace steward, Eliakim. The key of David is explained as possessing the unique authority to open and no one shut, and to shut and no one open. Although the elements of the identification here at Philadelphia are differently constructed than the previous letters, the common denominator is Jewish imagery about God himself and the royal house of David. A polemical context with the synagogue may be implied.

---

[126]Twelve cities devastated overnight included Sardis and Philadelphia; cf. Pliny *Nat. Hist.* 2.86; Tacitus *Annals* 2.47; Strabo *Geog.* 12.8.18; 13.4.10.

[127]Ignatius *Phil.* 6.

FIGURE 10.56. Philadelphia, Saint John's Basilica. The only evidence of Christianity today in Alaşehir, ancient Philadelphia, are the remains of the seventh-century Byzantine church, ironically called Saint John's Basilica.

Philadelphia Account (3:8)

Christ provides an "open door" to the Philadelphians that "no one is able to shut." The account pulls directly off the identification related to the key of David. Entrance into the royal house of David is through the true Messiah, not the synagogue. Since the synagogue has rejected the promised Messiah, she forfeits the right to speak for the Messiah. Perhaps a type of synagogue expulsion is between the lines here.

What is encouraging is that one can have "little power" yet can keep the gospel word of testimony and not have "denied my

FIGURE 10.57. Saint John's Basilica Inscription. This church inscription and the ruins of the ancient acropolis lie unexplored.

name." This denial likely is in the public context, and perhaps even could be court proceedings of the type suggested in Pliny's letter to Trajan. The Philadelphian church though small in size has effective witness, and this characteristic of faithful witness even without the help of size makes them a paradigm of true Christian testimony for John. One can note that of the seven churches, only two are without condemnation, Smyrna and Philadelphia, and yet these congregations are the most enfeebled in size, economic strength, and social status. This parallel characteristic between Smyrna and Philadelphia also adds weight to the idea of chiastic structure for the Seven Letters. Even though the sequence of Seven Letters makes a circuit along the major roads, John also seems to have composed the content of the letters so as to create a chiasm.

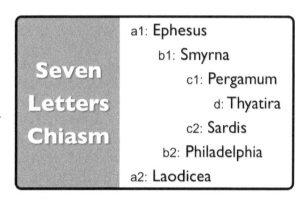

FIGURE 10.58. Seven Letters Chiasm. The structure emphasizes the parallels between Smyrna and Philadelphia, the only two churches receiving only positive commendation, and shows the central significance of Thyatira, which letter stigmatizes the false prophetess Jezebel.

Philadelphia Assessment (3:9–10)

With "those who say they are Jews but are not," John assesses that the Jewish community in Philadelphia is making an unfounded claim on Jewish identity. By this charge he cannot be referring to racial or social heritage. Rather he is referring to religious heritage of the true faith of Abraham on the pattern of Paul's teaching in Romans.[128] Again John uses the harsh "synagogue of Satan" rhetoric. God's true people are by the righteousness of faith witnessed in the life of Abraham and consummated in Messiah Jesus. As at Smyrna (2:9), Jesus is the litmus test of Judaism. If the Jews are acting like the synagogue of Satan by the nature of their response to the gospel, that is John's conviction of a

---

[128]Rom 2:17, 28–29; 3:29; 4:10–11, 16.

trajectory of behavior that, given free reign and power, would become lethal to believers, even as in the martyrdom of Polycarp. The rhetoric is harsh, but the reality harsher. Note that the only two references to "synagogue of Satan" in the Seven Letters are in those to Smyrna and Philadelphia, which are in chiastic parallel among the Seven Letters.

Causing opponents to "bow down at your feet" is ironic reversal of Gentiles bowing before Israel and Israel's God in the Old Testament.[129] The essential truth of this figure is to learn "that I have loved you." This love is God's covenant love as referenced in the prophets for Israel but ironically fulfilled in the Gentile church.[130]

What the Philadelphians have accomplished that garnishes praise from Jesus is that they "have kept my word of patient endurance." This word is gospel witness and this witness has to endure patiently because many oppose this testimony. John's faithful witness in persecution theme now is seen as one of the most consistent elements in the Seven Letters. Revelation's opening prologue starts this theme (1:5), and the Seven Letters make the theme core for the rest of the book. The church is to reflect the Son of Man pattern of the Inaugural Vision.

As the Philadelphians have kept their word, Jesus will keep his. He will keep them "from the hour of trial that is coming on the whole world to test the inhabitants of the earth." The hour of trial as a metaphor would be an intense but limited time. A misunderstanding is to read "from" as "away from," although that reading admittedly is a first impression. The impression is wrong because Antipas is dead. Jesus is not promising the church in Philadelphia what he failed to do for Antipas, or even John of Patmos for that matter. What Jesus is promising the Philadelphians is what he *did* do for Antipas. He gave Antipas the promise of resurrection life if he had to forfeit this life. He also gave Antipas a seal protecting from the second death sanctified by faithful testimony if he did not fear the first death. The emphasis is on Jesus keeping what he promises, and he does *not* promise witness without consequence. He also does not promise that some believers will be spared the responsibility of witness at any point in the story of the church, even including the "hour of trial coming on the whole world." Yes, read this as unequivocal rejection of rapture doctrine. Not only is

---

[129] Isa 45:14; 49:23; Ps 86:9.

[130] For example, Isa 43:4.

rapture doctrine a strange nineteenth-century innovation by a rogue Brethren prophet rejected by his own movement and alien to apostolic witness, the teaching ironically destroys the crucial point John has labored to establish throughout the Seven Letters with his theme of faithful witness: the hour of trial coming upon the whole world *is because the church refuses to give up her gospel testimony.* No church, no persecution; no persecution, no hour of trial.

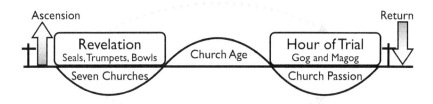

FIGURE 10.59. Hour of Trial. On the basis of his own experience and that of the seven churches, which John signifies in the Judgment Cycle of the Seals, Trumpets, and Bowls, John anticipates a coming "hour of trial" for the entire church and the world. This hour of trial will be the church's own passion story in following the Son of Man.

This "hour of trial" is John's allusion to a future he cannot see. John can anticipate, however, and imagine what that hour of trial will look like. He can see his own experience. John draws insight from his present situation and that of the seven churches of Asia Minor in their struggle with pagan idolatry and imperial ideology. He sees that struggle as a paradigm of the world's fundamental resistance to the gospel. This resistance is more than harmless apathy that only goes so far as to ignore. In emperor worship and pervasive pagan idolatry, John sees intimations of immorality that will unleash evil in such power as to be lethal to the existence of the church in the world.

If this perspective on John's understanding is correct, then one would have to conclude postmillennialism simply is entirely alien to John's core beliefs about the intransigence of evil in the world. Evil's intrinsic intransigence is the very reason for the inevitability of this "hour of trial." As for the Son of Man, whose story in history ends in passion, so for the church, whose story in history also will end in passion. Jesus charges his followers to take up their cross (plural) in order to follow him. With a pietistic emphasis on individual appropriation of this call, the application gets lost in personal life struggles of relationships, sickness, finances, and in-laws. ("I guess it's just my cross to bear.") Few note this charge is *corporate*, not just for daily witness, but to exhort the whole body of the church to embrace her own passion at the end of her story. In a way, futurists are right: a great tribulation is coming.

Dispensationalists, however, are wrong. Their nineteenth-century rapturist eschatology absolutely bungles Christology, ecclesiology, and soteriology. The truly sad legacy is that John's call to faithful witness both now and in the coming hour of trial is lost in the cacophony and chaos of competing end-time plots that seem absolutely clueless that the passion of Jesus means the passion of the church.

Philadelphia Exhortation (3:11)

Jesus' word that he "is coming soon" invokes a theology of presence. This coming and presence is the story of the one who stands "among the lampstands" (1:13). Believers are exhorted to "hold fast," which is faithful witness. Believers can hold fast because Jesus is with them and strengthens believers in the very task he calls them to perform. Jesus' assurance in Luke is evocative: "When they bring you before the synagogues, the rulers, and the authorities, do not worry about how you are to defend yourselves or what you are to say" (Luke 12:11).

"That no one may seize your crown" is the right to reign with Jesus, who is ruler of the kings of the earth. Following in the footsteps of the Son of Man will produce the same destination. "What you have" is present tense and is the crown not to let anyone seize. This idea is an intratextual allusion in the Seven Letters to the millennial reign.

Philadelphia Promise (3:12)

The promise to those who conquer is to be made a "pillar in the temple of my God." Of the possibilities, a pertinent one is the patronage system. Patrons always had memorial inscriptions with their names to identify their civic beneficence. Compare the imprint of Zoilos all over the ruins of Aphrodisias and the massive monument commemorating his vast patronage over a lifetime.[131] Temple columns also are possible when one sees the extraordinary attention given to building ancient temples. Whether monument or temple, the idea is honor and respect.

---

[131] See Fig. 9.6 and the discussion on p. 213.

FIGURE 10.60. Didyma, Apollo Temple Aerial. View of huge Apollo Temple complex.

FIGURE 10.61. Didyma, Apollo Temple. Rebuilt columns in upper right of aerial shot.

Ancient temples were famous for the size and number of their columns, such as the temple of Artemis at Ephesus, one of the "seven wonders" of the ancient world. That temple was rivaled by the temple of Apollo at Didyma, but the ambitious building project never was completed. Didyma means "twin" for the city's namesake of the story of the twin brothers, Apollo and Artemis, born to Zeus and Leto. At a total length of 394 feet with columns 82 feet high, the temple was enormous and impressive and third largest in the ancient world, behind only Ephesus and Samos. Striking architectural workmanship went into its features, especially decorative elements of the columns, though only 72 of the planned 122 columns were completed. Columns were set on bases of elaborate carvings, and front row columns included reliefs. Corner column capitals were distinctively carved with scenes between lion griffins and bull's heads. A series of Medusa heads at the apex of the tripartite architrave protected the temple from harm. This attention was given to this temple because the temple enclosed the oracle of Apollo associated with a sacred spring and rivaling even the oracle at Delphi. The temple also was the conclusion to the twelve-mile "Sacred Way" pilgrimage from Miletus down to Didyma for worshippers to participate in the annual spring festival there. Thus, pillars were one of the most impressive features of ancient buildings. The myth that Constantine after conversion closed the oracle of Apollo at Didyma and executed its priests is contradicted in ancient sources.[132]

FIGURE 10.62. Apollo Temple Drawing. Two front human figures show massive ratios.

FIGURE 10.63. Apollo Temple Workmanship. Medusa relief (left) and original corner capital of beautifully executed bull heads between lion griffins (right).

---

[132]Lactantius *Persecutors* 48. Cf. a history of Apollo oracles in Fontenrose, *Didyma*.

While the search for local references in each letter is legitimate and can illuminate the text, that "you will never go out of it" is a play on the city's history of abandoning buildings due to many earthquakes is not peculiar to Philadelphia. That metaphor applied to all cities of the ancient world that were subject to earthquakes. A more relevant idea is the problem of conquered temples, with their priests forced out or slaughtered, and the loss of sanctity, such as with the Jewish temple in the First Jewish War or the famous Apollo temple at Didyma by the Persians. This connection to conquered temples is stronger, because John actually alludes to the Jewish temple destruction in his imagery of not measuring the outer court of the temple as nations trample over the holy city in Rev 11:2. John would be saying God's heavenly temple never will be conquered nor its priests ever have to flee their sacred duty. A temple connection is stronger also because the next part of the promise alludes to the heavenly court.

Jesus will write on believers "the name of my God," which is possession. The "name of the city of my God" is habitation. Believers are promised they belong to God as God's own personal possession, and they dwell with God in God's own personal place. This city further is identified as the "New Jerusalem that comes down from my God out of heaven." New Jerusalem is the last vision of the book (Rev 21:2). That vision is about God's presence: "and God himself will be with them" (21:3). Once again we see how the promise sections of the Seven Letters are tied integrally to the ending of Revelation. The construction of these promise sections shows that Revelation starts with the seven churches, ends with the seven churches, is the seven churches.

Laodicea (3:14–22)

Laodicea was established about 261 B.C. by the Seleucid king Antiochus II (d. 246). He named the city for his wife Laodice. At an intersection of major trade routes, the city was prosperous commercially and became a large, money-lending center. Serious excavation finally began in 2003 directed by professor Celal Şimşek. The city boasts a stadium, two theaters, four bathhouses, four agoras, six fountains, two monumental entrances, a council house, temples, and monumental streets. Cemeteries surrounded the city on all four sides. Underground running below the streets was a sophisticated sanitation system.

FIGURE 10.64. Laodicea Stadium. Largest in ancient Anatolia, the stadium was dedicated to the emperor Titus, brother of Domitian.

The stadium south of the city, yet to be excavated, is visible as an oblong depression in the ground with some of the original seating exposed. At 919 feet long, the stadium now is believed to be the largest in ancient Anatolia. An inscription of dedication honors the patron who funded the project in the time of the Flavian emperor Titus (79–81), the brother of Domitian. A dedicatory inscription reads:

> This stadium was built with personal resources of Nicostratus, the youngest son of Lycias Nicostratus, for the people and the divine Emperor Titus Caesar Augustus Vespasian, son of Vespasian, and consul for the seventh time. The inheritor Nicostratus completed the missing parts and the people blessed the Proconsul Marcus Ulpius Traianus.

In the Greek period stadiums were venues for athletic competitions of sprinting, discus throwing, and long jumping. The Romans modified Greek stadiums in order to accommodate their popular animal combats (*venationes*) and gladiator fights (*munera*), and the Laodicea stadium was modified at one end in this manner. Adjoining public baths served not only the general public, but athletes of the stadium as well.

Laodicea had two main thoroughfares through the center of the city. The longest of these was the colonnaded Syria Street running over half a mile. Urban apartments (*insulae*) ran along both sides of this street. About 1312 feet of Syria Street from the Caracalla Fountain to the East Byzantine Gate is being restored.

FIGURE 10.65. Laodicea, Syria Street. Over half a mile long, Syria Street was a major thoroughfare of Laodicea, with shops and *insula*-type apartments along both sides.

FIGURE 10.66. Syria Street Tile Work. The street included beautiful tile work along side sections. All sanitation ran underground in channels under Laodicea's streets.

FIGURE 10.67. Laodicea, Central Temple Complex. An impressive temple is being restored in the central section of the city north of Syria Street.

An impressive temple on the north side of Syria Street is under excavation. The rectangular courtyard of this temple is surrounded by porticos, and the floor was laid with marble slabs.

The excavation team announced the discovery in 2010 of Laodicea's fourth-century church by underground radar. The plan is to excavate the church fully. The baptismal pool already promises to be as interesting as the pool of the Hagia Sophia in Istanbul.

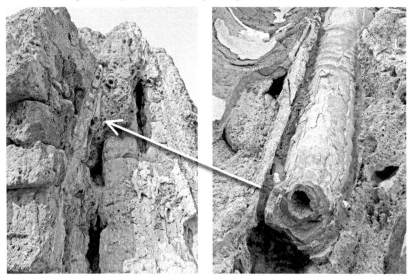

FIGURE 10.68. Water Distribution Terminal 1. Clay pipe system showing such extensive lime deposits in this particular pipe as almost to close off the flow entirely.

Laodicea had several water distribution terminals. Terminal 1 was located east of the stadium and South Baths complex. The base was about 20 feet by 66 feet, and the current preserved height is about 23 feet. The water source was the Başpinar spring in modern Denizli through twin travertine pipes. Terminal 2, to the north and larger than Terminal 1, is more complicated because this terminal supplied most of the city. Multiple supply pipes joined at a sedimentation pool that filtered impurities before going to the distribution pool.

Each terminal had a distribution tank on the top from which ran baked clay pipes of different diameters and at various heights from the bottom for distributing the water to various parts of the city, including nymphaeums (fountains or spring monuments dedicated to nymphs) and baths. Over sufficient time, the heavy lime deposits of the mineral water would encrust the interior of these pipes, like carotid artery disease, slowing water flow, eventually to the point of shutting off all flow entirely. Pipes would have to be replaced periodically. Even today the lime deposits are visible in exposed sections of the pipes from the remains of the terminal.

FIGURE 10.69. Terracotta Pipe System. Exposed underground system of terracotta pipe channeling water from the water distribution center to another part of Laodicea.

Laodicea formed part of a tri-city complex of Laodicea, Colossae, and Hierapolis in the Lycus valley. Colossae was eleven miles to the southeast at the foot of Mt. Cadmus. Her water was the pure snowmelt from the mountains, so, famously fresh, clear, and cool.

FIGURE 10.70. Colossae Tel. Eleven miles from Laodicea at the foot of Mt. Cadmus, Colossae's pure, snowmelt water was famous. The ancient site lies unexcavated.

Hierapolis was just across the valley from Laodicea a short four miles. Hot mineral springs made the city a famous health and healing center. The waters were medicinal, receiving visitors from around the world, and the god Asklepios and his daughter Hygeia were celebrated and worshipped in this place. The mineral springs cascade over a 300 foot cliff, covering the cliff surface with an impressive blanket of white lime deposits as the water evaporates that can be seen for miles.

FIGURE 10.71. Laodicea, West Theater. The west theater is poorly preserved but is notable for its view across the valley of the white cliffs of Hierapolis off in the distance.

FIGURE 10.72. Cliffs of Hierapolis. The lime deposits of the striking cliffs of Hierapolis are viewable for miles. This view is across the valley from the west theater of Laodicea.

The church at Laodicea probably was started as a part of Paul's Ephesian ministry on the third missionary journey in Acts 19. Our in-

FIGURE 10.73. Ancient Hierapolis Drawing. Four miles from Laodicea, Hierapolis was a medical center with hot mineral springs and famous white cliffs (HAMH).

FIGURE 10.74. Cliff View of Lycus Valley. View of the Lycus valley from the white cliffs of Hierapolis looking in the direction of the city of Laodicea.

formation is through the letter of Colossians. The surrounding regions of Ephesus apparently were evangelized by Paul's associates. Epaphras probably evangelized Colossae.[133] Paul orchestrated letter exchanges between Colossae and Laodicea and wrote the letter of Colossians in the New Testament.[134] The other two cities also were strong Christian centers. Hierapolis is notable for the church father and bishop, Papias (d. 155). Laodicea also was the seat of a bishopric and later hosted an important church council in the fourth century and produced the bishop Apollinarius (d. 390), famous as an opponent of Arianism.

[133] Col 1:7; 4:13.
[134] Col 4:13, 16 and 1:1; 2:1.

FIGURE 10.75. Frontinus Gate of Hierapolis. A patron dedicated the gate to Domitian.

FIGURE 10.76. Syrian Gate of Laodicea. Still hidden gate was dedicated to Domitian.

All three cities of the Lycus valley had strong relationships with the Flavian emperors. The main triple-gate entrance into Hierapolis was built about the time Revelation was written and was dedicated to Domitian. As noted already, the stadium at Laodicea was dedicated to Domitian's brother, Titus. Laodicea's Syrian Gate, a main triple-gate entrance into the city, like the one at Hierapolis, was built and dedicated to Domitian. Laodicea's Syrian Gate has yet to be excavated.

Laodicea eventually was granted the status of being a *neōkoros* city, or warden of the temple. This term originally referred to one who swept and cleaned temples, or to those in charge of caring for a temple or adorning for festivals and other activities. Especially in Asia Minor, the term came to be associated with imperial temples, and became an honorary title used particularly on coins to designate and honor cities who had achieved the privilege of hosting a center of imperial worship for the surrounding region.

FIGURE 10.77. Imperial *Neōkoros* Coin of Laodicea. The emperor receives the acclamation and worship of his legions (left) and the local provincial officials in Asia Minor (right). The functionaries in the care of the temple are between the pillars. The bottom inscription is LAODIKEŌN NEŌKORŌN ("Laodicea, Temple Warden"). The coin is dated 216–217 (PMB).

Of the Seven Letters, Laodicea seems to have an abundance of local references. One local reference is financial. The city was a banking center. Cicero (d. 43 B.C.), the famous philosopher, statesman, and lawyer, cashed his letters of credit in Laodicea while traveling through the region in 51 B.C.[135] The city had a significant Jewish population of some means as well. Cicero said that Flaccus, the Roman governor of Asia, issued an edict restricting the export of gold out of Asia Minor. Flaccus was convinced too much gold was leaving the province. Jews, however, continued trying to pay their annual temple tax to Jerusalem in gold. Flaccus got wind of the contraband and confiscated 20 pounds of gold in 62 B.C. from the Jewish shipment intended for Jerusalem.[136] The equivalent in half shekels means that approximately 7,500 male Jews lived in and around the city of Laodicea at this time.

---

[135]Cicero *Epis. Fam.* 3.5.4; cf. *Epis. Att.* 5.15.2. Also, cf. Hemer, *Letters*, 192.

[136]Cicero *Pro Flacco* 68. Cf. Josephus *Ant.* 14.241–43.

Another example of financial strength comes from the massive earthquake of A.D. 60 that did major damage to all three Lycus valley cities. The nearby cities of Hierapolis and Colossae were destroyed. Hierapolis was grateful for imperial rebuilding help. Colossae, however, after this massive quake devolved into a small peasant village that eventually went unoccupied after the eighth century. Such a result would mean that the early church in Colossae was lost to history within months or perhaps less than a year or so of receiving Paul's letter to them due to the A.D. 60 earthquake. In stark contrast to both Colossae and Hierapolis, however, even though Laodicea also was destroyed in the earthquake, her civic leaders refused emperor Nero's offer of financial aid for rebuilding. They preferred instead to rebuild out of their own resources.[137]

Another local reference is commercial. City industry included a major center for textile manufacturing (even as the modern city of Denizli today). The black wool from Laodicea widely was believed to be some of the finest in the world.[138]

FIGURE 10.78. Priestess of Isis. Other cults besides the imperial cult were active in Laodicea. One illustration is this 2nd cent. A.D. Roman statue of a priestess of Isis, which was found in Laodicea. Isis worship was popular among Romans (HAMH).

A third local reference is medical. Due to the proximity of the highly valued hot springs at Hierapolis just a few miles away, Laodicea was a medical center. In addition, the Phrygian god Mēn Karou was worshipped at a temple about thirteen miles northwest of Laodicea. This local god of healing later was associated with Asklepios. The temple maintained a medical school.

[137]Tacitus *Annals* 14.27. Laodicean wealth apparently had grown rapidly in the first century, because the city did accept financial assistance from Tiberius after the earlier earthquake of A.D. 17; see Strabo *Geog.*12.8.18.

[138]Strabo *Geog.* 12.8.16.

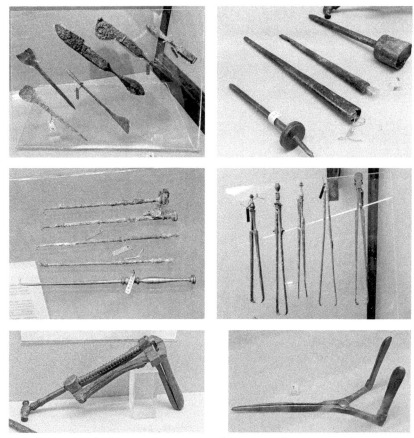

FIGURE 10.79. Medical Instruments. Preserved from Herculaneum are sophisticated tools of first-century Roman medical science. Pictured are scalpels, catheters and probes, dental tools, and retractors (NNAM).

First-century medical work was more sophisticated than some might imagine. Preserved tools of the trade easily still are recognizable today. One notable product of the medical school at Laodicea was the famous Laodicean eye salve, made from a "Phrygian powder" mixed with oil. The actual composition of this powder is unknown, probably kept a careful secret for commercial reasons. A connection between Laodicea and this famous eye salve can be established from surviving ancient works on ophthalmic medicine as well as numismatic evidence.[139]

---

[139] Ramsey's argument that *kollyrion* in Rev 3:17 is a reference to the Phrygian powder often is followed (cf. *Seven Churches*, 419, 429). Hemer, *Letters*, 196–97, however, rightly pointed out the weaknesses of that linguistic argument. Hemer, *Letters*, 197–99, then proceeded to put the argument on firmer ground, which is followed here.

FIGURE 10.80. Herculaneum, House of the Telephus Relief. With its large size (three stories) and situation on the edge of town overlooking Naples Bay, this house widely is believed to be that of the proconsul and patron Nonius Balbus.

FIGURE 10.81. Herculaneum, House of the Black Salon. A peristyle courtyard graces this home of a freedman who had grown wealthy in successful business ventures.

Probably due to the apostle Paul's ministry from Ephesus, Christian presence in Laodicea was significant. Christians met in a number of house churches. One house church at Laodicea met in the home of the patroness Nympha (Col 4:15).¹⁴⁰ Archippus also may have been from Laodicea (Col 4:17).

FIGURE 10.82. Herculaneum, House of the Corinthian Atrium. The roof to this atrium style home originally would have covered this area except for a rectangular opening in the center.

These patron homes would have been of the wealthy elite that had wide spaces able to accommodate a large gathering of people in one place. The peristyle was a columned porch surrounding a courtyard. The atrium was a square or rectangular space to greet guests entering a home with an opening to the sky, usually for collecting rain water. Homes in Herculaneum and Pompeii illustrate these Roman-style designs. Roman homes also had a large main dining room (*triclinium*) with smaller rooms adjacent to accommodate overflow. Romans ate in a reclining position, so not as many individuals could be in the same room around a table at meal times. The atmosphere was intimate.

---

¹⁴⁰The Greek spelling of the name technically could be masculine or feminine. The key is the following possessive pronoun. The KJV translators worked with only a few late Greek manuscripts, which had the masculine form of the pronoun ("his house"). The earliest and best manuscripts, however, render the pronoun as feminine ("her house"), which also is the more difficult reading, so more likely. Later scribes changed the pronoun, uncomfortable with the suggestion of women leaders in house churches.

Figure 10.83. Herculaneum, House of the Saminte. A multistory atrium style home.

Laodicea Identification (3:14)

Jesus is identified as the "Amen, faithful and true witness." This unusual "Amen" is the divine title given God in Isa 65:14. The emphasis is on God as a true witness to his redemptive acts in the overarching narrative of creation, salvation, Israel, and new creation. Jesus is key to the consummation of that plot, as publically declared by God through the eschatological event of resurrection.[141] Laodicea's challenge will be to become a true witness herself to God's redemption in Jesus. The following faithful and true witness expression is now a rhetorical *topos* in Revelation that shows the prologue wording in 1:5 to be setting this theme from the earliest verses of Revelation.

The next phrase, "origin of God's creation," is ambiguous. If the original creation, the thought would be similar to Col 1:18. If the new creation, the thought would be the resurrection, as in Rev 1:5. Either way, the thought is life. Jesus has the keys of Death and Hades (1:18) because he has the power of life. No one truly dies who dies in Christ. The thought of the entire power of creation resident in Jesus should be the assurance and guarantee of witness vindication.

Laodicea Account (3:15)

The account has no commendation at all. Laodicea is the only church to be castigated so completely. Even Sardis, who is "dead," has a few smoldering embers left in the fire of faith. Such a negative characterization of Laodicea is a calculated action by John for concluding the Seven Letters. Negative assessment is the last impression John intends to leave in the end. The overall situation is *that* serious, for those who will try to downplay John's urgent tone, as Jezebel or the Nicolaitans.

The charge is that they are "neither cold nor hot." Rather, they are "lukewarm." The key thought is usefulness for a purpose. John is comparing the usefulness of water sources in the Lycus valley region. The clear, cold water of Colossae is useful for drinking. The warm, mineral water of Hierapolis is useful for medicine. The tepid water of Laodicea is foul and worthless. Without filtration or a water system to precipitate out impurities, that water will make a person vomit.[142] This description is as strong in rhetorical impact as "synagogue of Satan," though this balance can be overlooked by critics of John's rhetoric.[143] Similar to Sardis, the Laodiceans are in a precarious spiritual state. In context of the other letters, they have compromised with idolatrous

---

[141] On the pattern of Paul's proclamation in Rom 1:3–4.

[142] The verb behind "spit you out" is *emeō* (ἐμέω), from which we get our adjective "emetic," an agent that induces vomiting.

[143] The charge that John is anti-Semitic is overdone, because the criticism is myopic. John is just as hard rhetorically on believers as anyone else.

trade guilds. They have worshipped the emperor. They are successful commercially but have a washed-out witness.

Laodicea Assessment (3:16–18)

Worse still, Laodicea is boasting in all the wrong things. The church boasts, "I am rich." She has the false security of wealth and a hubris to match. The city's response to the emperor's offer of assistance after the A.D. 60 disaster is reprised in the church, which does not bode well when King Jesus offers assistance. This boast is the very inference that John fears. Laodicea sees her wealth as a sign of God's blessing. John sees that wealth as possible only because of rank compromise with an ungodly commercial system. Beale offers the following insight.

> That some kind of boast about material welfare is in mind is likely from the observation that whenever πλούσιος ("rich") and πλουτέω ("I am rich") are used negatively in Revelation, the reference is to unbelievers who have prospered materially because of their willing intercourse with the ungodly world system (6:15; 13:16; 18:3, 15, 19). The same idea is present here. Indeed, the church is on the brink of becoming identified with such an ungodly system, as the second part of 3:17 bears out.[144]

Otherwise, had they maintained a genuine witness, Laodicean believers would be as the Smyrneans, financially distressed because they refused to play in the idolatrous trade guild racket necessary to be in imperial commerce. The House of the Black Salon in Herculaneum (Fig. 10.81) belonged to a former slave who had become wealthy as a freedman through suc-

FIGURE 10.84. Herculaneum Worship Shrine. In the House of the Skeleton (found in a room upstairs) is this ornate worship shrine (*lararium*). These shrines brought the sacred into Roman homes, and worship or veneration occurred on a weekly, sometimes even daily basis. Success or failure in life, and particularly in business, was understood in terms of piety and devotion to the proper divinities and powers controlling all areas of life. One of the main values of Roman character was *pietas*, devotion to the gods and ancestor worship.

[144]Beale, *Revelation*, 304.

cessful business. He likely boasted in imperial commercial power, and like many ancient homes, his probably included worship shrines for local gods and goddesses, Roman deities, and emperors. The freedman in Herculaneum probably belonged to a trade guild and showed necessary fidelity to the emperor, whose imperial peace fostered the good business fueling his ostentatious lifestyle. Even Roman soldiers, with their rare salaried pay, could be counted as relatively affluent.[145]

FIGURE 10.85. Herculaneum, House of the Augustals. The *augustals* in Herculaneum were a special group of priests dedicated to the worship of the imperial family. They conducted their meetings in this hall, which was filled with statues of emperors.

The problem is not exclusively Roman nor first century. A parallel with Hos 12:8 is strong in its content and context. Ephraim brags of a wealth he achieved without iniquity, but he is a merchant whose prosperity is by the hand of his oppression and his thinking pattern is so reprobate that he thanks self-made, mute and dumb idols for his commercial "blessing" (cf. Hos 2:5, 8; 12:8; 11, 13).

FIGURE 10.86. Herculaneum Augustals Plaque. Identifies benefactors of the college of priests.

---

[145]Domitian notably increased their pay; cf. Bingham, *The Praetorian Guard*, 68.

Jesus delivers a shocking newsflash, "You are wretched, pitiable, poor, blind, naked." The church could not have received a stiffer uppercut to the spiritual jaw. The spiritual metaphor is transparent. Laodiceans are opposite of what was thought. Local allusions come home to roost in these words. The combination wretched, pitiable, and poor is a triad of related terms that together offer stark contrast to their perceived commercial wealth. "Blind" is a play on the famous Laodicean eye salve. "Naked" is a play on the famous Laodicean wool.

Jesus counsels to "buy from me." Do commerce with Christ, not Caesar. True wealth is purified business activity. Coming to the praise of God with clean hands is more than some quick swipe of anti-imperial hand lotion before worship. First, buy "gold refined by fire." Metallurgy is a stock and trade Old Testament prophetic metaphor for spiritual purity, refining precious metal by fire.[146] True wealth is spiritual, exactly what Jesus indicated to the Smyrneans ("but you are rich," 2:9). Second, they should buy "white robes to clothe you and to keep the shame of your nakedness from being seen." White is stark contrast to the famous Laodicean black wool. Similar advice was given to believers in Sardis (3:4–5). This new purchase counters a current "naked" condition—ironic, because they are clothed in the very finest fashions imperial commerce could buy. Nakedness rhetoric will tie this Seven Letters material to the later Judgment Cycle. The shame of nakedness comes up again in Rev 16:15 in the Dragon, beast, and false prophet drama. The Laodicean letter prefigures the later storyline.

FIGURE 10.87. Clothing Finery. An exquisitely draped Roman woman (SMS).

[146]Ps 12:6; Isa 48:10; Jer 6:27; 9:7; Dan 11:35; 12:10; Zech 13:9; Mal 3:2–3.

Third, buy "salve to anoint your eyes." The famous Laodicean eye salve is no remedy for this condition. Only Christ can cure this type of blindness. In sum, the three elements of gold, garments, and salve are historical, local links.

Laodicea Exhortation (3:19–20)

Jesus reminds the Laodiceans that his reproof is an expression of his covenant love. The covenant love theme is precisely on target because of the story of Israel. She was judged because she was loved, and God was trying to save. Jesus, in like manner, is trying to save the church at Laodicea from its own hubris and false illusion of being a legitimate expression of the church. Jesus then exhorts, "Be zealous and repent." The proper response to the divine covenant love and effort to save is repentance. The carefully chosen verb "be zealous" is perfect for this context. Zealous is a hot condition, more like the hot springs of nearby Hierapolis that are soothing and salubrious. This zealous condition is the opposite of the current lukewarm state of the congregation. Significantly, the lukewarm condition is not permanent. Fortunately for believers in Laodicea, repentance is entertained as a possibility, which sets the stage for the invitation of the next verse.

"Behold, I stand at the door and knock." The present tenses of the verbs for standing and knocking create a realized eschatology. This reality happens the moment the Seven Letters are read in each church. Laodicea arrives at her eschatological crisis moment of decision as the "one who reads" (1:3) now gives the invitation directly to the church of the present, risen Lord standing among the lampstands.[147]

If Jesus is permitted entrance—an extremely ironic thought for a church—he will come in and "eat with you, and you with me." Rather than opining about social status and constantly jockeying to be on the invitation list to recline and dine with the social elite and wealthy of Laodicea for better position to make the next business deal, perhaps even a fortuitous meal with a provincial governor like Cicero on his

---

[147] This verse has been misused countless times as an evangelistic invitation to unbelievers in revival sermons. The use is wrongly applied. First, the original audience is believers, not unbelievers, so the exegetical point is renewal, not conversion. Second, the original crisis is eschatological judgment at the corporate level, not private individual struggle. That is, the issue is the church corporate as a body and involves her very destiny as an authentic, witnessing church in her own community.

way through the region, or perhaps daydreaming about the emperor's sumptuous dining halls, desire rather the table of the Lord. First-century social conventions did not mix social classes in sharing meals, which inherently would be a dishonor and loss of social status. Jesus, however, breaks these social conventions, the very social behavior that generated complaint against him by the scribes and Pharisees, which precipitated a triad of parables by Jesus, concluding with the parable of the lost older brother.[148] The shared community among all social classes that Jesus inspired was reflected in the early church "love feast" meal that accompanied the observance of the Lord's Supper.[149] This fellowship and meal around the table of Jesus was a powerful breaking of the power of the imperial beast to control the structure of society and the shared, intimate experience of human beings in communion.

FIGURE 10.88. Herculaneum Triclinium. Pictured above is the left wall of the summer dining room in the House of Neptune and Amphitrite, named for the main theme of the exquisite center mosaic on the richly-colored frescos of the center wall (right).

[148] Luke 15:1–2.

[149] The Christian love feast experience, however, was not without its own social tensions, which already had presented problems at Corinth; cf. 1 Cor 11:20–34.

Eucharistic overtones are strong in this invitation from Jesus to dine with the church at Laodicea, and, hence, to all the churches in Asia Minor. The Eucharistic overtones also show a duality of a present reality happening in church worship but a future reality as well anticipated in the observance.[150] The Eucharistic sense to this invitation in the letter to Laodicea once again confronts us with the question of the "coming" of Jesus. We are met time and again with a tension in New Testament perspective, even in the Gospels themselves. Ironically, the typical emphasis in preaching Revelation is on the future. Yet, these Seven Letters already have shown that *a future emphasis is not actually John's emphasis in the book of Revelation.* From the very first verse of the book John has not left the reader in the dark whatsoever about the timeframe of the content of this book ("what must take place soon," 1:1). We have seen that the Seven Letters simply cannot be understood in their proper context as true prophetic judgment oracles without a reality actually confronting the seven churches when first hearing the prophecy read in the context of weekly worship in house churches throughout Asia Minor. In his own discussion of this invitation to Laodicea as well as the thematic "coming" of Jesus to each of the seven churches, deSilva astutely points out, "Unless the congregations fall in line swiftly with his righteous demands . . . Christ's immediacy threatens swift judgment with no need to wait for the second coming."[151] Thus, focusing exclusively on a future nuance of the Rev 1:7 oracle of the coming of Jesus on the clouds simply does not cut the mustard on what John is doing in the very next chapters of the seven letters.

John's emphasis on the present "coming" of Jesus as Son of Man is witnessed in the Gospels. Matthew, for example, has present nuance much more than future when considered in context:

- "You will not have gone through all the towns of Israel before the Son of Man comes" (Matt 10:23), spoken of the evangelistic mission to Israel on which Jesus sends his disciples

- "Hosanna to the Son of David! Blessed is the one who comes in the name of the Lord!" (Matt 21:9), spoken by the Jerusalem crowds of the triumphal entry of Jesus into Jerusalem

---

[150] Luke 22:18–19; 1 Cor 11:24–25.
[151] deSilva, *Unholy Allegiances*, 81.

- "Now, when the owner of the vineyard comes, what will he do with those tenants?" (Matt 21:40), spoken by Jesus in a parable immediately after the Jerusalem crowds have acclaimed him as the one who comes to Jerusalem in the name of the Lord

- "For I tell you, you will not see me again until you say, 'Blessed is the one who comes in the name of the Lord'" (Matt 23:39), spoken by Jesus as a lament over Jerusalem after the triumphal entry, anticipating his resurrection glory through the cross (cf. Matt 27:53)

- "For as the lightning comes from the east and flashes as far as the west, so will be the coming of the Son of Man" (Matt 24:27), spoken by Jesus prophesying the destruction of Jerusalem and its temple

- "When the Son of Man comes in his glory, and all the angels with him, then he will sit on the throne of his glory" (Matt 25:31), spoken by Jesus of the judgment assize of the last day

The dominance of the present reality of the coming of the Son of Man in these sayings is obvious, even though a future component is not without voice, at least in the last example. When the matter is the coming of the Son of Man, the perspective of John of Patmos is similar to Matthew's own emphasis. John is no innovator in inaugurated eschatological rhetoric here in the Seven Letters. So, what is the bottom line being argued here? Our point is that *John's present perspective on the coming of the Son of Man as realized in the Seven Letters does not change in the following chapters of Revelation.*

What we are saying is that Jesus' invitation in Rev 3:20 to come and to dine with the Laodiceans if they repent anticipates the marriage supper of the Lamb in Rev 19:9. If the Laodiceans repent, the marriage supper of the Lamb is on. Revelation starts with the seven churches, ends with the seven churches, is the seven churches.

Laodicea Promise (3:21)

The promise to Laodicea if they "conquer" (repent and establish an authentic witness within the imperial commercial juggernaut) is "to sit with me on my throne." Here, John is reflective of Luke's emphasis on Jesus' ministry in terms of a kingdom, a meal, and a throne.[152] The

---

[152] Luke 22:29–30; cf. Moessner's excellent study of Luke in *Lord of the Banquet*.

promise of sitting on a throne anticipates in an intratextual echo the description of the millennial reign (Rev 20:4). As before in other letters, the promise section has eschatological overtones. Yet, John has set out these promises as realities obtainable by believers in first-century Asia Minor. The eschatology of the Seven Letters is inaugurated.

This promise statement's inaugurated eschatology is made clear in Jesus' following explanation, "even as I conquered and sat with my Father on his throne," a perspective of a strongly realized eschatology. Thus, Revelation has clear focus on Luke's ascension perspective on the realized glory of Jesus as the power presently energizing the nature and mission of the church through the Holy Spirit. That Jesus already has "conquered" echoes introduction expressions such as "firstborn of the dead" (1:5), "by his blood" (1:5), and "those who pierced him" (1:7). That Jesus already has "conquered" also anticipates expressions such as "a lamb slaughtered" (5:6), "souls of those slaughtered" (6:9), "they have conquered" (12:11), and "my reward is with me" (22:12). Probably the most revelatory verse and heartbeat of Revelation's conquering theme where the water hits the wheel is no more perfectly captured than in this one verse at the beginning of the Dragon drama:

> They have conquered him by the blood of the Lamb and by the word of their testimony, for they did not cling to life even in the face of death (12:11).

Suffused with pagan idolatry and sold out to imperial ideology, first-century Asia Minor is Satan's throne in the world. Here the church must live. In faithful, suffering witness, and in shared love feast and sacred supper, the church in Asia Minor has the daunting challenge in this deadly place to conquer this beast by expressing the present reign of the suffering Son of Man standing among the lampstands with head and hair white as snow, voice like the sound of many waters, eyes like flaming fire, mouth with a sword, a hand holding seven stars, feet as burnished bronze, and face like the sun.

SUMMARY

John uses two main visions to establish the theological foundation for a series of judgments that follows each vision. The first vision is the Son of Man in 1:9–20. This vision lays the foundation for the judgment of the church that follows in the Seven Letters in Rev 2–3. This vision occurs in the first chapter, which is divided into two literary units, an introduction (1:1–8) and the Inaugural Vision of the Son of Man (1:9–20). The introduction provides the christological key to Revelation. The Inaugural Vision provides the hermeneutical key.

The introduction is the christological key, because the focus is on Christ. The apocalypse of Jesus Christ means this book is from Jesus and about Jesus. The focus is on faithful witness, resurrection, and a kingdom. The path is sacerdotal, soteriological, and paradigmatic. So, Jesus is the sacrifice that saves and is to be emulated. These visions are communicated by signs and to be kept by obedience. The language is symbolic and metaphorical and the hearer is accountable. What is signed is soon. What is signed is specific to seven churches of Asia Minor. What is signed is authoritative. Jesus' coming in Danielic clouds of glory is realized in Jesus' present enthronement, not a future event. One cannot see this truth without eyes on the cross. The vision of Revelation rightly read is the gospel. God himself validates such a vision with the imprint of his own name.

The central vision of Revelation is the Inaugural Vision. This vision is the hermeneutical key to rest of the book. The central context is the church. The central figure is the Son of Man. This vision reveals how God expresses his supreme sovereignty over Caesar and his empire through Christ and his church. Jesus' suffering becomes the church's paradigm. The issue is corporate, not individual. The issue is present reality, but that reality is not without a future component.

John signs four truths about Jesus: who he is, where he is, how he is clothed, and what he looks like. Jesus is the Danielic Ancient of Days, judge of all the earth, but redefined by Jesus' own teaching about the Son of Man. This judge stands clothed as the perfect priest and king of Israel among the seven churches, which is the foundation of imminent judgment for those congregations. His sevenfold features show how perfectly he fulfills his identity as Son of Man and his functions as priest and king. The life Jesus brings is of an entirely different character than the life promised to Roman citizens subscribing to imperial ideology. Jesus has the keys of Death and Hades. He trumps all imperial death decrees. The only real death is the lake of fire, and Jesus is sovereign over the lake of fire like the emperor is not. Rev 1:19 is not the structural outline of the book.

The Seven Letters are not letters. They have neither the form nor content of first-century Greco-Roman letters, and calling them letters misconstrues their purpose. These Seven Letters are judgment oracles. They function together as a unit and represent the following judgment series that is based upon the opening vision of the Son of Man. The Ancient of Days executes judgment on his church. The letters read the first time are the coming of Jesus and play out the significance of an inaugurated eschatology. In structure, the letters are uniform and have the same sevenfold division. This uniform structure means all the letters are meant for all the churches, even though individual letters are tailored to each congregation. The letters mutually interpret each other and work in concert.

What unleashes the power of exegesis of the letters is to set them into two fundamental interpretive contexts. One context is historical. The historical context is first-century Asia Minor. Two literary elements use this historical context in discrete ways. One literary element using the historical context is the identification section. Specific features of each identification section build on the historical context of each city and function as thematic signals of what is to come in the following letter content. The other literary element of the letters using historical context is the following letter content itself. The letter content has allusions to features of a given city and its history that bring home the message in ways eminently pertinent to each church.

The other interpretive context is the Roman empire. An imperial ideology had constructed a powerful matrix of experience totally dominating political, religious, social, and commercial worlds. This matrix fused pagan and imperial idolatry and social patronage in ways powerfully dangerous, even lethal, to Christian confession. The threat was serious, even destroying the very mission and existence of the church. Sometimes Romans became so embedded into the imperial matrix, they were completely unaware of living an alternate reality, and breaking free would be like fighting a war with the very designer of the matrix.[153] The Son of Man has a sword in his mouth because this is a war of words—imperial ideology versus Christian truth.

---

[153]Yes, yes, of course, all allusions to the 1999 "Matrix" movie. Somehow, though, I cannot help but think Mr. Anderson's plight with the matrix and his nemesis, Mr. Smith, is the plight of the believer confronted with the ideology of the first-century Roman empire.

The point of the Seven Letters as judgment oracles is to identify and condemn the matrix and call believers to faithful witness. The true church on mission in a Roman world will be harassed and persecuted, but the church must conquer in this setting. The church must realize when they baptize believers, their paradigm is the baptism with which Jesus was baptized—and he died at the behest of Rome. In fact, the passion of Jesus means the passion of the church. The crucial hour of crisis for the seven churches confronted by the Roman imperial beast in first-century Asia Minor anticipates a future hour of trial coming on the whole world.

Each promise section of each letter offers eschatological reward to those who conquer through their faithful witness. This reward is repeated at the end of the book of Revelation. Such a literary *inclusio* for the book of Revelation seems entirely intentional. If asked to sum up this global literary structure in one thought, that thought would be this: Revelation begins with the seven churches, ends with the seven churches, is the seven churches.

11

Judgment of the World

The Sovereign God and His World

Is GOD SOVEREIGN OVER THE Roman world in which the seven churches have to live? This question is the one that haunts the churches of Asia Minor. Is God sovereign:

- when even a strong church has lost her first love?

- when believers refusing to compromise are poverty stricken?

- when believers lose their lives due to their confession?

- when false prophets advocate the Caesar worship guilds require?

- when the church is so dead only a few are keeping the faith?

- when synagogue Jews reject the very Messiah God had promised?

- when the church feels so self-sufficient not even Jesus is invited?

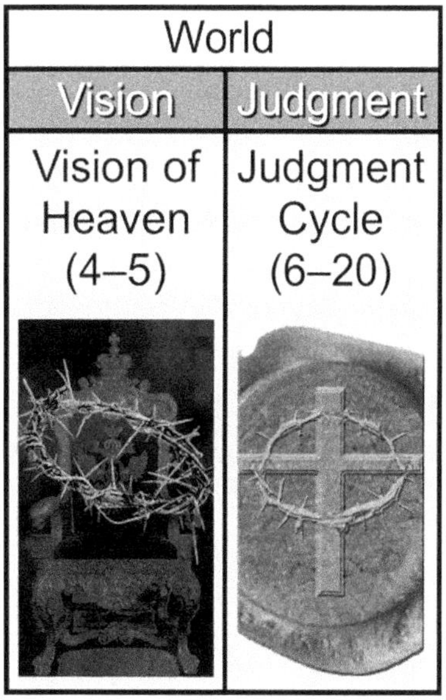

FIGURE 11.1. Revelation, Act 2. The Sovereign God and His World.

John uses a Vision of Heaven and its consequent Judgment Cycle to answer the question of God's sovereignty. His answer is absolutely yes. In giving this answer, John does not solve all the world's problems, but he does point to the mystery of God and how God conquers evil in the world. His answer, in other words, requires faith to see. The answer to the future is in the past. John is no voyeur beamed to the future in a Star Trek transporter, but he is a prophet of faith who has seen the cross as God's ultimate solution to dealing with evil. Thus, when the sovereign God in heaven rose up from his throne to deal decisively and conclusively with sin, as promised, he sent his only begotten Son to die on a cross. That is the gospel, and the gospel is the future. God conquers evil through the Son of Man and his churches.

VISION OF HEAVEN (REV 4–5)

Revelation 4–5 are two chapters that comprise one vision. As a literary unit, the two chapters work in unison and are mutually interpretive. The literary point is theological and pastoral. At the theological level, Christ is presented as fulfilling God's original creative purposes by subduing human rebellion. At the pastoral level, the vision reassures persecuted believers of God's sovereign control of the forces of human society and history and of faith's ultimate vindication.

The vision has three literary connections. The first connection is the imagery of the exalted Christ, which is a direct literary tie back to the last image of the Seven Letters in the promise section of the letter to Laodicea with the reference to sitting on a throne (3:21). Thus, this vision presents nothing new but simply expresses the heavenly reality behind the imagery of the Seven Letters. Another literary connection is linguistic. Numerous linguistic ties backward are in evidence:

- "receive" (2:28; 5:7–9)
- "conquer" (3:21; 5:5)
- "seven spirits" (3:1; 4:5; 5:6)
- "white clothing" (3:5, 18; 4:4)
- "saints, thrones" (3:21; 4:4)
- "crowns" (2:10; 3:11; 4:4)
- "open door" (3:8, 20; 4:1)

Finally, thematic ties are evident. The present reign of a kingdom and ruling in 1:5–6 is the very essence of the throne room scene of Rev 4.

The theme of overcoming ("to the one who conquers") that constitutes each promise section of all Seven Letters is recapitulated in Rev 5:5–6. Thus, whereas this Vision of Heaven opens up a new act in the drama of Revelation, multiple connections to the previous act of Rev 1–3 show they are related integrally. This point is crucial, because these types of literary devices compound together to give the impression that Revelation is all about the seven churches. Divorcing Rev 4–20 from Rev 1–3 destroys John's entire literary program and completely confounds interpretation.

The background for this Vision of Heaven is liturgical and Old Testament. One liturgical background is the synagogue morning liturgy. If so, John would seem to have some connection to the synagogue, as even his negative rhetoric in the Seven Letters shows in an oblique way. Another liturgical background is the Roman ceremonial cult. If so, John is creating a deliberate parody of emperor worship. Such background study is built on the observation that John's material in Rev 4–5 is expressed poetically, and is easily adaptable to liturgical use, which suggests John has composed the material with worship in mind. He even may be giving a heavenly pattern for the church to emulate.

Possible Old Testament settings include Dan 7, Ezek 1–2, and Isa 6. The Daniel background shows more than a dozen parallel elements, with Ezekiel only a few. The Isaiah background is the idea of a heavenly throne room and a heavenly temple, as in Isa 6:1–4, which also echoes in later portions of Revelation.[1] The connection to Old Testament portrayals of God's court, divine epiphany, and revelation is apparent, but only in allusive ways.

Revelation of God (4:1–11)

An Invitation (4:1)

The expression "after these things" is a literary shift, not sequential, to mark a different scene, not to enumerate the order of what is written as the sequence of what is experienced.[2] John says "I saw." What he

---

[1] The sanctuary and open door (11:19; 15:5); the flashing, lightning, and thunder (4:5; 11:19; 16:18); the seven lamps as temple lampstand (4:5); and the altar of incense (8:3; 9:13; 16:7).

[2] John does this regularly; cf. 7:1, 9; 15:5; 18:1; 19:1.

saw was heaven revealed. John saw "an open door in heaven," which prophetically signals revelation from God. John describes an epiphany of true divinity, which counters the blasphemous claims of emperors whose iconography perversely pretends divinity through billowing vestments.[3] John's imagery is anti-imperial, a direct shot across the bow of provincial authorities, trade guilds, and their false prophets supporting the idolatrous emperor cult.

This vision is tied to the Inaugural Vision, since the same voice addresses John, the one John earlier had heard speaking like a trumpet (1:10). This invitation is from the Jesus of the Inaugural Vision. This new scene is still about the heavenly realities behind the Son of Man vision. This same voice tying this vision back to the Inaugural Vision is the hermeneutical key that the "after these things" that John is to be shown continues to be related to an inaugurated eschatology. What John is shown continues to be those truths Jesus has established in his incarnation, death, and resurrection.

The "come up here" is not the rapture of the church.[4] All John says is, "I was in the spirit" (4:2). The point is not what happened, or where John went, how he got there, or even if he did not move an inch physically and this was all just a perceptual journey within his mind, which "in the spirit" certainly could imply. This spiritual state is the same condition leading to John seeing the Inaugural Vision of the Son of Man (1:10). The point is, John is being allowed access to the council room of God, mentally or physically, which puts his authority on par with the Old Testament prophets.

John is shown "what must take place after these things." This reference is the same as 1:19 with its allusion to Dan 2:28–29. Daniel's context is "the last days." John's context is Daniel inaugurated. John is talking about the eschatological realities Jesus has infused into human history as a result of the incarnation. The "after these things" are the things post the death, burial, and resurrection of Jesus. "These things" are ascension realities. Such realities are why John is invited by the voice with the sound of a trumpet, a metaphor for the risen Jesus.

---

[3]See Claudius depicted as divine master of land and sea (Fig. 9.23, p. 227).

[4]Revelation's language cannot be denied as metaphorical and then interpreted as metaphorical. If the seven churches are not seven literal churches but seven ages of church history, and John is not a literal prophet but the raptured end-time church, then Armageddon, the millennium, or any other figure also can be metaphorical!

FIGURE 11.2. Apocalypse Tapestry, Rev 4. Twenty-four elders in four panels of six each surround God, with the four living creatures near the throne. John auditions the scene on the left (Angers, France).

A Throne and A Sovereign (4:2–7)

John sees a throne and a sovereign—and not one trace of Domitian or his imperial court is to be found anywhere, not even in a tiny corner. In fact, nothing having anything to do with the Roman empire is part of this divine audience. The silence about Domitian and his imperial court is deafening and had to be stunning for the original audience. The occupied throne of heaven is the greatest of all signs of Revelation. The background is in Old Testament epiphanies, such as Ezek 1. The jasper, carnelian, and emerald stones and the rainbow all reflect God's glory (4:3).

John then describes the heavenly retinue surrounding the throne in two groups. Whatever these two groups figure individually, together they represent the combined worship of all creation in the praise of God. First mentioned are the twenty-four elders. These elders wear white robes, are crowned with golden crowns, and sit on thrones (4:4). Robes, crowns, and thrones are allusive to promises to conquerors in the seven churches, so these are probably reigning believers.[5]

---

[5] The real problem is the meaning of the number twenty four, which is debated as stars, angels, saints, patriarchs, apostles, Levite orders, and so forth. The meaning of the attire, on the other hand, is more clear as reigning believers, due to the immediately preceding material in the Seven Letters (Rev 2:26; 3:5, 21).

The "lightning, rumblings, thunder" (4:5) will have almost verbatim repetition in the conclusion of each of the three judgment septets of Seals, Trumpets, and Bowls.⁶ This wording at the end of each judgment series ties the source of the judgments back to the throne room of God. The Judgment Cycle is God acting in his sovereignty. The "seven flaming torches" are explained as the "seven spirits of God," which is a direct tie to the introduction (1:4).⁷ The seven torches figure the manifold operations of the Holy Spirit. The "sea of glass like crystal" (4:6) intends to reflect God's glory like the precious stones already mentioned.⁸

John then introduces "four living creatures" (4:6).⁹ Their depiction seems to combine Ezek 1 and Isa 6. They look like a lion, an ox, a human face, and an eagle. This imagery is apocalyptic zoomorphism. The creatures usually are taken to represent creation. More important as characters in the drama is not who they are but what they do. These four living creatures mediate God's judgments, and serve to tie the later Judgment Cycle back to the heavenly throne room vision.¹⁰

Heaven's Worship (4:8–11)

Heaven's unceasing worship is the believer's destiny. Believers in Asia Minor should be preparing for this destiny in their own worship from week to week. Pinching incense to Caesar insisting this worship action has no consequence for Christian confession not only is wrong at the personal level and for faithful witness, the action is denial of the very purpose of the church in preparing believers for eternity's worship.

---

⁶Rev 8:5; 11:19; 16:18.

⁷Cf. Zech 4:2–3, 10.

⁸Since sea imagery in ancient literature can be positive or negative, the nuance here in 4:6 is debated. The seas appear as chaotic powers that God must conquer later in Revelation, such that their fate is to be no more (21:1). However, the complexity of John's imagery and its sources probably means he uses the same imagery with different valences determined by context. Here, the context is positive and in concert with the purpose of all precious stones and reflective surfaces in augmenting the brilliance of God's glory.

⁹Perhaps inspired by the idea of the four angels standing at the four corners of the earth holding back the four winds (7:1). Early Catholic tradition turned these into the four evangelists, but that most assuredly is pure allegory and a flight of fancy. Cf. Augustine *Tr. John* 36.5.

¹⁰Rev 6:1–8; 15:7.

Four Creatures Worship (4:8). These creatures have "six wings." A winged creature or beast is not an uncommon idea in ancient times. Griffins often were pictured this way. Such creatures normally had distinctive faces as well. John's immediate image is taken from the seraphim description of Isa 6. "Full of eyes around and within" indicates their full spiritual insight and knowledge and function to reprise the eyes of the Son of Man like flaming fire. Like Jesus, all heaven sees through the idolatrous lies of emperor worship on earth. These creatures worship "day and night without ceasing," which is a fullness of veneration not even Domitian could command. The worship of God is the goal of all creation.

FIGURE 11.3. Griffin Artwork. Greek oinochoe pottery (wine), Smyrna, 620–610 B.C. Winged griffins, wild faces (IAMI).

We meet the first of Revelation's hymns in the context of the worship of the four living creatures. Revelation's hymns are crucial to the exegesis of the book, because they summarize its theology.[11] This triadic "holy, holy, holy" series echoes the expression of worship in the theophany experienced by Isaiah.[12] Thus, John views the God of the Old Testament prophets. The title, "the Lord God, the Almighty" (4:8) is a LXX motif with prophetic authority that is John's broadside to Roman imperial propaganda.[13] The "who is, who was, who is to come" verbal series echoes 1:4 and reflects Jewish exegetical tradition about the name of God. This Jewish formulation of God's name verbally puts emphasis on God's eternity and sovereignty. A reminder of God's sovereignty is meant to motivate persecuted believers in Asia Minor by reminding them that God controls history.

---

[11] Cf. Horn, "Hallelujah, the Lord our God, the Almighty Reigns."

[12] Isa 6:3. Scenes of the opening of heaven and dreams are vehicles of theophany; cf. Dan 7:1; Ezek 1:1.

[13] See the discussion on pp. 231–32. Cf. Amos 3:13; 4:13; 5:14–16; 9:5–6, 15; Hos 12:6; Nah 3:5; Zech 10:13; Mal 2:26.

FIGURE 11.4. Inscription, Praise of God Hymn. Record of a hymn of praise sung to the god "Men" of Axiolta, dated A.D. 57–58 (MMM).

Twenty-four Elders Worship (4:9–11). These living creatures give "glory, honor, and thanks" (4:9), which probably is meant as a parody of specific features of the ceremony for emperor worship.[14] From Augustus on the emperors wanted thanks for the benefits of empire they brought to the world.[15] This veneration by the four creatures, however, is enigmatic, as the praise is offered ambiguously to "the one who

---

[14] See the allusion to this ceremony, including prayers, incense, and wine offered to the genius of the emperor and statues of the gods in Pliny *Letters* 10.96.

[15] See the discussion of the *Res Gestae*, p. 299.

sits on the throne." This ambiguous phrasing probably is intentional by John to allow the mind to "fill in the blank" by habit from daily life with Domitian's name, but then mentally correct to the actual subject of this reference, who is God. Such a subtle rhetoric insinuates the problem in Asia Minor: buying into imperial rhetoric and its illusion that Domitian rules. Imperial propaganda has supplanted the proper object of human worship, and that action has become a habitual form of thought even for believers. Thus, "the one who sits on the throne" actually raises the question, Who sits on the throne?

The ambiguity is clarified immediately with "and who lives for ever and ever." Certainly not true of Domitian! That is the problem of all human claim to rule: impermanence. Impermanence is the impotency of human rule. Thus, John again mocks imperial propaganda of emperors who supposedly are "gods," and yet they are assassinated by their own Praetorian Guard, as was Caligula, or family members murder each other, as Agrippina murdered her husband, Claudius, to give her young son Nero the throne, or entire armies fight, as in the civil war that erupted upon Nero's suicide that brought three emperors to the throne in a year and a half in Roman dynastic struggles. Some emperors cannot stay on the throne even a few months! Even Domitian's own brother, Titus (79–81), fell ill suddenly and died of fever after just two years in office.

The elders fall down and "cast their crowns" (4:10). Falling down is common oriental behavior for acknowledging the king. Casting crowns derives from Hellenistic kingship traditions that the Romans inherited. Presenting golden crowns to the emperor was a part of ceremonies for accessions, consulships, victories, and anniversaries.[16] The symbol is one of complete submission and loyalty. John's depiction is another broadside against imperial ideology.

The elders declare, "you are worthy" (4:11). As will be made explicit in the second half of the verse, this worthiness is on the basis of God as creator. Augustus really did not make the world Romans live in. God made the world. The one truly worthy of worship is the creator God. Again, John strikes at the heart of imperial claims, because the next phrase, "our Lord and God" was a title that the historian

---

[16] Aune, "The Influence of Roman Imperial Court Ceremonial," 12. So also Reddish, *Revelation*, 101.

Suetonius said Domitian claimed.[17] The worthiness is because "you created all things." Creation theology is essential to eschatology. The One who creates is the One who consummates. God will achieve creation's goal. This consummation is how God realizes the Omega of the "Alpha and Omega" title (1:8). The Roman emperor is not even a smudge on that timeline.

In short, what John reveals in Rev 4 is a throne, a sovereign, and a song. These signal the truth of a sovereign controlling human destiny—the One who *will* be worshipped. The imagery is anti-imperial.

Revelation of Christ (5:1–14)

A Mysterious Scroll (5:1)

The expression "And I saw a scroll" is a continuation of the heavenly throne room vision and not really a new chapter. The scene transitions to a scroll. The contents of this scroll are not specified by John but are speculated by interpreters.[18] John emphasizes only three points about this mysterious scroll newly introduced into the vision: how the scroll is written, how the scroll is sealed, and who is worthy to open.

First, John emphasizes how this scroll is written. This scroll is "written on the inside and outside" (5:1). Whereas a codex (book with leaves bound at the edge, like modern books) can be written on both sides, a scroll, which is rolled inwardly from both ends or in one direction,

FIGURE 11.5. Scroll in Hand. Marble sculpture of a hand holding a rolled scroll, a symbol of education or administrative responsibilities (YMY).

---

[17]Suetonius *Dom.* 13.2. Suetonius is charged as unreliable as part of his program of deprecating the previous dynasty to aggrandize current ones (Trajan and Hadrian). See Thompson, *The Book of Revelation: Apocalypse and Empire*. For a response, see deSilva, *Introduction to the New Testament*.

[18]Speculation has included the messianic portion of the Old Testament applied to Jesus as fulfillment, the so-called Great Tribulation at the end of history, the record of human destiny, and the eschatological inheritance of saints. That the ideas are all over the map is a cautionary tale, but the contextual sense seems to be straight-forward, as we will suggest. Another minor question is whether the book is a scroll or a codex, but either form could take seals, so the matter is inconsequential. That John has in mind the background of Roman wills and contracts is interesting but not compelling.

normally is not written on both sides, but only on the inside, in order to protect the writing from exposure to handling, wear, and tear and, practically, to facilitate its reading in the act of unrolling. The practical matter of how a scroll had to be read meant that almost all two-sided documents in the ancient world were meant for private use, not public or commercial. Thus, this scroll is jammed full and for God's private use, a dramatic context setting up the apocalyptic moment (Rev 5:7).

FIGURE 11.6. Ancient Seals. Seals have been used for millennia. Top left is a Bronze Age (3000 B.C.) stamp seal of a horse (YMY). Top right is an Assyrian cylinder seal (2000 B.C.), that is rolled over impressionable material (KAM). Bottom is a Roman period relief seal of the profile of a man's head shown with corresponding impression (BMB).

Second, John emphasizes how the scroll is sealed. Seals in the ancient world were used to validate document contents, somewhat similar to the role of a notary public today. Instead of one seal, the normal procedure, this scroll has seven seals. The number is symbolic. Seven seals on a scroll within the inner sanctum of God's throne room means the scroll is divinely sealed. Only someone with God's own authority could open the scroll. Being divinely sealed is our clue that whatever is written in the scroll is God's will. Since opening the seals formally initiates the great Judgment Cycle (6–20), the scroll seems to carry the judgments of God that realize the divine conquering of evil in the world. The scroll is full because the divine judgments will be completed by the last septet of the Bowls.[19] These seven seals also provide an element of drama, because the contents of the scroll are revealed progressively with the sequential opening of each seal and not all at once.

Third, John emphasizes who is worthy to open the scroll. In the process, the drama hits the height of authorial pathos, as this scene is the only time John shows great emotion during his entire visionary experience. The burden of the scroll is great, and the angst of John is real. If the scroll is not opened, John's visionary experience is aborted prematurely, because John the prophet intuitively realizes the rest of the vision is in the scroll. Seeing the sovereign God on his throne is assuring, but not revealing. John the prophet already knows that God is sovereign. The scroll is why he has been invited to "come up here" in the first place. Somehow God's will has to be unleashed on creation, or the hymn to God just auditioned celebrating God as Almighty Creator is a hypocrisy. Somehow the scroll *must* be opened, or the letters to the seven churches just composed become false prophecy, and believers in Asia Minor live with false hope and suffer for naught.

A Cosmic Question (5:2–4)

An angel puts the question: "Who is worthy to open the scroll?" (5:2) so that John may have his Revelation. As "mighty," this angel has the necessary status for this special role. The call is cosmic. The entire universe is searched, which is advance notice that anyone found able to open the scroll will be unlike any other being in the universe. The one worthy has a unique role in all of creation, because this one accomplishes what no other can. All the known regions of habitation for living souls and spirits are searched, but in vain.[20]

That "no one was found" (5:3) is a serious cosmic conundrum. John the prophet is distraught: "and I was weeping much" (5:4).[21] His visionary experience appears to be short-lived. Further, the hymn to God just heard in Rev 4 appears now to be falsified. God's supposed sovereignty seems defeated, and the praise of his glory appears pre-

---

[19]"For with them the wrath of God is ended" (15:1).

[20]"In heaven, on earth, and under the earth" expresses a first-century world view of the habitation of beings and spirits.

[21]The verb is durative, so "I wept and wept" (NIV) is an excellent rendering.

mature. The drama is intense. The stage is set for a dramatic word of revelation. What is heard is the revelation in Revelation.

A Dramatic Answer (5:5–7)

One of the elders relieves the tension by answering the question. That one of the elders answers the question is symbolic. These elders probably represent the glorified saints in heaven. The symbolism is that being able to perceive who is worthy to open the scroll is a perspective of faith. Why is ability to see the one worthy so difficult and a matter of faith? Because false and pretentious claims to worthiness are rampant on earth and obscure the truth of who really is worthy. Roman emperors and other claimants to divine sovereignty have put out a lot of smoke and mirrors in the way of recognizing true worthiness of sovereignty and worship. Human hubris means the one truly worthy will not be known by some of earth's inhabitants until the scroll has been opened completely. What transpires with the unleashing of the scroll's contents will indicate why the one worthy has this honor, because the one truly worthy will effect God's will over the entire creation by executing God's judgments like no current pretender such as Domitian really can.[22] God, in effect, vindicates his own name against Domitian's slander and perfidy. Thus, an elder, one redeemed by the Lamb, knows the real score of worthiness and breaks the tension. God, in fact, is sovereign, even though that sovereignty momentarily seems challenged by Domitian. This part of the drama could function as a subliminal message to persecuted believers in Asia Minor.

In introducing the one worthy to John, the elder combines two titles. The titles together subvert and redefine worthiness versus first-century religious, social, and political conventions. John reconfigures the idea of worthiness based on gospel truths. Jesus himself rejected popular Jewish and Roman expectations of a worthy ruler.

Israel's prophets established the profile of Israel's Redeemer. The history of the Jews after the exile, however, distorted these prophetic expectations into militaristic images. Due to these distortions, Israel no longer could recognize in Jesus of Nazareth the original prophetic profile of Messiah. Neither could anyone write the correct script for how God would conquer evil in the world through Messiah. This fail-

---

[22]Running in perfect tandem with Paul's vision of the future in Rom 8:19–21.

ure was inevitable, since Messiah's person and Messiah's mission are inseparable. To distort the messianic profile is to pervert the messianic mission. This distortion and perversion is the very essence of Jesus' temptation in the wilderness.[23] Satan was attempting to redefine the person of Messiah in order to pervert the mission of Messiah. Jesus of Nazareth revealed to his disciples that the story of Messiah is the story of the suffering and dying Son of Man. This Son of Man profile is encapsulated in the Gospel of Mark. The picture is antithetical to a Maccabean warrior expectation, as in 1 Maccabees.[24]

Lion of Judah (5:5). The first title for the worthy one combines two Jewish traditions about Messiah. The one worthy is "the Lion of the tribe of Judah, the Root of David" (5:5). These are Jewish titles. The Lion of the tribe of Judah is a warrior image from Gen 49:9, taken messianically by Jews. The Root of David is a royal image taken from Isa 11:1, also taken messianically by Jews. The original context of each image is Israel overcoming her Jewish enemies, but John's context is vindicating God's sovereignty. With this title, the one worthy seems characterized as a typical warrior-king in Jewish messianic terms. This warrior-king illusion, however, will be demolished as quickly as the imagery has been spoken in the very next verse.

A reader might expect this title to be a Jewish counterpoint to Rome's imperial warrior-rulers who claimed to have conquered the whole earth, including wild barbarian regions. Rome's gospel is that victory is military conquest. Sovereignty is at the point of a sword. Might makes right. Triumph is glory, accolades, arches, and a parade down the streets of Rome. The mental image survives today in Roman statuary in the iconic, cuirassed, curly-haired, man-sculpted-like-a-god figure, the conquering general, so often carved in imperial marble. Jews just would be playing the same game by using the same themes, only with Jewish imagery and Jewish names for the rulers. Whether a Roman script or a Jewish script, John is going to destroy the imagery.

The royal Lion of Judah "has conquered" (5:5). Martial language such as "Lion of Judah" naturally predicates conquering language. A first-century reader would expect such martial verbiage if one were

---

[23]Mark 1:12-13; Matt 4:1-11; Luke 4:1-13.

[24]A history covering the Jewish revolt against the Syrians from 175–134 B.C. and extolling the Maccabean fighters as possible contenders to be the Messiah.

following the script of Jewish messianic expectations or Roman imperial ideology. However, as we have seen, John's conquering language is subversive rhetoric against both Jewish and Roman storylines. His ideology of victory is antithetical to the themes of Jerusalem or Rome, because John's ideology is driven by the gospel story. John's definition of "victory" is borne along through his early chapters by the wording of the prologue ("by his blood," 1:5), the suffering Son of Man figure of the Inaugural Vision (1:13), and the formulaic promise sections of the Seven Letters. In all these letters, the one who "conquers" receives promises couched in eschatological nuances but which also are translated into demands for daily sacrifice. The one worthy has led the way in this journey of daily sacrifice. He stands in the midst of the seven churches in order to show believers how they too can "conquer," even in their present difficult circumstances. They will live worthy if they follow in the steps of the one who is worthy. This "conquering" idea which plays out in confession and faithful living is the overcoming theme of Revelation that not only is established early in Revelation, but also globally binds the major sections of the book together from the beginning of the Seven Letters (2–3), through the Judgment Cycle (6–20), and on to the fulfillment theme of the final visions (21–22).

Slaughtered Lamb (5:6). John's second title is iconoclastic. He completely shatters the warrior-ruler icon he has just set up in the previous verse. John also shreds all first-century conquering scripts. John sees a "Lamb standing as slaughtered."[25] Here is our first encounter with the premier image for Jesus in Revelation, the Lamb. The noun "lamb" in Revelation is used 28 of 29 times to refer to Jesus. With this Lamb image John radically will redefine the Jewish messianic titles just enunciated. In the process, we have high Christology in the making.

John's slaughtered Lamb image is arresting, even staggering. The idea is abrupt, logically incongruous, even though the Old Testament backgrounds in Isa 53 and in Jewish Passover ritual quickly come to mind. The image is messy. Instead of a clean, shiny, marble statue, we have an animal at the moment of bloody sacrifice. A Roman reader

---

[25]"Slain" (NIV) simply is not strong enough for this context. Since the allusion is to the cross, "slaughtered" is necessary. The image is violent death. Why John had not seen or mentioned the Lamb, who is positioned even closer to the throne of God than the four living creatures, before this point is left unexplained.

would be convinced John had taken leave of his senses. No one dared to image victory in such a counterintuitive, illogical way. A lamb is weak, not strong. To make matters worse, this Lamb is slaughtered. In the Roman arena, death goes to the loser.

FIGURE 11.7. Apocalypse Tapestry, Rev 5:6. John on the left sees the twenty-four elders, who are situated in four panels of six elders each, which nicely correspond in layout symmetrically to the four living creatures. The slaughtered Lamb in the center carries the Christian banner gushing blood from his slit throat. The scheme for the layout had become traditional in the Medieval age (Angers, France).

<u>Slaughtered</u>. John, however, has qualified the image in two ways that indicate his gospel focus. First, the verb is the Greek perfect. The perfective aspect is completed action (like English), but includes ongoing consequences, that is, the continuing impact, of the completed action. John's language implies the sacrificial disposition of the Lamb is his eternal condition in heaven. Medieval art depicting the sacrificial imagery of a slaughtered Lamb as integral to the heavenly court scene around God's throne not only is faithful to the text of Revelation, this art communicates a crucial point in the universe of John's visionary symbolism about how God has expressed his sovereignty in regard to evil in the world. If God's sovereignty over evil is not expressed decisively and conclusively at the cross, any so-called battle of Armageddon is meaningless. The eternal sacrificial reality of the Lamb in heaven is the reason for his worthiness, the means of redemption (1:5) and a believer's paradigm for living (12:11). In terms of the pragmatics of Christian living for believers in Asia Minor, no image could be

more powerful or evocative of how to respond to persecution. The cross is like the black hole of theological space, so powerful that no theological thought can escape its gravitational force, not even the outer reaches of future eschatology. So, John's first qualification of the image to indicate his gospel focus is using perfective force for the verb in saying the Lamb is slaughtered.

FIGURE 11.8. Douce Apocalypse, Rev 5:6. Illumination of Ms. 180, Douce Apocalypse, at Rev 5:6 (*circa* 1270). This British manuscript shows the traditional Medieval depiction of the scene around the throne and the slaughtered Lamb (ADEVA).

Standing. John's second qualification of the image that indicates his gospel focus is to say that the Lamb is "standing" (5:6). This posture for a slaughtered Lamb logically is impossible, of course, so the image is meant to be dramatic, paradoxical, and emotive, not logical and rational. Once again, apocalyptic imagery proves its capacity to be innovative, even if defying normal logic for the purpose of theological point. A slaughtered Lamb simply cannot be "standing," by definition. Or, can he? This Lamb can! The posture of standing is John's symbol for resurrection. John now draws out the significance of characterizing Jesus as one "firstborn of the dead" in the prologue of Revelation (1:5), which idea is echoed in the Inaugural Vision (1:18) and then the Seven Letters (2:8). This idea is the theological key to the entire "conquering" motif, and transforms and transcends all Jewish messianic traditions. Messiah fulfills Israel's story, but not as expected. The Messiah died. The resurrection, however, is what transforms Jesus' death into a life-giving force unlike the death of any Jewish martyr on a first-century cross in Judea, and unlike even the noble death of a valiant gladiator in a Roman arena.[26] In Rev 5:6, traditional Jewish messianic imagery of the apocalyptic warrior lamb is transformed radically into a unique Passover Lamb who dies, but lives. In this powerful Passover nuance—a slaughtered Lamb standing—resides the heart of Christian faith and practice, the soul of the nature and mission of the church, and the hermeneutical key to Revelation's portrait of the eschatological future.

John adds two additional descriptions to his unique Lamb icon. This Lamb has seven horns (5:6). In apocalyptic, horns are the power to rule.[27] Seven is completeness, so all-powerful. Seven horns simply symbolizes the truth of the prologue description, "ruler of the kings of the earth" (1:5). Yet, this rule now has to be conceptualized within the given icon of a slaughtered Lamb. European monarchial concepts not only do not fit the mold, they contradict the point.

The Lamb also has seven eyes. The background is Zech 3–4. John leaves no doubt what he intends to symbolize, as he explains, "which are the seven spirits of God sent out into all the earth" (5:6). The seven spirits symbolize the Holy Spirit and echo the identification of the letter to Sardis (3:1). Here, the addition of "sent out into all the earth" emphasizes the divine presence of God in every nook and cranny of the world, including the world of Asia Minor. Nothing believers do and say in Asia Minor is hidden from Jesus' view and God's judgment. In their function as judgment oracles, the Seven Letters to the seven churches are the seven spirits going out into all the earth, and nothing of what has been confessed or denied by believers is off the heavenly radar screen and without accountability. Further, sent out into all the earth is the effective execution of God's redemptive plan. This Lamb is the agent of the messianic judgments in the Judgment Cycle (6–20).

---

[26] Josephus tells us that the Roman general Varus, governor of Syria, crucified 2,000 Jews at one time in Jerusalem after putting down a messianic revolt in Judea in 4 B.C., immediately following the death of Herod the Great (*Ant.* 17.10.10; *J.W.* 2.5.2). On a later occasion, Quadratus also crucified revolting Jews (*J.W.* 2.12.6).

[27] Dan 7:7—8:24.

Apocalyptic Moment (5:7). Jesus taking the scroll from the right hand of God in 5:7 is the precise meaning of the first verse of Revelation: "The revelation of Jesus Christ, which God gave him" (1:1). That is, this scroll holds the prophecies of Revelation that John is going to see and later write about. One can note that when the scroll begins to be opened with the breaking of its seals, the visions that launch the entire Judgment Cycle (6–20) are engaged, which are the bulk of the content of Revelation. John is called up to heaven in 4:1 to witness retrospectively the very act of God giving Jesus the revelation that Jesus gave John. God's private scroll Jesus receives.[28] John should not weep; his promised revelation will come, because the Lamb is worthy.[29]

The revelatory experience on Patmos might have been along the following lines. John, a prophet active in the orbit of seven churches of Asia Minor, perhaps himself from Pergamum, was on Patmos because of persecution. In the Spirit on the Lord's day, probably meaning in worship, while psalming a hymn of the redeemed from the common liturgy of the seven churches, John experiences an epiphany of the glorified Son of Man. The Son of Man commands John to write what he hears and sees. The Son of Man first issues judgment oracles to seven churches in Asia Minor and then gives John a vision of heaven that reveals the process of how the seven-sealed scroll in heaven becomes the book he writes through the slaughtered Lamb.

The scroll of John's prophecy is in the right hand of God like the prophets are in the right hand of Jesus (5:7). The taking of the scroll puts the power for executing the judgments of God in the hand of Jesus. Jesus is worthy because Jesus is the agent of the judgments of God. Fulfillment of these judgments is in the church guided by the Son of Man, who is John's equivalent for Daniel's Ancient of Days, who guides his church through his prophets and judges the world.[30]

---

[28]On scroll reading and the private nature of *epistographs* (double-sided scrolls), cf. Thompson, *Greek and Latin Paleography,* 49–50. Ironic that the vision futurists want to place into the future John carefully has placed retrospectively into the past. John is describing the very exchange between God and Jesus that created the book of Revelation in the first place, a process John explained in the first verse of Revelation. God's heavenly scroll transfigures into John's Apocalypse that the seven churches received.

[29]Beasley-Murray, *Revelation,* 126, suggests that having Jesus approach the throne of God and take the scroll is John's equivalent for New Testament exaltation language.

[30]Beale, *Revelation,* 356, points out that the only time in the Old Testament that a divine messianic figure is portrayed as approaching God's throne and receiving au-

Heavenly Worship (5:8–14)

When the Lamb takes the scroll, those in the heavenly council of God fall down prostrate before the Lamb, a bold act of worship (5:8). The Lamb receives worship that is due God, one of the highest moments of Christology in the New Testament. The worship due God is given to the Lamb, which does not provoke a rebuke. The elders hold harps and golden bowls of incense, which are interpreted as the prayers of the saints. Harps are the instruments accompanying worship hymns, and prayers are the corporately recited petitions that accompany the worship liturgy. This scene of heavenly worship is an obvious counterpoint to idolatrous acts in pagan temples, as well as in the emperor cult in first-century Asia Minor. The bowls and prayers encountered here will tie the Seal and Trumpet judgments together, showing how the entire Judgment Cycle flows out of this Vision of Heaven, not just the Seal judgments. The prayers of the saints imagery carries a theme of vindication, because they pray for vindication during the judgments.[31] Prayers activate the judgments of God, and the judgments of God vindicate the saints. Antipas, the paradigm witness in Revelation, will be vindicated for his faithful testimony even to the point of death (2:13) as the Lamb providentially directs history through the power of the cross and persevering believers to the consummation of God's kingdom.

FIGURE 11.9. Roman Incense Altar. Imperial priest burning incense in cultic worship (HAMH).

---

thority is Dan 7:13, the Ancient of Days vision, which has elements of a "son of man" and a scroll. John apparently intends this Lamb scene to correspond to the Daniel passage. That is, John portrays the fulfillment of Dan 7, an Old Testament theophany that has judgment nuances. Revelation preserves these judgment themes.

[31] Rev 6:9–11; 8:3–4.

The Redeemed Chorus (5:9–10). The redemptive action of the Messiah is celebrated by those most affected, the twenty-four elders (the saints), joined by the four living creatures (the creation), because redemption affects not only humans, but the entire cosmos. They sing a new song, which is the "song of the Lamb," and is equivalent to the song of Moses, because both songs celebrate the redemption of God's people.[32] The "new" characterizing this song is God's new creation in Christ through the cross and resurrection.

The song summarizes redemption theology. Key themes already expressed in the prologue in Rev 1:5 and the narrative introduction of the Lamb occur in each stanza of the hymn of the redeemed, indicated by the italicized words.

> You are worthy to take the scroll and to open its seals
>   because you were *slaughtered*
>   and you purchased for God *by your blood*
>   from every tribe and tongue and people and nation
>   and you made them a *kingdom and priests*
>   unto our God
>   and *they will reign* upon the earth (Rev 5:9–10)

Jesus' divine status finds allusion here. This status already has surfaced in the Inaugural Vision in 1:14, 16 and the letters to the churches in 3:14. The prologue wording in Rev 1:5 now can be seen to be taken from the lines of the hymn of the Lamb in 5:9–10. In this way we see that Revelation is imbued with the ethos of worship liturgy from the very beginning, and the original hearers probably had little trouble recognizing their own hymns sung in their house churches from one Lord's day to the next. Even as John had indicated, "I was in the spirit *on the Lord's day.*"[33] Singing such a hymn of the redeemed could have been the very activity that put John "in the spirit."

The reign of the saints in the hymn is future tense, but the question is whether this future is predictive or gnomic. An answer depends on one's eschatological presuppositions. Predictive would mean the reign is yet to be. Gnomic would mean the reign is now. The context of the just concluded Seven Letters argues for a gnomic future. In the Seven Letters, what is promised to "those who conquer" contemplates

---

[32]Later referenced in 15:3.

[33]Rev 1:10, emphasis added.

the present experience of the local churches as they deal with opposition and persecution right now. Thus, the eschatological language in which the promises are expressed are realities that bend back into the present living of believers in Asia Minor.

The crucial point theologically is that the action of Christ in dying on a cross is what effects the opening of the seals of the scroll. The Lamb is worthy to open the seals, because Christ's redemptive death is the very action that releases the content of the seals. The seals are like the undulating waves upon the surface waters of history of the death of Christ. Christ's death on a Roman cross is presented as God's victory, as ironic as such a thought might be.[34]

The enumeration of this fourfold sequence of metonyms (tribe, tongue, people, nation) is a symbolic way to speak inclusively of the impact of the redemptive death of Christ upon all humankind. The four corners of the earth and the four winds of heaven have their own counterpart here in this fourfold enumeration of humankind. This list represents the entire earthly sphere, thus God's consummated work among humanity. Priests who reign, already met in the prologue (1:5), seems allusive of an Exodus redemption theme, as in Exod 19:6.

The Angelic Chorus (5:11–12). John looks again, and an innumerable host of angels adds their own voice to the chorus.[35] This angelic chorus evokes Dan 7:10. The angelic chorus serves to reinforce the validity of the hymn of redemption sung by the elders and four creatures. John has fired another shot across the bow of imperial ideology: heaven is the best judge of praiseworthiness, not earth. The chorus of male choirs singing odes to the emperor in imperial temples sing in vain and offer a false worship to an unworthy subject who has usurped the sovereignty of God and the proper worship of the Lamb. Imperial hymns promote idolatrous lies. The angelic chorus echoes the elders' hymn that the Lamb is worthy, affirming that the elders' worship is properly addressed to the Lamb alone and for the right reason.

---

[34]But John in no way is unique in such theological reflection; cf. Phil 2:8.

[35]Their number, John says, is "myriads upon myriads, and thousands upon thousands" (5:11). Greeks had no cardinal units past ten thousand. After that unit, one just had "myriads." John then goes one further to continue to pile up more thousands even upon the myriads. This profusion of numbers is a way to say, "innumerable." Once again, John is going for dramatic impact, not a literal number.

> The Lamb who was slaughtered is worthy to receive
>   power, and riches, and wisdom
>   and strength, and honor, and glory, and blessing (Rev 5:12)

The enumeration has two characteristics. The first is that the elements are ripped from the headlines of imperial inscriptions incised on Roman statuary, monuments, buildings, acts of benefaction, and imperial cult temples throughout Asia Minor. These were characteristics that were claimed by and ascribed to the emperor. The second is that the elements number seven total. That number is intentional to symbolize not only the perfection of angelic worship in heaven but the perfected praise of the Lamb on earth.

FIGURE 11.10. Imperial Inscription, Sardis. The Marble Hall bathhouse of Sardis has this reconstructed imperial inscription over the main entrance evidencing various ascriptions such as "most excellent" with other typical phrases (Sardis, Turkey).

The Cosmic Chorus (5:13). The triadic offer of praise is completed by the entire cosmos. First comes the hymn of the redeemed in the innermost circle of heaven's court, closest to God. Then, the circle of praise widens to the chorus of heaven's angels affirming the hymn of the redeemed. Finally, the circle expands infinitely as all of creation joins all of heaven. The paean of praise reaches its crescendo.[36] Every creature in every conceivable place of habitation joins together to affirm the hymn of the worthy Lamb.[37] John probably intends for the reader to imagine the sound by now as deafening, which would be a

---

[36] The phrasing is James D. G. Dunn's characterization of Rom 8:31–39 in his commentary on Romans (*Romans 1–8*, 509). I think that Rev 5:9–14 is John's equivalent to Paul's thought in Rom 8:31–39.

[37] Conceivable habitation is the meaning of "every creature in heaven and upon the earth and under the earth, and in the sea, and all that is in them," 5:13. The entire cosmos is what John means. This company is the living, the dead, and the unknown. A similar thought is in Eph 3:10.

dramatic, even thrilling contrast to the worship experienced in small house church assemblies of first-century Asia Minor.

> To the One seated on the throne and to the Lamb be
> blessing and honor and glory and might,
> forever and ever (Rev 5:13)

The dual object of this praise is God and the Lamb, a stunning equality of divinity made explicit in this act of worship. Their functions merge. The Lamb is acting on behalf of God in the continued work of God's creation. The Lamb effects God's consummated creation on God's behalf as an integral expression of God's sovereignty over all his creation. Once again, the elements of the expression of praise are fourfold to represent the praise of all creation.

Concluding Affirmation (5:14). Typical worship liturgy allows for the affirmation of participants for what has been proclaimed. Thus, the proclamation of God's heaven joined by God's creation receives the "Amen!" of the four living creatures, and the elders fall down and worship (5:14). The worship liturgy is complete in a posture of prostration before God and the Lamb. This liturgy of triadic choruses that concludes the Vision of Heaven functions as an interpretive summary of the Lamb's redemption that consummates God's creation.

In summary, in Rev 5 we see a scroll, a savior, and a song. The truth is a salvation consummating all creation. In Rev 4 we have the sovereign God. In Rev 5 we have his saving Christ.

JUDGMENT CYCLE (REV 6–20)

As the Inaugural Vision functioned as the theological foundation upon which the Seven Letters were based, so the Vision of Heaven is the theological foundation upon which the Judgment Cycle is based. In parallel structure, Christ in his messianic role as Son of Man (Inaugural Vision) judges the church through his resurrected presence (Seven Letters). Similarly, God in his sovereign role as Creator (Vision of Heaven) judges the world through his slaughtered Lamb (Judgment Cycle). The slaughtered Lamb opens the sealed scroll. Judgments ensue. That is how God judges the world—through the cross.

The Judgment Cycle engages discussion of several hermeneutical issues. If the prophecies are assumed as foretelling, then what "fore" are they "telling"? Are they preterist, historicist, futurist, or idealist?

Or, what of the judgments as a series? Are they linear, telescopic, or recapitulation? Finally, one has to deal with millennium misery.[38] In terms of prophecy, our decision is John is not foretelling. Rather, he is forthtelling. He is challenging the churches of Asia Minor to live their gospel testimony in the face of intense religious, political, cultural, and social opposition. In the intricacies of the Judgment Cycle, John is dramatizing the consequences of releasing the power of the cross into the world through the slaughtered Lamb. The judgments recapitulate.

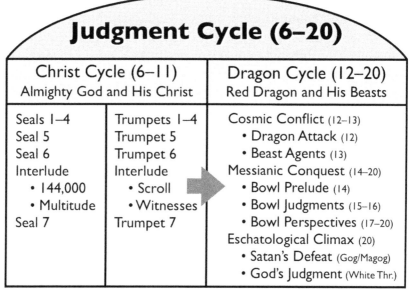

FIGURE 11.11. Judgment Cycle (Rev 6–20). Most of Revelation is the Judgment Cycle, with two major developments of the same material in its first-century context.

The Judgment Cycle has an interlocking triad of Seals, Trumpets, and Bowls unequally divided across two major halves of Revelation. The first half is the Christ Cycle (6:1—11:19) with a focus on God and his Christ. The second half is the Dragon Cycle (12:1—20:15), focused on the Dragon and his Beasts. The first half of the Christ Cycle tells the story of God's sovereignty through the Lamb from an earthly perspective. The second half of the Dragon Cycle retells the same story from a cosmic perspective. Two judgment heptads of Seals (6:1—8:1) and Trumpets (8:2—11:21) move the action forward in the first half. The Seal and Trumpet series have parallel structure, further showing

[38] See the "Historicizing Prophecy" section in this book, pp. 156–62.

their recapitulative nature. The third judgment heptad, the Bowls, extends the earlier two heptads of the Seals and Trumpets, but is delayed in order to make room for the introduction and development of new characters in the drama in the second half of the Dragon Cycle, and does not essentially move the plot along as do the Seals and Trumpets.

Christ Cycle (6:1—11:19)

The Seven Seals (6:1—8:1)

The Seals and Trumpets are constructed alike. The first four in each heptad are a sub-series of their own with uninterrupted movement, followed by the fifth and sixth judgments. In each heptad an interlude interrupts the movement before the seventh judgment. Each interlude has two parts. This repeated structure serves a recapitulation function.

The Seals are built on the eschatological woe traditions of the Synoptic Gospels, especially Mark 13, including even the basic sequence. Jesus used eschatological language to describe the destruction of Jerusalem, which was not the end of the world. This manner of speaking of historical events that are not the end of the world sets the precedent for reading John's usage, since he clearly is building his Seals series on Jesus tradition.

Mark 13	Rev 6
1. Wars	1. Wars
2. International strife	2. International strife
3. Earthquakes	3. Famines
4. Famines	4. Pestilence
5. Persecution	5. Persecution
6. Astronomical	6. Astronomical

FIGURE 11.12. Seals and Mark 13. The Seals are built on Jesus tradition.

Repeatedly, the Lamb opens a seal, one of the four living creatures introduced in the Vision of Heaven says, "Come!" and a rider on a colored horse appears. These Seal judgments inaugurate the Judgment Cycle, represent messianic action of the Lamb, and integrally are tied to the previous Vision of Heaven. Thus, the preaching of the gospel opens up these judgments into human history. The famous phrase, "four horsemen of the Apocalypse," is the first four of these Seals.

Seals 1–4. As representatives of creation, each of the four living creatures issues a command, "Come!" to bring forth four horsemen who ride the earth. Their command indicates earthly judgment. This "come" fulfills the opening promise of Jesus in the introduction of Revelation, "what must soon take place" (1:1) and echoes the prospect of threat and consolation hovering over the seven churches.[39] In these historical judgments, Jesus comes, as promised. He judges the world just as he judges the church. These historical judgments are not the "second coming" of Jesus, but they proleptically anticipate that event. Jesus comes in the witness of the church as the Word of God who has the two-edged sword coming out of his mouth, who wages a war of confession and ultimate loyalty for human hearts (19:11–21). This coming happens in history. In this series of judgments, only a fourth part of the earth is killed, a percentage that grows with each judgment series, indicating recapitulation but increasing intensity.

FIGURE 11.13. Luther Bible, Rev 6:1–8. Woodcut, four horsemen of Apocalypse (Taschen).

The judgments of the four horsemen are conquest, war, famine, and death (6:1–8). These elements together represent the ideology of empire. The spirit of conquest brings war. War brings famine. Famine brings death. So, kingdoms left to their own devices inevitably will implode on their own vices. No kingdom is forever. Inherent impermanence is the guarantee of the final victory of the kingdom of God over all the kingdoms of this world.

Seals 5–6. In the meantime, violent earthly kingdoms can do great violence to believers. The sixth seal reveals souls under the altar. They were "slaughtered" for the word of God and their testimony. Word of God and testimony echoes John's own self-description of the reason for his presence on Patmos (1:9). Further, the verb "slaughtered" is the same verb used to describe the worthy Lamb (5:6).[40] Thus, they follow the Lamb and share the Lamb's

---

[39] Rev 2:5, 16, 25; 3:3, 11, 20.

[40] The verb *sphazō* (σφάζω).

fate. These souls are believers in Asia Minor, such as Antipas, who have conquered Roman imperial ideology by their faithful confession even to death. These are those whom Pliny the Younger, governor of Bithynia, never could get to recant their faith.[41] That they were faithful to death already is the guarantee of their final victory. Their hearts and minds never were won by imperial lies. These souls cry out to a sovereign God on the basis of his holy and true character that their blood be avenged, indicating that their death was violent (6:10). Their blood will be avenged just like the blood of the Lamb was avenged—through the resurrection. They are given white robes as a symbol of their pure confession, and told to wait until the number of martyrs is complete (6:11). As Reddish noted, "John is telling the prospective martyrs that their deaths are a necessary part of God's plan for conquering evil. . . . John has already made clear that God's victory over evil has been accomplished by the death of the Lamb. Now he shows that the deaths of the faithful also contribute to victory."[42] Once again, we see that John's imagery is meant to interpret the context of the seven churches.

The sixth seal receives the greatest length of treatment because this seal brings the end (6:12–17). Nothing in this description would lead a reader to think otherwise. The imagery is climactic.[43] The language is quintessentially apocalyptic. If one were not aware beforehand of the book's actual content, this seal would communicate the end. The point, however, is not the end. The whole point of the drama of the sixth seal is to put in stark relief and emphasize the question raised at the end of the description in reference to God and the Lamb, "For the great day of their wrath is come, and who is able to stand?" (6:17). Indeed, who can stand? No one can. The only one "standing" is the Lamb (5:6). He stands in the power of the resurrection. Only those sealed in their death with the power of resurrection will "stand" in that day with the Lamb. Thus, the pointed question, "Who can stand?" sets the stage for an interlude of the sealing of the saints in order to answer that question. Only the saints can stand in the day of wrath. The point will be that God's security holds fast the persecuted.

[41] See the discussion of Pliny on pp. 314–18.

[42] Reddish, *Revelation*, 132.

[43] A strong argument for recapitulation of each series of judgments. See discussion of the climactic character of the sixth seal, p. 165.

Interlude (7:1–17). The interlude answers the question, "Who can stand?" by presenting a picture of the people of God from two compatible perspectives. The first perspective is Jewish with a focus on Israel. The second perspective is Gentile with a focus on the typical New Testament expansion of Israel to include Gentiles.

The 144,000 (7:1–8). The Jewish perspective is given in the imagery of the 144,000. The number symbolizes multiplied Israel (12 x 12) brought to divine fullness. Theologically this idea of completeness may include combining the twelve sons of Jacob with the twelve apostles of Messiah. The order of this enumeration of the twelve tribes is inconsequential, since lists in the Old Testament vary among themselves.[44] John's list has two distinctives, that Judah is first and Dan is omitted. Reuben is the firstborn of Jacob's sons, but to emphasize the tribe of Messiah, Judah is named first here. That Dan is omitted means nothing; even later Jewish traditions sometimes omit Dan.[45] Sealing indicates effective divine protection and corresponds to the sealing of the scroll the Lamb has taken from God. Only the divine can break open a seal, and only the divine can execute a seal. This sealing in this interlude has its parallel in the name of the Lamb and of God on the foreheads in the material of Rev 14:1. The three main theories on this group include converted tribulation Jews, all Jewish believers of all time, and all believers. Since the number 144 represents a doubling of Israel, the point seems to be the totality of the people of God, so all believers seems the most contextually driven. The point is that sealing protects *through* tribulation, not *from*. Antipas is a case in point. The sealing means ultimate destiny is in God's control.[46]

---

[44]Cf. Gen 29–30, 35; 35:22–36; 46:8–27; 49:1–27; Exod 1:1–5; Num 1:5–15; 1:20–54; 2:3–29; 7:1–88; 10:11–26; 13:4–15; 26:5–50; 34:19–28; Deut 27:12–13; 33:1–29; Josh 13–19; Judg 5:12–22; 1 Chr 2:1–2; 1 Chr 2–7; 12:24–38; 27:16–22; Ezek 48:1–29; and 48:30–34. No two lists correspond exactly. They differ in names, order, and number (some lists have more than twelve). We see some patterns. For example, Joseph tribes are combined when Levi is included, but divided into Manasseh and Ephraim when Levi is excluded. In contrast, Simeon always is counted, even after being absorbed into Judah, and Manasseh always counted as one even after spitting in two.

[45]Irenaeus, oblivious to Old Testament variation, deduced wrongly that omission of Dan meant that Antichrist would be a Jew from the tribe of Dan (*Adv. Haer.* 5.30.2). Irenaeus is the source of all "Antichrist is from Dan" traditions, which are latent anti-Semitism. The Dan idea adds to the biography (genealogy) of the so-called Antichrist.

[46]God's sealing the saints is not here only; cf. John 6:27; 2 Cor 1:22; Eph 1:13; 4:30.

FIGURE 11.14. Apocalypse Tapestry, Rev 7:9. The great multitude with white robes and palms in their hands (Angers, France).

The Great Multitude (7:9–17). This imagery recapitulates the 144,000, but from a different perspective with Gentile focus. The scene shifts from earth to heaven, and time shifts from persecution to end. A great multitude invokes the fulfillment of the promise to Abraham.[47] The enumeration, "nations, tribes, peoples, languages," is fourfold to represent every corner of the earth and indicates the different focus on Gentiles. White robes are for purity of confession, and palm branches suggest joyous festival, such as Sukkot (Tabernacles).[48] Another hymn summarizes the theology (7:10). Salvation belongs to God because he is "seated on the throne," which is a posture of divine sovereignty, and to the Lamb because he has been slaughtered and is standing; he has effected the resurrection. The judgments intimately are connected to the preceding throne room vision through characters introduced in that vision now renamed as participating in the act of worship (7:11). A combined chorus of angels, elders, and creatures (7:12) reiterates the sevenfold acclamation of the Lamb in the Vision of Heaven (5:12).

[47] Gen 12:2–3; 28:14.
[48] Cf. specifications in Lev 23.

The hymn of praise is proleptic of later developments in the Dragon Cycle. The beast demands praise that should go only to God. This praise issue is central to Revelation's second half: who should be worshipped? The beast controls buying and selling to have control of life in order to make demands of praise for himself. Already in this Seals interlude, John is showing us that the beast will not have the final say.

An elder interprets the scene as persecution and faithful witness. These have come out of the "great tribulation" (7:14). No definition is given; the reader is assumed to know this tribulation from context. The introduction to Revelation and the Seven Letters are our clue.[49] In these references, note that tribulation is a present experience for John himself. Believers in Smyrna are in such tribulation; even now they are reduced to poverty; further, that situation will not change, but even get worse to include imprisonment. The use of the adjective "great" in 7:14 is not unique, since this same adjective is used to describe the punishment of the false prophetess Jezebel and her spiritual children; further, in the Jezebel imagery, tribulation applies to opponents. We conclude that "great tribulation" in 7:14 contextually means present experiences of persecution of believers in Asia Minor as suggested in the Seven Letters and by John's description of his own experience that put him on Patmos. The robes are made white in the "blood of the Lamb" (7:14), which is logically incongruent but theologically symbolic of pure witness. The blood of the Lamb is a theme by now, having had prominence in the Prologue (1:5) and the Vision of Heaven (5:9). The significance is that the Lamb's path is the believer's paradigm.

They serve God continually in his temple (7:15), even though in the final vision, New Jerusalem has no temple (21:22), which means temple here is serving as a symbol for God's intimate presence, and builds on a wilderness theme of the tabernacle of God's presence with Israel. They hunger and thirst no more, because the Lamb provides sustenance of food and water for life. Neither are they exposed to the vicissitudes of unsheltered life, as the sun's heat no longer bears down (7:16), which evokes Isaiah's imagery.[50] Thus, the poverty-stricken life of believers such as at Smyrna is overcome, since faithful believers will have in the end what was denied in persecution.

---

[49] Rev 1:9; 2:9, 10, 22.
[50] As in Isa 49:10; 25:8.

God assuaging tears (7:17) is an expression repeated in the final vision of New Jerusalem (21:4). This "tears connection" between this interlude and the final vision of New Jerusalem reveals that this interlude is meant to show that the Judgment Cycle, while depicting present persecution and the outworking of the cross in history, also figures God's final victory. The great tribulation is part of God's redemptive plan. Mysteriously, in the end, everything that the great tribulation has attempted to do to threaten the sustainability of life for those who confess Jesus in reality God has controlled in his sovereignty to effect the consummation of the cosmos. God does not work in spite of the great tribulation. God works through the great tribulation. The great tribulation is the church recapitulating the passion of Christ, and in so doing finally and conclusively dealing with evil in the world. Faith in the slaughtered Lamb is vindicated, and God reigns sovereign over his universe. Whether the great tribulation is global persecution of believers throughout the church age or a concluding catharsis is not explicit. Functionally, the idea could be both realities: in time and end of time.

Seal 7 (8:1).[51] The last seal, strangely, is anticlimactic, as this seal opens to only a brief period of silence. No lights, no camera, no action. The end already has been described apocalyptically in Seal 6 and was followed by the interlude of the 144,000 and the great multitude. The climactic nature of the just narrated Seal 6 means that Seal 7 is not intended to be a climax and has some other literary function than portraying a judgment. This unusual nature of the content of Seal 7 gives support to the idea that the seventh in each series of Seals and Trumpets is not a judgment but rather a literary connecting device meant to "telescope" out to the next heptad of judgments.

The Seven Trumpets (8:2—11:21)

The Trumpets structurally repeat the Seals, showing the recapitulatory function of these judgment heptads. The first four are a unit, followed by the fifth and sixth. A two-part interlude interrupts the seventh. The trumpets continue the work of the Lamb effected through the church.

Seven Archangels (8:2). The Seals were inaugurated by the four living creatures. A new judgment series is inaugurated by archangels. They have seven trumpets to blow, but a throne room worship scene

---

[51]The chapter division is horrible. Not even an ounce of logic.

interrupts the action as a reminder of God's sovereignty in the course of all of his judgments as he moves creation to its ultimate goal.

FIGURE 11.15. Apocalypse Tapestry, Rev 8:2. The seven archangels are given trumpets to blow, which will inaugurate the second heptad of judgments. Before the series commences, a throne room worship scene interrupts the action (Angers, France).

Throne Room Worship (8:3–5). The action of an angel is used to symbolize that the prayers of God's people are received and answered. An incense altar is the equivalent of the Holy of Holies. An angel takes on hieratic function to mingle incense and prayers, which symbolizes prayers received. The angel casts the holy altar fire on earth, which symbolizes the prayers answered. The Trumpet judgments are God's response to the prayers of God's people. The impact of the altar fire is described apocalyptically as voices, thunderings, lightning, and earthquake. The description is fourfold to symbolize that the judgments affect the earth. The percentage of destruction in this Trumpet judgment series escalates to one third over the one fourth destruction with the Seal judgments, which shows recapitulation but heightening of intensity.

Egyptian Plagues	Rev 8
1. Blood (Nile)	1. Hail, fire, blood
2. Frogs	2. Blood (sea)
6. Boils	3. Bitter water
7. Thunder, hail	4. Darken (sun, moon, stars)
8. Locusts	5. Locusts
9. Darkness	6. Invading cavalry

FIGURE 11.16. Trumpets and Egyptian Plagues. The trumpets are built loosely on the Egyptian plagues of Exodus traditions.

Trumpets 1–4 (8:6–13). The Trumpet plagues are based loosely on the Exodus plagues, which alludes to the preeminent Old Testament paradigm of God's redemptive action on behalf of his people. Thus, the allusions are appropriate to the needs of believers in Asia Minor. The disasters of the first four trumpets—hail and fire mixed with blood, a huge mountain all ablaze thrown into the sea, natural waters poisoned by gases, and the sun, moon, and stars darkened—are all characteristics of a massive volcanic eruption, as in the A.D. 79 eruption of Vesuvius that buried for nearly two millennia the cities of Pompeii and Herculaneum on the Gulf of Naples. The huge ejected column of the stone, ash, and fumes reached twenty miles into the sky, and the hydrothermal pyroclastic flows killed as many as 16,000. We have detailed eyewitness accounts of this eruption in two letters Pliny the Younger wrote to Tacitus, his friend. Pliny's famous uncle, Pliny the Elder, a Roman naval officer stationed at Misenum in the Gulf of Naples near Vesuvius, died trying to rescue others during the course of this epic eruption.[52] Pliny's description of Vesuvius parallels the elements of the first four trumpets. Thus, while John is building on the imagery of the Exodus plagues, he also is innovating his language to correspond to natural disasters experienced in his own day. As a result, the Exodus allusions are somewhat loose.

FIGURE 11.17. Herculaneum, and Pompeii Victim. Vesuvius rises in the background with ancient Herculaneum in foreground. Bottom: plaster cast of a Pompeii victim.

[52] Pliny *Letters* 6.16 and 6.20.

A bird flying across midheaven creates a slight pause in the action for a grave announcement and ominous words.[53] Three woes are proclaimed. The impression is that the three woes go with the last three trumpets. A reasonable guess to explain the woes is that the object of the last three trumpets changes. The first four strike the earth. The last three strike humans directly.

Elements	Trumpet 1	
	Trumpet 2	
	Trumpet 3	
	Trumpet 4	
Humans	Trumpet 5	Woe 1
	Trumpet 6	Woe 2
	Trumpet 7	Woe 3

FIGURE 11.18. Trumpets: Three Woes.

Trumpets 5–6 (9:1–21). The fifth and sixth trumpets explicitly are associated with two of the three woes. An escalation of severity is the result. Humans directly are affected. One third are killed, which is the recapitulation scheme of increasing percentage of destruction. This imagery is dramatic, having more extended descriptions than any of the Seal judgments, which also increases dramatic tension.

The fifth trumpet opens the bottomless pit and releases a plague of locusts, who have fearsome, unimaginable descriptions, which takes the imagery well beyond the Egyptian plagues described in Exod 10:4–19. The description builds on Parthian warriors, the only enemy Rome ever feared because they gave Rome the worst defeat its army ever suffered in the Battle of Carrhae in eastern Syria in 53 B.C. Parthians represented the eastern border of the empire that the Romans never conquered. They were horsemen of renown. They invented the compound bow, which greatly increased range and power. They developed a style of shooting bow and arrow with such deadly accuracy that the method came to be know as the "Parthian shot." After an initial cavalry charge into infantry, as they rode away, the warriors would rise and turn backward in unison to fire a deadly volley into any pursuers. So, even from behind they could inflict a deadly sting like a scorpion's tail. Parthian warriors wore long hair, and their horses were heavily armored in a style called the *cataphract*, which later became the warhorse armament of feudal knights in the Medieval age.[54]

---

[53] Whether an eagle or a vulture is uncertain in the Greek manuscripts. The KJV has "angel," which is a scribal attempt to solve the problem from 14:6 that is found in later manuscripts.

[54] *Justin's History of the World* 41.2. That John with his fearsome locusts imagery is doing his best after teleportation into the future to view the battle of Armageddon to describe the modern warfare of helicopter gunships is exegetically senseless.

412 REVELATION: THE PAST AND FUTURE OF JOHN'S APOCALYPSE

FIGURE 11.19. Apocalypse Tapestry, Rev 9:1. Depicted from the fifth trumpet is the falling star, the key to the bottomless pit, smoke darkening sun, the fearsome locust cavalry, and their king, the destroyer angel, Apollyon (Angers, France).

The Parthian warrior imagery is clear. However, the frightening image of a fearsome Parthian cavalry swarming like locusts only sets the stage for the crucial point. The crucial point is the name of their leader, given as Abaddon in Hebrew, but immediately interpreted in Greek as Apollyon, "Destroyer" (9:11). This name plays off the name of the Greek god, Apollo, whom Roman emperors such as Nero and Domitian claimed to be.[55] Instead of gods, these emperors really are the very forces of evil sweeping over the earth. Rome does not civilize the world as in imperial propaganda. Roman legions destroy like swarming locusts.

FIGURE 11.20. Apollo Inscription. Imperial inscription of the *sebastion* cult temple of the emperor with reference to the god Apollo (MMM).

[55]See the discussion of the rhetoric of Apollyon, p. 230.

As with the sixth seal, this sixth trumpet is climactic. The locust swarms of the fifth trumpet pale in comparison to the numbers now released and the damage done. This unbelievable cavalry of two-hundred million kills a third of humankind (9:15–16). They are released from beyond the Euphrates where all Rome's feared enemies derived. By a threefold repetition in just three verses what is crucial in this new imagery is emphasized—that the power to do harm is in their mouths (9:17–19). What kills is what comes out of their mouths. This imagery in the sixth trumpet is meant to work in concert with that of the Son of Man, who has a sharp, two-edged sword coming from his mouth—*the war is over the truth of the gospel*. Revelation is a war of words. Belief and confession are how this battle is engaged. Thus, the imagery may be martial, but the point is the truth of words testified.

A passage now surfaces that reveals two crucial points about all John's martial imagery and all judgments in the Judgment Cycle.

> And the rest of humankind who were not killed by these plagues did not repent of the works of their hands, such that they not worship demons and idols of gold and silver and bronze and stone and wood, which neither see nor are able to hear or walk. They also did not repent of their murders, nor from their sorceries, or their fornication, or their thefts (Rev 9:20–21).

First, note what this passage shows about John's martial imagery. The passage interprets the innumerable cavalry just envisioned and the battle just engaged as not one of actual clashing armies. The combat is clashing confessions. The war is the worship of demons. The logistics are in the lies of idolatry institutionalized as a part of state policy such that murder can be committed in behalf of piety and politics, sorcery substitutes for truth, and property is confiscated from "criminals" who refused to pinch incense to Caesar. Ultimately, however, the enemies of the gospel hurt only those who do not have the seal of God on their foreheads, since that is the seal that secures the eternal future (9:4).[56]

Second, *repentance is sought in all of Revelation's judgments*. A similar repentance theme is sounded in the Bowl judgments, and this theme also occurs eight times in the Seven Letters.[57] That repentance

---

[56] A seal that presumably protects from the second death; cf. Smyrna, Rev 2:11.
[57] Bowls in Rev 16:9, 11. Letters in Rev 2:5 (2x); 2:21 (2x); 2:22; 3:3; 19.

is a theme of the judgments in Revelation, whether against the church or the world, indicates God's judgments are not punitive. They have redemptive intent. At the same time, God will undermine any empire with her worst fears without submission to his sovereignty. If not with the Parthians, then the Visigoths, in the great historical irony of the barbarian conquering the civilized and eternal Rome. The pattern will repeat in all stories of godless empire. They *will* fall. "Fallen, fallen is Babylon the great!" (18:2). As in Nebuchadnezzar's dream that Daniel alone could interpret above all the court sorcerers, the godless statue is shattered.[58]

Interlude (10:1—11:13). Just as with the Seal series, the Trumpet series has an interlude that breaks the movement before the last judgment in the series. Also like the Seals, the Trumpets interlude has two parts. The first part deals with John. The second part deals with the church. The purpose of the interlude is in the midst of the dramatic action of the Trumpet judgments to provide assurance to the faithful of God's sovereign control when historical events seem out of control and evil overwhelms believers.

We are presented with a number of minor interpretive issues in this interlude. One is the identification of the "mighty angel," who seems to echo the Son of Man imagery. Another is whether the "little scroll" is the same scroll as in the Vision of Heaven (5:1). Finally, the seven thunders are heard but refused interpretation, which seems odd and somewhat useless. Probably this angel is not the Son of Man, but acts in his authority. The little scroll is not the sealed scroll of the Vision of Heaven because its description, treatment, and function are altogether different. The purpose of the uninterpreted seven thunders is inscrutable.

<u>The Little Scroll (10:1-11)</u>. The important message of this unit is "no more delay" (10:6), which implies the seventh trumpet is the end. To this end, John is recommissioned, which reprises his original prophetic commission in 1:9-10. John is reaffirmed through this encounter in his prophetic authority. John may not be aware at this moment that the vision will continue past the seventh trumpet, but he soon will understand the intention to frame the same judgment of God over his creation from a new perspective of its cosmic forces and dimensions.

---

[58]See the discussion of Dan 2:31-45, pp. 12-15.

The mighty angel puts feet on sea and land (10:2). The order of mention—sea, then land—is significant. In the upcoming second half of the Judgment Cycle, the dragon comes from the sea, and his beasts come from the land. The mighty angel's legs like pillars of fire standing on both sea and land is an image that symbolizes God's authority over the major characters to arise in the second half of the Judgment Cycle to come. This authority over sea and land further is affirmed in the oath taken by the mighty angel, who swears by the creator God who made sea and land (10:6a).

The clarion call of the mighty angel indicates the imminent end of the judgments. The mighty angel declares:

> "Time no longer is, but in the days of the sound of the seventh angel when he is going to sound the trumpet, then the mystery of God is completed, as he promised to his servants the prophets" (Rev 10:6b–7).

No mistake here. The seventh trumpet is the end. The mystery of the creator God and his creation is completed, and the voice of prophecy is fulfilled. No statement of "the end" could be more climactic nor less ambiguous. Literarily, this angelic oath is one of the clearest indicators John gives that the series of three judgment heptads in the Judgment Cycle are recapitulatory, since the seventh trumpet is "the end," but Revelation obviously does not end after the seventh trumpet.

John then becomes personally involved in the action. He is told to take the little scroll and eat, which by all accounts is odd to be chewing on a document. The action is symbolic. Sweet in the mouth but bitter in the stomach is the word of prophecy. The word is God's, so sweet to receive, but the message is judgment, so sad to deliver. The good news of Christ's victory is sweet, but the bad news of persecution of God's people and rejection of God's salvation is bitter.

John then is told, "You must prophesy again" (10:11). This word extends his commission to write. This command is the bridge to the second half of the Judgment Cycle. John has witnessed the story of Almighty God and his Christ in the Seals and the Trumpets, but the story of the Red Dragon and his Beasts, the cosmic dimensions of this same story, is yet to unfold. The first part of the Trumpets interlude concerning John personally and his recommissioning, is complete. In the second part, John turns to the reality of the persecuted church in faithful witness.

Temple Measuring (11:1–2). The brief temple scene in 11:1–2 before the two witnesses come on stage presents several interpretive issues. The following questions have been asked about this material.

- Does this scene imply the Jerusalem temple still is standing at the time Revelation is written? Is this even the Jerusalem temple?
- If the Jerusalem temple, which courts are measured: Gentiles, Women, Israel, Priests, or Sanctuary?
- The unmeasured court represents whom: Christian apostates, the unbelieving world, or the persecuted church?
- What is the literary source: a prewar Zealot oracle about the Jerusalem temple, or Ezek 40–42, or Zech 2?
- Where is the first paragraph break: at verse 2 (GNT), or verse 3 (NRSV), or verse 6 (NIV), or none for the entire chapter (KJV)?
- Is this time of the forty-two months the same as the 1260 days of the two witnesses? (This answer depends on the paragraphing question above.)

Hard to avoid is the literary impression that John intends the temple scene to be the introduction of the two witnesses. A measuring of the temple is a prophetic sign of protection and praise to God.[59] The time period of the forty-two months or 1260 days seems to be the famous Danielic period of three and a half years of Dan 7:25. Daniel's context is a time of intense persecution for the people of God inspired by the historical event of the sacrilege of the Jerusalem temple by Antiochus IV Epiphanes, who sacrificed a pig on the Jewish altar, desecrating the holy place in 167 B.C. until the temple was recaptured and rededicated by Judas Maccabeus in 164 B.C. The historical period of three years of Syrian desolation was extended to three and a half years in apocalyptic traditions because of the symbolic value of half of seven. Thus, measuring the temple symbolizes that the people of God will be protected by God even though under severe duress by their enemies. Apparently, John has blended the Danielic image of duress for God's people with the historical reality of the destruction of the Jerusalem temple in A.D. 70, hence the giving over to the nations for "trampling" of the

---

[59] Ps 48:12–13; Ezek 40:3—42:20; Zech 2:1–5.

"outer courts" for this period of forty-two months, which most likely is not a literal time but a symbolic time, simply because almost all numbers in Revelation have symbolic value. John intends to say the people of God will be under severe duress but divinely sustained by God either over the entire duration of the church age or during an especially intense period of duress at the end. Either interpretation works and is faithful to the context of Revelation.

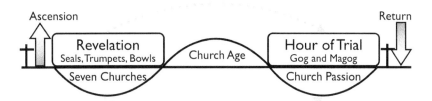

FIGURE 11.21. Hour of Trial. The Sardis "hour of trial" coming on the "whole world" (3:8) could be the same period as the "forty-two months" of the Trumpets interlude (11:2) and the Gog and Magog battle (20:8).

While the entire church age could be imaged here in the picture of the measuring of the temple, more likely John is functioning as a prescient prophet due to his own experience with Domitian in first-century Asia Minor about a future time of intense persecution for the church that brings her very existence in the world into question. Thus, this forty-two month time period presented in the Trumpets interlude is an alternate variation on the theme of the "hour of trial" to come on the whole world of Rev 3:10 in the letter to Sardis, and also should be equated with the intent of the Gog and Magog imagery of Rev 20:8. The persecution of the church during the church age simply would be the "early tremors" predicting a major earthquake to come. While Rev 11:1–2 in part could point to the church age, this imagery more likely is John's preliminary anticipation of the great "hour of trial" to come upon the whole world. Thus, 11:1–2 is Ezekiel's eschatological temple.

The Two Witnesses (11:3–13). These two witnesses are built on Zechariah's two seven-branched lampstands and the two olive trees.[60] These figures are anointed ones representing king and priest, which, in the original context of Zechariah was the issue of the rebuilding of

---

[60]Zech 4:2–3.

FIGURE 11.22. Elijah on Mount Carmel. This statue on Mount Carmel in Israel commemorates Elijah famously confronting the prophets of Baal in a showdown on Mount Carmel (1Kgs 18:19–40). Ahab's foreign princess wife, Queen Jezebel, had brought the idolatrous worship of Canaanite fertility deities into Israel's court, fostering 450 prophets of Baal and 400 prophets of the goddess Asherah at the royal table (1 Kgs 18:19). As prophesied, dogs ate Jezebel's corpse outside the city walls (2 Kgs 9:30–37). Elijah was expected to return to Israel as forerunner of Messiah (Mal 4:5).

FIGURE 11.23. Michelangelo's Moses. A Michelangelo marble masterpiece, this statue completed between 1513–16 is in the Church of San Pietro in Vincoli, Rome, commissioned by Pope Julius II for his tomb. Moses' horns are due to Jerome's Latin Vulgate, the Bible of the Roman Catholic Church. A difficult Hebrew original about Moses' face when coming down from Mount Sinai could be "horned" or "shining" (Exod 34:29–35). If taken as emitting rays as in a glorified state, then Jerome meant "horns" as a metaphor, but this subtlety was lost in later generations. Israel expected a future prophet to come who would be like Moses (Deut 18:18–19).

the temple with the return of Jews to Judea after the exile under king Zerubbabel and the priest Joshua.[61] Jewish traditions developed about a messianic king and anointed priest. Association with two Old Testament figures who were translated to heaven, Enoch and Elijah, would be natural. Some interpreters include Moses in the list of candidates. Elijah called down fire from heaven.[62] John, of course, has modified this imagery to suit his own point about testimony and witness in his symbols for his war of words, so these figures breathe fire from their mouths that "consumes their foes" (11:5). Elijah also induced drought, and Moses turned water to blood.[63] Finally, both Moses and Elijah anticipated God's future action on behalf of Israel, with a future prophet to come who would be like Moses, and a prophet to come who would be like Elijah to anticipate Messiah in Jewish traditions.[64] Note that their sackcloth clothing signals a prophetic call to repentance.

These witnesses are opposed by the beast out of the bottomless pit, who is Apollyon, the Destroyer. Apollyon fulfills the destiny of his name, because this figure destroys the church. Jerusalem is lumped in with Sodom and Egypt as with any who oppose Jesus. The witnesses are killed, which means the church is wiped out; the earth celebrates. The church's word of witness no longer pangs the conscience of the world. However, the celebration is premature. As in the gospel story of Jesus, God intervenes with the power of resurrection. Earth is judged. A great earthquake destroys a tenth of the city (not an unusual figure for a major earthquake, so the imagery is not outstanding).

The interlude makes clear that even wiping out the church does not wipe out God's plan or defeat God's sovereignty. God actually will use that event to bring about his final consummation of the kingdom, just as he used the death of Jesus to bring salvation and to express his sovereignty. As Reddish observed, "A strong *imitatio Christi* motif runs throughout the Apocalypse. The followers of the Lamb are to be imitators of him, As he was a faithful witness, they too are to be faithful witnesses. Like him they must expect persecution and suffering."[65]

---

[61] Zech 4:14; 6:13.
[62] 1 Kgs 18:38; 2 Kgs 1:10, 12.
[63] 1 Kgs 17:1; 18:41; Exod 7:14–25.
[64] Deut 18:15–18; Mal 4:5.
[65] Reddish, *Revelation*, 213.

Trumpet 7 (11:14–19). The interlocking three woes have their second explicit reference. Two have passed. Apparently, these two have been the fifth and sixth trumpets. The implication is that the seventh trumpet is the third woe, because the third woe is "coming soon" (11:14), but an explicit statement relating the third woe to the seventh trumpet is not made (unless John meant 11:14 that way). Thus, the third woe is either elsewhere (bowl judgments, etc.), or omitted by John (intentionally or unintentionally), or is trumpet seven.

The seventh trumpet is different in content and location. The first six trumpets were plagues on the earth. Trumpet seven really is a celebration in heaven. The setting is the throne room, and God's sovereignty rightly is recognized. Expressions such as "our Lord and his Messiah" evoke Ps 2:2, which is a royal enthronement psalm later taken messianically in Jewish tradition. All appearances are that the seventh trumpet intends to portray the end, because all statements are unequivocal, conclusive, and final.

> And the seventh angel trumpeted, and loud voices happened in heaven, which were saying:
> > "The kingdom of the world has become our Lord's and his Christ's,
> > and he will reign forever and ever."
> And the twenty-four elders who sit upon their thrones before God fell upon their faces and worshipped God and were saying:
> > "We bless you Lord God Almighty, who is and who was,
> > > because you have taken your great power and have begun to reign.
> > And the nations were enraged
> > > and your wrath came
> > > and the time for the dead to be judged
> > and to give the reward to your servants the prophets
> > > and to the saints and to those who fear your name
> > > the small and the great
> > and to destroy those destroying the earth" (Rev 11:15–18).

The verbal form of the divine title changes from three tenses of earlier references ("the one who is, who was, and who is to come," 1:4, 8; 4:8) down to two, "who is and who was"; a future tense, "is to come," now is missing (11:17). God has come in judgment as promised and he has "begun to reign." Yet, strangely, the judgment only is announced, not described. Since we already have had a grand finale at the end of the

Seal series in the sixth seal, this second grand finale is anticlimactic. This literary feature enhances the idea that the judgment heptads of the Seals, Trumpets, and Bowls are meant to recapitulate. Further, the announced judgment anticipates the second half of the Judgment Cycle, the Dragon Cycle, the story of the Red Dragon and his Beasts. The wording "your wrath came" (11:18) is proleptic of the entire Dragon Cycle itself with its integrated Bowl judgment heptad.

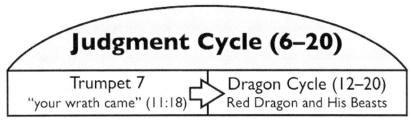

FIGURE 11.24. Trumpet 7 and Dragon Cycle. The announcement "your wrath came" (11:18) in the hymn of the elders in the seventh trumpet anticipates the Dragon Cycle.

Note the three players on the stage in this hymn: prophets, saints, and destroyers. The characters unfold from the historical context. The "prophets" are John and his circle of prophets preaching the apostolic gospel to the seven churches of Asia Minor. The "saints" are members of the seven churches under duress due to their confession of Jesus as Lord. The "destroyers" are Domitian (Apollyon) and his Roman empire, along with all complicit provincial officials enforcing the imperial cult and its commerce, exacerbated by rampant paganism. In short, these characters have first-century Asia Minor written all over them.

The seventh trumpet scene concludes with an apocalypse of the heavenly temple (11:19). God's temple in heaven is opened, meaning a revelatory scene. This opening is the divine response to the elders' victory hymn just sung (11:17–18). The ark of the covenant is revealed, which represents God's promised presence with his people. Jewish tradition speculated that the ark, though lost to the Babylonians in 587 B.C., would be restored by God's future Messiah.[66] Apocalyptic language features in the lightning, rumblings, thunder, earthquake, and hail. The point of this temple apocalypse is to put a "literary bow" on packaging the idea that the seventh trumpet means that the end time has arrived. Theologically, this scene is the divine "amen" to the recent song of victory by the elders still reverberating in the halls of heaven.

[66] 2 Macc 2:7; *2 Bar.* 6:1–9.

Dragon Cycle (12:1—20:15)

The Judgment Cycle now moves to its second half. The first half, comprised of Seals and Trumpets, tells the story of Almighty God and His Christ, in which the kingdom of the world becomes "the kingdom of our Lord and of his Christ" (11:15). This second half reprises the same story but emphasizing its cosmic dimensions, with new characters, the Red Dragon and his Beasts. As John was bringing the Christ Cycle to its end with the Trumpets interlude followed by the seventh trumpet, he dropped hints anticipating the Dragon Cycle. The first part of the interlude focused personally on John; his prophetic recommissioning included the charge to "prophesy again" (10:11), which anticipates the forthcoming Dragon Cycle. Then, the seventh trumpet proclaims in the concluding hymn "your wrath came" (11:18), which also anticipates the drama of the Dragon Cycle. The "your wrath came" expression at the end of the Trumpet series reveals why the language of wrath, already introduced in the climactic finale of the sixth seal ("the great day of their wrath has come," 6:17), becomes more prominent in this Dragon Cycle.

Dragon Cycle (12–20)
Red Dragon and His Beasts
Cosmic Conflict (12–13)
• Dragon Attack (12)
• Beast Agents (13)
Messianic Conquest (14–20)
• Bowl Prelude (14)
• Bowl Judgments (15–16)
• Bowl Perspectives (17–20)
Eschatological Climax (20)
• Satan's Defeat (Gog/Magog)
• God's Judgment (White Thr.)

FIGURE 11.25. The Dragon Cycle. This cycle plays out the seventh trumpet's "your wrath came."

Sections of the Dragon Cycle are tied by a repeated phrase, "and I saw a great sign in heaven," to introduce the Woman (12:1), Dragon (12:3), and Bowls (15:1). The story of *cosmic conflict* begins with the Dragon's attack (12), who calls up the Beasts as his earthly agents (13). *Messianic conquest* is anticipated in a proleptic prelude (14), followed by Bowl judgments (15–16) flowing seamlessly into four perspectives on them through further visions mediated by the seven Bowl angels (17–20). The *eschatological climax* is Satan's ultimate destruction as Gog and Magog and God's final judgment as a great, white throne (20).

Conflict: Dragon Attack (12:1–18)

In Rev 12, John is subverting pagan myth. To recognize his strategy, the reader of Revelation has to observe how John has had a creation focus all along. This focus is seen both in the descriptions of God and Christ and the words of the angels. God is celebrated as the Alpha and

Omega (1:8) and creator of all (4:11). In parallel, Christ is described as the origin of God's creation (3:14), while the angels use creation as the ground of oaths (10:6), and John will present a new creation in one of his final visions (Rev 21). John's own creation imagery uses the figures of four living creatures that are symbolic of creation in the Vision of Heaven (4:6–11). They are central to the worship of the Lamb (5:6), participate in the Seal judgments (6:1), and tie the vision of the great multitude in the Seals interlude in the first half of the Judgment Cycle. Now in the second half, these same four living creatures participate in the second 144,000 scene (14:3), inaugurate the climactic Bowl judgments (15:7), and join in the climactic hallelujah chorus (19:4).

Using all of this creation emphasis and imagery, John intends to subvert pagan myth, which he takes on in earnest in Rev 12. John will deconstruct pagan mythological language. He also will reinterpret the Jewish traditions that allude to these creation constructs. He subverts pagan myth and Jewish tradition with christological truth. He is re-imaging the church conflict revealed in the Seven Letters on a cosmic scale by saying the story has deeper characters. He is saying the story is critical because the issues have destiny implications. He is pointing out the story is cultural because of assimilation challenges. He uses Rev 12–14 to provide a detailed view of the assault on God's people by forces of evil before presenting the Bowl judgments on those forces. John evokes ancient creation myths to modulate his story into a cosmic key. His mythic language taps into the deep psyche of his Greco-Roman audience. Asia Minor churches can envision their struggles with arrogant Rome and her blasphemous emperors as nothing less than reincarnations of the strong, fearsome primeval chaos monster—the dragon, Greek Python, Babylonian Tiamat, Jewish Leviathan.

FIGURE 11.26. Revelation 12 Intercalation. The story of the Woman and Dragon split into two parts due to intercalating the combat story of Michael and the Dragon.

John's literary strategy is intercalation. He will interrupt the story of the Woman and the Dragon by intercalating a totally separate story, the Jewish combat myth of Michael and the Dragon. This intercalation splits the story of the Woman and the Dragon into two parts. The purpose of the intercalation is to provide the basis for presenting the most theologically important hymn of all of Revelation.

FIGURE 11.27. Marriage of Zeus and Leto. The Greek myth of Apollo starts with the marriage of the god Zeus to Apollo's mother, Leto, the daughter of the Titans Coesus and Phebe, depicted in this second-century A.D. relief. (HAMH).

Part 1: Woman/Dragon (12:1–6). John draws on ancient myth including the twelve signs of the Zodiac and the Greek birth of Apollo. In the Greek myth, Zeus impregnates Leto, whose offspring, Apollo, is destined to destroy the dragon Python. Python attempts to kill Leto and her child to thwart his own fatal end. Poseidon, however, intervenes by hiding Leto on the island Delos sunk under the sea until Leto secretly can give birth to Apollo. Her son eventually kills Python even as fated. Jewish reinterpretation already had rewritten the twelve signs of the Zodiac as the twelve tribes of Israel and the Python myth as the Lord slaying the sea dragon Leviathan. John's rewrite is to interpret the twelve tribes of Israel as the gospel story of Jesus and the twelve apostles. John then transposes the Apollo-Python conflict into the key of empire propaganda. He counters the emperor as Apollo by insisting the real "Apollo" hero defeating evil is Jesus. John's creation theology is applied to ancient chaos myth to deconstruct the pagan elements and reconstruct the christological truth. Precedent for such a reinterpretation already had been suggested to John through Jewish reformulations of ancient chaos myths using Leviathan, their own form of the seven-headed sea monster.

The description of the woman with child (12:1–2) is allusive of the Queen of Heaven, since she is "clothed with the sun," and has the "moon under her feet," and sports a "crown of twelve stars," which originally would have been the Zodiac, but reinterpreted as the twelve tribes of Israel in Jewish tradition. In Roman tradition, this Queen of Heaven was the goddess Roma, the city of Rome as the Queen Mother of the empire. The with child element is the allusion to the Apollo myth. Jewish tradition had adapted the woman in labor as Israel and the child as Messiah.[67] John's adaptation simply is to take the matter one step further christologically by identifying the Messiah as Jesus.

The great red dragon is introduced next (12:3–4). His description is as the creation/chaos monster. The seven heads are traditional, that is, already a standard feature of the ancient dragon myth. The diadems are traditional and indicate dominion, and the ten horns power. Also traditional is a tail dragging a third of the stars of heaven. Thus, the entire description of this monster is stereotypical and completely traditional. He is Python of Greek myth, Tiamat of Babylonian myth, and Leviathan of Jewish myth. No matter how traditional, the point is he is poised to kill the child.

The dragon is circumvented (12:5–6). The story is told first about the child and then about the woman. The child's story is reduced to three focal points: his birth, destiny, and ascension. As a male child, he subverts the traditional hero role of Apollo. This child of destiny rules the nations with a "rod of iron," which is a clear allusion to Ps 2, a Davidic royal enthronement psalm taken messianically both by Jews and Christians. The "rod of iron" rule is John's way of saying the figure of Apollo in the myth is Jesus in reality. His "reign," however, is

---

[67] Isa 26:17–18; enhanced if sun, moon, stars imagery also is allusive of Gen. 37:9.

not described. The story jumps to the ascension, expressed simply as the child being "snatched away" to heaven (12:5). An obvious lacuna in this retelling is that the death and resurrection climax in the gospel story is passed over; John's reworking perhaps is constrained by the plot in the mythic substructure underneath his presentation here. The woman part of the circumvention of the dragon then is related, but only briefly in terms of flight and refuge. Her refuge is in the wilderness for 1260 days. This period is the same length of time as the trampling of the outer court of the temple and the preaching of the two witnesses in the Trumpets interlude (12:2, 3).

FIGURE 11.28. Douce Apocalypse, Rev 12:6. The woman's child is snatched up to heaven away from the seven-headed red dragon (ADEVA).

Part 2: Michael/Dragon (12:7–12). Two principal characters are introduced, Michael, the archangel, and Satan, the devil. The Michael tradition is Jewish and postexilic. Michael was one of the seven archangels. His main features are as a warrior angel on behalf of Israel, who casts fallen angels into the fiery furnace, and who is the prince of light leading the apocalyptic battle.[68] Satan has no biblical biography. The idea of his primeval expulsion from heaven misunderstands Isa

---

[68] Dan 10:13, 21; 12:1; *1 En.* 54:6.

14:12; "Lucifer's" primeval fall is English literature, the imagination of John Milton (d. 1674) on display in the highly influential *Paradise Lost* epic. Gospel tradition records Jesus' metaphorical statement of seeing Satan fall, but the context is clear Jesus is speaking of the successful gospel mission of the returning seventy disciples who have reported to Jesus how even the demons submit to them in Jesus' name.[69]

FIGURE 11.29. Douce Apocalypse, Rev 12:7. The intercalation of the Jewish myth of combat between Michael and the Dragon in heaven (ADEVA).

The story now moves to war in heaven (12:7–9). The description is minimal, just the protagonist, the antagonist, and their angels. The battle is not even described, only that the dragon is defeated. Thus, the whole point of the war in heaven scene is to set up the background for the christological hymn that follows. Earthly events reflect heavenly counterparts. John already has made clear in Revelation through his description of Jesus as the Son of Man and the slaughtered Lamb that Satan's heavenly defeat is meant as the symbolic counterpart to the cross of Christ. Satan's descent down to earth is symbolic of the focus of the devil on the church after the ascension of Jesus, which is Part 2

---

[69]Luke 10:18. One should be careful also to note that Jesus speaks of "Satan falling" *in the context of a mission whose principal focus is witness.*

of the Woman/Dragon story. To nail the point of the identity of the dragon, John gives a quadruple nomenclature, the only character in Revelation so identified. This dragon is the "serpent," "Devil," "Satan," "Deceiver." This dragon of whom John speaks is the biblical adversary of God's people in both testaments of the Bible.

The victory hymn is sung (12:10–12). The whole point of John's Michael/Dragon intercalation is here. This hymn is about God's kingdom and Messiah's authority. Satan takes on his traditional role as the accuser of God's people, which once again emphasizes that Revelation is about a war of words (1:16) and that the operative theology in this cosmic conflict is witness and testimony. Believers take on their traditional role of conquering. This victorious conquest has two foci: "by the blood of the Lamb," which is sacrificial death, and "by the word of their testimony," which is faithful witness. This hymn celebrates the fulfillment of the Promise sections of the Seven Letters with their repeating phrase, "to the one who conquers," echoing seven times in the ears of believers in Asia Minor. Faithful testimony is the core of the war:

- Jesus, the faithful witness (1:5; 3:14)
- John, the faithful witness (1:2, 9)
- Antipas, the faithful witness (2:13)
- the church, the faithful witness (11:3; 12:11, 17; 19:10)

This faithful witness theme is in the context of persecution in all three judgment heptads. In the Seals, one has the martyred souls under the altar (6:9). In the Trumpets, one has the martyred witnesses (11:7). In the Bowls, one has the millennial reign, which is a martyr reign (20:4).

Thus, Rev 12:11 is the heart of this chapter, the center of John's cosmic stage in the Dragon Cycle, and the theological soul of the Apocalypse. John has engaged the ancient combat myth only to demythologize the story in a powerful way with gospel truth. Conquering "by the blood of the Lamb" is the thesis of Revelation, the believer's victory in persecution, the only path of true discipleship to the end of the age, and how God deals conclusively with evil in the world. No other battle wins that war. Verse 12:11 is the reason Revelation is canon.

The word of woe for the earth (12:12) anticipates the imagery of the rest of the Dragon Cycle to come (Rev 13–20). That "the devil has come down to you" is a transference of the cosmic struggle down to earth. This new arena already has been revealed in the situation of the seven churches of Asia Minor, as evidenced in the Seven Letters. The devil arrives on earth "with great wrath" because he knows his "time is short." This great wrath is released in the power of the beast and his false prophets (Rev 13), which provides the exegetical context for the famous mark of the beast (13:16–17), as well as the context for the later Babylon imagery (14:8; 18:3). The entire Dragon Cycle is about the seven churches of Asia Minor.

Part 3: Woman/Dragon (12:13–18). The opening storyline now is resumed. The wilderness theme derives from Exodus traditions. The eagles' wings for flight represents divine intervention, as in Exod 19:4. The wilderness itself is divine protection, as originally from Pharaoh's army. The nourishment is divine provision, as with the manna and the quail of the Exodus story.[70] The duration theme is on behalf of the preservation of the persecuted church. The "time and times and half a time" is three and a half years. This figure probably has the same symbolic significance as the sealing of the 144,000 in the Seals interlude (7:1–8) and the measuring of the temple in the Trumpets interlude (11:1–2). These several figures seem to be varied expressions for the same period. The idea is borrowed from Daniel.[71] Expressed as years, one has three and a half years of wilderness refuge (12:14); as months, one has forty-two months of trampling the outer court (11:2); as days, one has 1260 days of the preaching of the two witnesses (11:3) or of the wilderness refuge (12:6).

The point is, the Dragon's defeat in heaven is reprised on earth. The river flooding story has one innovation by John and one element from the mythical tradition. The river flooding story is innovated by John in terms of the notable source of the river: "from his mouth" (12:15). A close reading observes that the feature of the "mouth" is the same origin as the sword of the Son of Man in the Inaugural Vision (1:16). The same issue is insinuated: a war of words. The unusual nature of this war is a core feature of the action of the beasts that the Dragon calls up in the next chapter:

---

[70]Manna: Exod 16:31–35; Num 11:6–9; Deut 8:3–16; Neh 9:20; Ps 78:24; John 6:31, 49; Heb 9:4. Quail: Exod 16:13; Num 11:31–32; Ps 105:40; Wis 16:2; 19:12.

[71]Cf. Dan 7:25; 12:7.

> The beast was given a mouth uttering haughty and blasphemous words, and it was allowed to exercise authority for forty-two months. The beast opened its mouth to utter blasphemies against God, blaspheming his name and his dwelling, that is, those who dwell in heaven (13:5–6).
>
> Then I saw another beast that rose out of the earth; it had two horns like lamb, and it spoke like a dragon (13:11).
>
> And it was allowed to give breath to the image of the beast so that the image of the beast could even speak and cause those who would not worship the image of the beast to be killed (13:15).

The earth, however, swallows up the waters that are going to sweep away the woman. Flood and earth features are from the original myth. Of course, the Dragon goes off to make war on the rest of the woman's children, whose identity we do not know, because we were not told she had other children. John immediately gives the profile of this mysterious progeny: "who keep the commandments of God and hold the testimony of Jesus" (12:17). That was easy. This is John, who is on the island of Patmos "because of the testimony of Jesus" (1:9), and the martyrs under the altar, slaughtered for the "testimony they had given" (6:9), and the two witnesses, who are killed after they "finished their testimony" (11:7), and the saints in the period of the beasts who endure (14:12). Thus, we have the same, consistent picture of John, the prophets, and the churches of Asia Minor under persecution in their confessional conflict with the Roman empire and paganism.

The woman's background as derived from the Queen of Heaven imagery is obvious, but her identity in Revelation is unclear. In Jewish tradition she was Israel, and that background may be applicable, since John has woven so much Jewish material into his imagery. Yet, the identity as Israel quickly founders upon the lack of consensus about the complex relationship of the church and Israel in the New Testament. Christian traditions have gravitated to identifying the woman as either Mary as the mother of Jesus in Roman Catholic tradition, or the church as the mother of believers in Protestant tradition. A generic blend would be the faithful of all time. Since her exact identity seems illusive, perhaps precision was not part of John's intent.

While her precise identity is unclear, her literary function is. She forms the opposite contrast to Lady Harlot, the city of Babylon in Rev

17:5, the mother of whores. She is Lady Virtue, the city of New Jerusalem in Rev 21:2, the mother of saints. John gives us his own version of a "tale of two cities."

Transition to the Beasts (12:18). Once again, the chapter division is terrible. This verse really is the beginning of the story of the beasts. A textual issue is who stands on the seashore, John ("I stood," KJV), or the Dragon ("he stood," almost all modern translations). Strong arguments favor "he stood" (e.g., the Dragon). Thus, the Dragon calls for reinforcements for his war of words on those who keep the "testimony of Jesus." Two beasts will come forth to carry out the assault on the church in the next chapter. What will become evident in Rev 13 is that John sees the Dragon's attacks through the two beasts as embodied in Rome and its imperial ideology.

Conflict: Beast Agents (13:1–18)

Two beasts come on stage, one from the sea and one from land, because Domitian's empire from across the sea in Rome needs its local provincial enforcers in Asia Minor to ingratiate itself into the lives of people. John's dual beast imagery is straightforward to the situation of John and seven local churches and the imperial cult in Asia Minor and is easy to read.

John is being highly innovative with his apocalyptic imagery in several ways. First, he merges Daniel's four *separate* beasts representing four pagan empires into *one composite* beast representing one empire here in Rev 13. Second, he converts the ten horns of the fourth beast, which in Daniel are *sequential* kings prior to the arrival of the archenemy of God's people in Antiochus IV Epiphanes, to a *simultaneous* confederation allied with Rome. The point of John's innovations is that Rome, along with her commercial coterie

Daniel 7		Rev 13
1st beast	lion	
2nd beast	bear	one beast
3rd beast	leopard	
4th beast	ten horns	

Daniel 7		Rev 13
4th beast	ten horns	one beast
ten *sequential kings* of the Seleucid dynasty preceeding the infamous Antiochus IV Epiphanes		ten kings all contemporary with the sea beast

FIGURE 11.30. Rev 13 and Dan 7. John's freely innovative apocalyptic imagery.

out in the provinces, is the sum of ancient, evil empires rolled into one fearsome reality. In our colloquial slang, John is saying, "So, you think ancient pagan empires and Antiochus IV was something? You ain't seen nothing yet!"

The spirit of antigod empires was epitomized in Nebuchadnezzar and Babylon for Daniel, who viewed such empires as animated by a satanic spirit and marked by blasphemous speech.[72] This Babylonian spirit of antigod empire Daniel saw reprised in the infamous Syrian king Antiochus IV Ephiphanes.[73] John takes this basic viewpoint and applies the idea to the spirit of antigod Rome, because the parallels were obvious. The antigod forces of empire vivified by a satanic spirit were reprised in Rome's imperial control over society and commerce. Likewise, blasphemous speech was reprised in the blasphemous titles arrogated by Rome's Flavian dynasty.

	Sea Beast (Ch. 13)	Christ (Chs. 1, 5, 12, 19)
1	ten diadems-v1	many diadems-19:12
2	blasphemous name-v1	worthy name-19:11
3	causes worship of Satan-v4	causes worship of God-1:6
4	fatal wound, but lives-v3	fatal wound, but lives-1:18; 5:6
5	throne, power from Satan-v2	throne, power from God-12:5
6	receives human praise-v4	receives human praise-5:13

FIGURE 11.31. Sea Beast Parody of Christ. The features of the sea beast of Rev 13 form an intentional parody of Christ.

The Sea Beast (13:1–10). John reframes this spirit of antigod empire in this sea beast christologically. He intentionally sets up the sea beast as a parody of Christ feature for feature, including a parody of the death and resurrection through the idea of a mortal wound that was "healed."[74] To do this he uses recent Roman history and legends to inspirit his character with qualities of Roman imperial families for recognition by his Asia Minor audience.

---

[72] The fascinating story is recounted in Dan 4.

[73] Dan 7:8–25.

[74] Noted by Beasley-Murray, *Revelation*, 207–08.

FIGURE 11.32. Apocalypse Tapestry, Rev 13:1. The sea beast rising from the sea receives a scepter to rule from the Dragon as John looks on the scene (Angers, France).

Sea Beast Description (13:1–3). After Nero committed suicide in A.D. 68, he was rumored still to be alive and in hiding in Asia Minor awaiting his moment to return to retake Rome, or to have died, but to return to life again (*Nero redivivus*) to conquer Rome. With the beast's mortal yet healed wound, John builds on the power of *Nero redivivus* legends haunting the Roman political psyche. John sees in Domitian the spirit of Nero, the emperor infamous to Christians because of his persecution after the fire of Rome. Coming in the spirit of a past figure is similar to how Jesus framed John the Baptist as coming in the "spirit and power of Elijah" in Mark 9:13. Reddish observed, "John is warning his readers that the evil that was incarnate in Nero is not finished yet. In the figure of a future ruler (17:10), a particularly malevolent one, 'Nero' will return once more to wreak havoc on the people of God."[75] Beasley-Murray noted the extraordinary irony of John's scenario: "The Christ of God has risen, but the world declared it a lie (Mt. 28:13ff.), or madness (Ac. 26:24). The 'Christ' of the Devil comes from death—and the whole world worships him!"[76] The sea beast has the authority

[75]Reddish, *Revelation*, 251.
[76]Beasley-Murray, *Revelation*, 210.

of the dragon and is worshipped. The question, "who can fight against him?" parodies imperial ideology of invincible Roman generals subduing all empire enemies even on distant borders.

Sea Beast Agenda (13:4–8). The goal of the enterprise is worship of the beast as worship of the Dragon to usurp God's glory. Yet, all actions are under the sovereignty of God. Divine passives, in which the assumed agent is God, control the grammar. The sea beast is *given* a voice, *allowed* authority, *allowed* to make war. God controls history. Even when evil empires are in control, the sovereign God has not yielded control. God is the one who writes "The End" on any script.

Within this activity constrained by the sovereignty of God, the sea beast utters "haughty and blasphemous words" (13:5), which ties into the key theme of Revelation as a war of words. The object of his blasphemy is God, because he assumes divine titles and asserts sovereignty over humans. The period of his authority is the well-familiar forty-two months, by now known as John's standard figure for the time of the church's persecution. When he "makes war," the sea beast does so through imperial propaganda that promotes paganism and enforces emperor worship. True believers giving faithful testimony to Jesus will be conquered socially, culturally, politically, and religiously since their testimony either will be rejected if given clearly, or ignored if compromised ignobly. The impact of this war is global (the fourfold "every tribe and people and language and nation," 13:7), because empires by definition are global, and preeminently so Rome. The whole world worships the beast, except followers of the slaughtered Lamb (13:8). John now brings home the slaughtered Lamb truth of the Vision of Heaven that inaugurated this entire Judgment Cycle (5:6).

Call to Faith (13:9–10). In the midst of the drama of the sea beast, John the prophet delivers the prophetic call to faith, making clear this call is addressed to the seven churches by echoing the call section of the Seven Letters, "the one who has an ear, let them hear" (2:7) in the closely similar, "If anyone has an ear, let them hear" (13:9). Thus, without doubt John has made clear that the issues of Rev 13 are the issues of Rev 2–3. Here is where churches of Asia Minor are told their issues have cosmic dimensions. John concludes the call with his main point: he is calling for endurance and faith of the saints (13:10). This prophetic call for believers to endure is Revelation's theme of faithful endurance prominent both in the Seven Letters and in the conquest prelude.[77] The call implies that John expects the conflict to worsen. A minor issue with a textual variation does not need to be resolved, since John's main point of faithful endurance is explicit and clear.[78]

Land Beast (13:11–18). In the Dragon and his beasts, we are getting introduced to the characters who will be driving the plot in the second half of the Judgment Cycle. The first half of the Judgment Cycle (6–11) is driven not by characters but by two judgment heptads of the Seals and the Trumpets. The second half of the Judgment Cycle, in contrast, is character driven. These characters are the Dragon, his beasts, and Babylon. We do not meet Babylon until Rev 17 as one of four perspectives on the Bowl judgment series (15–16).

	Land Beast (Ch. 13)	Christ (Chs. 5, 7, 12)
1	horns as a lamb-v11	Lamb with seven horns-5:6
2	inspired speech as dragon-v11	has seven spirits of God-5:6
3	seals followers-v16	seals followers-7:3
4	causes sea beast worship-v12	causes worship of God-5:13
5	power/authority, sea beast-v2	power/authority, God-5:9; 12:10

FIGURE 11.33. Land Beast Parody of Christ. The features of the land beast of Rev 13 form an intentional parody of Christ.

Coordinated Strategy (13:11–13). The land beast works in concert with the sea beast. Their strategies are mutual and coordinated. These two beasts from sea and land called forth by the cosmic Dragon wage war on the progeny of Lady Virtue with whom the Dragon Cycle begins. This land beast has horns like a "lamb" but speaks like a "dragon" (13:11). This description reveals the attempt to usurp the Lamb's role as the object of worship, but one who is only masquerading as Satan's lackey. The earth beast, therefore, is a second parody of Christ. Even the descriptions echo the wording, such as Lamb with "seven

---

[77] Rev 1:9; 2:2, 3, 19; 3:10; 14:12.

[78] A textual variation on the verb for "kill" yields two different scenarios, either with scriptural support: (1) "is to be killed," which would be using Jer 15:2; 43:11 and make a good parallel to the first couplet of verse 10. The point would be the inevitability of God's punishment; (2) "must be killed," which is similar to Matt 26:52 as in those killing you will be killed. The point would be not to resist persecution by force.

horns" for Christ (5:6) and then "horns as a lamb" for the land beast (13:11), or that both seal their followers (7:3; 13:16) or that both cause worship (5:13; 13:12).

The beasts imitate prophetic powers by calling down fire from heaven like Elijah and performing signs that have deceptive intent.[79] John here pictures the religious charlatans who master sleight-of-hand trickery to fool a gullible public, such as at the famous oracles of Zeus at Delphi and Didyma—feigning the voice of the gods have spoken to humans about their fate when a pagan priest is only pretending a communication to relay. Likewise, the release of snakes in the Asklepion sleeping centers has absolutely nothing to do with healing. No power exists outside that of the sovereign God of creation, and no name exists under heaven whereby any person must be saved outside the name of the slaughtered Lamb. Pagan religion does all in its power to deny these two fundamental axioms of the spiritual universe, and Satan's sole purpose with any religion is to numb the spiritual mind to these truths of God the Almighty and his saving Christ.

<u>Enforced Worship (13:14–15)</u>. The crux of the issue with these two beasts is enforced worship. The role of this land beast is to enforce worship of the sea beast. To make clear he means Rome, the emperor, and the empire, John reiterates the idea of the healed mortal wound twice, first in "worship the first beast, whose mortal wound had been healed" (13:12), and then in the expression, "image for the beast that had been wounded by the sword and yet lived" (13:14). The legends of Nero live on in Roman psyche and Revelation's imagery.

In Roman terms this false worship is the emperor cult, with its genius of the emperor to which obeisance and offerings must be made, and its promoters in the provinces. Romans were quite serious about this cult. Pliny of Bithynia in his letter to Trajan only two decades after the composition of Revelation illustrates. We see the church impact in the Seven Letters, witnessed in problems created by the Nicolaitans, Jezebel, and the rest. All seven cities of the seven churches of Asia Minor had imperial cult temples, and five cities show evidence of an imperial altar and imperial priests performing regular sacrifices.[80] So, the second beast from the land is any provincial enforcer of imperial

---

[79] 1 Kgs 18:20–40.
[80] See the discussion, p. 211.

worship. Giving breath to the image of the beast to speak is empowerment of the cult of the emperor by local municipal authorities in Asia Minor. Pliny the Younger is a premier example of a local official "giving breath to the image of the beast." The matter is life and death, as those who refuse to worship the image of the beast are killed (13:15), which is precisely what Pliny indicates he did: "those who persisted I ordered executed."[81] John was prescient. Perhaps he had gained early intuition to this trajectory of Roman imperial cult worship because of the fate of Antipas (2:13).

FIGURE 11.34. Apocalypse Tapestry, Rev 13:15. Beast image is given breath to speak; worshippers worship before the beast; those refusing are beheaded by the sword; one decapitation is completed (Angers, France).

Controlled Commerce (13:16–18). Not only does Rome enforce worship, Rome controls commerce. This feature of imperial life in the first century is crucial to explaining the power and pervasive influence of the imperial cult in all levels of society. A mark is required to do business. This mark is the index of imperial worship for which Pliny was looking among those "ratted on" as believers by their neighbors. In the ancient world, a mark was a tradition of ownership customs, such as in branding. In the head and forehand is simply the obvious practicality of a conspicuous physical location in terms of a physical brand easily observed for proving ownership, and does not have to be

[81]See the context of Pliny's remarks in the full quote, pp. 315–16.

taken literally. John's simple point is that the "ownership" to which he alludes is conspicuous. The example of Pliny shows that Rome's "ownership" of those who participated in its imperial cult most certainly was conspicuous, and without that proper index of imperial worship, one could not do business in the Roman world. At the local level in Asia Minor, this mark would include belonging to the trade guilds who belonged to Rome, which was required for almost all occupations and for doing business. These trade guilds did not exist without strong ties to Rome and the cult of the emperor. To belong to a trade guild was to worship the emperor, the ultimate patron of all commerce in the Roman empire. We have contemporary, national counterparts.[82]

The mark is the name of the beast or the number of his name, which is 666. Name and number are equal because the ancient world used letters for numbers—our misery of "Roman numerals," Roman letters summed as numbers. Other languages such as Hebrew, Greek, and Latin were similar. One had a universe of possibilities for cute, inventive, praiseworthy, derogatory, or slanderous creations, riddles, and public graffiti between personal names and the numbers to which the letters of those names added up. Technical study of this phenomena is called gematria. The effort to come up with the name or slogan behind a number has only one trick—a trick ignored by everyone who does not comprehend gematria math: any given number has *infinite* solutions into names! *Thus, the only solution to a number riddle is one already known to the original readers.* You must know the name first. Contextually, John meant a Roman emperor. Which one was only for the original audience to know. Thus, all historical attempts to identify the beast will fail absolutely, because we furtively are trying to ignore the exegetical elephant in the room—we are not the original audience!

Even for extended application of the original meaning, interpretive issues surround this riddle. Is the mark conceptual abstraction or concrete reality? Is the beast conceptual abstraction or actual individual? Was the historical meaning only for John's time (preterist), or to be extended to the entire church age (idealist), or for a specific period at the end of the church age (futurist)? Finally, is extended application beyond the original historical context even permissible?

---

[82]Cf. the ideological national cult, cult statues, worship of millions, and complete economic control of North Korea by Kim Jong-un. No one has to have a literal mark!

The most common solution to the mark of the beast in Rev 13:18 within John's original context is the Nero cipher. Consult the critical commentaries for how this works. This Nero solution, however, is not straightforward. The solution requires starting with Hebrew letters and then shifting to Greek letters. John could have done something so convoluted, since he has used a Hebrew name and then given a Greek equivalent in the Abaddon, Apollyon cipher for the king of the Abyss (9:11). That nomenclature, however, was done in a straightforward manner and immediately and directly explained by John. Since one riddle of a number/name equivalency would come with infinite solutions, then two would be impossible: to bury a Greek number/name riddle inside a Hebrew number/name riddle would be an exercise in absolute futility of meaning—more like infinity times infinity.[83]

Even if the original audience probably knew the name, what is John's point if we never can solve his riddle? We can take a literary clue from the Dragon Cycle material in Rev 14. In that material the mark of the beast is the beast's parody of God's seal of believers. The beast promises his worshippers a kingdom full of commerce and life (13:15–17), but that claim is false and idolatrous. God holds the power of life, and God's power breaks the power of this inferior seal on human existence (14:10–11). Further, God's own seal that brings all of creation to its intended consummation never will be broken (14:1). Combining then the historical evidence of the first-century context of Roman emperors with the literary context of Rev 14, then John's mark of the beast seems to be a conceptual abstraction for participation in the imperial cult imperative for commercial and social success. John's beast likely was an actual individual, a Roman emperor who embodied idolatrous empire values and power attempting to usurp the sovereignty of Almighty God over his creation.

What about the preterist, futurist, and idealist options on Rev 13? Well, the idealist position is the least satisfactory of all, no more than a purposeless infinite loop, a weak philosophy of history with no goal and no end. Both preterist and futurist approaches represent a more

---

[83]The number/name riddle was discussed at length without definitive solution by Irenaeus *Adv. Haer.* 5.30.1–4. Interestingly, the Nero solution would explain the variant number 616 that occurs in some Latin manuscripts of Rev 13:18. For this story, see Cate, "The Text of Revelation," 128.

biblical philosophy of history.[84] The preterist approach, however, exhausts the full meaning of Revelation in one past context, a possibility exegetically, but just does not seem worth all the fuss of an elaborate apocalyptic drama that recapitulates multiple times. While a preterist reading may be all that God intended with this passage, some futurist reading just seems more in line with the purpose of the vast compass of the entire drama of Revelation.[85] One futurist reading could be that a certain power will arise arrayed against the church in the spirit of the blasphemous Nero/Domitian experience of first-century believers, one person in whom the power of satanic deception will be concentrated catastrophically for the church. He will exalt himself as God and demand total allegiance and worship as did the Roman emperors. He will control markets, natural resources, or commerce so as to enforce this allegiance as did the Roman emperors. The beast to come would be in some sense the fulfillment of the *Nero redivivus* legend. While not Nero, his impact would be of that character, only worse.[86]

One last exegetical caution needs to be registered: reading the beast specifically as an individual is not absolutely demanded. Even though a reasonable deduction from the original context, and the constant presumption of almost all futurists, the beast *could* be realized in an institutional system or group and not in one single individual. The bottom line is that, either way, whether an individual or abstraction, this beast will trigger the passion of the church that concludes the age. We will know him when we get there. Doubt about his identity will be impossible, because he will make life impossible for the church. No false or foolish Internet prophet will have to tell us who he is. Duh.

Conquest: Bowl Prelude (14:1–20)

The story of Messiah's conquest of the Dragon's Beasts begins with a proleptic prelude that anticipates the believer's final victory through the Lamb. This prelude integrates truths from both interludes of the Seals and Trumpets. The Seals paused to emphasize that God's people

---

[84]God as both creator and consummator, or, as John would say, Alpha and Omega.

[85]Whether John would have been aware of the future sense is altogether another issue of the hermeneutical question of multivalent prophecy.

[86]Yes, the profile resonates with Paul's "man of lawlessness" teaching in 2 Thess 2. Yet, the beast of Rev 13 is distinguished on multiple levels from the "antichrist" teaching in 1–2 John. Revelation has no "Antichrist" character. See the discussion on pp. 237–39.

are preserved through persecution. The Trumpets paused to recommission John to prophesy the upcoming Dragon Cycle and to portray symbolically as two witnesses the faithfully witnessing church in that Dragon Cycle. The idea of the protection of the people of God and the victorious witnessing church are recapitulated in this proleptic prelude to the messianic conquest. Protection means that whatever bad happens in this life is not the final word for the believer. The prelude has a repeating phrase, "then I saw," that suggests a tripartite division of three visions of Mount Zion, Angels, and Harvests on the theme of God's judgment as anticipated, announced, and executed.

The material of this prelude demonstrates the thematic unity of Revelation. As in the Inaugural Vision, we hear a heavenly voice that has the sound of many waters.[87] As in the Vision of Heaven, we have a throne, elders, great thunder, four living creatures, a Lamb, harps, a new song, and the company of the redeemed.[88] Again, as in the Seven Letters, we have the Father's name.[89] Finally, as in the Seals interlude, we have a symbolic 144,000 (7:4). These connections contribute to the literary and thematic unity of the whole narrative and integrate John's Judgment Cycle into those issues confronting the seven churches for which all of the Judgment Cycle is written.

Part 1: Vision of Zion (14:1–5). God's just judgment is anticipated. Mount Zion traditions had two streams in Jewish thought. The first was in the historical Davidic kingdom. The second was in prophecy as the place of God's deliverance. This Vision of Zion interprets the Seals interlude. The Lamb is the slaughtered Lamb of 5:6 who initiates the Judgment Cycle, and the 144,000 are the sealed saints of 7:4. We now realize that the 144,000 of the first half Seals interlude are victims of the Dragon and his beasts of chapters 12–13 in the second half. The contrast is the efficacy of the seal of God (14:1) versus the impotency of the mark of the beast (13:16). The saints share in defeating the Dragon through the Lamb's own triumph over the beast. The new song is a song of redemption, so only the redeemed know the lyrics. Sexual abstinence comes from Jewish holy war tradition.[90] Such sexual

---

[87] Rev 1:10, 15.

[88] Rev 4:2, 4, 5, 6; 5:6, 8, 9.

[89] Rev 2:17; 3:12.

[90] *Parthenoi* (παρθένοι) are male virgins; the idea is abstinence. Cf. Deut 23:9–10.

imagery is traditional prophetic symbolism of religious unfaithfulness, a contextual segue to the upcoming whore of Babylon figure in Rev 17.

FIGURE 11.35. Apocalypse Tapestry, Rev 14:1–6. Group (left) are the 144,000 singing a new song before the Lamb, four creatures, and twenty-four elders (right) surrounding heaven's throne. An angel (top) proclaims the eternal gospel (Angers, France).

The most crucial statement of this section is: "in their mouth no lie was found" (14:5). Revelation is a war of words. This truth-speaking is confessional, faithful witness in the context of persecution. The redeemed are blameless and deserve the symbolism of sexual purity because when drug into the court of a provincial governor with the worship of Caesar demanded, such as only a few years later with Pliny the Younger, they have denied the false claims of the Roman empire and chosen to die instead.

Part 2: Vision of Angels (14:6–13). God's judgment is announced. The first angel proclaims the eternal gospel in midheaven to broadcast to all points terrestrial (the fourfold "every nation and tribe and language and people," 14:6). The call is to fear *God* and give *him* glory, which distinctly is not the emperor. The emperor does not deserve the glory because the emperor did not create the world. Creation theology is invoked ("worship him who made heaven and earth," 14:7), which shows how the Vision of Heaven establishes the foundational theology of the Judgment Cycle (4:11). Creation is unfinished without redemption. Good news always is a two-edged sword, which is the meaning of the description of the two-edged sword in the mouth of the Son of

Man (1:16). If one considers the typical biblical narrative, salvation for some means judgment for others. The oppressed who need salvation have an oppressor who is the perpetrator. In the paradigm story of the Old Testament, salvation for Jewish slaves of Egypt meant judgment for Pharaoh. In first-century Asia Minor, salvation for oppressed believers will mean judgment for Domitian.

A second angel announces, "Fallen, fallen is Babylon the great!" (14:8). Babylon is a new character introduced rather abruptly here in the drama, and for whom the reader is unprepared. She will become the central character contrasting Lady Virtue, the woman figure that began the Dragon Cycle in Rev 12. With beasts in one section of the Dragon Cycle and Babylon in another, John is using multiple levels of symbols to figure the same issues of Rome, the emperor, and the empire. The use of Babylon applied to Rome already was a *topos* in Jewish literature after the First Jewish War, because this Rome historically reprised Babylon's destruction of Jerusalem and the temple.[91] Babylon also becomes a cipher for Rome in the New Testament.[92] Babylon's power and riches are enticing and intoxicating and draw in a league of allies. Rome's allies are complicit in Rome's idolatry, confederate in Rome's destiny, and condemned in Rome's judgment.

In this angel's cry of "Fallen, fallen!" we are advised in advance of the demise of Babylon. This prophetic word, which is announced in past tense as the surety of God's future judgment, will be the drama we encounter in the following chapters. The judgment will be pictured first in the Bowls heptad (15:1—16:21) and then a second time in the story of the city of Babylon, seen as a great whore that sits on many waters (17:1—19:21). We already know Babylon's end before her story even begins!

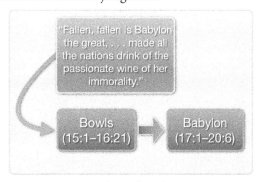

FIGURE 11.36. Second Angel's Babylon Announcement. Prophetic "Fallen, fallen!" anticipates Bowl and Babylon narratives of the following chapters.

---

[91] *2 Bar.* 11:1; *Sib. Or.* 5.143–45.
[92] Cf. 1 Pet 5:13.

In this judgment, Babylon gets what she gives. She gives the wine of the wrath of her fornication and gets the wine of God's own wrath. John's imagery comes from Jeremiah's words against ancient Babylon.

> For thus the Lord, the God of Israel, says to me: "Take the cup of the wine of wrath from My hand, and cause all the nations, to whom I send you, to drink it. And they shall drink and stagger and go mad because of the sword that I will send among them. . . . Babylon has been a golden cup in the hand of the Lord, intoxicating all the earth. The nations have drunk of her wine; therefore the nations are going mad" (Jer 25:15–16, 51:7, NASB).

This prophetic "you get what you give" theme on divine judgment is crucial in understanding how judgment works in history and how God's Messiah already is "ruler of the kings of the earth" right now and rules over the nations with a "rod of iron" in the present.[93] This concept is foundational to the insistence that Jesus' sovereignty over kings and nations does not await a second coming. Rome is her own worst enemy, and that is the essence of the wrath of God and the messianic judgments. Jesus is Lord over Rome, and Rome will find that out soon enough. None of the ancient emperors of Rome still sit on their throne today. Jesus does.

That the whole narrative of Babylon will recapitulate the story of the beasts is the essence of the third angel's announcement (14:9–13). The target of the wine of God's wrath are those with the mark of the beast, the story just told in 13:11–18. The wine is unmixed, meaning, not diluted with water, so full strength. Fire and brimstone (sulfur) evoke the Old Testament Sodom and Gomorrah story, which became a prophetic *topos*.[94] The idea of having no rest is deliberate contrast to the status of the saints. The third angel's declaration of the surety of judgment for the beast and those with the mark of the beast John uses to constitute a call for the endurance of the saints, defined in context as those who keep the commandments of God (in the context of Revelation, to fear him and worship him only) and who "hold fast to the faith of Jesus" (14:12), which is confessional courage in both public and political domains. A blessing on those who "from now on die in

---

[93] Rev 1:5; 2:27; 12:5; 19:15.

[94] Gen 19:24; Isa 34:8–10; as a debauched, infamous society divinely destroyed.

the Lord" immediately follows (14:13) because holding fast to the faith of Jesus as confessional courage implies imminent danger of death. This confession is the witness through tribulation theme of Revelation.[95]

The pronouncement of a blessing on those who "from now on die in the Lord" constitutes another of the continuously accumulating pieces of evidence in Revelation that believers are *not* raptured out of tribulation; instead, believers are promised a destiny of going *through* tribulation, just like Jesus had to go through Gethsemane, even though he prayed for a rapture out of the garden. Rapture theology is bogus ecclesiology, because this teaching aborts the eschatological mission of the end-time church. Dispensationalists obfuscate the clear message of Revelation and destroy John's clarion call to the church in Revelation to embrace her own historical destiny at the end of her life, as did Jesus, who himself declared unequivocally, "Whoever does not carry his own cross and come after me cannot be my disciple."[96]

Part 3: Vision of Harvests (14:14–20). God's judgment is executed. This material presents several interpretive difficulties. First, who is this figure? Do we have one like a "son of man," an angel, or one like a "Son of Man," that is, Jesus (1:13)? Commentators gravitate to the idea of Jesus, because the entire Judgment Cycle was initiated by the act of Jesus as the Lamb opening the seals (6:1). Second, are the harvests the same or distinct judgments? The imagery is taken from Joel 3:13 in which God's judgment is pictured as both grain and grape harvests. If one judgment is intended, as in Joel, then both harvests are negative. If the harvests are distinct, the first harvest is a positive image, that is, of the righteous, following in the New Testament pattern.[97] Even though the background is from Joel, John probably has integrated the New Testament harvest of the righteous theme into Joel's imagery, creating

---

[95]Rev 1:5, 9; 2:13; 3:14; 6:9; 11:17; 12:11. This blessing probably is an allusion to the imagery of the martyr's millennium that John will develop in Rev 20:4–6.

[96]Luke 14:27. Cf. Matt 10:38; 16:24; Mark 8:34; Luke 9:23. Paul makes the cross the essence of all Christian theology; cf. 1 Cor 1:17, "that the cross of Christ should not be made void," which is precisely what rapture theology does, voids the meaning of the cross for the church in history. Paul notes how those who are troubling the Galatians do so "that they may not be persecuted for the cross of Christ" (Gal 6:12). Not only the Gospels, but Paul also makes the path of the cross the paradigm of the church: "have this mind in you . . . becoming obedient to the point of death, even death on a cross" (Phil 2:5, 8).

[97]Luke 10:2; John 4:35–38.

FIGURE 11.37. Luther Bible, Rev 14:14–20. Grain and grape harvests (Taschen).

two distinct harvests, the first one positive, the second negative. Third, what is the context of the power over fire? Is this a specific angel's task, or is this the heavenly altar duty? In the context of Revelation, this altar fire in the present prelude may pick up on the image of the prayers of the saints in the prelude to the Trumpet judgments (8:3–5).

Thus, this action is the typical heavenly altar duty. Heaven's action always is focused on the saints on earth.[98] Fourth, what is the meaning of the expression, "outside the city," which is where the winepress of God's wrath is trodden (14:20)? If this is a generic expression, then this location simply is the normal place of execution for any ancient municipality. If this expression is specific location, then what city? Jerusalem? Elsewhere? If this expression is symbolic theologically, then is this evocative for the death of Jesus?[99] The context seems to call either for a generic or specific expression. If taken as a specific place, the only city mentioned in this material is Babylon. Fifth, how should we read the image of blood several feet deep for 1600 stadia, that is, about two-hundred miles? This image perhaps is the most gruesome in all of Revelation. Is this thought typical oriental hyperbole?[100] Further, what significance, if any, attaches to the number? The supposition that the expression is typical, oriental hyperbole does fit other New Testament rhetoric, even in the teaching of Jesus.[101] The image probably is hyperbolic. However, if the number is significant, its meaning is unknown.

The harvest judgments pause the action of the fearsome Dragon and his beasts story to speak to the inevitability of God's judgment. This judgment is faith's vindication of the testimony of the church in the Seven Letters (Rev 2–3) and the answer to the prayers of the saints in the Seals and Trumpets (6:9; 8:3, 5). God's judgment demonstrates God's sovereignty over the Dragon, his beasts, and their allies, fulfilling the Vision of Heaven's declaration that God is Almighty (Rev 4). God's judgment also reveals God's victory through the Lamb and his followers (Rev 5). Finally, the entire prelude itself shows that Rome as a beast and a harlot inevitably and divinely is doomed, even though its power over the church is great (Rev 17–18).

---

[98]Resonating with the idea of Eph 3:10: "So that through the church the wisdom of God in its rich variety might now be made known to the rulers and authorities in the heavenlies."

[99]Even as in the imagery of John 19:20 and Heb 13:12.

[100]Like Saddam Hussein declaring at the beginning of the Desert Storm war on Iraq that the "mother of all battles has begun" in a broadcast on Bagdad state radio, Jan. 17, 1991, as reported by the *Washington Post*, the BBC, and other news organizations.

[101]The statements of Jesus on plucking out an eye or cutting off a hand in the Sermon on the Mount always are taken as hyperbolic without even raising the question (Matt 5:29–30).

Conquest: Bowl Judgments (15:1—16:21)[102]

The great portent of the seven bowl angels is the third of three signs identified this way in the second half of Revelation. The first was the Woman (12:1). The second was the great Red Dragon (12:3). Now we have the seven bowl angels (15:1). The seven bowl angels represent the third and last in the triadic series of judgment heptads that span both halves of the Judgment Cycle of the Apocalypse (6–20). These Seals, Trumpets, and Bowls series, however, are not used equally in terms of literary function. The Seals and Trumpets drive the plot in the first half of the Christ Cycle (6–11). Characters, however, drive the second half of the Dragon Cycle (12–20). One easily could jump from the harvest images of God's judgment at the end of the prelude in Rev 14 past the Bowl judgments in Rev 15–16 straight to the portrayal of the judgment of the harlot Babylon in Rev 17 and not skip a beat.

So, why did John include a third heptad, even when that series is not necessary to drive the plot of the second half of the Judgment Cycle? Because John promised a climactic series of judgments that would display God's wrath and consummate all judgment. Before the end of the Christ Cycle first half of Revelation, John had promised to portray God's final wrath with these words, "Your wrath came, and the time came for the dead to be judged, . . . and to destroy those who destroy the earth" (11:18). The Bowl judgments are that final wrath promised at the end of the Christ Cycle. What has John gained by delaying the Bowl series? He now has made clear the object of final divine wrath in the Bowl series: the Dragon, the beasts, and Babylon, oppressors of the persecuted church. God conquers evil through messianic passion.

Bowls Introduction (15:1–8). The eight verses of Rev 15 open the Bowl series. This introduction clarifies the distinctive character of the judgments and their beneficiaries. In terms of their nature, these seven plagues "are the last, for with them the wrath of God is ended" (15:1). The judgments are last because they deal decisively with the Dragon, beasts, and Babylon, the main characters of the Dragon Cycle and the violent antagonists of the church. The beneficiaries of these judgments naturally are "those who had conquered the beast and its image and the number of its name" (15:2). Interestingly, just as with the Trumpet

---

[102]Chapter 15 is only eight verses and never should have been divided as a chapter. The material clearly is simply the prelude to the pouring out of the bowls.

series, the introduction of the Bowl angels is interrupted with another scene before the judgments actually begin.[103] The scene is one of the martyrs who in their martyrdom are conquerors. By refusing to recant their confession even to death, they deny the beast his object and win.

These martyr conquerors sing a hymn that summarizes the theological significance of the Bowl judgments. The hymn is styled as both the "song of Moses" as well as the "song of the Lamb" because the redemption story of Moses bringing God's people to the other side of the Red Sea safe from Pharaoh's armies is the redemption story of the Lamb bringing the church to the other side of the tribulation safe from the Dragon's beasts. Moses is described as a "servant" just like John (1:1). The song celebrates the Lord God Almighty as the only one to be worshipped by the nations, which is a dramatic rejection of the heart of imperial ideology and the cult of the Roman emperor.

> Great and amazing are your deeds,
>   Lord God the Almighty!
> Just and true are your ways,
>   King of the nations!
> Lord, who will not fear
>   and glorify your name?
> For you alone are holy.
>   All nations will come
>   and worship before you
> for your judgments have been revealed (Rev 15:3b–4).

Everything the Dragon and his beasts desperately were seeking, even on pain of death, now goes properly to God Almighty of free volition, with celebrative gratitude. Once again, John has used the appellation of God as "Almighty." This divine attribution is a powerful subversion of the name identifying the emperor in imperial inscriptions throughout the Roman empire.[104] So God is the Almighty versus the Roman emperor. God is king of the nations versus the Roman empire. Finally, God is worshipped by all nations versus the Roman beast.

---

[103] The Trumpet angels are introduced in 8:2, but a scene interruption occurs in 8:3–5, only to resume with the Trumpet angels in 8:6. Likewise, the Bowl angels are introduced in 15:1, but a scene interruption occurs in 15:2–4, only to resume with the Bowl angels in 15:5. These scenes really are not interruptions; they both function as literary preludes to each of the judgment heptads. The Seal judgments really are the odd man out from a literary point of view; yet, in a way, the Vision of Heaven is their prelude.

[104] See the discussion of the name "Almighty," p. 229.

John then sees the temple as the tent of witness opened in heaven (15:5). The tabernacle of witness occurs 130 of 150 times in the Old Testament just in Exodus to Deuteronomy.[105] Moses put the ten commandments in the ark of the tabernacle; the tabernacle preserved the testimony of God, and, thus, represented the standard of judgment.[106] That divine testimony now is summed up in Jesus (12:17). The angels are dressed in linen and golden sashes to reflect the Son of Man in the Inaugural Vision (15:6; 1:13); they act in his authority. They receive bowls from the four living creatures of the Vision of Heaven (15:7), so the Bowl heptad still is playing out the theology of the Vision of Heaven foundational to the Judgment Cycle (4:6). These same four living creatures begin the Seal judgments, which opens the entire Judgment Cycle, by calling forth the four horsemen of the Apocalypse (6:1–8). Thus, the four living creatures start and end the Judgment Cycle and create a literary *inclusio* over the entire Judgment Cycle movement.

FIGURE 11.38. Apollo Kylix. Apollo, crowned with a myrtle-leaf wreath, dressed in white peplos, red himation. Left hand plays lyre as right hand offers wine libation from a navel-phiale (AMAC). Credit: Jean M. Stevens.

[105] Beale, *Revelation*, 801.
[106] Exod 16:34; 25:21; 31:18; 32:15.

The bowls are the standard, flat, shallow cultic utensils for carrying altar ashes and libations. These particular bowls, however, carry the wrath of God, standard imagery in the Old Testament prophets.[107]

> Rouse yourself, rouse yourself!
> Stand up, O Jerusalem,
>   you who have drunk at the hand of the Lord
>   the cup of his wrath,
>   who have drunk to the dregs
>   the bowl of staggering.
> There is no one to guide her
>   among all the children she has borne;
>   there is no one to take her by the hand
>   among all the children she has brought up . . .
> Therefore hear this, you who are wounded
>   who are drunk, but not with wine:
> Thus says your Sovereign, the Lord,
>   your God who pleads the cause of his people:
> "See, I have taken from your hand the cup of staggering;
>   you shall drink no more
>   from the bowl of my wrath" (Isa 51:17–18, 21–22, NASB).

The intent of the wrath is remedial, but the desired repentance is not forthcoming. The execution of this judgment series is so monumental and significant that even normal temple activity is halted (15:8).

Seven Bowl Plagues (16:1–21). The Bowl series is not broken down into units of four and three like the Seals and Trumpets. All three judgment heptads are interconnected in various ways, but this Bowl series is distinctive. As in the Trumpets, the Exodus traditions clearly are echoed within the Bowls: plagues, a song of Moses, a crossing the sea, a tent of

Trumpets	Bowls
1. hail, fire, blood on earth	1. bowl poured on earth
2. blazing mountain into sea	2. bowl poured on seas
3. star into rivers, fountains	3. bowl on rivers, fountains
4. sun, moon, stars struck	4. bowl poured on sun
5. air darkened, torment	5. kingdom darkened, anguish
6. angels at the Euphrates	6. bowl poured on Euphrates
7. voices, lightning, hail, etc.	7. voices, lightning, hail, etc.

FIGURE 11.39. Plague Parallels. Both Trumpet and Bowl series are closely parallel and both reflect the Exodus plagues.

[107] Ps 75:8; Isa 51:17–18, 21–22; Jer 25:15–29; 49:12.

witness, even a refusal to repent, like Pharaoh. Also as in the Exodus story, God's actions have continual warnings, seeking repentance, but only resulting in a tragic, conclusive finale. John's narrative strategy is clear. He parallels divine intervention in redemptive history. The first redemption brought down God's judgment on Pharaoh. The last redemption brings down God's judgment on the beast. The purpose is to show eschatological redemption: God vindicates the Lamb's sacrifice and the church's testimony in history and at the end of history.

Bowl One (16:2). This bowl brings sores for those with the mark of the beast and who worshipped his image. This first bowl reveals the important contextual point that the Bowl judgments are directed spe-

FIGURE 11.40. Pollio Aqueduct. The Pollio family name appears on the inscription of the main aqueduct to the ancient city of Ephesus as the benefactors of the project.

FIGURE 11.41. Aqueduct at Antioch of Pisidia. This aqueduct system brought water from the snowmelt of nearby mountains into the high-altitude city using an ingenious siphoning system at the main water terminal. Paul preached in this city (Acts 13:14).

cifically at the conflict engaged by the new characters of the Dragon and his beasts that introduced and now drive the Dragon Cycle.

Bowl Two (16:3). This bowl turns the sea to blood. All are killed, not just a third, as in the Trumpets (8:7–12). An increasing percentage illustrates recapitulation among the judgment heptads but with intensification of the judgment effects; in the Bowls we arrive at the fullest extent. Indeed, these are the "seven plagues, which are the last" (15:1).

Bowl Three (16:4–7). This bowl turns all rivers and springs (fresh water) into blood. A key index of the Roman empire's civilization, surviving even to today, was the expert engineering of aqueducts running miles to bring a constant supply of fresh water from snowmelt mountain rivers and artesian springs to cities of the empire. Aqueducts were expensive projects (as all major public works) that required city benefactors to subsidize costs, such as the Pollio family in ancient Ephesus.

FIGURE 11.42. Nymphaeum at Perge. A fresh water stream flowed over this fountain and cascaded down a raised channel in the center of the colonnaded main street in steps that created pools in which fish were stocked. (See Figure 12.16.)

These aqueducts supplied the nymphaeums (fountains) that were city hallmarks. Such fountains were more than decoration. They supplied daily fresh water for city residents. One striking nymphaeum at Perge in Pamphylia had a fresh water stream flowing over the fountain and tumbling down a raised channel in the center of the colonnaded main street in a step fashion, creating dynamic pools stocked with fish.

454 REVELATION: THE PAST AND FUTURE OF JOHN'S APOCALYPSE

FIGURE 11.43. Trevi Fountain of Rome. The most famous fountain in the world, often seen in movies, Trevi has an ancient history and a role to play in the fall of Rome.

The world famous Trevi Fountain of Rome was at the junction of three roads[108] and marked the termination of one the aqueducts that supplied water to ancient Rome. The pure spring water source for this aqueduct was found by Roman technicians about eight miles outside the city (which is memorialized in the imagery on the front façade of the fountain), and the aqueduct fed the famous baths of Agrippa in Rome for 400 years. Germanic Goths besieging Rome in 537 cut off these fresh water aqueducts to the city, forcing inhabitants to draw water from polluted wells and the Tiber River. Mighty Rome finally fell to the Goths. The fall of Rome fundamentally in the end was the loss of her fresh water. This calamitous fall of the city to the Goths marks the transition from ancient Rome to Medieval Europe. The first image one sees after natural disasters like hurricanes and tornadoes is bottled water being shipped in. Life ceases without fresh, clean water.

An angel of the waters praises God for his just judgment on the fresh waters: "because they shed the blood of the saints and prophets, you have given them blood to drink" (16:6). This "you get what you

---

[108]Hence, the standard etymology of the name as *tre vie*, "three roads."

give" prophetic theme is announced by the second and third angels of the conquest prelude (14:8–10) and reiterates the martyr hymn of the Bowls prelude (15:3–4). The answer to the fifth seal's martyr vindication question ("How long?") is finally coming into view (6:10).

Bowl Four (16:8–9). This bowl is distinguished by its repentance theme, even though the "last" series. God still is seeking repentance, as with Pharaoh. The bowl releases the scorching heat of the sun. We already know from the Seals interlude that God's people are protected from this judgment (7:16). Tragically, the response of those affected is to curse God. They refuse to repent or give God glory.[109] Now we have the real reason these plagues are the "last": not because of an inexorable decree from God but because of intransigent human hearts.

Bowl Five (16:10–11). This bowl also is distinguished by a repentance note. The bowl is poured out on the throne of the beast, which plunges the beast's kingdom into darkness, with a gnawing of tongues in agony.[110] The throne of the beast as the object of the plague creates a clear intratextual echo with the letter to Pergamum, "where Satan's throne is" (2:13). Darkness probably is metaphor for spiritual condition in believing the lies of the beast and creates an intratextual echo of the Laodicean condition of blindness and needing eye salve (3:17). The problem is cozying up too closely to Rome's imperial propaganda. The testimony of Jesus is losing confessional integrity in Asia Minor churches such as Pergamum and Laodicea. That a note of repentance is mentioned a second time, unlike in any other judgment sequence, probably is to indicate that the Dragon rebellion has hardened into destiny and is reprising Pharaoh's role in the Exodus plagues.

Bowl Six (16:12–16). This bowl is the drying up of the Euphrates River. This action allows the "kings of the east" to cross over a boundary of the Roman empire to threaten the security of Rome. This great Euphrates is the traditional boundary between Roman and Parthian empires. The judgment seems to suggest an enemy invasion on Rome. This judgment is similar to that of the sixth trumpet (9:14).

Bowl six is distinguished by having three additional elements to strengthen its impact. The *first addition* is frogs (16:13–14), likely in-

---

[109]This wrath of God that hardens the unrepentant into deeper sin is parallel to the analysis of Paul in Rom 1:23, 25.

[110]Cf. Jesus tradition in Matt 8:12; 13:42, 50; 22:13; 24:51; 25:30. Also, Luke 13:28.

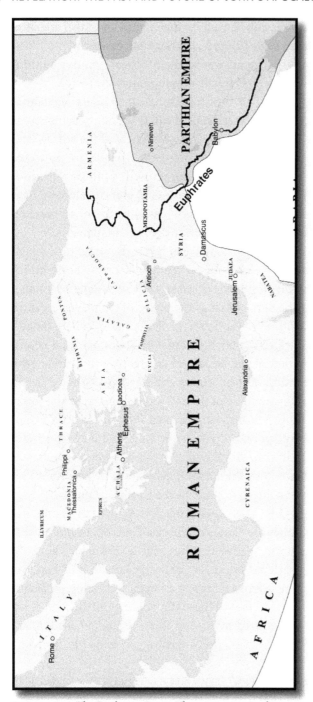

FIGURE 11.44. The Euphrates River. The great river Euphrates was the imaginary boundary between the Parthian empire in the east and the Roman empire in the west.

novated from the Egyptian plagues. The point is not the frogs but that unclean spirits come "from the mouth of the Dragon, from the mouth of the beast, and from the mouth of the false prophet." Once again, the "from the mouth of" deliberately repeated three times reiterates that Revelation is a war of words. Thus, what makes the unclean spirits "unclean" is what they say: these foul spirits are promoters of lies, Roman imperial propagandists deceiving people to their destruction.

This frog scene is significant because the second beast for the first time since being introduced in Rev 13 is given another identity. This second beast suddenly becomes the "false prophet." John puts this new prophetic angle on the second beast deliberately in order to produce a direct tie-in to the Seven Letters. The letter to Thyatira has an ominous warning at the start of its foreboding assessment: "But I have this against you: you tolerate that woman Jezebel, who calls herself a prophet and is teaching and beguiling my servants to practice fornication and to eat food sacrificed to idols" (2:20). Thus, with a new "false prophet" identity marker, the direct target of the Dragon Cycle's second beast imagery is revealed to be Thyatira's own false prophet Jezebel. The entire Judgment Cycle is about the seven churches of Asia Minor.

The purpose of the lying spirits is to rouse the kings of the world to battle. This king group is the second introduced in this chapter. We had the kings of the east in 16:12, but now we have the kings of the world in 16:14. By the time we hit ten confederate kings in 17:12–18, we will have had three king groups introduced in two chapters.[111] The exact relationship among the three king groups is not entirely clear. A possibility for the two groups in Rev 16 is that John has mixed two traditions, as he did with the harvest judgments. The tradition behind the kings of the east in 16:12 would be from Roman politics, Rome's feared destruction in its two strongest first-century forms, either the ever-present Parthian threat on the eastern boarder or the *Nero redivivus* legend kept alive in popular imagination. The tradition behind the kings of the world in 16:14 would be biblical, the gathering of the nations for the eschatological battle against God, as in Zech 14. John has

---

[111]Kings have shown up on occasion as minor characters in the Apocalypse. In the Seals, the "kings of the earth" hide in the caves (6:15), and in the Trumpets interlude, John must prophesy against "kings" (10:11). Later, we meet "kings of the earth" who commit fornication with Babylon (17:2). Such king references are minor and do not advance the plot. They function simply as background characters.

mixed historical and eschatological traditions. Why do this? John is driving at the multiple venues through which we need to understand God's judgments can take place: both in the process of history and in concluding history. The assurance for persecuted believers would be in the sure word that even the mightiest of kingdoms like Rome God can bring down, whether in history or at the end of history. As John has insisted on numerous occasions in the Apocalypse, God reigns as *pantokratōr*, the Almighty, and the *autokratōr*, the self-mighty emperor, is powerless to do anything about that.

The *second addition* enhancing the sixth bowl imagery is a warning followed by a beatitude (16:15). The impact of the exegesis of this second addition to the sixth Bowl on the interpretation of Revelation is huge but completely ignored by prophets of the Apocalypse. Grammar shifts to first person, creating a direct quote. English translations use quotation marks and sometimes parentheses for these words: "See, I am coming like a thief! Blessed is the one who stays awake and is clothed, not going about naked and exposed to shame."[112] Why is this warning and accompanying beatitude so significant? Well, the beatitude itself is not. Revelation actually has seven of these beatitudes.[113] What this warning and beatitude says is the big deal.

This warning followed by a beatitude creates another direct connection between the Bowl judgments and the Seven Letters. The first link is to Sardis. They were advised to wake up and strengthen what little remained of their dead confessional witness, building on the local setting that the impregnable Sardis fortress twice in her past had been conquered by stealth like a thief in the night (3:2). So, here in the Bowl judgments, a warning is pronounced of one who comes "like a thief," so hearers should "stay awake," as the assessment section had advised the church at Sardis. The second link is to the letter to Laodicea. The blessing spoken in this Bowl judgment not only is for the one who is "awake," but also for the one who is "clothed, not going about naked." This clothing imagery is a direct connection to the assessment portion of the letter to Laodicea, in which the church there is told they are not

---

[112] Cf. gospel and apostolic traditions; Matt 24:43; 1 Thess 5:2, 4; 2 Pet 3:10.

[113] Indeed, we have another series of sevens. Sevens populate the Apocalypse like mushrooms after a rain. Seems as though John was counting the beatitudes when he was putting them in. Cf. Rev 1:3; 14:13; 16:15; 19:9; 20:6; 22:7, 14.

rich, but naked, and they need to buy white garments from Christ in order "to keep the shame of your nakedness from being seen" (3:18). These links within the sixth Bowl judgment to very specific items in the Seven Letters are pronounced and blatantly obvious. Why does John do this? John makes direct connections between the sixth Bowl judgment and the Seven Letters *to contextualize the following imagery of Armageddon as applying to the seven churches of Asia Minor, not a fictitious future battle falsely invented by interpreters.* Armageddon is about Sardis, Laodicea, and the other churches of Asia Minor in John's original audience. Armageddon is no more than a subsidiary image meant only to enhance the sixth Bowl judgment. Armageddon has nothing to do with the incredible legends that have accumulated over the centuries of interpretation to one of the most minor images of the entire Apocalypse—indeed, mentioned only *one time*, and even then as only a *secondary* figure within a figure!

In the original context, the warning and beatitude of Rev 16:15 is directed at first-century believers in the churches of Asia Minor. John writes to encourage faithful living amidst powerful seduction of false prophets such as Jezebel at Thyatira, to resist the widespread idolatry of the beast. John writes out of concern for the dangerous spiritual condition of churches such as at Sardis that think they are alive but are dead, and at Laodicea that think they are rich but are naked. They are weak and easy prey for the Dragon and his beasts. They are at war in a clash of confessions and not even aware.

The *third addition* enhancing the sixth bowl imagery is an assembly at a place called Armageddon (16:16). This one verse has created more mass confusion than almost any other verse in the Bible. What is most curious from all the complex and detailed military and battle scenarios generated from this one verse is *what this verse does not say*. The verse does *not* say who—just "they." The verse does *not* say why—just "assembled." The verse does *not* say what—just "assembled." We are not even told what happened!

The only thing the verse says is *where*, and that is an enigma of its own, because *the where is nowhere known*. The term occurs nowhere else in the entire Bible. Even our Greek manuscripts are totally confused by the term, because they preserve two different words, Armageddon and Megiddo, that together present over a dozen different spellings.[114] The meaning in Hebrew is not certain. The usual sense given of "Mount Megiddo" is completely useless, because Israel never had a "Mount Megiddo." Israel *did* have a city of Megiddo, but the city of Megiddo was situated in a valley at the confluence of the Plain of Esdraelon and the Plain of Jezreel, not on a mountain. That location was strategic for linking two major highway systems, the main coastal road from the south and the main inland road leading to Damascus. That location also was notorious because King Josiah fatefully engaged Pharaoh Neco at Megiddo and was killed (2 Kgs 23:29). This meager history of Megiddo is no help at all, and does not touch on the etymology of John's word. In sum, the truth is, with Armageddon, we do not have any exegetical assurance of who, why, what, or even where.

Even without any specificity whatsoever to what John has written in this one verse, most interpreters immediately assume John is alluding to apocalyptic traditions about a great final battle. The most definitive traditions come from Persian Zoroastrianism. These type traditions were taken over in Jewish apocalyptic, such as at Qumran, with its *War of the Sons of Light and the Sons of Darkness*. In the Old Testament, as the prophets presented the Lord gathering the nations for the final judgment, the tradition of the place derived from Joel as the Valley of Jehoshaphat, but Joel actually does not indicate the location of this otherwise unknown valley.[115] The difficulty with this unquestioned assumption is that

FIGURE 11.45. Kidron Valley. The valley of Jehoshaphat traditionally has been associated with the Kidron Valley east of Jerusalem by Jews, Christians, and Muslims. Several burial grounds are located nearby to be first in the resurrection.

John may not have intended to imply any apocalyptic "final war" with his Armageddon image. The sixth bowl drying up the Euphrates for

---

[114]See Cate, "The Text of Revelation," 127.

[115]Cf. Joel 3:2, 11; Zeph 3:8; Zech 12:3; 14:2; Isa 13:4; specifically Babylon, Jer 50:29.

11—Judgment of the World 461

the kings of the east, and the frogs deceiving the kings of the world does build a contextual case for something combative and catastrophic intended with Armageddon, but none of the text or context prevents the original meaning from being about first-century Rome and her immediate political fears internally (Nero) or externally (Parthians).[116]

Exegetically, Armageddon's meaning is only to enhance the impact of the judgment of the sixth bowl. Contextually, John has tied this meaning to the Seven Letters. Interpretively, the meaning is directed at Thyatira, Sardis, and Laodicea in the confessional war with Rome in first-century Asia Minor.

<u>Bowl Seven (16:17–21)</u>. This bowl is a massive earthquake and huge hailstones. A loud voice from the temple cries, "It is finished!" This cry marks a conclusive end to the judgment heptads, fulfilling the words, "seven plagues, which are the last" (15:1). The "great city" split three ways is called "great Babylon" (16:19).[117] "Cities of the nations fell" as well. The following chapters make clear these are cities complicit with the idolatry and embedded commerce. Babylon especially gets "the wine-cup of the fury of his wrath." Islands fleeing away and mountains not found is apocalyptic rhetoric, but is realistic compared to actual tsunami tidal waves accompanying massive earthquakes and volcanic activity that can trigger along fault lines. Likewise, hailstones of a hundred pounds would be typical apocalyptic rhetoric, but again, would have a correlate in the real world with massive volcanoes. What is *not* said in this plague is important: repentance is missing. Instead, the human response is only to curse God (16:21). This response to God's last effort means no hope. Babylon's final doom is sealed.[118]

In the following chapters, John retells Babylon's final doom with different imagery. Thus, literally, the Bowl judgments are real, but they are symbolic. In John's new version he connects symbolic Baby-

---

[116]"Armageddon" is one gigantic mountain of exegetical ambiguity. How we can move instantly from complete exegetical obscurity to absolute interpretive clarity, to the tune of multivolume productions about this solitary word occurring nowhere else in the entire Bible is one sure credit to the incredible ingenuity of human imagination.

[117]The repetition of the same adjective, "great," in front of both seals the deal.

[118]God has responded in judging the world just as he responded in judging his own people. He has made every effort to be redemptive. He has shown extraordinary patience with human hubris. Yet, in the end, his wrath has been inevitable. The summary of the Chronicler would be appropriate here. Cf. 2 Chr 36:15–16.

lon to historical Rome. John's story throughout the Judgment Cycle is thoroughly consistent—Rome and the seven churches of Asia Minor.

Conquest: Bowl Perspectives (17:1—20:6)

The Dragon Cycle introduced a cosmic conflict fought by the Dragon and his beasts. They wreak havoc on the church. Messiah's conquest of the beasts has a prelude that assures the reader that the slaughtered Lamb and his followers are victorious. God's wrath will be poured out, crushing opponents like grapes in a vintage harvest. That wrath is pictured in the Bowl heptad of judgments. The Bowl series is the last and consummates the interwoven and recapitulating triad of judgment heptads in the Seals, Trumpets, and Bowls.

The Bowl judgments are finished, but John is not. He still wants to connect the cosmic force of the Dragon and the earthly power of Rome. He still wants to dramatize the fall of Rome. He yet has to show how a city's fall is the conquest of Christ and on what basis that conquest is won if this Christ mounts no land army of legions like Rome. Finally, he wants to honor martyrs of the confessional conflict through a unique reign with the reigning Christ. These perspectives are crucial.

Thus, John produces an extensive section that runs for four chapters to augment the Bowl judgments with four perspectives on them. These four perspectives are those of the prophet, heaven itself, Christ, and the martyr. John develops these perspectives with four scenes of the harlot, Babylon, the Rider, and the millennium.

Bowl Judgments—Perspectives	
Scene	Perspective
1. Harlot (Rev 17)	Prophet
2. Babylon (Rev 18)	Heaven
3. Rider (Rev 19)	Christ
4. Millennium (Rev 20)	Martyr

FIGURE 11.46. Bowl Judgments—Perspectives. John takes four chapters to continue augmenting the Bowl judgments with four additional perspectives.

Harlot: Prophet's Perspective (17:1–17). The harlot scene is the prophet's perspective on the Bowl judgments. One of the seven Bowl angels giving the invitation to John makes clear that the material of Rev 17:1—20:6 is intended to extend the Bowl judgment imagery. The Bowl angel's invitation to John is, "Come, I will show you the judgment of the great whore who is seated on many waters" (17:1). City imagery is transformed into the disgrace of a whore (prostitute), a title heard for the first time in Revelation, which was a rhetorical *topos* for spiritual idolatry in prophetic literature. Much of the propaganda of the Roman empire was expressed in the city goddess *Dea* Roma. She often was portrayed in military garb holding a scroll of justice, bringing conquest and justice to the empire. The goddess always was beautifully dressed. John's finely dressed harlot is a bold parody of *Dea* Roma. This evil prostitute is "seated on many waters," symbolizing the Roman empire spanning many seas in conquering many nations and peoples. John's "many waters" acknowledges the type of imperial ideology carved into the reliefs of the Sebastion at Aphrodisias that Rome had conquered many nations and peoples, including the Jews.[119] While we need to be careful with the image of women portrayed in Revelation, John's city as harlot imagery is thoroughly in concord with prophetic traditions, and John does have positive images of women.[120]

FIGURE 11.47. Claudius, Master of Land and Sea. (AMA).

The new imagery of a harlot will be used to make the case that Babylon, Lady Harlot (Rev 17), is a counterpoint to the Woman, Lady Virtue (Rev 12), the figure opening the Dragon Cycle. Later, we will learn that this

	Babylon (17)	Zion (12, 21)
1	desert home, demons	heavenly home, mountain of God
2	seated on beast = devil	gives self as God's throne
3	earthly pomp, pretense	adorned by stars, righteous
4	has cup of abomination = death	offers water of life
5	mother of harlots	mother of messiah
6	brings ruin, martyr blood	brings salvation to the world
7	end is a haunted place	destiny is a new creation

FIGURE 11.48. Babylon and Zion, New Jerusalem. This imagery has rhetorical force in the Apocalypse.

Woman as Lady Virtue is New Jerusalem coming down from heaven (Rev 21). These two cities are contrasted.[121] This city imagery would be a powerful message to the first-century mind. Futral makes a keen observation on Jerusalem as evil in Rev 11: 2, 8, 13.

---

[119] See the discussion and illustrations of the *Sebastion* at Aphrodisias, pp. 219–26.

[120] See the excellent essay by Hood, "Women and Warriors."

[121] See Beasley-Murray, *Revelation*, 250–51, for the contrast in the table above.

> These verses serve as a rhetorical turning point in the text which allowed John to accomplish his threefold objective. By referring to the historical Jerusalem as Sodom and Egypt, John opened a doorway which allowed the listeners to call into question the holiest of places, the most pristine of institutions, the most benevolent of cities. John startled his readers into the recognition that even the holy city of Jerusalem could become a location of evil, a place where the Lord was crucified. If Jerusalem, the renowned holy city, could be questioned, then John could help his own audience examine their own location in the cities of Asia Minor. This was a crucial step in relieving the rhetorical burden in that John must help the believing communities to search their own situation.[122]

Thus, when John makes his clarion call about Babylon to "Come out of her, my people!" (18:4), he has prepared the way for Roman citizens who are also believers to grasp the gravity of the issues at stake, even though their social identity is driven by their connection to Rome.

Babylon becomes paradigmatic as the ancient foe of Israel who first had destroyed the city and its temple. Babylon later became an apocalyptic symbol of all antigod forces. God's destruction of Babylon is pictured as a golden cup of intoxication, but wrath rather than wine. God's wrath is to make sure what one lusts for intoxicates until that intoxication itself becomes its very doom as evil implodes on its own obsessions. Ancient Babylon was built over canals of fresh water channeled from the Euphrates River. John uses this historical datum of Babylon sitting on "many waters" to symbolize the reality of the Roman empire's global reach. Other imagery sources for Rev 17 are:

- the city of Rome with its founding legends of a destiny of conquest and as a city of seven hills

- the *Nero redivivus* myth merged with the chaos monster imagery to provide the dead/alive theme for Rome's nemesis in either the Parthians or Nero

- the harlotry of the Oholah and Oholibah sibling whores whose lovers turn on them of Ezek 23

- the harlotry of Jezebel as the archetypical whore of Babylon devoured by dogs of 2 Kgs 9

---

[122] Futral, "The Rhetorical Value of City," 250.

Harlotry is traditional in the Old Testament for apostate cities.[123] That this city sits on many waters is not just historical memory. This feature is metaphorical for the corrupting influence on nations, "with whom the kings of the earth have committed fornication" (17:2); these "waters" are "peoples and multitudes, and nations, and languages," all in collusion with Rome's imperial ideology (17:15). These co-conspirators in sin include Jezebel of Thyatira, who teaches "my servants to practice fornication" (2:20).

John is carried away "in the spirit" to an undesignated wilderness to see a woman riding on a "red beast" (17:3). Images of riding on a beast were part of ancient mythology. For example, Dionysus often is pictured riding a panther, a tiger, or lion. The "Theban" style of this tradition is of a young Dionysus, sometimes with wings of divinity. (The name derives from his place of birth as Thebes.) One famous Theban Dionysus mosaic is from a Roman home in Pompeii, which illustrates that aristocratic homes were decorated proudly with such imagery, and such a scene of riding a beast is not unusual in John's world.

FIGURE 11.49. Theban Dionysus. Mosaic from a Pompeii villa (NNAM).

John's "red beast" in context is the Red Dragon (12:3), the only beast identified with red color in the Dragon Cycle. John means to say that Rome is carried by Satan's power, which undergirds and inspirits her idolatry and destructive imperial ideology that enslaves millions in the name of "civilization" and "manifest destiny." Rome and Satan are unified in purpose and destiny. Due to the source of its power and the evil spirit of its character, the beast is "full of blasphemous names, and it had seven heads and ten horns" (17:3). The blasphemous names are the manifold idolatries of Satan, which translate into the ascriptions of divinity to Roman emperors and worship of the emperor promulgated

---

[123]Tyre, Isa 23:16; Nineveh, Nah 3; Jerusalem, Isa 1:21; Jer 3; Ezek 16, 23.

by the imperial cult. This exegesis is clear, but Revelation's history of interpretation has clouded this clarity since the Reformation.

Constantine did change the church's character, even colors, signs, and emblems that reflect Roman empire days.[124] Yet, this same church also has suffered incredible persecution as well. So, the story of the church is not simple and has complicated turns. Luther's acerbic war with the Catholic church included succumbing to Antichrist slander against the pope. While this rhetoric is seen in Wycliffe, Luther took the polemic to new invective levels, from which Protestant exegesis never has recovered. If John is correct, Catholics will be dying just as much as will Protestants in the final passion of the church. This Antichrist slander is a foul heritage of perpetuating Antichrist legends. Sadly, such rhetoric all too often is confused with historical exegesis.

FIGURE 11.50. Luther Bible, Rev 17. This harlot wears the papal crown. Luther was none too subtle. Protestant exegesis never has recovered from his Antichrist slander (Taschen).

This woman is decked out, "adorned with gold and jewels and pearls" and also "clothed in purple and scarlet" (17:4). Modern readers are not in tune with how colors communicated status, wealth, and royalty in the ancient world. The Roman Sumptuary Laws were regulations pertaining to entertainment, clothing, jewelry, beverages, and food that were enacted to control behavior and to enforce boundaries of class structure. For example, only a Roman citizen was allowed to wear a toga. Four colors in particular communicated class and status. Purple, made from the extremely expensive Mediterranean Murex sea

---

[124]Cary and Scullard, *A History of Rome*, theorized against Mommsen and Gibbon that Rome did not fall but evolved into a Medieval feudal state unified by Catholicism.

shell, was restricted to the imperial family. Saffron yellow, indigo blue, and crimson red dyes were restricted to aristocrats and rich businessmen just below the imperial house in status. The opulent wealth of the Roman empire is infamous in Nero's extravagance.[125]

FIGURE 11.51. Roman Gold Jewelry. Fine jewelry was a fixture among Roman elite. Left to right: gold filigree bracelet with bull heads, Europos (TAM); gold filigree earring, Thessalonica (LP); jewel inlaid gold ring with insignia (HAM); gold and bronze serpentine bracelet, Corinth (LP).

FIGURE 11.52. Pompeii Aristocratic Woman. This sophisticated and elite Roman lady proudly displays an index of her wealth, a string of fine pearls. Her hairstyle aspires to that of the empress in Rome, showing this lady knows current fashions. The fine, delicate silks gracing her neckline come from the exotic, far reaches of oriental trade with China (NNAM).

[125]See on Nero's banquets, traveling entourage, and palace, pp. 300–301.

The great harlot holds a golden cup full of abominations and the impurities of her fornication, reprising Jeremiah's word to ancient Babylon.[126] Abomination terminology evokes the apocalyptic "abomination of desolation," a phrase made famous by Dan 9:27 in reference to the sacrilege by Antiochus IV. The phrase became a *topos* of apocalyptic lore, even entering Jesus tradition in Jesus' Olivet Discourse (Mark 13:14). John's use stigmatizes the imperial cult's idolatrous beliefs and practices. Imperial cult practices are not "harmless" paganism. They result in an empire satiated with martyr blood: "drunk with the blood of saints and the blood of the witnesses to Jesus" (17:6). These saints are those who loved not their lives to death celebrated in hymn at the beginning of the Dragon Cycle (12:11). John views the death of Antipas as the harbinger of things to come, the promise of more persecution, and the historical revisiting of Nero's infamous persecution of Christians after the fire of Rome.

FIGURE 11.53. Injured Aeneas. In this Pompeii fresco, a surgeon is treating Aeneas as the goddess Aphrodite rushes alongside to aid her wounded son, who leans on Ascanius (NNAM).

John supplies the beast's "biography," which is a subversion of Rome's founding legends, such as the story of the famous Trojan Aeneas's escape from Troy to Italy to become progenitor of the imperial family line with famous status and divine royal blood. Another is the story of abandoned twins, Romulus and Remus, who are suckled by a she-wolf, giving them aggressive and conquering natures, later raised to manhood by a shepherd and his wife. All such stories promulgated values of Roman imperial ideology.

John gives the empire's *true* story, which is not about divine heritage, royal blood, or manifest destiny to conquer peoples. The red beast "was, and is not, and is about to ascend from the bottomless pit and go to destruction" (17:8). This description plays off the *Nero redivivus* myth, which would sim-

---

[126]Jer 25:15–16, 51:7. See the quote, p. 444.

FIGURE 11.54. Hadrian Military Cuirass. Hadrian (117–38) was the emperor who put down the final Jewish revolt in the Second Jewish War under the Jewish rebel, Bar Kokhba (132–35). The failure of this revolt ended Jewish fascination with apocalyptic literature. This stylized military cuirass of a statue of Hadrian displays standard imperial propaganda. The goddess *Dea* Roma of the city of Rome, flanked at her thighs by an eagle of the empire's legions and the snake sacred to Apollo, is being crowned with a laurel wreath of victory as supreme ruler by supernatural beings. *Dea* Roma stands supported on the back of the legendary she-wolf that suckled the warrior brothers Romulus and Remus, founders of Rome (AMAC). Credit: Jean M. Stevens.

ply amaze the world were Nero to reappear as Rome's nemesis, and the very thought struck fear into the Roman heart. Romans should have contemplated the story of Nero's reign more intently than just fearing his return. Nero is the real story of Rome's character, which lies in the heart of evil—the bottomless pit. Nero was the dark side of true Rome. That is precisely why he acted the way he did. He was truly evil in a thoroughly Roman way and not even close to the ideology of Rome's founding legends. The storyline of divine and royal heritage propagandized in those legends blatantly was contradicted by Rome's own emperors such as Nero but conveniently ignored or suppressed.

Rome did not even pay attention to the obvious lie made of Roman ideology by Rome's own laws. The Roman senate's law, *damnatio memoriae*, "condemnation of memory," dishonored traitors or others who had brought discredit to the Roman state by removing any trace of their existence from official records. Such was the fate of some emperors, including Domitian. He was assassinated by court officials, and the senate enacted *damnatio memoriae* on him—his name erased off inscriptions, and his statues altered or defaced. Court writers and historians for emperor Trajan, such as Tacitus, Suetonius, and Pliny the Younger, also went to great lengths to caricature his predecessor Domitian in the most negative light in order to aggrandize Trajan's reign, which is why their depictions of Domitian have to be weighed carefully and substantiated with other evidence.

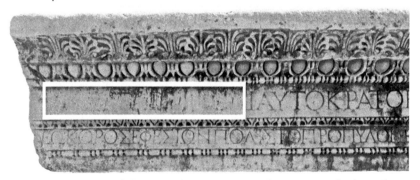

FIGURE 11.55. Domitian's *Damnatio Memoriae*. Imperial inscription of Ephesus from the imperial temple complex indicating the city officially as a *neōkoros* ("keeper of the temple"). Domitian's name, however, on the first line before *autokratōri* has been erased, which is the area indicated by the white rectangle.

The evil emperor is taken as the embodiment of the evil empire. The seven heads of the red beast are seven hills; these are the famous seven hills of Rome we already have discussed (17:9).[127] As John is wont to do, he innovates the traditional imagery of the seven hills of Rome by adding his own secondary twist beyond the commonplace idea of the seven hills. Of the seven heads, he says,

> also they are seven kings, of whom five have fallen, one is living, and the other has not yet come; and when he comes, he must remain only a little while. As for the beast that was and is not, he is an eighth but belongs to the seven, and he is going to destruction (Rev 17:9b–11).

Emperor									
Julius Caesar (44 B.C.)	1	1	1						
Augustus (27–A.D. 14)	2	2	2	1	1				
Tiberius (14–37)	3	3		2	2	1			
Caligula (37–41)	4	4		3	3	2	1	1	
Claudius (41–54)	5	5	3	4	4	3	2	2	
Nero (54–68)	6	6		5	5	4	3	3	1
Galba (68)	7			6		5	4		2	1
Otho (69)	8			7		6	5		3	2
Vitellius (69)				8		7	6		4	3
Vespasian (69–79)		7	4		6	8	7	4	5	4
Titus (79–81)		8	5		7		8	5	6	5
Domitian (81–96)			6		8			6	7	6

FIGURE 11.56. The Seven Kings of Rev 17. Clarity falters on basic issues of when to start counting and what to do with the period of the Roman civil war after Nero's suicide (adapted from Aune, *Revelation 17–22*, 947; Reddish, *Revelation*, 330).

The beast that was and is not is identified in the context as the Dragon under the alias of *Nero redivivus*. In this context, one would assume the kings are Roman. Contextually, what seems implied is that the fallen five is history past to John, and the one living is history current to John, and the coming seventh is John's near future. The eighth king is quite the enigma. His description varies from all the others. For one, he does not seem to be an actual king. For two, what is the meaning of "of the seven"? He seems a redux of them all, but he is a mystery.[128]

---

[127] See the discussion and image, pp. 231–32.

[128] The enigma of the eighth king is argued; check the critical commentaries.

One sure would think something concrete could come of all this counting, but, alas, such is not to be. We cannot agree on when to start counting, whether Julius Caesar as the founder of the Julio-Claudian dynasty, or Augustus as the founder of the Roman empire, or Tiberius as the emperor when Jesus was crucified, or Caligula as the emperor who infamously ordered his statue erected in the Jerusalem temple, or Nero as the first emperor to persecute Christians, or Galba as starting the civil war transition to the imperial dynasty in power when John wrote Revelation. Neither do we know what to do with Nero's suicide, in which Rome saw five emperors in two years, three of whom were dispensed in a year and a half of civil war (Nero, *Galba, Otho, Vitellius*, Vespasian). Do we not count the civil war emperors at all, count as a group, or count individually? What all these variables mean is that anyone sticking in the necessary assumptions when needed can get the list to wind up anywhere one has predetermined the list needs to wind up to prove whatever chronology one already has presumed for dating Revelation. Or, one can throw in the chronological towel and just take the whole list as symbolic in its entirety. What exact symbolism here would not be too clear, however, since the eighth "belonging to" the seven is a nebulous idea at best. Our only hope is that the original readers had a better clue as to John's meaning than do his later interpreters. This nut pretty much refuses to crack exegetically.[129]

Perhaps John's last word on the entire seven-kings escapade is the take home point: "and he goes to destruction" (17:11). This word is the bottom line on evil in the world: Evil will be destroyed. God is Almighty, and the less-than-almighty emperor should take note. Judgment means God holds all evil accountable.

Ten confederate kings then are identified. In Daniel, ten kings sequentially precede the fateful ruler, Antiochus IV. In John, the ten kings are simultaneous with the beast. Ten probably is not referential, but another symbolic number for humanity. These kings could be the kings of the east (16:12) or the kings of the world (16:14), but more likely in terms of the Roman imperial system are provincial governors and allied civic rulers supporting Roman ideology and rule. These leaders are clients of the emperor's patronage. Thus, these kings "yield

---

[129] We feel like the veritable fictional species character Scrat in the movie "Ice Age" (2002) going to death-defying extremes to possess the acorn.

their power to him" (17:13) in that they do not express free and independent rule but have to satisfy their client obligations to Rome in all aspects of society, politics, and religion. All Jewish rulers of Judea had to play this game, from Herod the Great down to his grandsons. Even Roman governors only ruled at the emperor's pleasure, such as when the procurator Felix was recalled to Rome and Festus took his place as governor of Judea while Paul was in prison in Caesarea (Acts 24:27).

The confederate kings make war on the Lamb (17:14). Since the only weapon the Lamb has is a sword out of his mouth (1:16), then this is a war of words, a war of confession. The war is not described, just as with the imagery of Armageddon (16:16), only its result. To a stunned Roman audience, the announcement is that the Lamb is the conqueror, not Rome! This word subverts all imperial ideology portraying the inevitability of the victorious Roman general on the field of battle. That this word of the Lamb's war and victory anticipates the Rider on the white horse scene (19:11–21) is made clear with the description that the Lamb is "Lord of lords and King of kings," the exact same identification we get in the Rider scene in 19:16. Thus, the Rider on the white horse scene in Rev 19, though clearly about Jesus, does *not* picture the second coming. *The Rider on the white horse scene in Rev 19 is a filling out of the war of the Lamb allusion here in 17:14.* This war and victory is the present confessional war the seven churches of Asia Minor are having with Rome, and the victory is the martyr's conquest of the beast through faithful testimony even to death. Thus, warriors accompanying the Lamb are "called and chosen and faithful." Antipas of Pergamum, for one, is part of this army of the Lamb.

A surprising mutiny takes place (17:15–18). Bracketed between the interpretation of the obvious symbolism of the waters as peoples of an empire and the woman as "the great city that rules over the kings of the earth" (17:15, 18)—all making clear Babylon is Rome—is a most shocking turn of events. The ten confederate kings and the beast turn on the whore, hate her, make her desolate and naked, then devour her flesh[130] and burn her up with fire. Such imagery also is similar to the story of the lovers turning on the twin sisters who are whores in Ezek 23. We are not advised why this stunning betrayal takes place. We do

---

[130]Like Jezebel was devoured by the dogs outside the city walls: 1 Kgs 21:23; 22:38; 2 Kgs 9:10, 36–37.

not need to know. John's purpose is to portray how God ultimately deals with evil: Evil inherently is self destructive. Greed, power, and violence breed their own ruin. John already enunciated this principle when the beasts first were brought onto Revelation's stage: Those who kill with the sword will be killed (13:10).[131]

The harlot's destiny of betrayal cannot be avoided, because her end is by God's sovereign will: "For God has put it into their hearts to carry out his purpose by agreeing to give their kingdom to the beast, until the words of God will be fulfilled" (17:17). Believers are challenged to believe that, even as evil empires persecute God's people for their confession of faith, God still walks among those palaces of power as God Almighty controlling fates of emperors and empires, directing all of history to the intended consummation of the kingdom of God. John concludes by repeating his symbolism: The woman "is the great city that rules over the kings of the earth" (17:18)—clearly, Rome.

Babylon: Heaven's Perspective (18:1—19:10). This Babylon scene is heaven's perspective on the Bowl judgments. John combines three Old Testament forms to compose this chapter picturing the ruination of Babylon—dirge, prophetic parable, and taunt song. He creates an effective, vicarious experience for his audience.[132] The point of the dirge is that Rome sums up and exceeds all past tyrants of Israel. The prophetic parable is the great millstone thrown into the sea. The common chord of prophetic taunt songs is derision of a fallen enemy.

Literarily, the laments on earth (18:9–24) are bounded on either side by two scenes from heaven. The opening scene is heaven's anticipation (18:1–8). The concluding scene is heaven's celebration (19:1–10). These two units form an *inclusio* that binds the laments to help in-

---

[131]This principle of evil's ruin is the Pauline understanding of the operation of the wrath of God as a divine and sovereign "delivering over" of sinners to the power of their own sin with the inevitable result of death in Rom 1:18–32. This principle of self-destructing sin also is the observation in Jas 1:14–15.

[132]An earnest, "That movie made me cry, and I'm a grown man," is the contemporary sense if you actually lived in your mind as a first-century reader the scene John portrayed. The Old Testament dirge background includes Babylon (Isa 13; Jer 51); Edom (Isa 34); Tyre (Ezek 26–28); and Nineveh (Nah 3). The prophetic parable has examples in Isaiah walking about the streets naked as though already a conquered and humiliated slave population (Isa 20), Jeremiah throwing his recorded prophecies into the Euphrates (Jer 13), and Ezekiel's actions before siege (Ezek 4). The form of taunt songs is not fixed but can be seen in Isa 23–24, Jer 50–51, and Ezek 26–27.

terpret the significance of the laments as God's judgment. The angel's authoritative word anticipates the judgment, and the final worship scene celebrates divine judgment executed on Babylon that is true and just.

18:1–8	18:9–24	19:1–10
Heavenly Anticipation	Earthly Lamentation	Heavenly Celebration
(Judgment Anticipated)	(Judgment Described)	(Judgment Celebrated)

FIGURE 11.57. Literary Form of Rev 18. Two scenes from heaven bind the lament on earth to give the lament its interpretation from divine perspective.

Heavenly Anticipation (18:1–8). The heavenly angel declares Babylon's doom: "Fallen, fallen is Babylon the great!" (18:2). The past tense conveys the surety of God's sovereign will.[133] The description of ancient Babylon's doom is the paradigm. Two groups here are in focus, kings of the earth who have fornicated with her and merchants of the earth who have grown rich through her (18:3). A third group, the seafarers, will be added in the laments. Rome and her luxury are the target. These groups share responsibility in Rome's commercial abuse of earth's resources to satisfy raw greed and lust. The poetic laments will dramatize these groups as the main auxiliary beneficiaries of Rome's sin. In this judgment, God's sovereignty and the saints' faithfulness are vindicated. This judgment answers the martyrs' cry of "how long, O Lord?" (6:10) and reverses Babylon's judgment against the saints.

What is heaven's perspective on imperial rule? First comes God's command to God's people in this confessional crisis, which also effectively becomes Revelation's central command to all seven churches: "Come out of her!" (18:4). Like the initial earthquake rumblings that presage the eruption of Mount Vesuvius in the hours leading up to the explosion, God gives due warning to his people. Participation in Rome's sins is loss of true confession and to share in Rome's plagues (the seven Bowl judgments just auditioned). This word is a direct word to the churches of Asia Minor. Emperor worship cannot be tolerated. The lampstand will be removed (Ephesus, 2:5).

The judgment is "you get what you give" (18:6). Her lifestyle, "glorified herself and lived luxuriously," is the Laodicean church: "I am rich and have prospered and have need of nothing" (3:17). This condition is like Sardis, who, though living in the security of Roman luxury, needs to "wake up" because they have "soiled their clothes" (3:3–

---

[133]The tense syntax is a prophetic aorist.

4). Again, like Pergamum, they participate in imperial cult and pagan idolatry, because they "eat food sacrificed to idols and practice fornication" (2:14)—exactly what the false prophetess Jezebel openly is advocating in Thyatira (2:20). This idolatry even in the seven churches is the fornication of Babylon, the Roman imperial patronage system.

Haughty hubris is the core: "I rule as a queen" (18:7), claiming the role of the mythical Queen of Heaven, imagery that kicked off this Dragon Cycle. The pride of Nebuchadnezzar, ancient king of Babylon, is reprised.[134] Yet, this queen is no queen; she is a spiritual harlot, a parody of Zion, New Jerusalem, true queen, the city of God coming down from heaven. In the end, she will be "burned with fire" (18:8), precisely the destruction revealed to John would be accomplished by the Dragon's betrayal along with ten confederate kings (17:16). The image is ancient siege warfare. "Pestilence, mourning, and famine" are conditions inside a besieged city. Josephus's vivid description of these very conditions in the fall of Jerusalem in the First Jewish War (A.D. 66–70) is particularly poignant and at times full of extraordinary pathos.[135] When any city falls, invaders loot and burn. God's judgment operates on a principle that evil inherently and inevitably collapses under its own weight.

FIGURE 11.58. Ephesus Ivory Panel Relief. From an Ephesus terrace home comes this exquisite but truly expensive furniture (EMS).

Earthly Lamentation (18:9–24). A series of three laments profile three groups profiting from a rapacious lust. The kings of the earth are first up (18:9–10). They are collaborators in the abusive power of Rome, promoters of empire propaganda and

---

[134]The story is told in Dan 4.

[135]Josephus wrote into the thirteenth year of the reign of Domitian (*Ant.* 20.267). On the war's famine and tragedy, cf. *Ant.* 18.8; *J.W.* 3.179; 4.361; 5.513; 6.1, 193; most especially the mother who roasted and ate her infant son, 6.201–14; 6.369, 405, 421, 430. Similarly in the Second Jewish War of Bar Kokhba, cf. Eusebius *H.E.* 4.6.3.

its idolatry. Provincial cities of the Roman empire competed to be honored with any privileged Roman status, such as to be the imperial temple warden or as the first to build an imperial cult temple, as for Ephesus, Smyrna, Pergamum, and Sardis of the seven churches.

Merchants of the earth are second up (18:11–17a). Their business is pandering to Roman opulence and the commerce of world empire. They are paid handsomely in their trade in lust. The listed cargo itemizes ship manifests bound for empire harbors and Roman homes, as in the palatial terrace homes of Ephesus and vacation villas of Herculaneum.[136] Demand for extravagance and ostentation in lucrative Roman lifestyles increased exponentially in the first century, and independent merchants and middlemen shifted to the hugely profitable trade of luxury items.[137] Often quoted is the characterization of Roman commerce by the second-century Roman, Aelius Aristides, in his eulogy to the city of Rome for the emperor.

gold, silver	Macedonia, Spain
jewels, pearls	India
fine linen	Egypt
purple	Tyre
silk, scarlet	China
scented, costly wood	North Africa
ivory	North Africa
bronze, iron	Britain, Spain
marble	Asia, North Africa
cinnamon, spice	South China, Arabia
incense, myrrh, frankincense	India, Media, Arabia
wine, olive oil	Italy, Spain, Gaul
choice flour, wheat	Egypt, North Africa
cattle, sheep	Asia, Europe
horses, chariots	Armenia, Gaul
slaves	Worldwide

FIGURE 11.59. Luxuries of an Empire. John chronicles ship manifests flowing into Rome's harbors from all points of the empire.

> Around that sea [Mediterranean] lie the great continents [Africa, Asia, Europe] massively sloping down to it, forever offering you in full measure what they possess. Whatever each culture grows and manufactures cannot fail to be here at all times and in great profusion. Here merchant vessels arrive carrying these many commodities from every region in every season and even at every equinox, so that the city takes on the appearance of a sort of common market for the world. One can see cargoes from India and even, if you will, from southern Arabia in such numbers that one must conclude that the trees in those lands

---

[136]See the illustrations, p. 291, 362–63. Cf. the empire commerce map in Reddish, *Revelation*, 355, which is adapted from Cary and Scullard, *A History of Rome*, p. 455.

[137]Cf. Koester, *Introduction to the New Testament*, 313.

have been stripped bare, and if the inhabitants of those lands need anything, they must come here to beg for a share of what they have produced. Your farmlands are Egypt, Sicily, and all of cultivated Africa. Seaborne arrivals and departures are ceaseless, to the point that the wonder is, not so much that the harbor has insufficient space for all these merchant vessels, but that the sea has enough space (if it really does). Just as there is a common channel where all waters of the Ocean have a single source and destination, so that there is a common channel to Rome and all meet here: trade, shipping, agriculture, metallurgy—all the arts and crafts that are or ever were and all things that are produced or spring from the earth. What one does not see here does not exist. So it is not easy to decide which is the greater: the superiority of this city relative to cities that presently exist, or the superiority of this empire relative to all empires that ever existed.[138]

FIGURE 11.60. Roman Glass Perfume Bottles. Roman elites had some of the rarest and most highly desired perfumes in the world. These 2nd/3rd cent. Roman bottles graced aristocratic dressing rooms across the empire (Left to right, #1–5: YMY; #6: KAM; #7: BMB; #8: EMS).

This is the same Aristides that wrote to emperor Marcus Aurelius to gain imperial assistance to rebuild Smyrna after the great earthquake of A.D. 178 destroyed his favorite city.[139]

The last item on John's list of Rome's commerce is the bottom of morality's barrel, the depravity of the ancient world's slave economy. Slaves comprised as much as one third of a city's population in the ancient world.[140] Remove slaves, and Roman life collapses in every arena, including in homes, economy, industry, business, landed estates, con-

---

[138] Aristides *To Rome* 11–13.
[139] See the discussion of Smyrna, p. 301.
[140] Bartchy, "Slavery (Greco-Roman)," 6:66–67.

struction, and management. John puts a barb to his point with his way of phrasing the last, climactic item: "bodies—even human souls."[141] Rome's trade in slaves was inhuman; they were not humans with personal names; instead, they were chattel to be counted as inventory on a market shelf ("bodies"). John has added the "human souls" to counter the callous treatment of human beings as slaves as the epitome of Rome's degradation and evil. In the ancient world of slavery, slave dealers were well known as lawless in acquiring their merchandise, untrustworthy in their sales, immoral in their sexual practices, and in clear violation of universal holiness codes and certainly Jewish law.[142] As his last word in his list of Roman commerce, John created his own iconic image of why this Babylon is a harlot that has passed on her golden goblet, and "all the nations have drunk of the wine of the wrath of her fornication" (18:3).

FIGURE 11.61. Relief of the Conquered Galatian. This replica is one of the most iconic images from Caesar's famous war in Gaul. The defeated Gaul is humiliated, stripped naked, hands bound behind his back, with a rope around his neck to lead him like an animal. He went from honored homeland soldier to dishonored empire slave in one day of battle (YMY).

The merchants lament the great city only for her commercial significance. Note how their lament simply repeats items from the list of cargo their ships have carried: "Alas, alas, the great city, clothed in fine linen, in purple and scarlet, and adorned with gold, with jewels, and with pearls" (18:16). All that they mourn is that "all this wealth has been

---

[141] The Greek is not the typical word for slave, *doulos* (δοῦλος), but rather, *sōmatōn* (σωμάτων), "bodies."

[142] Harrill, *Slaves in the New Testament*, 119–39.

FIGURE 11.62. Roman Glass Vase. Beautiful craftsmanship in this richly decorated glass vase, shown life size, probably Patara (AAM).

laid waste" (18:17). John could not be more blunt about the true motivation of the merchants. They could not care less about Rome itself.

Finally, seafarers are profiled (18:17b–20). These merchant marines are in collusion with supporting Rome's extravagant commerce. They throw dust on their heads in the ancient expression of grief or mourning.[143] Just like the merchants, their grief is over their economic loss, not any feeling for Babylon: "Alas, alas, the great city, where all who had ships at sea grew rich by her wealth" (18:19). This lack of loyalty is a fundamental contradiction of what Rome claimed in her imperial ideology. Nations did not love Rome. They only acquiesced to Rome's aggression due to political and military expediency. This superficial embrace of Rome is the basis of the quick turn around and rebellion of the ten confederate kings noted by the angel interpreting the figure of the harlot for John (17:16). Groups allied with Rome are loyal only superficially. Evil is its own demise.

All three of these groups illustrate those who are at the forefront of having the mark of the beast. The mark is precisely "so that no one can buy or sell who does not have the mark" (13:17), that is, the mark is for the market. Thus, in the context of the chapters that unfold immediately following Rev 13's introduction of the beasts, the mark of the beast is a first-century reality addressed specifically to the seven churches of Asia Minor. This commercial mark is played out in the Rome/Babylon commercial imagery in Rev 17–18 that expands the judgment of the Bowls in Rev 15–16. This context seems to suggest that the mark of the beast is not a physical mark but is an abstraction encoding the culpability of those who participate at all levels in first-century Rome's godless, dehumanizing, commercial enterprise.

Presumably the same voice as in 18:4 calls heaven to rejoice over Babylon's fall (18:20). Those called specifically are saints, and apostles and prophets, which are the persecuted church and her leaders. This call is the signal for the souls under the altar to realize their prayers for vindication are answered: "For God has given judgment for you against her." The fall of Babylon answers the saints' prayer of 6:10. In that context, the answered prayer means that the full number of church martyrs is complete. Herein lies another prophetic insinuation that while the entire Judgment Cycle pertains to the persecuted seven

---

[143] Josh 7:6; Job 2:12; Lam 2:10; Ezek 27:30.

churches of Asia Minor and Roman imperial idolatry and commercial harlotry, and that Babylon is first-century Rome, a proleptic element of the future passion of the church is encoded. While admittedly this understanding depends on implicit elements in the text, such a future encoding does seem contained within:

- the cryptic answer to the martyrs' cry of the fifth seal
- the extraordinary nature of the Dragon's beasts
- the multivalent capacity of the mark of the beast
- the strange enigma of the numbered seven kings
- the martyrdom motif of all imagery in every section

FIGURE 11.63. Douce Apocalypse, Rev 18:21. The great millstone (ADEVA).

The great millstone parabolic action reiterates the decisive nature of Babylon's judgment and gives John opportunity to dramatize further the fall of Babylon on the theme of silenced urban activity of what used to be the constant hubbub of city life (18:21).[144]

---

[144] I have to confess my own personal experience resonates deeply with this imagery. When I first returned to New Orleans after the total destruction of Hurricane Katrina,

FIGURE 11.64. Roman Street Players. Pompeii mosaic of minstrels entertaining with music and dance, signed by Dioscurides of Samos from the Villa of Cicero. "And the sound of harpists and minstrels and of flutists and trumpeters will be heard in you no more" (Rev 18:22; NNAM).

FIGURE 11.65. Roman Millstone at Pompeii. "And the sound of the millstone will be heard in you no more" (Rev 18:22). These millstones turned by animals or slaves ground out flour daily for the baking of the morning bread. Freshly baked bread for the day was carbonized by the pyroclastic flow of Mount Vesuvius after its eruption on Aug. 24, A.D. 79 and found by excavators nearly two millennia later at the nearby sister city of Herculaneum.

---

the absolute, total silence everywhere when I got out of my car sent a strange chill down my back. No birds, cats, dogs, squirrels, insects, animals. No barking, calling, talking. No central air conditioner motors kicking in. No horns, cars, trucks, vehicles. No lawn mowers, air blowers, sidewalk edgers. No sounds. Nothing. Total silence in a major city of the United States. The weirdest experience of silence I ever have had—and the destruction came in one day.

FIGURE 11.66. Roman Glass and Alabaster Krater. Surmounted rim collar, elegant sharp spines with particular virtuosity in the loops of articulated double volutes; used as furniture; later, used as a funerary urn. "An artisan of any trade will be found in you no more" (Rev 18:23; NNAM).

FIGURE 11.67. Roman Bronze Lamp. Oil lamp from Pompeii of fine bronze artistry with three tongues for brighter illumination meant to be hung from a ceiling with the attached chain and hook held by the figurine of a dancer. "And the light of a lamp will shine in you no more" (Rev 18:23; NNAM).

FIGURE 11.68. Roman Sarcophagus. This burial crypt depicts a home scene of husband, wife, and children. Man with roll of papers in hand symbolizing knowledge of science and the arts. "And the voice of the bridegroom and bride will be heard in you no more" (Rev 18:22; AAM).

All this tragic destruction in a day. The godless empire falls. Her commercial rapine is ended. Yet, the most egregious sin of all is last to be identified: "And in you was found the blood of prophets and of saints" (18:24). The church martyr theme ends the lament section. This is the theme that ties the past and future of the Apocalypse. The past of the Apocalypse is the clash of the church in first-century Asia Minor with the claims of imperial Rome that provides the context for an exegesis of all the images in the grand Judgment Cycle (6–20). The future of the Apocalypse is in the intimations of a future passion of the church that will complete the work of the cross of Christ in history. This future passion is embedded into Revelation's martyr theme.

John then concludes, "and of all who have been slaughtered on earth." This is John's final word on imperial ideology of conquest and manifest destiny to rule the world, the legends of the aggressive, wolf-like, warring brothers, Romulus and Remus. Rome has slaughtered thousands in order to realize her empire destiny and the so-called *pax Romana*, the "peace" of Rome. Jesus was one of those. The same verb is used here as is used to describe the slaughtered Lamb of 5:6. No one, however, has a true manifest destiny to rule the world except the one designated by the sovereign God who created this world and will consummate his purposes in the slaughtered Lamb—the Lord of Lords and King of Kings.

Heavenly Celebration (19:1–10). Once again, the chapter division is poor and misinforms the reader about the structure of the fall of Babylon section, as if this concluding hymn were extraneous somehow to the literary flow of Rev 18. These are the words that inspired part of Handel's "Hallelujah" chorus, and, indeed, they are the climax of the fall of Babylon scene. Two main sources for the imagery are marriage and banquet. Marriage imagery has a rich biblical tradition in both the Old and New Testaments.[145] Fine linen wedding imagery is given spiritual meaning as the righteous deeds of the saints and is intended as a dramatic contrast to the whore Babylon, church versus Rome. Banquet imagery also has biblical traditions in both Old and New Testaments.[146] A common banquet theme is kingdom joy and celebration.

---

[145]Isa 54:1–8; Jer 31:32; Ezek 16:8–14; Hos 1–3; Matt 25:1–12; Mark 2:18–20; John 3:29; 2 Cor 11:2.

[146]Isa 25:6–8; Matt 8:11–12; 22:1–14; 25:1–13; 26:29; Mark 14:25; Luke 13:29; 22:18.

After a focus on the earthly perspective, John returns the reader to a heavenly view on the fall of Babylon as a proper counterpoint to interpreting the event. One laments; the other rejoices. This hymn in its concentric circles of praise shows similar structure to the hymn of 5:6–14 in the Vision of Heaven. John is bringing us back to the vision that lays the theological foundation to God's judgment of the world in the Judgment Cycle.

Four hallelujahs punctuate the praise and structure the progression. A great multitude expresses the first two. This is the multitude in heaven encountered in the first half of the Judgment Cycle in the Seals interlude (7:9). They are the redeemed of all nations. Their "Hallelujah" is a rare biblical term, only here in the New Testament.[147] This Hebrew expression has its Greek equivalent in the "praise to our God" Greek expression in 19:5. Their "salvation, and glory and power to our God" (19:1) is anti-imperial and most certainly not what Domitian would have wanted to hear. God's judgments are true and just, and, unlike Rome's corrupted courts, cannot be persuaded by the faction yelling the loudest, as in the trial of Jesus before Pilate, or by the one willing to be bribed, as in Paul's dealings with governor Felix.[148] God is praised for avenging the "blood of his servants," which would include specifically, Antipas of Pergamum (2:13), for one.

The second hallelujah is revelatory. We learn Babylon's ruin is forever: "The smoke goes up from her forever and ever" (19:3). When an ancient city was sacked, the smoke of her downfall would rise on the horizon for days and even weeks. Surrounding populations would not be able to forget the conquered city's ruin for a long time. This truth has two correlates. One is historical. All kingdoms fall. Rome stood the longest, a thousand years. She gave the impression of being "eternal Rome," but she really was not. Rome is no more. However, even though true at the historical level, is this what John meant? Was he saying, "Don't worry, Antipas. In a thousand years, Rome is finished"? Possibly, but that does not seem to be a satisfying answer for those who have been left behind and currently are being persecuted.[149]

---

[147] Four times in this hymn. Cf. Pss 104–106; 111–113; 115–117; 135.

[148] Matt 27:16–26; Mark 15:7–15; Luke 23:18; John 18:40; Acts 24:26.

[149] Alas, the truth is, all true believers are "left behind." No passion of the church, no second coming of Jesus. Jesus comes most powerfully in his passion.

However, if this "destruction" of Babylon is not the literal fall of the city of Rome but the faithful witness of persecuted believers, as indicated in the hymn in 12:11 and in all promise sections of the Seven Letters, then the fall of Babylon imagery of Rev 18 could be metaphorical for the triumph of the believer in the courts of Rome in rejecting the demands of the imperial cult. In this sense, the fall of Babylon is the believer who says no to governor Pliny's demand for public show of emperor worship.[150] By definition, Rome never conquered a martyr. Thus, Babylon's fall could be located in the actual fall of Rome, but more likely is configured with Revelation's martyr theme to speak to faithful Christian confession in Caesar's court.

The other correlate is eschatological. For God to consummate his creation, all other kingdoms must be ended decisively and forever. All human kingdoms are corrupt, crippled by the Dragon's schemes to usurp the power and authority that belongs to God alone by getting humans to "worship the beast" (14:9, 11). Humans naturally like being thought of as gods (Gen 3:5), as did Caligula, Nero, Domitian, and so forth. Thus, the fall of Babylon has to have an eschatological correlate for the creator God to be the consummator. The fall of Babylon is a dramatic picture in Rev 18, but leaves us wondering the details of how the eschatological reality will correspond to any historical reality.

The third hallelujah coming from the twenty-four elders and four living creatures takes us directly back to the throne room scene of the Vision of Heaven that launched the entire Judgment Cycle in Rev 4. These characters are placed strategically to serve as a literary *inclusio* that binds the entire Judgment Cycle, as well as a unifying element in each of the three literary pauses within the Judgment Cycle:

- Vision of Heaven (4:4, 10; 5:5, 6, 8, 11, 14)
- Seals Interlude (7:11, 13)
- Trumpets Interlude (11:16)
- Conquest Prelude (14:3)
- Hallelujah Chorus (19:4)

---

[150]See p. 315 on Pliny's letter to Trajan: "I interrogated these as to whether they were Christians; those who confessed I interrogated a second and a third time, threatening them with punishment; those who persisted I ordered executed."

These literary features of these two sets of characters in the elders and four creatures signal that, whereas the Dragon Cycle (12–20) and the Christ Cycle (6–11) are not structured exactly alike internally as the two major subdivisions of the Judgment Cycle (6–20), John does intend these two major subdivisions mutually to interpret one another. The nature of the literary placement and function of these characters continues to add to the argument that the material in Revelation is recapitulatory, not sequential.

The fourth hallelujah comes from a great multitude. This characterization, "sound of many waters," occurs only three times in the Apocalypse: the description of the voice of the Son of Man in the Inaugural Vision (1:15); the description of the great multitude in the conquest prelude (14:2); and here in the description of the great multitude of the hallelujah chorus (19:6). In fact, this description here is almost verbatim the description in the conquest prelude:

14:2: ὡς φωνὴν ὑδάτων πολλῶν καὶ ὡς φωνὴν βροντῆς μεγάλης
19:6: ὡς φωνὴν ὑδάτων πολλῶν καὶ ὡς φωνὴν βροντῆς ἰσχυρῶν

14:2: hōs phōnēn hydatōn pollōn kai hōs phōnēn brontēs megalēs
19:6: hōs phōnēn hydatōn pollōn kai hōs phōnēn brontēs ischyrōn

14:2: "like the sound of many waters and like the sound of great thunder"
19:6: "like the sound of many waters and like the sound of strong thunder"

The only minor variation is use of synonymous adjectives at the very end of the phrase. John's point is that this great sound is the voice of the redeemed, and, as the redeemed, sounds like the Son of Man who redeemed them. The praise is carefully chosen anti-imperial rhetoric, phrase by phrase:

- "the Lord our God" counters Domitian's own claims[151]
- "the Almighty," *pantokratōr* counters Rome's imperator claims
- "has begun to reign" counters Rome's empire claims[152]

---

[151] According to Suetonius *Dom.* 13.2; Dio Cassius 67.4.7.

[152] The HCSB is one of the few English translations that catches that the aorist verb is an ingressive aorist. The better nuance is "begun to reign," the reality of Babylon's fall, not "reigns," which is an axiomatically true theological datum, so not a pertinent point for John to emphasize in this context.

The metaphor of the "marriage of the Lamb" is a literary device to offer an additional perspective of celebration of the fall of Babylon.[153] The device specifically is used to set the stage to focus on the element of clothing. The wedding attire of fine linen is to emphasize righteous character. This character-through-clothing emphasis of the marriage of the Lamb picks up on:

- the Inaugural Vision of the Son of Man dressed in a long robe (1:13)

- the very few persons in Sardis who have not soiled their clothes and walk with Christ dressed in white, who also are promised if they "conquer," they will be clothed in white robes (3:4–5), which is the promise to participate in this marriage of the Lamb

- the Laodiceans who are counseled to "buy" white robes from the Son of Man, for which now the occasion for this wardrobe has been provided, the marriage of the Lamb (3:18)

- the Sardis-style warning just before the battle of Armageddon scene about staying "awake" and "clothed" (16:15)

- the parody of the great city Babylon as clothed in "fine linen" when she really is full of filth and abominations (18:16), like those in Sardis who have "soiled" their clothes, showing that Sardis may be dressed in fine linen, but the church is dead, sold out to Rome

The metaphor of the fine linen is explained directly by John as "the righteous deeds of the saints" (19:8). In the context of Revelation these deeds are testimony in persecution.

The fourth benediction of Revelation is spoken upon those invited to the marriage supper of the Lamb, so the imagery shifts to a wedding banquet. The messianic banquet had become a stock metaphor for the kingdom of God among Jews. The gospel writer Luke probably has picked up on this tradition more than any other gospel writer.[154] The new metaphor of wedding guests at a wedding banquet mixes metaphors. The wedding party and the wedding guests merge into one figure. John is innovating and does not care to split hairs about the

---

[153] John's imagery is eschatological, similar to Paul in 2 Cor 11:2: "I promised you in marriage to one husband, to present you as a chaste virgin to Christ."

[154] See Moessner, *Lord of the Banquet*.

double metaphors. He just wants to emphasize the joy of the celebration of Babylon's fall. For the redeemed, the joy is like those getting married; for the redeemed the festivities are like being invited to the largest social event ever.

The hermeneutical point here is that this wedding banquet invitation in 19:9 reiterates Jesus' own banquet invitation in 3:20 spoken to the Laodiceans in the Seven Letters: "If anyone hears my voice and opens the door, I will come in to that person and dine with that one, and that one with me." As a conclusion to the entire Seven Letters unit, functionally this invitation is used to offer an open invitation to all the churches who hear Revelation read. Thus, once again, we see how the thoughts, ideas, and expressions within the Judgment Cycle resonate with features of the Seven Letters with hermeneutical significance.[155]

In either case, wedding or banquet, regardless of the mixed metaphor, these are the "true words of God" (19:9). That is, no believer's story ends in the grief and tragedy of martyrdom. God *will* vindicate. Believers may die as martyrs, but most assuredly as God lives, they will live for another day to celebrate a wedding and a banquet.

The drama of the visions of the Dragon Cycle have demonstrated why the Lamb is worthy to take the scroll of Revelation from the hand of the One seated on the throne and to discharge its contents as the Judgment Cycle (5:7; 6:1). John is overwhelmed by the reality of Babylon's fall, by the majesty of God that has accomplished this incredible judgment, and by the worthy Lamb of the Judgment Cycle. He falls down to worship at the feet of the angel bringing this marvelous revelation (19:10). He is warned against this action by the angel himself.[156] This "Worship God!" is the positive side of the earlier "come out of her" command (18:4). The angel protests he is only a "fellow servant" with John and with those who "hold the testimony of Jesus." This tes-

---

[155]Commentaries on Revelation often leave the Seven Letters disappearing in the rearview mirror of exegesis, an isolated unit quickly forgotten when reading the rest of the book. In contrast, we are using the Seven Letters systematically to disclose the Judgment Cycle's meaning. The local situation of the seven churches of Asia Minor is the immediate context for interpreting the Judgment Cycle.

[156]Exegetically, we cannot be sure whether John's reaction of falling down to worship is just an "honest to God" spontaneous and impetuous reaction of the moment without thinking, so without interpretive consequence, or whether this is a calculated scene to countermand some problem with angel worship in Asia Minor, on the order of the Colossian heresy (Col 2:18). Consult the commentaries.

timony of Jesus is confessional fortitude, and this holding fast to the confession of who Jesus is and what he has done is the very "spirit of prophecy." All New Testament prophecy is about Jesus, whose story is the gospel. All who speak a word about Jesus are "prophesying," because to tell someone about Jesus is to reveal to them their future.

	Vision of Heaven	Vision of Babylon
Sovereignty of God	Rev 4 Throne Vision	Rev 18 Fallen Babylon
Salvation of His Christ	Rev 5 Lamb Vision	Rev 19 Heavenly Rider

FIGURE 11.69. Parallel Structure. The Vision of Heaven and Vision of Babylon have parallel thematic structure on the sovereignty of God and the salvation of his Christ.

Rider: Christ's Perspective (19:11–21). The Heavenly Rider scene is Christ's perspective on the Bowl judgments. The story of Babylon conquered is an integral part of the fall of Babylon sequence.[157] The fall of Babylon has two angles. The first angle is the story of God's sovereign judgment, which Rome laments but heaven celebrates (Rev 18). The second angle is the story of God's saving Christ (Rev 19). Thus, literarily, the two-scene sequence involving God and Christ for picturing the fall of Babylon in Rev 18–19 structurally and theologically builds on a similar sequence involving God and Christ in the Vision of Heaven in Rev 4–5. John's unified literary strategy comes together. We conclude from this parallel literary structure that the Heavenly Rider scene of Rev 19 is *not* intended by John as a picture of the second coming of Jesus. Rather, *the Heavenly Rider scene of Rev 19 parallels the slaughtered Lamb scene of Rev 5 and, therefore, is a picture of the gospel impact of the first coming of Jesus.* Jesus in his incarnation, death, and resurrection (1:5) has released the power of the gospel into lives of believers whose faithful confession conquers the Dragon, his beasts, and their mark and brings about the fall of Babylon, most

---

[157]*Contra* a number of outlines that assume the Heavenly Rider scene is the *beginning* of a new unit unrelated to the fall of Babylon episode. This assumption is more forced by the *presumption* that John presents the second coming in Rev 19:11–21 than by narrative analysis, a presuppositional stance that needs to be challenged seriously to understand the integrated and consistent movement of the entire Dragon Cycle.

powerfully in martyrdom, which is the supreme act of "keeping" the "testimony of Jesus." The beast can kill the believer but not silence the voice. Further arguing against Rev 19:11–21 as John's portrayal of the second coming is the absence of resurrection, the preeminent event associated with the parousia in the New Testament.[158] Finally, a repeated sword out of the mouth clinches the argument: the same Jesus presently addressing John and the seven churches is the actor here.

The Heavenly Rider scene telling the story of Babylon conquered is based on Isaiah's divine warrior imagery for God (Isa 63:1–6). John, however, has completely inverted the imagery of the blood. In Isaiah, the blood is the smattered blood of God's enemies. John, however, has sublimated Isaiah's imagery to the gospel. The blood is the slaughtered blood of Jesus.[159]

The Rider Described (19:11–16). Throughout the scene that unfolds, the language used to describe the Rider shows intratextual echoes to other imagery for Jesus in Revelation, including the Son of Man (Inaugural Vision), the Lamb (Vision of Heaven), and the one speaking in the Seven Letters. The description alone of the Rider is the bulk of the entire scene, which indicates John's focus is the person of Jesus. Such descriptions build on existing themes and ideas in Revelation.

- "white horse" (19:11): parade animal; Roman triumph theme of a victory parade down the streets of Rome, such as Titus's triumph after the First Jewish War. Riding on a parade animal means the war already has been fought and won.

- "Faithful and True": witness theme (cf. 1:5; 3:14); characteristics of Jesus' followers; contradicts Roman lies about conquest and peace.

- "judges, makes war": Roman conquest theme; Christ's judgment in this conquest, however—unlike Rome's—expresses true righteousness and is the foundation for the later white throne of judgment.

- "eyes, flame of fire" (19:12): judgment theme (cf. 1:14; 2:18). This insight is the reason for the true judgment he can render.

---

[158]New Testament passages associated with the second coming of Jesus include Matt 16:28; 24–25; 26:64; Mark 13:26–27; 4:62; Luke 12:40; 17:22–37; 21:25–36; John 14:3; 1 Cor 1:7–8; 15:20–28; 2 Cor 1:14; Phil 1:6, 10; 2:16; 3:20; 1 Thess 4:16–17; 2 Thess 2:1–12; Heb 9:28; Jas 5:7–8; 1 Pet 1:7; 2 Pet 3:1–15.

[159]Arguments are given in discussing John's use of the Old Testament, pp. 232–35.

FIGURE 11.70. Triumphal Quadriga (Horses of St. Mark). This magnificent set of Roman bronze horses, originally a quadriga scene (four-horse carriage for chariot racing), was the façade of St. Mark's Basilica in Venice, Italy taken from the sack of Constantinople in 1204, and illustrates horses groomed for show as parade animals.

- "many diadems": sovereignty theme; "many" in contrast to the Dragon (12:3) and the beast (13:1). This supports the following "King of Kings, and Lord of Lords" language.

FIGURE 11.71. Gold Myrtle Wreath Crown. This gold crown from 330 B.C. was found in the cemetery of Pydna, Macedonia. Such crowns show centuries of heritage using crowns for political and religious symbols and signs of power, worn for public appearances and religious ceremonies (TAM).

- "unknown name": the name theme of the Seven Letters in terms of confession of Jesus (2:3, 13; 3:8, 12) that corresponds to the "new name" no one knows given to believers at Pergamum (2:17). This name probably is Jesus' own "new name" written on the Laodiceans (3:12). Name is power in the ancient world, which is the idea behind magical incantations, in which names are accumulated by the magician to gain mastery over other powers; this is the story of Simon the magician in Acts 8, Elymas the magician in the court of the proconsul Sergius Paulus on the island of Cyprus, whom Paul blinded temporarily in Acts 13, and the burning of "magic books" in Ephesus in Acts 19. Jesus' name is unknown to the magicians in the royal court of Rome, which makes him the higher power that breaks the power of their incantations, exactly how the Son of Man breaks the spell of Babylon's "sorcery" in 18:23.[160] These are the lies of the imperial cult, the worship of the beast, and unrestrained commercial lust, and is like Nahum's attack on Nineveh (Nah 3:4).

- "baptized in blood" (19:13): slaughtered Lamb theme; Christ's own blood (cf. 1:5; 5:6, 9, 12; 7:14; 12:11), a premier Revelation image.

- "Word of God": witness theme. The word of testimony is the sole weapon for conquering, which is the sword out of the mouth of the Son of Man (1:16; 2:12, 16; 19:15, 21). This thought as the Word of God also resonates with the prologue to the Gospel of John.[161] The Johannine Word theology has two characteristics that John of Patmos uses. First, Johannine Word theology of the prologue plays out a witness theme throughout the Gospel: "He came as a witness to testify to the light, so that all might believe through him" (John 1:7). Second, Johannine Word theology of the prologue is incarnational: "and the Word became flesh and tabernacled among us" (John 1:14). Thus, through this title's intertextual echo to Johannine Word theology, John of Patmos means to indicate that his Rider

---

[160] The word is *pharmakeia* (φαρμακεία) from which we obtain "pharmacy."

[161] Acknowledging an intertextual echo with the Gospel of John no more proves the author of Revelation was the author of the Gospel of John than does Revelation's final grace benediction in an epistolary form that exactly mimics the distinctive signature ending all of the apostle Paul's letters means the author of Revelation is the apostle Paul (22:21). Both mean John of Patmos worked in the same region where two of the most famous and literary apostles had long teaching ministries with major impact.

scene is to evoke Word theology of the Johannine prologue on two themes crucial to Revelation—witness and incarnation. The witness theme speaks to the needs of a confessional crisis in the churches of first-century Asia Minor. The incarnation theme is crucial to the Christology of Revelation and supports John's emphasis on the gospel as the revelation of Jesus Christ. What we need to know about the future is in the past. Any future victory is secured in the reality of the cross. Both John of Patmos and John the apostle are in agreement that the war with evil was fought in the incarnation. John of Patmos, however, will distinguish himself from the apostle by adding a layer of futurism to the realized eschatology of the Gospel of John with his theme of the future passion of the church.

- "heaven's armies " (19:14): a Roman conquest theme, but completely sublimated to gospel realities. The battle "armor" is priestly vestments of white linen. The "battle" horses are the customary white parade animals of a Roman triumph, an emulation of the Rider who leads them. This depiction is no army a Roman would recognize and is obviously metaphorical.

FIGURE 11.72. Arch of Septimius Severus. Dedicated A.D. 203, this massive arch in the Roman Forum commemorates Rome's final victories over the Parthians. The Arch of Titus is in the background of the central archway.

- "from his mouth a sharp sword" (19:15): Son of Man theme, precisely the description in the Inaugural Vision. This actor is exactly the same as the one presently addressing John and the churches.

- "rod of iron": messianic theme (cf. Ps 2:8–9), the fulfillment of messianic expectation in the Old Testament, but in unexpected ways. This sword, rod, and following winepress are three images giving three perspectives on the nature of this rule as God's judgment.

- "treads the winepress": a divine judgment theme, derived from Isa 63:1–6, but as already innovated by John in the conquest prelude in 14:17–20 that leads into the Bowl judgments. These Bowl judgments then are recapitulated as a bedecked harlot and then as doomed Babylon in two successive chapters in Rev 17–18. God's wrath is expressed as vindication. The winepress image is the third of three perspectives on the judgment nature of his rule. Thus, the Heavenly Rider is an expression of the judgment of God. Through such judgment images, the Rider scene recapitulates the fall of Babylon scene in Rev 18. Jesus is Rome's Armageddon.

FIGURE 11.73. Olive Press. Tread by a donkey attached to the arm, this olive press squeezed olives to release oil to be collected in urns. Olive and grape vineyards were key to ancient economy (KAM).

- "King of kings, and Lord of lords" (19:16): sovereign rule theme; earth's supreme power, God's supreme representative, and Rome's ultimate apocalypse; repeats Lamb's title in 17:14, securing identification of the Rider in Rev 19 as the slaughtered Lamb of Rev 5.

The Victory Described (19:17–21). Strangely, after all the lead up to the war by the extensive description of the Heavenly Rider and his armies, no war is described! This abrupt jump is precisely what we encountered with the Armageddon imagery in the Bowl sequence (16:16). All we get is a description of war *results*. Why? Like the Rider goes out from heaven to make war, but his vesture already is baptized in blood before the war even is described—*because the battle already has been fought*. This war is the war of the incarnation. This war was fought with Herod the Great slaying the infants of Bethlehem, Archelaus being too brutal for Jesus' parents to remain in Judea, Satan's temptations in the wilderness, the exorcism of demons, the curing of diseases, healing the blind and lame, the murderous opposition of Jewish leaders, the Garden of Gethsemane, and Roman crucifixion.[162]

---

[162] These indexes of the war of the incarnation are simply elements of the story preserved in the Gospels. Cf. Matt 2:16, 22; 4:1 (Mark 1:13; Luke 4:2); Matt 8:16; Mark 1:34; Luke 4:41; John 10:21; Luke 4:18–19; 7:20–23; John 11:46–53; Matt 26:39 (Mark 14:35–36); Mark 15:15 (Matt 27:26; Luke 23:24–25; John 19:16).

FIGURE 11.74. Second Crusaders Find First Crusader Remains. Crusaders come across the vanquished armies of Peter the Hermit and Walter the Penniless ravaged by scavenger birds who escape in startled flight at the sudden encounter with new troops. Woodcut by Gustave Doré (d. 1883).

An angel calls the scavenger birds to the "great supper of God" (19:17). This scene is the dark underside to the marriage supper of the Lamb. Instead of rejoicing, the image is tragic.[163] This graphic portrayal of ancient post-battle scenes is realistic. When whole armies were butchered, the dead were too many to bury. Corpses were left to the

[163]Modeled on Ezek 39:17–20, but with John's typical penchant for innovation.

birds and wild beasts. John's realistic war images have confused some, disappointed others, and distracted generally from his gospel message.

FIGURE 11.75. Douce Apocalypse, Rev 19:19. This unfinished illumination shows the Rider making war with the beast and kings of the earth. Notice the Saracen swords. This Medieval beast is the Muslim onslaught on Europe (ADEVA).

The beast and "kings of the earth" gather for war on the Rider (19:19). This false prophet is the second, land beast of Rev 13, who was renamed as the false prophet in the Bowl judgments in Rev 16:13. Narratively, the main characters of the Dragon Cycle are eliminated in the reverse order of their introduction. They entered the stage as Dragon, beasts, and Babylon. They depart as Babylon, beasts, and Dragon.[164] The issue is the same as Rev 13: false prophet, signs, deception, mark, worship. This scene seems to recapitulate other battles, such as Armageddon, though John makes no direct statement.

They gather, but no war is described, only that the beast and false prophet are "captured." Such brevity seems anticlimactic and is almost frustrating, because one would think the whole point dramatically is to describe the battle fought. At least, that is always the whole point in Hollywood—all the pyrotechnics and explosions computers can create

[164]Fiorenza, *Revelation: Vision of a Just World*, 103–04.

and budgets can afford. Clearly, the Hollywood emphasis on the actual battle fought is not John's. Why? Because John is compressing a story already told in the Gospels: this battle is the passion of Christ. Thus, John's focus is not on the historical battle fought outside Jerusalem at Golgotha, the place of the skull,[165] but on its *theological consequence*. The theological consequence of the cross is that evil in the world decisively is defeated. That decisive defeat worked by the cross is John's whole point, so he goes straight to the heart of the matter, the decisive defeat, which for John is imaged as the "lake of fire" (19:20). This lake of fire is the final disposition of evil in the world.[166] John alluded to the lake of fire by describing its characteristics without giving its name in the conquest prelude: "and they will be tormented with fire and sulfur . . . and the smoke of their torment goes up forever and ever" (14:10, 11). Jesus has similar statements, but he uses a different word that comes from a Hebrew background that English translators traditionally have used "hell" to translate.[167] While the words are different between Jesus and John, the ideas are parallel. Both ideas appear as irrevocable destinies, and both use the figure of fire.

The "rest" then are dealt with. Who exactly these are is not entirely clear. One may presume they are the kings of the earth and their armies of 19:19. Kings of the earth first enter the stage indirectly in the title of Jesus as "ruler of the kings of the earth" in the prologue (1:5). We have the "kings of the earth" who hide in the caves and rocks and mountains from the "wrath of the Lamb" in the climactic sixth Seal judgment (6:15–16). They do not reappear again until the harlot, Babylon sequence as those partnering with Rome's commercial enter-

---

[165] Matt 27:33; Mark 15:22; John 19:17.

[166] Our earlier statement applies: "Spiritually, the lake of fire is that reality to which sinful, incorrigible, unrepentant beings willfully have consigned themselves beyond which the redemptive efforts of God completely and eternally cease and to which no appeal ever can be made" (p. 307). The destiny is embraced willfully and entered irrevocably. In Revelation, no character consigned to the lake of fire ever reappears.

[167] Only in the Synoptics, but most occurrences in Matthew (only two in Mark and one in Luke); none in John. Cf. Matt 5:22, 29, 30; 10:28; 18:9; 23:15, 33; Mark 9:43, 47; Luke 12:5. James makes one reference discussing slander (Jas 3:6). The actual word translated "hell" is *Gehenna* (γέεννα), which is a Grecized form of a Hebrew word for the valley of the sons of Hinnom (Josh 15:8; 2 Chr 28:3; Jer 7:32). This valley was a ravine running south of Jerusalem and gained eschatological nuance as the place of God's final judgment in Jewish popular belief.

prise.¹⁶⁸ One might presume here that both the fall of Babylon and the Heavenly Rider scenes are other ways of playing out the conceptually odd "wrath of the Lamb" of the sixth Seal judgment. In the immediate context, the kings of the earth are part of the Babylon story. Yet, though they are destroyed completely here in this Rider scene, "kings of the earth" abruptly show up in the final vision bringing their "glory" to New Jerusalem (21:24).

In any case, "the rest were killed with the sword that came out of the mouth of the Rider" (19:21). That is some awkward way to fight. No, of course that is "obvious" metaphor. So how do we get from this "obvious" metaphor to a literal military engagement of tanks, planes, guns, and bombs? With the "sword out of the mouth" John is back to the core of the opening Son of Man imagery (1:16) and the realization of the victory anticipated in the hymn about how the Lamb and his followers conquer the Dragon (12:11). This metaphor speaks to the preaching of the gospel. The war in Revelation is a war of words. For Jesus, the words were the words of truth he revealed about his Father (John 12:49–50). For believers, the words are confessional. The words are the words of salvation and eternal life in Jesus (John 6:68). The sword out of the mouth is this battle of gospel truth. What destroys Babylon or any evil is the truth of the gospel. No other battle matters. What we get consistently in Revelation's martial metaphors is imagery of judgment, not any actual battle descriptions.

For many years I held the same assumption as almost anyone else that this passage of the Heavenly Rider has to be John's portrait of the second coming in Revelation. That this assumption needed to be questioned never occurred to me until I did a narrative analysis of the Dragon Cycle focused on character development. As a result of this analysis, the Dragon Cycle fell into place compositionally in a much more integrated and consistent manner, and the Rider scene suddenly was seen to go integrally with what just had been narrated rather than opening up a brand new topic in a sudden right turn. That is when the outline changed, and the Rider scene of Rev 19:11–20 became integral to the development of the Dragon Cycle and the fall of Babylon story and not this new topic coming as a sudden, unconnected, and abrupt "thrusting into the story" of a piece of Christian doctrine, as if John

---

¹⁶⁸Rev 17:2, 18; 18:3, 9.

were running out of papyrus and suddenly realized he had not included the second coming in his Apocalypse about the second coming.

Admittedly, New Testament imagery for the parousia[169] is quite diverse. The Synoptics gravitate to Danielic imagery of the Son of Man coming on clouds and gathering the elect (Mark 13:26–27). Paul gravitates to apocalyptic imagery, such as an archangel, with sounding the trumpet, and reference to resurrection (1 Thess 4:16–17). John prefers instead abiding metaphors and relationships like absence and return, preparing a place, anticipating a reunion (John 14:3). James leans on prophetic ideas such as the Old Testament Day of the Lord or coming of the Lord as the basis for his ethical admonitions (Jas 5:7–8). Then, to one-up everyone, 2 Peter uses Stoic imagery of the pyric dissolution of the elements, calling for a new heaven and a new earth (2 Pet 3:1–15). To these can be added other miscellaneous concepts.[170] The imagery is non-uniform, which insinuates we should not get too rigid in trying to visualize this truth. Elaborate scenarios deny this exegetical ambiguity, and most that are based on Revelation's martial imagery grossly have misunderstood John's point.

What I would like to add to the discussion is this: theologically, we must do a better job of integrating the first coming into our concept of the second coming. We have to come to terms with our obsession of Revelation as "about the future" and "the second coming" and drawing truly distorted, even perverted, images of the coming Messiah *when John's master image for Jesus is a slaughtered Lamb.* John uses the Rider image *only once* in Revelation. He uses the Lamb image over and over. The Lamb image is crucial and signals two important ideas for our theological reflection about the second coming. First, the slaughtered Lamb signals the nature of the struggle: faithful witness. Second, the slaughtered Lamb signals the nature of the victory: self-sacrifice. The first coming predicates the second coming. So, the first coming ended with Jesus on a cross. The second coming is triggered by the church on a cross. The two cannot be divorced functionally nor theologically, and both should be informed by a sound ecclesiology

---

[169]Which means "appearing," and is a transliteration of the Greek word *parousia*, παρουσία, used in the New Testament for the second coming of Jesus.

[170]1 Cor 1:7–8; 15:20–28; 2 Cor 1:14; Phil 1:6, 10; 2:16; 3:20; 2 Thess 2:1–12; Heb 9:28; 1 Pet 1:7.

and soteriology. Jesus will not be conquering evil any differently in the future than he did in the past. The future of Revelation is in the past.

Millennium: Martyr's Perspective (20:1–6). The millennial reign is the martyr's perspective on the Bowl judgments. Instead of the opening vision of the Son of Man, interpreters of the Apocalypse seized on the millennium as the crucial image. Major theories of the millennium have dominated and vexed eschatological thought for millennia. Entire eschatological systems receive their names as prefixes to the lexical root of the word millennium. Frustration with the entire enterprise is expressed in the wag, "All I know is, I'm definitely pro-millennial."

Why beat on this dead eschatological horse? Because fools rush in where angels fear to tread.[171] The history of interpretation from the chiliasts to Augustine to Protestant futurists says we will not end the discussion. Yet, we at least can insist on exegetical contextualization. What does *John* do with the image? He uses the imagery to continue to develop a full spectrum of perspectives on the Bowl judgments. The scene is presented in two short parts; the first is the binding of the Dragon; the second is the consequent millennial reign.

<u>Dragon Binding (20:1–3)</u>. John's structure throughout the Dragon Cycle is somewhat amorphous. Repeated expressions may not reveal much in terms of structure, since these might be simply minor scene transitions. For example, John's "Then I saw" that begins the Heavenly Rider scene might give the impression he now is punctuating major structural elements with this grammatical marker. However, careful observation shows he only loosely distributes this expression for scene transitions, three times each in Rev 19 and Rev 20, and once in Rev 21:

- "Then I saw heaven opened" (19:11)
- "Then I saw an angel standing" (19:17)
- "Then I saw the beast and the kings of the earth" (19:19)
- "Then I saw an angel coming down from heaven" (20:1)
- "Then I saw thrones" (20:4)
- "Then I saw a great white throne" (20:11)
- "Then I saw a new heaven and a new earth" (21:1)

---

[171] Alexander Pope (d. 1744), *An Essay On Criticism* (1711), line 625.

That John's "then I saw" is not really a structural marker probably is indicated in the narrow range of verses over which this expression occurs in these locations. The first three are over only nine verses, and the next three are over only eleven verses. The conclusion is that the millennium scene, even though this scene begins with a "Then I saw," is not actually a major break from the structural movement that has flowed fairly continuously throughout the entire Dragon Cycle. Such a continuous movement would make sense if the Dragon Cycle is character driven, and the characters never have changed.

FIGURE 11.76. Luther Bible, Rev 20:2. Woodcut in the 1522 Luther Bible of the angel with the key to the Abyss binding the Dragon. The binding of the Dragon is the prelude to the millennium, so they mutually interpret each other (Taschen).

An angel has a key to the bottomless pit (20:1). We know this pit from other places in Revelation:

- Trumpets: the bottomless pit of the fifth trumpet judgment that produces the locust army and their king, Apollyon (9:1–11)

- Two Witnesses: the bottomless pit that produces the beast who kills the two witnesses (11:1–7)

- Great Harlot: the bottomless pit that produces the beast upon which the harlot rides, but who goes to destruction (17:8)

We can deduce this pit is the cosmic abode of evil. This pit functions as the counterpart to heaven, but the reader never goes there. One never will see into the dark heart of evil, only its incarnation in beings who are evil to the core, whose hearts are as dark as the pit from which they derive. The Dragon character who launched the second half of the Judgment Cycle now comes back on stage. He has been offstage for four chapters, last heard from in the Bowl judgments, where, with beast and false prophet, he produced three unclean, demonic spirits like frogs to assemble the kings of the world for battle on the great day of God Almighty (16:13). With this Dragon character, John brings the reader back to the cosmic perspective on the local struggle of the seven churches, the core contribution of the Dragon Cycle.

The Dragon is seized, bound, and locked in the Abyss (20:2–3). His triple identity is serpent, Devil, Satan. John really wants to nail this character's identification to cover all the biblical bases from Genesis through Job on into the New Testament. Note that his multiple identification is repeated almost word for word from his introduction (12:9). The repetition forms a literary identity *inclusio* over the Dragon Cycle. The identity *inclusio* indicates the Dragon Cycle is drawing to a close.

Binding imagery comes from Jewish tradition.[172] A triple binding means the security of imprisonment. The triple binding is a metaphor for God's sovereignty. Incarceration denies the Dragon a chance to deceive the nations until a prescribed period of a thousand years is completed. We are told he will be released for a short while after the thousand years, but not why. Evil is powerful, but not unrestrained.

Martyr Reign (20:4–6). John then sees an ambiguous set of thrones of judgment (20:4). He does not say how many, nor does he even say where, such as earth, heaven, or elsewhere. Further, their occupants remain anonymous. The singular point John makes about the throne occupants is an authority to judge. However, again, who or what they judge actually is not explicitly stated. All of these factors leave the function of these thrones and their occupants in the scene ambiguous. Perhaps they participate in the judgment of martyrs, but such action is not explicit. Ambiguity with the thrones and their occupants means their function exegetically is not hugely important. They are like accessory furniture of a heavenly courtroom, so to speak. Perhaps their

---

[172] Isa 24:21:22; *1 En.* 10:4–6; *2 Bar.* 40; *Jubilees* 10:4–14; 2 Pet 2:4; Jude 6.

purpose is to help communicate a forensic setting. Thus, we at least know the scene unfolding is judicial.

John next sees the most crucial clue to the proper interpretation of this passage, almost always either overlooked or not fully integrated into the contextual meaning.

> Then I saw ... the souls of those who had been beheaded for their testimony to Jesus and for the word of God. They had not worshipped the beast or its image and had not received its mark on their foreheads or their hands. They came to life and reigned with Christ a thousand years (Rev 20:4).

We need to make several critical observations. First, *this reign is not focused on Jesus*. This reign is focused on martyrs of the beast. The reign is not new for Jesus. The reign is new for martyrs. Jesus has been reigning ever since the ascension. This is Luke's whole point with the double ascension narratives at the end of the Gospel (Luke 24:51) and the beginning of Acts (Acts 1:9). Further, this present reign of Jesus is acknowledged by every New Testament writer who mentions this or any related topic.[173] Thus, what is new about the millennial reign is not that Jesus suddenly has begun to reign. What is new is that martyrs from the beast persecution have joined Jesus in his present reign. The martyrs of the beast have been vindicated by the Messiah who initiated the Judgment Cycle. The millennial reign reverses the Dragon's actions, including the Dragon's false deception ("deceive no more," 20:3), and false verdict ("beheaded" to "came to life"). The coming of the kingdom of God could include the concept of an interim kingdom in Jewish apocalyptic writings. Messiah typically is involved, but the length of time varies considerably for symbolic significance.[174]

Second, *John provides no indication whatsoever of the location of this reign*. Jesus' present reign in glory is in heaven at the throne of God. Nothing whatsoever prevents this millennial reign of martyrs correspondingly being in heaven. Further, as for the emphasis in premillennial theories of a millennial reign on earth, besides a corruption

---

[173]Cf. Matt 27:53; Luke 1:33; Acts 7:55; 9:17; Rom 6:4; 1 Cor 2:8; 15:23, 25; 2 Cor 3:18; Eph 3:16; Phil 2:11; 3:21; 4:19; Col 3:4; 1 Thess 2:19; 3:13; 4:15; 5:23; 2 Thess 1:9; 2:1, 8; 1 Tim 3:16; 2 Tim 1:10; 2:12; 4:1, 8; Titus 2:13; Heb 1:3; 2:9; 9:24, 28; Jas 5:7, 8; 1 Pet 1:11, 21; 4:13; 5:1, 4; 2 Pet 1:16, 17; 3:4; 1 John 2:28; Jude 24.

[174]2 Esd 7:26–44; 12:31–34; *1 En.* 91:11–17; *2 Bar.* 29:1—30:5; 40:1–4; 72:2—74:3.

reformulating the spiritual idea of the kingdom of God into a Medieval European monarchy, repositioning Jesus' reign from heaven to earth is a *demotion* of status, not a promotion.

Third, *these are not all believers of all time.* John's specific details defy that identification. The context is fully first century; these are persecuted believers who experienced their confessional crisis in a Roman court that resulted in their death. Though under the weight of Roman criminalization, they kept their testimony to Jesus and the word of God. Their death is by beheading, which is Roman jurisprudence normally reserved for Roman citizens.[175] This death follows the paradigm of John the Baptist as the forerunner of the Messiah, and the tradition of the apostle Paul.[176] They refused to worship the beast, which is the Roman imperial cult. Neither did they receive the mark of the beast, which is Roman commerce. *These specifically are martyrs of the beast.* Twenty years after Revelation was written, these were believers hauled before the Roman governor Pliny and brought to a confessional showdown in his Roman court and then executed. Roman citizens Pliny remanded to Rome, who suffered the same fate almost by occasion of being remanded to the emperor. Even Pliny himself acknowledged that a similar scenario had repeated itself some "twenty years" earlier, which is the timeframe of the book of Revelation.[177] Thus, interpreting the "millennial reign" as another of John's vibrant images for the first-century Asia Minor crisis is fully congruent with the internal literary context of Revelation itself, as well as with the external historical context of Domitian, especially through the interpretive lens of Pliny and Trajan some few years later. John's millennial reign, taken in the larger context of the Seven Letters, seems to be John's theological portrayal of the probable fate of Antipas, "my faithful witness, who was killed among you, where Satan lives" (2:13).

The crucial declaration of the millennium is that martyrs of the beast currently reign with Christ (20:6). Thus, the witness victory of the martyrs is what binds the Dragon, who has been trying to deceive the nations through his special agents of the beasts. By having the

---

[175] Stevens, "Capital Crimes in the Roman Empire," 60–63. Justin Martyr *Dial.* 110.4; Livy 30.43.13; Josephus *Ant.* 20.117; Dio Cassius 66.15.4–5.

[176] Matt 14:1–12; Mark 6:14–28; Luke 9:7–9. Eusebius *H.E.* 2.25.

[177] Pliny *Letters* 10.96. The Latin reads twenty years. Twenty-five is an emendation.

beasts kill those who refused the mark of the beast, the Dragon sorely miscalculated. Martyr deaths only magnified their voice. The voice of Christian martyrs decisively exposes the deceit of the Dragon worked through imperial ideology of the Roman empire of the first century.[178] Martyr witness conquers the beast and binds the Dragon. The martyr millennial reign, in other words, is the story of the two witnesses dying and rising again in the Trumpets interlude (11:7–11); "finishing their testimony" is martyrdom, because their death immediately ensues.

With this millennial reign of martyrs, John reframes the situation of Antipas. Rome decreed death. God decreed life. Present martyrs of the beast have their reward immediately viewed from the perspective of the truth of the eternal gospel (14:6): "they came to life and reigned with Christ a thousand years." What the Son of Man promised earlier in the Seven Letters "to those who conquer," to Antipas is delivered:

- Ephesus: to eat of the tree of life in the paradise of God (2:7)

- Smyrna: shall not be hurt by the second death (2:11)

- Pergamum: hidden manna, white stone with new name (2:17)

- Thyatira: power over the nations, rule with rod of iron, morning star (2:26–28)

- Sardis: clothed in white garments, book of life, confessed before God (3:5)

- Philadelphia: pillar in God's temple, name of God, New Jerusalem, my own (3:12)

- Laodicea: sit with me on my throne (3:21)

Especially pertinent is the last promise to Laodicea, "to sit with me on my throne." This status is precisely the millennial reign of Rev 20:4.

John has set up an eschatological millennial reign with Jesus for martyrs of the Roman juggernaut, so this idea John has to relate in some way to resurrection doctrine. Whatever the philosophical and eschatological headaches John has induced among theologians, and against the best advice of his editors, he explained: "This is the first resurrection" (20:5). The "rest of the dead" make their debut after this

---

[178]Which has yet to be repeated in as virulent, idolatrous, and evil a form as in the imperial cult of Rome claiming to be God and in total control of all levels of society.

millennial reign of the beast's martyrs. This post-millennial raising apparently is the "second resurrection," even though John never actually says that. John's "dual resurrection" terminology is not easy to interpret, simply because resurrection always is just "the resurrection" in the New Testament outside this one passage in Revelation. The incident Matthew reports in Jerusalem is not a resurrection scene (Matt 27:52–53). Matthew's "out of the tombs" miracle is nothing more than a Synoptic correlate to the raising of Lazarus. The raising of Lazarus never is spoken of as a resurrection event. Lazarus came back from the grave only to die again, as with other raising from death miracles in the New Testament (cf. Mark 5:41). They are miracles of biological life but not eternal life. So, basically, we have nothing to work with by analogy in the New Testament. All we have is John and this context.

Perhaps what John means to say is that this "first resurrection," even without a corresponding mention of "second resurrection," is the first of two theological perspectives he presents on the one resurrecttion truth. For John, resurrection is a doctrine that addresses the realization of the promises of the Seven Letters for believers. Yet, John also believes that martyrs have a special place in heaven. His "first resurrection" seems to be an attempt to interrelate those two convictions. He simply wants to create a special place for martyrs of the beast and uses an innovation on resurrection to do so. For John, believers who give their lives particularly on behalf of their confession of Jesus are particularly close to the paradigm of the cross, the essence of discipleship, and the heart of Jesus. He might have chosen other ways to present this perspective, but that is our problem, apparently, not his.

Jewish traditions had multiple calculations on the length of the messianic reign based on the biblical significance of given numbers. Thus, forty is the time of wilderness wanderings, four hundred is the period of Egyptian slavery, and so forth. John's thousand years is a large number for a long time. The length of the church age is left indeterminate. Perhaps John did not think the period too long. Still, he chose a large number. Probably the logic and symbolic significance of his choice ever will remain as elusive as the number of the beast.[179]

---

[179]How a thousand-year reign for Jesus at the end of history compensates for a six thousand year reign of Satan in history (Adso's calculations) is just incomprehensible. Jesus got ripped off. He ought to ask for a new contract. The literal argument of a literal thousand years is specious. Clearly, the number is metaphorical in some way.

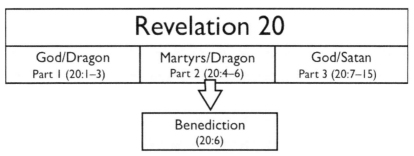

FIGURE 11.77. Millennium Intercalation. A literary technique similar to the beginning of the Dragon Cycle. The literary emphasis is put on the benediction's declaration.

The martyr millennial reign is intercalated between divine binding and loosing episodes in 20:1–3 and 20:7–15. Compare Michael's war intercalated into the story of the Woman and the Dragon (12:7–12). The literary burden of both of John's Dragon intercalations is to emphasize declarations made within them. The Michael declaration is the hymn's crux verse of 12:11. The martyr declaration is the benediction's crux verse of 20:6. (Note, however, that here the story changes radically with the Satan loosing episode—*the Dragon disappears.*)

The benediction is a blessing spoken on the martyrs resurrected to their special thousand-year reign with Christ (20:6). What we learn through this benediction is that these reigning martyrs have secured a destiny out of reach of the second death, which is the lake of fire. Further, we are told they are priests of God and of Christ. *Announcing a reign of priests in the millennium here is precisely the declaration in the introduction to Revelation,* that Jesus has "made us to be a kingdom, priests" (1:6). This declaration is reiterated in the Vision of Heaven as "made them to be a kingdom and priests" (5:10). So, in the millennial reign, we are back to the beginning of Revelation. The "made them to be a kingdom and priests" at the beginning of Revelation is a reference to the millennial reign of the martyrs at the end of the Dragon Cycle. The martyrs are "priests" because they faithfully have ministered the word of the gospel on earth and now minister in the eternal correlate of that kingdom in heaven.[180] While this martyr reign is conceived as *coincident* with the church age, the peculiar qualifications of the participants means the millennial reign is *not* the reign of the whole church in this age. Strictly speaking in Revelation, these are beast martyrs.

---

[180]Quite similar to Paul's imagery about himself in Rom 15:16.

Thus, the millennial reign is a review of the Dragon Cycle consequence from the perspective of the martyrs of the beast. John gives them special honor because they especially followed the path of the cross in the war with the Dragon. They victoriously defeated the Dragon's schemes to rob God of his glory on earth through an idolatrous imperial cult in the very manner of their death, choosing Christ over Caesar, ultimately forever denying the Dragon any confessional victory precisely by their martyr death. Words of truth live forever. If we speak the truth, Satan is defeated eternally.

Historically, what conquers Rome is the internal weight of her own sin and the external forces of evil she herself has inspired through the sorceries of her own imperial ideology. Spiritually, what conquers Rome is the gospel of Jesus Christ. The church will be one barbarian tribe on the spiritual fringes of the empire that Rome never will conquer. Instead, the church will conquer Rome. However, we must be clear that this victory most certainly is *not* the story of Constantine. This victory is the story of Antipas.

John is not advocating martyrdom or seeking martyrdom. John is just being realistic about what he already has seen from the beast in his world. He sees evil's dark heart has dark prospects for the church.

Climax: Satan's Defeat (20:7–10)

We now arrive at the probable place in Revelation where the future is contemplated. If John is foretelling in Revelation, Gog and Magog is probably that prophecy. Here is the end of the world for which everyone has been looking. John does not give us much when he addresses the end of history and the second coming of Jesus. This brevity about the actual event is par for the course with the New Testament pattern of comments on this topic, and John hardly gives us any more than we already have in other writers. This brevity and our frustration with the lack of detail may be why we scavenge around the rest of the book for anything else to substitute for the second coming, including the Rider scene in Rev 19. We just do not want to accept that John did not know any more about the second coming of Jesus than any other inspired New Testament writer. What John *does* do is to consolidate the idea that this event is the passion of the church that parallels the passion of the Son of Man and precipitates the parousia. This third unit of the Rev 20 intercalation is so distinct as to function almost independently.

Within John's context in Revelation, the Gog and Magog scene is the "hour of trial that is going to come upon the whole world in order to test the inhabitants of the earth" revealed to the Philadelphians in the Seven Letters (3:10). Thus, this Gog and Magog scene is intended by John to depict the end of the world, so is his eschatological climax.

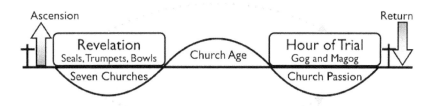

FIGURE 11.78. Gog and Magog as the Hour of Trial. This hour of trial is the church's own passion story in following the Son of Man revealed to the Philadelphians. John profiled this final crisis with Satan from his own first-century crisis with Rome.

The real solution in Revelation is *not* the millennium. We could destroy the beasts from the land and sea and still not take care of the problem of evil Revelation contemplates, because the Dragon always could stand on sea and land and bring forth more beasts. If we do not deal with the Dragon himself decisively, then we have not solved the problem of evil. Thus, the most important truth here is *not* the destruction of the Roman empire. Destroying Rome is not the solution to the problem that the book of Revelation posits. Satan must be destroyed, not Rome.

John harnesses Ezekiel's Gog and Magog imagery (Ezek 38–39), because this imagery typically was understood by Jewish interpreters to be situated on that prophetic horizon at the end of history. This traditional reading of the Gog and Magog imagery is what suggests that John here intends to foreshadow "the end" with his development of this scene. However, as usual, John innovates. In Ezekiel, Gog is the leader of the abstract nation Magog. John, however, converts Gog into another abstract nation. This move is helpful to his purposes, because by doing so he can globalize opposition from one nation in Ezekiel to all the nations in his own scene. Globalizing opposition to all the nations logically transforms Ezekiel's specific source of Magog as one nation attacking from the "north." In John's scene the source of the Gog and Magog confederacy of nations is all points of the compass.

Gog and Magog is the story of the final passion of the church. Her martyr witness to ultimate death will parallel the passion of Christ.

The loosing of Satan in 20:7 that kicks off the Gog and Magog conflict stands out on three counts. First, *John makes the timing ambiguous.* John just says "when" (20:7). The end of the thousand years is indeterminate, because the beginning never is specified. Further, John offers no sequence to facilitate detailed calculation of this beginning point, and, hence, end point. He intentionally is vague, which means calculation is not the point. He just starts a new episode at the end of the thousand years, but since the thousand years is unfixed, no linear timeline is established or even hinted. Ambiguity about the temporal location of the millennium allows the figure's one-thousand year time frame to serve the symbolic purpose for which the image was created to be coextensive with the church age, however long that age will be.

Second, *John shifts the tense from past to future.* The future tense means he is writing about something other than his own context. We no longer are in the first-century setting of imperial Rome. Even the immediately prior Dragon binding and millennial reign of the martyrs in 20:1–6 are consistently past tense. However, when John gets to the Gog and Magog story, he abruptly shifts to future tense: "When the thousand years are ended, Satan *will be released.*"[181] John has shifted the tense almost imperceptibly. Thus, Gog and Magog is not the ongoing tale of the first-century church but the trial of the future church.

Third, *John shifts the name from Dragon to Satan.* He noticeably changes his style of designation. This post-millennium story is about Satan. The Dragon designation used up to the start of the millennium is dropped precipitously. Dragon is used exclusively for the opponent of God's people throughout the Dragon Cycle. Even though associated with the Dragon at the beginning in 12:9, *the designation Satan never appears again throughout the rest of the Dragon Cycle.* Only in the Gog and Magog scene here in Rev 20 does the name Satan reappear to be a character that moves the plot. The Dragon character suddenly drops off the narrative radar—never to be mentioned or heard from again. Why? Because the Dragon character was John's special way to present the story of first-century Rome in particular, and John's story now no longer figures Rome and this first-century context. Thus, the Gog and

---

[181] Rev 20:7; emphasis added.

11—Judgment of the World   513

Magog scene brings the Judgment Cycle to a climax by way of using this past conflict of the church with Rome as a paradigm for the future conflict of the church with Gog and Magog. The unit moves into new territory uncovered by John to this point in his narrative. That new future dimension of the story is the meaning of Satan showing up suddenly again after an eight-chapter absence. Satan's appearance is prefigured in the Trumpets interlude's two witnesses: "when they have finished their testimony, the beast that comes up from the bottomless pit will make war on them and conquer them and kill them" (11:7).

Notice carefully what we do *not* have here. Given all the Twitter-like trending of end-timers: no end-time charts; not even a whisper of a so-called Antichrist; no schematics for battle plans of Armageddon. Nothing. Just Satan and Gog and Magog out in the indefinite future. Big clue: The crisis will be so huge the church will not have to guess!

FIGURE 11.79. Douce Apocalypse, Rev 20:7–8. Illumination of Satan released from the Abyss to lead Gog and Magog for the final assault on the church (ADEVA).

Satan is released by God's sovereignty. Somehow, Satan just never gets the picture that nowhere in the entire biblical storyline does he ever get to initiate. God always "allows." Satan never decides anything of which God is unaware nor ever acts unilaterally without God's consent. You would think he had gotten the message of sovereignty, but seems like some characters just never learn. He comes out to "deceive the nations" (20:8). We know what this looks like. This is some reality that reprises the features of Rome's empire, ideology, and cult. This is *not* a revived Roman empire that has to trace some genealogy, political or geographical, back to ancient Rome. This trial is not Great Britain or the United States or the United Nations or the European Common Market or the World Council of Churches or any other wild ideas of Internet peyote. This is worse. Confessing Christ out of fear one might die and go to hell is not enough of a confession. Those who only are buying divine fire insurance will capitulate their "faith" during the real fires of the Gog and Magog persecution. The Gog and Magog episode, therefore, will generate the great apostasy.[182]

These come from the "four corners of the earth" (20:8). This is global, like ancient Rome, only worse, because this trial is really global. (Rome was huge, but basically a broad extension of the Mediterranean basin.) A new character now is brought onto Revelation's stage: Gog and Magog. This verse is the *only* New Testament mention of Gog and Magog. These are Ezekiel's final opponents of the people of God. False etymologies "discovered" Gog and Magog to be communist Russia, which seemed to make a lot of sense at the time of the Cold War of the twentieth century, but this was before the Russian empire imploded in the 1980s. After that, this was Saddam Hussein and Iraq, but this was before Desert Storm and the "mother of all battles" of the 1990s. Then, this was Osama bin Laden and Islamic fundamentalists, but this was before he was killed in a raid in Pakistan in the 2000s. We keep trying. China's recent rise economically is waiting in the wings to keep end-timers blogging and happily preoccupied with gruesome thoughts.

Truth is, Ezekiel's figures are not a nation. They are Gog and Magog. That is, they are an abstraction—even for Ezekiel. For John's purposes, whoever and whatever persecutes the church qualifies. The real problem is, Satan gathers them, so they have considerable power, and "they are as numerous as the sands of the sea" (20:8). That figure pretty much means uncountable in the apocalyptic codebook.

They "march" over the whole breadth of the earth and "surround the camp of the saints and the beloved city" (20:9). John's language is

---

[182]John's Gog and Magog scene shares several thematic and descriptive similarities with Paul's great apostasy and the "man of lawlessness" (2 Thess 2:1–12).

just ambiguous enough to make his point. He is drawing on the Jewish background of Zion, King David's capital fortress, as the ever beloved, favored city of God, place of refuge and salvation.[183] John used Zion imagery in the conquest prelude of the Lamb standing on Mount Zion with the 144,000 (14:1). Now in this Gog and Magog scene, however, while wanting to use traditional Jewish Zion traditions to elicit ideas of God's favored protection for God's people in distress, John here distinctly avoids associating Ezekiel's Gog and Magog imagery with historical Jerusalem by avoiding the term Zion. John is not talking about Israel, and John is not talking about Jerusalem. John is talking about the church, because he says only vaguely, "the beloved city" and not specifically Zion, and then he uses the distinctive Pauline word for the people of God, "the saints."[184] This advance against the church then surrounds her hopelessly, like Jerusalem walled up by Sennacherib's Assyrian armies (2 Kgs 19:32–35). The Gog and Magog situation is hopeless because John has made absolutely clear that this is a huge army of incalculable numbers with the most formidable leader of all the forces of darkness from the depths of the Abyss. Against this awe-

---

[183] 2 Sam 5:7; Ps 2:6; 9:11; 14:7; 48:2, 11; 50:2; 53:6; 69:35; 76:2; 78:68; 84:7; 87:2; 102:13, 16, 21; 110:2; 125:1; 132:13; 146:10; Isa 1:27; 2:3; 4:5; 12:6; 14:32; 24:23; 28:16; 31:4; 34:8; 51:11; 52:1, 7; 59:20; 60:14; 62:11; Jer 31:12; 50:5; Joel 2:32; 3:17; Obad 17; Mic 4:2, 7, 8, 13; Zeph 3:14; Zech 1:14; 2:10; 8:3; 9:9. Some of these traditions are picked up in the New Testament; cf. Matt 21:5; John 12:15; Rom 9:33; 11:26; Heb 12:22; 1 Pet 2:6.

[184] That is, *tōn hagiōn*, τῶν ἁγίων. In the plural as a reference to God's people, only once in the Hebrew Scriptures (Ps 83:3 = 82:4, LXX), and only twice in the Apocrypha (Wis 5:5; 18:9, LXX). Even in the New Testament, occurrences outside of Paul are rare. Cf. Matt 27:52; Acts 9:32, 41; 26:10; Heb 6:10; 13:24; Jude 3. The term, however is frequent in Paul. Cf. Rom 12:13; 15:26; 16:2; 1 Cor 6:1; 14:33; 2 Cor 9:12; Eph 2:19; 4:12; 6:18; Col 1:12; 1 Thess 3:13; Phlm 7. Therefore, the extremely low incidence outside of Paul but high incidence inside Paul indicates that "the saints" is the premier Pauline term for the church in the New Testament and is quite distinctively Pauline. When one considers the prevalence of this term in Revelation (5:8; 8:3, 4; 13:7, 10; 14:12; 17:6; 19:8; 20:9), and adds John's use of the distinctive Pauline epistolary grace benediction (22:21), then one can conclude John of Patmos has been impacted by the Pauline ministry in Asia Minor. One even could speculate wildly that Paul's reference to a person who had had a vision and was exalted to the "third heaven" (2 Cor 12:2), which most commentators take as a modest self-reference by Paul—who, by the way, was not known among his peers for his modesty (Phil 3:4–6)—actually could be a possible reference to the visionary revelator, John of Patmos. Of course, as admitted, that is wild speculation, but what a fascinating kind of thought!

some scene, Armageddon from the Bowl judgments fades into insignificance like a pencil sketch on a dinner napkin. We hold our breath for the imminent slaughter of the saints.

Then, as always in every single martial metaphor in Revelation without exception—no actual battle ever is described! The massive siege of this mighty force boils down to one sentence: "And fire came down from heaven and consumed them" (20:9). The end. What? I demand a refund on my movie ticket. John may be worn out from writing by now and just wants to dispense with the script and call it a day.

FIGURE 11.80. Apocalypse Tapestry, Rev 20:9–10. The battle of Gog and Magog, fire from heaven, and the final lake of fire (Angers, France).

Or, maybe not. John has written nineteen chapters to give the profile of this war. This war is prefigured in all of Revelation, in the struggles of the seven churches of Asia Minor revealed in the Seven Letters and then through the grand Judgment Cycle revealed in the Seal and Trumpet judgments driving the Christ Cycle and the Dragon, beasts, and Babylon characters driving the Dragon Cycle. John has been prefiguring this final conflict all along. Thus, if one compresses all of Revelation's images of judgment into that one sentence noting fire from heaven, the Gog and Magog conflict has been designed by John to play out the passion of the church that presages the parousia of Christ. John does not say what this battle looks like for the church, but a vision of a bruised, battered, bleeding, scourged, naked, crucified Jesus hanging on a cross is suggestive. John's language of fire "from heaven" means the sovereign, creator God consummates his own final victory. Jesus was faithful, even to death on a cross, and God stunned the world with the resurrection of Jesus. With divine and unknowable wisdom (Rom 11:33–36), God will vindicate the church similarly, as implied in the story of the two witnesses in the Trumpets interlude who are killed and three and a half days later raised, similar to the death, burial and resurrection of Jesus (11:11–12). That vindication is tied up with the return of Christ (1:7).

John unfolds this scene in a way that has intimations of passion. He has gained prescient insight from his struggle to understand the Antipas incident in Pergamum and his own presence on the island of Patmos in the context of first-century Rome. He perceives that God sent him the vision of Revelation because his experience with Rome in the first century was to be the paradigm for the final assault of Satan on the church. The Dragon Cycle prospect is Gog and Magog, and Gog and Magog is the prospect of the passion of the church. What Rome accomplished as an empire never has been repeated in history, so John seems to be right on track with his forecast.

Recall that seal seven was silence to hear the prayers of the saints (8:1). These prayers come into focus with Gog and Magog and include the Lord's Prayer taught to the disciples, since that prayer is deeply eschatological in almost every line.[185] The opening line, "your kingdom come," will not find its final fruition until Gog and Magog. The "lead us not into temptation" has its most pertinent context in the Gog and Magog hour of trial. The plea, "deliver us from evil," is a redux of Jesus in Gethsemane. With this prayer, Jesus always has been training the church how to pray in her great Gog and Magog hour of trial.

For John, the result of the Gog and Magog conflict is God's final solution to evil. The heart of evil is consigned to the irrevocable lake of fire. There the Devil is cast to join his own beast and the false prophet (20:10). The cosmic forces of the Dragon Cycle have been consigned and consumed, never to appear again in John's drama. John does not ruminate on philosophical implications. Annihilation, however, is not supported by the language of "tormented day and night forever and ever" (20:10). Regardless these issues, John's singular point is simply that evil has its final solution in the outcome of the Gog and Magog affair. The bottom line is the lake of fire is irrevocable and forever.

[185]Matt 6:9–13; Luke 11:2–4.

Climax: God's Judgment (20:11–15)

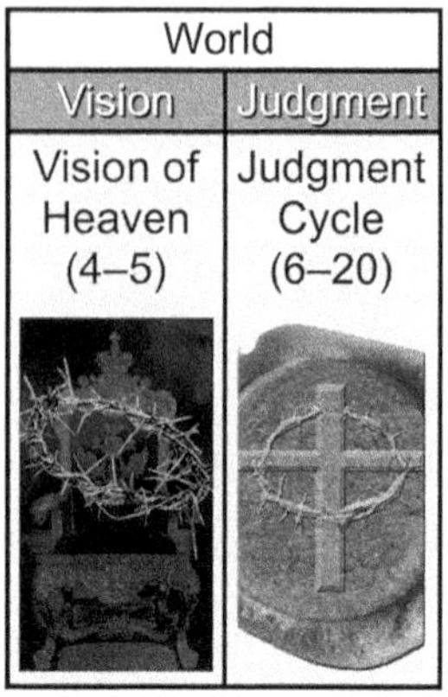

Time for final judgment. Narratively, John's great white throne vision in Rev 20 takes us all the way back to the throne room vision of Rev 4, which provided the theological foundation of the following Judgment Cycle. Thus, with this concluding vision of a great white throne of judgment, we have a throne room *inclusio* for the entire Judgment Cycle. John's complex drama started with God's throne and now intentionally ends with that same throne. The Judgment Cycle climaxes here. All that God is doing as both sovereign creator and saving redeemer is moving reality to final judgment in Christ. This great white throne is the last judgment in which God will consummate all creation's purposes. God brings creation to its intended Sabbath rest. God the Almighty is sovereign over all.

FIGURE 11.81. Judgment of the World.

That God is the one sitting on the throne is indicated by the reaction of the cosmos: "the earth and the heaven fled from his presence" (20:11). The language of cosmic disturbance, such as earth and heaven fleeing, is standard apocalyptic rhetoric. This scene appears similar to the cataclysmic and cosmic judgment depicted in the sixth seal:

> the sun become black as sackcloth, the full moon became like blood, and the stars of the sky fell to the earth as the fig tree drops its winter fruit when shaken by a gale. The sky vanished like a scroll rolling itself up, and every mountain and island was removed form its place (Rev 6:12b–14).

These similar descriptions reinforce the concept that the triadic heptads of the Seals, Trumpets, and Bowls recapitulate back to the same point of God's final judgment for dramatic effect. In addition, in the sixth seal, kings of the earth, magnates, generals, rich and powerful, and everyone slave and free (that pretty much covers all of society) tried to hide in caves and rocks of the mountains (6:15). We know now that those attempting to avoid this cataclysmic judgment in the sixth seal were not successful. That the judgment is inescapable is carried by the additional comment in this great white throne scene: "and no place was found for them." This inescapability is God's sovereignty.

John then sees the dead standing before this throne. The imagery of a judgment throne seems loosely based on Jewish tradition about Daniel's Ancient of Days and picked up in the New Testament.[186] He later explains these dead derive from any known place of the dead, including the sea, and Death and Hades (20:13). The judgment is inclusive in social rank (great, small) and circumstance (sea, Death, Hades). To be lost at sea was a terrible fate in the ancient world, since the spirit did not have proper dispossession of the body, and one would be separated in death from kin; further, performing proper burial was so important in society this deed was an act of piety.[187] John's point about the sea is that even those considered not properly buried and, therefore, supposedly lost forever are included in this great white throne. Mention of Death and Hades brings the story full circle back to the Inaugural Vision of the Son of Man, who has the keys of Death and Hades by the power of resurrection (1:18). To be sure, this great white throne is God's judgment, but Rev 4–5 indicates that this judgment is expressed through the slaughtered Lamb.

Judicial books of deeds done are opened, and the book of life (20:12). The book of life already has featured in Revelation,[188] which is also the book of the Lamb.[189] Judgment is on the basis of these books. The books are the royal court records important to the administration of any ancient kingdom.[190] This judgment is according to "what they had done" (20:13). At first blush, this judgment has the appearance of a works righteousness, but not contextually. All of Revelation has been about witness, testimony of Jesus, and word of God in a context of confessional conflict. The deeds done would relate to that context. For the seven churches of Asia Minor, these are the deeds of confessing the lordship of Christ, not Caesar. These are the deeds of worshipping Christ, not Caesar. These are the deeds of faithful living in a fatefully

---

[186] Dan 7:9–15, 27; e.g., Matt 19:28; Luke 22:30.

[187] Cf. 1 Kgs 13:21; 14:11; Jer 8:1–2; Tob 1–2.

[188] Letter to Sardis (3:5); the story of the great harlot (17:8).

[189] Beasts story of the Dragon Cycle (13:8), repeated in the New Jerusalem (21:27).

[190] In Jewish tradition, cf. Exod 32:32–33; Ps 69:28; Dan 12:1. In the Persian period, these are documents of administration and record keeping. In the later Greco-Roman period, we have the maintaining of city registers (cf. census of Augustus, Luke 2:4–5). The New Testament allusions include Luke 10:20; Phil 4:3; Heb 12:23. In Revelation, cf. 3:5; 13:8; 17:8; 20:12, 15; 21:27.

fallen world consumed by paganism and imperial ideology. For the church through history, the object may not be Caesar, but the issue is the same. Rejection of Christ and the failure properly to glorify God is the fountainhead of all deeds condemned at the great white throne. As Reddish observed about this final image, "What was inevitable since Easter morning has now become reality."[191]

FIGURE 11.82. Fresco of Christ's Judgment of the World. Magnificent fresco of Christ's judgment of the world by the Renaissance artists Fra Angelico and Benozzo Gozzoli on the ceiling of the Chapel of the Madonna di San Brizio in Orvieto, Italy.

Death and Hades are thrown into the lake of fire (20:14). This action is the symbolic equivalent of Paul's exclamation based on Hos 13:14, "O Death, where is your victory? O Death, where is your sting?" (1 Cor 15:55). Since death is the consequence of sin (Rom 1:32), then consignment of Death and Hades to the lake of fire is the end of sin. These realities of the old age are banished from the new creation. John explains the lake of fire as the "second death." For John, the first death is not a final adjudication of destiny. One still awaits being raised for the great white throne judgment. The great white throne of judgment is the "second death," meaning, "real death," since its consequence is irrevocable destiny in the lake of fire. This lake of fire image is unique to John. Satan, the beast and false prophet, and those who worshipped the beast are there, in John's image, in torment forever. John's picture sets up theological issues we leave to the systematic theologians.

[191] Reddish, *Revelation*, 390.

The only reality standing between the dead raised for judgment and the destiny of the lake of fire is being written in the Lamb's book of life (20:15). That enrollment would have required a decision before now. That enrollment would have required answering Jesus' question, "But who do you say that I am?" (Mark 8:29). The cross is judgment.

John's great white throne of judgment at the end of the book is the equivalent of the coming of the Son of Man in clouds of glory at the beginning of the book (1:7). This great white throne is the Danielic Ancient of Days conducting the great assize of the world. The passion of the church has triggered the parousia of Christ, and in that parousia the Son of Man (1:13) merges functions with the Ancient of Days (20:11), even as the description in the Inaugural Vision is intended to intimate (1:13–16). With head and hair white like snow, with eyes like a flame of fire, and with a face as the sun shining at noonday, the Son of Man is experienced as the Ancient of Days, and the dead are raised, and the world is judged. This majestic movement makes Revelation a supremely fitting book with which to end the Bible.

FIGURE 11.83. Mosaic of Christ's Last Judgment. Mosaic of Christ's last judgment of the world in the ceiling of the Florence Baptistery (Battistero di San Giovanni) by Coppo di Marcovaldo. At Christ's right hand, rewards of the saved leaving tombs in joy, and at Christ's left hand, punishments of the damned (cf. the parable of the sheep and the goats, Matt 25:31–46).

SUMMARY

The second act of John's drama is the judgment of the world. The act opens with a Vision of Heaven, which lays the theological foundation for the judgment of the world. Two great images occur in this vision, a throne and a slaughtered Lamb. These images convey the theology of the book as they contain in a nutshell the sovereignty of God and the salvation of his Christ. God expresses his sovereignty precisely through an incarnate Jesus who brings the gospel to reality in his life, death, and resurrection. This gospel unleashes forces of salvation and judgment on the world that eventually will conspire to bring history to a consummation. For those who follow Christ, the gospel is a call to faithful witness in the testimony of Jesus and the word of God that is a war of words against the lies of evil. This war is a confessional crisis in an assault on the fortresses of paganism and godlessness. For those who do not follow Christ, the gospel is judgment, being delivered over to the inherent self-destructive forces of evil that operate in history. God creates, creation rebels, Christ redeems. In this story, eschatology is creation theology consummated. Whatever we think of God's sovereignty, that truth must be conceptualized in a cruciform shape. What makes theology Christian is the cross. God never will present a fuller revelation of how all this works than Jesus dying on a cross.

The slaughtered Lamb is worthy to open the book, which inaugurates the messianic judgments of the Christ Cycle. These are followed by the cosmic judgments of the Dragon Cycle. These two recapitulating cycles create the Judgment Cycle, comprising the bulk of John's Apocalypse. The theme is the first-century Roman empire as paradigmatic of any empire that flaunts its power and might in God's face.

The structure of the Christ Cycle is based on a series of two judgment heptads, the Seals and the Trumpets. These two heptads parallel each other in structure. In each, the first four judgments are a unit. The sixth is a climactic finale evoking the end of the world, followed by an interlude before the seventh. The Seals interlude has two parts. These parts reassure the outcome for God's people because of God's sealing. The Trumpets interlude also has two parts. The first recommissions John to write more, which alludes to the upcoming Dragon Cycle. The second part symbolizes the witnessing church in her confessional crisis. The story of the two witnesses dying and rising figures the death and resurrection to millennial reign of martyrs in conflict with Rome. That story, however, also prefigures the final passion of the whole church in the final Gog and Magog battle that concludes the Judgment Cycle. The seventh judgment in both the Seals and the Trumpets is anticlimactic, due to the inherent climactic nature of the sixth. The seventh is discovered to be not as much a judgment as a narrative transition in a telescopic fashion to the next narrative unit.

The structure of the Dragon Cycle appears to be more like a kaleidoscope driven by characters. One keeps seeing different images but is turning the same cylinder. The contents in the cylinder lens never change. They just rearrange themselves in new and fascinating configurations with each twist of the cylinder. This Dragon goes after the Woman's child, then the Woman herself, then the Woman's other children after being cast down to earth. In this pursuit of the other children, the Dragon calls two beasts to his alliance. They all work idolatry through the sorcery of lies, deception, and demonic spirits.

This evil is judged through messianic conquest. The judgment is anticipated in a proleptic prelude that emphasizes the Lamb and his victorious followers. The judgment is portrayed as the Bowls of God's wrath. This Bowls series is presented as the third and final heptad of judgments, related to the Seals and Trumpets, but used differently as drama and not as a plot structuring device. The messianic conquest in the Bowls judgment is followed by four different perspectives on the judgment of the wrath of God in the Bowls within the context of their application to the first-century crisis of Rome and the church. These perspectives are those of the prophet, heaven, Christ, and the martyr.

The first perspective is how God's prophets, such as John and the prophets of Asia Minor with whom he mutually ministers to the seven churches, see the conflict: Rome as a great, idolatrous harlot seducing the world, riding on the back of this evil beast. The Bowls judgment then is presented from heaven's perspective on the conflict: Rome as a grand empire like Babylon of old—proud, mighty, master of all—yet from God's perspective doomed to a cataclysmic destruction, like its own Pompeii. The third perspective presents the Bowls judgment as how Christ sees the conflict: Rome as a confessional crisis for his churches who are to conquer as did he, with the sword coming out of his mouth, in their faithful gospel testimony. John turns the Dragon Cycle kaleidoscope one more time. A fourth perspective on the Bowls judgment presents how confessional martyrs see the conflict: Rome as declaring a sentence of death, but God invalidating this judgment with the martyrs' resurrection reign. In his martyr reign, John innovates on the idea of resurrection to make his point. He does not mean to invent two resurrections, which he knows is tautologous eschatologically. He intends to symbolize two theological truths about resurrection. One truth is that God especially honors faithfulness unto death even in the present reign of Jesus. The other truth is that God will judge the whole world. Yet, through Messiah, God already has. Without Jesus' death on the cross, we would not have a great white throne of judgment.

The Judgment Cycle is about gospel forces at work in history in God's Messiah and his church. This messianic story leads to an inevitable climax in Gog and Magog—the hour of trial coming upon the whole world and the passion of the church. The church is called to do what Jesus did, to carry a cross that ends life in this world. The good news in this ecclesial passion is that the church's faithfulness to her call will trigger a climatic resurrection event that ends history, as Jesus' own death triggered a resurrection event within history. This final resurrection is integral to the series of events related to the second coming of Jesus, which is the coming of the Ancient of Days, and the whole world is judged and consigned to eternal destiny. One destiny is the lake of fire. The other destiny is the New Jerusalem, a story yet to be told, the third and final act in John's drama.

A topical outline of the Dragon Cycle drama in the second half of the Judgment Cycle might be helpful. The following is suggestive:

    II. Dragon Cycle (12—20)
        A. Cosmic Conflict (12—13)
           a. Dragon Attack (12)
           b. Beast Agents (13)
        B. Messianic Conquest (14—20)
           a. Conquest Prelude (14)
           b. Bowl Judgments (15—16)
           c. Bowl Perspectives (17—20)
        C. Eschatological Climax (20)

12

Hope of Heaven

God and Christ and Their Victory

JUDGMENT IS COMPLETED, SO THIS Vision of Victory stands alone and is not prelude to a following story like the other two visions of the Son of Man in the Inaugural Vision is prelude to the Seven Letters and the Vision of Heaven is prelude to the crisis of the Judgment Cycle. The church has completed her gospel call to take up a cross, and her passion has transformed eternity as Jesus' passion transformed history, and God is sovereign over all.

What remains now is for John to wrap up his drama with a nice literary bow. He has purchased his present, but he needs to enclose his gift in some gorgeous wrapping paper of eternity tied off with a glittering bow of final justice and vindication before putting under the tree for the reader to discover on Christmas morning. His literary gift is to assure the follower of Jesus where the path of passion leads no matter how dark the journey.

FIGURE 12.1. Revelation, Act 3. A view of victory.

THE NEW JERUSALEM (21:1—22:5)

The master image of this new unit is the New Jerusalem. The new heaven and new earth are necessary only as a backdrop of a suitable symbolic space for the City of God. New Jerusalem descends (21:1–4), and God directly addresses his people. To hear directly from God in the Apocalypse is rare. Images of eternal life drive the passage (21:5–8). John's ecstatic experience offers a description of the eternal city in great detail with vivid metaphors (21:9–27). John then uses an Eden transcended motif to communicate creation consummated (22:1–4). A final image of New Jerusalem as the realization of the kingdom of God ties the entire biblical witness together and completes John's brilliant picture of eternity in his Vision of Victory (22:5). God wins.

The new material uses Jewish traditions. The new creation motif comes from Isa 65:17–19. The idea of "new" has two possibilities, and which one John means is not entirely clear. New can be renewed, as in the earth cleansed, or new can be recreated, as in the earth destroyed. Jewish opinion on the matter varied.[1] John does not provide us clarity because he does not really need to. This element is only necessary as suitable symbolic space preparing a special place for a special city.

The eschatological Jerusalem is another Jewish tradition. The historical city was glorified into a metaphorical city in apocalyptic literature and often seen in terms of bridal imagery of Zion as the wife of Yahweh, especially from Hosea.[2] Most significant in this regard is the symbolic use of the figure of a woman who suddenly transforms before the seer's eyes into the preexistent, heavenly Zion in an apocalyptic writer who was a contemporary of John.[3] Another tradition of the eschatological Jerusalem is the mountain of God.[4] Pagan myths told stories about a divine city of the gods in heaven, a significant feature in Babylonian legends with their emphasis on the astral sphere.

We also catch other bits and pieces from elsewhere in the Old Testament. Gates of pearl are reflected in Isa 54:12, and the Gentiles bringing their riches to Jerusalem in Isa 60:3–11. The jewels of a high priest's breastplate are emphasized in Ezek 18:12–14, and the river and tree of life in Ezek 47. One also is reminded of Solomon's temple being gold covered, or the importance of streams of water as sources of life.

---

[1] Renewed: *2 Bar.* 3:4–6; *Jub.* 4:26; 23:8. Recreated: 2 Esd 7:29–31; *Sib. Or.* 5.476–78; *1 En.* 83:3–4; 91:14–16. Human stewardship is integral to creation doctrine. A future destruction is not license to ravage earth's resources. How we behave toward God's creation reflects what we think of God. Cf. Cate, "How Green Was John's World?"

[2] Tob 13:16–18; Isa 49:14–16; 50:1–3.

[3] 2 Esd 10:25–27.

[4] On the pattern of Mount Olympus of the Greek gods; cf. Ezek 28:16; Isa 14:13.

John continues his innovations. Use of the number twelve illustrates. The twelve gates of the city originally derives from the twelve divisions of the Zodiac. John transforms them into the twelve tribes of Israel. Again, the twelve foundations normally would be a place of honoraria inscribed with names of public works benefactors in pagan temples, but John makes them into the twelve apostles of the Lamb. A final example is the heavenly city. Normally, this would have been conceived as the abode of the gods far off in heaven, absolutely inaccessible to humans, like crown prince Thor's Asgard in the superhero movie. John turns heaven's inaccessibility on its head by making no one have to go there; instead, his New Jerusalem comes down to earth, like circumventing Asgard's gatekeeper of the Bifröst time travel between the nine worlds. In this inventive and effective way, John has Jesus fulfill all human starry-eyed visions of a city of the gods.

New Jerusalem Descending (21:1–4)

Isaiah's famous image of a new heaven and new earth is the necessary setting for John for the New Jerusalem that will feature in a few verses. John's concern is not the how, when, why, but to set up the place for the heavenly city. The cosmos God finishes becomes the eternal residence where God lives. Sin's damage to the first heaven and the first earth is eradicated (21:1). Even though John will use great imagination to describe the place, his real point is not the place but the person. His real message is the intimate relationship between God and his people. No more sea is both mythic and Roman. The sea is dangerous, with its unpredictable, deadly storms such as the disciples and Jesus on the sea of Galilee, or Paul on journey to Rome, so an ancient religious symbol of chaos and rebellion. The sea, therefore, in Revelation is the source of the evil beast in Rev 13 and also supports the commerce of Rome, whose Roman merchants and seafarers thank the favor of the god Oceanus. God Almighty eliminates the sea as a source of evil and of the Roman empire.

New Jerusalem descends (21:2). Humans do not have to

FIGURE 12.2. Oceanus, Roman Sea God. Ancients thought of a world ocean (IAM).

scale the impossibly scalable mountain of God. Such mountains were too high to climb; thus, gods lived there. Instead, heaven comes down. The city is "as a bride adorned for her husband"; this new metaphor brings out the joyous intimacy of relationship. A voice declares:

> See! The tabernacle of God is among humans,
>   and he will tabernacle with them,
>   and they will be his people,
>   and God himself will be with them,
> And he will wipe away every tear from their eyes,
>   and death will not be anymore,
>   nor anymore mourning, crying, or pain.
>   The original age has passed away! (Rev 21:3–4)

FIGURE 12.3. Apocalypse Tapestry, Rev 21:2. John sees New Jerusalem descending from heaven to earth (Angers, France).

This proclamation is amazing to contemplate. Dwelling with God is the promise of a garden walk in the cool of the day (Gen 3:8). Jewish wilderness traditions of God's presence with his people in the pillar of cloud and fire and tabernacle traditions of God's resident Shekinah glory energize this entire motif. This word offers a new paradigm of relating to God directly without need for a mediating agent. God relating to humans above all creatures of the universe is the highest honor from the supreme patron of all of creation. An invitation to wicked Domitian's court is now revealed as disgraceful. "With humankind" is a theological axiom, the climax of biblical witness.

New Jerusalem Theophany (21:5–8)

A divine theophany ensues. The Creator announces the new creative act (21:5), which is what issues from the judgment of the world just narrated in the great white throne scene. Evil is eradicated. Faith is vindicated. Redemption power actually is inherent in creation power, even though hidden from normal view.[5] God promised heaven. God delivered heaven. All things God promised are delivered, and that fulfillment is why "these words are trustworthy and true" (21:5). John begins borrowing ideas from Isaiah and Ezekiel exactly at the point these prophets are dealing with the consummation of God's kingdom.

God then makes a second declaration: "It is done!" (21:6). The Greek tense indicates completed action with on-going consequences. The future already is accomplished from God's perspective. The point is the absolute surety of God's word. Creation is consummated in the Christ. This creation word will be played out more fully in 22:1–4.

God's third declaration is, "I am the Alpha and the Omega, the beginning and the end" (21:6). This word forms a divine title *inclusio* over the entire book (Rev 1:8). God bounds the book of Revelation with his own name. In his sovereignty he guarantees all the narrative in between those divine names, which is the whole book, the vision of the Son of Man, the Seven Letters, the Vision of Heaven, the Judgment Cycle, Gog and Magog. The end-game of the end-time is guaranteed. "The claim that God is Alpha and Omega, the beginning and the end, is not a vacuous or marginal statement for John. Indeed, this assertion is the major theological underpinning of John's entire Apocalypse."[6]

God's fourth declaration is the promise of the water of life. The allusion is to Isa 43:19. One first has to recognize the importance of access to fresh water in the ancient world, or today's world for that matter. Indoor plumbing simply did not exist—no sinks, bathtubs, showers, or running water just to turn on a spigot at will. The contrast here is with the third Bowl plague that struck the rivers and fresh water streams (16:4), and with Laodicea's emetic spiritual condition (3:15). Not only does God give life resources, God gives all life resources freely. This free access has prophetic nuance, as in Isaiah.[7]

---

[5] 2 Cor 5:17; Gal 6:15.
[6] Reddish, *Revelation*, 390.
[7] Cf. Isa 49:10; 55:1.

God's fifth declaration, "the one who conquers" (21:7), picks up the conquering theme of the promise section of the Seven Letters, unifying Jesus' word to the church at the beginning of Revelation with God's own word at the end. Once again, Roman ideology's conquest theme boomerangs back on the emperor and his empire. One problem with the Roman throne was its dynastic instability due to murders, plots, and schemes. Nero's suicide without an heir threw Rome into total chaos. The "will inherit" contrasts starkly the stability of God's people as heaven's heir, since the promise is from the sovereign God. Thus, a martyr's destiny never is heaven's question. Rather, God solemnly declares, "I will be God to that person, and they will be my child." The promise of an eternal relationship and the permanence of a heavenly inheritance is written in the blood of the slaughtered Lamb.

The contrast is the promise of eternal torment in the lake of fire, which is the second death (21:8). Second death and lake of fire metaphors now are integrated into divine relationship, which may provide insight into those metaphors—in or out of God's presence, conditions of before Eden and after Eden. Characteristics singled out for those relegated to the lake of fire are precisely those of the beast's followers: cowardly, faithless, polluted, murderers, fornicators, sorcerers, idolaters, liars. A progression surfaces. The cowardly are those who compromise with emperor worship as a matter of pragmatics but still want to pretend their faith is untouched. The faithless are worse; they are those whose faith is hypocrisy, completely absent a public confession. The liars are worse still; they are the false prophets who intentionally lead God's people astray, including Jezebel and the Nicolaitans. From beginning to end, Revelation is a war of words. John's conflict in Asia Minor with Rome and its perverted propaganda is not a local, temporary situation of no consequence. Rather, what needs to be heard in the seven churches is that what is going on in their congregations even in the moment Revelation is read has eternal consequences.

New Jerusalem Description (21:9–27)

John just will not let us forget the seven Bowl plagues. He transitions to a description of the New Jerusalem through one of the seven Bowl plague angels who invites him to see the bride and wife of the Lamb (21:9), just like John was invited by one of the seven Bowl plague angels to see the harlot riding on the beast (17:1). The connection is direct. The point is obvious. The seven last plagues are last because they are consummative. They finish God's work of judgment, and all that God is doing flows from his determination to make an end of evil. From them God judges Rome in history and Gog and Magog at the end of history.

John is carried away "in the spirit" (21:10).[8] He uses this expression only four times in Revelation: for the Inaugural Vision (1:10), the Vision of Heaven (4:2), the Babylon Vision (17:3), and the New Jerusalem Vision (21:10). Clearly, these are pivotal visions in the Apocalypse. The Babylon Vision of the harlot and the New Jerusalem Vision of the bride set up the contrast of Revelation as a tale of two cities.[9]

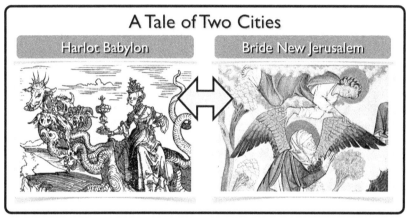

FIGURE 12.4. A Tale of Two Cities. The imagery between the Harlot City Babylon of Rev 17 and the Bride City New Jerusalem of Rev 21, when combined with the opening vision of the Woman clothed with the sun and the moon at her feet in Rev 12, is like a tale of two contrasting cities from the title of the classic Charles Dickens novel.

Verses 21:2 and 21:10 seem to repeat each other redundantly on the mention of the descending Jerusalem. However, John is using the descending Jerusalem image twice for introductory purposes, first to introduce the host and second to introduce the habitation. So, John now introduces the habitation by way of describing its appearance.

[8]The experience echoes Ezekiel's ecstatic state; cf. Ezek 40:1–2; 43:5. The echo may mean John intentionally is reconfiguring Ezekiel's eschatological temple.

[9]Beasley-Murray, *Revelation*, 315, many years ago was my first exposure to this idea playing off the classic 1859 Charles Dickens novel, *A Tale of Two Cities*, about London and Paris before and during the French Revolution.

The basic material is a "very rare jewel," a jasper-like crystal that is perfect to reflect God's glory uniformly throughout the city. The description parallels that in the Vision of Heaven (4:3). No surprise the city is a very rare jewel. Rome's trade in rare jewels (18:12) is now revealed as pathetic, tiny trinkets compared to an entire city built of gemstone. The symbol is that the whole city reflects God's very nature. This reflection carries forward the idea of a role fulfilled, the churches as seven lampstands being the only light in a dark world of evil (1:12).

FIGURE 12.5. Relief of Assyrian Assault on Lachish. The high walls are reflected in the steep angle of inclination. This relief from Sennacherib's palace in Nineveh chronicles in images Sennacherib's conquest of Lachish in his military campaign against King Hezekiah of Judah in the eighth century B.C., also recorded in 2 Kgs 18:13—19:37 and 2 Chr 32:1-23 (BML).

The city has a "great, high wall" (21:12). Walls were characteristic features of ancient cities. In the days before ballistic missiles and strategic bombers, strong, high walls were a city's best defense. The only offense was siege, and if a city could maintain her walls and her water, she could hold out for years. The extraordinary walls of Jerusalem that were fortified as part of Herod the Great's building projects was one of the reasons why the siege by Vespasian's troops in the First Jewish War took so long. The symbol of great, high walls is a way to represent the inviolable nature of fellowship with God that no force can break.

One of the greatest abilities of the Roman legions was in laying siege to a city. Roman engineers constructed ingenious siege engines, catapults, and battering rams, sometimes custom designed for particularly difficult challenges. One of their greatest conquests was of the

Jewish fortress of Masada at the Dead Sea after the First Jewish War. Jewish rebels fleeing Jerusalem led by the Zealot Eleazar held out in this Herodian fortress for three years. To get their siege engines up to the walls on the approachable west side, the Romans spent years making a ramp up which they could hoist their battering rams. The eroded ramp still is visible today after two thousand years, as well as outlines of Roman legion camps. However, no matter how hard they tried, not even the vaunted Roman legions could conquer New Jerusalem.

FIGURE 12.6. Masada Fortress. Tram leading up the steep incline to the precipice of Masada. Remains of a Roman army camp are in the lower right foreground.

FIGURE 12.7. Roman Siege. Left: aerial view of the outline of the remains of the eastern camp of the Roman legions attacking Masada. Right: the remains of the Roman siege ramp on the western side of the fortress still remaining to this day.

534 REVELATION: THE PAST AND FUTURE OF JOHN'S APOCALYPSE

John then symbolically combines historic and messianic Israel in descriptions of the gates and foundations. New Jerusalem has twelve gates, three gates each for the four compass points. The triple gate en-

FIGURE 12.8. Triple Arch Gate of Thyatira. The main entrance to the central agora of ancient Thyatira was through this triple gate.

FIGURE 12.9. Triple Arch Gate of Antioch of Pisidia. An artist's reconstruction of the main triple arch gate into ancient Antioch of Pisidia, one of the stops of the apostle Paul on the first missionary journey (Acts 13:14; YMY).

trance was a standard feature of Roman construction. Domitian recently had built a triple gate entrance for Laodicea's Syrian Street. A triple gate entrance was dedicated to Domitian at nearby Hierapolis by Frontinus.[10] Remains of Thyatira in modern Akhisar include the top arches of a triple gate into the central agora. John's innovation, in contrast to giving city gates the names of benefactors or emperors, is to give the New Jerusalem gates the names of Israel's twelve tribes. Thus, the heritage of the people of God from whom came the Messiah forever is honored and the imagery of the 144,000 in the Seals interlude (Rev 7) and in the vision of Zion in the conquest prelude (Rev 14) is integrated into the final vision of victory in the eternal city of God.

The city foundations are the twelve apostles as progenitors of the messianic people of God as the patriarchs were of the historical people of God. Israel's divine purpose from the beginning was fulfilled. For John, Jerusalem is one way to tell the two-stage story of the people of God, from nation to incarnation. The movement from historical Jerusalem to eternal Jerusalem is the story of the twelve tribes, Messiah, and the twelve apostles. John has inscribed this story into his imagery of New Jerusalem in the city gates and foundations.

FIGURE 12.10. Erastus Inscription at Corinth. The top line is ERASTVS PROAEDILI, "Erastus, Proaedile." The aedile was a public office in Rome for the supervision of public works. He also oversaw the organization of the ever-popular festivals and games. Thus, this office was highly sought after by career-minded politicians. Erastus previously had served in this role, hence, he is a "proaedile." Erastus donated the funds for paving this street that ran by the theater in ancient Corinth. This inscription in the paving stones honors this city benefactor who provided for this foundation for the traffic moving to and from the theater at Corinth. Credit: Jean M. Stevens.

The dimensions of the city are featured next (21:15–17). A measuring rod provided by an angel is similar to the measurement of the temple in the Trumpets interlude (11:1). While a simple form, from an

---

[10] See the illustrations, p. 358.

architectural point of view, the geometry is unclear. One cannot be sure whether the result is to be interpreted as cubic or trapezoidal. If cubic, the allusion may be to the Jewish holy of holies (1 Kgs 6:20). The city is so sacrosanct that its entire form is perfect holiness. If such an allusion is meant, the idea may be an alternate form of the kingdom and priests motif of the people of God John has used in the beginning (1:6), in the hymn of the slaughtered Lamb (5:10) and in the millennial reign (20:6). The symbol would represent a holy God's perfect presence with his holy people. If trapezoidal, the allusion might be in contrast to ancient Babylon's ziggurats. The building would be to contrast the pagan structures Babylon and Rome would feign to build.

FIGURE 12.11. Babylonian Ziggurat Model. One of several conceptualizations (PMB).

After the temple was destroyed by the Romans in the First Jewish War, Jews longed for its rebuilding, as after the Babylonian destruction. Postwar speculations on the dimensions were quite large, so that this temple could be conceived as glorious and a wonder of the world. No postwar Jewish temple speculation, however, even came close to approaching the dimensions John produces here for New Jerusalem—about 1500 miles in length, width, and height![11] The foundation would cover the Mediterranean basin, which might have been John's symbolic point: New Jerusalem swallows up the entire Roman empire in one city. Correspondingly, the wall, compared to normal ancient city walls, is disproportionately thick, at about 210 feet.[12] This city's eternal security is simply beyond any doubt.

The building material of the city as comprised of precious stones is described next (21:18–21). One can compare the description of Isa 54:11–12. The vision is fabulous beyond any imagination from anything ever seen even in the magnificent ancient royal cities. Romans adorned themselves with precious stones set into rings, bracelets, pendants, necklaces, and other jewelry. These gems were quarried all over

---

[11] An estimate for the 12,000 stadia measurement John gives (21:16).

[12] Using a Roman standard for the 144 cubits. Cubit measurement is ambiguous.

the world. Only a rich world enterprise could have fashioned them together so as to become the necklace of an elite Roman aristocrat. John takes what would have been one of such a series of small stones on a Roman necklace and transformed that small gem into entire walls and streets of this New Jerusalem. The picture would have been absolutely stunning to his audience. John does this, however, not to indulge his own commercial greed, but to put in the starkest terms the supreme superiority of what God offers to the believer over any little transient trinket of the empire.

FIGURE 12.12. Precious Stone Necklace. Jewelry of precious stones was highly prized among Romans. This beautiful piece from the terrace homes of Ephesus graced the neck of an elite Roman woman (EMS).

John puts a spiritual twist on every image to turn them into symbols of the reality of eternal relationship with God Almighty. The wall of jasper, for example, reflects God's own character when compared to the description of the throne room in the Vision of Heaven (4:3). The city itself of pure, transparent gold wildly surpasses all of Solomon's fabled glory. The foundations of precious stones may reflect the idea of the high priest's breastplate, but, if so, John innovates with different order and names (21:19–20).[13] Each city gate is a single pearl (21:21), which is inconceivable. The street, like the city in general, is pure gold, but transparent as glass—again, inconceivable, because gold is solid and opaque. This whole scene is so wonderful, which makes the hope of heaven the grandest hope for any human heart to hold.

The architecture is peculiar, even beyond Ezekiel's eschatological temple, because New Jerusalem has no temple (21:22)! John, however, does offer an explanation for the absence of a temple based on the tem-

---

[13] Cf. Exod 28:17–21; 39:10–14.

FIGURE 12.13. Jerusalem Temple Model. Ancient Jewish temple mount as rebuilt by Herod the Great on a scale of 1:50 (Holyland Model of Jerusalem, IMJ).

ple's function in historical Jerusalem to represent the presence of God with his people, where mediation between God and people took place to guarantee relationship and fellowship unbroken by sin. Since Death and Hades have been consigned to the lake of fire (20:14), then sin is eradicated. The need for a place of expiation to reconcile God and his people no longer is necessary. The slaughtered Lamb has made the sacrifice that has redeemed his own by his blood (1:5). Thus, John explains, "for its temple is the Lord God Almighty and the Lamb" (21:22). Such an image countermands Ezekiel and contradicts popular Jewish expectation about an eschatological Jerusalem. John's theological logic on the matter, however, is impeccable.

The cosmology likewise is peculiar (21:23–27). The original order of creation is transcended. No longer is the sun needed for light by day and the moon for light by night (Gen 1:16). Instead, light and lamp are God and the Lamb (21:23). This light motif serves to emphasize two ideas. One idea is the divine presence. God's glory outshines the sun, a brilliance that is intimated in the Inaugural Vision in the description of the face of the Son of Man (1:16). The prophet Isaiah had anticipated that the Holy One of Israel once again would glorify Jerusalem (Isa 60:19), and John has modulated this expectation to the New Jerusalem. Jesus had declared he was the "light of the world" (John 8:12), and John has modulated this gospel declaration into his imagery of New Jerusalem.

The light motif also serves to emphasize the prophetic expectation of the pilgrimage of Gentiles to Jerusalem bringing with them the wealth of the nations as an offering to God. John says, "The nations will walk by its light, and the kings of the earth will bring their glory into it" (21:24). The function here is clear. This action reverses the ruination of the nations and their resources by Rome. The proper use of all of earth's bounty returns to the God who created these resources to serve his purposes for life. This word is a role reversal of Babylon's sinful wealth, which only disguises perverted abuse. John reverses out the homage of the nations to harlot Babylon spelled out in detail in the dramatic lament of Rev 18. Homage to Jerusalem, in stark contrast to Babylon, is pure, unadulterated, and offered freely—the proper worship of the only God. In fact, God has no need of this wealth. All of creation already belongs to him.[14]

FIGURE 12.14. Sunrise on Cadillac Mountain. Morning sun first touches United States shores on Cadillac Mountain in Acadia National Park, highest point along the North Atlantic seaboard from October through March. John says God's glory means New Jerusalem has no need of the light of the sun.

The function is clear, but the storyline is not. The nations and the kings of the earth were the enemies of God and his people who were destroyed in the Gog and Magog scene (20:9). Their sudden reappearance here is mysterious, as that story did not leave any suggestions as

[14]Cf. Rev 4:7, 11.

to their possible rehabilitation or regeneration. Yet, the Gog and Magog scene itself also had its own character discrepancy, since the clear impression from the Heavenly Rider warrior scene is that "the rest were killed" (19:21). These apparent anomalies from scene to scene result from referential reading of martial imagery. We already have discussed how the Heavenly Rider scene has only one "weapon," and that weapon comes out of the mouth, and the warriors are clothed in thin, priestly linen. Thus, this conflict is no battle as fought by the legions of Rome. This battle is a war of words. John's metaphorical battle, in other words, is not to be pressed.[15] That this statement with its sudden appearance of the nations and kings destroyed in earlier episodes supports universal salvation in Revelation hyperextends John's metaphor illegitimately. At the same time, the "and they did not repent" recurring word in the Judgment Cycle does indicate that John is aware that God never judges such that he is not trying to save.[16] Further, the repeatedly expressed theme in the assessment and exhortation parts of the Seven Letters to the churches is the call to "repent."[17] Thus, in this life, even the churches have accountability to a sovereign God. No one is immune from God's judgment, and no one is stranded from God's grace. However, repentance is essential to access that grace. In the end, the sovereign God has the right to decide when grace is perverted into incorrigible indulgence and make a final and irrevocable consignment to the lake of fire. He has not chosen to allow a window into the divine wisdom that goes into that decision.

That the "gates never will be shut by day" (21:25) is the beautiful contemplation of the absence of rebellion anywhere in creation. The New Jerusalem never will take siege. No need for outlying villagers to rush madly to get inside the city at the approach of an invading army. The absence of night perhaps relates to deeds of darkness done under cover of night, so is the special season of evil. Evil simply does not exist and would not have opportunity to operate in any case. Enemies

---

[15] Hyperextension of metaphorical language is a classic mistake in reading and understanding. Notice the ubiquitous problem little children have with the adult metaphorical question, "Do you want to ask Jesus into your heart?"

[16] Rev 9:20, 21; 16:9, 11.

[17] All the churches except Smyrna and Philadelphia, who both receive only praise, conforming to each being at the same level in a chiastic arrangement of the letters. Cf. Rev 2:5, 16, 21, 22; 3:3, 19.

do not siege; evil does not assault. Instead, these inhabitants in this new heaven and new earth are only renewed people who bring the glory and honor of nations into New Jerusalem (21:26). This city has no "bad side of town." Presumably, Jezebel is not here.

Even though the gates of the city are open all the time (all day, and no night exists), "nothing unclean will enter it, nor anyone who practices abomination or falsehood, but only those who are written in the Lamb's book of life" (21:27). These evils are the characteristics of Babylon. The pollutions of the beast and idolatrous worship are gone. The falsehood of pagan idols who are no gods and the sorcerers' power that is no power is eliminated. Only those written in the Lamb's book of life have citizenship in the New Jerusalem. Jesus has delivered on his promise to Sardis: "and I will not blot your name out of the book of life" (3:5).[18]

New Jerusalem Consummation (22:1–4)

FIGURE 12.15. Apocalypse Tapestry, Rev 22:1. River of Life (Panel 6, Scene 82) shows God and the Lamb in their glory in a mandorla from which flows the water of life nourishing flowers and trees with abundant fruit evoking Eden before the fall. John is moving to join the Lord, and believers on the flank of the hill contemplate God's face (Angers, France).

John shifts to new imagery. John goes back to the past, because the future of Revelation is in the past. John now presents New Jerusalem as

[18] Cf. Rev 13:8; 17:8; 20:12, 15.

Eden transcended. Paradise renewal is a common apocalyptic motif, because this motif encompasses a premier reflection on a theology of creation. In essence, eschatology is just the last chapter in creation. Creation still has a Sabbath rest into which creation time is moving.[19] John's New Jerusalem is that Sabbath rest, or creation consummated. Garden of Eden imagery frequently is used to communicate these type of ideas in Jewish apocalyptic writers. John uses Eden imagery but innovates this imagery in three ways. These three ways involve the river of life, the divine curse, and divine fellowship.

Eden Image 1: River of Life (22:1–2)

FIGURE 12.16. Perge Canal. The main boulevard had a series of cascading pools of fresh water running down the middle of the street from the nymphaeum. Credit: Rzuwig, Creative Commons. (See Figure 11.42.)

John's first Eden innovation is the paradigmatic river of life. A river is integral to paradise imagery (Gen 2:10). This river is bright as crystal, indicating its purity. This "water of life" is the antidote to the problem of a lukewarm spiritual condition at Laodicea (3:16). John's river flows directly from God's throne, which innovates on Ezekiel's river, whose headwaters are in the eschatological temple on earth. New Jerusalem, however, has no temple, so its river flows directly from God, not from a piece of defunct architecture that used to represent God's presence

---

[19] A thought most fully developed in Heb 4–5 in the New Testament. Cf. Heb 4:9.

on earth. Flowing from the throne brings the narrative back to the throne of the Vision of Heaven (4:2).

That the river flows through the "middle of the street" means its access is immediate, easy, and universal. This easy water access right in the middle of the street is a counterpoint to the hundreds of miles of Roman aqueducts difficult to engineer and expensive to build and maintain necessary to supply fresh water to Rome's cities. One is reminded of the dramatic central boulevard of Perge that had cascading water pools down the middle of the colonnaded main street.

This river of the water of life supports the tree of life with twelve kinds of fruit for the twelve months of the year. Ezekiel had written about multiple trees (Ezek 47:7), but John brings this down to just one, probably on the idea of the one tree of life in Eden (Gen 2:9). Here in New Jerusalem, though, the fruit of this tree of life is not forbidden. This vision fulfills the promise of Jesus to Ephesus: "To him who overcomes I will give to eat of the tree of life, which is in the midst of the paradise of God" (2:7).

FIGURE 12.17. Date Palms of Galilee. Near Capernaum on the north shore of the Sea of Galilee always has yielded rich produce.

The leaves are for the "healing of the nations," an unusual idea on this other side of the great white throne, almost as suggesting something happened after Gog and Magog. John's nearest allusion comes in Rev 21:24, 26 in the discussion of New Jerusalem having no sun, but the nations walk by the light of God himself. At this point, we suddenly hear about nations when they had appeared to be wiped out only a chapter before. To ascribe the presence of the nations in New Jerusalem as "another of John's pointers to God's surprising and overwhelming grace,"[20] as if this might imply universalism, overworks the imagery of what John strictly never says and renders the entire Judgment Cycle no more than overwrought divine angst

[20] Reddish, *Revelation*, 420.

over incurable evil. Besides, if everyone gets saved, just snap the divine fingers now and be done with it. Phooey on plagues. What an absolute waste of time if everyone gets saved anyway. Rather than supporting universalism, a better contextual suggestion is that even though Gog and Magog was a global event among nations, this category does not mean all humans participated to a person. Further, if repentance truly was confessed by anyone during the Gog and Magog time, without doubt God would respond to save. Broad biblical testimony just does not support that God saves everyone regardless their own desire to be saved, most particularly the incorrigibly evil. Such a divine indulgence of sin was not true for ancient Jezebel, and probably was not true for Thyatira's Jezebel, and will not be true for any Jezebel of the future.

FIGURE 12.18. Bronze Relief, Creation of Adam and Eve. Panel on Gates of Paradise door of the Battistero di San Giovanni, Florence, Italy, by Ghiberti Lorenzo (d. 1455).

Eden Image 2: Divine Curse (22:3)

Eden is a tragedy ending in the divine curse (Gen 3:14–19). All of the salvation drama of the Old Testament is looking to reverse the curse, which is the pollution of human experience with transgression (Ezek

14:11). The curse disappears in New Jerusalem, because "the throne of God and the Lamb will be in it, and his servants will worship him" (22:3). Throne means power and sovereignty. That God is Almighty, declared over and over again in Revelation, means the God who sits on this throne has power and sovereignty to bring creation to its goal, which is the elimination of Eden's curse that facilitates the unhindered praise of God. That the Lamb sits on the throne with God means that God has chosen to achieve this goal of creation through a slaughtered Lamb. Servants worship God, which is the purpose of creation. The servant John of Patmos was engaged in worship when he received the vision of the Son of Man ("in the Spirit," 1:10). Then, as Paul said to the Corinthians, God becomes all in all (1 Cor 15:28).

Eden Image 3: Divine Fellowship (22:4)

The supreme experience of any human being is to look into the face of the Creator. While no human in the fallen state of humanity can look on the face of God and live,[21] that possibility is where all of life is heading. The blessing spoken on Israel in Numbers is, "The Lord make his face shine upon you, and be gracious to you" (Num 6:25). That blessing becomes a reality in the New Jerusalem. The metaphor of seeing God's face speaks to the promise of relationship, of walking with God. This truth is the ultimate biblical hope:

- the dream of prophets (Isa 52:8; 60:62)
- the desire of worshippers (Pss. 11:7; 27:4; 42:2)
- the beatitude of Jesus (Matt 5:8)
- the hope of the apostles (1 Cor 13:12)

John adds, "and his name will be on their foreheads." This mark is defeating the beast of Rev 13. This mark is a deliberate echo here in the New Jerusalem vision to show the final destiny of the sealing of the saints, which John dramatized in the Seals interlude (7:1–8), then referenced in the fifth trumpet plague spawning the locusts from the bottomless pit (9:4), and again in the conquest prelude vision of the Lamb on Mount Zion with the 144,000 (14:1). Here is another place in the New Jerusalem vision where the Seven Letters are drawn into the

---

[21] Exod 33:20–23; John 1:18; 1 Tim 6:16.

scene allusively, because this seal fulfills the promise of Jesus to believers in Philadelphia (3:12): "I will write upon him the name of my God, and the name of the city of my God, which is New Jerusalem, which comes down out of heaven from my God: and I will write upon him my new name."

New Jerusalem Reign (22:5)

John moves through his metaphors rapidly since he has spent twenty chapters to develop a literary foundation for them. He is winding up his work in a dramatic flourish with power and vigor, calling upon the prime themes of salvation history. One of those prime themes most certainly would be the kingdom of God. John taps into the sense of a kingdom reign in order to modulate the temporary truth of the millennial reign of martyrs of the beast into that of the eternal truth of the kingdom reign of all believers in the New Jerusalem. New Jerusalem is a reign that surpasses the millennial reign.

One cautionary note seems warranted. History has shown that any time a monarchial reign from Jerusalem has been attempted, war and destruction have followed. We ought to get the picture at some point. New Jerusalem is a metaphor. Truth be told, God is not really interested in a time-share condo on a small piece of real estate in the near east. He lays claim to the entire world.

John repeats the no need for sun or moon or lamp because God is their light he already has declared (21:23). This idea calls upon the full force of prophetic and praise motifs of the glory of God that run deeply in biblical testimony. Here, however, he yokes together God's glory with God's kingdom in an amazing economy of words: "and they will reign forever and ever." This brevity is amazing, because so much of the memorable action of Revelation has drawn on the martial metaphors of kings, their kingdoms, their armies, and their battles. These robust images provide the most iconic terms for which John's Apocalypse is known—Apollyon, Armageddon, millennium, Gog and Magog. And yet, when John concludes the matter in this denouement, he pares down the kingdom drama to just seven words: "and they will reign forever and ever." The composition of the plural "they," though indefinitely expressed, breaks out easily in context into two fundamental components. One is the composite God and the Lamb, who already have been identified as sitting in unity on the throne. The other would be the nations and the kings of the earth who stream into New Jerusalem with their tribute and wealth as a praise offering to God and the Lamb. So, we have God and the Lamb and the redeemed who reign forever and ever.

So, the redeemed need no light because God will be their light. This truth fulfills the beautiful Old Testament benediction over the people of God given in Num 6:24–26. This truth also consummates the reality of the Inaugural Vision of the Son of Man, whose face is "as the sun shining in its strength" (1:16). Revelation's narrative now has run full circle with the Inaugural Vision. What John saw, all see. Revelation's narrative also has run full circle with the Seven Letters. We are now back to the last promise in the last letter, a promise to reign with Christ as he reigns with God (3:21). In the end, the Seven Letters are consummated in Christ in eternity.

What is the rhetorical force of this New Jerusalem vision? One might think, rather obtusely, simply to promise pie in the sky by and by. However, John has set up a blunt antithesis contrasting the whore of Rev 17 with the bride of Rev 21. This rapid-fire burst of images on New Jerusalem comes as exhortation. John as prophet is forthtelling. He is exhorting the seven churches against compromise. He is urging believers to embrace the truth of the testimony of Jesus in a confessional stand against the beast, because believers must live according to their eschatological destiny to legitimize their witness. He is calling for decision like Joshua of old, "Choose you this day whom you will serve!" (Josh 24:15). He is calling for action like the voice from heaven over Babylon, "Come out of her!" (18:4). He has presented a tale of two cities, a tale of two women. Decide now, and live accordingly.

CONCLUSION (22:6–21)

John's deed is done. His prophecy has been written. Time to wrap up. John returns to the epistolary genre. This return forms a macro *inclusio* for the whole book, be-

FIGURE 12.19. Epistolary Genre *Inclusio*. John's literary form creates two interpretive corollaries.

ginning to end. The language here, therefore, will show numerous ties back to both the Introduction and to the Seven Letters. Two major narrative functions are achieved with this genre shift and the language connections. One function is to create two interpretive corollaries of unity and historical context. A literary unity is created that asks the reader to read the book as a whole and not to isolate one unit from all others as if independent in meaning. John also communicates with this genre that the book's meaning both in part and in whole is historically grounded in its first-century context. The meaning of Revelation is the seven churches of Asia Minor.

Motif	Prologue	Epilogue
1. revelation from God	1:1	22:6, 16
2. the one who testifies	1:1–2	22:20
3. John's identification	1:2	22:8
4. blessing on keeping	1:3	22:7, 9, 10
5. the time is near	1:3	22:10
6. the Seven Churches	1:4	22:16
7. coming soon	1:7	22:7, 12, 20
8. Alpha and Omega	1:8	22:13

FIGURE 12.20. Motif Connections. John intends to bring his readers full circle back to the beginning.

A second major narrative function is to allow the author to recapitulate crucial themes of his book for his readers. By connecting the words, phrases, and ideas of this epilogue in Rev 22 with the prologue in Rev 1, the reader's attention is drawn to the literary purpose of the author and his themes. He wants to characterize his words as words of prophecy, words of Christ, and words of warning, and to conclude with a word of amen and final benediction.

Words of Prophecy (22:6–11)

As words of prophecy, John has three emphases. His first emphasis is the authenticity of the revelation, that this revelation is "trustworthy" (22:6). The God who administers the spirits of the prophets, including John's, is the one authorizing this vision. Angelic mediators are divine signatures of the seriousness of God in this communication. John is fighting the lies of the beast and countering the lies of Jezebel, and this struggle can be effected only by God's help in revealing God's will and God's way to God's people. John does not fight alone nor on his own recognizance. He is not a maverick doomsayer walking the streets of Pergamum with a "The End" placard scribbled awkwardly.

His second emphasis is the nearness of fulfillment: "what must soon take place" (22:6). He thereby echoes the assessment portion of the Seven Letters and provides a stark reminder of the immediacy of the prophecy. His word of "soon" clearly means he is forthtelling, not foretelling. He said this same word at the beginning of Revelation (1:1, 3). So, beginning to end, John is not ambiguous on this point in the slightest. The interpreter ought to take John seriously. Exegesis ought to be affected. This word of "soon" puts us in the first century. Jesus reaffirms this very point: "See, I am coming soon!" (22:7). His coming translates into "keeping the words of the prophecy of this book" (22:7). The reader now knows "keeping the words of the prophecy" is a call to confessional integrity in the first-century crisis of the imperial cult.

In the context of the third emphasis on worship, we hear the name of the author for the fourth time, "I, John" (22:8).[22] His identity is clear to the original audience, but has to be argued by later readers. He is honest about his reaction to the revelation as a sense of awe and desire to worship before the revelatory angel (22:8). That action this angel rebukes (22:9). In a tangential way, we learn from the angel's remonstrance of John that the angel's role is as a "fellow servant" among the company of prophets and believers in general who "keep" the words of the book. This angelic comrade-in-arms role is unfamiliar to the reader of Revelation and not explained elsewhere in the New Testament.[23] The Seven Letters are addressed "to the angel of the church in," so John does suggest a direct connection to the seven churches. At least the "fellow servant" role apparently would include that relationship. Under that rubric, however, the angelic role seems to merge with

---

[22]Cf. Rev 1:1, 4, 9; 22:8.

[23]We have a few passages about angels in the New Testament, but little to fill in this concept of "fellow servant." Cf. nativity, Matt 1:20–24; 2:13, 19; Luke 1:11–19, 26–38; 2:10–15, 21; temptation, Matt 4:6, 11; Mark 1:13; Luke 4:10; reapers of judgment, Matt 13:39, 41, 49; parousia, Matt 16:27; 24:31, 36; 25:31; Mark 8:38; 13:27, 32; Luke 9:26; 12:8–9; 2 Thess 1:7; of children, 18:10; heavenly inhabitants, Matt 22:30; Mark 12:25; Luke 15:10; 16:22; 20:36; John 1:51; Heb 2:5–9, 16; 12:22; 1 Pet 3:22; 2 Pet 2:11; of the devil, Matt 25:41; cross, Matt 26:53; Luke 22:43; empty tomb, Matt 28:2, 5; Luke 24:23; John 20:12; miracle, John 5:4; Acts 5:9; 7:30, 35, 38; 12:7–15; law giving, Acts 7:53; Gal 3:19; Heb 2:2; messenger Acts 8:26; 10:3, 7, 22; 11:13; 27:23; death, Acts 12:23; judgment, 1 Cor 6:3; 2 Pet 2:4; Jude 6; worship, 1 Cor11:10; Col 2:18; Heb 1:6–13; Satan transformed, 2 Cor 11:14; unknown visitors, Heb 13:2.

the role of the actual local prophets. That blurring of the lines might be why commentators understandably have difficulty deciding whether the "angels" of the churches are heavenly beings or metaphors for the pastors or local prophetic leadership of the churches.

While his relationship with regard to the prophets is unclear, the angel's command is not. He rebukes John, "Worship God!" (22:9). If an actual inhabitant of heaven cannot be worshipped, Domitian plays the fool with his emperor cult. This "worship God" rebuke read in the churches functions as a call to the seven churches to confess Christ and reject all idolatrous claims to divinity, even when surrounded by a culture of embedded imperial worship. If one dare not worship angels, then most certainly not any emperors! The seven churches have been served notice to quit playing games with the imperial cult crisis.

John then offers a prophetic reprise on three counts. First, John reprises unsealing the words of prophecy (22:10). He is *not* to seal up the words, reversing Daniel's sealing up of prophetic words pointing to the messianic kingdom.[24] The incarnation unseals messianic prophecy. Allusion to Dan 2:45 recalls a great stone cut out of a mountain without hands that breaks in pieces the composite image of four successive empires, Daniel's iconic coming of the kingdom of God. So, what John has written is God fulfilling the prophecy of Daniel through Jesus Christ. Thus, Christ's death and resurrection unveils the future. The future is in the past.

Second, John reprises that what he writes is because "the time is near" (22:10). Soon is soon. Period. The bulk of what John writes is not about something two millennia distant. He explicitly says so, both at the beginning and end of the book. We have attempted to discover what happens exegetically when John is taken at his word. What was future for Daniel ("what must happen after these things") is present for John ("what must happen soon"). John implies a realized eschatology by making constant allusion to Daniel's prophecies and then contextualizing everything as Rome. Daniel's future is now for John.

Third, John reprises the core character of human beings (22:11). No matter how much God wants to save, he will not violate free will. Choice is embedded into the very structure of the universe. John makes clear that persistent evildoers will be judged. He also assures

---

[24] Cf. Dan 8:26; 12:4, 9.

that persistent righteous-doers will be rewarded. Use of "filthy" is related to ritual impurity.[25] Once again, the imperial cult is the target.

Words of Christ (22:12–16)

Jesus reiterates the truth of his coming (22:12). This promised coming is anchored in the second coming (1:7), but an obsessive focus on that future component exclusively blinds one to the complex dimensions of Jesus' coming portrayed in the Judgment Cycle. Once again, John is clear about what dimension of Jesus' coming he is talking, and that is not two millennia later. John says "soon." John of Patmos insists Jesus already has come, because the Rider already is blood-drenched as he rides out from heaven victoriously. All the Gospel writers completely agree. For Matthew, the Heavenly Rider already is blood-drenched because he already has come and has been baptized by the cross (Matt 20:22). For Mark, he already has come and been raised and glorified (Mark 16:6). For Luke, he already has come and ascended to heaven to reign at the right hand of God (Luke 24:51) and already has come and empowered the church to take up a cross and follow him (Acts 2:1). Luke thinks he already has come and eternally defeated the Dragon in the death of every martyr (Acts 7:55). For John, he already has come because the reality of the last judgment has broken into history and the prince of this world already has been cast out (John 12:31).

Thus, theologically, John is rehearsing gospel truth with his talk of the coming of Jesus communicated apocalyptically as the elaborate Judgment Cycle. Jesus is coming—soon. Jesus arrives in the powerful word of the gospel, simultaneously judgment and salvation, a two-edged sword coming out of his mouth. Jesus comes with his reward to repay everyone according to their "work." In Revelation, this "work" is the labor of being true to the testimony of Jesus in a confessional crisis. John speaks of the recompense of the eschatological judge and of destiny. On this motif, Thyatira is warned to beware Jezebel (2:23).

The Alpha and Omega divine title means that Jesus functions as the legitimate and authorized judge of humankind (22:13). The merg-

---

[25]The word is *hryparos* (ῥυπαρός), "soiled," "dirty," used only twice in the New Testament (Rev 22:11; Jas 2:2). James blasts being deferential to the rich with gold rings and fine clothes versus the poor in "dirty" clothes. The literal "filthy" became ethical and moral, as in Revelation, wicked people to avoid; cf. Plutarch *Quaes. Gr.* 25 (297a).

ing of the incarnational role of Jesus as Son of Man and the eschatological role of Jesus as the Ancient of Days becomes complete from beginning to end in Revelation. Revelation starts with Jesus as the Son of Man with only intimations of the Ancient of Days in the Inaugural Vision. Revelation then ends with the Gog and Magog final end-time drama, the passion of the church, which precipitates the second coming of Jesus and transitions directly into the great white throne of judgment conducted by the Ancient of Days. So Jesus really is Alpha and Omega, first and last, the beginning and end of Revelation.

John now augments the prologue blessing of Rev 1:3 (22:14). The blessing here picks up the clothing theme from the Seven Letters in the washing of robes metaphor.[26] John also picks up the tree of life and city gates motifs from the New Jerusalem vision. The tree of life also resonates back to the Seven Letters (2:7).

Using these motifs, John then proceeds to paint destiny in stark terms. One has either the redeemed or the dogs (22:15). The redeemed have "washed their robes," a common everyday laundering metaphor for the cultic act of redemption by the blood (3:4; 7:14). John then gives two beautiful metaphors for eternal life. One is the tree of life; the other is the privilege to enter by the city gates like all legitimate citizens of a city are allowed to do. In contrast, outside are the "dogs." The canine metaphor is harsh. The term is disparaging. Dogs were not pets in the ancient world. They were despised, and roamed fields and streets in scavenger packs. Their domestication was in the main utilitarian, such as serving as guard dogs at front entrances of affluent homes. The use of the term "dog" is blunt castigation of evil doers, hence John's last major word on the true character of evil. Evil degrades

FIGURE 12.21. *Cave Canem*. "Beware the dog!" warning on mosaic floor entrance to Pompeii's House of the Tragic Poet.

---

[26]Especially Sardis and Laodicea; cf. Rev 3:4, 5, 18.

humans into behaving like scavenging pack animals who would turn unpredictably and bite viciously in a moment. John is not abusively lobbing scurrilous epitaphs of mindless derision. Domitian's own true character is captured in this term. Give him a little leeway on the leash of God's sovereignty, and he will snap on you in a moment to tear you into pieces. The bad behavior list is a job description of participants in the imperial cult: "sorcerers and fornicators and murderers and idolaters, and every one who loves and practices falsehood" (22:15). The falsehood is imperial ideology.

Christ concludes with a divine asseveration that echoes the one already given in Rev 22:6 (22:16). Jesus sent his angel as mediator and interpreter of the vision. In this way, John emphasizes that God and Jesus always act in concert in Revelation. The "testimony" is the book of Revelation. This testimony is "for the churches." Once again, the plural value of the call section of the Seven Letters is reiterated. All of Revelation is for all the churches. Every letter is everyone's letter. The meaning and application of Revelation always is intended to be appropriated corporately.

Christ then identifies himself through a duality of titles that draw upon both Jewish and Roman worlds. From the Jewish world, Jesus is the root and descendent of David. This is the messianic emphasis of Christology, as is reflected in John's early merging of the slaughtered Lamb with the lion of the tribe of Judah (5:5).[27] The root of David term repeats the phrase from Rev 5:5. The reoccurrence of the term here is a reminder that we have to appraise this kingship in Israel accurately, which is to say, historically, and not put a naïve halo on the royal institution. Israel's experiment with its kingship

FIGURE 12.22. Tomb of David. A Jewish shrine at the traditional tomb of David in Jerusalem. The original tomb is unknown but thought to be in the old City of David on the narrow ridge running south of the temple mount.

---

[27]The idea is iconoclastic in its rejection of Jewish nationalism; see discussion, pp. 390–94.

was an abject royal failure.²⁸ God had to redeem the kingship. Jesus as the *root* of David seems to run the lineage question backwards. Jesus is inverting Isaiah's image of the *stem* of Jesse (Isa 11:1). Instead of Jesse as the origin (i.e., stem) of this Davidic line, *Jesus* actually claims to be the stem; he is the *root* of David, that is, the *source* of Davidic lineage. What does he mean? Jesus speaks messianically. What makes David's line truly royal and messianic, as God always intended for kingship in Israel, is not David. What really makes David's line royal and messianic according to God's original intentions is the Messiah, Jesus.²⁹ God allowed kingship, not because David would sire Messiah, but because God would send Jesus to save all Israel. This "reverse lineage" effect is a spiritual "backflow" idea that revolutionizes how to understand the messianic heritage of Jesus. In the terms God originally had intended for the function of Messiah in Israel, Israel has a royal line because of Jesus, not because of David.

Jesus is the "bright morning star." This title for Jesus is unique in the New Testament. Most commentators feel John here makes an allusion to Num 24:17, about the star descended from David and destined to reign over Israel and destroy her enemies. This text was taken messianically in Jewish traditions, and, in fact, was the text used by Rabbi Akiba to proclaim Simon ben Kosiba as messiah in the Second Jewish War (132–35), only fifteen years after John wrote Revelation.³⁰ Kosiba later was named "Bar Kokhba," or "son of the star" after Rabbi Akiba's doomed declaration.

Another allusion for "morning star" is to Venus, the star holding the fate of Roman generals on the field of battle. Venus also is the Roman equivalent of the Greek Aphrodite, and Aphrodite is a part of the founding legends of the line of the Roman emperor. Thus, the title is subverting Roman myth that attempted to seize honor and status for the imperial line by claiming divine heritage in the legends of imperial origins. This title links to Thyatira of the Seven Letters (2:28).³¹

---

²⁸On the failure of kingship in Israel, see the discussion, pp. 265–67.

²⁹This messianic reality is the origin of the conundrum Jesus presented to religious leaders: "How can David say, 'the Lord said unto my Lord?'" (Matt 22:44; Mark 12:36; Luke 20:42; Acts 2:34).

³⁰Jerusalem Talmud, *Ta'anit* 4:6 (68d–69a); Cf. Gruber, *Rabbi Akiba's Messiah*.

³¹Cf. promise section, Thyatira, pp. 330–31. Venus, of course, is a planet, but the ancients thought of that brightest of objects in the sky as a star. See Fig. 9.13, p. 218.

FIGURE 12.23. Temple of Aphrodite. The magnificent temple of Aphrodite (Venus) in Aphrodisias not far from Ephesus and Laodicea. Aphrodite (Venus) is the goddess of love, sex, fertility, and prosperity, and mother of the Romans through her son Aeneas.

Words of Invitation (22:17)

This material has a possible liturgical context.[32] Thus, this unit would be used in worship and provide antiphonal responses of the reader and congregation. This setting facilitates public confession of Christ. The church "practices" in worship what is to be lived in life. The act of worship also calls Rome into divine judgment as the Spirit and Bride join in the antiphony. In the antiphonal responses, three invitations of a call to "Come!" play out. All three of these calls are addressed to the warrior Rider. His "coming" will execute God's just judgment through the sword that comes out of his mouth. The sword is the word of the gospel spoken into existence, first through the incarnation, and now through the faithful witness of his followers who actualize the judgment of God by their testimony to

FIGURE 12.24. Heavenly Rider Motif. The heavenly warrior of Rev 19 is about the incarnation and the gospel (ADEVA).

---

[32]Beasley-Murray, *Revelation*, 343–44, outlines a nice series of call and responses.

Jesus. John of Patmos himself has engaged in this battle, which is his opening identification at the beginning of Revelation: "I, John, your brother and fellow partner in the tribulation and kingdom and perseverance in Jesus, was on the island which is called Patmos on account of the word of God and the testimony of Jesus" (1:9).

The first invitation is the Spirit and the Bride (22:17). This bride is the bride of the Lamb, the church.[33] Together, church and Spirit cry out a call to bring the kingdom of God to fulfillment. The *maranatha* cry of the early church became a standard part of her liturgy (1 Cor 16:22). This invitation to "come" is another occasion in Revelation when the cry of the martyrs under the altar is answered (6:9–11). John has reiterated that this martyr plea does not go unheeded by God. In historical judgments of Rome ("Fallen, fallen is Babylon!" 18:2), in the millennial reign of martyrs (20:4), and in the final, grand assize of the whole world (20:11–15), this cry has been answered.

The second invitation is of those hearing Revelation being read. These listeners themselves make a call, "Come!", which is their own congregational response to the call of the Spirit and the Bride. Thus, churches of Asia Minor in worship vocally affirm two truths with this response. First, these local congregations accept their own role as part of the universal Bride of Christ in their own formal acceptance of the corporate and eschatological marriage proposal of the Lamb. Second, these local congregations also vocally affirm God's calling Rome into judgment and accept responsibility for standing firm and loyal in that divine judgment process.

FIGURE 12.25. Herculaneum Fountain. A fresh water fountain in the middle of the street offered a cool, refreshing drink on a hot day in the main market area.

A third invitation is that of the evangelist. The call is to salvation. This offer is for any who are thirsty, reflecting John the apostle (John 7:37–38), the prophet Isaiah (Isa 55:1), and the recent invitation of the Alpha and Omega from the New Jerusalem (21:6). The "without price" grant of charity equals Paul's "saved by grace," and is

---

[33]Introduced in celebration of Babylon's fall (19:7), then New Jerusalem (21:2, 9).

a direct assault on Roman commerce for sordid self-gain and aggrandizement bleeding life out of empire subjects. Roman greed has gone mad, captured in the metaphor of a drunken stupor of compounded idolatries (17:2–6). Such water of life freely offered counters judgment scenes of famine, such as in the Seals (6:6) and the Bowls (13:17). This theme functions as John's equivalent to Paradise abundance themes. One should be careful not to emphasize this abundance too much, for fear of falling into the same materialistic perversions of the Chiliasts.

Words of Warning (22:18–19)

A curse formula is invoked about maintaining the integrity of the contents. In the ancient world, books were at the mercy of copyists, and formulaic endings like this were common to try to forestall temptation to tamper with the words. The *Letter of Aristeas* purports to relate the production of the Septuagint version of the Old Testament.

FIGURE 12.26. Ancient Scribes. All ancient manuscripts were hand copied. This made the integrity of the contents subject to unscrupulous scribes.

The author records the following at the conclusion of the project.

> And when the whole company expressed their approval, they bade them pronounce a curse in accordance with their custom upon any one who should make any alteration either by adding anything or changing in any way whatever any of the words which had been written or making any omission. This was a very wise precaution to ensure that the book might be preserved for all the future time unchanged (*Aristeas* 311).

Eusebius also preserves a colophon added at the end of Irenaeus's *On the Ogdoad*, written against the gnostic Valentinus.

> At the close of the treatise we have found a most beautiful note which we are constrained to insert in this work. It runs as follows: "I adjure you who may copy this book, by our Lord Jesus Christ, and by his glorious advent when he comes to judge the living and the dead, to compare what you shall write,

558 REVELATION: THE PAST AND FUTURE OF JOHN'S APOCALYPSE

and correct it carefully by this manuscript, and also to write this adjuration, and placed it in the copy" (*H.E.* 5.20.2).

John's warning is expressed in an add, subtract symmetry. Adding to the words is adding the plagues written within. Subtracting the words is subtracting from a share in the holy city.

John, however, may intend the formulaic warning to go deeper. Note carefully that this warning actually is not to scribes who copy but "to everyone who hears" (22:18). John is transforming this obligatory rhetoric traditionally about the activity of scribes into a subtle warning to believers in the seven churches themselves. With his "to everyone who hears," he is addressing behavioral reactions to the book in the local congregations. He already knows how Jezebel in Thyatira is going to feel about what to do with the book. He also can be highly suspicious what the Nicolaitans in both Ephesus and Pergamum will be inclined to do with the book. One does not have to take pen and ink in hand to change the words of the book. One can change the words in the book by the life one lives. So, adding of the plagues and exclusion from the tree of life and the holy city already are realized as the book is read. Predictable reactions of Jezebel and the Nicolaitans are precisely why John reprises the core character of human beings in 22:11: the evil doers will continue doing evil, and the filthy will continue being filthy. John is a realist. Jezebel most likely will continue being Jezebel, and the Nicolaitans will continue being Nicolaitans. Although he has warned Jezebel and the Nicolaitans, he knows the tragic word of the Bowl judgments probably will play out even for some within the seven churches: "they did not repent of their deeds" (16:11).

Words of Conclusion (22:20–21)

Word of Amen (22:20)

Jesus puts his own personal imprimatur on Revelation: "the one who testifies to these things" (22:20). Jesus puts his own stamp of approval on the entire Apocalypse. Jezebel and the Nicolaitans do not have a problem with John. They have a problem with Jesus. They had better come out of their drunken spiritual stupor induced by the harlot who has enticed them into idolatry before time runs out—and time is running out on these evil doers, because the one who testifies to these things immediately adds the announcement that is an assurance to believers but a threat to deceivers, the two-edged sword coming out of his mouth: "Yes, indeed, I am coming soon." This soon message is the constant refrain of Revelation:

- "what must soon take place" (1:1)
- "Repent then. If not, I will come to you soon and make war with them with the sword of my mouth" (2:16)
- "I am coming soon; hold fast to what you have, so that no one may seize your crown" (3:11)
- "what must soon take place" (22:6)
- "See, I am coming soon! Blessed is the one who keeps the words of the prophecy of this book" (22:7)
- "See, I am coming soon; my reward is with me, to repay according to everyone's work" (22:12)
- "Yes, indeed, I am coming soon" (22:20)

FIGURE 12.27. Church of the Holy Sepulcher. The site venerated as Golgotha where Jesus was crucified and buried. Pilgrims have trekked here since at least the fourth century. The place of the passion of Jesus is one of the most holy sites of Christendom.

The moment the book is read in the churches, the seals are opened, and Jesus comes. Surely, he is coming soon.

The coming of Jesus, both in time and at the end of time, is one of the profound truths of the Bible. The complete story requires Genesis to Revelation to tell. The reality of Jesus' coming plays out in the forces unleashed into human experience by the incarnation that proleptically anticipate the last judgment of the second coming. The mystery of the first coming is consummated by the passion of Jesus. The mystery of the second coming is consummated by the passion of the church. To contemplate these truths induces the fervent prayer of John himself, who consecrates the promise and then cries out in union with the voices of the souls under heaven's altar: "Amen! Come, Lord Jesus!" The word of amen is a liturgical conclusion that puts a worship bow on the book as the epilogue has called forth the final responses of Christ, the reader, and the congregation, and is a balanced, fitting end.

This most effective liturgical conclusion may be constructed to serve a dual function. The first time the book ever is read, John's amen and prayer function as his own personal word to the book he has written. Yet, in future readings, the congregation, once familiarized with this ending, could turn this expression into a fitting corporate conclusion. In this scenario, the lector (reader) first would pronounce the final "Amen." Then, the congregation would respond with their own resounding, "Come, Lord Jesus!"

"Come, Lord Jesus" is the early church Aramaic prayer *maranatha*.[34] The point would be crucial for the seven churches. By the very act of speaking the words in assembled worship, these seven churches activate the Judgment Cycle, and the worthy slaughtered Lamb comes to Asia Minor and begins opening the seals. As Lactantius observed,

> For it is related that the Egyptians, and Persians, and Greeks, and Assyrians had the government of the world; and after the destruction of them all, the chief power came to the Romans also. And inasmuch as they excel all other kingdoms in magnitude, with so much greater an overthrow will they fall, because those buildings which are higher than others have more weight for a downfall.[35]

Word of Benediction (22:20)

The benediction is the epistolary conclusion of the book. The words are given with a simplicity that belies their profundity:

> The grace of the Lord Jesus be with all.

---

[34]Two Aramaic dialects yield two different results. One form, *maran atha* would be a declarative, "Our Lord has (is, will) come." The other form, *marana tha*, would be the imperative, "Our Lord, come!" Consult the critical commentaries.

[35]Lactantius *Institutes* 7.15.

Alas, the final word of Revelation varies in the Greek manuscripts we have. John's proscription against tampering with the text did not fare well even in these last verses. Nothing serious is the result, as the tampering was innocent enough, creating minor variations on the three issues of the object, the pronouns, and the amen:

FIGURE 12.28. Codex Sinaiticus at Rev 22:21. Reads "with the saints" (METATWNAGI/WN, meta tōn hagiōn) and includes a final "Amen" (AMHN, *amēn*) at Rev 22:21 (Kirsopp Lake, 1911; by permission of Oxford University Press).

- Object: the question of the object of the preposition "with": whether the adjective "all," the noun "saints," the pronoun "us," the pronoun "you," or some combination, such as "all saints" (cf. 8:3).

- Pronouns: even if the "saints" option above is original, whether this noun is modified by an additional pronoun of either the second or the third person singular ("your" or "his").

- Amen: whether the final "Amen" is original.

Textual critical principles eliminate most of the varying options in favor of the translation given above. Even though the textual critical evidence is not in favor, the inclusion of the "Amen" is ubiquitous in English translation traditions, with exceptions, such as the CEB, CEV, NAB, NET, NLT, TEV, and Weymouth NT.[36]

---

[36] Beale's suspicion, *Revelation*, 1157, may be correct that John's original, unqualified "with all" was feared too open to being construed as universal salvation; all the variations were later additions trying to make clear only believers of the true church were included. Inconsistently, Aune, *Revelation*, 3:1239, uses the "more difficult reading" principle to accept the omission of the following "Amen" as original, but is unwilling to use the same principle to accept the omission of "the saints" as original; he seems to have the same problem as the scribes: "Yet it is difficult to accept the notion that John would have pronounced this concluding *charis*-benediction indiscriminately upon *all* without restricting its scope to Christians alone." The concluding "Amen" probably is not original on the stronger scribal likelihood of being added later rather than an original "Amen" later inexplicably being omitted.

Two elements bring gravity to understanding the significance of John's succinct conclusion. These two elements are an unexpected genre shift and an unusual linguistic content. The unexpected genre shift is from a prophecy-apocalypse form back to an epistle form. This genre shift back to the epistle parallels the opening greeting formula (1:4–6). As genre, the point is how highly irregular this ending is, most unusual for any apocalyptic literature. The interpretive corollary we drew from this deliberate and highly noticeable signal is how John in this way puts a historical anchor on his apocalyptic images. His meaning is specific, historical, and first century. After abiding by his literary signal to ground the apocalyptic images within the historical circumstance of the seven churches in first-century Asia Minor, we then have discovered how Revelation can be read thoroughly and consistently in this historical way as Rome—its empire, ideology, and cult—and that is probably what John intended.

However, we do have to recognize that *any* epistolary conclusion John would have composed would have given this exegetical result. We would see he enclosed his combined prophecy and apocalypse in this epistolary envelope. Thus, we immediately would conclude that issues of interpreting Revelation would become in this way the issues of interpreting epistles. Yet, something more seems hidden here, but only subtly in tantalizing suggestions.

The other element that brings gravity to this brief conclusion is its unusual linguistic content. This ending parallels the conclusion to all Paul's letters that is so invariably fixed his letters can be identified in this way. This distinctive Pauline ending has come to be called the "grace benediction." Its discovery became a key factor in determining the original form of the letter to the Romans.[37] John's conclusion is a close replica of a Pauline conclusion, a literary signature, so to speak, that belonged specially to Paul when he first was composing his mission letters. We can note that the Pauline grace benediction became an emulated form of concluding Christian epistles by later Paulinists following in the streams of Pauline Christianity.[38] Further, this particular word "grace" (*charis*, χάρις) occurs only twice in Revelation, once at the epistolary beginning (1:4), and once here at the epistolary con-

---

[37]Harry Gamble, Jr., *The Textual History of the Letter to the Romans*.
[38]Cf. *1 Clem.* 65:1.

clusion (22:21). This linguistic data is most unusual for its rarity in Revelation but its frequency in Paul as the centerpiece of his theological universe. Why does John use grace here when the word occurs nowhere else in Revelation outside once at the similar epistolary beginning? Probably *not* because he wanted to include a word of God's grace as central to his theological reflection, as suggested sometimes in commentaries.[39] No, this author's style clearly is to repeat what he regards important, even to the tune of recapitulating entire judgment cycles. Grace is not central to John's linguistic universe, at least not when he is in his apocalyptic-prophetic mode, as in the bulk of the Apocalypse.[40] Rather, John's use of grace, while not central to his core theological expression in Revelation, clearly evokes Paul.

FIGURE 12.29. Berea Paul Shrine. The apostle Paul had a tremendous impact on Asia Minor and Greece in his mission work. This mosaic of Paul is part of a plaza in modern Berea dedicated as a monument to the apostle Paul and the Macedonian Vision that sent him to Europe (Acts 16:9; 17:10).

FIGURE 12.30. Paul and Laodicea. The site of Colossae lies unexcavated in the Lycus valley near Laodicea, not too far from Ephesus on the western coast. Paul wrote letters to Ephesus, Colossae, and Laodicea (cf. Eph 1:1; Col 1:1; 2:1; 4:13, 15, 16).

What did John mean by ending his Apocalypse both looking and sounding like Paul, with Paul's concluding epistolary form and Paul's linguistic theological center? John's scores of allusions to traditions

---

[39] Typical examples would be Beasley-Murray, *Revelation*, 350; Reddish, *Revelation*, 431.

[40] The point is not that we think John does not believe in grace or does not know about grace. The point is asking, What are the core terms central to his theological expression in Revelation? Grace *de facto* simply is not one of them.

both biblical and non-biblical throughout Revelation present a hard time trying to determine intentionality and motive. The same would be true all the way to the last words of Revelation. In this form and this wording, was John of Patmos trying to evoke the spirit of one of the most famous Christian leaders of Asia Minor? We have several intersecting matrices of ministry between Paul and John:

- Paul's historic connections with the church of Ephesus (Acts 19:1; Eph 1:1)

- Paul's mission and letter connections to the churches of the Lycus valley tri-city complex of Colossae, Laodicea, and Hierapolis (Col 1:1; 2:1; 4:13–16)

- Paul's possible connection to the church at Thyatira through his patron Lydia at Philippi (Acts 16:14)

- Paul's uncontested martyrdom in Rome by beheading[41]

Was John trying to ingratiate himself into Pauline congregations in Asia Minor to encourage them to join forces with him and his seven churches in the confessional war with Rome? Is this what John meant when he chided the church at Ephesus that they had "lost your first love" (2:4), and then signed off the Apocalypse with a highly unusual epistolary form that imitated the apostle Paul? The case is speculative, but does provide some thought about trying to cognize the unusual ending of Revelation within its own literary and historical context.

Later scribes added the last word of Rev 22:21, the final "Amen." The word, while probably not original, is still in the spirit of John's intentions. This word can function two ways. One obvious way is as the scribe's own personal response to the antiphonal lines of the ending of Revelation he just has finished hand-copying word for word. Another way would be scripted for the appointed lector (1:3). This "Amen" puts the final touch to the actual act of reading the book in church worship. The reader's blessing arises out of the completion of his sacred liturgical duty. In his reading, he not only has blessed his listeners

---

[41]Cf. Rev 20:4. An interesting historical matrix exists between John's description of martyrs of the beast as having been beheaded and the strong and solid early church tradition that the apostle Paul was beheaded in Rome by Nero. We also have to take into account that Nero has legendary status in the book of Revelation as the spirit of the beast with a mortal wound healed returned in the form of Domitian.

(1:3), he also has sealed the servants of God with the testimony of Jesus and the word of God, just as the original author intended (7:2).

SUMMARY

Judgment is completed. The path of passion leads to New Jerusalem. John uses and innovates numerous biblical and non-biblical traditions of Zion and the astral city of the gods to communicate the blessedness of eternity. Rather than humans making the futile attempt to scale the heights, this city comes down. God is near and accessible. The real point is the person, not the place, the joyous intimacy of relationship. New Jerusalem is the assurance that the last judgment just depicted has been conclusive and irrevocable. Evil is eradicated. Faith is vindicated. God promised heaven, and he is faithful and true to his word. He has written in the blood of the slaughtered Lamb. The lake of fire as the second death is a metaphor for relationship, for being in or out of God's presence, and those issues currently are being decided in the confessional war with Rome in the seven churches.

New Jerusalem is described in ways that subvert Roman imperial ideology. This city is so huge, her footprint fills up the Mediterranean basin of the entire Roman empire. Further, Rome's trade in precious jewels transforms into paltry trinkets in the light of the gemstone of New Jerusalem. The precious gem image is more than succumbing to commercial hubris. New Jerusalem has a purpose for being complete gemstone—to reflect the brilliant glory of God throughout every crevice and corner. No matter the marvels of Roman engineering and filling valleys to create siege ramps to take a fortress down, New Jerusalem never will take siege: her walls are unfathomable in height and width. Her triple gates of solid pearl humiliate the triple-gate entrance to any Roman city, and the names of her heritage and benefactors, the twelve tribes of Israel, are inscribed eternally, never to be lost to natural disasters of earthquake or volcano. Likewise, her foundations are inscribed with the apostles of the gospel of the passion of Christ. This city, unlike any ancient city, has no temple. Such a thought is inconceivable to the ancient mind. No ancient citizen lived in a large city that did not have at least one temple. The need for mediation between divinity and humanity is transcended by the slaughtered Lamb.

The cosmology of the New Jerusalem also is theology. The glory of God and the Lamb outshines the sun, so New Jerusalem has neither sun nor moon nor night. To this divine light the kings of the earth are drawn, and the wealth of the nations flows into Jerusalem rather than the harbors of Rome. God, however, is the proper owner of the goods as Creator, and he properly will employ earth resources and wealth for his eternal beneficent purposes, unlike the commercial rape and pillage of creation by Rome on the exact pattern of Rome's military rape and pillage of kingdoms by forcible conquest. The gates of New Jerusalem never are shut, because rebellion never happens. These forever open gates means Babylon's pollutions and evils forever are gone.

The common paradise renewal motif of apocalyptic literature is John's biblical Eden transcended theme. Eschatology is creation consummated. The extensive system of Roman aqueducts covering the empire in a water web attempting to supply a constant source of fresh water necessary for life pales in comparison to an entire river gushing down the middle of New Jerusalem's main street from the very throne of God. A tree of life supplies fruits continually all year, not just in limited agricultural seasons of Italian landed estates. The leaves are for the healing of nations. Paradise also means Eden's curse is transcended. God and the Lamb sit on the throne of sovereignty over the world to work in concert to consummate creation. The presence of the Lamb on the throne means God's way of bringing creation to its Sabbath rest is through a slaughtered Lamb. Paradise imagery also means that all of life is moving back to walking with God face to face in the garden. The promise of relationship also can be symbolized by language of the mark of God written on the believer.

One of the prime themes of salvation history is the kingdom of God. John modulates the temporally-bound millennial reign of beast martyrs into the kingdom reign of all believers in the New Jerusalem.

All of these metaphors of New Jerusalem address the promise sections of the Seven Letters. Thus, Revelation is all about the seven churches. The New Jerusalem is exhortative rhetoric for these seven churches. John has set up the contrast of a tale of two cities as a tale of two women. John is calling for decision. A confessional crisis between a whore and a bride is confronting these churches. John wants to make clear that choosing between harlot and bride determines eternal destiny. Decide now, and live accordingly.

John's conclusion shows numerous ties with his beginning. Epistolary genre advises one to interpret as a unity and historically. He has written words of forthtelling prophecy that are authentic and authoritative. John is not a maverick doomsayer. He speaks for God and for Jesus. The time is near, so the immediacy of a response is unavoidable. The call is to keep the words of the prophecy, which is confessional in the context of the imperial cult. The angel's command to John is the command to all the churches of Asia Minor: "Worship God!" That present and timely call is why Daniel's sealing up of the words becomes John's unsealing of the words. The incarnation unseals messianic prophecy. Daniel's shattered image of kingdom is the coming of Christ. John constantly alludes to Old Testament prophecy and then contextualizes everything as Rome. The sad news is that people will continue to do evil in spite of all God is doing to save them.

Jesus already has come, because the Rider appears already blood-drenched coming from heaven. Jesus arrives in the powerful word of the gospel. Jesus is the Alpha and Omega because the Son of Man who elicits intimations of the Ancient of Days in the Inaugural Vision at the beginning of Revelation is the one who sits in judgment at the great white throne at the end of Revelation. John paints final destiny in stark terms of the righteous and dogs, but he only is describing realistically the emperor Domitian's true vicious character. John means for Revelation to be appropriated corporately by all Asian churches. Jesus sanctifies the messianic line of David and is the true source of a divine lineage even for Romans, who have mistaken the goddess Aphrodite as providing the honor and status of their imperial line.

Revelation ends with antiphonal responses that evoke a consciousness of liturgy and use in worship. The cry is for the Heavenly Rider of the eternal gospel to "come!" This cry calls Rome into judgment.

John converts the formulaic curse formula on tampering with the words of the book into a prescient forestalling of the rejection of the message of the book by John's opponents in Jezebel and the Nicolaitans by what they will advocate to undermine John's message. John reminds his listeners that how they live is how they preserve or destroy the words of his prophecy. Jesus is coming soon, because the moment Revelation is read in the seven churches, the seals are opened, and Jesus comes. John puts his own personal amen to that truth. What is anticipated in the Lord's Supper, the coming of Jesus, is celebrated and prayed for in worship. This prayer activates the Judgment Cycle in Asia Minor.

The final benediction form creates Revelation's epistolary ending. This genre shift has hermeneutical significance. John signals how to read his prophecy-apocalypse as unitary and historical. The final benediction form and words also are distinctively Pauline. John may be attempting to draw in various Pauline churches as reinforcements and "fellow-sharers in the tribulation and kingdom and perseverance in Jesus" (1:9) in the confessional conflict in Asia Minor of his seven churches. John seems confident were Paul still alive, on the pattern of Paul's death by beheading as a martyr of the beast, Paul would support him. Perhaps John is hoping he can persuade later Pauline generations to add their testimony with that of other churches of Asia Minor in a combined confessional stand against the fierce beast of Revelation. That Revelation was canonized by the church in Rome may show the signal success of this subtle appeal to Pauline churches.

Epilogue

The Future of John's Apocalypse

JOHN GAVE US HIS VISION IN THE NIGHT to exhort and encourage the seven churches of Asia Minor in their confessional conflict with Rome. In this war of words eternity was at stake. John presented the

Church		World		Heaven
Vision	Judgment	Vision	Judgment	Vision
Vision of Son/Man (1:9–20) 	Seven Letters (2–3) 	Vision of Heaven (4–5) 	Judgment Cycle (6–20) 	Vision of Victory (21–22) 

FIGURE E-1. Revelation: A Three-Act Play of God's Judgment.

conflict as a three-act play of God's judgment on evil in the world. God as sovereign Creator rules earth from heaven's throne. He brings all creation to its designed consummation through his slaughtered Lamb who is Son of Man, Ancient of Days, Lord of the church, ruler of the kings of the earth, final judge. The way is passion. The truth is gospel. The life is self sacrifice. The first coming is the apocalypse of the second coming. Christ or Caesar: choose this day whom to serve. The choice is radical, as martyrs will testify. One day the church will find out just how radical. That choice inevitably will bring history and church to an end. God in his infinite wisdom miraculously will turn death into life, as with Jesus, and thereby transform evil and eternity.

John's drama used martial and apocalyptic language. For an apathetic or anesthetized audience, that language just might have been the ticket to induce a visceral response from hearers primed for that kind of imagery in their culture, society, politics, religion, down to everyday life—artistry, design, decoration, temples, grave monuments, inscriptions, buildings, coins, mosaics, and frescos. Even common first-century inhabitants of the global Roman empire both spoke and thought in terms of griffins and gladiators. Images and ritual acts of life and death were commonplace.

FIGURE E-2. Gladiator Helmet. This artifact illustrates the Murmillo class gladiator and actually was found in the Colosseum of Rome (ROM).

FIGURE E-3. Griffins Galore. Fantastical beast—head of jaguar, horns of a bull, wings of an eagle, body of a lion, suckling mother—mercilessly eviscerates its helpless prey. This large-scale floor mosaic decorated the Great Palace of Constantinople and illustrates the dramatic use of griffin imagery in the ancient world (GPMM).

On the other hand, for an audience *not* primed for that kind of fantastical—but symbolic—communication, John's choice of language is a disaster. One quick trip to the Internet is easy proof that so many self-appointed prophets of the Apocalypse are clueless about historical exegesis or that Revelation has anything to do with the gospel. What is truly sad is that they do not cognize their own cataclysmic canonical problems, blithely proposing at the drop of a hat multiple messiahs, second salvations, and God glazed over about how exactly he wants to deal with evil. Doomsday websites suck the canonical life out of Revelation like spiders casting off a useless carcass. They destroy the book's true authority with insipid logic, bad exegesis, and constant falsification. All this interpretive trash is enough to convince one Revelation never should have been canonized. Perhaps the Eastern Church really has had the wisest course of approach to this book over the last two millennia: only begrudgingly acknowledging as in the Bible after the Western Church had preempted canonical options, but then requiring a strict quarantine from both doctrine and liturgy.

The Jews looked for the Messiah for hundreds of years. Yet, when God actually acted, no one knew what was happening or that God was involved. Village peasants having their first child in a stable, dislocated from home by an imperial decree, then fleeing for their lives and the life of the child from the wrath of the reigning Jewish monarch to hide far away in Egypt does not look much like anything any Jew expected. With all of the Jewish traditions about the Messiah, when the Messiah actually showed up, they rejected him because he did not meet their expectations. We should learn from this historical lesson. If the Jews messed up the first coming, then what is protecting prophets of the Apocalypse from royally messing up the second coming just as badly? Who says God is going to follow their script? He certainly did not seem to feel obligated to follow any Jewish script of the first century.

I wrote this book for my students who begged me, in spite of the spate of recent and excellent books and commentaries on Revelation, to have a record of what I was saying in class that they found challenging. In class over the years I have tried to persuade two take-home points to avoid the hermeneutical abyss of prophets of the Apocalypse. The first point is *our real job with Revelation is we must recanonize the book*, after its destruction by false prophets and truly wacko psychos. I know exactly what must happen to do so. The New Testament canon is based on the four Gospels. They are the authority and the bottom line. Even Paul must concord with the canonical Gospels, or he is not authoritative and inspired in any true New Testament sense. Thus, my second point is *we have to get Revelation integrated back into the four Gospels and a gospel message*. That message is the cross of Christ, and that is precisely why Paul is canonical (1 Cor 2:2) and the only way Revelation ever will be (Rev 11:8). If Revelation does not preach the gospel, whose message is a path of passion and victory by dying, then one should not preach Revelation. If God does not defeat Satan at the cross, why in the world would thermonuclear meltdown do the trick? Thus, I have to confess that I am not premillennial, postmillennial, or amillennial. I am "passion-millennial." I am the veritable mixed-breed yard dog that barks suspiciously at anything that tries to come inside the millennial gate. Whatever future Revelation sees is in the past. All eschatological truth is inherent in the incarnation. That is canon.

In this book, I tried to show how to go about the twin tasks of recanonization and gospel recentering of Revelation.[1] In order to see the future with Revelation, we have to revisit the past by traveling down four roads. First, we have to travel down the history of interpretation. To know where we are going, we have to know where we have been. Second, we have to travel down Christ's Via Dolorosa. To know what God is up to toward redeeming his world and resolving the problem of evil, we have to wrap our minds around what God did in Jesus Christ. Third, we have to travel down theological byways. The tail does not wag the dog. Eschatology is the tail and must be sublimated to Christology, ecclesiology, and soteriology. Fourth, we have to

FIGURE E-4. Emperor Trajan (98–117). Silver denarius, laureate wreath; IMP CAES NERVA TRAIAN AVG GERM; emperor to whom governor Pliny wrote (ASM).

---

[1] I personally am convinced the book is canonical. Prophets of the Apocalypse, however, need to be challenged to rethink what New Testament canonization theologically means. Revelation is not a *carte blanche* check for completely unrestrained craziness.

travel with John down the Roman roads of first-century Asia Minor. All of Revelation makes perfect sense when read using a first-century hermeneutic of seven churches in an inescapable confessional crisis with Rome. That John was prescient about Antipas as harbinger of storm clouds on the horizon is witnessed only two decades later in the Roman governor Pliny of Bithynia and his emperor Trajan on how to adjudicate the matter of Christians and their confession of Christ. We are only a half step from official state persecution.

Our commitment to stay with the text using an integrative close reading was paramount. I always have told my students, if you love the text, she will love you back. If John never mentions Antichrist, neither do we. If John connects the Hebrew name Abaddon to the Greek idea Apollyon, a pun on the name of Apollo, we follow him right to Domitian's doorstep. If John intratextually links a battle at a fictive location called Armageddon that exists on no real map to the crisis of the dead church at Sardis, we take his lead and go with him. If John links the rider warrior on the white horse in every conceivable way to the suffering Son of Man introduced in the Inaugural Vision and to the

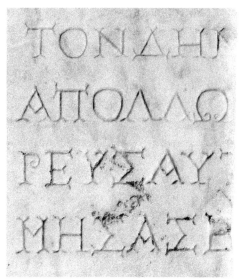

FIGURE E-5. Apollo Inscription. The name Apollo read in the second line (ΑΠΟΛΛΩ, *Apollō*) is part of this Apollo temple inscription (HAMH).

slaughtered Lamb of the Vision of Heaven, then we take his lead that he is symbolizing incarnation truth, not second coming. If John makes patently clear the millennial reign is reserved exclusively for martyrs of the beast as an alternate perspective on the meaning of the Bowl judgments against imperial idolatry and commercial harlotry, then we take his lead and interpret that reign as the direct result of the present empire crisis and concurrent with the reign of Jesus in his ascension glory, regardless terminological headaches of first and second resurrection John generates along the way to emphasize this conviction of immediately vindicated martyr witness. If John recapitulates the issues of the seven churches throughout the entire Apocalypse from the Seven Letters (2–3), through the broad stretch of the Judgment Cycle (6–20), and on into the Vision of Victory (21–22), we take his lead and say that Revelation is, start to finish, all about the seven churches of Asia Minor, not the future—even though the future of the church is intimated in that first-century crisis.

The future of John's Apocalypse is in the past. The past of *Christ and the cross* establishes the path of passion as God's sovereign way of dealing with evil that the church must live and at the end embrace as her own historical destiny. Thus, Revelation teaches that Christology and ecclesiology are inseparable and crucial for an adequate grasp of the eschatological dimensions of soteriology. We truly need to preach Revelation to prepare the church how to pray her Gethsemane prayer, not how to pack bags for an escapist rapture. We certainly want to be careful to think through just what motivates our escapist ideology and just what is the real end game of that ideology fully played out for real, most especially when confronted with the actions of the 39 members of the Heaven's Gate cult who committed mass suicide to book ticket on that space craft bound for the next world trailing the Hale-Bopp comet.[2] When Christ called the church to a cross, why do we preach rapture?

In terms of seeing the paradigm of the cross for the future, the past of *Christ and the Caesars* anticipates that future passion of the church. Apollyon and Armageddon are first-century Roman realities for the original seven churches. They will be reprised in the Gog and Magog mystery at the end of history—about which, ironically, we have very little information in Revelation. Even so, we most certainly will know we are there when we get there. No Internet prophet will have to tease out the "signs of the times" in a modern revival of a new Gnosticism, some special "secret knowledge" salvation reserved only for the elite end-time elect, most particularly those who sow the seed of that incessant financial contribution. Why the need to finance next month

---

[2]Marshall Applewhite's near-death experience after a heart attack convinced him he and his nurse at the time, Bonnie Nettles, were the two witnesses of Rev 11:3. Their lecture circuit garnered a small following with a tragic end. Cf. Gregory L. Reece, *UFO Religion: Inside Flying Saucer Cults and Culture*.

when the world ends tomorrow goes begging an explanation. In any case, those websites will be a pathetically moot point when Gog and Magog actually arise.

Finally, the past of *Christ and his coming* establishes the essence of the nature of his second coming, even if that coming is described as "revealed from heaven with his mighty angels in flaming fire" (2 Thess 1:6). The virgin Mary sings the Magnificat—her hymn of praise at the angel's news of the coming of Jesus (Luke 1:46–55)—couched in monarchial terms: "he has shown strength by his arm; he has scattered the haughty in the thoughts of their hearts; he has brought down the powerful from their thrones" (Luke 1:51–52). Yet, Jesus died on a Roman cross, and Pilate went on the next day with his regular business, as did Caiaphas and the rest. Just how has God shown "strength with his arm" and "brought down the powerful from their thrones" in Jesus dying on a cross? John's Apocalypse is simply another musical genre in which to sing Mary's Magnificat. The Apocalypse teaches that that future coming in glory, no matter what genre of words packages the truth, whether in Mary's monarchial kingdom language or John's apocalyptic drama

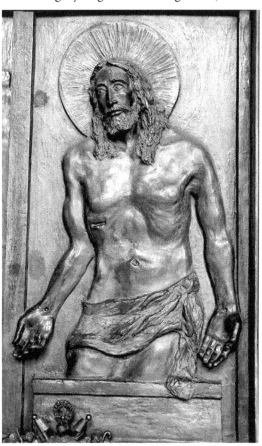

FIGURE E-6. The Risen Christ. Door of papal basilica, Santa Maria Maggiore, in Rome. The right panel is the risen Christ appearing to Mary pictured with a halo of glory but simultaneously bearing the marks of crucifixion. Sixtus III commissioned this basilica in Mary's honor after the Council of Ephesus (A.D. 431).

language, cannot be divorced from confessional witness in the present moment. Jesus' first coming and the second coming intersect at the point of testimony to Jesus, and that is why John was on the island of Patmos when he saw a vision of the Son of Man, ruler of the kings of the earth. The two comings together are the essential and mutual operations of how evil eternally is defeated and God's future kingdom comes. John teaches that the church must witness faithfully to her last breath for God's kingdom fully to come. He stands on gospel authority for his message (Mark 13:10).

The future of the Apocalypse also is in her interpreters. In these terms, the future is bleak if false prophets control, distort, and pervert the message. We need to be reminded that preaching an alien gospel message without an authentic apostolic core invokes a curse (Gal 1:6–8). On the other hand, the future is promising if John's message of indefatigable gospel faith and hope and courageous testimony to Jesus is proclaimed clearly and persuasively to a church that will need that message desperately in her hour of trial.

Bibliography

Abbott, Frank Frost. *The Common People of Ancient Rome: Studies in Roman Life and Literature*. New York: Biblo and Tannen, 1965.

Accordance, Version 10.1. OakTree Software Specialists, Altamonte Springs, Fla., 2013.

Aland, Barbara, Kurt Aland, Johannes Karavidopoulos, Carlo M. Martini, and Bruce M. Metzger, eds. *The Greek New Testament*. 4th Rev. ed. Stuttgart: United Bible Societies, 1993.

Aland, Barbara, Kurt Aland, Johannes Karavidopoulos, Carlo M. Martini, and Bruce M. Metzger, eds. *Novum Testamentum Graece*. 28th ed. Stuttgart: German Bible Society, 2012.

Aland, Kurt and Barbara Aland. *The Text of the New Testament*. 2nd ed. Translated by Erroll F. Rhodes. Grand Rapids: Eerdmans, 1989.

Aland, Kurt, ed. *Kurzgefasste Liste der griechischen Handschriften des neuen Testaments*. 2nd ed. Arbeiten zur neutestamentlichen Textforschung 1. Berlin: Walter de Gruyter, 1994.

Albrecht, Katherine and Liz McIntyre, *The Spychips Threat: Why Christians Should Resist RFID and Electronic Surveillance*. Nashville: Thomas Nelson, 2006.

"Apocalypse! The Story of the Book of Revelation." PBS Frontline Series. Directed by William Cran and Ben Loeterman, 120 min., PBS Home Video, 1999. Videocassette.

Aristeas. *The Old Testament Pseudepigrapha*. Accordance, Version 10.1.7. 2013. Print ed.: In vol. 1 of *Old Testament Pseudepigrapha*. Edited by R. H. Charles. 1913. 3 vols. Oxford: Clarendon Press.

Aristides, Aelius. *The Complete Works: Orations 1–16*. Leiden, The Netherlands: Brill, 1997.

Athenagoras. *The Ante-Nicene Fathers* on CD-ROM. Logos Research Systems Version 2.0. 1997. Print ed.: Athenagoras. In vol. 2 of *The Ante-Nicene Fathers*. Edited by Alexander Roberts, James Donaldson, and A. Cleveland Coxe. 1885–1896. 10 vols. New York: Christian Literature Company.

Augustine. *The Nicene and Post-Nicene Fathers of the Christian Church* on CD-ROM. Accordance Bible Software Version 10.1.5, 2013. Print ed.: Augustine. In vol. 1 of *The Nicene and Post-Nicene Fathers of the Christian Church*. Series 2. 1886–1889. Edited by Philip Schaff and Henry Wace. 14 vols. New York: Christian Literature Company.

Augustus. *Res Gestae Divi Augusti: The Achievements of the Divine Augustus*, with an introduction and commentary by P. A. Brunt and J. M. Moore. Oxford, New York: Oxford University Press, 1967.

Aune, David E. "The Influence of Roman Imperial Court Ceremonial on the Apocalypse of John." Biblical Research 28 (1983): 5–26.

———. *Revelation 1–5*. WBC, Vol. 52a. Dallas: Word Books, 1997.

———. *Revelation 6–16*. WBC, Vol. 52b. Nashville: Thomas Nelson, 1998.

———. *Revelation 17–22*. WBC, Vol. 52c. Nashville: Thomas Nelson, 1998.

Barclay, John M. G. "Deviance and Apostasy: Some Applications of Deviance Theory to First-Century Judaism and Christianity." Pages 110–23 in *Modeling Early Christianity: Social-Scientific Studies of the New Testament*. Edited by Philip Esler, New York: Routledge, 1995.

Barr, David L. "The Lamb Who Looks Like a Dragon? Characterizing Jesus in John's Apocalypse." Pages 205–20 in *The Reality of Apocalypse: Rhetoric and Politics in the Book of Revelation*. Edited by David L. Barr. SBLSymS, Num. 39. Edited by Christopher R. Matthews. Atlanta: Society of Biblical Literature, 2006.

———. "The Story John Told: Reading Revelation for Its Plot." *Reading the Book of Revelation: A Resource for Students*, 11–24. Resources for Biblical Study, No. 44. Edited by David L. Barr. Atlanta: Society of Biblical Literature, 2003.

———. *Tales of the End: A Narrative Commentary on the Book of Revelation*. Storytellers Bible, Vol. 1. Santa Rosa, Cal.: Polebridge, 1998.

———. "Towards an Ethical Reading of the Apocalypse: Reflections on John's Use of Power, Violence, and Misogyny." *Society of Biblical Literature 1997 Seminar Papers*. Atlanta: Scholars Press, 1997.

Bartchy, S. Scott. "Slavery (Greco-Roman)." *The Anchor Bible Dictionary*. Edited by David Noel Freedman. 6 vols. New York: Doubleday & Co., 1992. 6:66–67.

Bauckham, Richard. *The Climax of Prophecy: Studies on the Book of Revelation*. Edinburgh: T&T Clark, 1993.

———. *The Theology of the Book of Revelation*. Cambridge: Cambridge University Press, 1993.

Beale, Gregory K. *The Book of Revelation: A Commentary on the Greek Text*. NIGTC. Grand Rapids: Eerdmans, 1999.

Beard, Mary. *The Parthenon*. Cambridge: Harvard University Press, 2002.

Beard, Mary, et al. *Religions of Rome*. Vol. 1: *A History*. Cambridge: Cambridge University Press, 1998.

Beasley-Murray, George R. *Revelation*. NCBC. Grand Rapids: Eerdmans, 1981.

———. "Revelation." NBC21. Edited by G. J. Wenham, *et al*. Downers Grove: InterVarsity, 2004.

Beschlos, Michael. *Presidential Courage: Brave Leaders and How They Changed America 1789–1989*. New York: Simon & Schuster, Inc., 2007.

Bieber, Margarete. *The History of the Greek and Roman Theater*. Princeton: Princeton University Press, 1961.

Bingham, Sandra. *The Praetorian Guard: A History of Rome's Elite Special Forces*. Waco, Tex.: Baylor University Press, 2013.

Birdsall, J. Neville. "The Text of the Revelation of Saint John: A Review of Its Materials and Problems with Especial Reference to the Work of Josef Schmid." *Evangelical Quarterly* 33 (October 1961): 228–37.

Blaising, Craig A. and Darrell L. Bock, *Progressive Dispensationalism: An Up-to-Date Handbook of Contemporary Dispensational Thought* (Wheaton, Ill.: BridgePoint, 1993).

Blount, Brian K. *Can I Get a Witness? Reading Revelation through African American Culture.* Louisville, Ken.: Westminster John Knox, 2005.

Bock, Darrell L. *A Theology of Luke and Acts: God's Promised Program, Realized for All Nations.* Biblical Theology of the New Testament. Andreas J. Köstenberger, gen. ed. Grand Rapids: Zondervan, 2012.

Boring, M. Eugene. "The Theology of Revelation: 'The Lord our God the Almighty Reigns.'" *Interpretation* 40 (1986), 257–69.

Bouma-Prediger, Steven. *For the Beauty of the Earth: A Christian Vision for Creation Care.* Grand Rapids: Baker Academic, 2001.

Bowman, John Wick. *The Drama of the Book of Revelation.* Louisville: Westminster, 1955.

_____. "Revelation, Book of." IDB. Edited by George Arthur Buttrick. New York: Abingdon, 1962. 4:58–71.

Boxall, Ian. *The Revelation of Saint John.* BNTC. Peabody: Hendrickson; London: Continuum, 2006.

Boyer, Paul. *When Time Shall Be No More: Prophecy Belief in Modern American Culture.* Cambridge, Mass.; London: Harvard University Press, 1992.

Boyle, Anthony James. *An Introduction to Roman Tragedy.* New York: Routledge, 2006.

Braginton, Mary V. "Exile under the Roman Emperors." CJ. Vol. 39, No. 7 (Apr., 1944), 391–407.

Brant, Jo-Ann A. *Dialogue and Drama: Elements of Greek Tragedy in the Fourth Gospel.* Peabody: Hendrickson, 2004.

Bredin, Mark. *Jesus, Revolutionary of Peace: A Nonviolent Christology in the Book of Revelation.* PBTM. Carlisle, Cumbria: Paternoster, 2003.

Brouskari, Maria. *The Monuments of the Acropolis.* 3rd ed. Athens: Ministry of Culture, Archaeological Receipts Fund, 2006.

Brown, Dan. *The Da Vinci Code.* New York: Doubleday, 2003.

Burge, Gary M. *Jesus and the Land: The New Testament Challenge to "Holy Land" Theology.* Grand Rapids: Baker Academic, 2010.

Burge, Gary M., Lynn H. Cohick, and Gene L. Green. *The New Testament in Antiquity: A Survey of the New Testament within Its Cultural Context.* Grand Rapids: Zondervan, 2009.

Burkett, Delbert. *The Son of Man Debate: A History and Evaluation.* SNTSMS, Vol. 107. Cambridge: University Press, 1999.

Burrell, Barbara. *Neokoroi: Greek Cities and Roman Emperors.* CCSNS. Volume 9. Leiden: Brill, 2004.

Camille, Michael. "Visionary Perception and Images of the Apocalypse," *The Apocalypse in the Middle Ages.* Edited by Richard K. Emmerson and Bernard McGinn. Ithaca, NY; London: Cornell University Press, 1993.

Camp, John M. *The Archaeology of Athens.* New Haven: Yale University Press, 2001.

Carter, Warren. "Roman Imperial Power: A New Testament Perspective." *Rome and Religion: A Cross-Disciplinary Dialogue on the Imperial Cult*, 137–51. Edited by Jeffrey Brodd and Jonathan L. Reed. WGRWSS, No. 5. Atlanta: Society of Biblical Literature, 2011.

Cary, M. and H. H. Scullard. *A History of Rome: Down to the Reign of Constantine*. 3rd ed. Bedford: St. Martin's, 1976.

Casey, Maurice. *The Solution to the 'Son of Man' Problem*. New York: T&T Clark, 2009.

Cate, James Jeffrey. "How Green Was John's World? Ecology and Revelation." *Essays on Revelation: Appropriating Yesterday's Apocalypse in Today's World*, 145–55. Edited by Gerald L. Stevens. Eugene, Ore.: Pickwick Publications, 2010.

_____. "The Text of Revelation: Why neither Armageddon nor 666 May Be Exactly What You Think." *Essays on Revelation: Appropriating Yesterday's Apocalypse in Today's World*, 116–29. Edited by Gerald L. Stevens. Eugene, Ore.: Pickwick Publications, 2010.

Charles, R. H. *A Critical and Exegetical Commentary on the Revelation of St. John, with Introduction, Notes, and Indices; also the Greek Text and English Translation*. ICC. 2 Vols. Edinburgh: T & T Clark, 1920.

Chilton, Bruce. *Visions of the Apocalypse: Receptions of John's Revelation in Western Imagination*. Waco, Tex.: Baylor University Press, 2013.

Cicero. *Tusculan Disputations*. Translated by J. E. King. LCL 141. 1927. Cambridge, Mass.: Harvard University Press, 1960.

Clement of Alexandria. *The Ante-Nicene Fathers* on CD-ROM. Accordance Bible Software Version 10.1.5, 2013. Print ed.: Clement of Alexandria. In vol. 2 of *The Ante-Nicene Fathers*. Edited by Alexander Roberts, James Donaldson, and A. Cleveland Coxe. 1885–1896. 10 vols. New York: Christian Literature Company.

Clement of Rome. *The Ante-Nicene Fathers* on CD-ROM. Logos Research Systems Version 2.0. 1997. Print ed.: Clement of Rome. In vol. 1 of *The Ante-Nicene Fathers*. Edited by Alexander Roberts, James Donaldson, and A. Cleveland Coxe. 1885–1896. 10 vols. New York: Christian Literature Company.

Collingwood, R. G. and J. N. L. Myres. *Roman Britain and the English Settlements*. 2nd ed. OHE. Oxford: Oxford University Press, 1937.

Collins, Adela Yarbro. *The Apocalypse*. NTM. Collegeville, Minn.: Liturgical Press, 1990.

_____. *Crisis and Catharsis: The Power of the Apocalypse*. Philadelphia: Westminster, 1984.

Collins, John J. *The Apocalyptic Imagination: An Introduction to Jewish Apocalyptic Literature*. BRS. Grand Rapids: Eerdmans, 1998.

Cooper, David L. *When Gog's Armies Meet the Almighty in the Land of Israel*. Los Angeles: Biblical Research Society, 1940.

Cyril of Jerusalem. *The Nicene and Post-Nicene Fathers of the Christian Church* on CD-ROM. Accordance Bible Software Version 10.1.5, 2013. Print ed.: Cyril of Jerusalem. In vol. 7 of *The Nicene and Post-Nicene Fathers of the Christian Church*. Series 2. 1886–1889. Edited by Philip Schaff and Henry Wace. 14 vols. New York: Christian Literature Company.

Darby, John Nelson. *The Collected Writings of J. N. Darby*, 34 vols. Edited by William Kelly. London: G. Morrish, 1867–1900.

de Boer, Ielle Zeilinga and Donald Theodore Sanders, *Earthquakes in Human History: The Far-Reaching Effects of Seismic Disruptions*. Princeton, New Jersey: Princeton University Press, 2004.

Deissmann, Adolf. *Light from the Ancient East: The New Testament Illustrated by Recently Discovered Texts of the Graeco Roman World*. Lionel R. M. Strachan, trans. Eugene, Ore.: Wipf and Stock, 2004.

deSilva, David A. *Honor, Patronage, Kinship, and Purity: Unlocking New Testament Culture*. Downers Grove: InterVarsity, 2000.

_____. *An Introduction to the New Testament: Contexts, Methods and Ministry Formation*. Downers Grove: Intervarsity, 2004.

_____. *Seeing Things John's Way: The Rhetoric of the Book of Revelation*. Louisville: Westminster John Knox, 2009.

_____. *Unholy Allegiances: Heeding Revelation's Warning*. Peabody, Mass.: Hendrickson, 2013.

Douglas, Mary. *Purity and Danger: An Analysis of the Concepts of Pollution and Taboo*. New York: Routledge and Kegan Paul, 1966.

Duff, Paul B. *Who Rides the Beast? Prophetic Rivalry and the Rhetoric of Crisis in the Churches of the Apocalypse*. New York: Oxford University Press, 2001.

Dunn, James D. G. *Romans 1–8*. WBC, Vol. 38a. Dallas: Word Books, 1988.

Eisenstein, Elizabeth L. *The Printing Revolution in Early Modern Europe*. Cambridge: Cambridge University Press, 1993.

Elliott, Neil. *The Arrogance of Nations: Reading Romans in the Shadow of Empire*. PCCS. Minneapolis: Fortress, 2008.

Epictetus. *The Discourses as Reported by Arrian, the Manual and Fragments*. Vol. 2. Translated by W. A. Oldfather. LCL 218. 1926–28. Cambridge, Mass.: Harvard University Press, 1969.

Epiphanius. *The Panarion of Epiphanius of Salamis, Book I (Sects 1–46)*. 2nd Rev. Exp. Ed. Trans. by Frank Williams. Nag Hammadi and Manichean Studies (Book 63). Leiden: Brill Academic, 2008.

Eusebius. *The Nicene and Post-Nicene Fathers of the Christian Church* on CD-ROM. Accordance Bible Software Version 10.1.5, 2013. Print ed.: Eusebius. In vol. 1 of *The Nicene and Post-Nicene Fathers of the Christian Church*. Series 2. 1886–1889. Edited by Philip Schaff and Henry Wace. 14 vols. New York: Christian Literature Company.

Fanning, Bruce M. *Verbal Aspect in New Testament Greek*. Oxford: Clarendon Press, 1990.

Fee, Gordon D. and Douglas Stuart. *How to Read the Bible for All Its Worth*. Grand Rapids: Zondervan, 2003.

Ferguson, Everett. *Backgrounds of Early Christianity*. 3rd ed. Grand Rapids: Eerdmans, 2003.

Fiorenza, Elisabeth Schüssler. *Revelation: Vision of a Just World*. PC. Minneapolis: Fortress, 1991.

Fontenrose, Joseph. *Didyma: Apollo's Oracle, Cult, and Companions*. Berkeley: University of California Press, 1988.

Fox, Robert Lane. *Pagans and Christians*. New York: HarperCollins, 1986.

Friesen, Steven J. "The Beast from the Land." *Reading the Book of Revelation: A Resource for Students*, 49–64. RBS, No. 44. Edited by David L. Barr. Atlanta: Society of Biblical Literature, 2003.

_____. *Imperial Cults and the Apocalypse of John: Reading Revelation in the Ruins*. New York; Oxford: Oxford University Press, 2001.

Futral, James Robert, Jr. "The Rhetorical Value of *City* as a Sociological Symbol in the Book of Revelation." PhD diss., New Orleans Baptist Theological Seminary, 2002.

Galinsky, Karl. *Augustan Culture: An Interpretive Introduction*. Princeton: Princeton University Press, 1996.

_____. "The Cult of the Roman Emperor: Uniter or Divider?" *Rome and Religion: A Cross-Disciplinary Dialogue on the Imperial Cult*, 1–21. Edited by Jeffrey Brodd and Jonathan L. Reed. WGRWSS, No. 5. Atlanta: Society of Biblical Literature, 2011.

Gamble, Harry Jr. *The Textual History of the Letter to the Romans*. Studies and Documents 42. Edited by Irving Alan Sparks. Grand Rapids: Eerdmans, 1977.

Gates, Charles. *Ancient Cities: The Archaeology of Urban Life in the Ancient Near East and Egypt, Greece, and Rome*. London: Routledge, 2003.

Gonis, N., J. Chapa, W. E. H. Cockle, and Dirk Obbink, eds. *The Oxyrhynchus Papyri*. Vol. 66. London: Egypt Exploration Society, 1999.

González, Justo L. *Three Months with Revelation*. Nashville: Abingdon, 2004.

Greek Drama: From Ritual to Theater. DVD. Princeton: Films for the Humanities and Sciences, 2005.

Gregg, Steve, ed. *Revelation, Four Views: A Parallel Commentary*. Nashville: Thomas Nelson, 1997.

Grizzle, Raymond E., Paul E. Rothrock, and Christopher B. Barrett. "Evangelicals and Environmentalism: Past, Present, and Future." TJ. Vol. 18, No. 1 (Spring 1998): 3–27.

Gruber, Daniel. *Rabbi Akiba's Messiah: The Origins of Rabbinic Authority*. Kindle Edition. Elijah Publishing, 2012. ASIN: B00ACVN8MO.

Grudem, Wayne. *Bible Doctrine: Essential Teachings of the Christian Faith*. Edited by Jeff Purswell. Grand Rapids: Zondervan, 1999.

Gumerlock, Francis X. *The Seven Seals of the Apocalypse: Medieval Texts in Translation*. Translated with an Introduction and Notes. TCS. E. Ann Matter, Gen. Ed. Medieval Institute Publications. Kalamazoo, Mich.: Western Michigan University, 2009.

Hagee, John. "Countdown to Armageddon," DVD, Documentary, 2004, 100 min, A&E Television Networks.

Halsell, Grace. *Prophecy and Politics: Militant Evangelists on the Road to Nuclear War*. Westport, Conn.: Lawrence Hill, 1986.

Hanson, Anthony T. *The Wrath of the Lamb*. London: S.P.C.K., 1957.

Hanson, Kenneth C. "Blood and Purity in Leviticus and Revelation." *Listening: Journal of Religion and Culture* 28, 3 (1993): 215–30.

Hanson, Kenneth C. and Douglas E. Oakman, *Palestine in the Time of Jesus: Social Structures and Social Conflicts*. Minneapolis: Augsburg Fortress, 1998.

Harril, J. Albert. *Slaves in the New Testament: Literary, Social, and Moral Dimensions*. Minneapolis: Fortress, 2006.

Hauben, Michael. "The Expanding Commonwealth of Learning: Printing and the Net," accessed at http://www.columbia.edu/~rh120/ch106.x16 on Mar. 31, 2014.

Hays, Richard B. and Stefan Alkier, eds. *Revelation and the Politics of Apocalyptic Interpretation*. Waco, Tex.: Baylor University Press, 2012.

Hays, Richard B. *The Moral Vision of the New Testament: Community, Cross, New Creation. A Contemporary Introduction to New Testament Ethics*. Edinburgh: T&T Clark, 1997.

Heemstra, Marius. *How Rome's Administration of the Fiscus Judaicus Accelerated the Parting of the Ways Between Judaism and Christianity: Rereading 1 Peter, Revelation, the Letter to the Hebrews, and the Gospel of John in Their Roman and Jewish Contexts*. Doctoral Dissertation, September 2009, Rijksuniversiteit Groningen. Veenendal, the Netherlands: Universal Press, 2009.

Heim, S. Mark. *Saved from Sacrifice: A Theology of the Cross*. Grand Rapids: Eerdmans, 2006.

Heller, Matthew. "Psychological Perspectives on Peace: An Evangelical Analysis." *Sacred Tribes Journal*, Vol. 4, No. 2 (Fall 2009). Internet resource available from www.sacredtribesjournal.org.

Helyer, Larry and Ed Cyzewski, *The Good News of Revelation*. Eugene, Ore.: Cascade, 2014.

Hemer, Colin J. *The Letters to the Seven Churches of Asia in Their Local Setting*. JSNT Supplement Series 11. London: Sheffield Academic, 1986.

Herbert, A. S. *Historical Catalogue of Printed Editions of the English Bible 1525-1961*. Rev. and exp. ed. London: British and Foreign Bible Society, 1968.

Herodotus. *The Persian Wars*. Translated by A. D. Godley. 2 vols. LCL. Cambridge: Harvard University Press, 1921-1925.

Hildegard of Bingen: Scivias. Classics of Western Spirituality. Translated by Mother Columba Hart and Jane Bishop. Mahwah, New Jer.: Paulist Press, 1990.

Hippocrates. *On the Sacred Disease*. In *The Law, The Oath of Hippocrates, and On the Sacred Disease*. Translated by Francis Adams. Gloucestershire, UK: Dodo Press, 2009.

Hobson, Sarah and Jane Lubenenco. *Revelation and the Environment AD 95-1995*. Hackensack, N.J.: World Scientific Publishing Company, 1997.

Holmes, Michael W. *The Apostolic Fathers : Greek Texts and English Translations*. Updated ed. Grand Rapids: Baker, 1999.

Holmes. Arthur F. *War and Christian Ethics: Classic and Contemporary Readings on the Morality of War*. 2nd ed. Grand Rapids: Baker Academic, 2005.

Hood, Renate Viveen. "The Parthians." *Baker Illustrated Bible Dictionary*. Edited by Temper Longman III and Peter Enns. Grand Rapids: Baker Academic, 2013.

The Holman Illustrated Study Bible: Holman Christian Standard Bible. Nashville: Holman Bible Publishers, 2006.

_____. "Women and Warriors: Character Development in John's Apocalypse." *Essays on Revelation: Appropriating Yesterday's Apocalypse in Today's World*. Edited by Gerald L Stevens. Eugene, Ore.: Pickwick Publications, 2010.

Horace. *Satires, Epistles, and Ars poetica*. Trans. by H. Rushton Fairclough, LCL 194. Cambridge, Mass.: Harvard University Press, 1926, 1960.

Horn, Stephen N. "Hallelujah, the Lord our God, the Almighty Reigns: The Theology of the Hymns of Revelation." *Essays on Revelation: Appropriating Yesterday's Apocalypse in Today's World*, 41-54. Edited by Gerald L. Stevens. Eugene, Ore.: Pickwick Publications, 2010.

_____. "Let the One Who Has Ears: Hearing What the Spirit Says to the Church Today!" *Essays on Revelation: Appropriating Yesterday's Apocalypse in Today's World*, 175-87. Edited by Gerald L. Stevens. Eugene, Ore.: Pickwick Publications, 2010.

Hoskier, H. C. *Concerning the Text of the Apocalypse: Collations of All Existing Available Greek Documents with the Standard Text of Stephen's Third Edition Toge-*

ther with the Testimony of Versions, Commentaries and Fathers. 2 Vols. London: Bernard Quaritch, Ltd., 1929.

Humphrey, Edith M. "In Search of a Voice: Rhetoric Through Sight and Sound in Revelation 11:15—12:17." *Vision and Persuasion: Rhetorical Dimensions of Apocalyptic Discourse*, 141–60. Edited by Greg Carey and L. Gregory Bloomquist. St. Louis: Chalice, 1999.

_____. *The Ladies and the Cities: Transformation and Apocalyptic Identity in Joseph and Aseneth, 4 Ezra, the Apocalypse and the Shepherd of Hermas*. Ann Arbor, Mich.: UMI Research Press, 1993.

_____. "A Tale of Two Cities and (At Least) Three Women." *Reading the Book of Revelation: A Resource for Students*, 11–24. RBS, No. 44. Edited by David L. Barr. Atlanta: Society of Biblical Literature, 2003.

_____. *Surveillance Society: The Rise of Antichrist*. Toronto: Frontier Research Publications, 2000.

Hunt, Dave. *A Woman Rides the Beast: The Roman Catholic Church and the Last Days*. Eugene, Ore.: Harvest House Publishers, 1994.

Hylen, Susan E. "The Power and Problem of Revelation 18." *Pregnant Passion: Gender, Sex, and Violence in the Bible*, 205–20. SBLSS. Edited by Cheryl A. Kirk-Duggan. Atlanta: Society of Biblical Literature, 2004.

Ignatius. *Apostolic Fathers: English Translation* on CD-ROM. Accordance Bible Software Version 10.1.5, 2013. Print ed.: Ignatius. *The Apostolic Fathers: English Translation*. Translated by Michael W. Holmes. Grand Rapids: Baker Books, 1992, 1999.

Ioulis. *On Keos*. In *Sylloge Inscriptionum Graecarum*, Vol. 3. Edited by Wilhelm Dittenberger. Leipzig, Germany: Hirzel, 1920.

Irenaeus. *The Ante-Nicene Fathers* in *Accordance Bible Software*, Version 10.1.5. 2013. Print ed.: Irenaeus. In vol. 1 of *The Ante-Nicene Fathers*. Edited by Alexander Roberts, James Donaldson, and A. Cleveland Coxe. 1885–1896. 10 vols. New York: Christian Literature Company.

Jacobus, Lee A. *The Bedford Introduction to Drama*. 6th ed. New York: Bedford/St. Martin's, 2009.

Järvinen, Arto. "The Son of Man and His Followers: A Q Portrait of Jesus." *Characterization in the Gospels*, 180–222. David Rhoads and Kari Syreeni, eds. JSNTSup 184. Sheffield: Sheffield Academic, 1999.

Jeffrey, Grant R. *Final Warning: Economic Collapse and the Coming World Government*. New York: Random House, Inc., 1995.

Jerusalem Talmud. *The Jerusalem Talmud: A Translation and Commentary on CD*. Edited by Jacob Neusner. Trans. by Jacob Neusner and Tzvee Zahavy. Peabody, Mass.: Hendrickson, 2010. ISBN: 1598565281.

Johnson, Richard Warren. "Urban Persons: City and Identity in the Book of Revelation." *Essays on Revelation: Appropriating Yesterday's Apocalypse in Today's World*, 100–115. Edited by Gerald L. Stevens. Eugene, Ore.: Pickwick Publications, 2010.

_____. "Confronting the Beast: The Imperial Cult and the Book of Revelation." *Essays on Revelation: Appropriating Yesterday's Apocalypse in Today's World*, 130–44. Edited by Gerald L. Stevens. Eugene, Ore.: Pickwick Publications, 2010.

Jones, Brian W. *The Emperor Domitian*. Reprint edition. London: Routledge, 1993.

_____. *Suetonius: Domitian*. Bristol: Bristol Classic, 1996.

Josephus. Modules on CD-ROM. Accordance Bible Software. OakTree Software, Inc., Altamonte Springs, Fla. Greek text, ver. 1.5. 2005. Based on 1890 Niese edition, public domain. English text, ver. 1.3. 2005. Print ed.: *The Works of Flavius Josephus, Complete and Unabridged*. Updated edition. Translated by William Whiston. Peabody, Mass.: Hendrickson, 1987.

_____. Translated by H. St. J. Thackeray et al. 10 vols. LCL. Cambridge: Harvard University Press, 1926–1965; reprint 1968.

_____. *The Works of Josephus: Complete and Unabridged*. Updated edition. Translated by William Whiston. Peabody: Hendrickson Publishers, 1987.

Justin Martyr. *The Ante-Nicene Fathers* on CD-ROM. in *Accordance Bible Software*, Version 10.1.5. 2013. Print ed.: Justin Martyr. In vol. 1 of *The Ante-Nicene Fathers*. Edited by Alexander Roberts, James Donaldson, and A. Cleveland Coxe. 1885–1896. 10 vols. New York: Christian Literature Company.

Justin's History of the World. In *Justin's Epitome of The History of Pompeius Trogus, Literally Translated, with Notes and a General Index*. Translated by John Selby Watson. London: George Bell and Sons, 1886.

Kasher, Aryeh. *Jews, Idumeans, and Ancient Arabs*. Tübingen: J. C. B. Mohr, 1988.

Keener, Craig S. *Revelation*. NIVAC. Grand Rapids: Zondervan, 2000.

Keillor, Steven J. *God's Judgments: Interpreting History and the Christian Faith*. Downer's Grove: InterVarsity, 2007.

Kilpatrick, G. D. "Professor J. Schmid on the Greek Text of the Apocalypse." *Vigiliae Christianae* 13 (April 1959): 1–13.

Kim, Jean K. "Uncovering Her Wickedness: An Inter(con)textual Reading of Revelation 17 from a Postcolonial Feminist Perspective." JSNT 73 (1999), 61–81.

Klaus, Carl H., Miriam Gilbert, and Bradford S. Field Jr., eds. *Stages of Drama: Classical to Contemporary Theater*, 5th ed. Boston: Bedford/St. Martin's, 2003.

Klein, William, Craig Blomberg, and Robert Hubbard. *Introduction to Biblical Interpretation*. Rev. ed. Downers Grove: InterVarsity, 2004.

Koester, Craig R. *Revelation and the End of All Things*. Grand Rapids: Eerdmans, 2001.

Koester, Helmut. *Introduction to the New Testament. Volume 1: History, Culture, and Religion of the Hellenistic Age*, 2nd ed. New York: Walter de Gruyter, 1995.

Kohlenberger, John R. III, Edward W. Goodrick, and James A. Swanson. *The Exhaustive Concordance to the Greek New Testament*. Grand Rapids: Zondervan, 1995.

Kraybill, J. Nelson. "Apocalypse Now." *Christianity Today*, Oct. 25, 1999. Online: http://www.christianitytoday.com/ct/1999/october25/9tc030.html.

_____. *Imperial Cult and Commerce in John's Apocalypse*. JSNTSup 132. Sheffield: Sheffield Academic Press, 1996.

_____. *Apocalypse and Allegiance: Worship, Politics, and Devotion in the Book of Revelation*. Grand Rapids: Brazos Press, 2010.

Lactantius. *The Ante-Nicene Fathers* in *Accordance Bible Software*, Version 10.1.5. 2013. Print ed.: Lactantius. In vol. 7 of *The Ante-Nicene Fathers*. Edited by Alexander Roberts, James Donaldson, and A. Cleveland Coxe. 1885–1896. 10 vols. New York: Christian Literature Company.

Ladd, George E. *A Commentary on the Revelation of John*. Grand Rapids: Eerdmans, 1978.

LaHaye, Tim and Jerry B. Jenkins. *Left Behind: A Novel of the Earth's Last Days*. Wheaton, Ill.: Tyndale House, 1995.

Landes, Richard. "Lest the Millennium Be Fulfilled: Apocalyptic Expectations and the Pattern of Western Chronography 100–800 CE." *The Use and Abuse of Eschatology in the Middle Ages,* Werner Verbeke, Daniel Verhelst, and Andries Welkenhuysen, eds. (Leuven, Netherlands: Leuven University Press, 1988), 137–211. Grand Rapids: Eerdmans, 1978.

Lewis, Suzanne. *Reading Images: Narrative Discourse and Reception in the Thirteenth-Century Illuminated Apocalypse.* Cambridge: Cambridge University Press, 1995.

Lindsey, Hal, with C. C. Carlson. *The Late Great Planet Earth.* Grand Rapids: Zondervan, 1970.

Lindsey, Hal. *The 1980's: Countdown to Armageddon.* New York: Bantam Books, 1981.

_____. *Planet Earth—2000 A.D.: Will Mankind Survive? Revised, Updated Edition* (Palos Verdes, CA: Western Front, Ltd., 1994, 1996.

Livy. *History of Rome.* Translated by Frank Gardner Moore et al. 14 vols. LCL. Cambridge: Harvard University Press, 1919–1959; reprint 1965.

Longenecker, Bruce W. *The Lost Letters of Pergamum: A Story from the New Testament World,* with Extracts from Ben Witherington III. Grand Rapids: Baker Academic, 2003.

Lorein, G. W. *The Antichrist Theme in the Intertestamental Period.* JSPSS. London: T&T Clark, 2003.

Luther-Bibel von 1534, Die, Vollständiger Nachdruck. Vol. 2. Berlin: Taschen, n.d.

Luther's "September Bible" in Facsimile. Part I: Das Newe Testament Deützsch. Part II: Brief Historical Introduction by Kenneth A. Strand. Ann Arbor, Mich.: Ann Arbor Publishers, 1972.

Luther's Works. Vol. 35, Word and Sacrament. Edited by E. Theodore Bachmann. Philadelphia: Muhlenberg Press, 1955.

MacMullan, Ramsay. *Enemies of the Roman Order: Treason, Unrest, and Alienation in the Empire.* Cambridge: Harvard University Press, 1966.

Maier, Harry O. *Apocalypse Recalled: The Book of Revelation after Christendom.* Minneapolis: Fortress, 2002.

Malina, Bruce J. *Christian Origins and Cultural Anthropology: Practical Models for Biblical Interpretation.* Louisville: Westminster John Knox, 1986.

_____. *The New Testament World: Insights from Cultural Anthropology.* 3rd ed. Louisville: Westminster John Knox, 2001.

Malina, Bruce J. and John J. Pilch. *Social-Science Commentary on the Book of Revelation.* Minneapolis: Fortress, 2000.

Marshall, I. Howard. *New Testament Theology: Many Witnesses, One Gospel.* Downers Grove: InterVarsity, 2004.

Martyrdom of Polycarp. Apostolic Fathers: English Translation on CD-ROM. Accordance Bible Software Version 10.1.5, 2013. Print ed.: Martyrdom of Polycarp. *The Apostolic Fathers: English Translation.* Translated by Michael W. Holmes. Grand Rapids: Baker Books, 1992, 1999.

McGinn, Bernard. *Antichrist: Two Thousand Years of the Human Fascination with Evil.* New York: HarperSanFrancisco, 1994.

_____. "Moslems, Mongols, and the Last Days," *Visions of the End: Apocalyptic Traditions in the Middle Ages,* 149–57. Revised ed. New York: Columbia University Press, 1998.

McGrath, Alister E. *Christian Theology: An Introduction*. Oxford, U. K.; Cambridge, Mass.: Blackwell, 1994.

McKay, K. L. *A New Syntax of the Verb in New Testament Greek: An Aspectual Approach*. SBG, Vol. 5. New York: Peter Lang, 1994.

Melon, Michael P. *"Yet You Would Not Return to Me": Prophetically Speaking in an Age of Terror*. Longwood, Fla.: Xulon, 2004.

Metzger, Bruce M. *A Textual Commentary on the Greek New Testament: A Companion Volume to the United Bible Societies' Greek New Testament (Fourth Revised Edition)*. 2nd ed. Stuttgart: German Bible Society, 1994.

Michaels, J. Ramsey. *Revelation*. IVPNT. Downers Grove: InterVarsity, 1997.

Moessner, David P. *Lord of the Banquet: The Literary and Theological Significance of the Lukan Travel Narrative*. Minneapolis: Fortress, 1989.

Moffatt, James. *The Revelation of St. John the Divine*. EGT. Edited by W. Robertson Nicoll. Grand Rapids: Eerdmans, 1990.

Morris, Leon. *The Book of Revelation: An Introduction and Commentary*. Tyndale Rev. ed. Grand Rapids: Eerdmans, 1987.

Mounce, Robert H. *The Book of Revelation*. Rev. ed. NICNT. Grand Rapids: Eerdmans, 1997.

Moxnes, Halvor. "Honor and Shame." *The Social Sciences and New Testament Interpretation*, 19–40. Edited by Richard Rohrbaugh. Peabody: Hendrickson, 1996.

Müller, Mogens. *The Expression 'Son of Man' and the Development of Christology: A History of Interpretation*. CIS. Edited by Thomas L. Thompson. London, Oakville: Equinox, 2008.

Murphy, Frederick J. *Fallen Is Babylon: The Revelation to John*. NTIC. Edited by Howard Clark Kee and J. Andrew Overman. Harrisburg, Penn.: Trinity Press International, 1998.

_____. *Apocalypticism in the Bible and Its World: A Comprehensive Introduction*. Ada, Mich.: Baker Academic, 2012.

New Scofield Reference Bible, The. Edited by E. Schuyler English. New York: Oxford University Press, 1967.

Newport, John P. *The Lion and the Lamb*. Nashville: Broadman, 1986.

Neyrey, Jerome H. "The Idea and the System of Purity." *The Social Sciences and New Testament Interpretation*, 80–106. Edited by Richard Rohrbaugh. Peabody, Mass.: Hendrickson, 1996.

Niles, D. T. *As Seeing the Invisible*. London: SCM Press, 1962.

O'Leary, Stephen D. *Arguing the Apocalypse: A Theory of Millennial Rhetoric*. New York, Oxford: Oxford University Press, 1994

O'Rourke, John J. "The Hymns of the Apocalypse." *The Catholic Biblical Quarterly* 30 (1968), 399–409.

Oden, Thomas C. *The Rebirth of Orthodoxy: Signs of New Life in Christianity*. New York: HarperSanFrancisco, 2003.

Oilar, Forrest Loman. *Be Thou Prepared, for Jesus is Coming*. Boston: Meador Publishing Co., 1937.

Osborne, Grant R. *Revelation*. BECNT. Grand Rapids: Baker Academic, 2002.

Parker, David C. "A New Oxyrhynchus Papyrus of Revelation: P115 (P. Oxy. 4499), *New Testament Studies* 46 (2000): 159–74.

Parker, Robert. *Miasma: Pollution and Purification in Early Greek Religion*. New York: Oxford University Press, 1983.

Perriman, Andrew. *The Coming of the Son of Man: New Testament Eschatology for an Emerging Church*. Bletchley, Milton Keynes, UK: Paternoster, 2005.

Peterson, Eugene H. *Reversed Thunder: The Revelation of John and the Praying Imagination*. San Francisco: Harper and Row, 1988.

Petronius. Translated by W. H. D. Rouse and E. H. Warmington. LCL. Cambridge: Harvard University Press, 1913; updated by Michael Heseltine 1987.

Pippin, Tina. *Death and Desire: The Rhetoric of Gender in the Apocalypse of John*. Literary Currents in Biblical Interpretation. Louisville: Westminster John Knox, 1992.

Plevnik, Joseph. "Honor/Shame." *Handbook of Biblical Social Values*, 106–15. Edited by John J. Pilch and Bruce J. Malina. Peabody: Hendrickson, 1998.

Pliny the Younger. Translated by Betty Radice. 2 vols. LCL. Cambridge: Harvard University Press, 1969.

Plutarch. *The Parallel Lives*. Translated by Bernadotte Perrin et al. 28 vols. LCL. Cambridge: Harvard University Press, 1914–1969.

Polycarp. *Apostolic Fathers: English Translation* on CD-ROM. Accordance Bible Software Version 10.1.5, 2013. Print ed.: Polycarp. *The Apostolic Fathers: English Translation*. Translated by Michael W. Holmes. Grand Rapids: Baker Books, 1992, 1999.

Pope, Alexander. *An Essay On Criticism*. Amazon Kindle Edition, 2012. Page number source ISBN: 1419106406. ASIN: B0082ZGPCM2012.

Porter, Stanley E. *Verbal Aspect in the Greek of the New Testament, with Reference to Tense and Mood*. SBG. Vol. 1. New York: Peter Lang, 1989, 1993.

Price, S. R. F. *Rituals and Power: The Roman Imperial Cult in Asia Minor*. Cambridge: Cambridge University Press, 1984.

Ramsey, Sir William Mitchell. *The Letters to the Seven Churches of Asia: And Their Place in the Plan of the Apocalypse*. 4th ed. London, New York, and Toronto: Hodder and Stoughton, 1912.

Raquel, Sylvie. "Revelation as Drama: A Staging of the Apocalypse." *Essays on Revelation: Appropriating Yesterday's Apocalypse in Today's World*, 156–74. Edited by Gerald L. Stevens. Eugene, Ore.: Pickwick Publications, 2010.

Reddish, Mitchell G. *Revelation*. SHBC. Macon, Ga.: Smyth & Helwys, 2001.

_____, ed. *Apocalyptic Literature: A Reader*. Peabody, Mass.: Hendrickson, 1995.

Reece, Gregory L. *UFO Religion: Inside Flying Saucer Cults and Culture*. London, New York: I. B. Tauris, 2007.

Regev, Eyal. "Moral impurity and the temple in early Christianity in light of ancient Greek practice and Qumran ideology." Harvard Theological Review. 97. No. 4, 2004: 383–411.

Resseguie, James L. *The Revelation of John: A Narrative Commentary*. Grand Rapids: Baker Academic, 2009.

Rhoads, David M. *Reading Mark, Engaging the Gospel*. Minneapolis: Fortress, 2004.

Richardson, Peter. *Herod: King of the Jews and Friend of the Romans*. SPNT. Edited by D. Moody Smith. Columbia, S.C.: University of South Carolina Press, 1996.

Robbins, Ray Frank. *The Revelation of Jesus Christ: A Commentary on the Book of Revelation*. Nashville: Broadman Press, 1975.

Rossing, Barbara R. *The Choice Between Two Cities: Whore, Bride, and Empire in the Apocalypse*. HTS. Harrisburg, Penn.: Trinity Press International, 1999.

Routley, Erik. *Christian Hymns Observed: When in Our Music God is Glorified*. Princeton: Prestige Publications, 1982.

Schillebeeckx, Edward. *The Church: The Human Story of God*. London: SCM Press, 1990.

Schmid, Josef. *Studien zur Geschichte des griechischen Apokalypse-Textes*. 2 Vols. Munich: Karl Zink, 1955–56.

Schüssler Fiorenza, Elisabeth. "Babylon the Great: A Rhetorical-Political Reading of Revelation 17–18. " *The Reality of Apocalypse: Rhetoric and Politics in the Book of Revelation*, 243–69. Edited by David L. Barr. SBLSymS 39. Edited by Christopher R. Matthews. Atlanta: Society of Biblical Literature, 2006.

———. *The Book of Revelation: Justice and Judgment*. 2nd ed. Minneapolis: Augsburg Fortress, 1998.

Scrivener, Frederick H. A. *A Plain Introduction to the Criticism of the New Testament: For the Use of Biblical Students*. 4th ed. 2 vols. Edited by Edward Miller. London: George Bell & Sons, 1894.

Sibylline Oracles. *The Sibylline Oracles: Translated from the Greek into English Blank Verse*. Trans. by Terry Milton. Geneva: IPA, 2008.

Smalley, Stephen S. *The Revelation to John: A Commentary on the Greek Text of the Apocalypse*. Downers Grove: InterVarsity, 2005.

Smith, Uriah. *Daniel and the Revelation: The Response of History to the Voice of Prophecy; a Verse by Verse Study of These Important Books of the Bible* Nashville: Southern Publishing Association, 1897.

Spaeth, Barbett Stanley. "Imperial Cult in Roman Corinth: A Response to Karl Galinsky's 'The Cult of the Roman Emperor: Uniter or Divider?'" *Rome and Religion: A Cross-Disciplinary Dialogue on the Imperial Cult*, 61–81. Edited by Jeffrey Brodd and Jonathan L. Reed. WGRWSS, No. 5. Atlanta: Society of Biblical Literature, 2011.

Stagg, Frank "The Abused Aorist." JBL 91 (1972): 222–31.

Stevens, Gerald L. "A Vision in the Night: Setting the Interpretive Stage for John's Apocalypse." *Essays on Revelation: Appropriating Yesterday's Apocalypse in Today's World*, 1–15. Edited by Gerald L. Stevens. Eugene, Ore.: Pickwick Publications, 2010.

———. "One Like a Son of Man: Contemplating Christology in Rev 1:9–20." *Essays on Revelation: Appropriating Yesterday's Apocalypse in Today's World*, 16–40. Edited by Gerald L. Stevens. Eugene, Ore.: Pickwick Publications, 2010.

———. "Capital Crimes in the Roman Empire" *Biblical Illustrator*. Vol. 26, No. 2, (Winter 1999–2000), 60–63.

Stowers, Stanley K. "On the Comparison of Blood in Greek and Israelite Ritual." *Hesed Ve-Emet: Studies in Honor of Ernest S. Frerichs*, 179–96. BJS. Jodi Magness and Seymour Gitin, eds. Atlanta: Scholars Press, 1998.

Strabo. *The Geography of Strabo*. Vol. 2. Translated by Horace Leonard Jones. LCL 50, 1923. Cambridge, Mass.: Harvard University Press, 1988.

Strand, Kenneth. "'Overcomer': A Study in the Macrodynamic of Theme Development in the Book of Revelation." *Andrews University Seminary Studies* 28 (Autumn 1990), 237–54.

Suetonius. *The Lives of the Caesars*. Translated by J. C. Rolfe. 2 vols. LCL. Cambridge: Harvard University Press, 1914; reprint 1965.

Tacitus. Translated by M. Hutton et al. 5 vols. LCL. Cambridge: Harvard University Press, 1914–1937.
Talbert, Charles H. *The Apocalypse: A Reading of the Revelation of John*. Louisville: Westminster John Knox, 1994.
Taplin, Oliver. *Greek Tragedy in Action*. Berkeley: University of California Press, 1978.
Tertullian. *The Ante-Nicene Fathers* on CD-ROM. Accordance Bible Software Version 10.1.5, 2013. Print ed.: Tertullian. In vol. 3 of *The Ante-Nicene Fathers*. 1885–1896. 10 vols. Edited by Alexander Roberts, James Donaldson, and A. Cleveland Coxe. New York: Christian Literature Company.
Thomas, Scott Kevin. "A Sociological Analysis of Guilds in First-Century Asia Minor as Background for Revelation 2:18–29." PhD dissertation, New Orleans Baptist Theological Seminary, 1994.
Thompson, Edward Maunde. *An Introduction to Greek and Latin Paleography*. Burt Franklin: Bibliography and Reference Series #71. New York: Burt Franklin, reprint of Oxford, 1912 edition.
Thompson, Leonard. L. *The Book of Revelation: Apocalypse and Empire*. New York: Oxford University Press, 1990.
_____. *The Book of Revelation*. ANTC. Nashville: Abingdon, 1998.
Tödt, Heinz Eduard. *The Son of Man in the Synoptic Tradition*. NTL. Alan Richardson, ed. London: SCM Press, 1965.
Troeltsch, Ernst. *The Christian Faith*. Fortress Texts in Modern Theology. Minneapolis: Fortress, 1991.
Van Impe, Jack, with Roger F. Campbell, *Israel's Final Holocaust*. Nashville: Thomas Nelson, 1979.
Victorinus. *Scholia In Apocalypsin Beati Joannis*. Migne Patrologia Latina. Online: http://www.documentacatholicaomnia.eu/02m/0200-0300,_Victorinus_Petavionensis_Episcopus,_Scolia_in_Apocalypsin_Beati_Joannis,_MLT.pdf
Virgil. Translated by H. Rushton Fairclough. 2 vols. LCL. Cambridge: Harvard University Press, 1916.
Wainwright, Arthur W. *Mysterious Apocalypse: Interpreting the Book of Revelation*. Nashville: Abingdon, 1993.
Walhout, Edwin. *Revelation Down to Earth: Making Sense of the Apocalypse of John*. Grand Rapids: Eerdmans, 2000.
Weber, Timothy P. *On the Road to Armageddon: How Evangelicals Became Israel's Best Friend*. Grand Rapids: Baker Academic, 2004.
Whisenant, Edgar C. *88 Reasons Why the Rapture Could Be in 1988*. Nashville: The World Bible Society, 1988.
White, L. Michael. "Capitalizing on the Imperial Cult: Some Jewish Perspectives." *Rome and Religion: A Cross-Disciplinary Dialogue on the Imperial Cult*, 173–214. Edited by Jeffrey Brodd and Jonathan L. Reed. WGRWSS, No. 5. Atlanta: Society of Biblical Literature, 2011.
Wiersbe, Warren W. *Be Victorious (Revelation): In Christ You Are an Overcomer*. BEC. Wheaton: Victor Books, 1996, c1989.
Witherington III, Ben. *Revelation*. NCBC. Cambridge and New York: Cambridge University Press, 2003.
Wittmer, Michael E. *Heaven Is a Place on Earth: Why Everything You Do Matters to God*. Grand Rapids: Zondervan, 2004.

Wright, N. T. *Surprised by Hope: Rethinking Heaven, the Resurrection, and the Mission of the Church.* New York: HarperCollins, 2008.
_____. *Paul and the Faithfulness of God.* Christian Origins and the Faithfulness of God, Vol. 4. Minneapolis: Fortress Press, 2013.
Yamauchi, Edwin M. *New Testament Cities in Western Asia Minor: Light from Archaeology on Cities of Paul and the Seven Churches of Revelation.* Grand Rapids: Baker, 1980; reprinted Eugene, Ore.: Wipf and Stock, 2003.
Zanker, Paul. *The Power of Images in the Age of Augustus.* Ann Arbor, Mich.: University of Michigan Press, 1990.

Scripture Index

OLD TESTAMENT

Genesis

1:1	258
1:16	100, 101, 538
1:28	87
2:9	543
2:10	542
3:5	487
3:7	87
3:8	528
3:14–19	544
8:15	87
12:1	87
12:2–3	406n47
12:3	88
19:24	444n94
28:14	406n47
29–30	405n44
35	405n44
35:22–36	405n44
46:8–27	405n44
48:14	270n41
49:1–27	405n44
49:9	390

Exodus

1:1–5	405n44
4:22	280n63
7:14–25	419n63
10:4–19	411
15:6	270n41
16:13	429n70
16:31–35	429n70
16:32–34	320n94
16:34	450n106
19:1	87
19:4	429
19:6	398
19:16	253n5, 261, 270
24:4–8	253n5
25:21	450n106
25:31–40	264n163
27:14	261
28:17–21	537n13
29:20	270n41
31:18	450n106
32:15	450n106
32:32–33	519n190
33:20–23	545n21
34:29–35	273n52, 418
37:9	425n67
39:10–14	537n13
39:29	265n28

Leviticus

23	406n48

Numbers

1:5–15	405n44
1:20–54	405n44
2:3–29	405n44
6:24–26	547
6:25	545
7:1–88	405n44
10:11–26	405n44
11:6–9	429n70
11:31–32	429n70
13:14–15	405n44
22–24	319
24:17	26f2.1, 554
26:5–50	405n44
34:19–28	405n44

Deuteronomy

8:3–16	429n70
18:15–18	419n64
23:9–10	441n90
27:12–13	405n44
33:1–29	405n44
33:2	270n41

Joshua

7:6	481n143
7:13	280n63
13–19	405n44
15:8	499n167
24:15	150, 547

Judges

5:12–22	405n44
6:8	280n63

1 Samuel

2:27	280n63
4:21	264n22
8:7	265n30

2 Samuel

5:7	515, 482

1 Kings

2:19	270n41
2:27	280n63
6:20	5:36
11:31	280n63
13:21	519n187
14:11	519n187
17:1	419n63
18:19–40	418
18:19	418
18:20–40	436n79
18:38	419n62
18:41	419n63
21	325
21:23	473n130
21:25	325n103
22:38	473n130

7:8 — 280n63
7:16 — 266

2 Kings

1:10	419n62
1:12	419n62
2:21	280n63
2:27	280n63
9	464
9:10	473n130
9:22	325n103
9:30–37	418
9:36–37	473n130
18:13—19:37	532
19:32–35	515
23:29	460

1 Chronicles

2–7	405n44
2:1–2	405n44
12:24–38	405n44
17:7	280n63
27:16–22	405n44

2 Chronicles

11:4	280n63
16:9	268
28:3	499n167
32:1–23	532
36:15–16	266, 461n118

Nehemiah

9:20	429n70

Job

2:12	481n143
12:18	265n29
26:6	11
28:22	11
31:12	11

Psalms

2:6–7	265n30
2:6	515n183
9:11	515n183
12:6	368n146
14:7	515n183
16:8	270n41
16:11	270n41
17:7	270n41
18:35	270n41
20:6	270n41
44:3	270n41
45:9	270n41
48:2	515n183
48:11	515n183
48:12–13	416n59
50:2	515n183
53:6	515n183
60:5	270n41
63:8	270n41
69:28	519n190
69:35	515n183
73:23	270n41
75:8	451n107
76:2	515n183
78:24	429n70
78:68	515n183
80:17	270n41
82:4	515n184
83:3	515n184
84:7	515n183
86:9	346n129
87:2	515n183
88	251n2
89	251n3
89:7	251n2
89:13	270n41
89:37	251n2
90:4	33
98:1	270n41
102:13	515n183
102:16	515n183
102:21	515n183
104–106	486n147
105:40	429n70
108:6	270n41
111–113	486n147
115–117	486n147
118:15	270n41
110:2	515n183
125:1	515n183
132:13	515n183
135	486n147
138:7	270n41
139:10	270n41
146:10	515n183

Isaiah

1:24	280n63
6	379, 382, 383
6:1–4	379
6:3	383n12
6:6–10	298n76
11:1	390, 554
11:4	272, 272n49
14:12	426–27
22:20–22	265n29
22:22	343
25:8	407n50
26:17–18	425n67
27	148
30:8	261
34:8–10	444n94
40–66	125
41:10	270n41
42:6	88
43	148
43:4	346n130
43:10–13	253n5

Scripture Index   595

43:19	529	31:32	485n145	48:1–29	405n44
45:1	6	37:2	261	48:30–34	405n44
45:14	346n129	43:11	435n78		
48:10	368n146	49:12	451n107	Daniel	
48:13	270n41	50–51	474n133	2	278
49:6	88	50:5	515n183	2:18	279n62
49:10	407n50	50:29	460n115	2:19	279n62
49:23	346n129	51	148, 474n133	2:27	279n62
51:17–18	451	51:7	444, 468n126	2:28–29	233, 278, 380
51:21–22	451			2:28	279n62
52:8	545	Lamentations		2:29	279n62
53	391	1:1	4	2:30	279n62
53:7	102, 103	2:10	481n143	2:31–45	13, 414n58
54:11–12	536			2:45	233, 278, 550
54:12	526	Ezekiel		2:47	279n62
55:1	556	1–2	379	4	432n72, 476n134
60:3–11	526	1	381, 382		
60:3	88	1:1	383n12	7	148, 263, 279, 379, 396n28, 431
60:19	538	4	474n133		
60:62	545	4:13	280n63		
62:8	270n41	14:11	544–45	7:1	383n12
63	233	16	465n123	7:—8:4	394n27
63:1–6	233, 492, 495	16:8–14	485n145	7:9–15	519n186
63:3	233	18:12–14	526	7:9	267
65:4	340n121	23	464, 465n123, 473	7:10–12	341n123
65:14	364			7:10	398
65:17–19	526	26–28	474n133	7:13	233n38, 257, 396n28
65:17	125	26–27	474n133		
66	26, 123, 125, 126, 128, 148	27:30	481n143	7:18–25	432n73
		28:16	526n4	7:25	14, 416, 429n71
66:8	122, 124, 126	37	5, 126, 128		
66:10–11	125	37:23	126	8:26	550n24
		38:2	47	9:24	89, 90, 91, 124
Jeremiah		38:15	103	9:27	468
1:24	280n63	38:17	104	10	263, 279
3	465n123	38:18–32	103	10:13	426n68
2:2	280n63	38–39	258, 511	10:21—12:13	263n18
6:27	368n146	39:3	103	10:21	426n68
7:32	499n167	39:17–20	497n163	11:35	265n27, 368n146
8:1–2	519, 486	40–48	203		
9:7	368n146	40–42	416	12:1–2	341n123
13	474n133	40:1–2	531n8	12:1	426n68, 519n190
15:2	435n78	40:3—42:20	416n59		
25:15–29	451n107	43:5	531n8	12:4	131, 132, 133f5.3, 134f5.4,
25:15–16	444, 468n106	47	526		
31:12	515n183	47:7	543		

596 Scripture Index

	550n24
12:7	14, 270n41, 429n71
12:9	90, 91, 550n24
12:10	368n146
14:34	280n63

Hosea

1–3	485n145
2:5	367
2:8	367
11	367
12:6	383n13
12:8	367
13	367
13:14	520

Joel

2:28–32	115
2:32	515n183
3:2	460n115
3:11	460n115
3:13	445
3:17	515n183

Amos

1:16	280n63
3:13	383n13
4:13	383n13
5:14–16	383n13
9:5–6	383n13
9:15	383n13

Obadiah

| 1 | 280n63 |
| 17 | 515n183 |

Micah

2:3	280n63
4:2	515n183
4:7	515n183
4:8	515n183
4:13	515n183

Nahum

| 1:12 | 280n63 |

3	465n123, 474
3:4	494
3:5	383n13

Zephaniah

| 3:8 | 460n115 |
| 3:14 | 515n183 |

Haggai

| 1:2 | 280n63 |

Zechariah

1:3	280n63
1:14	515n183
2	416
2:1–5	416n59
2:10	515n183
3–4	394
4:2–3	382n7, 417n60
4:10	382n7
4:14	419n61
6	148
6:13	419n61
8:3	515n183
9:9	515n183
10:13	383n13
12:3	460n115
12:10–14	233n38
12:10	257
13:9	368n146
14	104, 113n24, 457
14:2	460n115
14:4	105
14:15	104

Malachi

1:4	280n63
2:26	383n13
3:2–3	368n146
4:5	418, 419n64

APOCRYPHA

Tobit

1–2	519n187
5:4	10
6:3–9	11
13:16–18	526n2

1 Maccabees

1:10	14
4:36–61	14
14:40–41	15

2 Maccabees

2:4–8	320n94
2:7	421n66
7:14	5

2 Esdras

7:26–44	505n174
7:28	147n3
7:29–31	526n1
10:25–27	526n3
12:31–34	505n174
14:12	14

NEW TESTAMENT

Matthew

1:4	280n63
1:20–24	549n23
2:13	549n23
2:16	496n162
2:19	549n23
2:22	496n162
4:1–11	390n23
4:1	496n162
4:6	549n23
5:8	545
5:15	66
5:22	499n167
5:29–30	447n101
5:29	499n167
5:30	499n167

Scripture Index

6:9–13	517n185	24:31	549n23	6:4–6	178
6:12	265n26	24:34	114, 118	6:14–28	506n176
8:11–12	485n146	24:36	549n23	6:30–34	176
8:12	455n110	24:42–43	339n118	6:45–52	177
8:16	496n162	24:43	458n112	6:49	177
10:15	195	24:51	455n110	6:52	177
10:23	371	25:1–13	485n146	8–10	176, 178
10:28	306n83, 499n167	25:1–12	485n145	8:1–10	177
		25:30	455n110	8:14–21	177
10:32	342n125	25:31–46	521	8:14	177
10:38	445n96	25:31	372, 549n23	8:15	178
12:36	195	25:41	549n23	8:17–18	178
13:9–17	298n76	26:29	485n146	8:22–26	178
13:39	549n23	26:39	496n162	8:24	178
13:41	549n23	26:52	435n78	8:25	178
13:42	455n110	26:53	549n23	8:27–38	179
13:49	549n23	26:64	270n41, 492n158	8:27	176, 180
13:50	455n110			8:29	180, 272, 521
14:1–12	506n176	27:16–26	486n148	8:31–38	180
16:17–19	180	27:26	496n162	8:32	180
16:24	445n96	27:33	499n165	8:33	181, 304
16:27	549n23	27:52–53	508	8:34	180, 295, 445n96
16:28	492n158	27:52	515n184		
17:1–2	273n52	27:53	372, 505n173	8:38	195, 549n23
18:9	499n167	28:2	549n23	9:1–32	182
19:28	519n186	28:5	549n23	9:1	181
20:22	551	28:16–18	267n35	9:3	273n52
21:5	515n183	28:18–20	186	9:7	174
21:9	111, 371	28:19	117, 253n6	9:13	433
21:12–27	266n34			9:30–32	182
21:40	372	**Mark**		9:33	182
22:1–14	485n146	1:1	174	9:47	499n165
22:13	455n110	11:9–10	111	10:32–34	182
22:30	549n23	1:11	174	10:38	234
22:44	554n29	1:12–13	175, 390n23	10:46–52	183
23:39	372	1:13	496n162, 549n23	10:52	183
23:15	499n167			11–16	176, 182
23:33	499n167	1:24–25	175	11:1–11	183
24–25	492n158	1:34	175, 496n162	11:15–18	266n34
24	117, 118	2:7	175	12:25	549n23
24:2	18n7	2:18–20	485n145	12:35–37	267
24:3	116	3:22	175	12:36	554n29
24:6	128, 130, 131	4:1	176	13	402
24:7	128, 130	4:9	298n76	13:2	18n7
24:27	372	5:41	508	13:4	115
24:30	258	6–8	176	13:8	128, 130

Reference	Page(s)
13:10	575
13:14	468
13:26–27	492n158, 501
13:27	549n23
13:29	132
13:30	114
13:32	549n23
14:25	485n146
14:35–36	496n162
14:50	183
14:62	181
14:66–72	184
15:7–15	486n148
15:13–14	111
15:15	496n162
15:22	499n165
15:34	184
15:59	184
16:1–8	185
16:6	551
16:7	185
16:8	185, 186
16:9–20	185n1
16:17–19	180

Luke

Reference	Page(s)
1:11–19	549n23
1:26–38	549n23
1:33	505n173
1:46–55	575
1:51–52	575
2:4–5	519n190
2:10–15	549n23
2:14	294n73
2:21	549n23
2:25–35	186
2:26	186
2:32	88, 187
3:21–22	191
4:1–13	390n23
4:2	496n162
4:10	549n23
4:18–19	496n162
4:41	496n162
7:20–23	496n162
8:8	298n76
9:7–9	506n176
9:23	192, 445n96
9:26	549n23
10:2	445n97
10:18	427n69
10:20	519n190
11:2–4	517n185
11:17	268n38
12:4	306n83
12:5	499n167
12:8–9	549n23
12:11	348
12:40	492n158
13:28	455n110
13:29	485n146
14:27	445n96
15:1–2	370n148
15:10	549n23
16:22	549n23
17:22–37	492n158
19:45–48	266n34
20:36	549n23
20:42	554n29
21:6	18n7
21:7	115
21:11	128, 130
21:20	115
21:25–36	492n158
21:32	114
22:18–19	371n150
22:18	485n146
22:29–30	372n152
22:30	519n186
22:43	549n23
22:69	270n41
23:18	486n148
23:21	111
23:24–25	496n162
24:23	549n23
24:51	551

John

Reference	Page(s)
1:2	267n36
1:14	196
1:18	545n21
1:29	196
1:48	268n38
1:51	549n23
2:11	196
2:13–22	266n34
3:13	267n36
3:19	113
3:29	485n145
3:36	193
4:35–38	445n97
5:4	549n23
5:22–30	113
5:25	270
6:27	405n46
6:31	429n70
6:35	320
6:48	320
6:49	429n70
6:68	500
7:37–58	556
8:12	538
9:39	111
10:21	496n162
11:46–53	496n162
12:15	515n183
12:23	196
12:29	270
12:31	113, 195, 551
12:49–50	500
13:31	196
14:3	501, 492n158
16:11	113
18:10	183
18:36	168, 253, 297
18:40	486n148
19:6	111
19:16	496n162
19:17	499n165
19:20	447n99
20:12	549n23
20:21	186
20:25–29	196
20:31	193
21:19	196

Acts

Reference	Page(s)
1–12	117

Scripture Index 599

1:1	186	12:12	318n91	5:10	198
1:3	188, 189, 190	12:23	549n23	5:12	198
1:6–8	21	13–28	117	6:4	505n173
1:6	188, 189, 190	13:14	452f11.41,	6:10	265n25
1:7	117, 190		534f12.9	8	162
1:8	117, 191, 253n6	14:22	188, 260	8:19–21	389n22
		15:14	88	8:24	196n6
1:9	505	16:9	563f12.29	8:31–39	399n36
1:11	104	16:14–15	287f10.9, 324	8:34	270n41
2:1–4	295	16:14	564	9–11	155
2:1	87, 551	17:6	304	9:33	515n183
2:14–21	115	17:10	563f12.29	11:26	155, 515n183
2:16–21	258n10	17:28	148	12:13	515n184
2:22–36	192	19	290n66, 356	13:11	196n6
2:33	270n41	19:1	564	15:16	265n27, 509n180
2:34	554n29	19:8	188		
2:38	265n26	19:10–20	293n68	15:26	515n184
5:1–10	268n38	19:23–40	154, 154f7.6	16:2	515n184
5:9	549n23	20:25	188		
5:31	270n41	22:25	341	**1 Corinthians**	
6:5	208	23:8	6	1:7–8	492n158, 501n170
7:30	549n23	24:26	268n39, 486n148		
7:35	549n23			1:17	445n96
7:38	549n23	26	187	1:18–25	112
7:53	549n23	26:10	515n184	2:2	572
7:55–56	250n1, 258n9	26:18	187	2:8	505n173
7:55	270n41, 505n173, 551	27:2	187f8.4	6:1	515n184
		27:23	549n23	6:3	549n23
8:12	188	28:11	187f8.4	11:10	549n23
8:26	549n23	28:23	188, 189	11:20–34	370n149
8:28–34	102	28:31	188, 189	11:20	262
9	187			11:24–25	371n150
9:1	250n1	**Romans**		11:26	88
9:3–5	273n52	1–11	155	12:2	250n1
9:3	187	1:3–4	262n17, 365n141	12:28–29	150n4
9:15–17	187			13:12	545
9:15	88	1:18–32	474n131	14:29	150n4
9:17	505n173	1:23	455n109	14:32	150n4
9:32	515n184	1:25	455n109	14:33	515n184
9:41	515n184	2:17	345n128	14:37	150n4
10:3	549n23	2:28–29	345n128	15:1–11	330n113
10:7	549n23	3:21	258n10	15:10	88
10:22	549n23	3:29	345n128	15:20–28	501n170
11:13	549n23	4:10–11	345n128	15:23	505n173
12:1–17	266	4:16	345n128	15:25	505n173
12:7–15	549n23	5:9	196n6	15:28	545

15:32 295f10.17
15:42–53 196
15:55 520
15:58 268
16:15 275n57
16:22 556

2 Corinthians

1:14 492n158, 501n170
1:22 405n46
3:18 505n173
5:17 529n5
9:12 515n184
11:2 485n145, 489n153
11:14 549n23
12:2 515n184

Galatians

1:6–8 576
3:19 549n23
6:12 445n96
6:15 529n5

Ephesians

1:1 563f12.30, 564
1:13 405n46
1:20–21 267n35
1:20 270n41
2:19 515n184
3:6 88
3:10 399n37, 447n98
3:16 505n173
4:12 515n184
4:30 405n46
6:10 268
6:18 515n184

Philippians

1:6 492n158, 501n170
1:10 492n158, 501n170
2:5 445n96
2:8 398n34, 445n96
2:9–11 267n35
2:12 196n6
2:16 492n158, 501n170
3:20 492n158, 501n170
3:21 273n53

Colossians

1:1 357n134, 563f12.30, 564
1:7 357n133
1:12 273n53, 515n184
1:13–14 265n26
1:17 267n36
1:18 365
1:24 192, 295
2:1 357n134, 563f12.30, 564
2:9 273n52
2:18 490n156, 549n23
3:1 270n41
3:3–4 273n53
3:4 505n173
4:12–13 29f2.3
4:13 357n133n134, 563f12.30
4:13–16 564
4:15 363, 563f12.30
4:16 287f10.9, 357n134, 563f12.30
4:17 363

1 Thessalonians

2:19 505n173
3:13 505n173, 515n184
4:15 505n173
4:16–17 492n158, 501
4:16 270, 267n36
4:17 91
5:2 458n112
5:4 458n112
5:9–10 196
5:9 196n6
5:23 505n173

2 Thessalonians

1:6 575
1:7–8 198
1:7 273n52, 549n23
1:9 198, 505n173
2 440n86
2:1–12 492n158, 501n170, 514n182
2:1 505n173
2:3 40, 238
2:6–7 35, 49
2:8 272n49, 505n173

1 Timothy

3:16 505n173
6:16 545n21

2 Timothy

1:10 505n173
2:12 505n173
4:1 505n173
4:8 505n173

Titus

2:13 505n173

Philemon

7 515n184

Hebrews

1:1–4 112
1:1–2 258n10
1:2 198
1:3 270n41, 273n52, 505n173
1:6–13 549n23

Scripture Index 601

2:2	549n23	1:20	112	1:1–6	257
2:5–9	549n23	2:5–10	253n6	1:1	50, 145, 244, 251, 253, 255, 271, 303, 341, 371, 402, 449, 549, 549n22, 559
2:9	505n173	2:6	515n183		
2:16	549n23	3:18	265n25		
4–5	542n19	3:22	270n41, 549n23		
4:12	272				
4:13	268	4:13	505n173		
4:14	265n25	5:1	505n173	1:2	261, 428
4:15	267n36	5:4	505n173	1:3	145, 151, 235, 254, 255n8, 271, 280, 280n64, 303, 314, 320, 342, 369, 458n113, 549, 552, 564, 565
4:19	542n19	5:13	443n92		
6:10	515n184				
7:24–26	267n36	**2 Peter**			
7:27	265n25	1:1	267n36		
7:28	267n36	1:16	505n173		
8:1	270n41	1:17	505n173		
9:4	429n70	2:4	504n172, 549n23	1:4–6	562
9:12	265n25			1:4	145, 152, 210, 244, 252n4, 256, 257, 337, 382, 420, 549n22
9:24	505n173	2:11	549n23		
9:26	265n25	3:1–15	492n158, 501		
9:28	501n170, 505n173	3:4	505n173		
		3:10	458n112		
10:2	265n25				
10:10	265n25	**1 John**		1:5–7	233n38
10:12	270n41	2:18–19	238	1:5–6	251, 378
12:2	270n41	2:18	238	1:5	150, 155, 228, 261, 262, 264, 265, 268, 275, 292, 303, 313, 314, 346, 365, 373, 391, 392, 393, 407, 428, 444n93, 445n95, 491, 492, 494, 499, 538
12:22	515n183, 549n23	2:19	238		
		2:22	238		
12:23	519n190	2:28	505n173		
13:2	549n23	4:3	238		
13:12	447n99				
13:24	515n184	**2 John**			
		7	238, 239		
James					
1:14–15	474n131	**Jude**			
1:14	239	3	515n184	1:6	228, 253, 260, 264, 265, 509, 536
2:2	551n25	6	504n172, 549n23		
3:6	499n167				
5:7–8	501, 492n158	24	268, 505n173	1:7–8	257
5:7	505n173			1:7	182, 320, 371, 373, 517, 520, 551
5:8	505n173	**Revelation**			
		1–11	241, 242		
1 Peter		1–3	277, 379		
1:7	492n158, 501n170	1	149f7.3, 156, 242, 548	1:8	229n34, 256, 257, 258, 265, 267, 274, 303, 386, 420, 423,
1:11	505n173	1:1-8	249, 250, 259, 279, 374		
1:21	505n173				

602 Scripture Index

	529		278	2:14	203, 318n90,
1:9–20	7, 23, 155, 249,	2–3	48, 149, 155,		476
	259, 273f10.4,		157, 202, 242,	2:15	151, 154f7.6,
	276, 279, 373,		255, 261, 263,		203, 293, 325
	374		270, 276, 373,	2:16	254, 319,
1:9–11	260		391, 434, 447,		327n107,
1:9–10	414		573		403n39, 494,
1:9	206, 207, 209,	2:1—3:20	280		540n17, 559
	244, 260, 261,	2:1-7	287	2:17	253, 282n65,
	271, 403,	2:1	280, 287f10.9,		320, 441n89,
	407n49, 428,		291, 337		494, 507
	430, 435n77,	2:2–3	291	2:18–29	321
	445n95,	2:2	260, 435n77	2:18	324, 492
	549n22, 556,	2:3	435n77, 437,	2:19	292, 324,
	568		494		435n77
1:10	250n1, 261,	2:4	564	2:20–23	325
	380, 441n87,	2:5–6	292, 318	2:20	151, 203,
	531, 545	2:5	254, 255,		318n90, 457,
1:11	210, 256, 262,		327n107,		465, 476
	276		403n39,	2:21	327, 327n107,
1:12–16	262		413n57, 475,		413n57,
1:12	263, 532		540n17		540n17
1:13–16	520	2:6	154f7.6, 203,	2:22	327, 327n107,
1:13	155, 251, 263,		325		407n49,
	264, 348, 391,	2:7	253, 282n65,		413n57,
	445, 450, 489,		294, 297, 298,		540n17
	520		434, 507, 543,	2:23	328, 551
1:14	267, 492		552	2:24–25	328
1:15	268, 270,	2:8–11	298	2:24	318n90, 325
	441n87, 488	2:8	303, 393	2:25	255, 403n39
1:16	156, 261, 270,	2:9	260, 303,	2:26–28	328, 507
	271, 272,		318n90, 345,	2:26	253, 381n5
	272n49, 337,		368, 407n49	2:27	330, 444n93
	340, 428, 429,	2:10	254, 305, 306,	2:28	330, 378, 554
	443, 473, 494,		378, 407n49	2:29	282n65
	500, 538, 547	2:11	253, 282n65,	3:1–6	332, 340
1:17–18	274		306, 306n83,	3:1	337, 338, 378
1:17	271, 303		327, 413n56,	3:2	255, 338, 458
1:18	274, 343, 365,		507	3:3–4	339, 475
	393, 519	2:12–17	307	3:3	327n107,
1:19–20	276	2:12	313, 494		403n39,
1:19	276, 277,	2:13	154, 202, 313,		413n57,
	277f10.5, 278,		318n90, 428,		540n17
	303, 374, 380		445n95, 486,	3:4–5	368, 489
1:20	149, 270,		494, 506	3:4	552, 552n26
	271n42, 274,	2:14–15	318	3:5	253, 340, 378,

Scripture Index   603

	381n5, 507,		518		403, 404, 423,
	519n190, 541,	4:1–11	379		434, 436, 441,
	552n26	4:1–8	382		441n88, 485,
3:6	282n65	4:1	93, 157,		487, 494
3:7–13	342		280n64, 378,	5:7–9	378
3:7	318n90, 343		379	5:7	387, 395, 490
3:8	344, 378,	4:2–7	381	5:8	441n88, 487,
	417f11.21, 494	4:2	380, 441n88,		515n184
3:9–10	345		531, 543	5:9	252n4, 407,
3:9	292, 318n90	4:3	381, 532, 537		441n88, 494
3:10	417, 435n77,	4:4	340n122, 378,	5:10	509, 536
	511		381, 441n88,	5:11	487
3:11	255, 348, 378,		487	5:12	406, 494
	403n39, 559	4:5	378, 379n1,	5:13	436
3:12	253, 348,		382, 441n88	5:14	487
	441n89, 494,	4:6–11	423	6–20	242, 326, 391,
	507, 546	4:6	142, 382,		393f11.11, 485,
3:13	282n65		382n8, 441n88,		488, 573
3:14–22	351		450	6–11	155, 305, 435,
3:14	364, 423,	4:7	539n14		488
	445n95, 492	4:8	229n34, 257,	6–9	263
3:15	365, 529		383, 420	6	57, 105, 148,
3:16–18	366	4:9–11	384		155, 157, 241
3:16	542	4:9	275n55,, 384	6:1–11:19	402
3:17	361n139, 366,	4:10	385, 487, 499	6:1–8:1	393f11.8, 402
	455, 475	4:11	229n35,	6:1–8	382n10, 403,
3:18	255, 340n122,		259n11, 385,		403f11.13, 450
	378, 459, 489,		423, 499,	6:1	423, 445, 490
	552n26		539n14	6:6	557
3:19–20	369	5	155, 156, 447,	6:9–11	556
3:19	327n107,		496	6:9	207, 373, 428,
	413n57,	5:1–14	386		430, 445n95,
	540n17	5:1	386, 414		447
3:20	255, 372, 378,	5:2–4	388	6:10	202, 252n4,
	403n39, 490	5:2	388		404, 455, 475,
3:21	253, 372, 378,	5:3	388		481
	381n5, 507,	5:4	388	6:11	340n122, 404,
	547	5:5–7	389		448
3:22	282n65	5:5–6	112, 155, 379	6:12–17	165, 404
4–22	276, 277, 280	5:5	267, 318n90,	6:12–14	518
4–20	270, 379		378, 390, 487,	6:12	252n4
4–19	64		553	6:15–16	499
4–5	155, 378, 379,	5:6–14	486	6:15	275n58, 366,
	491, 519	5:6	341, 373, 378,		457n111, 518
4	381f11.2, 386,		391, 392f11.7,	6:17	404
	388, 447, 487,		393, 393f11.8,	6:20	387, 448

Scripture Index

7–8	57		318n90, 412, 439	11:18	420, 445n95 421, 421f11.24, 422, 448
7	241	9:13–21	165	11:19	379n1, 382n6, 421
7:1–17	405	9:13	379n1		
7:1–8	405, 429, 545	9:15–16	413	12–20	240, 241, 242, 305, 326, 448, 488
7:1	379n2, 382n9	9:17–19	413		
7:2	565	9:17	47f2.17		
7:3	436	9:20–21	413	12–14	423
7:4	147, 318n90, 441	9:20	327n108, 540n16	12–13	240, 241, 441
7:5–10	318n90	9:21	327n108, 540n16	12	148, 240, 241, 422, 423, 423f11.26, 443, 531f12.4
7:9–17	406				
7:9	340n122, 379n2, 406f11.14, 486	10	57		
		10:1—11:13	414		
7:10	406	10:1–11	414	12:1—20:19	422
7:11	406, 487	10:2	415	12:1—20:15	393f11.8
7:12	229n35, 406	10:6–7	415	12:1–18	422
7:13	487	10:6	259n11, 414, 415, 423	12:1–6	424
7:14	252n4, 260, 407, 494, 552			12:1–2	425
		10:11	275n58, 415, 422, 457n111	12:1	422, 448
7:15	407			12:2	426
7:16	407, 455	11	57, 60f3.6	12:3–4	425
7:17	408	11:1–2	416, 417, 429	12:3	422, 426, 448, 465, 493
8:1	163, 408, 517	11:1–7	503		
8:2—11:21	393f11.8, 408	11:1	535	12:5–6	425
8:2—11:19	252	11:2	351, 417f11.21, 429, 463	12:5	426, 444n93
8:2	408, 409f11.15, 449n103			12:6	46, 46n16, 122, 426f11.28, 429
		11:3–13	417		
8:3–5	409, 446, 449n103	11:3	46n16, 428, 429, 574n2	12:7–12	426, 509
				12:7–9	427
8:3	447, 515n184, 561	11:5	419	12:7	318n90, 427f11.29
		11:7–11	507		
8:4	515n184	11:7	428, 430, 513	12:9	9, 305, 318n90, 504, 512
8:5	382n6, 447	11:8	463, 572		
8:6–13	410	11:9	135	12:10–12	428
8:7–12	453	11:11–12	517	12:10	229n35
8:6	449n103	11:13	463	12:11	155, 156, 193, 252n4, 253, 292, 305, 373, 392, 428, 445n95, 468, 487, 494, 500, 509
8:7	252n4	11:14–19	420		
8:8	252n4	11:14	420		
8:11	318n90	11:15–19	163		
8:13	379n1	11:15–18	420		
9:1–21	411	11:15	260, 422		
9:1–11	503	11:16	252n4, 487		
9:1	412f11.19	11:17–18	421	12:12	428
9:4	413, 545	11:17	229n34, 229n35, 257,	12:13–18	429
9:11	12, 230,			12:14	429

Scripture Index 605

12:15	429	13:18	439, 439n83	15:7	275n55, 382n10, 423, 450
12:17	428, 430, 450	14	240, 241, 435, 439, 448, 535		
12:18	431	14:1–20	440	15:8	229n35
13–20	428	14:1–6	442f11.35	15:13	229n34
13	57, 148, 203, 240, 326, 429, 431, 431f11.30, 432f11.31, 434, 435f11.33, 439, 440n86, 457, 481, 498, 527, 545	14:1–5	441	16	340, 457
		14:1	405, 422, 439, 441, 515, 545	16:1–21	451
				16:1–8	450
		14:2	488	16:2	452
		14:3	423, 487	16:3	252n4, 453
		14:4	340n121	16:4–7	453
		14:5	320, 442	16:4	252n4, 529
13:1–18	431	14:6–13	442	16:5	257
13:1–10	432	14:6	442, 507	16:6	252n4, 454
13:1–3	433	14:7	442	16:7	229n34, 379n1
13:1–2	240f9.33	14:8–10	455	16:8–9	455
13:1	422, 433f11.32, 493	14:8	22, 429, 443	16:9	22, 327n108, 413n57, 540n16
		14:9–13	444		
13:2	436	14:9	487		
13:4–8	434	14:10–11	439	16:10–11	455
13:2	436	14:11	442, 487, 545	16:11	327n108, 540n16, 558
13:4	436	14:12	427, 430, 435n77, 444, 515n184		
13:5–6	430			16:12–16	455
13:5	434			16:12	275n58, 457, 472
13:7	434, 515n184	14:13	445, 458n113		
13:8	341n124, 434, 519n189, 519n190, 541n18	14:14–20	445, 446f11.37	16:13–14	455
		14:17–20	241, 495	16:13	498, 504
		14:20	103, 252n4, 447	16:14	229n34, 275n58, 457, 472
13:9–10	434	15–16	57, 241, 422, 435, 448, 481		
13:9	434			16:15–16	339
13:10	260, 434, 474, 515n184	15	448, 448n102	16:15	368, 458, 458n113, 459, 489
		15:1—16:21	443		
13:11–18	435, 444	15:1–8	448		
13:11–13	435	15:1	165, 242, 388n19, 422, 448, 449n103, 453, 461	16:16	8, 459, 473, 496
13:11	430, 435, 436				
13:12	436			16:17–21	461
13:14–15	436			16:18	148, 379n1, 382n6
13:15–17	439	15:2	142, 448		
13:15	430, 437, 437f11.34	15:2–4	449n103	16:19	461
		15:3–4	449, 455	16:21	461
13:16–18	437	15:3	318n90	17–18	57, 303, 447, 481, 496
13:16–17	429	15:5—16:21	252, 448		
13:16	77, 366, 436, 441	15:5	379n1, 379n2, 449n103, 450	17	60f3.7, 203, 240, 241, 243, 326, 435, 448,
13:17	481, 557	15:6	450		

606 Scripture Index

	464, 466f11.50, 471f11.56, 531f12.4, 547	18:3	275n58, 366, 429, 475, 479, 500n168	19:11–21	403, 473, 491, 491n157, 492
17:1—20:6	462	18:4–24	474, 475	19:11–20	500
17:1—19:21	443	18:4	464, 475, 481, 490, 547	19:11–16	492
17:1–14	462			19:11	234, 272, 492, 502
17:1	241, 462, 531	18:6	475	19:12	492
17:2–6	557	18:7	476	19:13	155, 156, 233, 234, 252n4, 272, 494
17:2	275n58, 457n111, 465, 500n168	18:8	476		
		18:9–10	476		
		18:9	275n58, 500n168	19:14	265, 340n122, 495
17:3	465, 531				
17:4	466	18:10	22	19:15	156, 229n34, 272, 494, 495
17:5	22, 431	18:11–17	477		
17:6	252n4, 468, 515n184	18:12	532	19:16	473, 479, 496
		18:15	366	19:17–21	496
17:7–9	231	18:16	489	19:17	497, 502
17:8	341n124, 468, 503, 519n188, 519n190, 541n18	18:17–20	481	19:18	275n58
		18:17	481	19:19	275n58, 498, 498f.11.75, 499, 502
		18:19	366, 481		
		18:20	481		
17:9–11	471	18:21	22, 482, 482f11.63	19:20	499
17:9	275n58, 471			19:21	272, 494, 500, 540
17:10	433	18:22	483f11.64, 483f11.65, 484f11.68		
17:11	472			20	57, 64, 167, 168, 170, 171, 240, 328, 428, 502, 512, 518
17:12–18	457				
17:12	275n58	18:23	484f11.66, 484f11.67, 494		
17:13	473				
17:14	275n58, 473, 496	18:24	252n4, 485	20:1–6	502, 512
		19	57, 156, 234, 240, 272, 473, 491, 496, 502, 510, 555f12.24	20:1–3	502, 509
17:15–16	473			20:1	502, 503
17:15	465, 473			20:2–3	504
17:16	476, 481			20:2	318n90, 503f11.76
17:17	474	19:1–10	474, 485		
17:18	275n58, 473, 500n168	19:1	229n35, 379n2, 486	20:3	505
				20:4–6	166, 166f7.14, 445n95, 504
18–19	491	19:2	252n4		
18	148, 158, 212, 240, 326, 328, 485, 487, 491, 496	19:3	486	20:4	35, 87, 148, 168, 207, 373, 502, 504, 505, 507, 556, 564n41
		19:4	423, 487		
		19:5	486		
		19:6	229n34, 488		
18:1—19:10	474	19:7	556n33		
18:1–3	474, 475	19:8	265, 489, 515n184	20:5	35, 507
18:1	379n2			20:6	306, 306n83, 458n113, 506, 509, 536
18:2	15, 22, 414, 475, 556	19:9	458n113, 490		
		19:10	428, 490		

20:7–15	509, 510		531, 556n33	22:4	545
20:7–10	511	21:3–4	528	22:5	526, 546
20:7–8	513f11.79	21:3	351	22:6–21	547
20:7	318n90, 512, 512n181	21:4	408	22:6–11	548
		21:5–8	526	22:6	255, 298, 337, 548, 549, 559
20:8	47, 417, 417f11.21, 514	21:5	529		
		21:6	259, 529, 556	22:7–19	341
20:9–10	516f11.80	21:7	530	22:7	255, 280, 341, 342, 458n113, 549, 559
20:9	292, 514, 515n184, 516, 539	21:8	306, 306n83, 530		
		21:9–27	526, 530	22:8	244, 549, 549n22
20:10	517	21:9	530, 556n33		
20:11–15	518, 556	21:10	66, 531	22:9	298, 341, 549, 550
20:11	502, 518, 520	21:12	318n90, 532		
20:12	341, 341n124, 519, 519n190, 541n18	21:15–17	535	22:10	341, 550
		21:16	536n11	22:11	550, 551n25, 558
		21:18–21	536		
20:13–14	275	21:19–20	537	22:12–16	551
20:13	519	21:21	537	22:12	280, 373, 559
20:14	306, 306n83, 520, 538	21:22	229n34, 407, 537, 538	22:13	259, 551
				22:14	458n113, 552
20:15	341n124, 444n93, 519n190, 520, 541n18	21:23–27	538	22:15	552, 553
		21:23	538, 546	22:16	318n90, 331, 551, 553
		21:24	500, 539, 543		
		21:25	540	22:17	555, 556
21–22	242, 391, 573	21:26	541, 543	22:18–19	557
21	148, 423, 502, 531f12.4, 547	21:27	341n124, 519n189, 519n190, 541	22:18	341, 558
				22:19	341
21:1—22:5	525			22:20–21	558
21:1–4	525, 527	22	548	22:20	558, 559, 560
21:1	259n11, 382n8, 502, 527	22:1–4	526, 529, 541	22:21	152, 494n161, 515n184, 561f12.28, 563, 564
		22:1–2	542		
21:2	35, 351, 431, 527, 528f12.3,	22:1	541f12.15		
		22:3	544, 545		

Scripture Index 607

Ancient Documents Index

1 Clement

65:1	562n38

1 Enoch

54:6	426n68
10:4–6	504n172
83:3–4	526n1
91:11–17	505n174
91:14–16	526n1

2 Baruch

3: 4–6	526n1
6:1–9	421n66
11:1	443n91
29:1—30:5	505n174
40	504n172
40:1–4	505n174
72:2—74:3	505n174

Aristides
Encomium of Rome

11–13	478n138

Athenagoras
Embassy for the Christians

3	304n82

Augustine
Tractates on John

36.5	382n9

Augustus
Res Gestae Divi Augusti

25	299n77

Cicero
Epistulae ad Atticum

5.15.2	359n135
6.5	231n36

Epistulae ad Familiares

3.5.4	359n135

Pro Flacco

68	359n136

Clement of Alexandria
Quis Dives Salvetur

42	208n16

Cyril of Jerusalem
On the Mysteries. II. Of Baptism

2	340n120

Catechetical Lectures

4.36	204n8

Dio Cassius
Historia Romana

43.22.1–2	331n115
51.20.6–8	293n69
66.15.4–5	506n175
67.4.7	488n151

Epictetus
The Discourses

3.13.9	299n77

Epiphanius
The Panarion of Epiphanius of Salamis

51.33.1	202n2

Eusebius
Historia Ecclesiastica

2.25	506n176
3.39	29
3.20.9	208n16
3.23.3	208n17
3.23.6	210n20
3.25.2–4	204n9
4.6.3	476 n135
5.20.2	558
7.25.7–27	205n10
7.25.4	205n11

Herodotus
The Histories

1.79–84	333n116

Horace
Carmen Saeculare

7	231n36

Epistularum liber secundus

2.1.15	272n50

Justin Martyr
The First Apology

5	304n82

Dialogue with Trypho

33.3	26n3
80–81	29
81.4	204n7
110.4	506n175

Ignatius
To the Ephesians

9.1	292n67

To the Philippians

6	343n127

Irenaeus
Against Heresies

5.33.3–4	29
5.32–36	29
5.30.1–4	439n83
5.30.2	405n45
5.30.3	202n5
2.22.5	208n17

Jerusalem Talmud
Moed Ta'anit

4:6	554n30

Josephus
Jewish Antiquities

13.14.2	103n10
14.241–43	359n136
17.10.10	394n26
18.8	476n135
20.117	506n175
20.267	476n135

Jewish War

2.5.2	394n26
2.7.8	266n32
2.12.6	394n26
3.179	476n135
4.361	476n135
4.9.3	266n32
5.513	476n135
6.1	476n135
6.193	476n135
6.201–14	476n135
6.369	476n135
6.405	476n135
6.421	476n135
6.430	476n135

Lactantius
Divine Institutes

7.15	560n35

On the Manner in which the Persecutors Died

48	350n132

Livy
History of Rome

30.43.13	506n175

Martial
Epigrams

4.64	231n36

Martyrdom of Polycarp

2.3	271n44, 297n75
5	318n91
13	319n93

Petronius
Satyricon

119.1–12	212n28

Pliny the Elder
Natural History

2.86	343n126
3.66	231n36

Pliny the Younger
Epistulae

6.16	410n52
6.20	410n52
10.96	261n14, 316n88, 384n14
10.96.5	319n92

Plutarch
Antony

58.5	311n86

Quaestiones Graecae

25 (297a)	555n25

Polybius
Histories

7.15–18	333n117

Polycarp
To the Philippians

11.3	202n2

Propertius
Elegies

3.9	231n36

The Sibylline Oracles

5.143–45	443n91
5.476–78	526n1

Strabo
Geographica

3.2.5	299n77
12.8.16	360n138
12.8.18	343n126, 360n137
13.4.10	343n126

Suetonius
Domitianus

13.2	386n17, 488n151

Nero

25.1	233n40
31.1–2	301n79

Tacitus
The Annals of Tacitus

2.47	343n126

4.30	209n19	*De Praescriptione Haereticorum*		Virgil	
4.37	293n70			*Aeneid*	
4.55–56	293n71	32.2	302n81	6.784	231n36
14.27	360n137			*Eclogae*	
15.44	202n4, 304n82	Victorinus		4	272n50
		Scholia in Apocalypsin		*Georgics*	
Tertullian		10.11	210n20	2.535	231n36
Against Marcion					
3.24.4	30				

Modern Authors Index

Abbott, Frank Frost, 322n97
Albrecht, Katherine and Liz McIntyre, 108
Aune, David E., 264n24, 267n37, 271n42, 275n56
Barr, David L. 271n48
Bartchey, S. Scott, 478n140
Bauckham, Richard, 205n12
Beale, Gregory K., 201n1, 202n2, 205n12, 232n37, 264n24, 276n59, 329, 329n111, 366, 366n144, 395n28, 450n105, 562n36
Beasley-Murray, George R., 259n12, 264n24, 395n29, 432n74, 433, 433n76, 463n121, 531n9, 555n32, 563n39
Beschlos, Michael, 92n9
Bingham, Sandra, 211n26, 367n145
Blackstone, William E., 126–27, 127n36
Blaising, Craig A. and Darrell L. Bock, 96n12
Bowman, John Wick, 236n41
Boyer, Paul, 9n4, 65n9, 66n11, 107n19, 128n39, 136n45
Braginton, Mary V., 207n14
Brown, Dan, 80n4
Burge, Gary M. 191, 191n3

Burge, Gary M., Lynn H. Cohick, Gene L. Green, 266n31
Burrell, Barbara, 229n33
Camille, Michael, 59n4, 61n5
Carter, Warren, 227n32
Cary, M. and H. H. Scullard, 466n124, 477n136
Cate, James Jeffrey, 439n83, 460n114, 526, 526n1
Charles, R. H., 241n45
Chilton, Bruce, 35n9, 37n11, 50n20, 65n10
Collins, Adela Yarbro, 202n3
de Boer, Ielle Zeilinga and Donald Theodore Sanders, 129n40
deSilva, David A., 202n4, 212n29, 264n24, 271n46, 371, 371n151, 386n17
Dunn, James D. G., 399n36
Eisenstein, Elizabeth L., 131n42
Elliott, Neil, 270n40
Fanning, Bruce M., 277n60
Fee, Gordon D. and Douglas Stuart, 102n9
Ferguson, Everett, 261n14, 272n50
Fiorenza, Elizabeth Schüssler, 498n164
Fontenrose, Joseph, 350n132
Friesen, Steven J., 294n73

Futral, James Robert, Jr., 463, 464n122
Gaebelein, Arno C., 126–27
Galinsky, Karl, 212n29, 227n32
Gamble, Harry Jr., 562n37
Gruber, Daniel, 554n30
Gumerlock, Francis X., 102n8
Hagee, John, 105n18, 130n41
Halsell, Grace, 92n9
Hanson, Anthony T., 271n47
Hauben, Michael, 131n42
Helyer, Larry, and Ed Cyzewski, 199n7
Hemer, Colin J., 208n15, 211n23, 262n16, 324n101, 359n135, 361n139
Hood, Renate Viveen, 6f1.5, 463n120
Horn, Stephen N., 224n31, 383n11
Humphrey, Edith M., 250n1
Hunt, Dave, 61n6
Jeffrey, Grant R., 108
Johnson, Richard Warren, 22n9, 210, 210n21, 211n24, 212, 212n27
Jones, Brian W., 202n4
Klein, William, Craig Blomberg, and Robert Hubbard, 16n6, 102n9
Koester, Helmut, 477n137

Kraybill, J. Nelson, 254n7, 270n40, 294n72, 297n74, 299n78, 317, 317n89
Landes, Richard, 33n8
LaHaye, Tim and Jerry B. Jenkins, 8, 9, 9n3
Lewis, Suzanne, 46n17
Lindsey, Hal, 63, 76n1, 91, 92n8, 96, 99n1, 100n3, 100–102, 103n11, 104–05, 104n14, 105n16n17, 110, 110n22, 112–13, 112n23, 113n24, 118n27, 118–19, 119n28n30, 120f5.2, 121–22, 121n31, 122n32, 126n35, 126–27, 127n37, 136n45
Longenecker, Bruce, 199n7, 210n22
Lorein, G. W., 35n10, 40n12
MacMullan, Ramsay, 322n98
McGinn, Bernard, 35n10, 40n12, 47n18
McKay, K. L., 277n60
Moessner, David P., 372n152
Murphy, Frederick J., 146n1, 265n28, 275n57

Oden, Thomas C., 271, 271n45
Oilar, Forrest Loman, 9, 9n4
O'Leary, Stephen D., 33n8, 76n1, 109n21
Osborne, Grant R., 264, 171
Pentecost, Dwight, 95
Perriman, Andrew, 272n50
Porter, Stanley E., 277n60
Price, S. R. F., 211, 211n25
Ramsey, Sir William Mitchell, 209n19, 323n100, 361n139
Raquel, Sylvie, 235, 236, 236n41, 236n42, 237
Reddish, Mitchell G., 203n6, 272n51, 404, 404n42, 419, 419n65, 433, 433n75, 471f11.56, 477n136, 520, 520n191, 529n6, 543n20, 563n39
Reece, Gregory L., 574n2
Resseguie, James L., 264n24, 273n53
Robbins, Ray Frank, 263n20, 273n54
Ryrie, Charles, 95
Smalley, Stephen S., 202n5, 205n12, 233n39, 264n24, 321n95
Spaeth, Barbett Stanley, 227n32
Stagg, Frank, 277n60
Stevens, Gerald L., 7n2, 209n18, 233n38, 259n13, 263n19, 263n20, 266n32, 266n33, 271n42, 275n56, 506n175
Thomas, Scott Kevin, 322n96, 323n99, 326, 326n105
Thompson, Edward Maunde, 395n28
Thompson, Leonard L., 202n4, 386n17
Van Impe, Jack, 123n34
Wainwright, Arthur W., 25, 25n1, 27n5, 42n13, 64n8, 128n38, 166
Walvoord, John, 95
Weber, Timothy P., 137
Whisenant, Edgar C., 119n29, 120f5.2
White, L. Michael, 227n32
Wright, N. T. 270n40
Zanker, Paul, 270n40

Subject Index

666, 147, 438
1260, 46, 46n16, 51, 64, 122, 416, 426, 429
144,000, 83, 127, 147, 159, 240, 241, 405, 406, 408, 423, 425, 429, 441, 442f11.35, 515, 535, 545
Abaddon, 11, 230, 318n90, 321, 412, 439, 573
Abyss, 12, 329, 503f11.76, 504, 513f11.79, 515
acropolis, 229f9.25, 307, 308, 308f10.30, 309f10.32, 311f10.35, 314, 314n87, 322, 332, 332f10.46, 333, 336, 336f10.53, 344f10.57
Adam, 161, 194, 198, 544f12.18
Adso, 40–41, 44, 45, 50, 237, 508n179
Advent, First, 39, 88, 98n14, 110, 119
Advent, Second, 98, 100, 110, 112
Adventism, 76–78, 83, 97, 141
Aeneas, 212–13, 212f9.5, 330, 330n114, 468, 468f11.53, 555f12.23
agora, 213, 301f10.25, 321f10.40, 351, 534f12.8, 535

Agrippina, 225, 226, 226f9.22, 385
Ahab (king), 325, 325n103
AIDS, 108f5.1, 130
Akiba, Rabbi, 26f2.1, 111, 554
Alaric I, 36
Alcazar, Luis de, 64
Alexander (of Cleopatra), 103n10
Alexander the Great, 9, 9f1.8
Alien (movie), 147n2
allegory, 39, 100–101, 105–06, 262, 382n9
Almighty, 224n31, 229, 245, 256, 257, 259, 265, 383, 388, 415, 420, 422, 436, 439, 447, 449, 458, 472, 474, 488, 504, 527, 537, 538, 545
Alogi, 31
Alpha and Omega 256, 258, 259, 267, 303, 386, 422–23, 440n84, 529, 551, 552, 556, 567
Altar of Peace, 294
Altar of Zeus, 307, 308f10.31, 310, 310f10.33, 310f10.34, 314n87
Amen, 364–65, 400, 548, 558, 560, 561, 567
America(n), 8, 27, 40, 63, 65, 65n9f3.5, 66–67, 68, 69, 69f3.11, 71, 72, 73, 76, 79, 80, 81, 84, 85, 86, 87, 92, 92n9, 94, 95, 96f4.13, 97, 111, 127, 128, 135, 136, 137, 141–42, 161, 167, 169
American Indians, 71
American Messianic Fellowship, 127
amillennial(ism), 37, 46, 49, 50, 55, 57, 68, 100, 140, 165–66, 167–68, 170, 171, 572
amphora, 329f10.43
Anabaptist, 27, 37, 62–63, 62n7, 68
Ancient of Days, 263, 267, 268, 273f10.4, 279, 280, 303, 307, 374, 375, 395, 519, 521, 524, 552, 567, 569
Andreas, 32
angel, xxiifP-1, 9–12, 18, 24, 57, 64, 71, 104, 147, 149, 163, 165, 185, 195, 198, 241, 242, 251, 255, 265, 270, 271, 271n42, 271n43, 274, 279, 281, 287f10.9, 294n73, 298, 318, 371, 372, 381n5, 382n9, 388, 398, 399, 406, 408, 409, 409f11.15, 411n53, 412f11.19, 414, 415, 420, 422, 423, 426, 427,

615

616 Subject Index

441–50, 442f11.35, 443f11.36, 449n103, 454, 455, 462, 474, 475, 481, 490n156, 496, 497, 501–03, 503f11.76, 530, 535, 548–50, 549n23, 553, 567, 575
Anglican, 85, 89
annihilation, 307n84, 517
Anno Domini, 39
Anno Mundi, 33
anti-Semitic, 42, 51, 365n143, 405n45
Antichrist slander, 45, 51, 54, 55, 56, 58–59, 66, 68, 466, 466f11.50
Antichrist, 9, 35, 35n10, 36, 40–45, 41f2.13, 43f2.15, 47, 51, 54, 55, 56, 58–61, 66, 68, 77, 78, 78n2, 79, 107, 136, 140, 159, 160, 199n7, 237–39, 246, 256, 292, 320, 326, 405n45, 440n86, 466, 466f11.50, 513, 573
Antioch of Pisidia, 260, 452f11.41, 534f12.9
Antiochus II, 351
Antiochus III, 333, 339
Antiochus IV, 14, 14f1.14, 40, 416, 431, 432, 468, 472
Antipas, 154, 202, 294, 300, 314, 317, 318, 320, 332, 346, 396, 404, 405, 428, 437, 473, 486, 506, 507, 517, 573
Antonius Pius, 337
Aphrodisias, 212–27
Aphrodite, 212, 212f9.5, 213, 213f9.7, 214, 215f9.10, 218f9.13, 330, 330n114, 330f10.44, 331, 331f10.45, 468f11.53, 554, 555f12.23
Apocalypse Tapestry (An-

gers, France), 59, 59f3.5, 240f9.33, 254f10.2, 273f10.4, 287f10.9, 381f11.2, 392f11.7, 406f11.14, 409f11.15, 412f11.19, 433f11.32, 437f11.34, 442f11.35, 516f11.80, 528f12.3, 541f12.15
apocalypse, 21, 23, 24, 25, 27, 41, 50, 56, 58, 59, 66, 83, 101, 105, 107, 139, 145–50, 152, 154, 156, 166, 169, 170, 174, 181, 185, 192, 198, 199, 201, 206, 227, 237, 249, 251, 252, 262, 297, 374, 421, 496, 562, 568, 570
apocalyptic traditions, development, 69f3.11
Apocrypha(l), 58f3.4, 279n62, 515n184
Apollinarius, 357
Apollo, 12, 148, 230, 230f9.27, 245, 324, 349, 349f10.60, 349f10.61, 350, 350n132, 350f10.62, 350f10.63, 351, 412, 412f11.20, 424, 424f11.27, 435, 450f11.38, 469f11.54, 573, 573fE-5
Apollyon, 12, 23, 79, 150, 230, 245, 318n90, 321, 412, 412n55f11.19, 419, 421, 439, 503, 546, 573, 574
apostasy, 40, 48, 49, 78n2, 514, 514n182
Applewhite, Marshall, 574n2
Aquinas, Thomas, 90n6
Aramaic, 560, 560n34
Arch of Constantine, 32f2.7
Arch of Septimus Severus, 495f11.72
Arch of Titus, 20, 20f1.24,

21f1.25, 495f11.72
archangel, 270, 408, 409f11.15, 426, 501
Archelaus, 266, 496
Archippus, 363
Arias(rianism), 57, 357
Aristides (Aelius), 477–78
ark of the covenant, 26f2.1, 163, 264n22, 320n94, 421, 450
Armageddon, 8, 24, 46, 79, 82, 83, 103, 110, 111, 119, 137, 256, 339, 340, 380n4, 411n54, 459–61, 461n116, 473, 489, 496, 513, 516, 546, 573, 574
Armenia, 222
Armstrong, Garner Ted, 80–81, 81f4.5
Armstrong, Herbert W., 78–80
Artaxerxes I, 73
ascension, 102, 104, 150, 190, 251, 258, 373, 380, 425, 426, 427, 505
Asia Minor, 22, 24, 25, 29f2.3, 30, 30f2.5, 32, 48, 49, 63, 139, 148, 151, 153, 154, 158, 169, 185, 202, 202n5, 203n6, 204, 205, 206, 210f9.4, 211, 228, 229, 236f9.31, 244, 245, 251, 255–56, 259, 262, 272, 274, 276, 277, 279, 337f10.54, 343, 359, 359f10.77, 375, 376, 377, 385, 395, 399, 421, 429, 431, 433, 437, 438, 459, 473, 490n155, 490n156, 515n184, 563f12.29, 564, 568, 569, 573
Asklepio(s)(n), 308f10.30, 311–12, 311f10.36, 312f10.37, 313f10.38, 356, 360, 436

Subject Index 617

Aspendos, 236f9.31
astronomical, 115, 116, 159
atheism, 304n82
Athena, 311f10.35
Attalus II, 342
Attalus III, 307, 342
auctoritas, 212n29
augustals, 367f10.85, 367f10.86
Augustine, 34–37, 38, 39, 46, 47, 48, 49, 50, 55, 59, 68, 84, 101, 165, 166, 167, 171, 502
Augustus, 175f8.2, 203, 222, 253, 256, 272, 293, 294, 299, 299n77f10.22, 352, 385, 472, 519n190
Aurelius, Marcus, 299f10.21, 301, 301f10.25, 308f10.30, 312, 478
autokratōr, 238, 458, 470f11.55
Babylon, 3, 4f1.1, 13, 15, 22, 37, 62, 93, 124, 125, 148, 150, 158, 203, 212, 231, 234, 235, 240, 241, 242, 256, 303, 321, 326–28, 414, 421, 422, 429, 430, 432, 435, 442–48, 443f11.36, 457n111, 460n115, 461, 462–64, 463f11.48, 473–91, 474n133, 488n152, 491n157f11.69, 492, 494, 496, 498, 500, 516, 523, 531, 531f12.4, 536, 539, 541, 547, 556, 556n33, 566
Balaam, 203, 318n90, 319, 320
Balfour Declaration, 123
banishment, 207–08
Bar Kokhba (Simon), 26f2.1, 140, 180, 469f11.54, 476n135, 554

Bartimaeus, 183
basilica, 321f10.40, 344f10.56, 344f10.57, 493f11.70, 575fE-6
Bataille, Nicholas, 59f3.5
Battle Hymn of the Republic, 67
Battle of Carrhae, 411
Battle of Lipany, 54
beast, 24, 25, 31, 35, 37, 43f2.15, 44, 46, 49, 51, 57, 59, 60f3.6, 60f3.7, 62, 64, 66, 67, 67f3.10, 77, 78, 78n2, 106, 108, 140, 147n2, 148, 158, 161, 168, 201, 231, 240, 240f9.33, 241, 256, 305, 318, 326, 327, 332, 368, 370, 373, 376, 401, 407, 415, 419, 421, 422, 429–40, 437, 11.34, 440n86, 441–44, 442f11.31, 433f11.32, 435f11.33, 437m f11.34, 447–53, 455, 457, 459, 462, 465, 470–74, 481, 482, 487, 491–94, 498, 498f11.75, 502–11, 513, 516, 517, 519n189, 520, 523, 527, 530, 531, 541, 545–48, 564n41, 566, 568, 570fE-3, 573
Bede, 33–34, 33f2.8, 39–40, 39f2.12, 46, 50, 61, 73, 89, 140, 159
Beth Shean, 300
Bethsaida, 178, 181, 183
Bickersteth, Edward, 27
biometric cryptology, 108f5.1
Birks, Thomas, 27
Bithynia, 208, 261, 314, 315f10.39, 404, 436, 573
Black death, 38, 38f2.11, 130
Blackstone, William E., 126–

27
bless(ing), 26, 38f2.11, 254, 270n41, 274, 291, 320, 339, 341, 342, 352, 366, 367, 371, 372, 399, 400, 420, 444, 445, 445n95, 458, 509, 545, 552, 559, 564, 565
blood, 21, 103, 115, 150, 155–56, 165, 193, 202, 228, 233–34, 252, 270n41, 295, 373, 391, 392f11.7, 397, 404, 407, 410, 419, 428, 447, 453–54, 468, 485, 486, 492, 494, 496, 518, 530, 538, 551, 552, 565, 567
Bockelson, John (of Leyden), 62n7, 63, 68
Bolsheviks, 123
Book of Mormon, 72, 72f4.1
Branch Davidians, 82–84, 141
Braveheart (movie), 272
bride, bridegroom, 44, 265, 484f11.68, 528, 530, 531, 531f12.4, 547, 555–56, 566
Britannia, 222, 225, 225f9.21
British Israelism, 79–80
Brookes, James H., 94
bubonic plague, 38, 50, 62, 63
Burrus, 226, 226f9.22
Byzantine, 344f10.56, 352
Cadillac Mountain, 539f12.14
Caesarea Maritima, 299, 300f10.23, 473
Caesarea Philippi, 176, 178–83, 182f8.2, 185
Caiaphas, 575
Caligula, 14, 15f1.16, 385, 472, 487
Calvin, John, 53, 59, 90n6
Campus Crusade for Christ,

618 Subject Index

105n17
canon(ical)(ize)(ization), xxiii, xxiifP-1, 23, 28, 31–32, 37, 50, 89, 116, 142, 150–52, 158, 174, 195, 199, 199n7, 201, 202, 205, 253n6, 259, 279n62, 428, 571, 572, 572n1
Caracalla, 343, 352
Cave of the Apocalypse, 206, 207f9.2, 209, 209f9.3
CBS (television), 113n25
Chafer, Lewis Sperry, 94
chiasm, 239, 239n44, 240, 322, 345, 345f10.58, 346, 540n17
chiliasm, 25–30, 25n2, 37, 49, 140, 154, 167, 502, 557
Christ Cycle, 401, 402, 422, 448, 488, 516, 522
Christology, 110–13, 138, 160, 173, 199, 238, 239, 250, 253, 267, 279, 292, 348, 391, 396, 495, 553, 572, 573
Church of England, 65, 85
Church of God International, The, 80
Church of Ireland (Anglican), 85, 89
Cicero, 359, 369
civic millennialism, 65, 65f3.9, 66, 67, 72, 141, 169, 171
Civil War, American, 67, 84, 141
Civil War, Roman, 18, 18f1.20, 203, 289f10.13, 294, 385, 471f11.56, 472
Claudius, 222, 225, 225f9.21, 226, 227f9.23 235, 256, 380n3, 385, 463f11.47
clean (unclean), 265n27,
266n34, 359, 368, 391, 454, 457, 504, 526, 541
Clement of Alexandria, 208
Clement VII (pope), 55
Cleopatra, 103n10
client 15, 15f1.17, 16, 211, 266, 299, 472, 473
CNN, 108f5.1, 135
codex, 386, 386n18, 561f12.28
Cold War, 63, 67, 96, 105n16, 135, 136n45, 514
colonial, 65–66, 65f3.9, 67, 67f3.10, 68, 84, 129, 140, 141, 167, 169
Colossae, 29f2.4, 355, 355f10.70, 357, 360, 365, 563f12.30, 564
Colosseum, 20f1.24, 32f2.7, 231f9.28, 295f10.16, 301, 570fE-2
commerce (commercial), 8, 17, 67, 96, 107, 122, 138, 141, 153, 211, 212, 220, 289f10.12, 290, 298, 303, 305, 329f10.43, 330, 330n112, 332, 342, 351, 360, 361, 366, 367, 368, 372, 375, 421, 431, 432, 437–40, 461, 475–82, 477n136, 485, 499, 506, 527, 537, 557, 565, 566, 573
communist, 61, 63, 136, 514
confession(al), 150, 151, 174, 175, 178–84, 202, 234, 265, 303, 317, 320, 323, 328n109, 338, 339, 342, 375, 377, 382, 391, 403–06, 413, 421, 430, 442, 444, 445, 449, 455, 458, 459, 461, 462, 473–75, 487, 491, 494, 495, 500, 506, 508, 510,
514, 519, 522–23, 530, 549, 551, 555, 564–69, 573, 575
Constantine, 31, 31f2.6, 32f2.7, 33, 34, 35n9, 37, 48, 49, 50, 51, 64, 68, 121, 140, 158, 167, 350, 466, 510
Corinth(ians), 153, 153f7.5, 154, 206, 227n32, 268, 321f10.40, 330n113, 363f10.82, 370n149, 467f11.51, 535f12.10, 545
corona civica, 222
Council of Ephesus, 37, 50, 575fE-6
Cranach, Lucas, the Elder, 56f3.3, 59
creation, 33, 45, 100, 125, 147, 158, 161, 162, 164, 258, 259, 275, 279, 364, 365, 382, 383, 386, 388, 397, 399, 400, 402, 409, 414, 415, 422, 423, 425, 436, 438, 439, 442, 487, 518, 520, 522, 526, 526n1, 528, 529, 538, 539, 540, 542, 544f12.18, 545, 566, 569
Croesus (king), 333
Crusade(r), 37, 42, 46, 51, 497f11.74
cult(us), 8, 16, 179, 217f9.12, 235f9.30, 290, 322, 324, 360f10.78, 438n82, 552, 574, 574n2
Cumming, John, 127
Curetes Street, 154f7.6, 289f10.18
curse, 264, 266, 316, 320, 455, 461, 542, 544–45, 557, 566, 567, 576
Cybele, 334
cyborg, 107

Subject Index   619

Cyril of Jerusalem, 204, 340n120
Cyrus Cylinder, 6f1.5
Cyrus, 6, 6f1.5, 83, 158, 333, 339
Dallas Theological Seminary, 95
Damascus (Road), 187, 273n52, 460
damnatio memoriae, 470, 470f11.55
Dan (tribe of), 40, 51, 405, 405n45
Daniel, 13–15, 22, 73, 89–92, 117, 124, 148, 233, 233n38, 257–58, 263, 265n27, 267, 273f10.4, 278, 279n62, 341, 380, 396n28, 416, 429, 431–32, 519, 521, 550, 567
Darby, John Nelson, 85–98, 85f4.9, 87f4.10, 90n6, 93n10, 94f4.11, 106, 110, 117, 141
Darbyism, 84–96, 97, 141
Dark Ages, 38, 59, 130, 131
David, Davidic (kingdom), 4, 5, 79, 80, 80n3, 83, 112, 183, 252n150, 266, 272, 318n90, 325, 343, 344, 371, 390, 425, 441, 515, 553–54, 554n29, 553f12.22, 567
Day of the Lord, 261, 262, 262n15, 501
Dead Sea Scrolls, 8, 16, 16f1.18, 17, 18
death rays, xxiifP-1
Delphi, 350, 436
demon(ic), 9, 10, 10f1.9, 11, 11f1.10, 12, 24, 41, 51, 64, 169, 175, 413, 427, 496, 504, 523
De Soto, 128
devil, 10, 44, 175, 240, 305, 426, 427, 428, 429, 433,
504, 517, 549n23
Diana (Ephesian), 290, 290f10.14
Didyma, 349–50, 349f10.60, 349f10.61, 351, 436
Diggers, 127
Dionysius of Alexandria, 35, 204–05, 244
Dionysius, 35, 204, 205, 244
disciple(ship), 26, 62, 63, 104, 114–19, 173, 175–85, 187–90, 196, 200, 204, 234, 258, 263, 272, 304, 371, 390, 427, 428, 445, 508, 517, 527
Dispensationalism, 13n5, 48, 63, 76, 84–96, 85f4.9, 87f4.10, 91n7, 94f4.11, 95n11, 96n13f4.13, 97–98, 99, 102, 110, 111, 112, 117, 126, 127, 128, 135, 137, 141, 157, 159, 160, 167, 348, 445
Dispensations, 86–87, 87f4.10, 98
Domitian, 12, 12f1.11, 12f1.12, 14, 22, 29f2.4, 40, 148, 149, 151, 158, 185, 201, 202, 202n4, 202n5, 208, 210n20, 211, 211n25, 230, 235, 243, 245, 256, 261, 274, 287, 288f10.10, 288f10.11, 293, 296f10.18, 317, 318, 352, 352f10.64, 358, 358f10.75, 358f10.76, 381, 383, 385, 386, 389, 417, 421, 431, 433, 440, 443, 470, 470f11.55, 476n135, 486, 487, 488, 506, 528, 535, 550, 553, 564n41, 567, 573
Donatists, 57
Dragon Cycle, 401, 402, 407, 421, 421f11.24, 422,
422f11.25, 428, 429, 435, 439, 440, 441, 443, 448, 453, 457, 462, 463, 465, 468, 476, 488, 490, 491n157, 498, 500, 502, 503, 504, 509, 509f11.77, 510, 512, 516, 517, 519n189, 522, 523
dragon, 9, 148, 149, 169, 193, 240, 240f9.33, 241, 256, 305, 318, 341, 368, 373, 401, 402, 415, 421–31, 421f11.24, 422f11.25, 423f11.26, 426f11.28, 427f11.29, 433f11.32, 434, 435, 439, 440, 441, 443, 447–49, 453, 455, 457, 459, 462, 463, 465, 468, 471, 476, 482, 487–91, 491n157, 498–507, 503f11.76, 509–12, 509f11.77, 516–17, 519n188, 519n189, 522–24, 551
drama, 9, 88, 90, 114, 126, 139, 140, 147, 149, 175, 235–39, 236f41, 241, 242n46, 245, 249, 250, 257, 259, 272, 275, 279, 306, 379, 382, 388, 389, 402, 404, 422, 434, 440, 443, 490, 518, 522, 523, 525, 544, 546, 570, 575
dualism, 7, 37, 314
Dürer, Albrecht, 59, 61
eagle, 296f10.18, 334, 334f10.48, 382, 411n53, 429, 469f11.545, 570fE-3
earthquakes, 129–31, 129n40, 163, 165, 298f10.21, 301f10.25, 302f10.26, 323f10.41, 343, 351, 360, 360n137, 409, 417, 419, 421, 461,

620 Subject Index

475, 478, 565
ecclesiology (ecclesiastical), 47, 50, 98, 110, 113, 138, 160, 169, 173, 186–92, 199, 260, 279, 340, 348, 445, 501, 572, 573
Eck, Johann Maier von, 57
Eden, 298, 526, 530, 541f12.15, 542–45, 566
Edict of Milan, 31, 32f2.7, 49, 158, 167
Edom, 233, 474n133
Edwards, Jonathan, 66
Eleazar, 533
Eli, 264n22
Eliakim, 265, 343
Elijah, 79, 325, 418f11.22, 419, 433, 436
Elymas, 494
emperor worship, 12f1.12, 22, 24, 211, 219, 226, 293, 294, 301f10.25, 303, 316, 328, 336, 340, 347, 359, 359f10.77, 366, 367f10.85, 377, 379, 396f11.9, 438, 440, 442, 475, 487, 494, 519, 530
Emser, Jerome, 57
Enoch, 419
Enron, 109
Epaphras, 29f2.3, 357
Ephesus, 12f1.12, 29f2.3, 37, 50, 154f7.6, 189, 203, 204n7, 206, 208, 210, 211, 211n25, 211n26, 226, 228, 228f9.24, 244, 254, 280, 287–98, 288f10.10f10.11, 289f10.12, 290f10.14, 291f10.15, 296f10.19f10.20, 298, 305, 307, 312, 318, 319, 324, 325, 331f10.45, 337, 338, 349, 357, 362,

452f11.40, 453, 470f11.55, 475, 476f11.58, 477, 494, 507, 537f12.12, 543, 555f12.23, 558, 563f12.30, 564, 575fE-6
Ephraim, 80, 367
Epimenides, 148
Episcopal, 66
epistle (epistolary), 145, 151, 152–56, 152f7.4, 157, 161, 169, 189, 204, 205, 238–39, 243, 494n161, 515n184, 547f12.19, 560–64, 568
epistograph, 395n28
Erastus, 535f12.10
Eros, 214, 216f9.11, 218f9.13
Ethiopian Eunuch, 102, 104
Ethiopian Orthodox Church, 21
Eucharist, 53, 62, 371
Eumenes II, 29f2.4, 307, 311
Euphrates River, 47f2.17, 165, 413, 455, 456f11.44, 460, 464, 474n133
European Common Market, 108f5.1, 514
Eusebius, 29, 35n9, 204, 204n7, 557
Eve, 544f12.18
exorcism, 10, 11f1.10, 175, 496
Ezekiel, 5, 126, 128, 203, 232, 257, 258, 379, 417, 474n133, 511, 514, 515, 529, 531n8, 537, 538, 542, 543
Faber, 57
Faustina, 301f10.25, 337
Felix (governor), 268n39, 473, 486
female, 225, 316
Festus (governor), 473
First Jewish War, 17–22,

19f1.21, 19f1.22, 20f1.23, 20f1.24, 21f1.25, 24, 61, 111, 115, 224, 244, 290, 291, 295f10.16, 351, 443, 476, 492, 532, 533, 536
first missionary journey, 189, 260, 534f12.9
first resurrection, 35, 507–08
Flaccus, 359
Flavian, 287, 293, 295f10.16, 352, 358, 432
four creatures, 381f11.2, 382, 383, 384, 391n25, 392f11.7, 397, 398, 400, 402, 408, 423, 441, 442f11.35, 450, 487, 488
four horsemen, 105–06, 148, 402–03, 403f11.13, 450
Franciscans, 50n20
Frederick II, 36
futurism, 64, 68, 89, 92, 93, 94, 108, 159–61, 238, 252, 261, 328, 340n119, 348, 395n28, 400, 438–40, 495, 502
Gaebelein, Arno C., 126–27
Gaius of Rome, 31
Galba, 18, 18f1.20, 203, 472
Galen, 308f10.30, 312
Gallio, 153
gematria, 438
gender, 333
genetic engineering, 108f5.1
Genghis Khan, 47
genocide, 108f5.1
genre, 32n7, 47, 55, 56, 101–02, 137, 145–56, 146f7.1, 152f7.4, 169–70, 189, 227, 245, 250, 262, 278, 547–48, 547f12.19, 562, 567, 568, 575
George III (England), 66
Gethsemane, 182, 183, 251,

Subject Index 621

445, 496, 517, 574
Gigantomachy, 307, 310f10.33, 314
gladiator(ial), 214, 295, 295f10.16, 295f10.17, 296f10.19, 296f10.20, 297, 312, 352, 394, 570, 570fE-2
global warming, 108f5.1
Gog and Magog, 47, 57, 256, 282, 321, 328, 417, 417f11.21, 422, 510–17, 511f11.78, 513f11.79, 514n182, 516f11.80, 523, 524, 529, 531, 539, 543, 544, 546, 552, 574, 575
gold(en), 264, 265, 265n28, 272f10.4, 280, 301, 332, 359, 368, 369, 381, 385, 396, 413, 444, 450, 464, 466, 467f11.51, 468, 479, 493f11.71, 526, 537, 551n25
Golgotha, 499, 559f12.27
Google, 114n26
grace, 44, 87, 152, 540, 543, 556, 560, 562, 563, 563n40
grace benediction, 152, 494n161, 515n184, 562
Grant, James, 127
Great Disappointment (Millerite), 74, 75, 77, 86
Great Parenthesis (Dan 9:24), 89–90
great tribulation, 253, 280n64, 348, 386n18, 407, 408
great white throne, 273f10.4, 492, 502, 518–21, 524, 529, 543, 552, 567
Greek heroic style, 222, 222f9.18, 225
Greek Orthodox Church, 32, 49, 78, 142

Gregorian calendar, 73
Grotius, Hugo, 64
Gulf of Naples, 410
Gulf War, 7
Gutenberg printing press, 58, 108, 131, 131n42
Hades, 275, 275n56, 276, 365, 374, 519, 520, 538
Hadrian, 268, 269f10.3, 386n17, 469f11.54
Hale-Bopp comet, 574
Hammond, Henry, 64
harlot(ry), 22, 60f3.7, 241, 242, 245, 303, 327, 422, 430, 447, 448, 462–65, 466f11.50, 468, 474, 476, 479, 481, 482, 496, 499, 503, 519n188, 531, 531f12.4, 539, 558, 566, 573
Hasmonean, 15, 16, 266, 266n31, 267
heaven, 10, 36, 44, 74–75, 88, 93, 104, 112, 114, 125, 147, 148, 155, 160, 163, 174, 181, 187, 242, 246, 250n1, 256, 259n11, 267, 330, 341, 377, 378, 379, 380, 381, 383, 383n12, 392, 395, 398, 399, 399n37, 400, 402, 406, 407, 414, 421, 423, 425, 426, 426f11.28, 427f11.29, 427, 429, 430, 434, 436, 442, 450, 462, 474, 475f11.57, 481, 486, 487, 491, 491f11.69, 496, 501, 502, 505, 506, 509, 516, 518, 523, 525, 527, 528, 528f12.3, 531, 532, 537, 541, 543, 546, 547, 550, 551, 555, 574
Heaven's Gate cult, 574
Heavenly Tabernacle, 74–75, 80n3, 82, 92, 97

Hekate, 275n56, 310f10.34
hell, 10f1.9, 81, 499, 499n167, 514
Hellenism, 9, 13, 14, 24, 111, 266, 300, 308, 310f10.33, 314, 321n95, 336, 385
Hemera, 223, 223f9.19
Henry VIII, 65
Herculaneum, 177f8.1, 361f10.79, 362f10.80, 362f10.81, 363, 363f10.82, 364f10.83, 366, 366f10.84, 367, 367f10.85, 367f10.86, 370f10.88, 410f11.17, 477, 483f11.65, 556f12.25
Herod Agrippa I, 266, 318
Herod Antipas, 300
Herod Philip, 179f8.2
Herod the Great, 5f1.3, 15, 15f1.17, 46, 179f8.2, 299, 300f10.23, 394n26, 473, 496, 532, 538f12.13
Herzl, Theodore, 92n9
Hezekiah, 265, 532f12.5
Hierapolis, 28, 29f2.3, 29f2.4, 355, 356, 356f10.71, 356f10.72, 357, 357f10.73, 357f10.74, 358, 358f10.75, 360, 365, 369, 535, 564
high priest(hood), 16, 17, 181, 184, 526, 537
Hildegard of Bingen, 42–45, 43n14, 44n15
Hitler, Adolf, 123n34, 203n6
Hoffmann, Melchior, 62, 68
holocaust, 108f5.1, 123, 123n34, 261
Holy Commonwealth, 65
Holy Spirit, 31, 45, 45f2.16, 46, 56, 142, 190–91, 250n1, 261, 264, 266,

271, 281, 282, 337, 338, 373, 382, 394, 395, 545, 555–56
holy war, 441
honor(able), dishonor, 17, 29f2.4, 43, 138, 179f8.2, 182, 205, 214, 214f9.8, 215f9.10, 224, 225, 228, 229, 270, 270 n41, 287, 289f10.13, 293, 294, 307, 311, 323, 338, 342, 348, 352, 359, 370, 384, 389, 399, 400, 462, 470, 477, 479f11.61, 510, 524, 527, 528, 535, 535f12.10, 541, 554, 567, 575fE-6
Houteff, Victor, 82
Howe, Julia Ward, 67
Howell, Vernon Wayne (David Koresh), 82–84
Huss, John, 53
Hussein, Saddam, 7, 447n100, 514
Hussites, 53
Hygeia, 312f10.37, 356
hymn, 67, 193, 234, 294, 310, 383, 384f11.4, 388, 395–99, 406, 407, 421, 421f11.24, 422, 424, 427, 428, 449, 455, 468, 485, 486, 486n147, 487, 500, 509, 536, 575
Ice Age (movie), 472n129
Ichabod, 264n22
identity, 10, 79, 112, 173–76, 177, 179, 180, 182, 183, 184, 186, 190, 211, 262, 263, 267, 304, 322, 324, 345, 374, 428, 430, 440, 457, 464, 504, 549
ideology, 65, 94, 139, 223f9.19, 224, 224n31, 224f9.20, 226, 255, 270n40, 287, 291f10.15, 293–95, 294n73, 297,

297n74, 299f10.22, 303, 347, 373, 374, 375, 375n153, 385, 391, 398, 403, 404, 431, 434, 439, 463, 465, 468, 470, 472, 473, 481, 485, 507, 510, 514, 520, 530, 553, 562, 565, 574
idolatry, 179, 203, 228, 265, 314, 317, 319, 325, 340, 347, 373, 375, 413, 443, 459, 461, 463, 465, 476, 477, 482, 523, 558, 573
Ignatius, 202n4, 291, 292, 343
imitatio Christi motif, 419
immoral(ity), 319, 320, 325, 327, 340, 347, 479
imperial (emperor) cult, 12f1.12, 22, 22n9, 25, 151, 211–12, 211n26, 214f9.8, 219, 227n32, 228, 228f9.24, 229f9.25, 230f9.26, 287, 288f10.11, 291f10.15, 293–94, 294n73, 301f10.25, 303, 307, 314, 317, 325, 343, 379, 380, 396, 396f11.9, 399, 412f11.20, 421, 431, 436–38, 439, 449, 466, 468, 476, 477, 487, 494, 506, 507n178, 510, 514, 549, 550, 551, 553, 562, 567
impure, 354, 365, 468, 551
inaugurated eschatology, 194–95, 233, 257, 278, 295, 328, 372, 373, 375, 380, 408, 434
inclusio, 276, 342, 376, 450, 474, 487, 504, 518, 529, 547, 547f12.19
inscription, 14f1.14, 214, 220, 221f9.17, 229, 230f9.26, 253, 259,

262n16, 270, 299f10.22, 302f10.26, 304, 304f10.28, 311f10.36, 312, 323f10.41, 334, 334f10.49, 337f10.54, 344f10.57, 348, 352, 359f10.77, 384f11.4, 399, 399f10.10, 412f11.20, 449, 452f11.40, 470, 470f11.55, 535f12.10, 573fE-5
intercalation, 423f11.26, 424, 427f11.29, 428, 509, 509f11.77
interlude, 57, 241, 402, 404, 405, 407, 408, 414, 415, 417, 417f11.21, 419, 422, 423, 426, 429, 440–41, 455, 457n111, 486, 487, 507, 513, 517, 522, 535, 545
international terrorism, 108f5.1
Internet, 16, 82, 97, 108f5.1, 109, 131, 131n42, 132, 138, 160, 440, 514, 571, 574
iPad, 132
Irenaeus, 29, 66, 90n6, 202, 202n5, 208, 302, 405n45, 439n83, 557
Iron Man (movie), 237
Ishmael, 128
Ishtar, 4f1.1
Isis, 323f10.41, 360f10.78
island, 67n13, 165, 206–08, 206f9.1, 207, 207n13f9.2, 209, 209n19f9.3, 221f9.16, 245, 318, 424, 430, 461, 494, 517, 518, 556, 575
Israel, 8, 15–18, 45, 78–80, 88–92, 92n9, 96, 98, 104, 110, 116, 117, 120f5.2, 121–28, 136,

Subject Index   623

137, 147, 158, 183, 188, 190, 232, 233, 233n38, 253, 253n5, 257, 258, 261, 264–67, 264n22, 266n32, 270, 318n90, 319, 325, 326, 343–46, 364, 369, 371, 374, 389, 390, 394, 405, 407, 416, 418f11.22, 418f11.23, 419, 424–26, 430, 444, 460, 464, 474, 515, 527, 534, 535, 538, 545, 553, 554, 554n28, 565
James, brother of Jesus, 499n167, 501, 551n25
James, son of Zebedee, 182, 266
Jaws (movie), 147n2
Jehoshaphat (valley of), 460, 460f11.45
Jehovah's Witnesses, 82, 141
Jeremiah, 80, 320n94, 444, 468, 474n133
Jerusalem, 4f1.2, 15f1.17, 17, 17f1.19, 18, 19, 19f1.21, 22, 28n15, 29, 30, 42, 62, 73, 79, 80, 83, 104, 111, 115–16, 121, 125, 158, 168, 183, 203, 231, 295f10.16, 359, 371–72, 394, 325, 416, 419, 464, 465n123, 499n167, 508, 515, 533, 538
Jesus Christ, 39, 50, 71, 72, 73, 80, 110, 117, 145, 149, 150, 152, 155, 174, 188, 189, 196, 198, 238, 250, 251, 292, 317, 374, 395, 460f11.45, 495, 510, 550, 553f12.22, 557, 572
Jesus Movement, 96
jewelry, 466, 467f11.51, 536, 537f12.12
Jews, 4, 5, 6, 6f1.5, 9, 13–21, 20f1.24, 24, 26, 42, 45,

83, 103, 105, 111, 113, 115, 123n34, 126–27, 137, 159, 224, 251n3, 298, 302, 304, 319, 320n94, 333–34, 345, 359, 377, 389, 390, 394n26, 405, 419, 460f11.45, 463, 489, 536, 571
Jezebel, 151, 154, 203, 271, 274, 318n90, 322, 324–30, 325n102, 325n103, 345f10.58, 365, 407, 418f11.22, 436, 457, 459, 464, 465, 473n130, 476, 530, 541, 544, 548, 551, 558, 567
Joachim of Fiore, 37, 45–48, 45f2.16, 50, 51, 61, 73, 89, 106, 122, 140, 159
John of Patmos, 22–23, 116, 200, 203–09, 243–45, 292, 346, 372, 494, 494n161, 495, 515n184, 545, 551, 556, 564
John Paul II (pope), 199f8.7
John the Apostle, 26, 193–99, 202n5, 203–09, 207f9.2, 209f9.3, 210n20, 238–39, 243–45, 290, 291, 302, 320, 344f10.56, 344f10.57, 495, 556
John the Baptist, 16, 17, 176, 433, 506
John the Elder, 204n7
John the Zealot, 111
John, son of Zebedee, 182
Jonathan Maccabeus, 111
Joseph (tribe), 405n44
Josephus, Flavius, 394n26, 476, 476n135
Josiah (king), 45, 460
Judas Iscariot, 183
Judas Maccabeus, 14, 17, 111, 180, 183, 416
Judgment Cycle, 145, 162–

66, 164f7.13, 170, 241, 249, 257, 261, 326, 327, 339, 341, 347f10.59, 368, 377, 382, 387, 391, 394, 395, 396, 400, 401, 401f11.11, 408, 413, 415, 422, 423, 434, 435, 441, 442, 445, 448, 450, 457, 462, 481, 485, 486, 487, 488, 490, 490n155, 504, 505, 513, 516, 518, 522, 523, 524, 525, 529, 540, 543, 551, 560, 563, 568, 573
Julius Caesar, 203, 293, 331, 472, 479f11.61
Julius II (pope), 418f11.23
Jurassic Park (movie), 147n2
Justin Martyr, 26, 29, 66, 203, 244
Karaite calendar, 73
King James Version, 21, 91, 131, 132, 150, 363n140, 411n53, 416, 431
kingdom of God, 7, 8, 17, 21, 111, 159, 167, 170, 181, 188–90, 191, 195, 200, 251, 252, 260, 278, 298, 403, 474, 489, 505, 506, 526, 546, 550, 556, 576
kingdom of priests, 228–29, 245, 252–53, 258, 397, 509
Korean Air Flight 007, 67n13
Koresh, David, 82–84, 84f4.8
Lachish, 532f12.5
Lactantius, 560
Lady Harlot, 430, 463
Lady Virtue, 431, 435, 443, 463
lake of fire, 57, 275, 306, 307, 327, 374, 499, 499n166, 509, 516f11.80, 517, 520, 521, 524, 530, 538, 540, 565
Lamb, 112, 155, 165, 193,

224n31, 234, 252n4, 265, 340n122, 341, 342, 372, 373, 389, 391–408, 391n25, 392f11.7, 393f11.8, 396n28, 419, 423, 427, 428, 430, 434, 435, 436, 441, 442f11.35, 445, 447, 449, 452, 462, 473, 485, 489, 490, 491, 492, 494, 496, 497, 499, 500, 501, 515, 519, 521, 522, 527, 532, 536, 538, 541, 541f12.15, 545, 546, 547, 553, 556, 560, 565, 566, 569, 573
Laodicea, 29f2.4, 48, 210, 212, 226, 255, 287f10.9, 304, 330f10.44, 351–73, 352f10.64, 353f10.65, 353f10.66, 353f10.67, 355f10.69, 355f10.70, 356f10.71, 356f10.72, 357f10.73, 357f10.74, 359f10.77, 360n137, 360f10.78, 378, 455, 458, 459, 461, 475, 489, 490, 494, 507, 529, 535, 542, 552n26, 555f12.23, 563f12.30, 564
Last Emperor Myth, 35–36, 40, 49
Latin Vulgate, 91, 91n7, 418f11.23
League of Nations, 67
Leto (myth), 148, 349, 424, 424f11.27
Levellers, 127
Leviathan, 423, 424, 425
Library of Celsus, 154f7.6
linear theory, 35, 39, 48, 51, 75, 162–63, 162f7.11, 170, 242n46, 401
linen, 214f9.9, 265, 323n100, 450, 479, 485, 489, 495, 540

lion, 9f1.8, 112, 147, 148, 182–85, 234, 267, 334, 334f10.48, 350, 350f10.63, 382, 390, 465, 553, 570fE–3
literal dictum, 99–101
Lord's day, 261, 262, 395, 397
Lord's supper, 262, 370–72, 373, 567
Louis I (of Anjou), 59f3.5
Louis IV (of West Francia), 41
Louis IX (of France), 42f2.14
Luke, the Evangelist, 21, 114–17, 176, 186–92, 200, 253n6, 258, 264, 290n66, 294n73, 295, 324, 348, 372, 373, 489, 505, 551
Luther, Martin, 50n20, 51, 53, 54, 55–61, 56n1f3.3, 57n2, 57n3, 62, 68, 82, 84, 90n6, 101, 101n6, 101n7, 142, 152, 156, 157, 157n5, 159, 466, 466f11.50
LXX, 232, 262n15, 280, 329n110, 340n121, 383, 515n184
Lydia (of Thyatira), 287f10.9, 324, 564
Maccabe(es)(an), 5, 12, 14, 15, 17, 111, 117, 180, 266, 390, 390n24, 416
Magnificat hymn, 575
male, 294, 307, 359, 398, 425, 441n90
Mamertine Prison, 20f1.23
man of lawlessness, 40, 49, 238, 440n86, 514n182
Manasseh, 80
Manicheans, 57
manna, 320, 320n94, 321n95, 429, 429n70, 507
Marble Hall, 335f10.50, 336,

336f10.52, 342f10.56, 399f11.10
Marcion, 57
mark of the beast, 67, 67f3.10, 77, 108, 429, 437–40, 438n82, 441, 444, 452, 481, 482, 498, 505, 506, 507, 545
martial (imagery), 8, 79, 111, 140, 155, 183, 252, 271, 390, 413, 500, 501, 516, 540, 546, 570
martyr(dom), 29, 30, 168, 202, 252n4, 268, 271, 292, 297, 302, 302n80, 303, 306, 314, 318, 319, 332, 340n122, 343, 346, 394, 404, 428, 430, 445n95, 449, 455, 462, 468, 473, 475, 481, 482, 485, 487, 490, 492, 502–10, 512, 523, 524, 530, 546, 551, 556, 564, 564n41, 566, 568, 570, 573
Martyrdom of Polycarp, 302n80
Marx, Karl, 61
Mary (mother of Jesus), 430, 575, 575fE-6
Masada, 533, 533f12.6, 533f12.7
Mather, Cotton, 66
Mather, Increase, 128
Matrix (movie), 375n153
Mattathias, 111
Matthys, Jan, 62–63, 62n7, 68, 72
Maxentius, 31, 31f2.6
Mayan, 107
McDonald, Larry, 67
Mede, Joseph, 65n10
medical, 311–12, 312f10.37, 356, 360–61, 357f10.73, 361f10.79, 365
Mediterranean, 15, 236f9.31,

Subject Index 625

466, 477, 514, 536, 565
Medusa, 350, 350f10.63
Megiddo, 8, 8f1.7, 459–60
menorah, 20, 21f1.25, 264, 264n21
messiah, 6, 26f2.1, 87, 88, 89, 90, 98n14, 99, 110–13, 115, 125, 127, 138, 140, 142, 147, 151, 170, 175, 177–88, 190, 194, 195, 198, 200, 238, 263, 266, 279, 302, 304, 320n94, 343, 344, 345, 377, 389, 390, 390n24, 394, 397, 405, 418f11.22, 419, 420, 421, 425, 428, 444, 501, 505, 506, 535, 554, 571
messianic secret, 175
Michael, 318n90, 423f11.26, 424, 426–28, 427f11.29, 509
Miletus, 189, 206, 206f9.1, 230f9.27, 350
millennium, 3n1, 23, 25, 25n1, 27, 28, 30, 32, 33, 33n8, 34, 35, 35n9, 36, 37, 39, 41, 48, 50, 54, 55, 65n10, 66, 68, 92, 107, 108, 127, 139, 142, 145, 166–69, 170, 199n7, 237, 256, 380n4, 401, 445n95, 462, 502, 503, 503f11.76, 506, 509, 509f11.77, 511, 512, 546
millennium theories, 166–69
Miller, William, 73–74, 73f4.2, 75, 76, 82, 93, 122, 141
Millerism, 73–76, 97, 141
Milton, John, 427
Milvian Bridge, 31, 31f2.6, 32f2.7
Minerva, 12, 12f1.11
misogyny, 61n6

Mohammed, 57
Monastery of St. John, 206, 207f9.2
Mongols (empire), 47, 51, 158
monotheism, 7, 305
Montanus, 23, 30–31, 30f2.5, 37, 49, 57, 68, 72, 98, 106, 136
Mormon(ism), 71–72, 72f4.1, 97, 141
morning star, 330, 331, 507, 554
Moroni (angel), 71
Mount Carmel, 82, 83, 84f4.8
Mount of Olives, 4f1.2, 104, 105, 105n17, 114
Mount Olympus, 305, 526n4
Mount Sinai, 261, 270, 273n52, 418f11.23
Mount Zion, 240, 241, 441, 515, 535, 545
Münster Rebellion, 62–63, 62n7
Müntzer, Thomas, 54, 61–63, 62n7, 68, 83
Muslim, 40, 42, 46, 46n17, 47, 47f2.17, 51, 63, 136, 158, 343, 460f11.45, 498f11.75
mystery, 45, 90, 91, 128, 278, 279, 323f10.41, 378, 415, 471, 559, 560, 574
myth(ology), 40, 41, 128, 148, 149, 203, 225, 239, 256, 275n56, 305, 314, 330, 350, 422–30, 424f11.27, 427f11.29, 464, 465, 468, 476, 526, 527, 554
narrative, 10, 11, 40, 165, 174, 176, 178, 180, 181, 184, 185, 189, 190, 192, 251, 297, 319, 364, 397, 408, 443, 443f11.36, 444, 452, 491n157, 498,

500, 505, 512, 513, 518, 523, 529, 543, 547, 548
Nathan, 266, 267
Nazareth, 300f10.24
Nazi Socialist Party, 123
Nebuchadnezzar, 4f1.1, 13, 14, 414, 432, 476
neōkoros, 228, 336, 343, 359, 359f10.77, 470f11.55
Nero redivivus myth, 203, 433, 440, 464, 468, 471
Nero, 14, 15f1.16, 18, 40, 201, 202, 202n4, 203, 203n6, 222, 225, 226, 226f9.22, 235, 243, 256, 300, 304, 360, 385, 412, 433, 436, 439, 439n83, 440, 461, 464, 467, 467n125, 468, 470, 471f11.56, 472, 487, 530, 564n41
Nerva, 208
New Jerusalem, 4–5, 23, 30, 30f2.5, 31, 35, 62, 63, 66, 67, 68, 69, 72, 141, 169, 351, 407, 408, 463, 463f11.48, 476, 500, 507, 519n189, 524, 525–47, 528f12.3, 531f12.4, 539f12.14, 552, 556, 556n33, 565–66
New World, 65–66, 69, 71, 128, 140, 169
Niagara Bible Conference, 94
Nicaea, 293n69
Nicolaitans, 151, 154, 154f7.6, 203, 271, 274, 293, 294, 318, 319–20, 365, 436, 530, 558
Nicomedia, 293n70
Nineveh, 93, 465n123, 474n133, 494, 532f12.5
Novatus, 57
nuclear, 103–04, 108f5.1, 112, 136, 138, 156, 160,

626 Subject Index

198, 234, 256, 261, 572
numbers (symbolic), 147–48,
    240, 387, 398, 399, 400,
    406, 409, 417, 434, 442,
    458n113, 504, 505, 508
numerology, 148
Nympha, 363
nymphaeum, 354, 453,
    453f11.42, 542f12.16
occasional literature, 156
Oceanus, 223, 223f9.19, 527,
    527f12.2
odeon, 313f10.38
Oecumenius, 32
Old Testament, 79, 102, 110,
    205, 206, 232–35,
    233n39, 243, 245, 251–
    52, 257–58, 261, 262,
    274, 278, 298, 318, 340,
    379, 380, 381, 383,
    386n18, 391,
    395(396)n30, 405,
    405n45, 410, 443, 444,
    450, 451, 465, 474,
    474n132, 492n159, 495,
    501, 526, 544, 547, 557,
    567
oracle, 280–81, 298, 342, 350,
    350n132, 371, 375, 376,
    394, 395, 416, 436
Origen, 35, 57, 90n6
Osama bin Ladin, 136, 514
Otho, 18, 18f1.20, 203, 472
overcome, 264, 273, 275n57,
    276, 407, 543
Palatine Hill, 32f2.7,
    231f9.28
Palmyra, New York, 71
Pan(ias), 179, 179f8.2
Panacea, 312f10.37
pandemic, 108f5.1
pantokratōr, 229, 458, 488
papal (papacy), 50n20, 51,
    54, 55, 55f3.2, 57, 59,
    61, 62, 64, 68, 77, 78,
    108f5.1, 575fE-6

Papias, 28, 29, 29f2.3, 29f2.4,
    66, 204n7, 357
papyrus, 311, 501
Paradise Lost, 427
paradise, 140, 297, 507, 542,
    543, 544f12.18, 557,
    566
parchment, 311
parody, 379, 384, 432,
    432f11.31, 435,
    435f11.33, 439, 463,
    476, 489
Parthian, 411, 412, 414, 455,
    456f11.44, 457, 461,
    464, 495f11.72
passion, xxiv, 176, 180–85,
    188, 263, 303, 347,
    347f10.59, 348, 376,
    408, 440, 448, 466, 482,
    485, 486n149, 495, 499,
    510–17, 511f11.78, 521,
    523, 524, 525, 552,
    559f12.27, 560, 565,
    569, 572, 574
Patmos, 18, 22, 24, 116, 200,
    206–10, 206f9.1,
    207f9.2, 208n15,
    209f9.3, 210n20, 244,
    245, 270, 292, 318, 346,
    372, 395, 403, 407, 430,
    494, 494n161, 495,
    515n184, 517, 551, 556,
    564, 575
patristic, 25–28, 39, 167, 202,
    243
patron(age), 15, 16, 17, 22,
    24, 211, 213–14,
    213f9.6, 213f9.7,
    214f9.8, 217f9.12, 253,
    266, 268, 275, 287f10.9,
    293, 296f10.19, 297,
    299, 300f10.23,
    301f10.25, 302f10.27,
    303, 304, 319, 322, 324,
    326, 334f10.49, 348,
    352, 358f10.75,

    362f10.80, 363, 375,
    438, 472, 476, 528
Paul(ine), 29f2.3, 35, 40, 49,
    66, 91, 112, 117, 148,
    150, 152–54, 154f7.6,
    187, 187f8.4, 188, 189,
    191, 192, 194, 196,
    196n6, 198, 206, 238,
    250n1, 260, 262,
    262n17, 268, 268n39,
    270, 273n52, 275n57,
    287f10.9, 290, 293n68,
    295, 295f10.17, 304,
    324, 330n113, 341, 345,
    356, 357, 360, 362,
    365n141, 389n22,
    399n36, 440n86,
    445n96, 452f11.41,
    455n109, 473, 474n131,
    486, 489n153, 494,
    494n161, 501, 506,
    509n180, 514n182, 515,
    515n184, 520, 527,
    534f12.9, 545, 556,
    562–64, 563f12.29,
    563f12.30, 564, 564n41,
    568, 572
Peasants' Revolt, 61, 65
penal colony, 209–10
Pentecost, 115, 116, 191, 264
perceived crisis, 202n3
Pergamum library, 310–11,
    311f10.35
Pergamum, 29f2.4, 203, 210,
    211, 229, 229f9.25, 254,
    287, 293, 294, 307–21,
    307f10.29, 308f10.30,
    308f10.31, 309f10.32,
    310f10.33, 310f10.34,
    311f10.35, 313f10.38,
    314n87, 322, 325, 332,
    338, 342, 395, 473, 476,
    477, 486, 494, 507, 517,
    548, 558
periodizing, 45f2.16, 46, 47,
    48, 51, 56, 57, 64, 68,

87f4.10, 89, 102, 138, 140, 159f7.8
persecution, 30, 31, 46, 63, 64, 72, 154, 192, 202, 202n3, 202n4, 207, 243, 252, 259, 260, 263, 268, 275, 279, 303, 323, 347, 393, 395, 398, 406, 407, 408, 415, 416, 417, 419, 428, 430, 433, 434, 435n78, 440, 442, 466, 468, 489, 505, 514, 573
pesher, 16, 16n6, 113, 126
pestilence, 108f5.1, 130, 476
Peter the Hermit, 497f11.74
Peter, 115, 116, 117, 179–82, 183–84, 192, 208, 253n6, 266, 318, 501
Petronius, 211, 212
Pharisee, 5, 10, 178, 370
Philadelphia, 210, 210f9.4, 255, 342–51, 342f10.55, 343n126, 344f10.56, 345f10.58, 507, 511, 511f11.78, 540n17, 546
Philip (the evangelist), 103
Philippi, 287f10.9, 324, 564
Phineas, 264n22
Phoenix, 109
Phrygian powder, 361, 361n139
Pilate, 168, 252, 253, 297, 303, 486, 575
plague, 31, 32, 38, 38f2.11, 50, 62, 63, 104, 128, 129–31, 165, 232, 242, 252, 341, 409f11.16, 410, 411, 413, 420, 448, 451, 451f11.39, 453, 455, 457, 461, 475, 529, 530, 531, 544, 545, 558
Plain Truth, The 78–79
platonic, 37
Pliny the Elder, 410
Pliny the Younger, 202, 202n4, 261, 314, 315,

315f10.39, 317, 318, 319, 345, 404, 410, 436, 437, 437n81, 438, 442, 470, 487, 487n150, 506, 573
Plymouth Brethren, 84–87, 141
pneuma(tic), 31, 49, 238
polis, 210, 211
pollute, 17, 454, 530, 541, 544, 566
Polycarp, 271, 302, 303, 318, 319, 346
Pompeii, 14f1.15, 177f8.1, 323f10.41, 329f10.43, 363, 410, 410f11.17, 465, 465f11.49, 468f11.63, 483f11.64f11.65, 484f11.67, 523, 552f12.21
Pompey, 331
pope, 51, 53, 54, 58, 61, 64, 65, 68, 77, 466
Pope, Alexander, 502n171
Poseidon, 424
postmillennial(ism), 27n6, 28n15, 65, 65f3.9, 66, 67, 72, 84, 140, 141, 167, 169, 170, 347, 572
power rays, xxiifP-1, xxiii, 138, 198
praetorian guard, 211n26
premillennial(ism), 25–28, 27n4, 27n6, 27f2.2, 28n15, 54, 62, 68, 100, 127, 136n45, 140, 167, 168, 169, 170, 572
preterism, 64, 68, 151, 153, 157–58, 162, 170, 400, 438, 439–40
priest(ly), 8, 16, 17, 17f1.19, 38f2.11, 53, 181, 184, 184f8.3, 211, 211n26, 214, 214f9.8, 215f9.10, 217f9.12, 228–29,

228f9.24, 245, 252–53, 263, 264–65, 264n24, 265n27, 265n28, 266, 267, 273f10.4, 312, 337f10.54, 350, 351, 360f10.78, 367f10.85, 367f10.86, 374, 396f11.9, 397, 398, 416, 417, 419, 436, 495, 509, 526, 536, 537, 540
Priestly, Joseph, 27
Prochorus, 208–09, 209f9.3, 245
proconsul, 153, 287, 289f10.12, 289f10.13, 337f10.54, 352, 362f10.80, 494
Progressive Dispensationalism, 96, 96n12
prophecy, 33, 64, 65n9, 80n3, 85, 88, 100, 103, 126, 150–52, 156–62, 157f7.7, 169–70, 186–88, 254, 259, 267, 280, 280n64, 337, 341, 342, 372, 395, 401, 415, 440n85, 441, 491, 510, 547, 548–50, 562, 567, 568
Protean quality, 107–09
pure, 8, 17, 26, 44, 46, 47, 65, 265n27, 267, 276, 301, 355, 355f10.70, 368, 404, 407, 454, 537, 539
Puritans, 65–66, 65n10, 69, 128
purity, 273f10.4, 368, 406, 442, 468, 542, 551
Python, 423, 424–25
Quakers, 127
Queen of Heaven, 425, 430, 476
Qumran, 7, 8, 8f1.6, 16, 16n6, 16f1.18, 61, 83, 113, 252, 460
Ranch Apocalypse, 83

628 Subject Index

Ranters, 127
Raphael, 10, 11f1.10
rapture (secret), 27, 91–92,
  93, 97, 108, 110, 117,
  138, 160, 192, 253,
  280n64, 306, 346, 347,
  380, 380n4, 445,
  445n96, 574
Reagan, Ronald, 67, 136
realized eschatology, 194,
  194f8.5, 196, 197, 238,
  251, 257, 258, 267, 278,
  328, 369, 373, 374, 550,
  558
recapitulation theory, 35, 48,
  164–66, 164f7.13, 170,
  242n46, 257, 401, 402,
  403, 404n43, 408, 409,
  411, 415, 421, 440, 453,
  462, 488, 518, 563
Renaissance, xxiifP-1, 41, 59,
  196, 199f8.7, 312,
  520f11.82
Res Gestae Divi Augusti,
  299n77, 299f10.22,
  384n15
resurrection, 5–6, 6f1.4, 7,
  24, 29, 35, 116, 117,
  149, 150, 167, 176, 180,
  181, 182, 185, 186, 189,
  190, 192, 193, 194, 196,
  200, 204, 235, 250n1,
  251, 258, 262, 263, 268,
  274, 275, 297, 306, 332,
  346, 365, 372, 374, 380,
  393, 394, 397, 400, 404,
  406, 419, 426, 432,
  460f11.45, 491, 492,
  501, 507, 508, 509, 517,
  519, 523, 524, 550
Revere, Paul 66
RFID technology, 108
rhetoric (subversive), 227–
  32, 270, 271, 295, 391
rhetoric(al), 27n6, 32, 32n7,
  47, 51, 56, 61, 62, 63,
  67, 68, 69, 74, 76, 85,
  92, 97, 100, 105n17,
  106, 107, 109, 109n21,
  118, 119, 120f5.2, 123,
  124, 130, 136, 138, 141,
  160, 205, 224, 227, 230,
  245, 256, 257, 270, 271,
  274, 295, 304, 319, 325,
  326, 339, 345, 346, 365,
  365n143, 368, 372, 379,
  385, 391, 412n55, 447,
  461, 463, 463f11.48,
  464, 466, 488, 518, 547,
  558, 566
Ribera, Francisco, 48, 64
Robbins, John 127
robe, 155, 233, 264, 273f10.4,
  340, 340n122, 368, 381,
  404, 406, 406f11.14,
  407, 489, 552
Roden, Lois and George, 83
Roma (*Dea*), 223, 224f9.20,
  232f9.29, 293, 298, 425,
  463, 469f11.54
Roman Catholic Church, 21,
  32, 48, 50, 53, 55, 61, 65
  77, 78, 91, 91n7, 121,
  167, 418f11.23, 430,
  466
Roman Forum, 20f1.24,
  231f9.28, 331,
  495f11.72
Roman standards, 296f10.18
Rome (city), 20f1.23, 28, 29,
  29f2.3, 31, 31f2.6, 36,
  45, 65, 185, 187f8.4,
  189, 202, 203, 203n6,
  231–32, 231f9.28,
  232f9.29, 244, 253, 264,
  292, 295f10.16, 315,
  343, 425, 454,
  454f11.43, 467f11.52,
  469f11.54, 477f11.59,
  492, 506, 527, 530,
  535f12.10, 564, 564n41,
  570fE-2, 575fE-6
Rome (empire), 15–22,
  15f1.17, 34–35, 36f2.10,
  49, 111, 115, 140, 194,
  208, 209–10, 211–28,
  214f9.8, 224f9.20,
  225f9.21, 245, 251, 256,
  293, 297n74, 299–301,
  299f10.22, 301f10.25,
  303, 307, 322, 330,
  330n112, 342, 390, 411,
  413, 414, 423, 431–40,
  443–44, 454, 458, 462–
  91, 495f11.72, 511–14,
  511f11.78, 523, 527,
  531, 555, 566, 569, 573
Romulus and Remus,
  232f9.29, 468,
  469f11.54, 485
root of David, 390, 553–54
Rosh Hashanah, 119n29
Russell, Charles T., 78, 81–
  82, 81f4.6, 92, 93
Russian empire, 514
Russian Orthodox Church,
  78
Rutherford, Joseph F., 82
sacramentum, 317
Sadducee, 6, 15, 16, 17
Saint John's Basilica,
  344f10.56, 344f10.57
Saladin, 46, 136
Salt Lake City, 68, 72, 141
Saracens, 57
Sardis, 210, 211, 255, 322,
  332–42, 332f10.46,
  333f10.47, 334f10.48,
  334f10.49, 335f10.50,
  335f10.51, 336f10.52,
  336f10.53, 337f10.54,
  343n126, 365, 394,
  399f11.10, 417,
  417f11.21, 458, 459,
  461, 475, 489, 507,
  519n188, 541, 552n26,
  573
Satan(ic), 12, 35n10, 41, 46,

Subject Index 629

61, 64, 82, 175, 181, 239, 304, 305, 313–14, 314n87, 318, 318n90, 319, 325, 326, 328, 345, 346, 365, 373, 390, 422, 426–28, 427n69, 432, 435, 436, 440, 465, 496, 504, 506, 508n179, 510, 511, 511f11.78, 512–14, 513f11.79, 517, 520, 549n23, 572
scaenae fons, 236f9.31, 237f9.32
schizophrenic messiah, 98n14, 99, 110–13, 138, 151, 199
Scofield Reference Bible, xx, 48n19, 87, 87n5, 94–95, 94f4.11, 95n11, 95f4.12, 100, 100n4, 101, 101n5, 110n22, 141
Scofield, Cyrus I., 87, 94, 94f4.11, 95–96, 100, 101
Scrat (character), 472n129
scribe(s), 175, 176, 185n1, 208, 209f9.3, 245, 266, 363n140, 370, 557f12.26, 558, 561n36, 564
scroll, 359–89, 386n18, 386f11.5, 395–400, 395n29, 395(396)n30, 405, 414–15, 463, 490, 518
Scythopolis, 300, 300f10.24
seal, 90, 91, 153, 233, 241, 320, 332, 341, 346, 386, 386n18, 387, 387f11.6, 395, 398, 400, 404–05, 405n46, 413, 413n56, 429, 436, 439, 441, 522, 545, 546, 550, 565, 567
Sebastion, 219–27, 219f9.14, 220f9.15, 221f9.16, 221f9.17, 412f11.20,

463, 463n119
second coming, 27, 27n4, 46, 62, 64, 68, 73, 75, 84, 91, 93, 97, 110, 111, 112, 113, 136, 160, 166f7.14, 167, 168, 169, 181, 193, 194, 199, 257, 258, 319, 320, 371, 403, 444, 473, 486n149, 491, 491n157, 492, 492n158, 500, 501, 501n169, 510, 524, 551, 552, 559, 560, 570, 571, 573, 575, 576
second death, 306, 327, 338, 346, 413n56, 507, 509, 520, 530, 565
Second Jewish War, 111, 476n135, 469f11.54, 554
second missionary journey, 287f10.9, 324
second resurrection, 167, 508
Seleucus I, 321
sēmainō, 253–54
Seneca, 226, 226f9.22
Sennacherib, 515, 532f12.5
Sepphoris, 300, 300f10.24
Septuagint, 557
Sergius Paulus, 494
Servant Song (Isaiah), 102–03
servant, 112, 184, 251, 255, 341, 415, 420, 449, 457, 465, 486, 545, 549, 549n23, 565
seven (symbolic), 22, 33, 34, 46, 48, 60f3.7, 89, 102, 147, 149, 158, 231, 249, 256, 262, 267, 270, 273f10.4, 274, 279, 281–82, 281f10.6, 291, 306, 327, 337, 374, 380n4, 382, 387, 394, 399, 414, 416, 425, 426f11.28, 458, 458n113, 465, 470–71,

471f11.56, 482
seven churches, 22, 24, 145, 147, 149, 153, 154, 155, 157, 201, 210, 210f9.4, 243, 245, 249, 253, 254, 255, 256, 258, 259, 262, 270, 273f10.4, 274, 279, 280, 282, 287f10.9, 290, 293, 298, 306, 320, 327, 337, 339, 342, 345, 347, 347f10.59, 351, 371, 372, 374, 376, 377, 379, 380n4, 381, 388, 391, 394, 395, 403, 421, 429, 434, 436, 441, 457, 459, 462, 473, 475, 476, 477, 481, 482, 490n155, 492, 504, 516, 519, 523, 530, 547, 548, 549, 550, 558, 560, 562, 564, 565, 566, 567, 568, 569, 573, 574
seven hills (of Rome), 231–32, 231n36, 231f9.28, 232f9.29, 245, 464, 470, 471
seven kings, 471–72, 471f11.56
seven lampstands, 7, 23, 139, 149, 249, 251, 255, 263, 264, 268, 270, 273, 279, 280, 291, 292, 305, 313, 338, 348, 369, 373, 417, 475, 532
seven letters, 48, 202, 224, 234, 242, 244, 249, 255, 256, 263, 271, 276, 280–86, 281f10.6, 282f10.7, 283–86f10.8, 490, 490n155
seven seals, 402–08
seven spirits, 147, 337, 378, 383, 394
seven trumpets, 408–21
Seventh-day Adventist, 13f1.13, 61, 73, 76–83, 77f4.3, 92, 97, 98, 132,

133f5.3, 134f5.4, 141, 157, 160
sexual abstinence, 441–42
Shekinah, 528
Sheol, 230, 275
shepherd, 329n110
Sigismund, King, 54
signs of the times, 46, 47, 48, 51, 75, 76, 93, 96, 97, 99, 100n2, 109, 113–38, 114n26, 141, 160, 574
Simeon (tribe), 405n44
Simeon the prophet, 186–88, 191
Simon ben Giora, 19, 20f1.23, 224
Simon bar Kokhba, 26f2.1, 140, 180, 469f11.54, 476n135, 554
Simon Maccabeus, 111
Simon the magician, 494
sin, 112, 198, 266, 327, 455n109, 465, 474n131, 485, 510, 520, 538, 544
Sinai, 261, 270, 273n52, 418f11.23
Sinaiticus, 561f12.28
Six Day War, 96, 128
Sixtus III (pope), 575fE-6
Smith, Joseph, Jr., 71–72, 141
Smith, Uriah, 77–78, 77f4.3
Smyrna, 202, 202n5, 210, 228, 254, 271, 287, 293, 298–307, 299f10.21, 301f10.25, 302f10.26, 302f10.27, 319, 322, 325, 327, 328, 338, 342, 345, 345f10.58, 346, 383f11.3, 407, 413n56, 477, 478, 478n139, 507, 540n17
social(ism), 9, 30, 54, 61, 62, 63, 68, 82, 96, 107, 123, 135, 136, 139, 161, 207, 208, 210, 210n21, 211, 213, 214f9.8, 214f9.9,
217f9.12, 228, 243, 245, 253, 255, 268, 304n82, 305, 317, 322, 323, 324, 326, 332, 334, 345, 369, 370n149, 375, 389, 401, 434, 439, 464, 490, 519
society, 9, 24, 54, 61, 81, 92, 211, 212, 234, 245, 293, 294, 297, 326, 370, 378, 432, 437, 444n94, 473, 507n178, 518, 519, 570
Solomon(ic), 125, 264n21, 526, 537
Son of God, 45, 174–76, 184, 193, 258, 270, 324, 326, 329, 332
Son of Man, 23, 114, 116, 139, 149, 150, 155, 156, 173, 174, 179–82, 183, 184, 185, 190, 194, 198, 200, 234, 241, 242, 249, 250n1, 251, 257, 258, 259–63, 263n19, 264, 265, 267, 268, 270, 271, 272, 276, 279, 280, 281, 282, 291, 304, 339, 340, 341, 346, 347, 348, 371–75, 378, 380, 383, 390, 391, 395, 396n28, 400, 413, 414, 427, 429, 442, 445, 450, 488, 489, 492, 494, 495, 500, 501, 502, 507, 510, 519, 521, 525, 529, 538, 545, 547, 552, 567, 569, 573, 575
song of Moses, 397, 449, 451
song of the Lamb, 397, 449
sorcery, 234, 293, 325, 413, 414, 494, 510, 523, 530, 541, 553
soteriolog(y)(ical), 86, 110, 113, 138, 150, 155, 160, 173, 193–99, 279, 348, 374, 502, 572, 574
sovereign(ty), 13, 14, 15, 24, 39, 147, 162, 164, 227,
228, 229, 242, 246, 256, 259, 275, 279, 280, 337, 374, 377, 377f11.1, 378, 381, 382, 383, 386, 388, 389, 390, 392, 398, 400, 401, 404, 406, 408, 409, 414, 419, 420, 434, 436, 439, 444, 447, 451, 474, 474n131, 475, 485, 491f11.69, 493, 496, 504, 513, 516, 518, 522, 525, 529, 530, 540, 545, 553, 566, 569, 573
Stamp Act (British), 66–67, 67f3.10
Star Trek, xxiifP-1
Stephen, 250n1, 258n9
Suetonius, 386, 386n17, 470
Sylvester II (pope), 41, 50
symbol(ic), 7, 14, 21–25, 32, 34, 46, 49, 55, 56, 68, 101, 137, 140, 146, 147, 148, 156, 158, 161, 161f7.10, 165, 166, 167, 168, 169, 171, 183, 205, 218f9.13, 222, 223, 223f9.19, 225, 226, 231, 244, 250, 253–54, 262, 265, 267, 279, 298, 306, 312f10.37, 314, 321, 334, 337, 340, 340n120, 341, 374, 385, 387, 389, 392, 393, 394, 398, 399, 404, 405, 407, 409, 415, 416, 417, 419, 423, 427, 441, 442, 443, 447, 461, 463, 464, 472, 473, 484f11.68, 493f11.71, 505, 508, 512, 520, 522, 524, 525, 526, 527, 532, 534, 536, 537, 566, 571, 573
synagogue, 178, 188, 189, 302, 304, 304f10.28, 319, 325, 332f10.46, 333, 333f10.47, 334,

Subject Index 631

334f10.48, 334f10.49,
  335, 335f10.50,
  335f10.51, 338, 343,
  344, 345, 346, 365, 377,
  379
tabernacle, 232, 264n21, 407,
  450, 528
tabernacle (heavenly), 74–75,
  80n3, 82, 92, 97
Tabernacles (Sukkot), 406
Taborites, 53, 54
Tacitus, 410, 470
Tany, Thomas, 127–28
Tatian, 57
telescopic theory, 163–64,
  163f7.12, 170, 401, 523
temple measuring, 416–17,
  426, 429, 535
temple warden, 336, 359
temple
  Aphrodite, 213, 213f9.7,
    330n114, 555f12.23
  Apollo, 349–50,
    349f10.60, 349f10.61,
    350f10.62, 350f10.63,
    351, 573fE-5
  Artemis, 290, 290f10.14,
    336, 336f10.53, 337,
    349
  Asklepios, 313f10.38
  Athena, 311f10.35
  Augustus, 179f8.2, 293
  Dea Roma, 293, 298
  Domitian, 287, 288f10.10,
    470f11.55
  Ezekiel, 5, 417, 530n8, 542
  heavenly, 379, 407, 421,
    450, 451, 461, 537, 538,
    565
  imperial, 211, 219f9.14,
    228, 287, 288f10.11,
    293, 298, 307, 316, 359,
    359f10.77, 398, 399,
    412f11.20, 436, 477
  Isis, 323f10.41
  Jerusalem, 4, 4f1.2, 5f1.3,

8, 15–22, 17f1.19,
  21f1.25, 24, 26f2.1, 73,
  111, 114, 115, 116, 118,
  125, 131, 163, 186, 203,
  231, 232, 264, 264n21,
  266n34, 295f10.16,
  320n94, 351, 359, 372,
  379n1, 416, 443, 464,
  472, 526, 536,
  538f12.13, 553f12.22
  Julius Caesar, 293
  Mēn Karou, 360
  pagan, 231f9.28, 314, 348,
    349, 351, 353f10.67,
    354, 396, 527
  Telesphorus, 313f10.38
  Tiberius, 293, 298
  Trajan, 229f9.25, 307,
    308f10.30
  Venus, 331
tent of witness, 450, 451–52
Terminator (movie), 107,
  132
Tertullian, 30, 90n6, 207n13,
  302
textual variation, 431, 435,
  435n78, 459–60, 561,
  562n36
theophany, 261, 383, 383n12,
  396n28, 529
Third Advent, 75, 82, 92, 97–
  98
third heaven, 515n184
third missionary journey,
  189, 290, 356
throne, 14, 15, 28n15, 79,
  112, 142, 147, 165,
  224n31, 226, 228, 256,
  266, 267, 273f10.4, 281,
  313–14, 314n87, 329,
  340n122, 372, 373, 378,
  381–82, 381f11.2, 385,
  391n25, 393f11.8,
  395n29, 400, 409,
  409f11.15, 420,
  442f11.35, 455, 492,

502, 504–05, 507, 518–
  21, 529, 530, 543–45,
  552, 566, 569, 575
Thyatira, 202, 203, 210,
  202n5, 210f9.4, 255,
  287f10.9, 292, 321–32,
  321f10.40, 323f10.41,
  338, 345f10.58, 457,
  459, 461, 465, 476, 507,
  534f12.8, 535, 544, 551,
  554, 554n31, 558, 564
Tiamat, 423, 425
Tiberius, 222, 225, 225f9.21,
  256, 293, 360n137, 472
Titus, 18, 20, 20f1.24,
  21f1.25, 114, 224, 256,
  264, 287, 293,
  295f10.16, 352,
  352f10.64, 358, 385,
  492, 495f10.72
Tobias, 10
Tobit, 10, 11, 11f1.10
toga, 222, 466
topos, 32, 32n7, 45, 51, 56,
  109n21, 224, 365, 443,
  444, 463, 468
trade guilds, 211, 214,
  214f9.8, 290, 319, 322,
  323, 324, 325, 326, 328,
  330, 366, 367, 377, 380,
  438
Trajan, 202n4, 208, 229f9.25,
  261, 289f10.13, 307,
  308f10.30, 314, 315,
  318, 345, 386n17, 436,
  470, 487n150, 506,
  572fE-4, 573
transfiguration, 174, 181,
  182, 273n52
tree of life, 297, 341, 507,
  526, 543, 552, 558, 566
tribulation, 27, 27n4, 91, 117,
  159, 160, 161, 163, 189,
  207, 252, 253, 260,
  280n64, 303, 304, 307,
  338, 348, 386n18, 405,

407–08, 445, 449, 556, 568
triumph(al), 20, 20f1.24, 21f1.25, 224, 231f9.28, 264, 390, 441, 487, 492, 493f11.70, 495
triumphal entry, 111, 182, 183–84, 371, 372
Truman, Harry, 92n9
Turk(ish), 42, 57, 62, 127, 158
twenty-four elders, 163, 340n122, 381, 381f11.2, 384, 392f11.7, 397, 420, 442f11.35, 487
Twitter, 146, 513
two ages, 7, 193–94, 194f8.5
two covenants, 88
two witnesses, 416–19, 426, 428, 429, 430, 503, 507, 513, 517, 522, 574n2
Tyconius, 35, 167
Tyre, 465n123, 474n133
unclean, 457, 504, 541
United Nations, 120f5.2, 122, 123, 126, 128, 514
United States, 3, 72, 133f5.3, 133f5.4, 293, 483n144, 514, 539f12.14
universal bar code, 108f5.1
Urban II (pope), 42
Urban VI (pope), 55
urban, 208, 210
Valentinus, 557
Van Gogh, 250
Varus, 103n10, 394n26
velarium, 236f9.31
Venus, 330–32, 554, 554n31, 555f12.23
Vespasian, 8, 18, 19f1.22, 22, 61, 202n5, 232f9.29, 256, 289f10.13, 293, 295f10.16, 352, 472, 532
Vesuvius, 177f8.1, 323f10.41, 410, 475, 483f11.65

Victorinus, 35, 48, 164, 165, 209, 210n20
Victory (goddess), 224, 224f9.20, 302f10.27
Virgil, 272
virgin, 441n90, 489n153, 575
Visigoths, 36, 414
Vitellius, 18, 18f1.20, 203, 472
votive, 311f10.36, 312
Walnut Street Presbyterian Church, 94
Walter the Penniless, 497f11.74
war imagery, 8
war of words, 156, 234, 271, 292, 298, 320, 375, 413, 419, 428, 429, 431, 434, 442, 457, 473, 500, 522, 530, 540, 569
warrior, 47f2.17, 103, 156, 182, 225, 233–35, 272, 390, 391, 394, 411, 412, 426, 469f11.64, 473, 492, 540, 555, 555f12.24, 573
wash, 11, 129, 366, 552
Watchtower Bible and Tract Society, 81
water(s), 11, 22, 116, 119, 129, 177, 179f8.2, 241, 270, 274, 311, 354–56, 354f10.68, 355f10.69, 355f10.70, 363, 365, 373, 407, 410, 419, 430, 441, 443, 444, 452f11.41, 453f11.42, 453–54, 462–65, 473, 478, 488, 526, 529, 532, 541f12.15, 542–43, 542f12.16, 556f12.25, 557, 566
Wesley, John, 90n6, 129
white robe(s), 340, 340n122, 368, 381, 404, 406f11.14, 486, 489

White, Ellen G., 76–77
whore(dom), 325, 326, 431, 442, 443, 462, 464, 473, 485, 547, 566
Wilson, Woodrow, 67
witness(es), 60f3.6, 117, 135, 150, 154, 155, 156, 169, 184, 188–92, 204, 234, 235, 251, 255, 260, 261, 271, 272, 274, 279, 292, 294, 297, 305, 306, 314, 328, 338, 339, 340, 342, 345–48, 364–66, 379n148, 372, 373, 374, 376, 382, 395, 396, 403, 407, 415, 427n69, 428, 441, 442, 445, 458, 468, 487, 492, 494, 495, 501, 506, 507, 522, 547, 555, 573, 575
woman, 11, 22, 44, 147, 222, 287f10.9, 368f10.87, 422–31, 423f11.26, 426f11.28, 443, 448, 457, 463, 465, 466, 467f11.52, 473, 509, 523, 526, 531f12.4, 537f12.12
Word of God, 152, 156, 207, 234, 260, 272, 403, 494, 505, 506, 519, 522, 556, 565
World Council of Churches, 108f5.1, 514
World Tomorrow, The 78–79
World War I, 67, 108f5.1, 123
World War II, 123
World Zionist Congress, 92n9
Worldwide Church of God, 78, 79, 141, 159, 160
Wormwood, 318n90, 321
worship, 8, 18, 77–78, 78n2, 168, 179f8.2, 220f9.15,

Subject Index 633

296f10.18, 311, 317, 319, 323f10.41, 324, 325, 327, 330, 331, 331f10.45, 332, 336, 336f10.53, 337, 341, 356, 360, 366f10.84, 367, 371, 381, 382–86, 389, 395, 396–400, 406, 408, 409, 409f11.15, 413, 418f11.22, 420, 423, 430, 433–40, 437f11.34, 438n82, 442, 444, 449, 452, 465, 474, 475, 487, 490, 490n156, 505, 506, 519, 520, 539, 541, 545, 549, 549n23, 550, 555, 556, 560, 564, 567, 568

wrath, 126, 156, 165, 193, 196, 241, 242, 265, 304, 388n19, 404, 420–22, 429, 444, 447, 448, 451, 421f11.24, 422, 422f11.25, 455n109, 461, 461n118, 474n131, 462, 464, 479, 496, 499, 500, 523, 571

Wycliffe, John, 50n20, 53, 54–55, 55f3.2

Y2K crisis, 107, 108f5.1

Young, Brigham, 72

YouTube, 79f4.4, 81f4.5, 146

Zealot, 20f1.23, 111, 224, 266, 416, 533

Zedekiah, 80

Zerubbabel, 419

Zeus, 14f1.14, 307, 308f10.31, 309f10.32, 310, 310f10.33, 310f10.34, 314n87, 324, 336, 336f10.53, 337, 349, 424, 424f11.27, 436

Zeus Altar, 307, 308f10.31, 310, 310f10.33, 310f10.34, 314n87

Zion (city of), 67, 72, 240, 321, 463f11.48, 476, 515, 526, 565

Zionism(ist), 92, 92n9, 123

Zodiac, 424, 425, 527

zoomorphism, 146, 382

Zoroas(ter)(trianism), 5, 6, 7, 111, 314, 460

Zwingli, 53, 90n6

Lightning Source UK Ltd.
Milton Keynes UK
UKHW052047040821
388321UK00008B/1656